Frameworks for Multi-Tiered Systems of Support for Trauma-Informed Educational Settings

Jennifer Lauren Aniano
National University, USA

IGI Global
Scientific Publishing
Publishing Tomorrow's Research Today

Vice President of Editorial	Melissa Wagner
Director of Acquisitions	Mikaela Felty
Director of Book Development	Jocelynn Hessler
Production Manager	Mike Brehm
Cover Design	Phillip Shickler

Published in the United States of America by
IGI Global Scientific Publishing
701 East Chocolate Avenue
Hershey, PA, 17033, USA
Tel: 717-533-8845
Fax: 717-533-7115
Website: https://www.igi-global.com E-mail: cust@igi-global.com

Library of Congress Cataloging-in-Publication Data

Names: Aniano, Jennifer, 1986- editor
Title: Frameworks for multi-tiered systems of support for trauma-informed educational settings / edited by: Jennifer Aniano.
Description: Hershey, PA : IGI Global Scientific Publishing, [2025] | Includes bibliographical references and index. | Summary: "The purpose of this book is to offer an MTSS framework for the PK-12 educational setting that is built from the lens of trauma-informed care and integrates principles of anti-racist education and social-emotional learning while also addressing the needs of multiple subgroups of students, including but not limited to BIPOC, LGBTQIA+, Female, students living with ACEs, etc"-- Provided by publisher.
Identifiers: LCCN 2025000742 (print) | LCCN 2025000743 (ebook) | ISBN 9798369390207 hardcover | ISBN 9798369390214 paperback | ISBN 9798369390221 ebook
Subjects: LCSH: Education--Social aspects | Educational sociology
Classification: LCC LC191 .F728 2025 (print) | LCC LC191 (ebook) | DDC 306.43--dc23/eng/20250415
LC record available at https://lccn.loc.gov/2025000742
LC ebook record available at https://lccn.loc.gov/2025000743
British Cataloguing in Publication Data
A Cataloguing in Publication record for this book is available from the British Library.

This book is dedicated with love to the educator who understands the importance of holistic education and has the bravery and fortitude to build trauma-informed systems. You truly make the world go round.

Editorial Advisory Board

Table of Contents

Detailed Table of Contents

and families. The transformative model developed empowers students with learning disabilities for successful postsecondary transitions, persistence, and completion, underscoring that tailored interventions are key to improving postsecondary outcomes, boosting parental and student involvement, institutional collaboration, and access to key critical resources.

Dr. Brandy Shooks presents a comprehensive exploration of how trauma-informed practices, when integrated with Multi-Tiered Systems of Support (MTSS), can effectively address the unique challenges faced by multilingual learners (MLs). These students often navigate intersecting barriers, including trauma, language acquisition, cultural adjustment, and systemic inequities, making a multifaceted approach essential for fostering resilience and academic success. This chapter delves into the critical need for trauma-informed educational settings that prioritize safety, trust, and collaboration while providing MLs with the tools to thrive academically and emotionally.

Children of Immigrant parents, regardless of being born in the USA, face additional challenges. Even though young children have a higher level of resilience, some live traumatic events vicariously. Chronic stress of the parents due to language barriers, cultural differences, social influences, and legal status can permeate the children. Clinical interventions with the family can reduce the negative impact of acculturation on the parents and help them understand their children's cultural differences. The challenge is that many of these families are afraid to utilize the available resources, or they are unaware that such resources exist. Promoting such interventions in educational facilities can inform migrant families and help them adjust to a new society.

This chapter delves into several key topics that are essential to understanding and supporting English Language Learners (ELLs) in K-12 education, including the distinctions between adult ELLs and native English speakers, diversity, language diversity, cultural awareness, cultural competence, strengths, challenges, and the complexities of cultural integration. By addressing these areas, the chapter seeks to illuminate the unique needs of ELLs and provide actionable strategies to foster their academic success and overall well-being. This chapter's primary objective is to explore ELLs' critical needs and identify motivational strategies to empower them. These strategies include implementing well-resourced

Preface

INTRODUCTION

Education is a dynamic and ever-evolving field, requiring continuous reflection and adaptation to meet the diverse needs of students. While Multi-Tiered Systems of Support (MTSS) have long served as a foundational framework for intervention and support in PK-12 educational settings, integrating a trauma-informed lens remains underdeveloped. Even fewer frameworks explicitly incorporate anti-racist principles, crucial in fostering equitable educational environments. This book seeks to bridge that gap by offering a comprehensive and inclusive approach to MTSS that is both trauma-informed and anti-racist.

The contributors to this volume are esteemed educational professionals with extensive experience across PK-12 settings. Their expertise spans various disciplines, including special education, school psychology, social-emotional learning, diversity, equity, and inclusion. Each chapter presents valuable insights into implementing trauma-informed and anti-racist MTSS practices, addressing the multifaceted needs of all students within a school district.

The purpose of this book is to provide a robust MTSS framework that integrates trauma-informed care with principles of anti-racist education and social-emotional learning. Furthermore, this framework acknowledges and addresses the needs of various student subgroups, including but not limited to BIPOC, LGBTQIA+, female students, and students experiencing Adverse Childhood Experiences (ACEs). By centering these perspectives, we aim to create educational environments that are inclusive, responsive, and supportive for all students.

This book is intended for a broad audience, including PK-12 educators, school administrators, educational policymakers, higher education professionals, social workers, and child psychologists. Whether you are a classroom teacher seeking to support your students better, a school leader striving for systemic change, or a researcher exploring the intersection of trauma, race, and education, this book offers critical insights and practical applications to enhance the educational experience for all learners.

I hope this work serves as a meaningful contribution to the ongoing efforts of creating trauma-sensitive, anti-racist, and student-centered educational environments. By collectively embracing these principles, we can build a more just and equitable education system that supports the holistic development of every child.

ORGANIZATION OF THE BOOK

This edited volume critically explores contemporary challenges and innovations in education, particularly through the lens of trauma-informed, culturally responsive, and equity-focused practices. The chapters in this book provide a multidimensional understanding of the complex interplay between social-emotional learning (SEL), Multi-Tiered Systems of Support (MTSS), and culturally responsive pedagogy. By examining these topics, the contributors offer actionable insights for educators, policymakers, and researchers committed to fostering inclusive and supportive learning environments.

Chapter 1, "The Travesty of Traditional Tiers and Positive Behavior Intervention Supports," examines the widespread adoption of Positive Behavior Intervention Supports (PBIS) and their integration into MTSS. While these systems were designed to close opportunity gaps, the chapter critiques their inherent biases and unintended consequences, which often exacerbate inequalities rather than resolve them.

Chapter 2, "Culturally Responsive Trauma-Informed Training for Educators and School Counselors," highlights the necessity of trauma-informed, anti-racist approaches in education. It provides a historical overview of trauma-informed practices, an analysis of children's trauma experiences, and key training components. The chapter also addresses staff wellness and administrative support, emphasizing the critical need for comprehensive educator training.

Chapter 3, "MTSS and SEL: Behavior," offers a metaphorical analysis of MTSS and SEL, likening the framework to the layers of a cake. It presents a tiered approach to intervention, focusing on integrating SEL into all levels of support. The chapter underscores the importance of early detection, individualized assistance, and a holistic strategy for addressing behavioral challenges in students.

Chapter 4, "Minneapolis Trauma-Informed School Practices," presents a qualitative study of trauma-informed education in a Minneapolis high school. Through interviews and classroom observations, the study identifies the significance of empathy-driven practices and teacher well-being in sustaining trauma-informed approaches, advocating for a structured, multi-tiered strategy.

Chapter 5, "Cultural Competence Social-Emotional Learning," explores the intersection of cultural competence and SEL within an MTSS framework. It discusses the role of SEL in promoting emotional and academic success in diverse communities, offering practical strategies and recommendations for effective implementation in educational settings.

Chapter 6, "Integrating Anti-Racist Education into Social-Emotional Learning with a Trauma-Informed MTSS Framework," critiques the Eurocentric underpinnings of SEL and advocates for incorporating anti-racist principles. The chapter discusses systemic inequities in education and presents strategies for embedding culturally sustaining practices, professional development, and community partnerships within SEL frameworks.

Chapter 7, "Social-Emotional Learning as a Strategy for Addressing Math Anxiety in High School Students," examines the impact of math anxiety and the role of SEL in mitigating its effects. By incorporating trauma-informed and anti-racist principles, the chapter outlines strategies such as differentiated instruction and restorative practices to create inclusive learning environments and improve academic outcomes.

Chapter 8, "Heart and Mind — Empathy in Action: The Power of Social and Emotional Learning," delves into the transformative potential of SEL. It highlights the role of empathy, resilience, and interpersonal skills in academic and personal development, offering case studies and psychological insights to support its arguments. The chapter provides practical strategies for integrating SEL into school curricula to foster inclusive communities.

Chapter 9, "A Hidden Oasis of Care: Trauma-Informed Educational Practices and Teachers of Less Commonly Taught Content Areas (LCTCA)," explores the unique position of LCTCA educators in supporting marginalized students. It examines the intersection of trauma-informed practices, culturally responsive teaching, diversity, equity, and inclusion, arguing for the vital role of specialized educators in fostering safe and supportive learning environments.

Chapter 10, "Addressing Commercial Sexual Exploitation of Children: The Role of Trauma-Informed Practices in Schools," sheds light on the critical issue of commercial sexual exploitation and the responsibilities of schools in identifying and supporting affected children. The chapter highlights the necessity of trauma-informed practices in creating safe, educational spaces and addressing the stigma and lack of awareness surrounding exploited youth.

Chapter 11, "Ensuring Inclusive K-14 Classrooms for LGBTQIAA+ Students When Teachers Implement Equitable Practices by Using the Growth Heartset Theory," discusses the application of the Growth Heartset Theory in fostering inclusive learning environments for LGBTQIAA+ students. The chapter presents best practices for supporting this diverse student population and ensuring their validation and well-being within educational contexts by focusing on empathy, belonging, and respect.

Chapter 12, "Beyond the Frontlines: The Importance of Trauma-Informed Care for Military Children in the K-4 Setting," describes the all-volunteer military force (AVF) as a foundational element of the United States' defense strategy since 1973. However, its success has come with challenges, particularly for military-connected families. Frequent relocations, known as Permanent Change of Station (PCS) moves, and parental deployments place significant academic, social, and emotional strain on military children. Despite the necessity of strong support systems, research on the specific needs of these children within the K-12 educational framework remains scarce. This chapter examines the integration of Multi-Tiered Systems of Support (MTSS) and Trauma-Informed Care (TIC) as critical interventions to promote resilience and academic success for military children. By exploring the intersection of military culture, developmental needs, and evolving family support structures, this chapter underscores the urgent need for specialized educational strategies tailored to this unique student population.

Chapter 13, "The Evolution of Special Education and the Framework to Support Struggling Students," explores the evolution of special education has been marked by landmark legal cases and policy developments, beginning with Brown v. Board of Education and progressing through contemporary legislative efforts. This chapter presents a historical and analytical perspective on the transformation of special education, emphasizing the development of equitable practices that foster inclusive learning environments. It explores essential frameworks such as Multi-Tiered Systems of Support (MTSS), Positive Behavioral Interventions and Supports (PBIS), and Universal Design for Learning (UDL), all of which contribute to more effective educational outcomes for students with diverse learning needs. By examining emerging trends and future directions in special education, this chapter highlights the ongoing commitment to ensuring that all students receive the support necessary to thrive academically and socially.

Chapter 14, "Reimagining Inclusivity and Access: A Transformative Model to Empower Students with Learning Disabilities," describes the impact of more students with learning disabilities enrolling in higher education institutions on a concerning gap in degree attainment. This chapter presents a qualitative case study exploring parental perceptions of postsecondary transitions for students with learning disabilities, guided by Schlossberg's transition theory. The study reveals that a successful transition from high school to college requires a holistic collaboration between schools, disability services, outreach programs, and families. Effective Individualized Education Programs (IEP) and 504 plans facilitate these transitions. The chapter introduces a transformative model that enhances institutional collaboration, increases parental and student engagement, and provides access to essential resources, ultimately improving postsecondary outcomes and degree completion rates for students with learning disabilities.

According to Chapter 15, "Frameworks for Multi-Tiered Systems of Support for Trauma-Informed Educational Settings: Supporting Multilingual Learners, " Multilingual learners (MLs) face a complex array of challenges, including trauma, language acquisition barriers, cultural adaptation, and systemic inequities. This chapter, authored by Dr. Brandy Shooks, explores how trauma-informed practices integrated with Multi-Tiered Systems of Support (MTSS) can effectively support MLs in educational settings. Triangulation-informed frameworks create environments where MLs can thrive academically and emotionally by prioritizing safety, trust, and collaboration. The chapter presents practical strategies for educators to address the unique needs of MLs while fostering resilience and success through culturally responsive pedagogy and targeted interventions.

Chapter 16, “A Comprehensive Approach Combining the Education System with Family Therapy to Help Immigrant Families with Acculturation: Guide for Educators and Clinicians,” explores The challenges of acculturation extend beyond immigrant parents to their children, who often experience the stressors of cultural integration vicariously. Language barriers, cultural differences, social influences, and legal status create a landscape of chronic stress that can negatively impact children's development and educational outcomes. This chapter explores the role of educational institutions and clinical interventions in mitigating these effects by supporting parents and children through acculturation. It emphasizes the importance of accessible resources and proactive engagement to help immigrant families adapt to their new environment, ultimately fostering improved academic achievement and long-term success for their children.

According to Chapter 17, “Whole Human Family Support in K-12 Education: Exploring the Divide,” understanding the unique needs of English Language Learners (ELLs) requires a multifaceted approach considering language diversity, cultural awareness, and the complexities of cultural integration. This chapter delves into the distinctions between adult ELLs and native English speakers, highlighting the strengths and challenges of language acquisition in a K-12 setting. It presents motivational strategies and well-resourced interventions designed to empower ELLs, equipping educators with the tools to foster inclusive and effective learning environments. By addressing attendance, graduation rates, and overall well-being, this chapter advocates for a holistic approach that ensures the academic success of ELLs and prepares them for future opportunities.

According to the last chapter, “Education Without Borders: Ramping up Support for Refugee, Migrant, and Immigrant Learners, PK-12,” education is a fundamental right, yet refugee, migrant, and immigrant children often face significant barriers to accessing quality learning environments. With approximately 1.6 million migrant children residing in the United States and a growing number of unaccompanied minors, the need for equitable and inclusive educational support has never been more urgent. This chapter explores the interconnected experiences of different migrant groups, examining their educational, environmental, health, and socioeconomic challenges. Through a theoretical lens, it analyzes factors contributing to child migration and the varying levels of institutional support available. The chapter concludes with actionable recommendations for enhancing educational opportunities for migrant learners, ensuring that every child has access to the tools necessary for academic and personal growth.

Collectively, the chapters in this book provide a robust analysis of the challenges and opportunities in contemporary education. Through trauma-informed, culturally responsive, and equity-driven approaches, the contributors offer invaluable insights into fostering inclusive learning environments that prioritize student well-being, academic success, and social justice.

CONCLUSION

As we navigate the evolving landscape of education, it becomes increasingly clear that a one-size-fits-all approach is no longer sufficient to meet the diverse needs of today's learners. The chapters within this volume collectively underscore the urgency of fostering inclusive, trauma-informed, and culturally responsive educational environments. From military-connected children and students with learning disabilities to multilingual learners and refugee students, each chapter offers critical insights into the barriers these populations face and the innovative frameworks that can help dismantle them.

By integrating Multi-Tiered Systems of Support (MTSS), trauma-informed care, and family-centered interventions, educators and policymakers can cultivate environments where all students—regardless of background or circumstance—can thrive. Moreover, the research presented here highlights the essential role of collaboration between schools, families, and community stakeholders in shaping a more equitable education system.

Ultimately, this book serves as a call to action and a guide for reimagining education beyond traditional boundaries. The knowledge and strategies shared by our contributing authors illuminate a path forward where inclusivity, accessibility, and holistic support are the cornerstones of academic success. We hope this work informs and inspires meaningful change in educational practice and policy, ensuring that every learner receives the support they need to reach their full potential.

Acknowledgments

To Derek Allen, the first person to show me the powers of trauma-informed teaching and trauma-informed education. The first individual to introduce me to the dangers in the ignorance of an uniformed Positive Behavior Supports System lacking an integrated Multitiered System of Supports.

Ms. J. Goodrich, for believing in my leadership potential before I knew I had the potential to lead and be a change agent.

Thank you to Dr. Maggie Broderick for propelling me forward in my publishing journey out of the kindness of her heart. Thank you to Dr. Linda Bloomberg for wanting nothing more than to empower the next generation of strong women scholars to speak intelligently, proudly, and often. Thank you to Dr. Brianna Parsons for allowing me to find my small space and become what I never knew I needed to be. Thank you to Dr. Lisa St. Louis, who has shown me what genuine kindness in leadership can do to ensure growth and organizational change. National University has given me the courage to be a voice for change in education. I can never truly thank this community enough for what you have done for me.

More appreciation than can be written goes to the authors, editors, and contributors of this book, especially Dr. Brandy Shooks, Dr. Samira Galvao, and Dr. Chisato Hotta, who tirelessly hung in there with me, recruiting authors, editing more manuscripts than I can count, and being the support I needed the most. You all are the true heroes of this publication.

And I must thank my husband for understanding my desire to research and publish to change the educational landscape for the better. It takes a special type of person to carry the people who research, write, and educate for a living. I am grateful to have him.

Last but certainly not least, I must thank the people who showed me ***how not to lead.*** I have had many poor examples of leadership in my 16 years in education. Perhaps those examples drove me onto the path of trauma-informed care, social-emotional learning, and into studying leadership when obtaining my doctorate. So, thank you for inspiring me to be a better teacher, a better coworker, a better leader, a better friend, and a better human being.

Section 1
Building Trauma-Informed School Communities

Chapter 1
The Travesty of Traditional Tiers and Positive Behavior Intervention Supports

Jennifer Aniano
https://orcid.org/0009-0000-6567-432X
National University, USA

ABSTRACT

For the last several decades, Positive Behavior Intervention Supports (PBIS) structures have been where many school districts across the United States have invested time, training, resources, and staff and allocated millions of dollars (Kim, R. M., & Venet, A. S., 2023; Funar, 2022; Dorado et al., 2016). In addition, these PBIS have been integrated through the Multitiered Systems of Support (MTSS), which have academic and social implications within the school climate and culture and intervention structures (Kim, R. M., & Venet, A. S., 2023; Funar, 2022; Dorado et al., 2016). What most systems and institutions have failed to recognize is the inherent racism, classism, and bias the very PBIS and MTSS structures meant to bridge the opportunity gap for our most marginalized students are not only widening the gap but also further traumatizing the students they are meant to serve the most (Osta & Vasquez, 2024).

SYSTEMIC TRAUMA/COMPLEX TRAUMA AND HISTORICAL TRAUMA IN K-12 EDUCATION

Trauma in this context is any disturbing experience causing negative consequences for a k-12 student or staff's daily functioning (APA, 2022; Kaufman & Diliberti, 2021; Kim, R. M., & Venet, A. S., 2023; Osta & Vasquez, 2024). Traumatic events will change an individual's perspective of the world, causing feelings of unpredictability (APA, 2022). A Trauma Trigger in this context is an antecedent to a reaction causing an escalation in behaviors, disobedience, disruption, etc. (APA, 2022). Historical Trauma/Intergenerational Trauma is an epigenetic form of trauma, which means the trauma is not only shared on a societal level but also on a genetic level from generation to generation (APA, 2022; Kaufman & Diliberti, 2021; Kim, R. M., & Venet, A. S., 2023; Osta & Vasquez, 2024). The American Psychological Association (2022) listed the following in the cited definition:

DOI: 10.4018/979-8-3693-9020-7.ch001

Research on intergenerational trauma concentrated initially on the children, grandchildren, and great-grandchildren of survivors of the Holocaust and Japanese American internment camps, but it has now broadened to include the impact of slavery and structural racism on Black people, as well as the historical trauma experienced by American Indian communities, the families of Vietnam War veterans, and others. Also called historical trauma; multigenerational trauma; secondary traumatization (APA, 2022).

Adverse Childhood Experiences (ACEs) are traumatic events that occur in children and young adults from birth to age 17 (CDC, 2024). The United States Center for Disease Control (2024) lists the following examples as ACEs: (a) experiencing violence, abuse, or neglect; (b) witnessing violence in the home or community; (c) having a family member attempt or die by suicide. The United States Center for Disease Control (2024) lists growing up in a household with the following examples as ACEs: (a) substance use disorder; (b) mental health issues; (c) instability and parental separation; (d) instability due to the criminal justice system. Unsurprisingly, children who have suffered from ACEs or other forms of trauma during their formative years and k-12 education career are 2.5 times more likely to be retained in one or more grade levels and, by default, will have lower test scores (Williams, 2017). These students may also experience more failures within the opportunity gap continuum, experience academic and behavioral issues, have trouble with cognitive functioning and executive skills, and be given labels, especially in the school district MTSS programs (APA, 2022; Kaufman & Diliberti, 2021; Kim, R. M., & Venet, A. S., 2023; Osta & Vasquez, 2024). These are the students who may be labeled in the Tier 3 intervention block of both the behavioral and academic MTSS program; there are often correlations for students in these areas (APA, 2022; Kaufman & Diliberti, 2021; Kim, R. M., & Venet, A. S., 2023; Osta & Vasquez, 2024).

Systemic Trauma/Complex Trauma are the policies, procedures, practices, etc., implemented by institutions that cause harm to individuals or specific groups of people (Wilson, K. & Pressley, J., 2024). These policies, procedures, practices, etc., perpetuate inequality, injustice, marginalization, exploitation, and oppression through denial of opportunities, exclusionary tactics, preferential advancement, disenfranchisement, forced displacement, isolation, or separation from family, resources, or other supports (Wilson, K. & Pressley, J., 2024). As previously discussed, Historical Trauma/Intergenerational Trauma is an epigenetic form of trauma, which means the trauma is not only shared on a societal level but also on a genetic level from generation to generation (APA, 2022; Kaufman & Diliberti, 2021; Kim, R. M., & Venet, A. S., 2023; Osta & Vasquez, 2024), that means that students coming to school may be facing these traumas on top of other traumas related to ACEs or traumas that may be a part of the school day (Osta & Vasquez, 2024).

To deepen the struggle students may face, families may keep trauma, criminal justice involvement, and domestic or community violence a secret from the school (Williams, 2017). These traumas are all contributors to trauma triggers and are antecedents to student academic issues and missed opportunities (Williams, 2017). The National Education Association's Trauma-informed Toolkit for Educators (2017) listed the following as possible adverse effects of trauma on children in the k-12 education system: (a) cognitive delays, (b) difficulty concentrating or paying attention, (c) increased frustration with complex tasks, (d) noncompliance with directions, (e) challenges with executive function – especially planning and problem-solving, (f) inability to process relationships and emotions, (g) difficulty forming or maintaining relationships, (h) reading social cues, (i) trusting others, (j) inability to predict and make inferences, (k) lessoned understanding of cause and effect, (l) difficulty understanding that they can influence what happens to them (Williams, 2017).

The Opportunity Gap is created when students lacking privilege lack equal access to resources and learning opportunities (Jean-Pierre & Parris-Drummond, 2018). Punitive measures disproportionately affect marginalized students, reducing access to said opportunities (Jean-Pierre & Parris-Drummond, 2018). Arwine (2017) reported that students from historically marginalized groups perform lower academically in comparison to their white peers, and that includes economically disadvantaged students. The conversations of systemic inequities are incomplete when the only discussion of marginalization is race instead of intersectionality (Arwine, 2017; Jean-Pierre & Parris-Drummond, 2018; Williams, 2017). While recognition of the Opportunity Gap led to more good intentions like the federal legislation No Child Left Behind (2000), the attention to the disparities led to tracking and grouping students, further marginalizing and ostracizing our most vulnerable students through the well-intended PBIS and MTSS programs that have manifested today. (Arwine, 2017; Jean-Pierre & Parris-Drummond, 2018; Williams, 2017).

> Special analyses by the National Center for Education Statistics in 2011 show that African American and Hispanic students trailed their White peers by an average of over twenty test score points on the NAEP math and reading assessments at the fourth and eighth grade levels. Twenty test score points is a difference of approximately two grade levels (Arwine, 2017).

Beard et al. (2023) cited the COVID-19 Pandemic as a turning point in the United States for pushing the Opportunity Gap to the forefront of the conversation regarding the inequities in the American Education System. Students in districts highly populated with students from marginalized groups and low-income communities lacked the technology, supplies, academic support, and mental health support they needed to thrive working from home (Beard et al., 2023; Conner, 2023). While the COVID-19 Pandemic highlighted the deep-seated issues systemic racism and institutional marginalization have caused in the American k-12 educational system, the problems have existed since the institution began (Ben-Asher, 2020; Gomez, 2021; Osta & Vasquez, 2018).

> According to Editorial Projects in Education Research Center's annual Diplomas Count report, while each major racial and ethnic group had more students graduate in the class of 2008, massive graduation achievement gaps remained among students. While 82.7% of Asian students and 78.4% of White students in the class of 2008 graduated on time, only 57.6% of Hispanic students, 57% of African American students and 53.9% of American Indian students graduated on time (Arwine, 2017).

Osta and Vasquez (2018) recommended that leaders, educators, and Americans reflect on structural racism and implicit bias through reflective considerations. Leaders can also use these considerations to build a reflective self-practice for growth and understanding, a practice with staff to build cultural competence and connection, and a teaching tool for instructors to build community with students toward truth and racial healing (Jean-Pierre & Parris-Drummond, 2018; Osta & Vasquez, 2018). The following are the considerations Osta and Vasquez (2018) recommended, explaining how they can be implanted with leadership self-reflection, staff collaboration, and classroom community building.

Consideration #1: Situate learning about implicit bias in a historical and socioeconomic political context (Osta & Vasquez, 2018). Betrayal trauma occurs when one person violates the trust of another person in a contextual situation (Gomez, 2021). Since a school is a community, there are opportunities for relationship betrayal on many occasions. Those betrayals can occur between adults, adults, and students, between students, the school community, the larger community, and various other combinations. There are also varying levels of betrayal trauma depending on the seriousness of the relationship and the type of relationship, meaning the power dynamic in the relationship (Gomez, 2021; Osta & Vasquez, 2018).

Cultural Betrayal trauma occurs when a perpetrator with privilege violates the trust of someone lacking privilege in that context (Gomez, 2021; Osta & Vasquez, 2018).

Self-Reflection. Cultural Competence training should be mandatory in all school districts and buildings (Ben-Asher, 2020). Self-reflection should be a large part of this process (Ben-Asher, 2020; Williams, 2017).

Staff Collaboration. Cultural Competence training should be mandatory in all school districts and buildings (Ben-Asher, 2020). This training should be done yearly and, on a continuum and advancing basis, in conjunction with Implicit Bias training and teambuilding and community-building activities to embrace both old and new additions to the team (Ben-Asher, 2020; Gomez, 2021; Osta & Vasquez, 2018; Williams, 2017). Retention of staff is a national problem in the k-12 education system. It cannot be ignored when considering the cultural competence of staff and the school community (Williams, 2017).

Classroom Community. Given that schools are complex organisms with diverse communities filled with interactional power structures, the staff and students must understand implicit and explicit bias and the true history surrounding them (Gomez, 2021; Osta & Vasquez, 2018). The curriculum and teaching must reflect these concepts (Gomez, 2021; Osta & Vasquez, 2018).

Consideration #2: We are all connected – our fates are linked. Working for social justice is not about "helping those kids" or "those communities" but dismantling structures that exclude, increasing access to opportunity, and building healthy, inclusive communities where we all belong and can thrive (Osta & Vasquez, 2018). Trauma-centered social justice is becoming an increasingly recognized principle in psychology, sociology, anthropology, philosophy, and education (Ben-Asher, 2020). The abuse of power and privilege is necessary for the perpetuation of trauma caused by the institution of the k-12 school system (Ben-Asher, 2020). A commitment to a Critical Race Theory approach to dismantling this inequitable system and rebuilding the trauma-informed system built on antiracist principles meant to heal and repair harm to all students will take the entirety of the school community and society (Ben-Asher, 2020; Gomez, 2021; Osta & Vasquez, 2018).

Self-Reflection. Recognizing that power constructs like race and gender are societal creations and not natural is the first step in recognizing that privilege is a *subordination-centered approach* and an *abuse-of-power and exploitation* tactic leading to law-making (Ben-Asher, 2020). Committing to reflecting on your place in this system, your role in this system, and your power to change this system is necessary for both your growth and dismantling (Williams, 2017).

Staff Collaboration. Consider beginning to analyze, revise, and evaluate your curriculum through appropriate, research-based protocols built on philosophies and theories like Critical Race Theory (Conner, 2023). Empowering students through truthful teaching and learning and disrupting the empowerment narrative of a whitewashed curriculum is important, which can further add to the systemic generational institutional trauma in America (Ben-Asher, 2020; Conner, 2023).

Classroom Community. Commit to being a culturally competent antiracist educator and classroom instructor willing to repair harm, learn, and grow (Ben-Asher, 2020; Conner, 2023). A culturally competent antiracist instructor often employs an asset-based pedagogy to include all students, can apologize and repair harm, places truth and relationships above all else, and is brave in the commitment to removing whitewashing from the curriculum to promote social justice and racial healing (Ben-Asher, 2020; Conner, 2023).

Consideration #3: Any effort to interrupt implicit bias and its impacts must be accompanied by efforts to dismantle structures that exclude and build structures that provide access to opportunity or create new opportunities (Osta & Vasquez, 2018). Schools are institutions and thereby are a place where implicit and explicit bias occurs on a micro-aggressive and macro-aggressive level whether those aggressions are adult-to-adult, peer-to-peer, adult-to-student, or any combination of these (McAdoo et al., 2023). School districts must be willing to commit to creating opportunities to close the gaps created by these systemic biases so that all students are given an equitable chance at success (Ben-Sher, 2020).

Self-Reflection. Implicit bias training should be mandatory in all school districts and buildings (Ben-Asher, 2020). Self-reflection should be a large part of this process (Ben-Asher, 2020; Williams, 2017).

Staff Collaboration. Implicit bias training should be mandatory in all school districts and buildings (Ben-Asher, 2020). This training should be done yearly and, on a continuum and advancing basis, in conjunction with cultural competence training and teambuilding and community-building activities to embrace both old and new additions to the team (Ben-Asher, 2020; Gomez, 2021; Osta & Vasquez, 2018; Williams, 2017). Retention of staff is a national problem in the k-12 education system. It cannot be ignored when considering the cultural competence of staff and the school community (Williams, 2017).

Classroom Community. Implicit bias training should be mandatory in all classrooms as part of a research-based curriculum program (Ben-Asher, 2020). This training should be done yearly and, on a continuum and advancing basis, in conjunction with cultural competence training and teambuilding and community-building activities to embrace the new school year and in secondary education the new semester or trimester (Ben-Asher, 2020; Gomez, 2021; Osta & Vasquez, 2018; Williams, 2017).

MULTITIERED SYSTEMS OF SUPPORT

While Multitiered Systems of Support (MTSS) are intended to serve the most vulnerable population of students in the United States, the repercussions over the past few decades have demonstrated that the opposite effect may be coming to fruition (APA, 2022; Kaufman & Diliberti, 2021; Kim, R. M., & Venet, A. S., 2023; Osta & Vasquez, 2024). These MTSS programs are generally universally structured through three tiers (see Figure 1). These tiers have a behavioral and academic intervention component (Funar, 2022; Dorado et al., 2016). Tier 1 is where most students will fall and will be school-wide interventions and supports (Funar, 2022; Dorado et al., 2016). Tier 2 will be intermediate intervention and support with a smaller set of students (Funar, 2022; Dorado et al., 2016). Tier 3 will have an intensive support program and a small group of students (Funar, 2022; Dorado et al., 2016). A Positive Behavior Intervention Support Program (PBIS) often accompanies these tiered systems (Kim, R. M., & Venet, A. S., 2023; Funar, 2022; Dorado et al., 2016).

Figure 1. The traditional depiction of a tiered model in a MTSS program

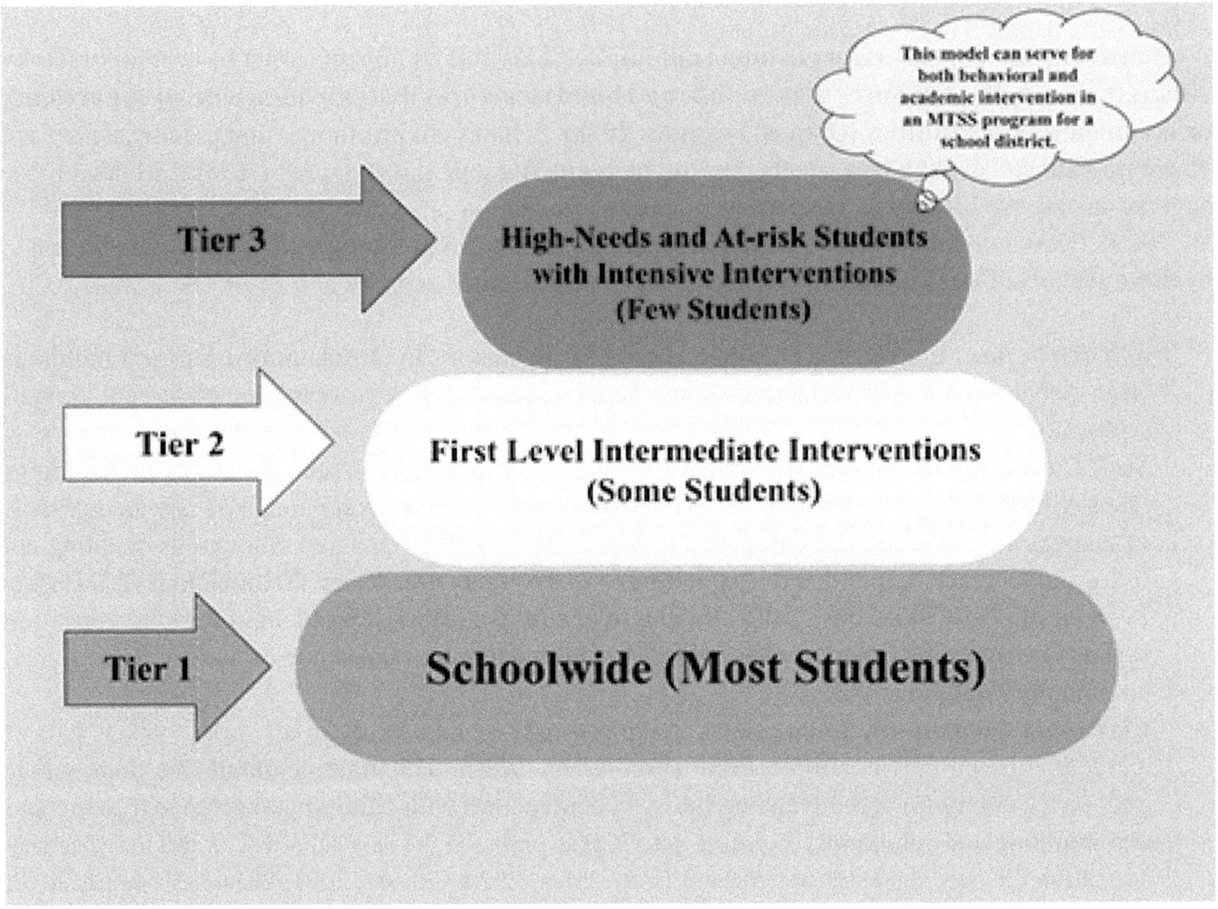

Chafouleas et al. (2016) recommended that if tiered interventions are the framework of choice for a given school district for MTSS, and if PBIS is also necessary for the educational leaders in that MTSS program, then a trauma-informed approach must also be integrated to equitably serve all stakeholders in the school community (Chin, (2023); Comas-Diaz et al., (2019); Graphenreed & Poe (2022); Pewewardy & Smith, (2019). Chin (2023) suggested systemically colorblind institutions to transform into antiracist equitable institutions, teachers and educators with privilege must challenge racial inequities and power hierarchies; in this case, MTSS and PBIS programs that disproportionately discriminate against BIPOC and marginalized student populations, as well as break the White Cannon in curriculum, conversation, community, and culture, in this case point out the inequities and injustices and bring in the materials relevant to truth and racial healing (Chin, (2023); Chafouleas et al. (2016); Comas-Diaz et al., (2019); Graphenreed & Poe (2022); Pewewardy & Smith, (2019).

PBIS in K-12 Education

The biggest failure of positive intent may be the Positive Behavior Intervention Support (PBIS) framework (see Figure 2) the United States Education system has developed to support MTSS programs (APA, 2022; Kaufman & Diliberti, 2021; Kim, R. M., & Venet, A. S., 2023; Osta & Vasquez, 2024). The PBIS models are a framework for managing student behavior described as part of a Multi-Tiered System of Support (Kim, R. M., & Venet, A. S., 2023; Funar, 2022; Dorado et al., 2016). Some state laws require the framework, and some federal funds support the use (Kim, R. M., & Venet, A. S., 2023; Funar, 2022; Dorado et al., 2016).

Figure 2. Stigmatizing tiers and economizing grades and behaviors

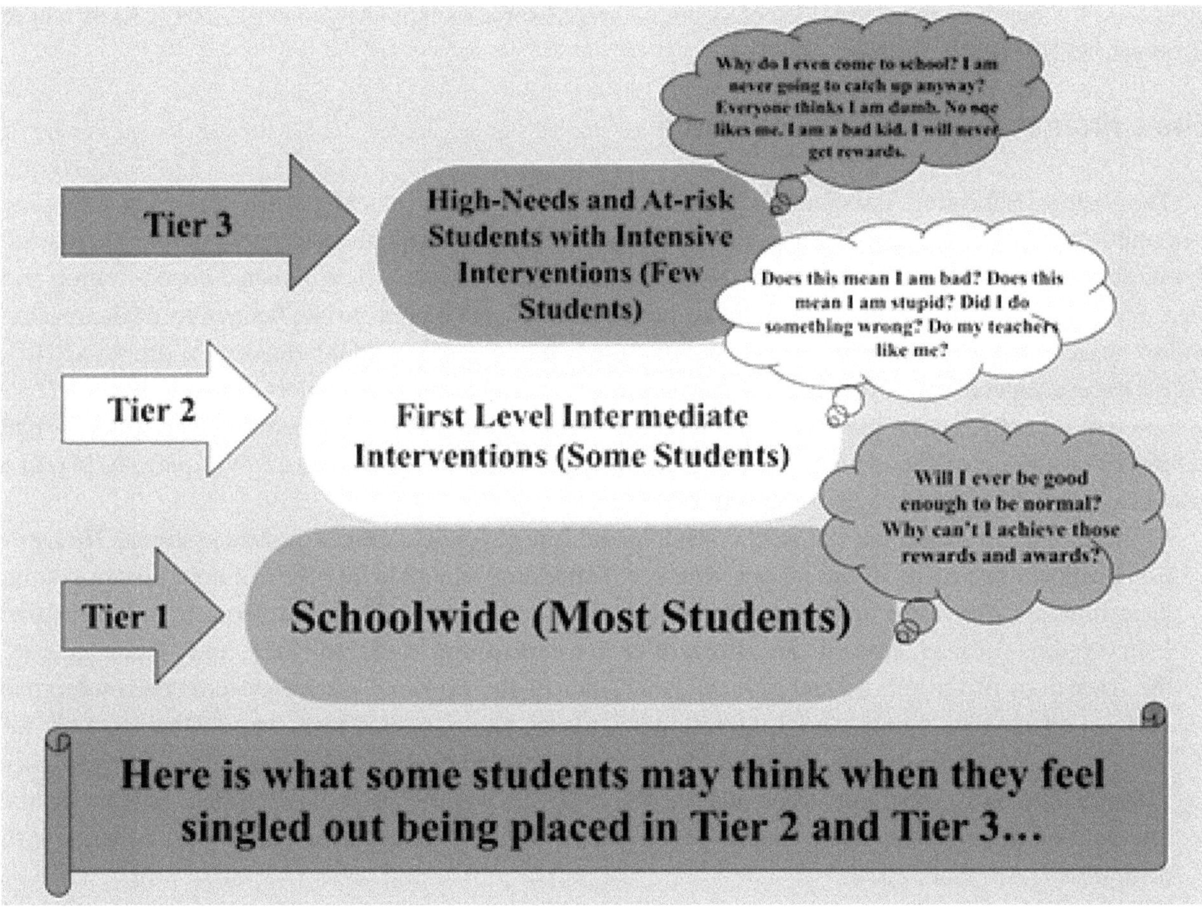

In a review of the literature on school discipline, Anyon et al. (2018) reported that the *zero-tolerance era* swept the American education system in the early 1990s as the *gun-free school zone* and the *anti-gun lobby* began rallying against guns in and around school zones. Anyon et al. (2018) define *zero-tolerance policies* in k-12 schools as the following:

Policies that rely on exclusionary discipline practices, including out-of-school suspension or expulsion, to remove students from the classroom or school as a form of punishment, usually for minor offenses like disruption, defiance, and disrespect.

These exclusionary practices can further traumatize students by disconnecting them from school and, thereby, the greater community and higher education into adulthood (Anyon et al., 2018; Kaufman & Diliberti, 2021). Students who are frequently disproportionately affected by exclusionary discipline are less likely to achieve a high school diploma, often repeat grades and fail classes, and students who have faced three or more traumatic events, in addition, are more than three times more likely to have severe attendance issues (Arnwine, 2019). These students may face a greater disposition toward the criminal justice system and toward dropping out of school before completing a k-12 education (Anyon et al., 2018; Kaufman & Diliberti, 2021; Osta & Vasquez, 2024). Racial and socioeconomic disparities demonstrate vast disproportionality in who is on the receiving end of these exclusionary disciplinary measures, further deepening the tides of systemic and historic racism (Anyon et al., 2018; Kaufman & Diliberti, 2021; Osta & Vasquez, 2024).

The Criminalization of Consequence

The National Education Association's Trauma-informed Toolkit for Educators (2017) listed the following as manifestations of trauma in students, especially those who have faced historic and systemic trauma due to marginalization and intergenerational trauma or epigenetic trauma: (a) diminished concentration and memory, (b) decreased organizational and language abilities, (c) inappropriate behavior, (d) depression and/or anxiety, (e) perfectionism, (f) self-destructive behavior, (g) suicidal behavior (Williams, 2017). These trauma antecedents often lead to manifestations in behavior that subject students to an MTSS system that monetizes good grades and good behavior and criminalizes manifestations described as bad behaviors (Anyon et al., 2018; Arnwine, 2019Kaufman & Diliberti, 2021; Osta & Vasquez, 2024). In a law review article, Arnwine (2019) reported:

> Children are 'Tunneled out" of public schools and into juvenile criminal justice systems. This section proposes that many of the schools that are 'Tunneling" students into the criminal justice system have students who suffer from untreated complex trauma and would benefit from trauma-sensitive interventions. Instead, students are isolated for not performing well, punished, and 'Tunneled out" the back door of the school and into the front door of the criminal justice system. Zero-tolerance policies criminalize minor school infractions, while on-site police officers criminalize students for behavior that should be handled inside the school. Students from inner-city communities are especially vulnerable to the "funnel out" trend and the discriminatory application of discipline. Student-police interactions disproportionately impact low-income students, students of color, and students with disabilities (Arnwine, 2019)

The Danger in Resiliency. According to the National Education Association's Trauma-informed Toolkit for Educators (2017), the most fundamental needs of students who have faced trauma, especially those who have faced historic and systemic trauma due to marginalization and intergenerational trauma or epigenetic trauma, are the following: (a) safety, (b) Caring adults / positive relationships, (c) A feeling of accomplishment and/or success, (d) Choices and options in daily tasks, like assignments, that help develop their sense of agency and control over their lives (Anyon et al., 2018; Kaufman & Diliberti, 2021; Osta & Vasquez, 2024; Williams, 2017). An educator who can fulfill these fundamental needs and provide this safety net must understand the danger of grit and resilience. Students are often taught that grit and resilience can be learned or acquired and that they have an equal opportunity to gain access to these skills. However, they do not have equitable access to attaining these skills. Students who bring trauma to school that other students have not experienced and suffered will have a more difficult time than their peers in developing the skills of grit and resilience; therefore, expressing that the skills can and should be acquired and expecting all students to learn them can itself be retraumatizing and systemically traumatizing (Anyon et al., 2018; Kaufman & Diliberti, 2021; Osta & Vasquez, 2024; Williams, 2017).

Telling a student to *pick themselves up by their bootstraps* can be further traumatizing if one student has *boots with laces long enough to tie*, another student's *laces are too short*, another is *missing one lace*, another is *missing both laces* and still yet, another *has no boots*. Many students suffering from trauma have little to no understanding of self-worth, self-image, self-identity, or self-esteem (see Figure 3) (Anyon et al., 2018; Kaufman & Diliberti, 2021; Osta & Vasquez, 2024; Williams, 2017). They need the adults in school to help empower them to build this confidence, image, and agency and then teach them the tools and vocabulary to build healthy social skills and relationships (Williams, 2017). Comas-Diaz et al. (2019) warned against educators further perpetuating the idea of white supremacy by teaching inaccurate history, neglecting to teach with content reflective of the student population, dismissing student voice or student empowerment, existing by seeing the world from a colorblind lens, failing to recognize the existence of privilege and one's axis within, among other ways to unintentionally inflict racial trauma not including intentional ways to inflict trauma (Chin, (2023); Chafouleas et al. (2016); Comas-Diaz et al., (2019); Graphenreed & Poe (2022); Cross et all., (2019). Cross et al. (2019), in a literature review of decolonization, restoration, and reconciliation, artfully concluded:

> Leadership education can be irrelevant or restorative, deculturizing or decolonizing. In Dugan's words, this is the "radical importance of now" (2018, p. 10). Indigenous leaders, scholars, researchers, and students are already moving toward a preferred future in which the Indigenous mind is freed from the fear of persecution and deculturalization. Leadership education can join in and assist or unwittingly sit back and resist.

Figure 3. Trauma-informed tier example

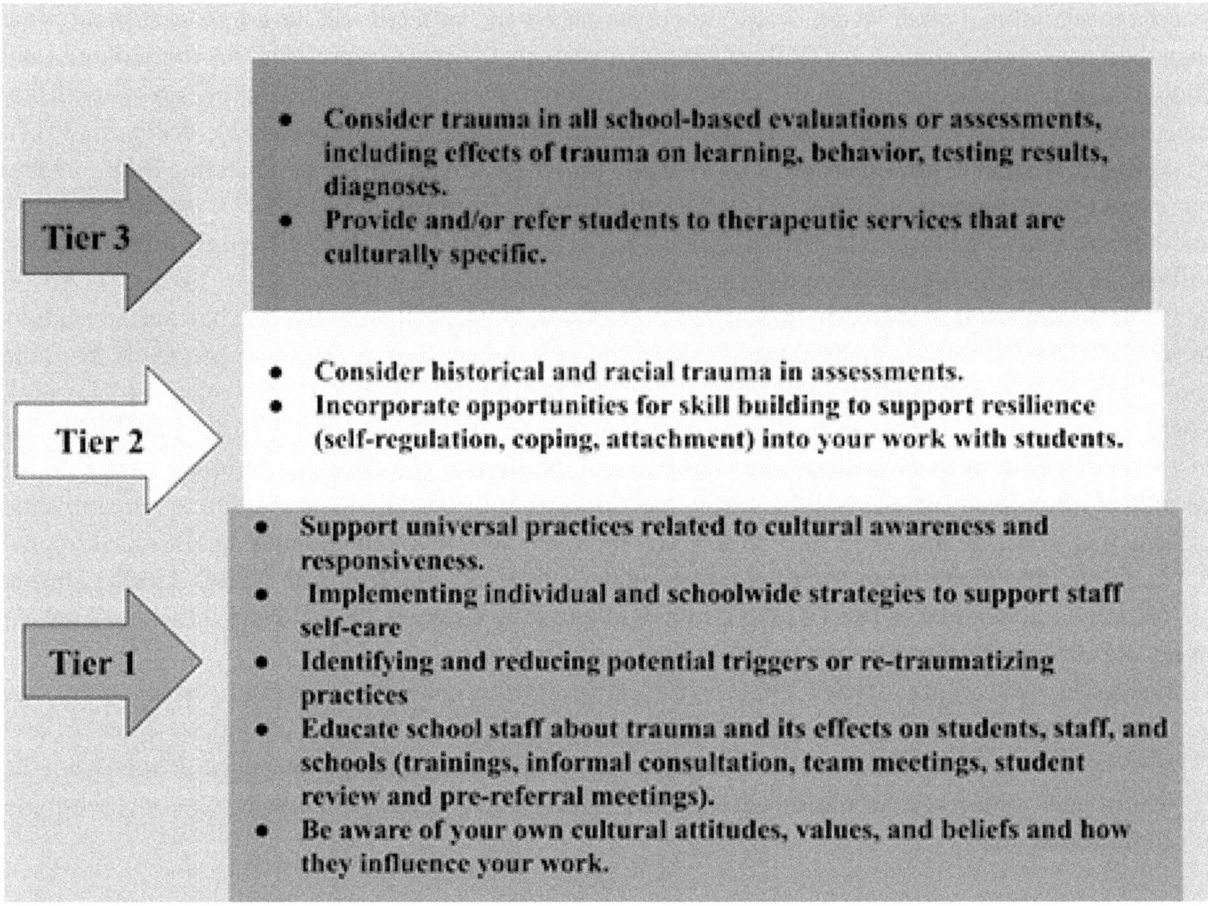

Note: This Tiered System was adapted from the National Center for Safe Supportive Learning Environments (2024). Trauma-sensitive schools. The U.S. Department of Education, Office of Safe and Supportive Schools to the American Institutes for Research. https://safesupportivelearning.ed.gov/building-trauma-sensitive-schools

UNDERSTANDING TRAUMA TRIGGERS AND MAPPING INTERVENTIONS

Trauma triggers can be subtle or dramatic (National Center on Safe and Supportive Schools, 2024). For example, an instructor may force students to make eye contact (National Center on Safe and Supportive Schools, 2024). This may be triggering to some students because of past trauma, cultural misunderstanding, or cultural insensitivity. A larger example may be a car backfiring in the parking lot, causing a student from a refugee community to have a flashback to an experience of a civil war event (National Center on Safe and Supportive Schools, 2024). Trauma triggers can also be implicit and explicit or aggressive on a macro or micro level (National Center on Safe and Supportive Schools, 2024). The perpetrator of the trigger can behave intentionally or unintentionally in the cause of the harm (National Center on Safe and Supportive Schools, 2024). Sometimes, a thing or an idea can be a trigger, but the trigger is not always a person (National Center on Safe and Supportive Schools, 2024). These are common trauma triggers listed by the National Center on Safe and Supportive Schools (2024): (a) odors, (b) chaotic environments, (c) threatening gestures, (c) loud environments, (d) physical touch, (e) confinement, (f) uncertainty about expectations, (g) change in routine, (h) situations involving authority figures and limit setting, even appropriate limits, (i) body gestures that appear threatening, (j) witnessing violence between other individuals, such as peers fighting, (k) areas of the school experienced as unsafe, such as bathrooms or less well-monitored areas, (l) emergency vehicles and police or fire personnel, (m) feelings such as anger, sadness, or fear in response to common school conflicts—getting in trouble, doing poorly on a test, arguing with another student— (Such feelings may trigger an intense reaction related to past trauma.).

Phase 1: Baseline

The baseline is how students behave on a typical day with consistent routines and no disruptions (National Center on Safe and Supportive Schools, 2024). The baseline is not the same for all students. Some students will suffer from more trauma than other students, as trauma is a continuum (Anyon et al., 2018; Kaufman & Diliberti, 2021; Osta & Vasquez, 2024; Williams, 2017). Students suffering from little to no trauma will have a more even baseline personality each day with few to no triggers (National Center on Safe and Supportive Schools, 2024). The more trauma a student experiences, the more heightened their baseline personality (National Center on Safe and Supportive Schools, 2024). Students with extremely heightened baselines will often exhibit signs of triggering and will also often exhibit signs of the flight, flight, or freeze response (National Center on Safe and Supportive Schools, 2024).

Interventions

- Be calm, clear, and consistent
- Be responsive and respectful
- Have daily routines
- Incorporate social-emotional learning and mindfulness into daily routines
- Have trauma-informed plans for each phase that students know and understand (plan and practice; be ready to act)
- Arrange the physical space to avoid and eliminate trauma triggers

Note: These interventions were adapted from Dorado et al. (2016), Funfar (2022), the Maryland State Education Association, the National Center on Safe and Supportive Schools, and The National Education Association.

Phase 2: Triggering Phase

In this phase, something or someone has triggered the student and activated the stress response (National Center on Safe and Supportive Schools, 2024). Some responses may include: (a) shorter responses, (b) tearfulness, (c) moving or pacing, (d) raised voice, (e) becoming quieter, (f) withdrawing, (g) unresponsiveness (National Center on Safe and Supportive Schools, 2024). The behavior of the student who has been triggered by someone or something will most likely seem to be an overreaction to peers and adults, but remember, the fight, flight or freeze response has been activated, and the chemical response in the brain is causing this overreaction (National Center on Safe and Supportive Schools, 2024). The role of the adult in charge is to manage the situation and their behavior and de-escalate.

Interventions

- DO NOT ARGUE OR CONFRONT
- Be calm, clear, and consistent
- Be responsive and respectful
- Validate the student's feelings
- Listen to what the student is saying
- Use encouraging statements
- Provide a space for the student to calm down.
- Avoid threatening punishment

Note: These interventions were adapted from Dorado et al. (2016), Funfar (2022), the Maryland State Education Association, the National Center on Safe and Supportive Schools, and The National Education Association.

Phase 3: Escalation Phase

Students who have escalated likely will not listen to reason because the emotional center of their brain has taken over, and rationality is diminished (National Center on Safe and Supportive Schools, 2024). Some signs of this phase are: (a) increased agitation and intense, emotionally driven, survival-based responses; (b) fight, flight, or freeze responses; (c) yelling, swearing, posturing, running away, refusing to talk, spacing out, or appearing disconnected (National Center on Safe and Supportive Schools, 2024). For the adult in this situation, de-escalation using nonverbal cues is extremely important (National Center on Safe and Supportive Schools, 2024). Students are more likely to gather information from body language and proximity than verbal language and tone (National Center on Safe and Supportive Schools, 2024).

Interventions

- DO NOT ARGUE OR CONFRONT
- Be calm, clear, and consistent
- Be responsive and respectful
- Validate the student's feelings
- Listen to what the student is saying
- Use encouraging statements
- Pay attention to your body language, gestures, and physical proximity to the student
- Maintain boundaries
- allow for a reasonable "comfort zone" to offer space
- Use grounding techniques (e.g., breathing, providing something to hold or squeeze).
- Provide choices
- Refrain from giving many directions
- Check your level of stress

- Get support as needed

Note: These interventions were adapted from Dorado et al. (2016), Funfar (2022), the Maryland State Education Association, the National Center on Safe and Supportive Schools, and The National Education Association.

Phase 4: Outburst Phase

Everything from the escalation phase applies here with an increased potential for dangerous behavior (National Center on Safe and Supportive Schools, 2024). The safety of all individuals involved and de-escalation are the goals in this face and are the role of the adult (National Center on Safe and Supportive Schools, 2024).

Interventions

- DO NOT ARGUE OR CONFRONT
- Be calm, clear, and consistent
- Be directive while maintaining a respectful tone
- Validate the student's feelings
- Listen to what the student is saying
- Use encouraging statements
- Pay attention to your body language, gestures, and physical proximity to the student
- Maintain boundaries
- allow for a reasonable "comfort zone" to offer space
- Use grounding techniques (e.g., breathing, providing something to hold or squeeze).
- Provide choices
- Set clear limits
- Refrain from giving many directions
- Set the tone that you expect the student will regain control
- Check your level of stress
- Get support as needed

Note: These interventions were adapted from Dorado et al. (2016), Funfar (2022), the Maryland State Education Association, the National Center on Safe and Supportive Schools, and The National Education Association.

Phase 5: Recovery Phase

The student returns to baseline, and restorative practices repair the relationship between the adult and the student triggered by trauma and the student and the school or classroom community (National Center on Safe and Supportive Schools, 2024). The student needs to believe they are and identify as a valued member of the school community (National Center on Safe and Supportive Schools, 2024).

Interventions

- Debriefing with colleagues can help you reduce your stress
- Re-establish a connection with the student
- Clarify the chain of events
- Identify triggers
- Develop a plan (identify possible triggers, early warning signs, and helpful strategies)
- Teach new coping skills
- Help the student practice new behaviors

Note: These interventions were adapted from Dorado et al. (2016), Funfar (2022), the Maryland State Education Association, the National Center on Safe and Supportive Schools, and The National Education Association.

APPLYING THE CORE PRINCIPLES OF TRAUMA-INFORMED TEACHING AND EDUCATION

Any trauma-informed Multitiered System of Support in any k-12 school district aims to create a safe and inclusive environment for all students to equitably access all daily opportunities (National Center on Safe and Supportive Schools, 2024). To do that, all staff must be trained in, committed to, and practice efficacy trauma-informed care, social-emotional learning, cultural competence, and antiracism (Crosby, (2015); Crosby et al., (2020); Cours, (2024); Christopher, (2024). A common misnomer regarding trauma and social-emotional learning in the k-12 setting is that only certain students or certain classroom environments require the training and tools (Arnwine, 2019; Dorado et al., 2016; Gomez, 2021; McAdoo et al., 2023). The chronic stress accompanying the chronic trauma impacting school districts and buildings negatively affects everyone in the community, which means all stakeholders (Arnwine, 2019; Dorado et al., 2016; Gomez, 2021; McAdoo et al., 2023). Building genuine relationships of respect between leadership and staff, staff and students, students and leadership, and the community stakeholders and the district are immensely important to the regulation of daily life in every school building (Anyon et al., 2018; Kaufman & Diliberti, 2021; Osta & Vasquez, 2024). Knowing and effectively integrating and implementing the Core Principles of Trauma-informed Care in Education (see Table 1) is the main ingredient of the MTSS of the future (Williams, 2017).

Table 1. The core principles of trauma-informed education

Believe that healing happens in relationships
Ensure emotional and physical safety
View students holistically
Support choice and empowerment
Cultural competence
Collaboration
Mindfulness and Self-control—Not Classroom Management
Social-emotional Learning
Restorative Justice
Antiracism

Note: These Core Principles were adapted from Crosby (2015), Crosby et al. (2020), Cours (2024), Christopher (2024), Dorado et al. (2016), Funfar (2022), Gomez (2021), McAdoo et al., (2023), the Maryland State Education Association, the National Center on Safe and Supportive Schools, and The National Education Association.

Classroom management is not the control of student behavior or misbehavior; this is the ability of the teacher to be consistent, clear, and manage expectations (Dorado et al., 2016; Gomez, 2021; McAdoo et al., 2023). One can only control one's behavior (Dorado et al., 2016; Gomez, 2021; McAdoo et al., 2023). Do not mistake classroom management for the management of people (Dorado et al., 2016; Gomez, 2021; McAdoo et al., 2023). Building genuine relationships and community in the school and the classroom will help to secure emotional regulation throughout the day (Anyon et al., 2018; Kaufman & Diliberti, 2021; Osta & Vasquez, 2024). Replace classroom management with the trauma-informed teaching principles of building relationships, *the people-centered piece*, and ensuring emotional and physical safety, *the environment-centered piece* (Williams, 2017). Some examples of *Trauma-informed Strategies and Actions* can be found below in *Table 2*. According to the National Center on Safe and Supportive Schools:

> Students who have experienced trauma have a primary need to feel safe. When someone is threatened, or perceives a threat, they will have a fight, flight, or freeze response. Children who have experienced trauma may perceive threats when others do not. This can trigger them to have the same fight, flight or freeze response in situations that are not dangerous, but because of trauma, the child perceives it as such. Creating a safe environment and reassuring students that they are out of harm's way is essential to helping them learn both academic and social and emotional skills (National Center on Safe and Supportive Schools, 2024).

Table 2. Trauma-informed strategies and actions

Strategies	Actions	Students Who May Need Intervention
Help students identify an area where they feel successful	Create a display of things students do well (be sure every single student can achieve a space)	Keep an eye out for any student who has a difficult time identifying one thing they do well. This could be a signal that this student needs more positive and caring relationships with adults and peers.
Make sure that each student in your class has a strong relationships	Create a safe space in your school or classroom that students can visit when they need to calm down and process their emotions.	Students who are in need of this space often or have trouble building relationships may be in need of team intervention. Refer your student to the school counselor for support. Healing from a traumatic experience is a process.
Help students recognize how their emotions affect their bodies and give students tools to change their state of mind	The 5-4-3-2-1 coping technique is often used by therapists to help traumatized individuals connect to the present moment through their senses in times of acute stress.	
Create a safe classroom environment		

Note: These key strategies and correct actions were adapted from Crosby (2015), Crosby et al. (2020), Cours (2024), Christopher (2024), Dorado et al. (2016), Funfar (2022), Gomez (2021), McAdoo et al., (2023), the Maryland State Education Association, the National Center on Safe and Supportive Schools, and The National Education Association.

RECOMMENDATION FOR THE HOLISTIC MODEL OF THE FUTURE

Kaufman and Diliberti (2021), in conjunction with the Rand Corporation and Insights from the American Educator Panels (2021), performed a self-reported survey of fully remote teachers during the COVID-19 pandemic. Kaufman & Diliberti (2021) reported, "Students who needed academic support most might not have gotten It in the 2020–2021 school year." One key recommendation based on the findings of the survey was:

> When making decisions about how to spend federal funds, district and school leaders should rely on multiple data points collected now and in the next year, including those related to absenteeism, performance on formative assessments, and students' potential nonacademic needs (p. 16).

Noting this finding, since many students living with the most trauma are those relying on the most federal and state funding, lawmakers, elected school board officials, superintendents and their cabinet members, community stakeholders, and educational leaders who have any influence over school funding allocation and daily operations must be willing to advocate for holistic Multitiered Systems of Support removing the idea of economized incentives for good grades, good behavior, and good attendance, but rather created from the lens of Trauma-informed care incorporating cultural competence, antiracism, Restorative Justice, Social-emotional Learning, mental health supports, truth and racial healing, and emphasizing safety, empowerment, and relationship building above all (Crosby, (2015); Crosby et al., (2020); Cours, (2024); Christopher, (2024).

Crosby (2015) referred to the school as an ecology of students. If this is true, then it is the responsibility of those charged with the decisions of this ecology to understand the evolution of the k-12 education system and adapt their leadership and decision-making to fit this new and evolving ecosystem. Perhaps it is not a failure of our schools, educators, and students today but the failure of our policy, systems, and institutions to evolve and adapt to our society and students (Crosby, (2015); Crosby et al., (2020); Cours, (2024); Christopher, (2024). The first commitment the American k-12 community must make is to remove the tiered system of support from the vernacular and remove the monetization of good grades, good behavior, and good attendance. The proposal is a multilayered system of support whereby all students have an equitable chance to achieve all opportunities within the district (see Figure 4).

Figure 4. Multilayered system of support

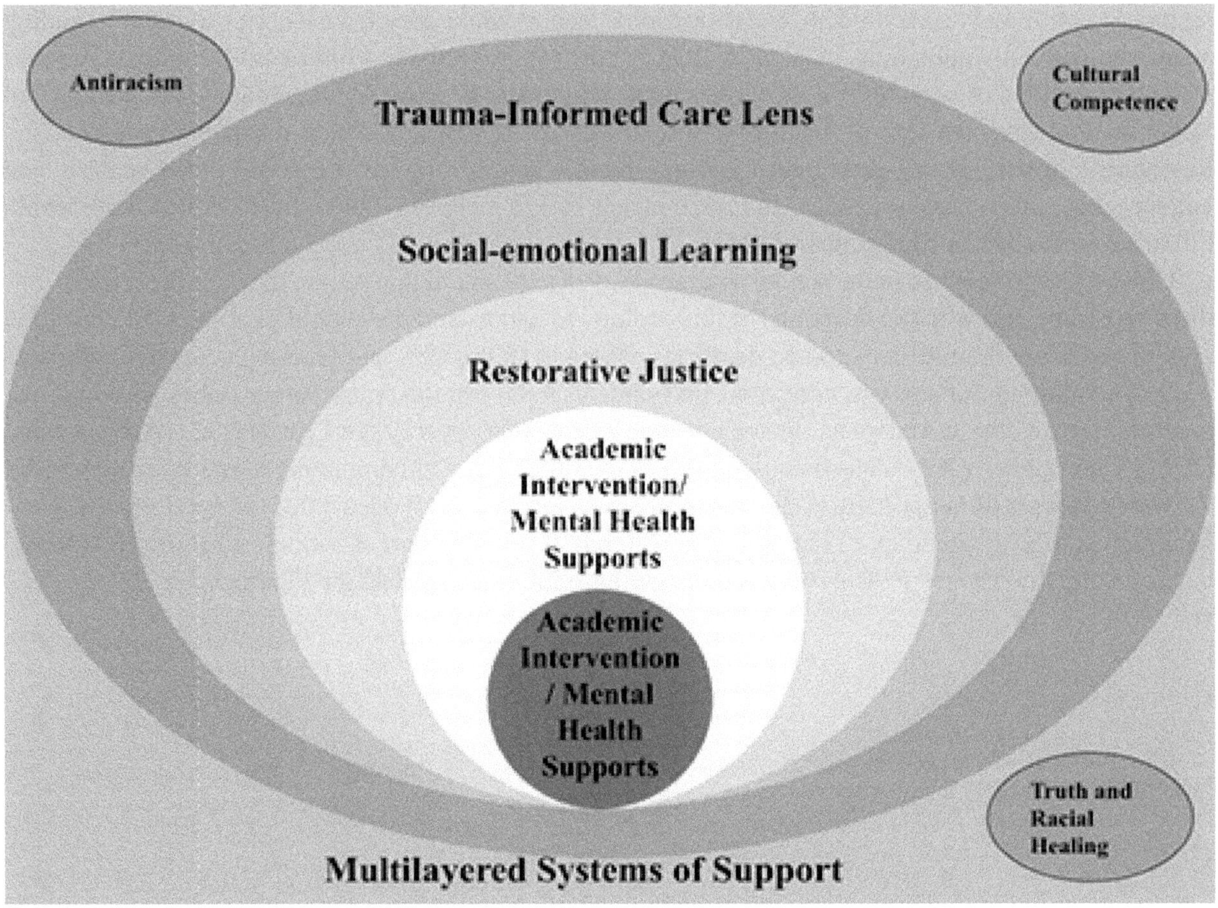

Note: This model was adapted from Crosby (2015), Crosby et al. (2020), Cours (2024), Christopher (2024), Dorado et al. (2016), Funfar (2022), Gomez (2021), McAdoo et al., (2023), the Maryland State Education Association, the National Center on Safe and Supportive Schools, and The National Education Association.

People are holistic, complex beings, not linear; therefore, the traditional tiered intervention system is inappropriate for the k-12 school system students. Integrating trauma-informed teaching practices and antiracist truth and racial healing curriculum into every school in the k-12 school system will help the American school system advance into a space where equitable education for all students is possible (Avery et al., 2020). Adding courses to the k-12 curriculum in every school, such as social-emotional learning through dance, character building and development, leadership, literature of BIPOC writers, history of the oppressed, etc., the institution begins to transform into a holistic education system supporting the learning and development of the whole student (Avery et al., 2020; Campbell, 2019). A true Multilayered System of Support (Avery et al., 2020; Campbell, 2019; Crosby, (2015); Crosby et al., (2020); Cours, (2024); Christopher, (2024).

REFERENCES

American Psychological Association. (2022). *APA Dictionary of Psychology*. American Psychological Association.

Anyon, Y., Atteberry-Ash, B., Yang, J., Pauline, M., Wiley, K., Cash, D., Downing, B., Greer, E., & Pisciotta, L. (2018). “It’s all about the relationships”: Educators’ rationales and strategies for building connections with students to prevent exclusionary school discipline outcomes. *Children & Schools*, *40*(4), 221–230. DOI: 10.1093/cs/cdy017

Arnwine, M.Jr. (2019). Trauma and learning: Creating a culture of educational access for inner-city communities. *University of San Francisco Law Review. University of San Francisco. School of Law*, *53*(1), 77–116.

Avery, J. C., Morris, H., Galvin, E., Misso, M., Savaglio, M., & Skouteris, H. (2021). Systematic review of schoolwide trauma-informed approaches. *Journal of Child & Adolescent Trauma*, *14*(3), 381–397. DOI: 10.1007/s40653-020-00321-1 PMID: 34471456

Beard, K. S., Vakil, J. B., Chao, T., & Hilty, C. D. (2023). Time for Change: Understanding Teacher Social-Emotional Learning Supports for Anti-Racism and Student Well-Being During COVID-19, and Beyond. *Education and Urban Society*, *55*(7), 825–843. DOI: 10.1177/00131245211062527

Ben-Asher, N. (2020). Trauma-Centered social justice. *Tulane Law Review*, *95*(1), 95–142.

Broderick, M., & Lyn, A. E. (2022). Integrating social-emotional learning into the formative development of educator dispositions. In von Hohenberg, S. C. (Ed.), *Dispositional development and assessment in teacher preparation programs*. IGI Global. DOI: 10.4018/978-1-6684-4089-6.ch004

Campbell, B. (2019). Past, present, future: A program development project exploring post-traumatic slave syndrome (PTSS) using experiential education and dance/movement therapy-informed approaches. *American Journal of Dance Therapy*, *41*(2), 214–233. DOI: 10.1007/s10465-019-09320-8

CASEL. (2023). Fundamentals of SEL. https://casel.org/fundamentals-of-sel/

CDC. (2024). About Adverse Childhood Experiences (ACEs). Centers for Disease Control and Prevention. https://www.cdc.gov/aces/about/index.html

Chafouleas, S. M., Johnson, A. H., Overstree, S., & Santos, N. M. (2016). Toward a blueprint for trauma-informed service delivery in schools. *School Mental Health*, *8*(1), 144–162. DOI: 10.1007/s12310-015-9166-8

Chin, C. (2023). Facilitating the Journey From Color-Blind to Antiracist Art Teacher. *Art Education*, *76*(6), 18–23. DOI: 10.1080/00043125.2023.2234793

Christopher, G. (2024). Truth, racial healing, and transformation: Implementation guidebook. Truth, Racial Healing, and Transformation: The Kellog Foundation (Battle Creek, MI). https://wkkf.issuelab.org/resource/truth-racial-healing-transformation-implementation-guidebook.html

Comas-Díaz, L., Hall, G. N., & Neville, H. A. (2019). Racial trauma: Theory, research, and healing: Introduction to the special issue. *The American Psychologist*, *74*(1), 1–5. DOI: 10.1037/amp0000442 PMID: 30652895

Conner, C. J. (2023). Whitewashing U.S. History: The Marginalization of Latinxs in the Georgia Standards of Excellence. *Journal of Latinos and Education*, *22*(3), 1299–1315. DOI: 10.1080/15348431.2021.1951735

Cours, S. (2024). Aces and trauma: Healing with the use of social-emotional learning. *Better Kids*. Retrieved from https://betterkids.education/blog

Crosby, S. D. (2015). An ecological perspective on emerging trauma-informed teaching practices. *Children & Schools*, *37*(4), 223–230. DOI: 10.1093/cs/cdv027

Crosby, S. D., Howell, P. B., & Thomas, S. (2020). Teaching through Collective Trauma in the Era of COVID-19. *Trauma-informed Practices for Middle Level Learners.*, *6*, 7.

Cross, T. L., Pewewardy, C., & Smith, A. T. (2019). Restorative education, reconciliation, and healing: Indigenous perspectives on decolonizing leadership education. *New Directions for Student Leadership*, *163*(163), 101–115. https://pubmed.ncb. DOI: 10.1002/yd.20350 PMID: 31385660

Dorado, J. S., Martinez, M., McArthur, L. E. & Leibovitz, T. (2016). Healthy environments and response to trauma in schools (HEARTS): A whole-school, multi-level, prevention and intervention program for creating trauma-informed, safe and supportive schools. *School Mental Health: A Multidisciplinary Research and Practice Journal,* 8(1),163-176.

Funfar, M. G. (2022). Out of trauma comes strength: The trauma-informed positive education (TIPE) model. In Bernadowski, C. (Ed.), *Strategies and Methods for Implementing Trauma-Informed Pedagogy* (pp. 208–224). IGI Global., DOI: 10.4018/978-1-7998-7473-7.ch011

Gomez, J. M. (2021). Cultural betrayal as a dimension of traumatic harm: Violence and PTSS among ethnic minority emerging adults. *Journal of Child & Adolescent Trauma*, *14*(3), 347–356. DOI: 10.1007/s40653-020-00314-0 PMID: 34471453

Graphenreed, T., & Poe, M. (2022). Antiracist Genre Systems: Creating Non-Violent Writing Classroom Spaces. *Composition Studies*, *50*(2), 53–76.

Jean-Pierre, J., & Parris-Drummond, S. (2018). Alternative school discipline principles and interventions: An overview of the literature. *McGill Journal of Education*, *53*(3), 414–433. DOI: 10.7202/1058410ar

Kaufman, J. H., & Diliberti, M. K. (2021). *Divergent and Inequitable Teaching and Learning Pathways during (and Perhaps Beyond) the Pandemic: Key Findings from the American Educator Panels Spring 2021 COVID-19 Surveys. Data Note: Insights from the American Educator Panels. Research Report. RR-A168-6*. RAND Corporation.

Kim, R. M., & Venet, A. S. (2023). Unsnarling PBIS and trauma-informed education. *Urban Education*. Advance online publication. DOI: 10.1177/00420859231175670

McAdoo, G., Williams, K., & Howard, T. C. (2023). Racially just, trauma-informed care for black students. *Urban Education*. Advance online publication. DOI: 10.1177/00420859231175668

National Center for Safe Supportive Learning Environments. (2024). Trauma-sensitive schools training package: 1. Applying the core principles worksheet. *The U.S. Department of Education, Office of Safe and Supportive Schools to the American Institutes for Research.*https://safesupportivelearning.ed.gov/building-trauma-sensitive-schools

Osta, K., & Vasquez, H. (2024). Implicit bias and structural racialization. National Equity Project. https://www.nationalequityproject.org/frameworks/implicit-bias-structural-racialization

Southwest, R. E. L. (n.d.). Handout: Alternatives to exclusionary discipline. *U.S. Department of Education's Institute of Education Sciences (IES).*https://ies.ed.gov/ncee/ rel/regions/southwest/pdf/sw_handout_110322_4.pdf

Williams, J. (2017). *Trauma toolkit*. Maryland State Education Association.

Wilson, K., & Pressley, J. (2024). Glossary of terms: Systemic Trauma. Complex Trauma Resources. *The Foundation Trust*. https://www.complextrauma.org/glossary/ systemic-trauma/

ADDITIONAL READING

Biggers, S. (2016, February). *TedTalk: An artist's unflinching look at racial violence* [Video]. YouTube. https://youtu.be/MO0L_LY2hRA

Brown, B. (2018). *Dare to lead: Brave work, tough conversations, whole hearts*. Random House.

Crnobori, M. (2019, January 10). *Why all schools should be trauma-informed* [Video]. TEDxVanderbiltUniversity.

Crenshaw, K. (2016, October). *The urgency of intersectionality.* [TEDWomen 2016]. TedTalk. https://www.ted.com/talks/kimberle_crenshaw_the_urgency_of_intersectionality?subtitle=en&trigger=30s

Dixon, T.M., & Garrison, V. (2017, April). The trauma of systematic racism is killing Black women. A first step toward change. [TED2017]. TedTalk.

Edutopia. (N/A*). Students learn the skill of conflict resolution in a multi-age class* [Video]. YouTube.

Fairfax County Public Schools. (N/A). *Restorative justice at Mountain View Alternative High School* [Video]. YouTube.

Jefferies. (2020, October 28). *Why we must confront the painful parts of US history* [Video]. TED.

Kendi, I. (2019). *How to be an antiracist*. Bodley Head.

Teachers' Democracy Project. (2017, November). *Restoring schools* [Video]. YouTube.

KEY TERMS AND DEFINITIONS

Adverse Childhood Experiences (ACEs): Adverse Childhood Experiences (ACEs) are traumatic events that occur in children and young adults from birth to age 17 (CDC, 2024). The United States Center for Disease Control (2024) lists the following examples as ACEs: (a) experiencing violence, abuse, or neglect; (b) witnessing violence in the home or community; (c) having a family member attempt or die by suicide. The United States Center for Disease Control (2024) lists growing up in a household with the following examples as ACEs: (a) substance use disorder; (b) mental health issues; (c) instability and parental separation; (d) instability due to the criminal justice system.

Antiracist Education: Antiracist Education offers a voice to all students through a set of methods to improve our teaching in ways that acknowledge interactions and classroom spaces are shaped by power and privilege (Gomez, J. M., 2021; Graphenreed, T., & Poe, M., 2022). Antiracist Educators focus on providing safety, choice, sharing, collaboration, trust, clarity, consistency, clear boundaries, validation, and empowerment (Gomez, J. M., 2021; Graphenreed, T., & Poe, M., 2022).

Criminalization of School Discipline: Criminalization of School Discipline includes exclusionary and punitive disciplinary measures in schools, such as zero-tolerance policies, physical searches, locks, fences, cameras, closed campuses, suspensions, and expulsions (Jean-Pierre, J., & Parris-Drummond, S., 2018). Punitive measures disproportionately affect marginalized students, thereby reducing their opportunities (Jean-Pierre, J., & Parris-Drummond, S., 2018).

Cultural Competence: Cultural Competence is the ability to collaborate with diverse populations through recognition of the diversity both between and within cultures (APA, 2022). Culturally competent individuals have a capacity for self-assessment and a willingness to adapt, which has become a central concept in education (APA, 2022).

Exclusionary Discipline: Exclusionary Discipline excludes a student from the least restrictive or typical learning environment and opportunity (REL Southwest, n.d.). This type of discipline is negative, with little evidence of its effectiveness (REL Southwest, n.d.).

Historical Trauma/Intergenerational Trauma: Historical Trauma/Intergenerational Trauma is an epigenetic form of trauma, which means the trauma is not only shared on a societal level but also on a genetic level from generation to generation (APA, 2022). The American Psychological Association (2022) listed the following in the cited definition: Research on intergenerational trauma concentrated initially on the children, grandchildren, and great-grandchildren of survivors of the Holocaust and Japanese American internment camps, but it has now broadened to include the impact of slavery and structural racism on Black people, as well as the historical trauma experienced by American Indian communities, the families of Vietnam War veterans, and others. Also called historical trauma; multigenerational trauma; secondary traumatization (APA, 2022).

Multitiered Systems of Support (MTSS): Multitiered Systems of Support (MTSS) are generally universally three tiers. These tiers have a behavioral and academic intervention component. Tier 1 is where most students will fall and will be school-wide interventions and supports. Tier 2 will be intermediate intervention and support and will have a smaller set of students. Tier 3 will have an intensive support program and a small group of students (Dorado, J. S., Martinez, M., McArthur, L. E. & Leibovitz, T., 2016). A Positive Behavior Intervention Support Program (PBIS) often accompanies these tiered systems.

Positive Behavior Intervention Support (PBIS): Positive Behavior Intervention Support (PBIS) is a framework for managing student behavior described as part of a Multi-Tiered System of Support (Kim, R. M., & Venet, A. S., 2023). Some state laws even require the use of the framework, and some federal funds support the use (Kim, R. M., & Venet, A. S., 2023).

Privilege: Privilege is granted to the dominant social identity group for no other reason than membership in this group (APA, 2022). Privilege includes societal advantages and immunities (APA, 2022).

Resiliency: Resiliency is adapting to life experiences and external and internal demands (APA, 2022). The American Psychological Association lists several factors that greatly impact the way resiliency can play a role in the life of an individual, chief among them is access to privilege, (a) how individuals view and engage with the world, (b) the availability and quality of social resources, and (c) specific coping strategies (APA, 2022).

Restorative Justice: Restorative Justice in this context is an alternative to exclusionary discipline that emphasizes repairing the harm done to victims and building community and relationships (APA, 2022).

Systemic Trauma/Complex Trauma: Systemic Trauma/Complex Trauma are the policies, procedures, practices, etc., implemented by institutions that cause harm to individuals or specific groups of people (Wilson, K. & Pressley, J., 2024). These policies, procedures, practices, etc., perpetuate inequality, injustice, marginalization, exploitation, and oppression through denial of opportunities, exclusionary tactics, preferential advancement, disenfranchisement, forced displacement, isolation, or separation from family, resources, or other supports (Wilson, K. & Pressley, J., 2024).

Social-Emotional Learning (SEL): In this context, Social-emotional Learning (SEL) is the dedication to teaching students the skills and tools necessary to build healthy and appropriate relationships with peers, staff, family members, mentors, and other community stakeholders (CASEL, 2023).

The Opportunity Gap: The Opportunity Gap is created when students lacking privilege lack equal access to resources and learning opportunities (Jean-Pierre, J., & Parris-Drummond, S., 2018). Punitive measures disproportionately affect marginalized students, reducing their opportunities (Jean-Pierre, J., & Parris-Drummond, S., 2018).

Trauma: Trauma in this context is any disturbing experience causing negative consequences for a k-12 student or staff's daily functioning (APA, 2022).

Traumatic Events: Traumatic events will change an individual's perspective of the world, causing feelings of unpredictability (APA, 2022).

Trauma-Informed Care in Education: Trauma-informed Care in Education is where adults are educated and trained to recognize and respond to trauma as well as understand and know their trauma and trauma triggers (Williams, J., 2017). The adult can then respond with a trauma-informed approach in a school culture that supports the approach closely associated *with Trauma-informed Teaching Practices* (Williams, J., 2017). Those practices include (a) creating a safe classroom environment, (b) incorporating consistent routines and rituals, (c) taking a zero-tolerance stance on bullying, (d) helping students identify an area of competence, (e) helping students identify an area where they feel successful, (f) supporting positive relationship development with students (Williams, J., 2017).

Trauma Triggers: A Trauma Trigger in this context is an antecedent to a reaction causing an escalation in behaviors, disobedience, disruption, etc. (APA, 2022).

Truth and Racial Healing: Truth and Racial Healing is the dismantling of the privileges of the governmental institutions in the United States, including the k-12 educational system (Christopher, G., 2024). In the *Truth, Racial Healing, and Implementation Guidebook* from the Kellog Foundation, Christopher (2024) defined this process as: Dismantle[ing] the hierarchy of human value—the widespread, centuries-old belief that some people and groups of people are innately more valuable than others and, therefore, more deserving of the rights and benefits afforded by a democracy. Creating the conditions for equitable opportunity means cultivating a deeper capacity to see ourselves in one another while working to transform the structural and systematic manifestations of this devastating belief.

White-Washing Curriculum: White-washing Curriculum is the exclusion or alienation of marginalized students in the context of the daily school curriculum (Conner, 2023). This can also include learning as an oppressive experience when students *continually do not see themselves or see themselves depicted as depicted as alternatively lazy, incompetent, or ungrateful* (Conner, 2023).

Chapter 2
Culturally Responsive Trauma-Informed Training for Educators and School Counselors

Jennifer M. Foster
https://orcid.org/0000-0003-1574-7863
Western Michigan University, USA

Jennifer A. Meador
https://orcid.org/0009-0004-4458-5626
Aquinas College, USA

Aneesh Kumar
https://orcid.org/0000-0003-1081-7201
Christ University, India

ABSTRACT

Educational systems must become trauma-informed, anti-racist, and multi-tiered systems of support for all students, which requires comprehensive training for educators and school counselors. This chapter begins with an introduction to the history of trauma-informed approaches. Second, the chapter discusses children who have experienced trauma and the critical need for trauma-informed training in schools. Third, an anti-racist framework for culturally responsive approaches is provided. Fourth, key components of trauma-informed training are discussed, specifically building relationships and establishing safety. Fifth, research-based recommendations for successful training of educators and school counselors are provided. Sixth, the wellness needs of school staff to minimize occupational burnout and combat indirect trauma, which includes vicarious trauma, secondary traumatic stress and compassion fatigue are discussed. Finally, the importance of increased support from administration and community partners for the implementation of trauma-informed practices is emphasized.

DOI: 10.4018/979-8-3693-9020-7.ch002

INTRODUCTION

Culturally sound trauma-informed (TI) approaches are critically needed as children continue to experience high levels of adversity (Thomas et al., 2019). By definition, TI practices apply knowledge about trauma and its effects on children to foster school environments that proactively respond to students' needs (Venet, 2021). Some researchers have suggested the broader term adversity-informed teaching to include students who do not meet the clinical definition of trauma but have experienced adversities (e.g., deportation or migration, housing instability, community violence, loss of a parent due to death, foster care placement, discrimination due to race, sexual orientation, place of birth, disability or religion; Compton et al., 2023). Trauma and adversity affect numerous school-aged children, yet few educators and school counselors have received comprehensive culturally responsive TI training (Honsinger & Brown, 2019). The field of education is known for a continual shift to the next new thing, and some may consider TI practices a passing trend. Yet, the extensive research-based positive outcomes suggest that TI approaches may withstand the test of time. For example, studies on TI interventions have indicated improved academic outcomes, behavior, attendance, graduation rates, and lowered trauma symptomology for students (Baker et al., 2018; Brunzell et al., 2016; Cafaro et al., 2023; Crosby et al., 2016; Day et al., 2017; Herrenkohl et al., 2019; Ijadi-Maghsoodi et al., 2017; Plumb et al., 2016; Roseby & Gascoigne, 2021). Additionally, students are more likely to be engaged in a TI learning environment (Alvarez et al., 2022).

While research with students is widespread, fewer studies have focused on educators' experiences with and uses of TI practices. In a meta-analysis, the few studies that included educators noted increased TI knowledge following training (Cafaro et al., 2023). Only two known qualitative studies have examined perceptions of training. The first was a phenomenological study that explored Australian educators' lived experiences during a year of exposure to TI literature (Brunzell et al., 2021). The educators reported perceived personal benefits to their wellness, relationships, and regulation skills. A second study used case methodology and held interviews and focus groups with educators in the United States during and after a yearlong TI training (Foster et al., under review). The findings included a meta-theme, the centrality of the educator-student relationship, and four other themes: the importance of safety, educator changes, resistance, and thriving. The study highlighted the importance of training and the challenges for educators during the training process.

In addition to limited studies on TI training for educators, scant research exists on school counselors' experiences with TI practices (Grimes et al., 2023; Howard et al., 2022). While they are expected to be TI, their roles and responsibilities are new and undefined (Howard et al., 2022). Additionally, they require up-to-date knowledge, such as the neurobiology of trauma and its effect on the developing brain (Howard et al., 2022). Despite the evidence-based benefits of TI practices for students and school staff, TI training is rarely required for educators or school counselors before entering the field (Brown et al., 2022; Honsinger & Brown, 2019). Moreover, those working in schools often have had scant exposure to TI practices. A community needs analysis revealed that only 54% of school staff had any prior in-service training on trauma, and yet staff voiced a desire for access to comprehensive training (Aragón et al., 2024). Therefore, for schools to be TI, lack of training must be recognized as a barrier for educators and school counselors who are key stakeholders (Brown et al., 2022; Honsinger & Brown, 2019; Van Asselt et al., 2016).

Educational systems must become TI, anti-racist, and multi-tiered systems of support for all students, which requires staff training followed by implementation and evaluation. This chapter begins with a discussion of the historical background of TI approaches. Second, the chapter discusses children who have experienced trauma and the critical need for training in schools. Third, an anti-racist framework for culturally responsive TI approaches is provided. Fourth, key components of TI training are discussed, specifically the importance of building relationships and establishing safety to facilitate learning and prevent re-traumatization. Fifth, research-based recommendations for successfully training pre-service and in-service educators and school counselors are provided. Sixth, the wellness needs of school staff to minimize occupational burnout and combat indirect trauma, which includes vicarious trauma, secondary traumatic stress, and compassion fatigue, are discussed. Finally, the importance of increased support from administration and community partners for implementing TI practices school and community-wide is emphasized.

HISTORY OF TRAUMA-INFORMED APPROACHES

While trauma has been documented throughout all of human history, the development of trauma-informed work is fairly recent. Research and treatment, predominately with combat survivors, informed the first diagnosis of post-traumatic stress disorder (PTSD) that was published in the Diagnostic and Statistical Manual of Mental Disorders (DSM-1) in 1952. PTSD captured what physicians observed as survivors' stress reactions to disaster or war. Despite increasing evidence to support the diagnosis, PTSD was not included in DSM-II and was replaced with Adjustment Reaction to Adult Life. In 1980, the DSM-III returned the diagnosis of PTSD, which stemmed from extensive research on Vietnam veterans, Holocaust survivors, sexual abuse/assault survivors, and others.

In the decades to follow, research on survivors found that the experience of trauma, especially multiple traumas (polyvictimization), alters the brain and nervous system and may result in coping strategies that are maladaptive (e.g., substance use, anger, avoidance, dangerous behaviors, social withdrawal, emotional numbing, and overworking; National Center for PTSD, 2025). In 1997, the groundbreaking Adverse Childhood Experiences (ACE) study brought global attention to trauma and polyvictimization through a national sample of 17,000 adults who were asked 10 yes/no questions about common types of adversity (Felitti et al., 1998). After two years of data collection using the ACE survey, physical exams, and health data, the researchers reported a strong correlation between trauma in childhood and an increased risk of poor health, including the potential of early death in adulthood. The findings indicated that adversity in childhood is common and corresponds with a host of long-term negative outcomes, especially for those with four or more types of adversity.

In 2001, researchers, clinicians, educators, and community stakeholders started to focus on trauma-informed practices in medicine and education with the development of the Donald J. Cohen National Child Traumatic Stress Initiative and the National Child Traumatic Stress Network. These initiatives have helped practitioners learn about the effects of trauma, particularly on child development. This information helped pediatricians, educators, and others who provide direct services to children and families shift from solely focusing on children's poor health, behaviors, and academics to a wider acknowledgment of contextual factors such as poverty and trauma, crises, and disasters on children's wellbeing.

CHILDREN'S EXPERIENCES OF TRAUMA THE IMPACT ON SCHOOLS

Schools are critical in helping children thrive after adversity (Foster & Kumar, 2022; Meador & Foster, 2025). This requires that educators and school counselors have a comprehensive understanding of trauma. While there have been significant advances in neurobiology and a growing body of trauma-related research, there continues to be a lack of agreement on the definition of trauma. One of the most frequently cited definitions is from SAMHSA (2014) and refers to trauma as:

> An event, series of events, or set of circumstances that is experienced by an individual as physically or emotionally harmful or life-threatening and that has lasting adverse effects on the individual's functioning and mental, physical, social, emotional, or spiritual well-being (p. 7)

This chapter used a broader, nonclinical definition: "Trauma is in the eye of the beholder. Each individual assigns meaning to their own experiences" (Clark, 2024, p. 21). With this definition, trauma can be individual, familial, systemic, generational, and/or historical (e.g., European and American enslavement of Africans, genocide and colonization of Indigenous peoples in the United States, the Nazi mass murders of ethnic Jews, and others during the Holocaust). While trauma and other adversities are experienced by individuals of all races, ethnicities, genders, and socioeconomic statuses, those with identities that have been historically marginalized and oppressed are more likely to experience multiple adversities (e.g., BIPOC, LGBTQIA+, women).

In the past year, up to 1 billion youth from across the globe have been abused or neglected (Hillis et al., 2016). Thus, schools regularly engage with children who have experienced trauma and other forms of adversity. Most children experience abuse by a known perpetrator, which is referred to as complex trauma. Their experience may also be a betrayal trauma if it was perpetrated by someone that they depended on for survival, such as a primary caregiver (Freyd, 1996). Complex and betrayal traumas such as sexual abuse have an increased risk of future victimization, and the experience of multiple traumas before age 18 has been referred to as polyvictimization (Wolfe, 2018).

ACE research on children reported that physical abuse was most common (28%), followed by familial substance abuse (27%), emotional neglect (25%), parental separation/divorce (24%), sexual abuse (21%), having a family member with mental illness (20%), and witnessing domestic violence (13%; Nickerson & Jimerson, 2015). Yet, ACE scores alone do not account for factors such as age of onset, chronicity, duration, and relationship to the offender of the abuse. In school settings, higher ACE scores correlate with the potential for various challenges (e.g., below grade-level reading and math scores, lower GPA, chronic absenteeism, greater rates of dropout, more individualized special education plans, higher frequency of grade retention, and increased number of suspensions/expulsions; Bethell et al., 2014; Blodgett et al., 2018; Kiesel et al., 2016; Morrow & Villodas, 2018; Stempel et al., 2017; Stewart-Tufescu et al., 2022; Tan et al., 2017). Furthermore, school-aged children who have experienced two or more ACEs were twice as likely to be disengaged in their school environments than their peers with no ACEs (Bethell et al., 2014). In a retroactive sample of urban youth, researchers found that exposure to 4 or more ACEs increased the odds of learning, behavioral problems, and obesity by 33% compared to children with 0 or 1 ACE (Burke et al., 2011).

Traumas and adversities do not occur in a vacuum, and systemic factors must be examined. Research using expanded ACE inventories that included community violence, race-based discrimination, and foster care placement found that ACE scores were higher for BIPOC adults and youth (Bernard et al., 2020; Cronholm et al., 2015; Maguire-Jack et al., 2020). Racism has been recommended as an ACE exposure risk factor to be added as a category on the ACE inventory and used as a factor when examining long-term outcomes (Bernard et al., 2020). The decades of ACE studies yielded an important conclusion: abuse is preventable and requires systemic, community-based approaches (Centers for Disease Control and Prevention [CDC], 2024).

Educators and school counselors know that trauma affects the children and families that they serve, yet many lack comprehensive training in TI (Brown et al., 2022; Honsinger & Brown, 2019; Van Asselt et al., 2016) and anti-racist practices (Ieva et al., 2021; Legette et al., 2023; Stickl Haugen et al., 2023). Additionally, while some children may have abuse or neglect documented in their records, many children have not previously disclosed their experiences. Educators and school counselors need to know the warning signs of abuse and neglect so they can properly report when it is suspected. They also need effective preventative and responsive strategies in their classrooms and school environments. School staff can be prepared to create TI school systems through evidence-based, culturally informed approaches.

ANTI-RACIST FRAMEWORK FOR CULTURALLY RESPONSIVE TRAUMA-INFORMED APPROACHES

TI practices cannot be discussed without addressing how trauma is embedded within systems of oppression and racism. This starts with acknowledging that experiences of historical trauma, intergenerational trauma, and race-based trauma are all specific forms of trauma and can interact with and/or increase the effect of traumatic experiences. For TI work to be successful, school counselors and educators need an anti-racist framework. Race is a social construct that was created to separate groups of people into a hierarchy. In the United States, this system carries an anti-Black bias and disadvantages individuals who are BIPOC along with other historically marginalized populations. An important first step for school counselors and educators is understanding historical and current racism and how this applies to PK-12 education today.

Many BIPOC students experience chronic racial trauma due to institutionalized racism, which has been linked to poor academic achievement, increased disciplinary actions, lower graduation rates, and disproportionately higher placements in special education (Kohli et al., 2017; NCTSN, 2017). The school-to-prison pipeline is in part due to higher disciplinary referrals of students of color, reports by school officials to law enforcement, and the criminalization of students (Nance, 2017; U.S. Department of Education, 2018). Anti-blackness, implicit biases, microaggressions, White saviorism, color-blind, and culture-blind ideologies all cause harm to BIPOC students. Unfortunately, instead of seeing flaws in the system, educators and school counselors may believe problems reside in BIPOC children and their families and view them through a deficit lens. Schools are racialized institutions, and disparities in educational outcomes are often due to systemic racism and barriers rather than deficiencies in students or families (Williams et al., 2020). As educators and school counselors seek to understand trauma using an anti-racist lens, they must also consider children's unique perspectives and how those intersect with their culture, including race, gender, and sexual identity, and socioeconomic status (Ford et al., 2015; Foster & Hagedorn, 2014ab; Foster, 2017b). For children, disclosure of abuse is particularly difficult, and if they do reveal abuse, they may experience shame, stigma, secrecy, and fear of family disruption (Carson et al., 2014). Cultural betrayal trauma theory captures the complicated experience when the victim and offender share at least one marginalized identity, which may limit disclosure (Gómez & Gobin, 2024).

Adults within a school setting need to understand their role as mandated reporters. They must be prepared to handle disclosures, including how to respond with belief and support, as well as how to manage their reactions. Discipline must be distinguished from abuse, and school staff would benefit from training that helps educators gain cultural competence (Adkison-Johnson, 2021). Thus, trauma must be understood through an anti-racist, anti-oppression framework to employ prevention and intervention strategies within schools that are culturally sound and do not cause further harm.

Key Components of Trauma-Informed Training

According to the National Child Traumatic Stress Network, there are essential components of TI schools. First, educators must be able to recognize and attend to trauma, and schools must promote awareness through training. Second, educators must connect with students and their families to create environments that promote social/emotional well-being in a culturally responsive manner. Third, schools must have plans for emergency and crisis response and mitigate the risk of secondary traumatic stress by providing staff with support and encouraging self-care. Fourth, schools need to evaluate approaches to discipline and employ TI policies. Finally, schools need to foster connections with community stakeholders. TI schools must prioritize building safe relationships and environments to accomplish these aims. Likewise, all staff require a comprehensive TI knowledge base. The following sections discuss (1) how to build safe relationships and atmospheres and (2) TI knowledge, focusing on two key concepts: the window of tolerance and emotional regulation.

Building Safe Relationships and Environments

A primary component of TI practices is establishing safe relationships between adults and the students they serve. While school leaders have long known the importance of building relationships with students, recent literature has framed this as a protective factor for children who have experienced trauma (Keane & Evans, 2022). Educators and school counselors need to learn specific strategies to connect with students who may present with difficulty trusting and being vulnerable due to their lived experiences.

Safe relationships and environments are proactive and set students up for success. These relationships are built one day at a time through consistency and care, knowing that trust cannot be rushed. Educators must employ a strengths lens and empathy, genuineness, and unconditional positive regard to help students reach their fullest potential (Rogers, 1957). For some children, adults at school may be the first people who have affirmed them and believed in their capacity for growth. These positive, consistent relationships instill hope and help students begin to believe in themselves.

Trauma-informed work also centers on the value of belonging. In a classroom where students are fully accepted, they realize they are not alone. Hearing from adults at school that they are important, cherished learning community members is vital. It is important that this status is not earned through good behavior or performance; it must be true and constant because of their worth and dignity. As students experience love and acceptance, they build the tools to connect with others. Furthermore, an environment of belonging also reduces the need for children to compete for attention and nurtures greater empathy for their classmates.

A vital need for children who have experienced trauma is safety, both within the relationship (e.g., appropriate boundaries) and the environment (e.g., calm, predictable, clear expectations). Students feel safe when they know that (1) the adults during the school day will be able to regulate their own emotions, and (2) adults will be there to help students when they experience dysregulation (hyper- or hypo-arousal). Yet, many educators and school counselors have not been taught skills in regulation and co-regulation. With training, adults can learn, model, and teach regulation to children, which increases feelings of safety and security in the school environment (Healy, 2023).

Another important consideration for relational and environmental safety is the process in which conflict is managed. Restorative justice approaches have been identified as culturally responsive methods that promote responsibility, elevate students' voices, and focus on solutions in the school setting. These approaches tend to be less punitive and focus on accountability and making amends. Conversely, zero-tolerance policies often negatively impact students of color and result in harsh punishments with no opportunities for learning or restoration. For students who have experienced trauma, conflict can be triggering for students. If the conflict becomes physical, the safety of the students and staff is of primary importance, and de-escalating methods must be quickly employed. When considering school-wide approaches to discipline, educators need to consider if the methods are TI, culturally, and relationally sound. All students need to experience connection and care at school. They also need to feel safe in those relationships and the school environment. When staff are trained in TI approaches, they can meet these foundational needs.

Trauma-Informed Knowledge and Practices

There is a myriad of TI approaches. Thomas and colleagues (2019) published a review of 30 TI practices in schools. Additionally, The National Child Traumatic Stress Network (2017) published a guide on getting started for schools new to TI. Regardless of the framework selected, most include the following components: (1) acknowledging how trauma affects children and how they recover, (2) recognizing and responding to signs and symptoms of victimization, (3) applying knowledge about trauma in the school environment, and (4) reducing re-traumatization by adults through preventative strategies and TI procedures, and practices. These components are multi-tiered, preventative, and responsive. This section highlights two concepts that educators have reported as immediately useful in understanding and responding to students: the window of tolerance and emotional regulation (Foster et al., under review).

Window of Tolerance

The window of tolerance model developed by Siegel (1999) is based on neuroscience and explores optimal functioning and stress management. When children function within their tolerance window, they can play, connect with others, and learn. When triggered, they leave the window and enter hypo-arousal or hyper-arousal. Hypo-arousal is a stress response characterized by withdrawal, shutting down, exhaustion, depression, disconnection, freezing, and/or feeling numb. Conversely, hyper-arousal is marked by excess energy, such as anxiety, anger, irritability, outbursts, being easily startled, difficulty concentrating, and/or flight/fight responses. While each child has a window of tolerance that is influenced by trauma history, neurobiology, social support, environment, and existing coping skills, it is not fixed. Windows can be widened to tolerate stress better. With greater self-awareness and coping strategies, students can become equipped to recognize distress in their bodies and respond proactively. Students can also learn how being hungry, not getting enough sleep, and lack of time outdoors or movement can narrow their window of tolerance.

Additionally, students can be taught to recognize personal triggers such as sensory overload, feeling excited, peer conflict, struggling with an assignment, or having to focus for long periods of time. As students increase their awareness and listen to their bodies, they can learn to employ mindfulness and breathing strategies to cope with stress both during and outside of the school day. Furthermore, adults can provide environmental support to help widen the window of tolerance. Classrooms can use a quiet corner stocked with fidgets, breathing and grounding prompts, blankets, and other tools for self-soothing. Educators can also create predictable learning environments with posted schedules and routines. They can also provide notice, when possible if the routine must change. Educators are tools when they develop a strong rapport with students, and they can assist them in regulating their emotions, which is referred to as co-regulation. Thus, students can build resilience and expand their stress tolerance through internal student strategies (e.g., increased self-awareness and mindfulness) and external strategies (calming corners, routines, supportive adults).

Emotional Regulation

Trauma-informed trainings provide educators with strategies to become aware of and respond to dysregulation. Educators can learn the Three R's of Reaching the Learning Brain (regulate, reconnect, and reason), developed by neuroscientist Bruce Perry. In this model, the educator's first job is to help a dysregulated student regulate, helping them calm their fight/flight/freeze trauma responses. A child often needs space and somewhere quiet and safe. The next task is to reconnect with the student. This interaction communicates that the educator is present and continues to hold them with positive regard and care. Educators can say, "I am here to help." They may narrate briefly what happened and what may happen next. They can also reflect how the student may have felt dysregulated (e.g., scared, angry, overwhelmed). Educators can also empathize and share that they know how it feels that way.

The third step is to help the child reason. This only begins when the child has returned to baseline and is calm and attentive. Often, adults start on this step and try to get a dysregulated child to talk about the behavior and what they need to do instead. This is ineffective because their brain cannot think clearly when students are in survival mode. After children are regulated and experience re-connection, they are ready to reflect and learn from what happened. The process of regulating must occur within the context of a supportive, caring relationship. This requires adults to utilize strategies when they feel dysregulated because "a dysregulated adult cannot regulate a child" (Desautels, 2020). Adults must be aware of their needs and attend to those daily (e.g., nutrition, sleep, stress and pain management, social support, time for movement and play, and time in nature).

When adults are having a difficult day, they can actively model regulation strategies. For example, they may tell their class, "I feel frustrated and stressed today. My body feels tense so that I will do some progressive muscle relaxation. Anyone who wants to join me is welcome to follow along." If a teacher feels down and sad, they might say, I'm realizing I am feeling sad today. I think some music and movement would help. You are welcome to join in while I take this brain break." Educators can also model for students to take calming breaths before responding when irritated or overwhelmed. They can also model how to step away by asking another staff member to cover their class so they can have a brief break.

RECOMMENDATIONS FOR TRAINING SUCCESS

Pre-Service Educators

National standards for training educators and administrators do not require training in trauma or TI practices (Council for Exceptional Children, 2022; National Policy Board for Educational Administration, 2018). Teacher preparation programs primarily focus on pedagogy, content mastery, assessment, and learning science. This is no longer enough. Educator preparation programs must equip their students to be culturally responsive and TI. Comprehensive training for pre-service educators includes the following components: (1) knowledge about trauma, (2) TI skills to use with students, and (3) personal coping strategies to mitigate the impact of indirect trauma. As educators-in-training are introduced to trauma, they need to learn how to define trauma and adversity, recognize and respond to warning signs, and avoid re-traumatization (SAMHSA, 2014). They also need to develop knowledge and awareness of historical and current systems of oppression. Moreover, they must learn evidenced-based, culturally informed approaches and practice application through role play and case study examples. Students need opportunities to engage in reflective work that provides an opportunity to examine their biases or assumptions. During training, students may disclose their own lived experiences of trauma, and for some, this may be their first time to share these experiences with others. Counseling to process one's own lived experiences of trauma and adversity should be made available to all students. Faculty members can reduce stigma by encouraging students to engage in counseling as a form of self-care and as a part of their healing journeys.

Pre-Service School Counselors

School counseling has existed in American schools for more than a century, and the training of school counselors has evolved by moving away from deficit-based language about students to working towards antiracist (Holcomb-McCoy, 2022) and TI school counseling (Matthews et al., 2023). School counselors are expected to hold a holistic view of students (ASCA, 2019), foster a trauma-sensitive environment (ASCA, 2022b), serve as social justice change agents, and affirm all students (ASCA, 2022a). Recently, ASCA (2021) implemented The School Counselor and Anti-Racist Practices, which tasks school counselors to work toward cultural competence and engage in anti-racist actions. Yet, most school counselors-in-training do not have specific preparation for antiracism (Ieva et al., 2021; Legette et al., 2023; Stickl Haugen et al., 2023). Additionally, many trainees are inadequately prepared to address trauma (Foster, 2017a; Mathews et al., 2023). These training deficits may improve with The Council for Accreditation of Counseling & Related Educational Programs (CACREP, 2024) new standard for school counseling training programs to teach and assess "techniques of social-emotional and trauma-informed counseling in school settings." An important consideration is that the faculty need continuing education in culturally responsive TI work. Faculty have expressed discomfort, lack of training, changing standards, and lack of joy in TI content (Van Asselt et al., 2016), yet this training is necessary to increase competence. It may decrease vicarious trauma during clinical work (VanAusdale & Swank, 2020).

In-Service Staff

In previous research, school staff, including teachers, paraprofessionals, counselors, and other key personnel, have reported little or no training in TI approaches; therefore, in-service trainings are urgently needed (Aragón et al., 2024; Shooks, 2020). Training conducted within the school setting should include all adults who work in the building. Implementing TI work school-wide requires a paradigm shift and a unified effort by all staff to maximize the effectiveness (Maddox et al., 2024). Before launching training, there are important considerations to optimize effectiveness and engagement. Additionally, there are specific challenges to consider that can be addressed proactively by trainers and administration (Foster et al., under review).

Preparing for Trauma-Informed Training

To start, readiness for change must be considered. In one study, higher self-reported readiness to learn TI strategies correlated with more positive TI attitudes and use of the skills following training (Blanton et al., 2022). For trainers, it is important to gauge staff's attitudes about TI approaches and willingness to learn new strategies. An anonymous quantitative pre-test could be used to capture pre-training perspectives. This format allows for honesty without fear of repercussions. Qualitative group discussions could also invite staff to share initial thoughts about the proposed training, including specific needs, concerns, and logistical considerations such as timing and delivery format. While this approach is not anonymous, it shows care for the staff's perspectives, and efforts should be made to incorporate their recommendations. In addition to assessing readiness, exploring initial resistance, and understanding the needs of the trainees, trainers could consider sharing research-based evidence of the effectiveness of the TI approaches in schools, particularly those with similar demographics. The research presented should include quantitative and qualitative outcomes (e.g., decreased absences, fewer disciplinary referrals, greater sense of belonging reported by students, greater self-efficacy reported by teachers). The research could be bolstered by inviting guest speakers from other schools to share their own training and implementation experiences. The educators could share their initial resistance and ways that changed as they learned the science behind TI practices and implemented strategies. They could also respond to questions from the staff. It is possible that establishing increased staff trust and commitment before training could yield higher engagement throughout the process as well as better implementation results.

Another important consideration for any staff development is time investment. Becoming TI is involved, and a single workshop is not sufficient. It may be beneficial to spread the training over an academic year, allowing content to be taught thematically and skills to build over time. It also prevents an information dump, which can be overwhelming and ineffective for promoting school-wide cultural change. Given the extent of burnout educators are experiencing and the increased demands on their time, all training should be conducted during establishing professional development hours onsite in which staff are paid for their attendance. Requiring staff to complete training on their own time is counterproductive and could build resentment and create resistance. Becoming TI is a process, and educators need to think differently about their work. Some are challenged to reconsider what they were taught and have done things for many years. This shift requires significant support as staff gain TI knowledge and skills along with strategies for wellness and protection from indirect trauma.

Potential Training Challenges. While most educators have reported personal and professional benefits from TI training, some educators have experienced challenges (Foster et al., under review). Foster and colleagues' study indicated that trainers must be prepared to help educators needing additional support or supervision. In their yearlong qualitative study of receiving TI training, they identified three types of adverse responses: (1) burdened, (2) triggered, and (3) jaded. The educators who felt burdened were overwhelmed with the content, found it difficult to establish boundaries between work and school, and were resentful for having to complete the training on their own time. Overwhelmed educators will likely benefit from increased administrative support and peer mentorship. Additionally, as discussed earlier, training should be delivered during paid professional days to reduce the burden of completing it on one's own time.

In the second category, educators who were triggered had unprocessed trauma histories, and the content caused those memories to resurface. The participants hurried through the content, had difficulty recalling what they learned, and shared feeling overwhelmed by their students' experiences of trauma. Staff experiencing re-traumatization would benefit from encouragement to seek counseling along with engaging in other forms of self-care. Then, in the final category, one participant was jaded. They found the training unhelpful and believed trauma had ruined the children's lives and placed blame on their families. Staff with such views may cause harm, and increased supervision is warranted. Overall, the educators who struggled with the TI training each showed signs of distress, which may be due in part to indirect trauma (Foster et al., under review). Thus, trainers need to be prepared to support those who are struggling and are at risk for secondary traumatic stress, compassion fatigue, vicarious trauma, and occupational burnout (Aragón et al., 2024). In sum, no single approach exists for TI work within schools (Maddox et al., 2024). Numerous trainings, models, and resources are available, and each school leadership team must determine the training is appropriate for their community based on demographics, resources, and readiness. Once training is started and an implementation plan is in place, evaluation of adherence to the model and effectiveness of the strategies is needed (Fye et al., 2023). As leaders and advocates within their schools, school counselors can administer a measure, such as the Trauma Informed Practice Scales - School Counseling Programs Version (TIPS-SCP). This tool assesses TI practices and assists stakeholders in making data-driven decisions and program improvements. Qualitative feedback about the training and TI practices could also be gathered to monitor knowledge, attitudes, and skills and respond with necessary support.

PREVENTATIVE WELLNESS FOR SCHOOL STAFF

School staff are often the drivers of TI programs in schools. Their active engagement and support determine the success of any TI programs (Wassink-de Stigter et al., 2022). School teachers experience burnout and stress, reporting that these are major causes of leaving the workforce. The well-being of adults in the school is directly associated with the school climate. Adults who are victims of trauma or abuse are at higher risk of being abusive. Additionally, they may be more susceptible to indirect trauma, including vicarious trauma, secondary traumatic stress, and compassion fatigue. Hence, the mental health and well-being of school staff is a serious concern. Educating and equipping adults with self-care and TI practices helps personal and professional lives (Kumar et al., 2018). There are many evidence-based and culturally competent practices to enhance staff wellness. While understanding that school staff need professional training and support in TI and wellness programs, it is important to ensure that such programs do not add to the burden and workload of school staff (Crotwell, 2011). Some key aspects to consider as part of preventive wellness for staff include creating safe spaces and providing wellness facilities and programs.

Creating Safe Spaces

Along with prioritizing safety for children in TI schools, staff safety is vital. School leadership must create an environment where all staff feel safe and are treated with dignity and respect. An important aspect is creating opportunities for open conversations and constructive feedback. Additionally, feedback should be provided from staff and administration about their wants and needs. School leaders can survey staff to understand key concerns and generate ideas for positive change. Developing a climate of trust and a sense of safety fosters well-being and faculty retention. Supportive leadership can create a culture to break trauma cycles and foster resilience and empathy (McKinley, 2024).

Wellness Facilities and Programs

Staff wellness programs should be embedded into school daily routines and calendars, addressing physical and emotional concerns. Health aspects, including nutrition, exercise, and paid personal days, can be carefully planned, ensuring overall health and productivity (Neves et al., 2020). Schools can partner with community healthcare facilities and encourage staff to prioritize their health and wellness and know when to seek support. Mental health wellness facilities, including access to counselling support for staff, respond to the needs of adults who are survivors of trauma and/or have been impacted by indirect trauma (Beames et al., 2023). Professional development activities can include wellness as a key focus, which helps staff value wellness, thereby making it easier to transact the same in their classrooms.

ADMINISTRATIVE AND COMMUNITY SUPPORT

Everyone in the school ecosystem plays a role in creating and supporting a TI approach. "There is recognition that healing happens in relationships and the meaningful sharing of power and decision-making" (Foreman et al., 2021, p. 6). There are various levels of power within a school community and between school leaders and community organizations. Recognizing this power and the diverse resources and perspectives each entity can offer strengthens relationships and the potential for partnerships (Manian & Sorensen, 2024). Despite increasing interest and research about TI approaches within schools and communities, empirical evidence about how leaders support whole-school approaches is limited (Avery et al., 2020; Matlin et al., 2019). Even so, the following section discusses principles of collaboration, successful examples of school leadership, and community involvement in supporting TI initiatives and efforts.

Principles of Collaboration

The National Child Traumatic Stress Network (NCTSN), Schools Committee (2017) outlined four strategies for partnering and collaborating effectively. First, consistent and coordinated messaging among all partners (e.g., federal agencies and school leaders) is essential to support and sustain TI policies, laws, and resources. SAMHSA (2014) emphasizes that regardless of the partnership, each service sector must share an understanding of trauma and adversity. For instance, if a student is at school, in an after-school program (e.g., YMCA), around the community, or at home, they should ideally receive consistent information and support. A second strategy from NCTSN is to provide a comprehensive resource catalog highlighting available services at school and community levels. This resource can promote access for families and students to receive services, appropriate referrals, screening, and assessment. Third, NCTSN recommends establishing a multidisciplinary team of staff and community members to help with decision-making and continuous evaluation of TI policies and practices. This could include inviting stakeholders and local agencies to 1) address the severity of an issue or event (e.g., natural disaster, poverty, transience), 2) discuss how it influences the school climate, and 3) provide intentional and consistent resources that provide support from diverse angles (e.g., mental health, housing, academic). Finally, according to NCTSN, ongoing communication and consultation should be maintained to promote and provide wraparound services for youth safety in various settings (e.g., residential, justice).

School Leadership

School leadership includes administrators, district personnel, and other stakeholders who are typically more likely to provide essential resources like money, time, and staff (Garcia et al., 2023). SAMHSA (2014) states that dedicated support from school leaders is key to developing, implementing, and sustaining TI approaches. If leadership is not committed to creating or sustaining a TI school environment, then time, energy, and resources will be directed elsewhere, leading to missed opportunities to prevent and support trauma and adversity intentionally. A systematic review from 2008 and 2019 of TI school-wide approaches echoed that readiness and motivation are essential for implementing a TI school, as mentioned earlier, but also emphasized leadership buy-in and adequate systems (infrastructure) as paramount to building and sustaining a TI community (Avery et al., 2020). Similarly, Garcia and colleagues (2023) analyzed a two-year state-wide initiative program (Trauma-Informed Practices for Educators and School Personnel; TIPE), highlighting the importance of leadership support. School leaders who participated in this program learned about trauma, TI strategies, and ways to teach and support other educators. Results of implementing TI classroom strategies and techniques showed a significant increase between pre- and post-analysis when leaders were fully involved. Put, commitment, and leadership buy-in promote school-wide TI efforts.

Furthermore, Kataoka and colleagues (2018) provided three case studies highlighting district and community involvement (finances, leveraging of school policies), school-wide initiatives (restorative practices), and principal leadership from the Los Angeles Unified School District (LAUSD). This district serves approximately 664,774 students in grades K-12. One case example highlighted an elementary school principal. To support students dealing with trauma, the principal, in a Latino neighborhood affected by violence and poverty, provided specific training to staff about understanding the emotional needs of students while also fostering trust with parents through conversations. SAMHSA (2014) echoed the importance of training and said that ongoing training about trauma and peer support is essential. However, training staff without other learning and advocating is often insufficient; thus, this principle and school continued its efforts. To address concerns about neighborhood safety, the principal organized community walks to assess local conditions and gather opinions. This information and parent experiences were shared with city officials and leaders. Over time, family engagement ratings, academic benchmarks, and student participation in trauma interventions increased (Kataoka et al., 2018). Without the knowledge and commitment of school leadership, this case example would not have been possible.

Schools must regularly evaluate TI practices, services, and partnerships to provide effective and reliable support. Evaluation ensures that these initiatives function well and that evidence-based trauma screenings, assessments, and treatments are applied appropriately (SAMHSA, 2014). In addition to specific program evaluations, schools can utilize general assessments to evaluate overall systems. One example is the Trauma Responsive Schools Implementation Assessment (TRS-IA), an online self-assessment developed by the Treatment and Services Adaptation Center for Resilience, Hope, and Wellness in Schools in collaboration with the Center for School Mental Health. This evidence-informed tool includes eight domains of trauma-responsive schools and districts. It evaluates planning for whole-school safety, prevention strategies, trauma-informed classroom practices, targeted early interventions, staff self-care, and family and community engagement. The survey takes less than 20 minutes and provides automatic and specific feedback to enhance district and school-wide efforts (School Health Assessment and Performance Evaluation System, 2023).

Community Partnerships

Schools are members of a larger society, and though a school can provide rich resources, including evidence-based and culturally appropriate interventions, community involvement and referral to community services are often necessary to bridge support gaps (Manian & Sorensen, 2024; SAMHSA, 2014). Schools can boost their resources by working with community organizations, and active community members across all sectors are essential to foster resilient TI schools. Partnerships allow for a more comprehensive (multitiered) approach and system to supporting students (Manian & Sorensen, 2024). Community support looks different for each district, as contextual factors like resources and geographic location influence access; however, partnerships could involve community agencies, such as mental health services, law enforcement, advocacy/support groups (e.g., LGBTQ, violence prevention, homelessness, refugee), university-based clinics, trauma survivors willing to get involved, after-school programs, and so on (National Child Traumatic Stress Network, Schools Committee, 2017; SAMHSA, 2014).

Along with targeted partnerships (e.g., screening, referral, and support for specific issues and populations), districts have adopted a whole district or community-school approach to address various student needs, as highlighted in three examples (Manian & Sorensen, 2024). First, Oakland Community Schools partners with multiple organizations to provide resources for family engagement and addressing ACEs, going beyond a traditional academic focus (Manian & Sorensen, 2024). Second, the San Antonio Independent School District collaborates with Community in Schools (Communities in Schools of Appalachian Highlands, 2021) to support social and emotional needs through on-campus counseling, mental health services for families, and college readiness programs across 81 schools (Manian & Sorensen, 2024). Lastly, the Pottstown School District in Pennsylvania focuses on creating a TI environment through partnerships that address mental health and ACEs, engaging over 100 organizations to tackle community trauma, especially for low-income, underrepresented families (Matlin et al., 2019). For instance, monthly meetings were held to increase communication and consistent messaging to explore ACEs, TI practices, community engagement strategies, and evaluation approaches that would further support community-building efforts.

CONCLUSION

It is time for schools to become culturally responsive, anti-racist, and TI by providing support, connection, and safety for all children. These TI practices "create more responsive and effective learning environments" for students (Maddox et al., 2024, p. 511). This approach requires all staff to understand how trauma and adversity affect the children they serve (Meador & Foster, 2025). From individual relationships to classrooms to building and community-wide practices, safety must be prioritized, and re-traumatization must be prevented to foster resiliency and help students thrive (Perry & Daniels, 2016). As discussed, no single approach works the same for schools when implementing TI programs. For example, some schools already have resources and initiatives that can be integrated into a TI system, while others do not. Some may expand a specific initiative or program, while others may follow a different direction. Regardless, schools can enhance their TI systems by forming partnerships in the community. Collaborative efforts provide resources, create practical tools, fill support gaps, and can more fully evaluate the effectiveness of school and district changes (Garcia et al., 2023; Kataoka et al., 2018; National Child Traumatic Stress Network, Schools Committee, 2017; SAMHSA, 2014). Regular evaluation of TI practices is essential. It should include ongoing assessment, tracking, and monitoring of TI principles and the effective use of evidence-based trauma-specific screenings, assessments, and treatments (SAMHSA, 2014). Altogether, it is essential for all stakeholders to engage in continuous learning and show their support and advocate for school and community TI initiatives. Partnering together with determination, clear goals, evaluation practices, and a willingness to learn is key to the success of these efforts.

REFERENCES

Adkison-Johnson, C. (2021). *Child discipline in African American families: Culturally responsive policies*. Lexington Books. DOI: 10.5771/9781793620941

Alvarez, J. M., Saunders, R., Neubauer, E., & Brown, C. H. (2022). School counselors Implementing a trauma-informed approach through evidence-based practice. *Professional School Counseling*, *26*(1), 2156759X221086742. Advance online publication. DOI: 10.1177/2156759X221086742

American School Counselor Association. (2019). *The ASCA National Model: A framework for school counseling programs* (4th ed.).

American School Counselor Association. (2021). *Position statement: The school counselor and anti-racist practices.*https://www.schoolcounselor.org/Standards-Positions/Position-Statements/ASCA-Position -Statements/The-School-Counselor-and-Anti-Racist-Practices

American School Counselor Association. (2022a). *ASCA ethical standards for school counselors.*https:// www.schoolcounselor.org/getmedia/44f30280-ffe8-4b41-9ad8-f15909c3d164/EthicalStandards.pdf

American School Counselor Association. (2022b). *The school counselor and trauma-informed practice.* https://www.schoolcounselor.org/StandardsPositions/Position-Statements/ASCA-Position-Statements/ The-SchoolCounselor-and-Trauma-Informed-Practice

Aragón, K. M., Mullin, A. C., Felix, E. D., Appel, O., & Sharkey, J. D. (2024). Identifying what educators need to support trauma-informed practices in the schools: A community needs assessment. *School Psychology*, *39*(5), 520–529. DOI: 10.1037/spq0000621 PMID: 38330316

Avery, J. C., Morris, H., Galvin, E., Misso, M., Savaglio, M., & Skouteris, H. (2020). Systematic review of school-wide trauma-informed approaches. *Journal of Child & Adolescent Trauma*, *14*(3), 381–397. DOI: 10.1007/s40653-020-00321-1 PMID: 34471456

Baker, C. N., Brown, S. M., Wilcox, P., Verlenden, J. M., Black, C. L., & Grant, B. E. (2018). The implementation and effect of trauma-informed care within residential youth services in rural Canada: A mixed methods case study. *Psychological Trauma: Theory, Research, Practice, and Policy*, *10*(6), 666–674. DOI: 10.1037/tra0000327 PMID: 29016153

Beames, J. R., Spanos, S., Roberts, A., McGillivray, L., Li, S., Newby, J. M., O'Dea, B., & Werner-Seidler, A. (2023). Intervention programs targeting the mental health, professional burnout, and/or wellbeing of school teachers: Systematic review and meta-analyses. *Educational Psychology Review*, *35*(1), 26. DOI: 10.1007/s10648-023-09720-w PMID: 36876289

Bernard, D. L., Calhoun, C. D., Banks, D. E., Halliday, C. A., Hughes-Halbert, C., & Danielson, C. K. (2020). Making the "C-ACE" for a culturally-informed adverse childhood experiences framework to understand the pervasive mental health impact of racism on Black youth. *Journal of Child & Adolescent Trauma*, *14*(2), 233–247. DOI: 10.1007/s40653-020-00319-9 PMID: 33986909

Bethell, C. D., Newacheck, P., Hawes, E., & Halfon, N. (2014). Adverse childhood experiences: Assessing the impact on health and school engagement and the mitigating role of resilience. *Health Affairs*, *33*(12), 2106–2115. DOI: 10.1377/hlthaff.2014.0914 PMID: 25489028

Blodgett, C., & Lanigan, J. D. (2018). The association between adverse childhood experience (ACE) and school success in elementary school children. *School Psychology Quarterly*, *33*(1), 137–146. DOI: 10.1037/spq0000256 PMID: 29629790

Brown, E. C., Freedle, A., Hurless, N. L., Miller, R. D., Martin, C., & Paul, Z. A. (2022). Preparing teacher candidates for trauma-informed practices. *Urban Education*, *57*(4), 662–685. DOI: 10.1177/0042085920974084

Brunzell, T., Stokes, H., & Waters, L. (2016). Trauma-informed positive education: Using positive psychology to strengthen vulnerable students. *Contemporary School Psychology*, *20*(1), 63–83. DOI: 10.1007/s40688-015-0070-x

Brunzell, T., Waters, L., & Stokes, H. (2021). Trauma-informed teacher wellbeing: Teacher reflections within trauma-informed positive education. *The Australian Journal of Teacher Education*, *46*(5), 91–107. Advance online publication. DOI: 10.14221/ajte.2021v46n5.6

Burke, N. J., Hellman, J. L., Scott, B. G., Weems, C. F., & Carrion, V. G. (2011). The impact of adverse childhood experiences on an urban pediatric population. *Child Abuse & Neglect*, *35*(6), 408–413. DOI: 10.1016/j.chiabu.2011.02.006 PMID: 21652073

Cafaro, C. L., Molina, E. G., Patton, E., McMahon, S. D., & Brown, M. (2023). Meta-analyses of teacher-delivered trauma-based and trauma-informed care interventions. *Psychological Trauma: Theory, Research, Practice, and Policy*, *15*(7), 1177–1187. DOI: 10.1037/tra0001515 PMID: 37166916

Carson, D. K., Foster, J. M., & Tripathi, N. (2014). Child sexual abuse in India: Current issues and research. *Psychological Studies*, *58*(3), 318–325. DOI: 10.1007/s12646-013-0198-6

Centers for Disease Control and Prevention. (2024, October 8). *Preventing adverse childhood experiences*. https://www.cdc.gov/aces/prevention/index.html

Clark, D. (2024). *Counselor education doctoral student supervisors' preparedness to address indirect trauma: Compassion fatigue, secondary traumatic stress, and vicarious trauma.* [Doctoral dissertation, Western Michigan University]. ScholarWorks Dissertations. https://scholarworks.wmich.edu/dissertations/4107

Communities in Schools of Appalachian Highlands. (2023). B*uilding social emotional competencies through integrated student supports.*https://cisofah.org/wp-content/uploads/2022/04/Building-SEL-Competencies-through-ISS.pdf

Council for Exceptional Children. (2022). Initial special education standards preparation standards. https://exceptionalchildren.org/standards/initial-special-educationpreparation-standards

Cronholm, P. F., Forke, C. M., Wade, R., Bair-Merritt, M. H., Davis, M., Harkins-Schwarz, M., Pachter, L. M., & Fein, J. A. (2015). Adverse childhood experiences: Expanding the concept of adversity. *American Journal of Preventive Medicine*, *49*(3), 354–361. DOI: 10.1016/j.amepre.2015.02.001 PMID: 26296440

Crosby, S. D., Somers, C. L., Day, A. G., & Baroni, B. A. (2016). Working with traumatized students: A preliminary study of measures to assess. *Journal of Therapeutic Schools & Programs*, *8*(1), 65–76. DOI: 10.19157/JTSP.issue.08.01.08

Crotwell, W. G. (2011). *Elementary school teachers' experience of professional workload and time.* Walden University.

Day, A. G., Baroni, B., Somers, C., Shier, J., Zammit, M., Crosby, S., Yoon, J., Pennefather, M., & Hong, J. S. (2017). Trauma triggers: Students' perspective on enhancing the classroom experiences at an alternative residential treatment-based school. *Children & Schools, 39*(4), 227–237. DOI: 10.1093/cs/cdx018

Desautels, L. L. (2020). *Connections over compliance: Rewiring our perceptions of discipline.* Wyatt-MacKenzie Publishing.

Felitti, V. J., Anda, R. F., Nordenberg, D., Williamson, D. F., Spitz, A. M., Edwards, V., Koss, M. P., & Marks, J. S. (1998). Relationship of childhood abuse and household dysfunction to many of the leading causes of death in adults: The adverse childhood experiences (ACE) study. *American Journal of Preventive Medicine, 14*(4), 245–258. DOI: 10.1016/S0749-3797(98)00017-8 PMID: 9635069

Ford, J. D., Grasso, D. J., Elhai, J. D., & Courtois, C. A. (2015). *Social, cultural, and other diversity issues in the traumatic stress field. Posttraumatic Stress Disorder* (2nd ed.). Academic Press., DOI: 10.1016/C2013-0-19408-1

Foreman, C., Grossman, H., Graham, M., & Seymour, M. (2021). A trauma-informed resources for strengthening school family partnerships. Los Angeles, CA, and Durhan, NC: National Center for Child Traumatic Stress.

Foster, J. M. (2017a). A survey of students' knowledge about sexual abuse and perceived readiness to provide counseling services. *The Journal of Counselor Preparation and Supervisor*, *9*(1), 1–31. DOI: 10.7729/91.1165

Foster, J. M. (2017b). The fears and futures of boy victims of sexual abuse: An analysis of narratives. *Journal of Child Sexual Abuse, 26*(6), 710–730. DOI: 10.1080/10538712.2017.1339223 PMID: 28836930

Foster, J. M., & Hagedorn, W. B. (2014a). A qualitative exploration of fear and safety with child victims of sexual abuse. *Journal of Mental Health Counseling*, *36*(3), 243–262. DOI: 10.17744/mehc.36.3.0160307501879217

Foster, J. M., & Hagedorn, W. B. (2014b). Through the eyes of the wounded: A narrative analysis of children's sexual abuse experiences and recovery process. *Journal of Child Sexual Abuse, 23*(5), 538–577. DOI: 10.1080/10538712.2014.918072 PMID: 24819252

Foster, J. M., & Kumar, A. (2022). Understanding the impact of trauma on school-age children and their families. In Kramer, B., & McKenzie, J. (Eds.), *Children and trauma: Critical perspectives for meeting the needs of diverse educational communities* (pp. 93–110). Myer Education Press.

Foster, J. M., Shooks, B., & Cate, H. (under review). This changes everything: Educators' perspectives from a yearlong trauma-informed training program.

Freyd, J. J. (1996). *Betrayal trauma: The logic of forgetting childhood abuse.* Harvard University Press.

Fye, H. J., Wind, S. A., & Cook, R. M. (2024). Development of the Trauma-Informed Practice Scales – School Counseling Programs Version (TIPSSCP). *Measurement & Evaluation in Counseling & Development*, *57*(3), 211–230. DOI: 10.1080/07481756.2023.2243263

Garcia, A., Sprang, G., & Clemans, T. (2023). The role of school leaders in cultivating a trauma-informed school climate. *Children and Youth Services Review*, *146*, 106816. Advance online publication. DOI: 10.1016/j.childyouth.2023.106816

Gómez, J. M., & Gobin, R. L. (2024). "It will always feel worse because it comes with that added 'betrayal'": Intersectionality praxis and Black young women survivors' perspectives on cultural betrayal trauma theory. *Journal of Trauma & Dissociation*, *25*(5), 656–673. Advance online publication. DOI: 10.1080/15299732.2024.2383197 PMID: 39093694

Herrenkohl, T. I., Hong, S., & Verbrugge, B. (2019). Trauma-informed programs based in schools: Linking concepts to practices and assessing the evidence. *American Journal of Community Psychology*, *64*(3–4), 373–388. DOI: 10.1002/ajcp.12362 PMID: 31355976

Hillis, S., Mercy, J., Amobi, A., & Kress, H. (2016). Global prevalence of past-year violence against children: A systematic review and minimum estimates. *Pediatrics*, *137*(3), e20154079. Advance online publication. DOI: 10.1542/peds.2015-4079 PMID: 26810785

Holcomb-McCoy, C. (2022). *School counseling to close opportunity gaps: A social justice and antiracist framework for success* (2nd ed.). Corwin. DOI: 10.4135/9781071854969

Honsinger, C. J., & Brown, M. H. (2019). Preparing trauma-sensitive teachers: Strategies for teacher educators. *Teacher Educators'. Journal*, *12*, 129–152.

Howard, J., L'Estrange, L., & Brown, M. (2022). The school counsellor's role in trauma-aware education. *Journal of Psychologists and Counsellors in Schools*, *32*(2), 243–253. https://doi-org.libproxy.library.wmich.edu/10.1017/jgc.2021.32. DOI: 10.1017/jgc.2021.32

Ieva, K. P., Beasley, J., & Steen, S. (2021). Equipping school counselors for antiracist healing centered groups: A critical examination of preparation, connected curricula, professional practice and oversight. *Teaching and Supervision in Counseling*, *3*(2), 7. Advance online publication. DOI: 10.7290/tsc030207

Ijadi-Maghsoodi, R., Marlotte, L., Garcia, E., Aralis, H., Lester, P., Escudero, P., & Kataoka, S. (2017). Adapting and implementing a school-based resilience-building curriculum among low income racial and ethnic minority students. *Contemporary School Psychology*, *21*(3), 223–239. DOI: 10.1007/s40688-017-0134-1 PMID: 29686938

Kataoka, S. H., Vona, P., Acuna, A., Jaycox, L., Escudero, P., Rojas, C., Ramirez, E., Langley, A., & Stein, B. D. (2018). Applying a trauma informed school systems approach: Examples from school community-academic partnerships. *Ethnicity & Disease*, *28*(Supp), 417–426. DOI: 10.18865/ed.28.S2.417 PMID: 30202195

Kiesel, L. R., Piescher, K. N., & Edleson, J. L. (2016). The relationship between child maltreatment, intimate partner violence exposure, and academic performance. *Journal of Public Child Welfare*, *10*(4), 434–456. DOI: 10.1080/15548732.2016.1209150

Kohli, R., Pizarro, M., & Nevárez, A. (2017). The "new racism" of K–12 schools: Centering critical research on racism. *Review of Research in Education*, *41*(1), 182–202. DOI: 10.3102/0091732X16686949

Kumar, A., Bhagyalakshmi, K. C., & Foster, J. M. (2018). Child sexual abuse: Evaluating the school-based prevention programs in India. In *Social, Psychological, and Forensic Perspectives on Sexual Abuse* (pp. 166-178). IGI Global.

Legette, K. B., Iruka, I. U., Halberstadt, A. G., & Forte, A. B. (2023). Teachers' awareness of systemic and individual racial bias as a first step towards anti-racist schools. *Teaching and Teacher Education, 132*, 104213. DOI: 10.1016/j.tate.2023.104213

Maddox, R. P., Rujimora, J., Nichols, L. M., Williams, M. K., Hunt, T., & Carter, R. A. (2024). Trauma-informed schools: Implications for special education and school counseling. *Teaching Exceptional Children, 56*(6), 510-520. https://doi-org/DOI: 10.1177/00400599221107142

Maguire-Jack, K., Lanier, P., & Lombardi, B. (2020). Investigating racial differences in clusters of adverse childhood experiences. *The American Journal of Orthopsychiatry*, *90*(1), 106–114. DOI: 10.1037/ort0000405 PMID: 30816722

Manian, N., & Sorensen, C. (2024). *Building school community partnerships for mental health supports and services*. National Comprehensive Center at Westat.

Matlin, S. L., Champine, R. B., Strambler, M. J., O'Brien, C., Hoffman, E., Whitson, M., Kolka, L., & Tebes, J. K. (2019). A community's response to adverse childhood experiences: Building a Resilient, Trauma-Informed Community. *American Journal of Community Psychology*, *64*(3-4), 451–466. DOI: 10.1002/ajcp.12386 PMID: 31486086

McKinley, J. A. (2024). *"Trust Us to Teach It": Examining the Associations Among Leadership, Organizational Trust, and Well-being in Educational Settings* (Doctoral dissertation, Illinois State University).

Meador, J. A., & Foster, J. M. (2025). The role of school counselors in preventing child sexual abuse. *Journal of School-Based Counseling Policy and Evaluation*, *7*(1).

Morrow, A. S., & Villodas, M. T. (2018). Direct and indirect pathways from adverse childhood experiences to high school dropout among high-risk adolescents. *Journal of Research on Adolescence*, *28*(2), 327–341. DOI: 10.1111/jora.12332 PMID: 28736884

Nance, J. P. (2017). Student surveillance, racial inequalities, and implicit racial bias. *Emory Law Journal*, *66*, 765–838. https://scholarship.law.ufl.edu/cgi/viewcontent.cgi? article=1793&context=facultypub

National Center for PTSD. (2025). History of PTSD in veterans: Civil War to DSM-5. *U.S. Department of Veteran Affairs*. https://www.ptsd.va.gov/understand/what/history_ptsd.asp#:~:text=PTSD%20became%20a%20mental%20health,to%20create%20the%20PTSD%20diagnosis

National Child Traumatic Stress Network. (2017). *Addressing race and trauma in the classroom: A resource for educators.* National Center for Child Traumatic Stress. Retrieved from: https://www.nctsn.org/sites/default/files/resources//addressing_ race_and_trauma_in_the_classroom_educators.pdf

National Child Traumatic Stress Network. Schools Committee. (2017). *Creating, supporting, and sustaining trauma-informed schools: A system framework.* Los Angeles, CA, and Durham, NC: National Center for Child Traumatic Stress. Retrieved from: https://www.nctsn.org/sites/default/files/resources/creating_supporting_sustaining_traum a_informed_schools_a_systems_framework.pdf

National Child Traumatic Stress Network. (n.d.). *Essential elements.*https://www. nctsn.org/trauma-informed-care/traumainformed-systems/schools/essentialelements

National Policy Board for Educational Administration. (2018). *National Educational Leadership Preparation (NELP) program recognition standards building level.* https:// www.npbea.org/wp-content/uploads/ 2018/11/NELP-Building-Standards.pdf

Neves, I. C., Amorim, F. F., & Ribeiro Salomon, A. L. (2020). Burnout syndrome on teachers and its relation to nutrition: An integrative review. *Current Psychiatry Research and Reviews, 16*(1), 31–41. DOI: 10.2174/1573400515666191202113523

Nickerson, A., & Jimerson, S. R. (2015). *Supporting students experiencing childhood trauma: Tips for parents and educators.* National Association of School Psychologists. https://www.nasponline.org/ resources-and-publications/resources-and-podcasts/school-climate-safety-and-crisis/mental-health -resources/trauma/supporting-students-experiencing-childhood-trauma-tips-for-parents-and-educators

Perry, D., & Daniels, M. (2016). Implementing trauma-informed practices in the school setting: A pilot study. *School Mental Health, 8*(1), 177–188. DOI: 10.1007/s12310-016-9182-3

Plumb, J., Kersevich, S. E., & Bush, K. A. (2016). Trauma-sensitive schools: An evidence-based approach. *School Social Work Journal, 40*(2), 37–60.

Roseby, S., & Gascoigne, M. (2021). A systematic review on the impact of trauma-informed education programs on academic and academic-related functioning for students who have experienced childhood adversity. *Traumatology, 27*(2), 149–167. DOI: 10.1037/trm0000276

School Health Assessment and Performance Evaluation System. (2023). *Trauma responsive schools: What is the TSR-IA.*https://theshapesystem.com/trauma/

Shooks, B. A. (2020). *The impact of trauma-informed pedagogical practices on teacher self efficacy.* (Publication No. 28025831) [Doctoral dissertation, Cornerstone University]. ProQuest Dissertations & Theses.

Siegel, D. J. (1999). *The developing mind: Toward a neurobiology of interpersonal experience.* Guilford Press.

Stempel, H., Cox-Martin, M., Bronsert, M., Dickinson, L. M., & Allison, M. A. (2017). Chronic school absenteeism and the role of adverse childhood experiences. *Academic Pediatrics, 17*(8), 837–843. DOI: 10.1016/j.acap.2017.09.013 PMID: 28927940

Stewart-Tufescu, A., Struck, S., Taillieu, T., Salmon, S., Fortier, J., Brownell, M., Chartier, M., Yakubovich, A. R., & Afifi, T. O. (2022). Adverse childhood experiences and education outcomes among adolescents: Linking survey and administrative data. *International Journal of Environmental Research and Public Health, 19*(18), 1–17. DOI: 10.3390/ijerph191811564 PMID: 36141833

Stickl Haugen, J., Bledsoe, K. G., & Springfield, J. (2023). The development and evaluation of the Anti-racist School Counseling Inventory. *Professional School Counseling, 27*(1), 2156759X231218907. https:// doi-org.libproxy.library.wmich.edu/10.1177/2156759X231218907. DOI: 10.1177/2156759X231218907

Substance Abuse and Mental Health Services Administration (SAMHSA). (2014). SAMHSA's concept of trauma and guidance for a trauma-informed approach (HHS Publication No. 14-4884). https://ncsacw.acf.hhs.gov/userfiles/files/SAMHSA_Trauma.pdf

Tan, T. X., Wang, Y., & Ruggerio, A. D. (2017). Childhood adversity and children's academic functioning: Roles of parenting stress and neighborhood support. *Journal of Child and Family Studies*, *26*(10), 2742–2752. DOI: 10.1007/s10826-017-0775-8

Thomas, M. S., Crosby, S., & Vanderhaar, J. (2019). Trauma-informed practices in schools across two decades: An interdisciplinary review of research. *Review of Research in Education*, *43*(1), 422–452. DOI: 10.3102/0091732X18821123

U.S. Department of Education. (2018). 2015-16 - Civil rights data collection: School climate and safety. https://www2.ed.gov/about/offices/list/ocr/docs/school-climate-and-safety.pdf

Van Asselt, K. W., Soli, L. L., & Berry, E. L. (2016). Crisis fearlessness: A call for trauma competencies in counselor education. *Journal of Individual Psychology*, *72*(3), 200–213. DOI: 10.1353/jip.2016.0017

Venet, A. S. (2021). *Equity-centered trauma-informed education*. W.W. Norton & Company.

Wassink-de Stigter, R., Kooijmans, R., Asselman, M. W., Offerman, E. C. P., Nelen, W., & Helmond, P. (2022). Facilitators and barriers in the implementation of trauma-informed approaches in schools: A scoping review. *School Mental Health*, *14*(3), 470–484. DOI: 10.1007/s12310-021-09496-w

Williams, K. L., Coles, J. A., & Reynolds, P. (2020). (Re) creating the script: A framework of agency, accountability, and resisting deficit depictions of Black students in P-20 education. *The Journal of Negro Education*, *89*(3), 249–266. https://muse.jhu.edu/article/802542

Wolfe, D. A. (2018). Why polyvictimization matters. *Journal of Interpersonal Violence*, *33*(5), 832–837. DOI: 10.1177/0886260517752215 PMID: 29411694

ADDITIONAL READING

Alexander, J. (2019). *Building trauma-sensitive schools: Your guide to creating safe, supportive learning environments for all students*. Paul H. Brookes Publishing Co.

Center for Safe & Resilient Schools and Workplaces. (2024). *Trauma aware schools*.https://traumaawareschools.org/

Forbes, H. T. (2012). *Help for Billy: A beyond consequences approach to helping challenging children in the classroom*. Beyond Consequences Institute.

Forbes, H. T. (n.d.). *Beyond Consequences Institute: Trauma-informed solutions for schools, parents, and professionals*. Beyond Consequences. https://www.beyondconsequences.com/

Forbes, H. T., & Sporleder, J. (2019). *The trauma-informed school: Administrator's guide a step-by-step implementation guide for administrators and school personnel*. Beyond Consequences Institute.

Healy, G. (2023). *Regulation and co-regulation: Accessible neuroscience and connection strategies that bring calm into the classroom*. National Center for Youth Issues.

National Child Traumatic Stress Network. (2024). *Defining child traumatic stress*. https://www.nctsn.org/

Souers, K., & Hall, P. (2016). *Fostering resilient learners: Strategies for creating a trauma-sensitive classroom*. Association for Supervision and Curriculum Development (ASCD)

van der Kolk, B. A. (2014). *The body keeps the score: Brain, mind, and body in the healing of trauma*. Viking.

Venet, A. S. (2023). *Equity-centered trauma-informed education (Equity and Social Justice in Education Series)*. Routledge.

KEY TERMS AND DEFINITIONS

Compassion Fatigue: The mental and physical exhaustion felt by helping professionals when working with survivors of trauma.

Indirect Trauma: An inclusive term that includes compassion fatigue, secondary traumatic stress, and vicarious trauma and is the natural result of proximity to trauma.

Occupational Burnout: The workplace experience in which stressors are chronic and are not addressed effectively, which results in physical and mental exhaustion, cynicism, decreased morale, and low productivity.

Post-Traumatic Stress Disorder (PTSD): According to the Diagnostic Statistical Manual of Mental Disorders V-TR (DSM5TR; American Psychiatric Association [APA], 2022), the criteria for post-traumatic stress disorder includes "exposure to actual or threatened death, serious injury, or sexual violence" (p. 670). This includes direct experiences as a victim or witness, learning the incident occurred to a close family member, or repeated exposure to the event's details.

Secondary Traumatic Stress (STS): Stress that manifests from knowledge about trauma that another individual or group experienced. This can occur immediately after a single exposure. Symptoms correlate with those of PTSD and include avoidance, intrusive thoughts, and a heightened state of arousal.

Shared Trauma (ST): when the helper (school counselor or teacher) and clients (students or colleagues) are both exposed to the trauma-causing experience (e.g., death of a classmate due to gun violence, suicide, or experience of a natural disaster).

Trauma: One or more experiences that are physically, mentally, sexually, spiritually, or emotionally harmful or life-threatening and have lasting effects. It is best and most accurately defined by the individual who experienced it.

Vicarious trauma (VT): The emotional effect from proximity to another's trauma. It changes their schema or worldview due to exposure to victims' lived experiences. A belief in a mostly good, safe world may change to one of distrust and feelings of unsafety. VT can increase over time if not addressed, and it is related to burnout and leaving the field.

Chapter 3
MTSS and SEL:
Behavior

Michael Ellison
https://orcid.org/0009-0000-7803-7063
National University, USA

ABSTRACT

MTSS and Social emotional learning are not just a group of tiers and layers. This can be compared to a cake. Within MTSS there are certain issues that have to be discussed that are layered within the process of helping a child. The Base (Tier 1): Starts with high-quality instruction for all, with SEL baked in. This creates a positive learning environment where students feel valued and can develop crucial social-emotional skills. Adding Flavor (Tier 2): Involves early detection of students needing extra help. Targeted interventions address specific needs, like executive functioning, early childhood development, and ADHD. The Finishing Touch (Tier 3): Provides highly individualized support, like one-on-one instruction or therapy. Strong collaboration between educators, families, and specialists is key. Holistic Approach: MTSS weaves SEL throughout all tiers, recognizes the impact of trauma, and emphasizes family engagement. It's about nourishing the whole child, academically, socially, and emotionally.

SOCIAL-EMOTIONAL LEARNING, MULTI-TIERED SYSTEMS OF SUPPORT, AND TRAUMA-INFORMED CARE

Plato (375 BC) professed that social justice, encouraging student talents, and good citizenship were important for student development. Society should support children to create people who want to support society (Dussault & Thompson, 2024). Thus, Plato (375 BC) may have begun the social-emotional movement in education (Dussault & Thompson, 2024). According to the American Psychological Association (2024), Social emotions include interactions with others and how we perceive their thoughts and feelings towards us, and there is a process of getting through these interactions called social-emotional learning. Social-emotional learning is how people manage emotions and behavior consciously and unconsciously (APA, 2024). Adolescence is a critical development period; obtaining and utilizing social-emotional tools and skills is crucial (APA, 2024). The World Health Organization (2024) stated that adolescent phases between childhood and adulthood are from 10 to 19. There are five competencies in social-emotional learning (Jackson et al., 2024).

DOI: 10.4018/979-8-3693-9020-7.ch003

Figure 1. Social-emotional learning competencies

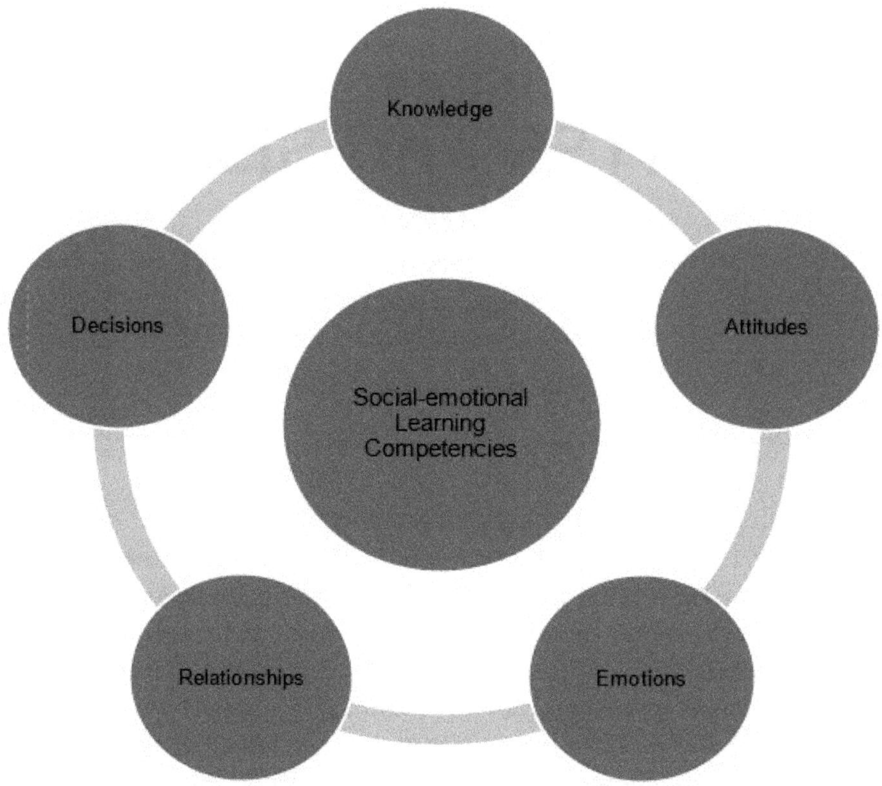

Figure Note: Adapted from Jackson et al., 2024 and the American Psychological Association

- Attitudes are enduring and relatively objective to a person, individual, or group. The concept of attitude ranges from negative to positive. Attitude derives from specific beliefs, emotions, and past behaviors (APA, 2024).
- Knowledge is a state of being familiar with something and aware of its existence, usually resulting from experience. It can also refer to an individual's understanding/ information range (APA, 2024).
- Skills to recognize and manage their emotions- These fall under emotional intelligence, which is the processing of emotional information and its use, as well as the processing of reasoning and cognitive activities. Emotional intelligence has more to do with the individual's development than age (APA, 2024).
- Establish and maintain positive relationships- an association or connection between two or more people. relationships are often thought of when you think of family, friendships, partnerships, marriages, etc. An individual's relationships, especially in adolescence, are crucial to their development (APA, 2024).

- Make responsible decisions- decision-making is a process that involves two or more alternatives, and decision-making can be clear-cut or complex. All definitions are checked and come from the (APA, 2024).

Multi-Tiered Systems of Support

Multi-Tiered System of Support MTSS is a proactive and comprehensive approach to supporting all students' academic and social-emotional needs. It has three levels of support. This data-driven system allows students to be identified and given the proper help. Data is processed through cycles and periodically given assessments (Vetter et al., 2024). Multi-tiered systems of support and social-emotional learning trauma-informed care fall into Trauma-Informed Care. Trauma-informed care is bringing about such programs as restorative justice and restorative classrooms and promoting relationship safety and agency (Parameswaran et al., 2024). Multi-tier systems of support and social-emotional learning, as well as mental health, play a crucial part in framing how these programs are being shaped. There is an increasing demand for intervention and therapy due to the trauma that our youth is facing in schools today.

Figure 2. Tiered intervention systems

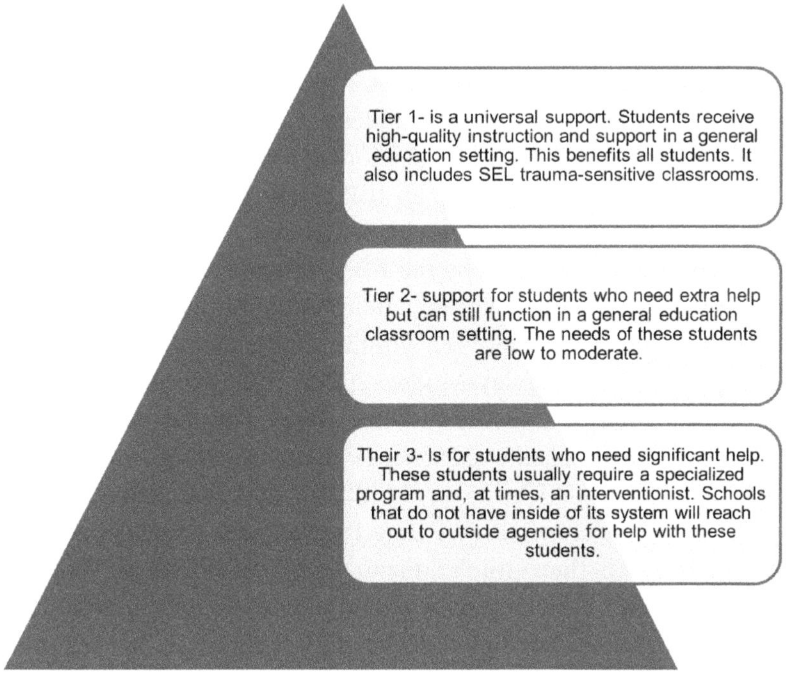

Functional Behavior Assessments (FBA)

The COVID-19 virus caused a significant emotional impact on students. Many students were isolated during COVID-19, creating a mental effect in many classrooms in the United States and worldwide (Hamilton, 2024). The need for a multi-tiered system and social-emotional learning Is also linked to socioeconomic status. Students from poverty and economic backgrounds where the household struggles financially carry the stress that their parents bring home due to trying to keep a roof over their family's head and food on the table (Parameswaran et al.,2024).

Trauma such as bullying, identity issues, and other trauma issues have given way to a significant need for trauma-informed care at schools. Establishing the child's needs is key to deciding how to serve them best (Toa et al., 2024). The function-based approach of a Functional Behavior Assessment (FBA) is a powerful tool for understanding why a child behaves in a certain way (F.B.A, 2024). Instead of simply addressing the behavior itself, it delves into the root causes, identifying the behavior's function for the child. This understanding is crucial for developing effective strategies that address those underlying needs and lead to positive change Christensen (2024).

A Functional Behavior Assessment (FBA) can be conducted by the Individualized Education Program (IEP) team, which includes educators, specialists, and parents who work collaboratively. In some cases, an expert like a Board Certified Behavior Analyst (BCBA) may be brought in to provide specialized expertise in assessing and developing behavior intervention plans (F.B.A, 2024). The Individuals with Disabilities Education Act (IDEA) recognizes the importance of addressing behavior in the educational setting. It mandates that the IEP team consider various strategies, including Positive Behavioral Interventions and Supports (PBIS) and FBAs when a student's behavior impedes their learning or disrupts the learning of others (ACT, 2025). If a child's behavior becomes a barrier to their educational progress or creates a disruptive environment, requesting an IEP team meeting is essential. The team can then determine whether a formal FBA is necessary and whether specific behavioral goals should be included in the child's IEP. These goals, informed by the FBA, provide a roadmap for supporting the child's behavioral needs and fostering a positive learning environment for everyone.

A Holistic Approach. Cooperation between families and educators can achieve a holistic understanding of the child (Schwind & Handley-Moore, 2024). This can develop a more comprehensive understanding of the child's strengths, needs, and challenges. Families provide valuable insights into the child's development, preferences, and experiences outside of school, while educators offer observations and data from the school setting (Chacko et al., (2024). This shared understanding allows for more effective and targeted interventions. Increased Parent Engagement is important for strong partnerships encouraging parent engagement in their child's education and development. When parents and students feel supported and informed, they are more likely to actively participate in interventions and carry over strategies at home, leading to better outcomes for the child (Hamilton, 2024). This partnership fosters open communication and collaboration between families and school staff. This allows for ongoing sharing of information, progress monitoring, and adjustments to interventions as needed. Empowerment and advocacy can be accomplished with strong partnerships that empower families to advocate for their children's needs and actively participate in decision-making processes (Schwind & Moore, (2024). This collaborative approach ensures that the child's voice is heard, and their needs are met.

Families can share information about the child's interests, routines, and experiences at home. Attending meetings and conferences is important for parents, administration, and teachers. The best possible plan can be implemented and adjusted by actively participating in parent-teacher conferences, IEP meetings, and other collaborative meetings to share information and develop goals (Chacko et al., 2024). Fostering strong family and school partnerships, education systems can maximize the impact of their interventions within the MTSS framework. This collaborative approach ensures that students receive comprehensive and consistent support, leading to improved academic, behavioral, and social-emotional outcomes and setting the stage for future success. Academic, behavioral, and social-emotional aspects of a student's development are interconnected (Guest et al., 2024). This connection and utilizing a holistic approach to intervention addresses the whole child and their unique needs.

School-Based Occupational Therapy Practitioners Sbotp's Have Changed

An important part of the Multi-Tiered System of Support MTSS and student success is the evolving role of School-Based Occupational Therapy Practitioners (SBOTPs) and their crucial contribution to supporting students' overall well-being and academic success. (Schwind & Handley-Moore, 2024). While SBOTPs have traditionally focused on students with disabilities, their expertise is increasingly considered valuable for all students, including those in general education. School-Based Occupational Therapy Practitioners (SBOTPs) are uniquely positioned to address many student needs within the school setting. Their expertise extends beyond traditional motor skills and sensory processing to encompass areas such as Activities of Daily Living (ADL). School-Based Occupational Therapy Practitioners (SBOTPs) can be vital in supporting students who struggle with ADL tasks, such as feeding, dressing, and hygiene. Difficulties with feeding can affect a child's focus, attention, and energy levels, impacting their ability to learn and participate in the classroom (Hintz et al., 2024). These skills are essential for independence and can significantly impact a child's development. SBOTPs can contribute to mental health initiatives by addressing issues like anxiety, stress management, and emotional regulation through activities that promote self-regulation and coping skills. Also, by addressing underlying sensory, motor, or cognitive challenges, SBOTPs can help students improve their focus, attention, and overall academic performance (Schwind & Handley-Moore, 2024). Addressing ADL within MTSS emphasizes integrating ADL support within the Multi-Tiered System of Supports (MTSS) framework. This means that SBOTPs can provide interventions at various levels.

Figure 3. School-based occupational therapy practitioners tiered support

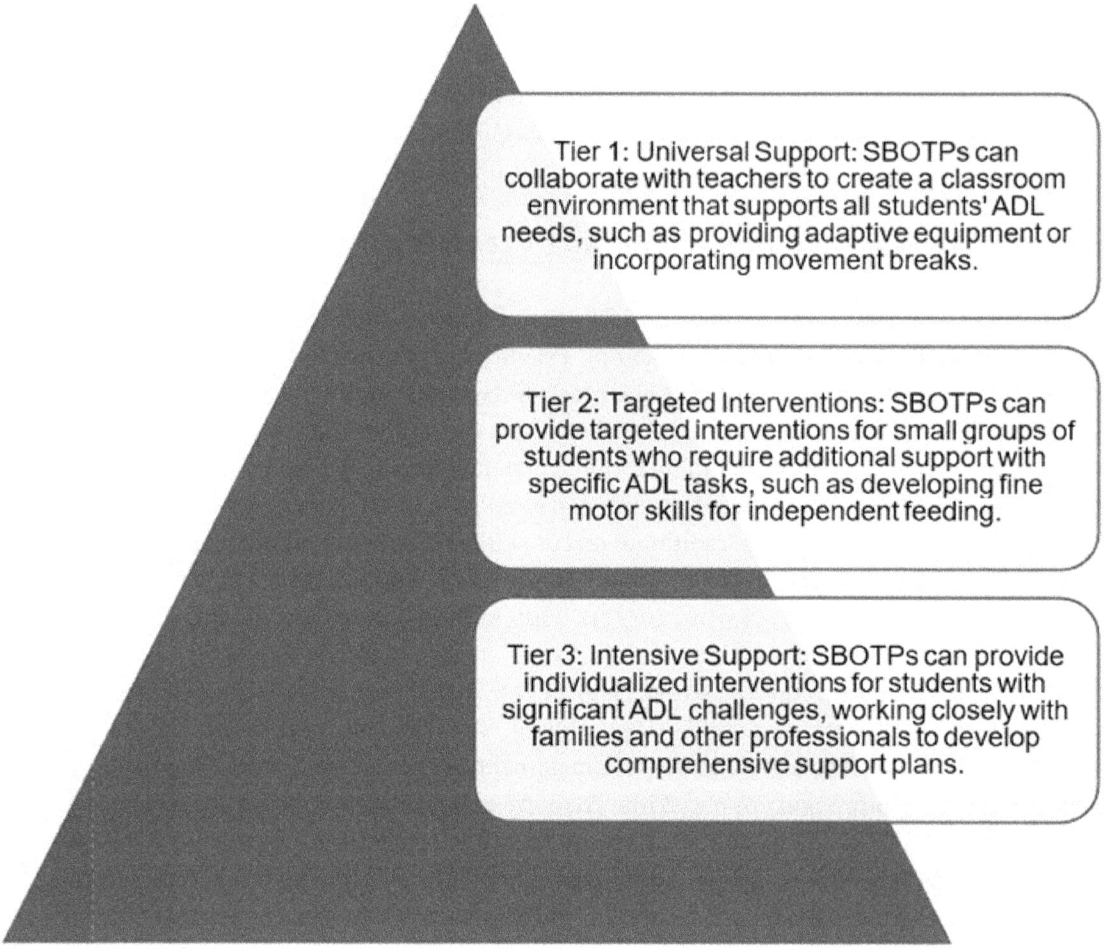

Figure Note: Add a citation and any necessary information

The impact of Activities of Daily Living (ADL) on Student Success can impact academic skills. Difficulties with Activities of Daily Living (ADLs) can be associated with behavioral manifestations such as frustration and anxiety, which may present as challenging behaviors that could disrupt the learning environment and affect social interactions (Chacko et al., 2024). Challenges with ADLs can have social-emotional considerations that can impact a child's self-esteem, confidence, and social interactions and possibly contribute to social isolation or bullying experiences (Guest et al., 2025). By recognizing the interconnectedness of ADL, academic performance, and social-emotional well-being, schools can utilize the expertise of SBOTPs to provide comprehensive support for all students (Ray et al., 2024). This holistic approach can improve student outcomes, creating a more inclusive and supportive learning environment where every child can thrive. This is a valuable contribution of occupational therapy practitioners (OTPs), particularly school-based OTPs (SBOTPs), in fostering student success across academic, behavioral, and social-emotional domains. OTPs can effectively support students within the Multi-Tiered System of Support (MTSS) framework by implementing targeted interventions and utilizing their expertise in activity analysis and adaptation.

A study conducted by Waldron (2024) showed that 50% of administrators reported using a workload model for occupational therapy (OT) services, while 83% reported effective integration of OT services within their district. Additionally, 75% of administrators identified administrative support as a top five factor impacting the successful implementation of OT services. Individual and group services were perceived as more effective than contextual group and individual services. Direct services were perceived as highly effective, whereas preventative programming and screenings were reported as the least successfully implemented. Directors of Special Education reported a higher overall perceived value and effectiveness of occupational therapy services compared to Principals. Participants were surveyed about their familiarity with the role of occupational therapy in school-based practice as outlined by the Individuals with Disabilities Education Act (IDEA) and the Every Student Succeeds Act (ESSA) (see Figure 4). No significant difference in reported familiarity with IDEA and ESSA was observed between the two participant groups. Regarding the inclusion of occupational therapists in Multi-Tiered Systems of Support (MTSS) in their districts, participant responses were never (n=1, 3%), sometimes(n=26, 90%), and always (n=2, 7%) (Figure 9). The most frequently reported factor impacting the inclusion of occupational therapists in MTSS was that OT services are based on the needs indicated in the Individualized Education Program (IEP) (n=8, 29%).

Occupational Therapy

Implementing Tier 2 and Tier 3 interventions, including occupational therapy services and sensory strategies, has demonstrated significant positive outcomes for students. These interventions have led to addressing underlying sensory needs, motor challenges, or emotional regulation difficulties, and they can help students manage their behavior more effectively. This also includes improved academic attention (Hamilton, 2024; O'Donnell, 2024). Occupational therapy can support students' ability to focus, attend, and engage in learning activities, leading to improved academic performance. It also includes increased participation and engagement. Addressing barriers to participation, such as sensory sensitivities or motor challenges, students are more likely to actively engage in classroom activities and social interactions. Occupational therapists possess specialized training and expertise in activity analysis, which involves breaking down activities into their component parts to understand the skills required for successful participation (Schwind et al., 2024). They represent a bridge to successfully understanding a student's needs and implementing an intervention. This expertise allows OTPs to scaffold skills. Occupational Therapy Practitioners (OTPs) can decompose complex skills into smaller, more manageable components, offering support and guidance to facilitate a student's progressive skill development. This can involve adapting tasks to enhance accessibility and incrementally increasing the level of challenge as the student advances (Stodden et al., 2023). Educational activities can be adjusted in difficulty to align with a student's capabilities, aiming to provide appropriate challenges without being overwhelming.

In a study by Schwind and Handley-Moore (2024), school-based occupational therapy practitioners (SBOTPs) proved to be valuable in supporting general education students with Activities of Daily Living (ADL) tasks, like feeding Within a Multi-Tiered Systems of Support (MTSS) framework the findings indicate that a tiered approach to addressing ADL tasks may contribute to improvements in academic, behavioral, and social-emotional skills. Additionally, the study demonstrates the effectiveness of a tiered approach, incorporating occupational therapy and sensory strategies, in supporting students with behavioral challenges in the cafeteria to promote self-regulation and academic outcomes. Modifying tasks and creating adaptations: OTPs can promote independence and successful participation. This may involve using adaptive equipment, modifying the physical environment, or adjusting teaching strategies. The Occupational Therapy Practice Framework - 4th edition (OTPF-4) aligns with the MTSS framework (AOTA, 2020). This means that SBOTPs can effectively contribute to all tiers of intervention.

Figure 4. Occupational therapy tiered intervention

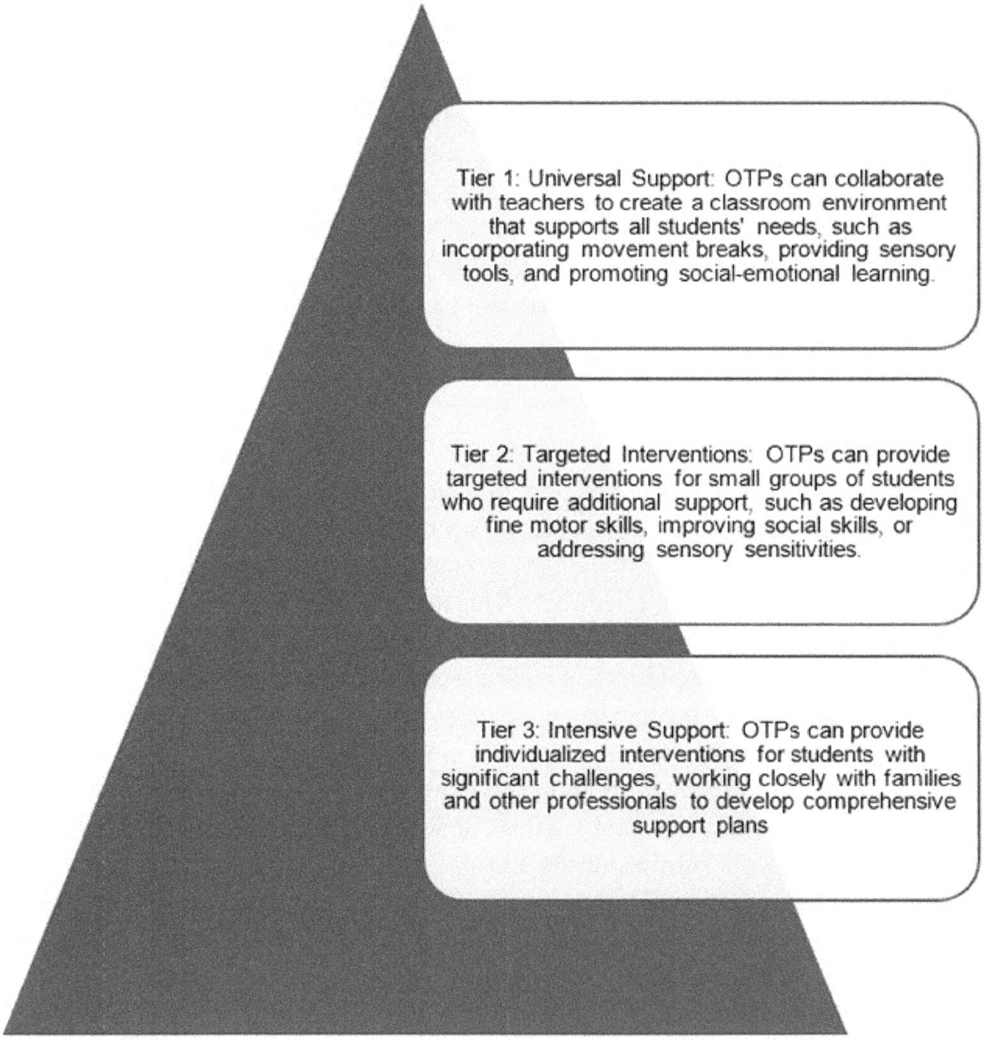

Figure Note: American Occupational Therapy Association (AOTA, 2020a), 4th edition (2020)

By utilizing their expertise in activity analysis, adaptation, and the Multi-Tiered System of Support (MTSS) framework, OTPs can play a crucial role in supporting students' success across all areas of development. This collaborative and holistic approach can improve student outcomes, creating a more inclusive and supportive learning environment where every child can thrive (Schwind & Handley-More,

2024). Strong family and school partnerships are essential when Occupational Therapy Practitioners (OTPs) work within the Multi-Tiered System of Support (MTSS) framework to support students. This collaborative approach is crucial for building the academic, behavioral, and social-emotional skills that pave the way for future success. When families and schools work together, they can create a consistent support system for the child across home and school environments (Stodden et al.,2023). This consistency reinforces learning and skill development, leading to greater progress and generalization of skills. Developing and implementing home programs using OTPs can work with families to develop and implement home programs that reinforce skills learned at school. This might involve improving fine motor skills, developing sensory strategies to manage challenging behaviors, or practicing social skills (Chacko, 2024). Occupational Therapy Practitioners (OTPs) can collaborate with teachers and other school staff to coordinate interventions and ensure consistency across environments. This might involve adapting classroom activities, providing sensory breaks, or implementing behavioral support plans.

Executive Function and Digital Technology

A student's Multi-Tiered System of Support MTSS tier Executive Function (EF) must be addressed to implement an intervention. Executive function (EF) skills are important in childhood education, especially for students with special educational needs (SEN) (Gunners, 2024). Executive functions, encompassing abilities like planning, working memory, and self-regulation, are fundamental for academic success and overall well-being (Gunnars, 2024). The review emphasizes that children with SEN often face challenges with these skills, making targeted support crucial. This plays an important role in MTSS. Game-based learning: Engaging games can be designed to specifically target and strengthen different EF skills in an interactive and motivating way (Hamilton, 2024). Targeted EF skills training and digital tools can deliver structured exercises and activities that improve specific executive functions like attention, inhibition, or cognitive flexibility (Guest, 2025). Classroom management tools can assist educators in monitoring student behavior and engagement, allowing for timely interventions and adjustments to the learning environment. Tailoring teaching strategies to individual needs is essential for effectively supporting EF development in all students, particularly those with SEN (Stodden et al., 2023). Digital tools can facilitate personalized learning by providing adaptable and differentiated instruction. Digital technology as an EF support: The review provides evidence for the effectiveness of digital interventions in enhancing EF skills training, notably in areas like mathematics, language acquisition, and coding. These tools offer engaging and interactive ways to practice and strengthen these crucial cognitive abilities (Gunnars, 2024). Teacher beliefs and motivation for students' EF development can significantly impact their success. Teachers knowledgeable about EF and utilizing effective strategies, including digital tools, play a vital role in fostering these skills in their students. It advocates for a thoughtful and strategic approach to integrating technology in the classroom, emphasizing personalized learning and teacher support (Gunnars, 2024).

Executive Functioning

The importance of foundational Executive Function EF skills can be linked to inhibiting eye movement (Chan et al., 2022; Zhou et al., 2021). This ability to control impulsive eye movements is a fundamental building block for broader inhibitory control, a key component of executive function. As Bishara & Kaplan (2022) explain, the capacity to inhibit dominant reactions begins developing in infancy with the control of eye movements, highlighting the significance of supporting these foundational skills early on. Digital technology holds immense potential for supporting EF development and improving educational outcomes for students with Special Educational Needs (SEN). Interactive games, targeted exercises, and assistive technologies can provide engaging and personalized learning experiences that cater to individual needs and learning styles. EF helps to explore challenges faced by students with, or at risk for, Emotional and Behavioral Disorders (EBD) (Chacko et al.,2024). These students often exhibit lower EF and academic performance levels than their typically developing peers. This finding underscores the importance of early identification and intervention for these students. There is a link between EF, academic success, and stress. Stronger EF skills predict better academic performance, while perceived stress negatively impacts EF and academic outcomes. This suggests that addressing stress and promoting emotional well-being are crucial for supporting EF development and academic achievement, especially in students with (EBD) (Hintz et al., 2024). Specifically, students with, or at risk for, Emotional and Behavioral Disorders (EBD) reported significantly higher levels of perceived stress compared to their peers. This heightened stress was particularly prominent in the family and peer domains, suggesting that these students may face greater challenges in their relationships and social interactions (O'Donnell, 2024).

There is an interconnectedness of individual EF, stressors within the home and school environments, and students' overall ability to succeed academically. Students with or at risk for EBD exhibited lower scores on EF tasks and displayed a heightened sensitivity to experienced stress (Chan et al., 2022). This suggests that these students may be more vulnerable to the negative impacts of stress on their cognitive functioning and academic performance. There is a critical need for early identification and effective interventions that address the underlying factors contributing to academic success in students with, or at risk for, Emotional and Behavioral Disorders (EBD) (Hamilton, 2025). Focusing on these foundational elements can significantly improve their educational outcomes and well-being. Intervention is crucial in executive function (EF) skills and stress management in academic competence. Students with EBD often exhibit weaker EF skills, such as planning, working memory, and self-regulation, which can hinder their learning and academic performance (Bishara & Kaplan, 2022). Additionally, they experience heightened levels of stress, particularly within the family and peer domains, which can further impede their cognitive functioning and academic success. Therefore, effective interventions should target both (EF) development and stress reduction. This might involve implementing evidence-based programs that enhance EF skills through targeted exercises and activities, and strategies to promote coping mechanisms and stress management techniques (Lambert et al.,2024). Furthermore, creating a supportive and understanding school environment that minimizes stressors and fosters a sense of belonging is crucial for these students (Waldren, 2025).

Special Populations

When designing educational interventions, it is important to consider the individual needs of students with special educational needs (SEN), including those with EBD. A one-size-fits-all approach is unlikely to be effective. Instead, personalized strategies that cater to specific strengths and challenges are necessary to optimize learning and development (Sodden et al., 2023). By recognizing the interconnectedness of (EF), stress, and academic achievement and tailoring interventions accordingly, educators can empower EBD students to overcome challenges, build resilience, and reach their full potential (Christensen, 2025). This approach benefits the individual student and contributes to a more inclusive and supportive learning environment. Many students with (SEN), including those with EBD, experience difficulties with EF, which can hinder their learning and progress. Therefore, targeted interventions that strengthen these essential cognitive abilities are crucial (O'Donnell, 2024). Findings revealed significant differences between students with or at risk for EBD and their peers without behavior problems in terms of perceived stress, EF, and academic outcomes. Students with EBD reported higher levels of perceived stress, particularly in the family and peer domains, indicating they may face greater challenges in their social and emotional lives. Moreover, they demonstrated poorer performance on EF tasks, specifically in working memory and cognitive flexibility, which are vital for learning and problem-solving (Guest, 2025). These difficulties in EF were, in turn, related to lower academic outcomes.

A strong link exists between perceived stress, EF, and academic performance. Higher levels of perceived stress were negatively associated with EF performance, indirectly impacting academic outcomes. This underscores the importance of addressing stress and promoting emotional well-being in students, especially those with EBD, as it can significantly affect their cognitive functioning and academic success (Waldren, 2024). On the other hand, a comprehensive approach is needed to support students with SEN in primary education. This involves careful consideration of the impact of digital technology, targeted interventions to enhance EF skills, and strategies to address stress and promote emotional well-being. By addressing these interconnected factors, educators can create a more inclusive and supportive learning environment where all students can thrive (Brant, 2024). Students face challenges with, or at risk for, Emotional and Behavioral Disorders (EBD) in schools, highlighting the interconnectedness of executive function (EF), stress, and academic performance.

Students with Emotional and Behavioral Disorders (EBD) demonstrate challenges in key areas of executive functioning (EF), specifically working memory and cognitive flexibility, when compared to their typically developing peers. These EF skills are fundamental to the learning process and academic success, enabling students to retain information, transition smoothly between tasks, and adapt to changing demands within the classroom (Dussault& Thompson, 2024). Furthermore, these students exhibited lower performance on standardized academic measures in mathematics and English Language Arts (ELA), suggesting a correlation between their EF difficulties and academic struggles. Recognizing and addressing the unique needs of students with EBD is important (Donohue, 2025). Their heightened sensitivity to stress and difficulties with EF can create a cycle of vulnerability that hinders their academic progress. Early identification and intervention are crucial to break this cycle and foster resilience.

To improve outcomes for students with EBD, there is a need for targeted interventions that address the underlying factors contributing to their academic challenges. This includes programs that strengthen (EF) skills through engaging activities, exercises, and strategies to manage stress and promote emotional well-being (Gunnars, 2024). By focusing on these foundational elements, educators can empower students with EBD to overcome obstacles, build resilience, and achieve academic success. Specifically, the study indicates that students with EBD tend to perceive higher levels of stress in their lives, particularly within the family and peer domains. This heightened stress can negatively affect their EF skills, such as working memory, cognitive flexibility, and inhibitory control, which are essential for learning and problem-solving (Stodden, 2023). As a result, these students may struggle academically, demonstrating lower performance in areas like math and language arts. It is important to address perceived stress and EF in interventions to improve academic outcomes for students with EBD. A two-pronged approach is necessary. Implementing strategies to help students manage and cope with stress, such as mindfulness techniques, relaxation exercises, and social-emotional learning programs, can create a more conducive learning environment and improve their overall well-being (Stodden, 2023). Strengthening EF by providing targeted interventions that enhance EF skills, such as cognitive training exercises, working memory games, and organizational strategies, can empower students to regulate their thoughts and behaviors better, leading to improved academic performance (Donohue, 2025).

Educators can create a more supportive and effective learning environment by addressing the emotional and cognitive factors contributing to academic challenges in students with EBD. This holistic approach recognizes the interconnectedness of stress, EF, and academic achievement and aims to provide students with the tools they need to thrive academically and emotionally. Behavioral Parent Training (BPT) is an important intervention (Chacko et al., 2024). BPT is recognized as a well-established and extensively studied psychosocial intervention for children with various mental health disorders, including ADHD. This approach equips parents with effective strategies to manage their child's behavior, improve communication, and foster positive parent-child interactions (Nikolašević et al., 2022). BPT programs typically involve parent education, skill-building exercises, and ongoing support to help parents implement these strategies daily. There is a need for Adolescent-Focused BPT. BPT has demonstrated significant benefits for children with ADHD, as adolescents with ADHD face unique challenges and require tailored interventions to address their developmental needs. There is also a need to enhance the potency and effectiveness of BPT programs. This may involve exploring innovative delivery methods, such as incorporating technology or group-based formats, to increase accessibility and engagement. Additionally, tailoring BPT programs to address specific challenges faced by adolescents with ADHD, such as academic difficulties, social skills deficits, and emotional regulation issues, is crucial.

Evidence-based psychosocial interventions, particularly BPT, in the treatment of ADHD in children and adolescents call for these interventions and ensure that they are accessible, engaging, and effective for all young people with ADHD. By equipping parents and families with the knowledge and skills to support their children, psychosocial interventions can significantly improve the quality of life for those affected by ADHD and help them reach their full potential. Key components of implementing (BPT) and interventions include: (1) Clear Goals and Rules- Establishing clear expectations for behavior and academic performance helps students with ADHD understand what is expected of them and reduces ambiguity; (2) Clear Feedback- Providing immediate and specific feedback on student behavior, both positive and corrective, helps them learn from their actions and adjust as needed; (3) Rewards and Consequences- Implementing a system of rewards and consequences, such as token economies or privilege systems, can motivate students to meet behavioral goals and reinforce positive behaviors; (4) Daily Report Cards- The article highlights the daily report card as a cost-effective and efficacious positive behavior support tool. This allows for consistent communication between teachers and parents, providing regular feedback on the student's progress and facilitating collaboration between home and school, creating a learning environment that promotes positive character traits, providing opportunities for students to practice these traits, and incorporating character-building activities into civics lessons. Also, integrating character education into school education provides a strong foundation for students' personal and social development. It cultivates positive attitudes, such as respect, empathy, and fairness. It instills important civic values like justice, equality, and responsibility. This equips students with essential social skills like communication, cooperation, and conflict resolution. By nurturing these qualities in young learners, we pave the way for a future generation of responsible, engaged, and compassionate citizens (Gustina, 2024).

Oh et al. (2024) discuss and describe new and emerging interventions. These are emerging interventions for ADHD, including EndeavorRX: This FDA-approved video game treatment showed initial promise but ultimately failed to demonstrate superior improvements in ADHD behavioral symptoms compared to a control condition. This highlights the need for further research and development in digital therapeutics for ADHD. Cenextra: This intervention, which combines cognitive training with physical activity, showed promising results in improving working memory and reducing objectively assessed hyperactivity in children with ADHD. This suggests that integrating physical activity into interventions may enhance their effectiveness. CogMed: While initially believed to improve working memory, further research indicates that CogMed primarily enhances specific components of short-term memory rather than working memory capacity. This underscores the importance of accurately understanding the mechanisms and effects of interventions.

The Family Peer Advocate (FPA) ADHD Model highlights delivering evidence-based psychosocial interventions, particularly for reaching underserved populations. FPAs, who are parents of children with ADHD, provide support, guidance, and advocacy to other families navigating the challenges of ADHD (Waldron, 2024). This peer-to-peer approach can be particularly valuable in building trust and fostering engagement. Technology-based approaches emphasize the potential of technology to improve access to evidence-based interventions. This includes online self-directed behavioral parent training programs, which can offer flexibility and convenience for families. By embracing a multi-faceted approach that combines established and innovative interventions, we can provide more effective and accessible support for individuals with ADHD and their families (Gustina, 2024).

INTEGRATED SYSTEMS

MTSS is a comprehensive approach to supporting students with or at risk of learning disabilities and emotional/behavioral disorders. It advocates for integrating academic and behavioral support within a tiered intervention system, recognizing the interconnectedness of these two domains and the importance of addressing both to foster student success (O'Donnell et al., 2024). Integrated Support System: The purpose of a multi-tiered support system that seamlessly integrates academic and behavioral interventions. This approach recognizes that academic and behavioral difficulties often co-occur and influence each other. By addressing both simultaneously, schools can create a more comprehensive and effective support system for struggling learners (Hamilton, 2024). There are significant behaviors. These fundamental behaviors have a ripple effect on other areas of behavioral functioning. These include academic engagement, Active participation in learning activities, attentiveness, and task completion. Demonstrating consideration for others, following rules, and engaging in positive social interactions. Persisting in challenging tasks, demonstrating a willingness to learn, and putting forth effort to achieve goals. Educators can create a positive classroom environment by focusing on these behaviors and laying the foundation for academic and social-emotional growth (Parameswaran et al., 2024). Self-regulation techniques emphasize the importance of equipping students with self-regulation techniques. These strategies empower students to manage their emotions, behaviors, and attention, fostering independence and resilience. Examples include Mindfulness exercises, Promoting self-awareness, and emotional regulation. Cognitive behavioral strategies: Identifying and challenging negative thoughts and behaviors. Relaxation techniques: Managing s There are potential long-term consequences of unaddressed academic and behavioral difficulties. These can include academic failure, social isolation, low self-esteem, and an increased risk of mental health challenges (Chacko, 2024; Stodden, 2023).

Schools can mitigate these risks and promote positive student outcomes by implementing early and effective interventions. A proactive and holistic approach to supporting students with learning and behavioral challenges. By integrating academic and behavioral supports, targeting behaviors, and empowering students with self-regulation techniques, schools can create a more nurturing and effective learning environment that fosters success for all learners. This has a powerful impact on integrating self-regulation strategies and behavioral supports into academic interventions for students integrating reading and mathematics. By simultaneously addressing academic and behavioral factors, this approach offers a more comprehensive and effective pathway to improve student achievement (Bishara &Kaplan, 2022).

Synergistic Effects combine self-regulation of behaviors (such as academic engagement, respect, and effort) with academic interventions, creating a synergistic effect. This integrated approach simultaneously tackles multiple factors influencing student achievement, leading to more significant improvements than addressing either area in isolation. Efficient Integration of behavioral interventions can be seamlessly woven into the fabric of existing reading and mathematics interventions. Educators can efficiently incorporate behavioral support without additional time or resources (Bishara &Kaplan, 2022; Chan et al., 2022). This integrated approach maximizes efficiency and ensures that academic and behavioral needs are addressed within the learning context. Self-monitoring as a key strategy highlights the effectiveness of self-monitoring as a tool to promote self-regulation and improve student outcomes. Self-monitoring involves teaching students to track their behavior and academic progress, fostering self-awareness and accountability. This strategy empowers students to take ownership of their learning and behavior, leading to increased academic engagement and improved behavioral outcomes. Evidence-based approaches are supported by multiple randomized controlled trials involving students with academic difficulties. This rigorous research methodology provides strong evidence for the effectiveness of integrating self-regulation and behavioral support into academic interventions (Dussault & Thompson, 2024).

By incorporating self-regulation strategies and behavioral supports into their existing interventions, educators can Address multiple needs simultaneously. This integrated approach allows educators to efficiently address academic and behavioral challenges within the context of learning. Empower students: Self-monitoring strategies promote student agency and ownership of their learning and behavior. Maximize efficiency: Behavioral supports can be seamlessly integrated into existing academic interventions, minimizing the need for additional time and resources. Improve student outcomes: This approach has significantly improved academic engagement, behavior, and overall achievement in students with learning difficulties (Gunnars, 2024).

Educators can create a more supportive and effective learning environment that fosters student success by adopting this integrated approach. This is important in prioritizing behavioral expectations and procedures in the initial days of implementing a classroom intervention, even if it temporarily reduces time dedicated to academic instruction. This upfront investment in establishing clear routines and expectations pays dividends by fostering a learning environment conducive to rapid and effective integration of academic interventions (Hamilton, 2024). The successful integration of academic and behavioral support within a classroom employs self-regulation techniques designed to benefit students with, or at risk of, learning disabilities and emotional/behavioral disorders (Stodden, 2023). This approach underscores the interconnectedness of academic and behavioral learning, recognizing that students need support in both areas to thrive.

There is a significant improvement in students' self-regulation of academic engagement, a factor strongly correlated with academic achievement. By providing students with the tools and strategies to manage their learning behaviors, the intervention empowered them to take ownership of their academic success. This influences students' self-awareness and honesty regarding their behavior. Students demonstrated an increased ability to recognize and acknowledge their actions and a desire to improve their academic engagement. Interventions have fostered a sense of responsibility and agency within the students (Suharnadi et al., 2024). Beyond self-regulation, interventions also produced tangible improvements in classroom behavior. Students exhibited greater attentiveness and on-task behavior, specifically during the intervention block, indicating the efficacy of implementing strategies to promote a focused learning environment.

There is an effectiveness of integrating academic and behavioral support in a classroom setting. Educators can create a learning environment that fosters academic success and positive behavioral development by prioritizing establishing clear expectations and procedures and empowering students with self-regulation techniques. This approach holds promise for students with learning disabilities and emotional/behavioral disorders, who often require tailored support to reach their full potential (Suharnadi et al., 2024). There is a profound impact of a holistic approach to education, one that recognizes the intricate interplay between academic learning and behavioral development. By integrating academic and behavioral support within a tiered intervention system, educators can effectively address the diverse needs of students, particularly those with or at risk of learning disabilities and emotional/behavioral disorders (Stodden et al., 2023).

This highlights the transformative potential of this integrated approach. Specifically, studies focusing on behaviors – such as academic engagement, respect, and effort – can yield widespread benefits, creating a ripple effect that positively influences various aspects of student learning and behavior. There is a significant influence of behavioral intervention on students' ability to self-regulate their academic engagement (Hamilton, 2024). This carries substantial weight and correlates strongly with self-regulated academic engagement and achievement. By equipping students with the skills to monitor and manage their learning behaviors, this intervention empowers them to take ownership of their academic success. It champions a comprehensive approach that addresses the academic and behavioral facets of learning, recognizing that these two domains are intrinsically linked and mutually reinforcing.

Self-monitoring is a highly effective strategy for enhancing academic engagement and overall behavior. By encouraging students to actively reflect on and track their actions, self-monitoring fosters a sense of responsibility and agency, enabling them to make more conscious choices and strive for continuous improvement (Vetter et al., 2024). There is a paradigm shift in education that moves beyond a solely academic focus to embrace a more holistic approach that nurtures the whole child. By integrating academic and behavioral supports and empowering students with self-regulation strategies, educators can create a learning environment that fosters academic success, promotes positive behavior, and unlocks the full potential of every student.

School Counselors

Learning, and academic intervention and support. This dual approach to education ensures students are not merely recipients of knowledge and cognitive skills but also acquire the crucial interpersonal skills, emotional intelligence, and resilience necessary to navigate the complexities of an ever-evolving world (Donohue, 2024). They learn to effectively communicate, build meaningful relationships, manage their emotions, resolve conflicts constructively, and adapt to challenges with grace and determination. By fostering this comprehensive skill set, we significantly increase the likelihood of students successfully completing their high school education and transitioning seamlessly into their chosen postsecondary pathways (O'Donnell, 2024). Whether they pursue higher education, embark on vocational training, or enter the workforce directly, these students have the foundational skills to excel in their chosen fields and contribute meaningfully to society.

This holistic approach to education recognizes that academic success is but one piece of the puzzle. By nurturing students' social and emotional well-being and intellectual development, we empower them to lead fulfilling lives marked by personal growth, strong relationships, and meaningful contributions to their communities (Stodden, 2023). This investment in their holistic development yields dividends that extend far beyond the classroom walls, impacting their overall quality of life and prospects. The focus of this resource centers specifically on the cultivation of these essential social-emotional and academic competencies. Research consistently demonstrates that students with these skills are better prepared to face challenges, overcome obstacles, and thrive in diverse settings. By prioritizing these areas, we lay the foundation for students to flourish academically and personally (Bashira & Kaplan, 2022). It is important to recognize that early intervention is key. Students who receive the necessary support, particularly in their formative years, develop a stronger foundation for coping with the inevitable challenges accompanying adolescence and young adulthood. This early investment in their development can have a profound and lasting impact on their overall well-being and future success. To effectively foster these skills, we must adopt a targeted approach. Small group interventions tailored to specific developmental stages provide a supportive and focused environment for skill-building. This allows educators to address students' unique needs and challenges at different points in their development (Waldren, 2024).

The benefits of Tier 2 interventions extend far beyond the individual students participating in the groups. These interventions contribute to a positive school climate by equipping students with the skills to navigate social interactions, manage their emotions, and resolve conflicts constructively (Chacko et al., 2025). This, in turn, fosters a more supportive and inclusive learning environment for all school community members. A holistic approach to education that prioritizes social-emotional learning and academic development is essential for preparing students for success in all aspects of their lives. Investing in these key competencies and providing targeted support through interventions like small groups can empower students to thrive academically, socially, and emotionally while creating a more positive and harmonious school environment. School counselors and school-based mental health professionals possess a unique and invaluable skill set that makes them ideally suited to spearhead the development and implementation of targeted interventions, such as small group or Tier 2 supports, within the K-12 educational setting (Chacko et al., 2025). Their specialized training and expertise in child development, mental health, and counseling equip them to address the diverse needs of students comprehensively and effectively.

These professionals deeply understand the developmental stages and challenges students across different grade levels face. This knowledge allows them to design interventions tailored to specific age groups and address students' unique social, emotional, and behavioral needs at each stage of their educational journey. Furthermore, school counselors and mental health team members are adept at identifying and addressing the root causes of students' struggles. They can assess students' needs, identify barriers to success, and develop targeted interventions that build critical skills and foster resilience (Hamilton, 2024). This may include interventions focused on improving social skills, emotional regulation, conflict resolution, stress management, and academic self-efficacy. Their group dynamics and facilitation expertise enable them to create a safe and supportive environment where students can learn, grow, and practice new skills. They are skilled at fostering open communication, building trust among group members, and creating a sense of belonging, all of which are essential for effective group interventions.

The collaborative approach ensures that interventions are integrated seamlessly within the school's support system. They work closely with teachers, administrators, and families to coordinate support and ensure that students receive consistent and comprehensive care. School counselors and school-based mental health professionals play a vital role in promoting the academic, social, and emotional well-being of K-12 students. Their expertise in child development, mental health, and group dynamics makes them uniquely qualified to develop and implement effective Tier 2 interventions that address the diverse needs of students and equip them with the skills necessary for success in school and beyond (Donohue, 2025).

Absenteeism and Avoidance

A worrying trend in the post-pandemic educational landscape that is adding to MTSS. There is a significant rise in anxiety and school absenteeism among students of all ages. Disturbingly, levels of persistent absence, such as extended school absence (EBSA), where students miss a substantial amount of school, have more than doubled compared to pre-pandemic figures. This highlights the lasting impact of the pandemic on students' mental health and well-being, with implications for their academic progress and social development (Hamilton, 2024).

Anxiety from the pandemic has fueled a surge in anxiety among young people, with school often becoming a source of stress and worry. This can manifest in various ways, from separation anxiety and social anxiety to generalized anxiety and panic attacks. Bullying remains a significant problem in schools, and the pandemic may have exacerbated its impact. Students who experience bullying are more likely to withdraw from school to avoid further victimization. For some students, particularly those with sensory sensitivities or neurodevelopmental conditions like autism, the school environment can be overwhelming and distressing Brant (2024). This can lead to avoidance behaviors and school refusal. Autistic pupils are particularly vulnerable to experiencing school-related distress and anxiety, which can contribute to EBSA. Additionally, girls appear to be especially prone to experiencing EBSA, highlighting the need for gender-specific interventions and support. Extended School Absence (EBSA) is often linked to deeper issues such as anxiety, bullying, and a lack of belonging in the school community. This highlights the need to address not just the absence but also the underlying factors contributing to it. Multi-tiered support system: The researchers recommend a multi-tiered system of support to address EBSA. This involves providing universal support for all students, targeted interventions for those at risk of absence, and intensive support for students experiencing chronic absenteeism. Creating a school environment where students feel safe, accepted, and valued is crucial for preventing EBSA. Furthermore, empowering students with agency and control over their learning can promote engagement and reduce school avoidance. There is a positive shift in policy towards prioritizing school attendance. This renewed focus is particularly important given that existing educational inequalities are often exacerbated by extended school absences, disproportionately affecting disadvantaged groups. By addressing the root causes of EBSA and providing comprehensive support for struggling students, we can create a more equitable and inclusive educational system where all students can thrive (Jackson & Ettekal, 2024).

There is a complex relationship between mental health and school attendance in the post-COVID-19 landscape, with a particular focus on the challenges faced by neurodivergent students, including those with autism, in mainstream school settings (Hamilton, 2024). It emphasizes the need for comprehensive strategies to address extended school absences (EBSA), recognizing that a one-size-fits-all approach is insufficient. Here is a dual approach to tackling EBS. Implementing whole-school initiatives that promote positive mental health, acceptance of differences, and anti-bullying interventions can create a more inclusive and supportive environment for all students (Stodden et al., 2023). This includes fostering a culture of respect and understanding, providing mental health education and support, and implementing effective anti-bullying programs. Targeted Interventions In addition to universal strategies, targeted processes are necessary for individual children who are at risk of chronic EBSA. This may involve individualized support plans, counseling services, and close collaboration between school staff, parents, and mental health professionals.

Here are key findings regarding the experiences of neurodivergent pupils in mainstream schools. Autistic students face a disproportionately high risk of bullying from their peers (Hamilton, 2024). This can lead to feelings of isolation, anxiety, and school avoidance. Sensory Challenges: the physical school environment is often overwhelming with sensory input (noise, lights, crowds). This can be particularly challenging for autistic students with sensory processing differences. This can contribute to feelings of discomfort, anxiety, and a desire to avoid school. Understanding the Student Perspective: The study emphasizes the importance of a holistic understanding of the factors contributing to a student's perception of school as a hostile environment (Stodden, 2023). This involves listening to students' experiences, considering their needs and challenges, and working collaboratively to create a more positive and supportive school experience.

EBSA Key Findings: Underlying Causes

Often linked to underlying mental health issues, such as anxiety and depression. Bullying and feelings of not belonging in the school community are also significant contributing factors. Multi-tiered Support: A multi-tiered support system is recommended to address EBSA effectively. This involves providing universal support for all students, targeted interventions for those at risk, and intensive support for students experiencing chronic absenteeism. Promoting belonging and agency while creating a school environment where all students feel safe, accepted, and valued is crucial for preventing EBSA. Additionally, empowering students with agency and control over their learning can promote engagement and reduce school avoidance Parameswaran et al., 2024).

By combining universal and targeted strategies, schools can create a more inclusive and supportive learning environment that addresses the complex needs of all students, including neurodivergent students. This will improve mental health, reduce absenteeism, and improve academic and social-emotional outcomes for all. There is a need for a deeper understanding of the complex factors contributing to extended school absence (EBSA), particularly the psychological barriers preventing students from attending school regularly. It calls for a compassionate and collaborative approach to addressing EBSA, recognizing the importance of working closely with students, families, and school staff to develop effective solutions. Six highlighted keys are: Understanding Psychological Barriers: EBSA is often rooted in underlying psychological factors, such as anxiety, depression, and social difficulties (Hamilton, 2024; Schwind and Handley-Moore, 2024)

It is essential for educators and mental health professionals to identify and address these psychological barriers to support students experiencing EBSA effectively. This may involve providing access to mental health services, implementing social-emotional learning programs, and fostering a school climate that promotes mental well-being. Collaboration and Compassion: Addressing EBSA requires a collaborative and compassionate approach that involves working closely with students, families, and school staff. Open communication, empathy, and a shared commitment to finding solutions are crucial.

This may involve establishing strong relationships with families, conducting home visits, and creating individualized support plans that address the unique needs of each student.

Focus on Autistic Pupils. The study emphasizes the urgent need to understand better the specific barriers to school attendance faced by autistic pupils. This includes recognizing the challenges they may experience with social interaction, sensory processing, and communication and developing targeted supports to address these issues. This may involve providing sensory accommodations, implementing social skills training, and creating a more inclusive and accepting school environment. **Holistic Understanding.** The research highlights the importance of a holistic understanding of the factors contributing to a student's perception of school as a hostile environment. This involves considering not only individual factors, such as mental health and learning difficulties, but also systemic factors, such as bullying, discrimination, and a lack of support. By addressing individual and systemic factors, schools can create a more welcoming and inclusive environment for all students (Suharnadi et al., 2024). Psychologically Informed Intervention concludes that EBSA is a complex issue that requires a psychologically informed approach to intervention. This means that interventions should be based on an understanding of the psychological factors that contribute to EBSA and should be tailored to the individual needs of each student. A multi-tiered system of support (MTSS) is suggested for effectively addressing emotional, behavioral, and social adjustment (EBSA) (Schwind & Handley-More, 2024). This involves providing universal support for all students, targeted interventions for those at risk of EBSA, and intensive support for students experiencing chronic absenteeism (Brant, 2024). MTSS provides a framework for early identification and intervention, ensuring that students receive the appropriate level of support based on their individual needs.

Brant (2024) gives a better view of the need for an MTSS approach to absenteeism. This was accomplished using a current example of a rural school showing a concerning trend in how school districts address student absenteeism. While communication and incentives are frequently employed strategies, there appears to be a significant disconnect between these efforts and the underlying social and economic factors contributing to chronic absenteeism.

Current Approaches

School districts heavily rely on communication-based strategies to combat absenteeism. This typically involves conveying the importance of regular school attendance to students and their families through various channels, such as parent-teacher meetings, newsletters, phone calls, and school-wide announcements. While emphasizing the value of education is crucial, this approach alone may not address the complex reasons behind student absences. Incentivizing attendance is another common tactic that districts and school principals employ using incentives to encourage regular attendance. This can include offering rewards, recognition, or privileges to students with good attendance records. While incentives can be motivating in the short term, they may not address the root causes of absenteeism and may lose their effectiveness over time. Some districts and principals prioritize providing resources and social services that address the barriers preventing students from attending school regularly. These barriers often stem from social and economic inequalities, such as

- Lack of reliable transportation: Students may struggle to get to school due to inadequate public transportation, financial constraints preventing access to private transportation, or unsafe walking routes (Brant, 2024).
- Socioeconomic challenges: Families facing poverty, housing, or food insecurity may struggle to prioritize school attendance when basic needs are unmet (Brant, 2024).
- Lack of access to healthcare: Students with chronic health conditions or limited access to healthcare may experience increased absences due to illness or medical appointments (Brant, 2024).

Recommendations for Improvement

Relying solely on communication and incentives is unlikely to substantially reduce absenteeism, particularly for students facing significant social and economic disadvantages. Without addressing the root causes of their absences, these students may struggle with attendance, hindering their academic progress and overall well-being. Failing to address the social and economic factors contributing to absenteeism can perpetuate inequalities in educational opportunities and outcomes. Students from disadvantaged backgrounds may face additional barriers to success if their basic needs and challenges are not addressed.

- **Adopt a Holistic Approach:** School districts must move beyond a narrow focus on communication and incentives and adopt a more holistic approach to attendance interventions. This involves integrating strategies that address the social and economic factors affecting students and their families (Stodden, 2023).
- **Strengthen Community Partnerships:** Collaborating with community organizations and social service agencies can provide essential wraparound services for students and families. This may include connecting families with resources for housing, food assistance, healthcare, and mental health support (Stodden, 2023).
- **Invest in Early Intervention:** Identifying and supporting students at risk of chronic absenteeism early on is crucial. This may involve implementing early warning systems, providing targeted support for struggling students, and fostering strong relationships between schools and families (Stodden, 2023).
- **Promote Equity and Inclusion:** Creating a school environment that is welcoming, inclusive, and supportive of all students is essential. This includes addressing issues of discrimination, bullying, and cultural insensitivity that may contribute to absenteeism for some students (Stodden, 2023).

School districts can create a more equitable and supportive learning environment where all students can succeed by shifting from a primarily communication-based approach to a more comprehensive strategy that tackles the root causes of absenteeism. There is a critical gap in how school districts address the pervasive problem of chronic absenteeism. While investing in new infrastructure and communication strategies is a step in the right direction, the study emphasizes that these efforts alone are insufficient to reduce absenteeism significantly. A more comprehensive and nuanced approach is necessary, one that acknowledges and addresses the complex social and economic factors that contribute to student absences.

- **Infrastructure and Personnel:** Many districts are focusing on building new organizational infrastructure and hiring additional personnel to tackle attendance issues. This may involve creating new attendance tracking systems, hiring specialists, or implementing new attendance policies.

While these efforts can improve efficiency and data collection, they may not address the root causes of student absences.

- **Communication Strategies:** Some districts continue to rely heavily on communication-based strategies, such as emphasizing the importance of attendance to students and families. However, the study indicates that these communication efforts are unlikely to yield substantial improvements without addressing the underlying social and economic inequalities that often lead to absenteeism.
- **Addressing Root Causes:** The study underscores the urgent need for districts to shift their focus from simply monitoring attendance to understanding and addressing the root causes of absenteeism. This requires a deeper dive into the social, economic, and environmental factors that prevent students from attending school regularly.
- **Ecological Approach:** The researchers advocate for an ecological approach to attendance interventions. This involves recognizing the interconnectedness of various factors that influence student attendance, including individual, family, school, and community-level factors. By addressing these interconnected factors, districts can create a more supportive ecosystem that promotes regular attendance.
- **Prioritizing Barrier Removal:** A key component of an ecological approach is prioritizing identifying and alleviating barriers to attendance. This may involve providing transportation assistance, connecting families with social services, addressing health-related barriers, and creating a more welcoming and inclusive school climate.
- **Collaboration and Partnerships:** The importance of forging external partnerships and cross-sector collaborations to address attendance issues effectively. This includes working with community organizations, healthcare providers, social service agencies, and other stakeholders to provide wraparound support for students and families.

This is a call to action for policymakers and educators to rethink current attendance practices. Investing in new infrastructure and communication strategies will not significantly reduce chronic absenteeism. Instead, a more holistic and comprehensive approach is required, prioritizing understanding and addressing the root causes of absenteeism, removing barriers to attendance, and fostering strong community partnerships. By adopting this ecological perspective, districts can create a more equitable and supportive learning environment where all students can thrive.

Being an Agent for Change

Motivation is undeniably important in learning and profoundly impacts student academic achievement. Motivated students demonstrate a greater thirst for knowledge, exhibiting higher enthusiasm and a willingness to invest effort in their studies (Suhamadi et al., 2024). This intrinsic drive fuels their persistence in facing challenges, leading to improved problem-solving skills and a deeper understanding of the subject matter. Motivation is not merely a peripheral factor in education but a cornerstone of the learning process. When students are motivated, they are more engaged, attentive, and receptive to new information. This heightened engagement translates to increased effort, persistence, and a genuine desire to learn and master new skills.

While various factors contribute to a conducive learning environment, motivation is a primary catalyst for academic success. Direct observation of students in learning settings confirms this assertion. Motivated students are easily identifiable by their active participation, eagerness to ask questions, and willingness to take on challenges. The impact of motivation extends far beyond the classroom. A person's level of motivation influences their behavior in various aspects of life, driving them to pursue goals, overcome obstacles, and achieve their full potential. Fostering learning motivation is paramount for improving student academic achievement. Teachers and parents play a crucial role in cultivating this motivation by creating a supportive and stimulating learning environment. This involves Promoting a growth mindset, encouraging students to embrace challenges, and viewing mistakes as opportunities for learning. Providing meaningful feedback: Offering constructive criticism and praise, focusing on effort and progress. Setting realistic goals. Helping students set achievable goals and celebrate their accomplishments. Fostering a sense of autonomy. Allowing students to have some control over their learning experiences and choices. Creating a sense of belonging. Building a positive and inclusive classroom community where students feel supported and valued. Educators and parents can unlock their potential by nurturing intrinsic motivation in students and fostering a lifelong love of learning and academic success.

CONCLUSIONS

There is a need to embed social and emotional learning (SEL) comprehensively within the educational landscape. SEL must be woven into daily teaching practices and permeate all aspects of school life to effectively address students' escalating mental health crises (Guest et al., 2024). A clear and universally understood conceptualization of (SEL) is an important start for successful implementation. This clarity is essential to avoid confusion among school stakeholders and ensure the effective delivery of services and support. Trauma-informed practices can have a positive impact on both teacher and student outcomes. These practices improve classroom organization, enhance emotional and instructional support, and improve academic performance. Similarly, SEL interventions have been shown to boost academic outcomes, particularly for disadvantaged students. The proposed TI-SEL MTSS model advocates for adopting evidence-based SEL programs that utilize a whole-school approach, systematically integrating SEL skill development into every facet of daily school life. This model emphasizes the synergy between trauma-informed practices, SEL, and a multi-tiered support system (MTSS) to provide students with comprehensive mental health prevention and intervention services.

These are keys to the impact of SEL implementation: Teachers' understanding of SEL skills, curricula, pedagogy, and practical application. This highlights the need for professional development to equip educators with the knowledge and confidence to effectively implement SEL in their classrooms. The TI-SEL MTSS model demonstrates the profound impact of establishing SEL as a foundational element of learning. This foundation strengthens the effectiveness of multi-tiered support structures. It facilitates the seamless integration of school mental health services, trauma-informed services, and SEL into a cohesive system that addresses prevention and intervention needs. Trauma-informed practices and SEL interventions yield positive student outcomes, including enhanced academic performance, improved classroom behavior, and stronger social-emotional skills. After receiving individualized support from the school counselor, the TI-SEL MTSS model shows promise in supporting students' social and emotional growth and progress in emotional regulation and empathy.

Embedding SEL in daily teaching practices and throughout the school environment is crucial to mitigate the growing student mental health crisis. A well-defined and shared understanding of SEL is necessary to prevent confusion among stakeholders and ensure the effective implementation of support services. Integrating trauma-informed practices and SEL within an MTSS framework is essential to support students who have experienced trauma effectively. This integrated approach can potentially generate positive outcomes for students across various domains. The TI-SEL MTSS model provides a comprehensive and holistic approach to fostering students' social and emotional development. Embedding SEL skills into the daily fabric of school life establishes a strong foundation for future mental health and trauma services. The TI-SEL MTSS model offers a practical framework for supporting students by establishing a robust foundation of SEL skills and clear pathways for accessing additional mental health services as needed. Pre-service and in-service professional development in SEL is crucial to equip educators with the knowledge and skills to implement SEL in their classrooms effectively.

This positively impacts students with ADHD and other disabilities. There is an urgent necessity to improve access to and availability of evidence-based psychosocial interventions for Attention-Deficit/Hyperactivity Disorder (ADHD) in children and adolescents (Chacko, 2024). While significant strides have been made in developing and evaluating effective interventions, the challenge lies in translating these advancements into real-world benefits for the broader population of youth with ADHD. Despite decades of research demonstrating the effectiveness of psychosocial interventions for ADHD, many individuals still face barriers to accessing these vital services. This gap between research and practice needs to be addressed to ensure that all young people with ADHD can benefit from evidence-based support. By integrating trauma-informed practices, SEL, and MTSS, schools can create a nurturing and supportive learning environment that empowers students to thrive academically, socially, and emotionally.

REFERENCES

ACT. D. E. (2025). Building and sustaining inclusive education practices_https://www.ed.gov/media/document/inclusive-practices-guidance-109436.pdf

American Occupational Therapy Association (AOTA). (2020). Occupational Therapy Practice

An, F. B. A. (2024). Functional behavior assessment.

APA. (2024) American Psychological Association. https://dictionary.apa.org/

Bishara, S., & Kaplan, S. (2022). Inhibitory control, self-efficacy, and mathematics achievements in students with learning disabilities. *International Journal of Disability Development and Education*, *69*(3), 868–887. DOI: 10.1080/1034912X.2021.1925878

Brant, C. S. (2024). *Chronic Absenteeism: The Journey Toward Improved Attendance and Achievement in a Rural Elementary School* (Doctoral dissertation, The University of Nebraska-Lincoln).

Chacko, A., Merrill, B. M., Kofler, M. J., & Fabiano, G. A. (2024). Improving the efficacy and effectiveness of evidence-based psychosocial interventions for attention-deficit/hyperactivity disorder (ADHD) in children and adolescents. *Translational Psychiatry*, *14*(1), 244.

Chan, A. S., Lee, T. L., Sze, S. L., Yang, N. S., & Han, Y. M. (2022). Eye-tracking training improves the learning and memory of children with learning difficulty. *Scientific Reports*, *12*(1), 13974.

Donohue, P. (2025). Setting The Table for Tier 2 Small Group Social And Emotional Learning And Academic Interventions For K 12 Students.

Dussault, M., & Thompson, R. B. (2024). Fundamental Themes in Social–Emotional Learning: A *21*(4), Theoretical Framework for Inclusivity. *International Journal of Environmental*

AOTA. (2020a). Framework: Domain and Process (4th ed.). https://www.aota.org/practice/domain-and-process/framework

Guest, J. D., Ross, R. A., Childs, T. M., Ascetta, K. E., Curcio, R., Iachini, A., & Griffiths, L. (2024, July). Embedding social-emotional learning from the bottom up in multi-tiered services and supports frameworks. *Psychology in the Schools*, *61*(7), 2745–2761. DOI: 10.1002/pits.23183

Gunnars, F. (2024). A systematic review of special educational interventions for student attention: Executive function and digital technology in primary school. *Journal of Special Education Technology*, *39*(2), 264–276.

Gustina, N. (2024). Integration of character education in citizenship education learning to develop the character of elementary school students. Int. J. Students Educ, 390-397.

Hamilton, L. G. (2024). Emotionally based school avoidance in the aftermath of the COVID-19 pandemic: Neurodiversity, agency and belonging in school. *Education Sciences*, *14*(2), 156.

Hamilton, L. G. (2024a, February 02). Pandemic: Neurodiversity, agency and belonging in school. *Education Sciences*, *14*(2), 156. DOI: 10.3390/educsci14020156

Hintz, L. A., Maas, C., Bliss, J. R., & Pizarro, E. (2024). School-based occupational therapy and multitiered systems of support in the United States: A scoping review. *Journal of Occupational Therapy, Schools & Early Intervention*, *17*(3), 605–623.

O'Donnell, K. E., Shen, L., Stratford, D. C., Candelaria, P. Y., & Clemens, N. H. (2024). Integrating a Self-Regulation Intervention Within a Tier-2 Academic Intervention. *Intervention in School and Clinic*, *60*(1), 17–27.

Nelson Christensen, A. C. (2025). Rethinking trauma-sensitive schools from an anti-racist lens. International Journal of School &amp. *Educational Psychology*, *13*(2), 156–169. DOI: 10.1080/21683603.2025.2483931

Jackson, D., Prochnow, T., & Ettekal, A. V. (2024). Programs Promoting Physical Activity and Social-Emotional Learning for Adolescents: A Systematic Literature Review. *The Journal of School Health*, *94*(10), 994–1004. DOI: 10.1111/josh.13486 PMID: 38962813

Lambert, M. C., Katsiyannis, A., Maag, J. W., Mason, W. A., & Epstein, M. H. (2024). Long-Term Trends in Socially Maladjusted Behavior of Students With and Without Emotional and Behavioral Disorders: A 22-Year Repeated Cross-Sectional Study.

Nikolašević, Ž., Krstić, T., Rajšli, A., & Bugarski Ignjatović, V. (2024, June). The Relationship Between Behavior Aspects of Executive Functions and Personality Traits in Healthy Young Adults. *Psychological Reports*, *127*(3), 1317–1335. DOI: 10.1177/00332941221132996

Parameswaran, U. D., Molloy, J., & Kuttner, P. (2024). Healing Schools: A Framework for Joining Trauma-Informed Care, Restorative Justice, and Multicultural Education for Whole School Reform. *The Urban Review*, *56*(1), 186–209. DOI: 10.1007/s11256-023-00666-5

Ray, S. A., Hollenbeck, J. K., Ankomahjr, P., Giacopelli, T., Link, G., Ruckdaschel, T., & Runge, J. (2024). Effects of Occupational Therapy Professional Development Training on School-Based Practice. *Journal of Occupational Therapy, Schools & Early Intervention*, *17*(4), 979–993. DOI: 10.1080/19411243.2024.2326212

Schwind, D. B., & Handley-More, D. (2024). Utilizing MTSS for the occupation of feeding: A case study. *Journal of Occupational Therapy, Schools & Early Intervention*, *17*(2), 193–200.

Stodden, D. F., Pesce, C., Zarrett, N., Tomporowski, P., Ben-Soussan, T. D., Brian, A., Abrams, T. C., & Weist, M. D. (2023, June). synthesis with a focus on a multi-tiered system support structure. *Clinical Child and Family Psychology Review*, *26*(2), 343–361. DOI: 10.1007/s10567-023-00428-5 PMID: 36826703

Stodden, D. F., Pesce, C., Zarrett, N., Tomporowski, P., Ben-Soussan, T. D., Brian, A., & Weist, M. D. (2023). Holistic functioning from a developmental perspective: A new synthesis with a focus on a multi-tiered system support structure. *Clinical Child and Family Psychology Review*, *26*(2), 343–361.

Suharnadi, P., Neviyarni, S., & Nirwana, H. (2024). The Role and Function of Learning Motivation in Improving Student Academic Achievement. *Manajia: Journal of Education and Management*, *2*(1), 1–8.

Tao, J., Xu, Y., & Gao, X. A. (2024). Teacher emotions and agency enactment in online teaching. *Teaching and Teacher Education*, *137*, 104389.

Vetter, J. B., Fuxman, S., & Dong, Y. E. (2024). A statewide multi-tiered system of support (MTSS) approach to social and emotional learning (SEL) and mental health. *Social and Emotional Learning: Research, Practice, and Policy*, *3*, 100046.

Waldron, S. M. (2024). Administrators' Perspectives on Successful Implementation of Occupational Therapy Services in the School-Based Setting.

Zhou, W., Cui, X., Shi, B., Su, M., & Cao, M. (2021). The development of brain functional connectome during text reading. *Developmental Cognitive Neuroscience*, *48*, 100927.

APPENDIX

Key Terms

- **Multi-tiered system of support (MTSS):** This framework provides targeted support to students based on their needs. It typically operates on three levels or tiers, with Tier 1 being universal instruction for all students, Tier 2 providing targeted interventions for students needing additional support, and Tier 3 offering intensive, individualized interventions for students with the most significant needs (Common understanding in education).
- **Activities of daily living (ADLs):** These are the basic self-care tasks that individuals perform daily to function independently. They typically include eating, bathing, dressing, toileting, and mobility (Common understanding in healthcare and occupational therapy).
- **School-based occupational therapy practitioners** are occupational therapists (OTs) and occupational therapy assistants (OTAs) who work in school settings. They use meaningful activities (occupations) to help children and youth participate in academic, social, and daily life activities within the school environment. They address performance's physical, cognitive, psychosocial, and sensory components (American Occupational Therapy Association - AOTA).
- **Functional Behavior Assessment (FBA):** This is a systematic process to understand why a student engages in a challenging behavior. It involves gathering information about the behavior, including what happens before (antecedents) and after (consequences) the behavior and the function or purpose the behavior serves for the student (Common understanding in special education).
- **Early childhood development:** This refers to the period of rapid physical, cognitive, social, and emotional growth that occurs from infancy through approximately age 8. Experiences during this period lay the foundation for future learning, behavior, and health (Common understanding in developmental psychology and education).
- **Attention deficit hyperactivity disorder (ADHD):** This is a neurodevelopmental disorder characterized by persistent inattention and/or hyperactivity-impulsivity that interferes with functioning or development (*APA Dictionary of Psychology* and Common Understanding in Psychology and Psychiatry).
- **Individualized Education Program (IEP):** This is a legally binding document created for a student with a disability who is eligible for special education services. It outlines the student's unique educational needs, measurable goals, and specific services. It supports the school will provide to help them achieve them (Common Understanding in Special Education, related to the Individuals with Disabilities Education Act).
- **Individuals with Disabilities Education Act (IDEA):** This is a United States federal law that governs how states and public agencies provide early intervention, special education, and related services to children with disabilities. It ensures that all children with disabilities have a free appropriate public education (FAPE) emphasizing special education and related services designed to meet their unique needs and prepare them for further education, employment, and independent living (*APA Dictionary of Psychology* and common understanding in education law).
- **Positive Behavioral Interventions and Supports (PBIS):** This is a proactive, systems-level framework used to create safe and effective school environments and to support the behavioral, social, emotional, and academic success of all students. It emphasizes teaching and reinforcing

positive behaviors and using data to make decisions about school-wide and individualized support (Common Understanding in Education).

- **Occupational therapy:** This healthcare profession helps people across the lifespan participate in the things they want and need to do through the therapeutic use of everyday activities (occupations). Occupational therapists enable people of all ages to live life to its fullest by helping them promote health and prevent—or live better with—injury, illness, or disability (Source: American Occupational Therapy Association - AOTA).
- **Every Student Succeeds Act (ESSA):** This United States federal law reauthorized the Elementary and Secondary Education Act (ESEA). It aims to ensure that all students receive a high-quality education and includes accountability, standards, and support for struggling schools and diverse student populations, including students with disabilities (U.S. Department of Education and Common Understanding in Education Policy).
- **Executive function:** Higher-level cognitive processes control and regulate other abilities and behaviors. They include planning, working memory, attention, problem-solving, inhibition, cognitive flexibility, and self-monitoring skills. These processes are often associated with the frontal lobe of the brain (Source: *APA Dictionary of Psychology* and common understanding in psychology and neuroscience).
- **Special education needs:** This broad term refers to the unique learning and developmental requirements of students with disabilities or other conditions that necessitate modifications to standard educational practices. These needs are addressed through special education services and support (Common Understanding in Education).
- **Emotional and behavioral disorders (EBD):** This category encompasses a range of conditions characterized by difficulties in social-emotional functioning that significantly impact a student's ability to learn and interact with others. These disorders may manifest as internalizing problems (e.g., anxiety, depression) or externalizing problems (e.g., aggression, defiance) (Common understanding in special education and the *APA Dictionary of Psychology,* which refers to "mental disorder" encompassing emotional and behavioral disturbances).
- **Social and Emotional Learning (CASEL) defines SEL** as acquiring and applying the knowledge, skills, and attitudes to develop healthy identities, manage emotions, achieve goals, show empathy, maintain relationships, and make responsible decisions. This framework encompasses five core competencies: self-awareness, self-management, social awareness, relationship skills, and responsible decision-making, all crucial for success in various aspects of life (CASEL).

Chapter 4
Minneapolis Trauma-Informed School Practices

Tetiana Holovatenko
https://orcid.org/0000-0002-7545-3253
V.N. Karazin Kharkiv National University, Ukraine

ABSTRACT

This study explores trauma-informed practices at a high school in Minneapolis, aiming to create a supportive ecosystem for students. Using a qualitative design, it incorporates semi-structured interviews and classroom observations. Participants included five school staff members, such as teachers, social workers, and an assistant principal, with varying levels of experience. The study examines participants' understanding of trauma-informed education, strategies used, challenges faced, and views on sustainability. The study identifies two key themes: the role of empathy-driven practices in supportive classrooms and the importance of teacher well-being. Findings emphasize the need for a multi-tiered approach and the critical role of teachers' emotional well-being in implementing trauma-informed practices. Ethical considerations, including informed consent and confidentiality, were maintained throughout.

INTRODUCTION

Currently, there is a rising number of children experiencing trauma. According to the U.S. Department of Veterans Affairs, up to 43% of children experience at least one trauma, and from 3% to 15% of girls and 1% to 6% of boys experience PTSD (U.S. Department of Veterans Affairs, 2024). Additionally, the World Health Organization says people, on average, have 3.2 traumas per life (Kessler, et al., 2017). This statistic highlights a growing issue of childhood trauma. Trauma can lead to difficulties in concentration, reduced academic performance, and disruptive behavior in educational settings. Children dealing with trauma may display symptoms such as anxiety, depression, hypervigilance, or emotional numbness (van der Kolk, 2000). Consequently, schools and educators must focus on trauma-informed practices, creating environments that foster safety, trust, and emotional resilience.

With the full-scale Russian invasion in Ukraine and increasing instability in Ecuador and Venezuela, there are an unprecedented number of newcomers in the Twin Cities metropolitan area. For instance, according to the Minnesota Department of Education data, in the 2021/22 academic year, 325 students identified their primary home language as Ukrainian; in 2022/23 – 508 students and 2023/24 – 725

DOI: 10.4018/979-8-3693-9020-7.ch004

students (Minneapolis Department of Education). This rapid increase in newcomers, coupled with the traumatic experiences many have experienced due to war and displacement, presents unique challenges for schools in the Twin Cities. In addition to the trauma of conflict that led them to resettle in the first place, many of these Ukrainian students also experience resettlement trauma. Significantly affected by trauma are English language learners; the majority of students resettling in the United States, whose language proficiency is not enough to express themselves in English, are left to navigate traumatic events without peer or teacher support (Mora-Flores & Dewing, 2023). Schools must adapt to not only support these students academically but also foster a learning environment that acknowledges and addresses the profound impact of trauma.

People have various reactions to stress and traumatic experiences. All types of trauma influence the body. Neurobiologically, trauma affects the brain. Particularly the amygdala, hippocampus, and prefrontal cortex, which play key roles in emotional regulation, memory, and executive functioning (van der Kolk, 2014). As a result, traumatic experiences can impair school performance. Reupert (2020), based on a holistic analysis, has proposed theoretical models outlining the dynamic relationship between mental health and academic performance. The author has distinguished the adjustment erosion model, according to which externalizing problems directly affect learning; the academic incompetence model, according to which academic failure leads to inconfidence and involvement in risk behaviors; the shared risk model, according to which risk factors in the children's background history impacts their academic performance and mental health (Reupert, 2020). The third model is the core to understanding the influence of traumatic experiences on students' ability to learn. Students who have gone through trauma often struggle with memory retention, have a limited attention span, face challenges in understanding language, experience difficulties with logical reasoning and recognizing cause-and-effect relationships, and may find it hard to build relationships or trust others (Dehn, 2022; Matte-Landry et al., 2023).

The aftermath of coping with trauma is shaped by a complex set of factors, such as what the stressful event was, access to internal and external resources, and reinforcing inner neural networks to cope with stress (Berardi & Morton, 2019). Recently, teachers have reported a growing number of students with signs of trauma in their classrooms, seeing behavioral problems, academic challenges, stress and anxiety, and mental health issues (Berardi & Morton, 2019). Venet, Berger & Martin write that it is crucial for teachers not to treat students from the standpoint of the one who is looking for traumatized individuals to help them but rather create an environment where students know it is safe to be who they are and be assured they can get the support they are looking for regardless of the fact they had trauma (Venet, 2021). The driving principle of trauma-informed practices is the assumption that every individual has experienced some trauma in their life, but the impact of the trauma differs from case to case (Berardi & Morton, 2019). Some teachers have implemented trauma-informed practices to address the needs of a diverse cohort of students.

Consequently, implementing trauma-informed practices in schools is important in creating a welcoming environment for those who have previous traumatic experiences. Educational implications of creating a trauma-sensitive classroom environment cover scaffolding the material and reducing the cognitive load (Dehn, 2022), changing the physical environment to reduce distractions, incorporating regulatory strategies, and providing transitional support to students (Forbes & Maki, 2020). Venet (2021) categorizes these changes into developing the trauma-informed lens in terms of practice, transforming classrooms by shifting the pedagogy towards being more trauma-informed and changing the policies implemented. However, the lack of a shared understanding of trauma-informed instruction and no system to disseminate practical approaches has resulted in far too many instructors being unable to recognize behavior impacted by trauma, the inability to access resources necessary to support students, inability to find the balance between teaching academic skills and fulfilling their role as social workers or psychologists; finding the balance between students' individual needs and group needs, focusing on traumatic experiences or on everyday life (Alisic et al., 2012).

Previous scholarly research has focused on ways to ensure a trauma-informed culture in brick-and-mortar environments. However, it is worth mentioning researchers have also delved into the ways to create a trauma-informed online environment using technology. It has emerged as a critical approach to supporting students during lockdown. The safety principle is implemented through cybersecurity and creating an emotionally safe environment (Moses et al., 2023; Schmidt, 2024). Trust and transparency are ensured by allowing students to control their learning, learning pace, and content using online tools (Howard, 2024). The principle of collaboration is ensured through using shared platforms (Ahmadpour et al., 2023). Scholars argue technology can be instrumental in processing trauma and promoting emotional regulation, teaching students self-reflection, meditation, and mindfulness (Ahmadpour et al., 2023; Apgar, 2023; Ruiz, 2021).

Schools around the world, in their attempt to create trauma-informed environments, have introduced trauma-informed pedagogy. In the USA, the trauma-informed approach is grounded in the following principles: physical, emotional, social, and academic safety; trustworthiness and transparency; support and connection; collaboration and mutuality; empowerment, voice, and choice; social justice; resilience, growth, and change (Fallot & Harris, 2006). Organizing the school environment according to these principles ensures the creation of an atmosphere that is welcoming and respectful and avoids triggering students who potentially have previous traumas.

One of the programs aiming to create a school-wide trauma-sensitive environment is the Trauma and Learning Policy Initiative (TLPI). It is an inquiry-based program supporting teachers in collaboratively designing trauma-informed school environments. The process is rooted in organizational change theory and involves continuous learning, coalition-building, prioritization, action planning, reflection, and evaluation. Instead of offering ready-made solutions for schools, it suggests schools a sustained inquiry plan designed by school team members based on four questions ("Why do we feel an urgency to become a trauma-sensitive school?, How do we know we are ready to create a trauma-sensitive action plan?, What actions will address staff priorities and help us become a trauma-sensitive school?, How do we know whether we are becoming a trauma-sensitive school?") (Jones et al., 2018, p. 23-26). The key tools to gauge educators' understanding of how to implement trauma sensitivity into school activities and agree on a clear vision of what trauma-sensitive actions and priorities are questionnaires. According to the program, the readiness indicators to build trauma-sensitive school environments are understanding, urgency and motivation, support and barriers to implementation, time, alignment with other initiatives, and leadership commitment. The report on the implementation of the program showed that creating a trauma-sensitive school environment requires a substantial amount of basic resources and guidance at the initial stage, as well as the active involvement of school leadership (Jones et al., 2018). The case of the TLPI model showed that implementing trauma-informed pedagogy requires building a common vision of a systemic, school-wide transformation rooted in shared understanding, reflective practice, and strong leadership.

Another example of a school-wide program is Positive Behavioral Interventions and Supports (PBIS). This evidence-based, multi-tiered framework is designed to create a safe and welcoming school environment by promoting positive student behavior and enhancing academic and social outcomes. The framework is structured across three tiers. Tier 1 provides universal supports for all students to encourage positive behavior and prevent problems before they arise. Tier 2 targets students who are at risk of developing behavioral challenges, offering additional support to help them succeed in the school environment. Tier 3 offers individualized, intensive interventions for students with significant behavioral or academic needs, guided by formal assessments. These tiers form a comprehensive approach to fostering a positive, inclusive, and supportive school climate (PBIS, 2025).

The TLPI and the PBIS are examples of the whole-school approach, which prioritizes approach rather than isolated interventions that address students' needs. Programs aim to create a safe and supportive school environment that reduces negative behaviors and promotes emotional well-being through data-driven decision-making, reflection, assessment, and evaluation. However, the PBIS is focused primarily on positive behavior and is based on behavioral psychology and prevention science. The TLPI aims at building trauma-sensitive school environments rooted in organizational change theory and trauma research. The PBIS is more structured with clear tires and behavior expectations, while the TLPI is flexible and depends on educators creating context-specific solutions.

One example of a trauma-informed initiative in the UK is the Trauma-Informed Schools UK (TISUK) program. Its goal is to foster a trauma-sensitive school culture by transforming everyday practices. The program includes comprehensive training for the entire school community, including both leadership and frontline staff, promotes the use of supportive strategies, and offers guidance for educators in managing their own trauma or secondary traumatic stress. At the heart of this framework are insights from neuroscience and trauma psychology, focusing on how trauma affects behavior, cognitive functioning, relationship-building abilities, and overall mental health. The TISUK program provides research-informed solutions for creating a school-wide trauma-informed culture. It is distinguished by a comprehensive approach to providing materials and assistance to schools.

Implementing trauma-informed practices in school environments has evidence of positive outcomes for both students and educators. Schools adopting trauma-informed practices have improved student performance and social-emotional skills and reduced behavioral issues at schools, fostering a more welcoming and supportive environment (Mukherjee & Horton, 2024; Somers & Wheeler, 2022). Additionally, the implementation of trauma-informed practices in schools raises awareness among educators on self-care and support strategies; educators feel more job satisfaction due to feeling more equipped to overcome trauma-related issues in their classrooms (Sharkey et al., 2024; Stokes, 2022).

However, there is a gap in scholarly research and practice on how educators and leaders create the trauma-informed school climate in their capacity and what their lived experiences are.

This chapter **aims** to identify and disseminate multi-tiered interventions and experiences of teachers, administrators, and support staff to structure trauma-informed choices in content teacher and English language learner classrooms in Minneapolis Public Schools.

Researcher Positionality

Tetiana Holovatenko, a teacher trainer from Ukraine, experienced the Russian full-scale invasion first-hand in February 2022 with its personal and social impacts. Her experience as a refugee abroad has further shaped her research positionality. While observing various emergency measures to support Ukrainian schoolchildren overseas and sustain the educational process in Ukraine during the war, she noted the critical role of trauma-informed practices. Inspired by high school subject teachers fostering trauma-sensitive environments in an American school, she became interested in equipping teachers to apply similar approaches when teaching in Ukraine. Additionally, her identity is shaped by her experience as civilian enduring Russian missile attacks on infrastructure and living under constant threat.

Currently, the author teaches courses on the trauma-informed approach and social and emotional learning in Ukraine to pre-service teachers. Her identity is also affected by being a civilian who experiences Russian missile attacks on civilian infrastructure and living under continuous life threats. These lived experiences have influenced her positionality and impacted the study.

In the next section, the author locates the study in relation to scholarly research on trauma-informed teacher training, providing its brief overview.

METHODOLOGY

This study sought to understand practices implemented at one school to build a trauma-informed ecosystem of support. It employs a qualitative research design, extensively using semi-structured interviews and observations. Similar studies have adopted this methodology to explore teachers' experiences with students having traumatic experiences. For instance, Ellison and Walton-Fisette (2022), as well as Jacobson (2021) utilized semi-structured interviews to understand the impact of trauma-informed practices on student engagement. These studies underscore the value of qualitative methods for fostering a deeper understanding of educational interventions within real-world contexts. Additionally, the author has also used observations to gain insight into the practical implementation of trauma-informed practices.

Participants and Recruitment

Participants were recruited through invitations sent to a high school in Minneapolis. The inclusion criteria for the study required participants to be a content area teacher, an English Language Learner (ELL) teacher, and school staff in leadership or support roles, all of whom were implementing a trauma-informed approach. Additionally, all participants had to be employed at the same school within the Minneapolis Public School District. Participants were enrolled in the study after the confirmation that they met the inclusion criteria.

Participants (*n=5*) represented a convenience sample, including two participants who were Science and ELL teachers with over 15 years of teaching experience; two of the participants were social workers with over 10 and over 25 years in the field; the assistant principal is a novice in the leadership role, but has approximately 20 years of teaching experience.

Data Collection and the Tool

Potential participants were invited to take part in the study through email communication. The research team then conducted semi-structured, in-depth interviews. This focus was chosen to outline a structured, multi-tiered approach towards building the trauma-informed environment of a school on various levels.

The author developed an interview guide that was grounded in scholarly research. Participants were asked to talk about: 1) their background (e.g. licensure preparation, trauma-informed training and practices, and professional development); 2) their understanding and experience with the concept of 'trauma-informed education'; 3) strategies they use to create a trauma-informed environment in their capacity; 4) their efficacy in implementing trauma-informed practices; 5) difficulties and barriers they faced regarding implementing the trauma-informed approach; and 6) how participants see the sustainability of these practices. Participants were also allowed a degree of flexibility to craft their own lines of discussion.

Two interviews were conducted via Zoom, and two were conducted face-to-face. Interviews and observations were conducted in December, 2022 - March, 2023. The interview started with the interviewer introducing themselves to the teachers and explaining the study's purpose. They provided details on the methods for data collection, analysis, and storage and informed participants of their rights, including the option to withdraw from the study. The researchers also outlined the measures to ensure confidentiality, such as assigning pseudonyms to all participants. Participants provided written consent to participate and verbal consent to record interviews and were assured of the anonymity of interview reporting. Each interview ranged from 45 to 60 min and was based on a semi-structured, in-depth interview guide developed by the author that was grounded in scholarly research. Participants were asked to talk about: 1) their background (e.g. licensure preparation, trauma-informed training and practices, and professional development); 2) their understanding and experience with the concept of 'trauma-informed education'; 3) strategies they use to create a trauma-informed environment in their capacity; 4) their efficacy in implementing trauma-informed practices; 5) difficulties and barriers they faced regarding implementing the trauma-informed approach; and 6) how participants see the sustainability of these practices. All discussions were audio-recorded, transcribed verbatim by the author, and stored online in a double-factor identification folder. Interviews were transcribed using Otter.ai, and any identifying information was deleted.

Ethical Considerations

Ethics approval for the study was secured from the Institutional Review Board of the University of Minnesota (STUDY00018360). The informed consent form provided participants with the researcher's contact details and encouraged them to reach out via phone or email with any concerns or questions. Interviewers highlighted that participation was entirely voluntary, and participants could withdraw consent and exit the study at any time. This information was explicitly outlined in the consent form and reiterated verbally throughout the process. During interviews, interviewers remained attentive to subtle nonverbal signs of discomfort, conducting regular checks to ensure participants' physical and emotional well-being. They offered breaks and refrained from pressuring participants to answer any uncomfortable questions. Notably, all participants answered every question posed.

During recruitment, the researcher underscored the importance of confidentiality and assured participants that their information would remain anonymous. The informed consent form, written in clear and accessible language, specified that participants' personal details would be kept confidential and their names would not appear in any publications. To safeguard privacy, data was anonymized by assigning unique codes, which were securely stored separately from the main data set.

Throughout the interviews, researchers maintained open and approachable body language, using a friendly and reassuring tone. They honored pauses, allowing participants to respond in their own time without pressure. Trust and rapport were fostered through warmth, empathy, and genuine interest in participants' narratives and perspectives. Researchers actively listened, providing encouragement and displaying patience during moments of hesitation. At every stage, participants were thanked for their contributions and insights. Additionally, researchers built trust by briefly sharing their positionality, creating common ground, and fostering mutual understanding.

Data Analysis

The data analysis is grounded in critical thematic analysis (Lawless & Chen, 2018). First, the author read the transcript numerous times to structure the data according to the initial six codes they attempted to elicit. Next, they discussed and reflected on initial readings of the data and possible changes to the codes. Hence, researchers have used inductive and deductive approaches. Line-by-line coding was done using NVivo and Excel. The author grouped 20 codes into two main higher-order themes — empathy-driven trauma-informed practices in building supportive classroom environments and teacher well-being.

RESULTS

Study participants offered thoughtful insights about their understanding of trauma-informed classrooms and schools, how they learned being trauma-informed in their position, and the challenges of becoming trauma-informed. Two overarching themes emerged from the interviews. First, participants shared various dimensions of creating supportive classrooms to build student safety and promote resilience. Second, they shared the key aspect of being able to provide trauma-informed support for others - taking care of their mental health. Additionally, the author will delve into the challenges participants shared regarding the creation of the trauma-informed school environment.

Creating Supportive Classrooms

One of the overarching themes identified in the data was the importance of the multi-tiered approach toward creating a safe and welcoming environment at school by changing disciplinary and instructional practices to empathy-driven responses.

Participants often reiterated that they did not receive formal training on trauma-informed education at universities, but their actions were informed by their willingness to tailor the school environment and instruction to the needs of dysregulated students. Additionally, participants have stated it was rewarding to work with students having previous experience of trauma. In the words of some participants,

> *I think of it as having an awareness of how trauma impacts children or people and how it might manifest, especially in educational settings, how it might cause certain behaviors or responses or reactions to things and so that I, as an educator, can proactively or reactively respond to a student who I know has had trauma or if I think I'm in a situation I know, it's likely something that I'm dealing with* [KS1].

> *We have to come up with a place for them to go besides the bathroom and smoke weed* [KS1].

> *I love them. I think they're so great. I think they're so resilient. They're so brave. And they have such rich gifts to offer, like gifts of empathy, and [...] strategic thinking. And advocacy, I think they are just so great.* [TS1]

> A lot of it [approach the instructor uses] stems from living being a child in a war-torn country. [TS2]

Another piece informing educators' actions was their understanding of trauma and stress and its effects on children.

> *So I think to me, being trauma-informed means A): having an understanding of what trauma is, what the definition is. I appreciate that you're already making a distinction between acute trauma and chronic stress. I think in one of those trainings that I went to, she did a really great job explaining the difference, but they can have similar effects on a child's brain, or a human's brain, and their*

physiological response. So I think it's a working definition of trauma. B): That physiological piece, understanding that it's things happening in a human body. For me, that's really important because it C) removes personal blame or any sense that something is wrong with the person. These are natural processes that happen in human brains and bodies in response to certain events or experiences. That is a really core understanding for me in terms of trauma-informed practice [TS1].

I think that the behaviors students exhibit, or the ways things manifest at school that might be considered problematic, are likely adaptive responses to their prior or current life experiences related to trauma. Many of the kids—and even the parents—we work with have experienced multiple traumas, often complex trauma. [KS3]

Considering this, it is essential to foster a safe and inclusive environment within the school setting. The participants provided insights into their diverse experiences and strategies for achieving this.

Creating a "Homey" Classroom

One of the participants shared their personal experience of surviving hard times and referred to keeping their space clean and neat as one of the important factors in their lives. Consequently, they strived to create a welcoming space in their classroom. The instructor added an abundance of colors to the classroom, plants, posters, and calming corners for students to regulate themselves. These adjustments to the classroom environment are aligned with previous scholarly research (Aduwo et al., 2017; Bucholz & Sheffler, 2009; Granito & Santana, 2016; Xu, 2015). The neurobiological underpinning of this process lies in the fact that the environment, perceived by an individual as threatening or unpredictable, activates the sympathetic nervous system, which is responsible for the "fight, flight, or freeze" response (Forbes & Maki, 2020; Osuch & Engel, 2004). Hence, creating a clean, clutter-free environment can reduce anxiety and promote healing by fostering comfort, acceptance, and a sense of agency in individuals.

I don't know what home situation they may have. I want them to be here and feel like … [at home, where it] *… smells good. There's light, there's color.* [TS2]

And that's the other piece of creating a space for them to deal with the trauma, too. They don't have to guess where they can find materials. When they come to the classroom, they know where they can find things. [TS2]

Another effective strategy highlighted by participants was the creation of calming corners—dedicated spaces within the classroom designed to help students self-regulate during moments of heightened stress or emotional dysregulation. These areas, often equipped with soft seating, sensory objects, and calming visuals, provide students with an alternative to punitive measures or removal from the learning environment. One participant described how the calming corner in their classroom became a transformative tool, allowing students to re-enter the learning process after a brief period of self-regulation.

I'm working with them so that they feel like, 'You know what, right now I can't concentrate on this task, so I'm going to step into this area of the classroom where I can draw.' I have drawing boards—those Buddha boards where you just use water and a brush—and they can draw, take a break, and come back. They can stand up; they don't have to sit the whole time. We're not a military school where they have to stay in one spot. They can move to any part of the classroom as long as they're still paying attention. [TS2]

This practice aligns with trauma-informed frameworks, which emphasize the importance of empowering students and offering choices as a means of restoring autonomy and reducing the likelihood of retraumatization (Craig, 2016; Forbes & Maki, 2020; Perry, 2009; Venet, 2021). Observations of these calming corners (Figure 1) revealed the incorporation of various art therapy techniques, such as coloring books, Zen gardens, and materials for beading bracelets. Additionally, the spaces included simple wooden building blocks, brain teasers, bean-filled stuffed animals, stress-relief fidgets, Hoberman breathing spheres, affirmation cards, and cognitive-behavioral therapy solution cards. Incorporating such spaces underscores the broader ethos of trauma-informed education—where relationships, environment, and emotional awareness intersect to create classrooms that facilitate academic learning and promote healing and resilience.

By integrating calming corners, educators signaled to students that their emotional well-being was a priority. This approach also reinforced the notion that emotional regulation is a skill to be developed, not a behavior to be punished.

> *With any strategy I use in the classroom, I always explain why. [...] I have games, cards, coloring books—small things like Zen gardens. I tell them, 'These are here for when you need them.' I'm upfront about my own experiences. [...] I try to make mental health feel natural, not something taboo. I share that I deal with anxiety and depression.* [TS2]

Figure 1. Calming corner setup

By normalizing conversations about mental health and openly sharing personal experiences, the educator fosters an environment of trust and empathy. This self-disclosure helps break down the stigma surrounding mental health, encouraging students to feel safe acknowledging their own emotional struggles. In doing so, the teacher models vulnerability, demonstrating that seeking support and utilizing coping strategies is acceptable. This transparency humanizes the educator and creates a classroom culture grounded in understanding, compassion, and mutual respect—key pillars of a trauma-informed approach.

Additionally, one of the participants shared that they teach their students units on mindset, brain science, and neuroscience. However, they tend to omit triggering phrases like "trauma" and "stress" yet explaining students they are going to get accommodations in the classroom.

I probably wouldn't use the word "trauma" because it might feel triggering. I might not even use "chronic stress," though I might consider it. What I used to say to students was, "I will do my best to make sure you get what you need. And what you need may look different from what your peers need. In this classroom, not everyone will always be doing the same thing, and that's intentional. It's not about being unfair—it's about ensuring that each of you receives the support necessary for your success. [TS1]

However, as one participant mentioned, there is a rising awareness among students about their mental health and state. This leads to the need to allocate resources to create calming corners and quiet zones at schools, as the number of those willing to use one is greater than the capacity. Additionally, one of the participants shared they created a calming corner out of their own expenses, as no additional funding was given.

Schools aren't set up to provide quiet rooms for every student who needs one. The dilemma now is that there's a greater awareness of what students are struggling with, and schools want to respond to that. But how do you decide who gets support, and how do you secure the resources to go beyond just being a kind listening ear? [KS1]

Building on this foundation of trust, establishing classroom rules further reinforces a sense of psychological safety and predictability. Clear, consistent expectations—such as showing respect, making good decisions, and solving problems. In this way, classroom rules become more than procedural guidelines; they serve as a framework for nurturing mutual care and reinforcing the importance of collective well-being. The instructor explains:

Because three is enough. They have seven classes learning to navigate the different rules in different classrooms. It is way too much. So, just those three rules apply to everything. So that's one area in terms of high academic expectations paired with being caring. [TS2]

Another dimension of creating a safe and predictable environment, according to the instructor, is creating routines. Routines are repeated actions and regime activities aiming at reducing distractions disrupting students' attention in the classroom (Buckley & Sullivan, 2023). Routines give a sense of organization, stability, and reliability for stressed or traumatized students. They create a sense of safety and stability, which is necessary to develop students' resilience (Craig, 2008; Gaines & Hutson, 2021; Koslouski et al., 2023). In the words of one of the participants:

Spacing out learning and revisiting content over time enhances retention. One simple and effective method is the Pomodoro technique. For example, I set a timer and tell students, "We will work for five or ten minutes." With ninth graders, I often use shorter cycles, such as five minutes of work followed by a one-minute break, as they benefit from more frequent pauses. Starting with small, attainable goals and Start with a small goal that can be attainable and then start increasing that little by little. And so they know that they're going to have a time where they can decompress where they can take time off from everything and just shut off their brains, and they have a space in the classroom where they can do that. [TS2].

Another intend the instructor uses this technique is to build up students' self-confidence and empower their agency. Student empowerment is closely connected to enhancing student responsibility for their learning and personal growth (Hooper et al., 2023). By gradually guiding students to take ownership of their progress, the instructor helps them build essential skills such as time management, goal setting, and self-assessment. This process enhances academic performance and equips students with tools to navigate challenges independently. Additionally, creating opportunities for self-advocacy encourages students to express their needs, seek support when necessary, and reflect on their strengths and areas for growth, fostering a more active and engaged approach to learning.

finding [...] strategies that help students manage their time, advocate, and do a lot of self-advocacy [TS2].

Additionally, students are encouraged to take a wider perspective on their individual learning as a part of the learning community they are in. To achieve this goal, one of the participants created a poster with each student as a scholar with their individual learning goal and a shared goal for the year. Another participant shared they created mindfulness posters with motivating and affirmatory phrases to keep students moving towards their goal as well as regulate.

We're a community where we take care of each other. [...] And so I think it was a balance of using that individualized approach, but also showing we're a community where we look out for each other. [TS1]

A key aspect of fostering agency in the classroom is ensuring clarity and consistency in instructional materials and communication. One participant highlighted that providing students with clear instructions, explicit expectations, and a well-defined purpose for each task removes ambiguity. It allows students to engage more confidently with the content. This structured approach supports students in managing their responsibilities and reinforces the notion that they can meet high standards. The balance of clear guidance and high expectations—what the participant describes as "tough love"—encourages students to rise to challenges, fostering resilience and a sense of accomplishment. This alignment between instructional clarity and empowerment creates a learning environment where students are equipped to take ownership of their progress while feeling supported throughout the process.

One of the keys underpinning of building a supportive environment is providing students with the necessary resources, clear guidance, and emotional safety to navigate their learning experiences confidently and effectively. Building a system of support and accommodations for students ensures the creation of a trauma-informed environment. One of the participants says,

In a nine-week quarter, I dedicated the first and last weeks to individual conferences with students. I found this approach to be highly valuable. Additionally, I conducted a mid-quarter check-in, which didn't take a full week but lasted a couple of days. I made the conscious decision that investing time in building individual relationships was worthwhile, as it helped bridge students' dreams and their understanding of concrete steps, reinforcing the relevance of school. [TS1]

The insights shared by participants underscore the potential of skillfully designed classroom environments. These efforts are not only concerned with redecorating the classroom or changing the procedures; they are deeply rooted in neurobiological and pedagogical research that validates the role of the environment in regulating students. Fostering trust, developing students' agency, and building a culture of empathy and mutual respect in classroom environments develops students' resiliency.

Interventions

The second tier of the multi-tiered system of trauma-informed support is provided by expert psychologists or mental health practitioners in a group or individual setting. However, an important aspect before suggesting students refer to practitioners is to regulate them. Teachers are at the forefront of dealing with the dysregulated behavior of students. Hence, it is important for them to follow the safety protocol and provide first psychological aid.

Instructors shared they immediately stopped the class and separated a dysregulated child from the environment they were in. In a quiet space, they aim to regulate the student. Participants say,

I've learned that I can't push them into a corner [...] I've learned to back off and reach out for someone else who has a good relationship with them to help or even just to follow them back [to their classroom] [KS1]

I physically intervened and put my body between that student and the other students around them. [...] I'll ask them to go into the hall. I'll tell the rest of the class I need to chat with that student. [TS1]

Supporting students in managing their emotions involves skills in de-escalation, along with a thorough understanding of the neurobiology behind stress and trauma. One participant highlighted that their initial approach focuses on acknowledging and validating students' experiences in the moment. Once students are calm, educators can engage their higher-order thinking by prompting reflection and encouraging logical reasoning.

She sat on a chair; I sat on the floor so that I was below her and trying to be nonthreatening. [KS1]

I typically take students out of the room, help them calm down, and then work with them to create a plan for returning—either later that day or the next. It often involves having a conversation with the student and then addressing the class by saying something like, "Hey, so-and-so is coming back and has something they'd like to say." If the student feels ready, they might apologize to the class by saying, "I'm sorry for disrupting our learning." [TS1]

At the second and third tiers of trauma-informed support, there is more targeted assistance from psychologists, mental health practitioners, or social workers. Their strategies are centered around mindfulness and cognitive and behavioral therapy and being active listeners.

In an individual setting, when I'm working with the student, I try to employ solution-focused strategies. I am trying to be present in the moment, using mindfulness strategies... [KS2]

Interventions provide chances for collaboration between educators and mental health professionals in responding to students' emotional needs. While specialized intervention is often delivered by psychologists or counselors, teachers remain the first responders in moments of acute dysregulation. Their ability to recognize signs of distress, provide immediate psychological first aid, and safely de-escalate situations is foundational to a trauma-informed ecosystem. Participants' reflections reveal thoughtful, compassionate strategies—from physically protecting students and others to using non-threatening body language and offering space for reflection and repair. These moments, though often challenging, are deeply relational and underscore the importance of trust, emotional attunement, and regulation before redirection. Ultimately, when teachers are equipped with trauma-informed skills and supported by a coordinated network of care, the classroom becomes a bridge—not a barrier—to healing and resilience.

Teacher Well-Being

Another overarching idea in the research is teacher well-being. The ability of educators to manage their own stress and emotional regulation directly impacts their effectiveness in supporting students, particularly those affected by trauma. When teachers prioritize their mental health, they model healthy student coping strategies and create a more stable, empathetic classroom environment. Research highlights that burnout and compassion fatigue are common among educators working in high-stress environments, making self-care and peer support essential to sustainable teaching practices. The school has implemented a school-wide mindfulness program. In the words of some participants,

Developing the practice of deep listening—listening without simultaneously thinking or planning a response—has been something I've found to be really important in my professional life. This is also something we've worked on in mindfulness training as well. [KS3]

Many participants have also re-interacted that they participate in a meditation program, where the group meets every two or three weeks with follow-up 20-minute 1:1 meetings with involved participants to decompress.

We have a community of practice, which is like a sangha, where we meet together as a group in the school. And at Roosevelt we have two of those groups. [KS2]

One participant mentioned that students are a great source of motivation and inspiration for them. It is also a way of regulating themselves by reminding them of their purpose, taking a regular walk, and being with nature.

How do I help myself? So, I have a drawer in my office where I keep all the cards that the students give me. You know, like little notes or those little things that I have there. I have a card in here where students drew for Christmas. [TS2]

Teacher well-being emerges as an essential component of trauma-informed education. Educators' emotional presence and self-regulation shape the classroom climate and serve as powerful models for students learning to navigate their stress responses. Equally vital is that educators prioritize their own mental and physical health while also engaging in school-wide initiatives that normalize conversations around mental health, address trauma, and foster strong communities of professional support.

Challenges in Creating the Trauma-Informed Environment

Analysis of the data would be incomplete without paying attention to the challenges participants mentioned regarding the implementation of the trauma-informed school environment. These challenges are different in their nature. For instance, challenges related to the lack of facilities in schools. There are not enough calming corners and quiet zones for students, as the number of students requiring them is rising.

But then they say "I can't go to class". And we're not really set up to have individual quiet rooms for everyone who needs them. I think the dilemma for schools now is we have kids with this greater awareness, and we have this greater awareness of possibly all the things that they're struggling with, and we want to be responsive to that. But how do you decide? And how do you get the resources to be able to do something with that besides just being a kind listening ear? [KS1]

Another issue related to the implementation of the trauma-informed approach is the resistance of some educators. The participant explains that such resistance is due to the lack of professional development and competencies necessary to implement the trauma-informed approach. In some cases, the reason is the quality of the training provided and its content or the heavy workload teacher have.

I think there's some resistance from teachers, but [name of school], not dramatically. No one is "These kids, they just need to come and learn". I think the biggest resistance is just they quietly don't do the thing. [KS1]

Like the teacher PD version of the Body Keeps the Score, like what's happening in kids' brains? And what are some actual strategies that I could use when they are elevated? Or when they are hallucinating? Or when they are... Those are things I just genuinely don't know. But I would genuinely love to learn. But not like fluffy PD. I don't need to learn how to hold hands and sing in a circle. I want to learn psychology, biology, and history; I want to learn what medical students learn in psychology. I don't want the watered-down version. [KS1]

But we can't send all of our staff to it [PD training], even if we had the money, because we don't have the time built into our schedule. [KS1]

Another dimension of the challenging problem is staffing. One of the participants points out the problem of teacher retention. When teachers leave school, most students are left without a trusted adult who is able to counsel or regulate them. Additionally, another participant mentioned that the current support staff is insufficient to meet the growing needs of students, as there is a high volume of student inquiries and requests for assistance from a diverse cohort of students. It is important to build rapport with students, which is easier is they are counseled by somebody to them.

I think we need to tackle the teacher retention problem in general because I think kids just do better when there's stability. [KS1]

[...] *my point is having folks providing mental health services who look like the students that we work with would be really helpful* [KS2]

DISCUSSION

This study aimed to enhance the overall understanding of the multidimensional face of multi-tiered trauma-informed systems of support in schools. The study used a qualitative methods approach to analyze the data. Qualitative interview analyses provide detailed information about participants' experiences as educators in a trauma-informed school in Minneapolis, having implemented a multi-tiered trauma-informed approach. This finding is consistent with prior research on trauma-informed approach (Forbes & Maki, 2020; Venet, 2021). In this paper, these themes are discussed through the lens of the neurobiology of trauma (van der Kolk, 2000).

Trauma-Informed Practices in Building Supportive Classroom Environments

Many teachers lack formal training in trauma-informed approaches, leaving them to rely on observation and intuition to address students' needs. One participant shared, "I do not recall having any class that addressed that area (trauma-informed teaching) specifically, which is unfortunate. Because I think in these times that we live in, it is extremely important." [TS2] Without structured guidance, teachers navigate a challenging educational landscape by independently developing methods to address the impact of trauma on students' cognitive abilities. Ultimately, these teachers rely on pedagogical intuition over structured programs to support their students' emotional and cognitive well-being.

Van der Kolk argues that safety is essential for building connections with others and recovering from previous traumatic experiences (van der Kolk, 2000). The participant shares, "We had kids who had emigrated from Iraq and experienced war. I started to piece together that some of these behaviors aren't just bad or annoying, but tied to something bigger and greater they've experienced" [TS1]. Aligned with what van der Kolk writes, educators prioritize building trustful relationships with students. Additionally, as a part of building trustful relationships educators set a predictable environment, explaining students "where we're headed, what we're doing, feeling really grounded, and that things are predictable". Additionally, they preface the year and course for their students and give trigger warnings and alternative assignments for students.

However, building trust with students is a matter of time. Meanwhile, when educators feel they are not yet in such relationships, they "back off, and reach out for someone with a good relationship with them to help or even follow them". Another important thing to keep in mind is to track the mental state students are in. If they feel aroused or threatened, having conversations with them is not the best time.

According to the Triune Brain theory, only when students are regulated can they reason and assess the consequences of their decisions due to the neocortex being responsible for that function. Hence, what participants did is "when they've calmed down, then have the conversation".

FUTURE RESEARCH DIRECTIONS

Future research is suggested to identify perspectives of disseminating practices of the trauma-informed approach of the school across a wider community of practitioners.

CONCLUSION

In conclusion, the study revealed insights into the experiences of educators working within trauma-informed classrooms. Participants demonstrated a clear commitment to fostering environments where students feel supported, safe, and empowered. Their strategies focused on the importance of creating spaces that promote emotional well-being, such as calming corners and clear, structured routines, which align with trauma-informed principles of safety, predictability, and emotional regulation. Additionally, educators emphasized the value of mental health care, both for themselves and their students, highlighting the necessity of self-care to provide effective support.

The participants' experiences also shed light on the challenges faced in implementing trauma-informed practices, particularly in under-resourced schools. The lack of formal training in trauma-informed education was noted, yet participants demonstrated a strong drive to adapt and tailor their teaching approaches to meet the needs of students who have experienced trauma. The study also illuminated the broader importance of fostering a community-centered classroom that empowers students and provides them with the tools to advocate for themselves.

Ultimately, the findings underscore the need for continued investment in trauma-informed education, not only in terms of resources but also in ensuring that educators are supported and equipped to navigate the complexities of working with students who have experienced trauma. The educators' reflections reveal the transformative potential of trauma-informed practices in enhancing student resilience and fostering a supportive, inclusive learning environment that prioritizes mental health and well-being.

ACKNOWLEDGMENT

This research received no specific grant from any funding agency in the public, commercial, or not-for-profit sectors.

This study was made possible with the informational support of libraries of the University of Minnesota Twin Cities, where the author was a Visiting Scholar in 2022-2023.

Thank you to the participants of this study, who shared their time, insights, and practices with the author. Additionally, the author would like to express sincere gratitude to Martha Bigelow, who supported the author's aspiration to do this research, and to Christopher Sanville, who assisted in providing invaluable support at the initial phase of the research process.

The author would like to express her gratitude to Beyond Consequences Institute for providing the author with access to the book Classroom 180 and accompanying resources.

REFERENCES

Aduwo, B., Mutfwang, T., Umoren, E., Chima, O. N., & Williams, O. A. (2017). The effect of the classroom's environment on the learning experience of primary and secondary school students in Ota, Ogun state. *EDULEARN17 Proceedings*, 8802-8806. DOI: 10.21125/edulearn.2017.0651

Ahmadpour, N., Loke, L., Gray, C., & MacDonald, C. (2023). Understanding how technology can support social-emotional learning of children: a dyadic trauma-informed participatory design with proxies. *International Conference on Human Factors in Computing Systems*. DOI: 10.1145/3544548.3581032

Alisic, E., Bus, M., Dulack, W., Pennings, L., & Splinter, J. (2012). Teachers' experiences supporting children after traumatic exposure. *Journal of Traumatic Stress*, *25*(1), 98–101. DOI: 10.1002/jts.20709

Apgar, D. (2023). Video narratives as a trauma-informed pedagogical tool in remote social work education. *Social Work Education*, 1–17. DOI: 10.1080/02615479.2023.2229862

Berardi, A., & Morton, B. (2019). *Trauma-Informed School Practices: Building Expertise to Transform Schools*. Open Textbooks.

Bucholz, J. L., & Sheffler, J. L. (2009). Creating a Warm and Inclusive Classroom Environment: Planning for All Children to Feel Welcome. *Electronic Journal for Inclusive Education*, *2*(4), 1–14.

Buckley, S., & Sullivan, P. (2023). Reframing anxiety and uncertainty in the mathematics classroom. *Mathematics Education Research Journal, 35*(2021), 1–14. DOI: 10.1007/s13394-021-00393-8

Craig, S. E. (2008). *Reaching and teaching children who hurt : strategies for your classroom*. Paul H. Brookes Pub.

Craig, S. E. (2016). *Trauma-sensitive schools: Learning communities transforming children's lives*. Teachers College Press.

Dehn, M. J. (2022). *Assessing and Intervening with Children who have Difficulties with Learning and Memory*. DOI: 10.1002/9781119790563.ch30

Ellison, D., & Walton-Fisette, J. (2022). "It's more about building trust": Physical education teachers' experiences with trauma-informed practices. *European Physical Education Review*, *28*(4), 906–922. DOI: 10.1177/1356336X221096603

Fallot, R. D., & Harris, M. (2006). *Trauma-informed services: A self-assessment and planning protocol.* Community Connections. https://children.wi.gov/Documents/CCTICSelf-AssessmentandPlanningProtocol0709.pdf

Forbes, H., & Maki, D. (2020). *Classroom180: A Framework for Creating, Sustaining, and Assessing the Trauma-Informed Classroom*. Beyond Consequences Institute.

Granito, V., & Santana, M. (2016). Psychology of Learning Spaces: Impact on Teaching and Learning. *Journal of Learning Spaces*, *5*(1), 1–8.

Hooper, A., Hyder, M., Colclough, T., & Mann, D. (2023). Re-Envisioning Learning through a Trauma-Informed Lens: Empowering Students in their Personal and Academic Growth. *The Journal of Scholarship of Teaching and Learning*, *23*(3). Advance online publication. DOI: 10.14434/josotl.v23i3.35234

Howard, A. (2024). Is Your Syllabus Trauma Informed? *Journal of Trauma Studies in Education*, *3*(2), 69–89. DOI: 10.70085/jtse.v3i2.6436

Jacobson, M. R. (2021). An exploratory analysis of the necessity and utility of trauma-informed practices in education. *Preventing School Failure*, *65*(2), 124–134. DOI: 10.1080/1045988X.2020.1848776

Jones, W., Berg, J., & Osher, D. (2018). *Trauma and Learning Policy Initiative (TLPI): Trauma-Sensitive Schools Descriptive Study Final Report*. American Institutes for Research. https://traumasensitiveschools.org/wp-content/uploads/2019/02/TLPI-Final-Report_Full-Report-002-2-1.pdf

Kessler, R., Aguilar-Gaxiola, S., Alonso, J., Benjet, C., Bromet, E., Cardoso, G., & Haro, J. (2017). Trauma and PTSD in the WHO World Mental Health Surveys. *European Journal of Psychotraumatology*, *8*. Advance online publication. DOI: 10.1080/20008198.2017.1353383

Koslouski, J. B., Stark, K., & Chafouleas, S. M. (2023). Understanding and responding to the effects of trauma in the classroom: A primer for educators. *Social and Emotional Learning: Research, Practice, and Policy*, *1*, 100004. DOI: 10.1016/j.sel.2023.100004

Lawless, B., & Chen, Y. W. (2018). Developing a Method of Critical Thematic Analysis for Qualitative Communication Inquiry. *The Howard Journal of Communications*, *30*(1), 92–106. DOI: 10.1080/10646175.2018.1439423

Matte-Landry, A., Grisé Bolduc, M. È., Tanguay-Garneau, L., Collin-Vézina, D., & Ouellet-Morin, I. (2023). Cognitive outcomes of children with complex trauma: A systematic review and meta-analyses of longitudinal studies. *Trauma, Violence & Abuse*, *24*(4), 2743–2757. DOI: 10.1177/15248380221111484

Minneapolis Department of Education. (n.d.). *Data Reports and Analytics.* Retrieved from Minneapolis Department of Education: https://public.education.mn.gov/MDEAnalytics/DataTopic.jsp?TOPICID=2

Mora-Flores, E., & Dewing, S. (2023). *Teaching and Supporting English Learners: A Guide to Welcoming and Engaging Newcomers*. Shell Education.

Moses, J., Bayne, H. B., & Moore, R. L. (2023). *Guiding Course Development: Trauma-Informed Rubrics for Asynchronous Online Learning Environments*. DOI: 10.59668/722.13025

Mukherjee, D., & Horton, K. B. (2024). A Trauma-Informed Approach to School Mental Health Workforce Development. *Best Practices in Mental Health*, *20*(1), 1–16. DOI: 10.70256/033599dyxpgc

Osuch, E., & Engel, C. C.Jr. (2004). Research on the treatment of trauma spectrum responses: The role of the optimal healing environment and neurobiology. *Journal of Alternative and Complementary Medicine (New York, N.Y.)*, *10*(Suppl 1), S211–S221. DOI: 10.1089/1075553042245944

PBIS. (2025). PBIS. https://www.pbis.org/

Perry, B. D. (2009). *Born for love: Why empathy is essential—and endangered*. HarperCollins.

Reupert, A. (2020). *Mental Health and Academic Learning in Schools : Approaches for Facilitating the Wellbeing of Children and Young People* (1st ed.). Routledge. DOI: 10.4324/9781315310930

Robertson, C. A., & Robertson, C. L. (2021). Trauma and the Middle School Brain: Impacts and Instructional Strategies. In Gaines, C., & Hutson, K. (Eds.), *Promoting Positive Learning Experiences in Middle School Education* (pp. 66–86). IGI Global Scientific Publishing. DOI: 10.4018/978-1-7998-7057-9.ch004

Ruiz, R. E. (2021). *Delivering Interventions to Individuals With Trauma-Induced Behaviors Through Immersive Virtual Learning Environments*. IGI Global. DOI: 10.4018/978-1-7998-4222-4.CH012

Schmidt, H. (2024). *Survivors of Complex Trauma as Adult Online Learners*. DOI: 10.18357/otessac.2024.4.1.378

Sharkey, J. D., Mullin, A. C., Felix, E. D., Maier, D., & Fedders, A. (2024). Supporting Educators and Students: A University–Community Partnership to Implement Trauma-Informed Practices in Schools. *School Mental Health*. Advance online publication. DOI: 10.1007/s12310-024-09667-5

Somers, J. W., & Wheeler, L. (2022). A Blueprint for Collaborative Action to Build a Trauma-Informed School: A Case Study. *Professional School Counseling*, *26*. Advance online publication. DOI: 10.1177/2156759X221134670

Stokes, H. (2022). Leading Trauma-Informed Education Practice as an Instructional Model for Teaching and Learning. *Frontiers in Education*, *7*. Advance online publication. DOI: 10.3389/feduc.2022.911328

U.S. Department of Veterans Affairs. (2024). *PTSD: National Center for PTSD*. U.S. Department of Veterans Affairs. https://www.ptsd.va.gov/understand/common/common_children_teens.asp

van der Kolk, B. (2000). Posttraumatic stress disorder and the nature of trauma. *Dialogues in Clinical Neuroscience*, *2*(1), 7–22. DOI: 10.31887/DCNS.2000.2.1/bvdkolk

Van der Kolk, B. (2014). *The body keeps the score: Mind, brain and body in the transformation of trauma*. Penguin Books.

Venet, A. (2021). *Equity-centered trauma-informed education*. W.W. Norton & Company.

Xu, M. (2015). Discussion of the Influence Mechanism of Psychological Environment in Classroom for Effective Teaching. *Creative Education*, *6*, 1573–1577. DOI: 10.4236/ce.2015.614157

ADDITIONAL READING

Filio, S. (2020). *Responding to student trauma. A toolkit for schools in times of crisis.* Free Spirit Publishing.

Forbes, H., & Maki, D. (2020). *Classroom180: A Framework for Creating, Sustaining, and Assessing the Trauma-Informed Classroom.* Beyond Consequences Institute.

Holovatenko, T. (2024). *Pre-service teachers' perceptions on implementing the trauma-informed approach in educational institutions.* In *Proceedings of the 4th International Conference on History, Theory and Methodology of Learning (ICHTML)* (pp. 130–137). SciTePress. DOI: 10.5220/0012648000003737

Holovatenko, T. (2025). Rethinking Competences for Initial Language Teacher Training Through Trauma-Informed Lens. In Rahmat, M., & Osborne, A. (Eds.), *Pedagogies of Compassion and Care in Education* (pp. 337–370). IGI Global Scientific Publishing. DOI: 10.4018/979-8-3693-3613-7.ch015

KEY TERMS AND DEFINITIONS

Supportive Trauma-Informed Environment: Regulating environment designed to recognize the impact of trauma and stress on students and ensure students can gain control over their lives without being re-traumatized. This environment is grounded into trust, emotional safety, collaboration, empowerment, and cultural sensitivity. In educational contexts, it also promotes academic engagement, social-emotional learning, and resilience.

Trauma-Informed Pedagogy: A pedagogic approach grounded in the recognition of the prevalence of traumatic events and their influence on learners, aimed at assisting instructors in establishing an inclusive environment that caters to the diverse needs of learners with various traumatic backgrounds.

Section 2

The Intersection of Social-Emotional Learning and Trauma-Informed School Communities

Chapter 5
Cultural Competence Social–Emotional Learning

Ranjit Singha
https://orcid.org/0000-0002-3541-8752
Christ University, India

Alphonsa Diana Haokip
https://orcid.org/0000-0003-2578-0114
Don Bosco College, Maram, India

Surjit Singha
https://orcid.org/0000-0002-5730-8677
Kristu Jayanti College, India

Jishamol Thomas
https://orcid.org/0000-0002-2912-9188
Christ University, India

Melita Stephen Natal
https://orcid.org/0009-0004-1240-7817
Amity University, Greater Noida, India

Mibi Riba
Dera Natung Government College, India

ABSTRACT

This chapter delves into the integration of cultural competence and social-emotional learning (SEL) within trauma-informed educational settings, proposing a multi-tiered systems of support (MTSS) framework. The chapter examines the theoretical and conceptual foundations of cultural competence and SEL, emphasizing the importance of these components in supporting students' emotional and academic success, particularly in diverse and trauma-affected communities. Practical strategies and challenges for implementing culturally responsive SEL practices are discussed, along with recommendations for educators, policymakers, and future research directions.

INTRODUCTION

Integrating cultural competence and social-emotional learning (SEL) within trauma-informed educational settings has emerged as a critical focus area for enhancing students' emotional and academic outcomes. As educational institutions strive to address the diverse needs of learners, particularly those from historically marginalized and trauma-affected backgrounds, the necessity of adopting frameworks that foster inclusivity, equity, and holistic well-being has become increasingly evident. A multi-tiered system of support (MTSS), rooted in trauma-informed principles, offers a structured approach to achiev-

DOI: 10.4018/979-8-3693-9020-7.ch005

ing these goals by embedding cultural responsiveness and SEL practices at every level of intervention (Al-Hroub & Al-Hroub, 2024; Jackson, 2017).

Cultural competence is understanding, appreciating, and interacting effectively with individuals from different cultural backgrounds. It involves recognizing and valuing students' unique cultural identities, experiences, and perspectives within educational settings. Cultural competence extends beyond surface-level awareness to include meaningful engagement with the systemic inequities that may affect students' learning experiences. For students from diverse cultural backgrounds, the presence or absence of culturally competent practices can significantly influence their sense of belonging, academic performance, and emotional well-being (Arruzza & Chau, 2021).

Trauma-affected students, in particular, often face compounded challenges related to cultural dissonance, systemic biases, and socio-economic disparities. Teachers and school staff who lack cultural competence may inadvertently perpetuate these inequities, resulting in a lack of trust, engagement, and support. Conversely, culturally responsive practices enable educators to build stronger relationships with students, validate their lived experiences, and foster an environment where all learners feel seen, heard, and valued (Matalon & Clauss-Ehlers, 2023).

Social-emotional learning (SEL) focuses on developing critical skills such as self-awareness, self-regulation, social awareness, relationship building, and responsible decision-making. These competencies are essential for students to navigate the complexities of academic and interpersonal life. In trauma-informed settings, SEL provides a foundation for fostering resilience and emotional regulation among students who may struggle with the lingering effects of (ACEs) adverse childhood experiences (Al-Hroub & Al-Hroub, 2024).

The intersection of SEL and cultural competence is particularly relevant in supporting diverse learners. Traditional SEL frameworks may fail to account for the cultural contexts that shape students' emotional and social development. For example, behaviors interpreted as disruptive or defiant in one cultural framework may hold entirely different meanings in another. Embedding cultural competence within SEL ensures that these programs are sensitive to cultural nuances, fostering deeper connections and understanding between educators and students (Katzman & Stanton, 2020).

Trauma-informed education is rooted in the recognition that many students carry the invisible burden of trauma, which can manifest in various ways, including difficulties in concentration, emotional regulation, and social interactions. By integrating cultural competence and SEL into trauma-informed practices, schools can create learning environments that are both supportive and transformative. Trauma-informed approaches prioritize safety, trust, collaboration, and empowerment—elements that are inherently aligned with SEL and cultural competence (Matalon & Clauss-Ehlers, 2023).

The Multi-Tiered Systems of Support (MTSS) framework offers a scalable and structured approach for implementing culturally competent social-emotional learning (SEL) within trauma-informed educational settings by addressing students' diverse needs at varying intervention levels. **Tier 1** encompasses universal strategies designed to create inclusive and equitable classroom environments through culturally responsive teaching practices, SEL curricula, and school-wide policies that promote diversity and inclusion. **Tier 2** involves targeted interventions for students requiring additional support, such as small group counseling sessions or culturally adapted SEL workshops tailored to address specific needs. **Tier 3** focuses on individualized, intensive interventions for students with significant challenges, integrating trauma-informed care with culturally relevant therapeutic approaches. By embedding cultural competence across all tiers of the MTSS framework, educators can create environments that respect and incorporate students' cultural identities, fostering emotional safety, academic engagement, and overall well-being (Hossain & Mumu, 2024).

Despite the growing awareness of the importance of cultural competence and SEL, many schools struggle to implement these practices effectively. Challenges such as limited resources, insufficient training, and systemic biases can hinder progress. Cultural intersection and dynamics necessitate ongoing learning and adaptation. Educators and policymakers must work collaboratively to overcome these barriers, leveraging research-based strategies and community partnerships to create sustainable change. This chapter addresses these challenges by proposing a comprehensive framework integrating cultural competence and SEL within an MTSS approach. It explores theoretical and conceptual foundations, highlights practical strategies, and examines the opportunities and obstacles in implementing culturally responsive SEL practices. By doing so, it aims to empower educators and policymakers to create trauma-informed educational settings that are inclusive, supportive, and transformative for all learners.

Background

Integrating cultural competence and social-emotional learning (SEL) in educational settings has evolved significantly over the past decades, reflecting broader societal shifts toward diversity, equity, and inclusion. Historically, educational systems were often designed with a one-size-fits-all approach, overlooking students' cultural and emotional needs from diverse backgrounds. The growing recognition of these elements as fundamental to student success and well-being has spurred a transformation in how schools address the challenges faced by diverse populations. This section examines the historical context and evolution of cultural competence and SEL, highlighting their increasing significance in modern education (Kohli et al., 2010). Cultural competence in education emerged in response to the growing diversity within classrooms, particularly in countries with high immigration levels and multicultural populations. Initially rooted in healthcare and social work, cultural competence was introduced to education to address the inequities experienced by students from marginalized and underrepresented communities. Early efforts focused on increasing educators' awareness of cultural differences, reducing biases, and improving communication with students and families from diverse backgrounds.

During the 1960s and 1970s, the civil rights movement in the United States and similar social justice movements worldwide brought attention to systemic inequities in education. Scholars and activists emphasized the importance of acknowledging students' cultural identities to promote equity and inclusion. The multicultural education movement emerged during this period, advocating for curricula reflecting diverse cultural groups' histories, experiences, and contributions (Banks, 2013). In the 21st century, the concept of cultural competence expanded beyond awareness to include actionable skills and behaviors that educators could adopt to create more inclusive and supportive learning environments. This shift was driven by research demonstrating that culturally responsive teaching practices positively impact students' academic performance, emotional well-being, and sense of belonging. Educational frameworks such as Gloria Ladson-Billings' concept of culturally relevant pedagogy and Geneva Gay's work on culturally responsive teaching provided practical strategies for integrating cultural competence into classroom practices (Gay 2018).

Social-emotional learning (SEL) has its roots in developmental psychology and educational philosophy, particularly in the work of theorists such as John Dewey, Jean Piaget, and Lev Vygotsky, who emphasized the importance of social and emotional development in learning. However, SEL as a formalized concept began to gain traction in the late 20th century (Vygotsky, 1978). The Collaborative for

Academic, Social, and Emotional Learning (CASEL), founded in 1994, was instrumental in defining SEL and advocating its integration into education. CASEL identified five core competencies—self-awareness, self-management, social awareness, relationship skills, and responsible decision-making—essential for students' academic and personal success. SEL programs were initially introduced as stand-alone initiatives, focusing on building students' emotional intelligence and interpersonal skills. Over time, the scope of SEL expanded to address broader issues such as bullying prevention, mental health, and school climate. Research revealed that SEL enhances students' emotional and social development, improves academic outcomes, reduces behavioral problems, and fosters resilience. As a result, SEL became an integral part of educational reform efforts to create holistic and supportive learning environments.

The intersection of cultural competence and SEL represents a natural progression in the evolution of these concepts. Both aim to create inclusive and equitable learning environments that address the diverse needs of students. However, traditional SEL programs often lacked cultural responsiveness, failing to account for the ways in which students' cultural identities influence their social and emotional experiences. In recent years, there has been growing recognition of the need to embed cultural competence within SEL frameworks. Culturally responsive SEL involves adapting SEL curricula and practices to reflect students' cultural values, norms, and experiences. This approach ensures that SEL programs are relevant and meaningful, fostering deeper connections and engagement among students.

The integration of cultural competence and SEL is particularly important in trauma-informed educational settings, where students from diverse backgrounds may face unique challenges related to their cultural identities and experiences. By combining these elements, schools can create environments that support students' academic and emotional needs and celebrate their cultural strengths and resilience. Today, cultural awareness and emotional intelligence in education are widely acknowledged. Research has shown that these elements foster positive relationships, reduce achievement gaps, and promote overall well-being. Policymakers, educators, and researchers continue to advocate for integrating cultural competence and SEL into educational frameworks, emphasizing their role in preparing students for success in an increasingly diverse and interconnected world. Despite these advancements, challenges remain in implementing culturally responsive SEL practices on a large scale. Issues such as limited resources, lack of training, and systemic biases can hinder progress. However, the ongoing efforts to address these barriers reflect a commitment to creating inclusive, equitable, and supportive educational systems for all learners. Understanding the historical context and evolution of cultural competence and SEL, educators and policymakers can build on past successes and address current challenges, paving the way for future more effective and sustainable practices.

THEORETICAL FRAMEWORK

Integrating cultural competence and social-emotional learning (SEL) within trauma-informed educational settings requires a robust theoretical foundation to understand the complex interplay of cultural and emotional factors influencing learning and development. This section explores key theories that underpin these concepts, providing a basis for creating inclusive and supportive educational environments. The primary theoretical frameworks include Vygotsky's Social Development Theory, Bronfenbrenner's Ecological Systems Theory, and Banks' Multicultural Education Theory.

Vygotsky's Social Development Theory

Lev Vygotsky's Social Development Theory (1978) emphasizes the fundamental role of social interaction in cognitive and emotional development. According to Vygotsky, learning is inherently a social process that occurs through interactions with more knowledgeable others, such as teachers, peers, and family members. His concept of the **Zone of Proximal Development (ZPD)** highlights the gap between what a learner can do independently and what they can achieve with guided support. In the context of cultural competence and social emotional learning (SEL), Vygotsky's theory (year) underscores the importance of culturally responsive interactions in fostering students' social and emotional growth. Educators can use culturally relevant scaffolding techniques to build students' self-awareness, social awareness, and interpersonal skills, aligning with SEL's core competencies. Vygotsky (year) emphasized language as a tool for cognitive development resonates with the need to consider students' linguistic and cultural backgrounds in designing SEL activities and curricula.

Bronfenbrenner's Ecological Systems Theory

Urie Bronfenbrenner's Ecological Systems Theory provides a holistic framework for understanding how various environmental factors influence a child's development. This theory posits that development is shaped by the interactions between the individual and their surrounding systems, which are organized into five levels:

1. **Microsystem**: Immediate environments such as family, school, and peers.
2. **Mesosystem**: Interconnections between microsystems, such as the relationship between home and school.
3. **Exosystem**: External environments that indirectly affect the individual, such as parental workplace policies.
4. **Macrosystem**: Broader cultural and societal influences, including norms, values, and laws.
5. **Chronosystem**: The dimension of time, capturing changes in the individual and their environment over time.

Bronfenbrenner's theory highlights the significance of cultural and social contexts in shaping students' emotional well-being and learning outcomes. Educators must consider how students' microsystems and mesosystems interact with larger societal and cultural factors in a culturally competent SEL framework. For example, trauma-informed practices should address the impact of systemic inequities and cultural barriers on students' development, ensuring that interventions are responsive to their unique experiences and needs.

Banks' Multicultural Education Theory

James A. Banks' Multicultural Education Theory focuses on integrating students' cultural identities into the educational process to promote equity and inclusion. Banks outlines five dimensions of multicultural education:

1. **Content Integration**: Incorporating diverse cultural perspectives into the curriculum.

2. **Knowledge Construction**: Helping students critically examine how cultural assumptions influence knowledge.
3. **Prejudice Reduction**: Implementing strategies to reduce biases and stereotypes.
4. **Equity Pedagogy**: Adapting teaching methods to accommodate diverse learning styles.
5. **Empowering School Culture**: Creating an environment that supports all students' academic and social success.

Banks' theory aligns closely with the goals of cultural competence and SEL by emphasizing the need for educators to acknowledge and value students' cultural identities. For instance, culturally responsive SEL practices can involve using culturally relevant materials, addressing implicit biases, and fostering an inclusive classroom climate. By integrating Banks' dimensions into SEL frameworks, schools can ensure that all students feel seen, heard, and supported.

Integration of Theories

These theories provide a comprehensive framework for understanding the interplay between cultural and emotional factors in education. Vygotsky's Social Development Theory emphasizes the role of social interactions and culturally relevant scaffolding in SEL. Bronfenbrenner's Ecological Systems Theory highlights the broader environmental and cultural contexts that shape students' development. Banks' Multicultural Education Theory provides practical strategies for embedding cultural competence into educational practices. By drawing on these theoretical foundations, educators and policymakers can design trauma-informed educational settings that effectively integrate cultural competence and SEL. This integration ensures that students' cultural identities and emotional needs are addressed, fostering academic success and emotional well-being. Applying these theories also underscores the importance of creating systemic changes in educational environments to support diverse learners, offering a roadmap for future research and practice.

CONCEPTUAL FRAMEWORK

The conceptual framework for integrating cultural competence and social-emotional learning (SEL) into a multi-tiered system of support (MTSS) provides a roadmap for addressing the diverse needs of students in trauma-informed educational settings. This framework emphasizes a holistic approach that combines the principles of MTSS, cultural competence, and SEL to create inclusive, supportive, and equitable learning environments.

Components of Intersectional Multitiered Systems of Support

This tiered framework is designed to provide differentiated support to students based on their unique needs. Each tier builds on the foundation of the previous one, ensuring a continuum of care that addresses academic, social, emotional, and behavioral needs. Cultural competence involves recognizing, valuing, and integrating students' cultural identities into education. SEL focuses on developing students' self-awareness, self-management, social awareness, relationship skills, and responsible decision-making.

Integrating these components into MTSS ensures effective, culturally responsive, and trauma-informed interventions.

Figure 1. Integrating cultural competence and social-emotional learning

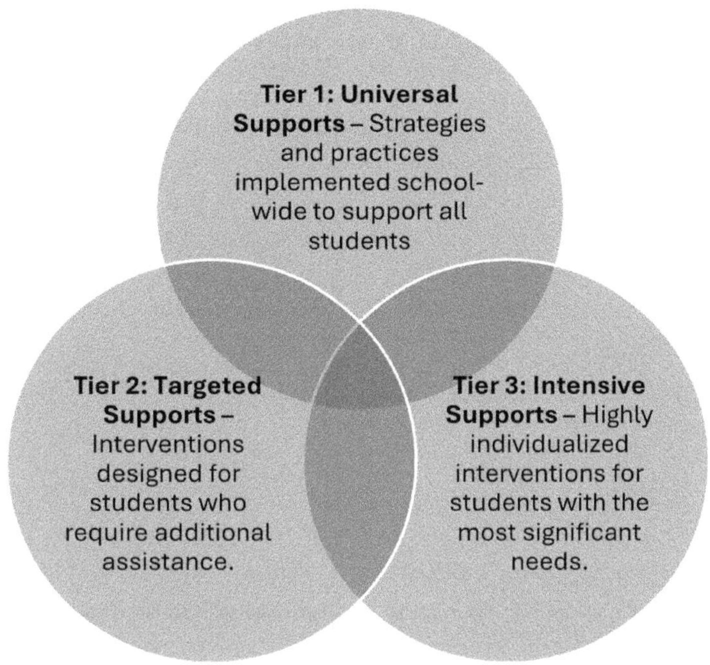

Tier 1: Culturally Responsive Universal Supports

The universal level focuses on creating an inclusive school culture that promotes diversity and fosters emotional well-being.

- **Culturally Responsive Practices**: Incorporate students' cultural backgrounds into the curriculum and teaching methods to make learning relevant and engaging.
- **SEL Curriculum**: Implement school-wide SEL programs that address core competencies, such as empathy, emotional regulation, and conflict resolution.
- **Professional Development**: Train educators in cultural competence and trauma-informed practices to enhance their ability to support diverse learners.
- **Inclusive Policies**: Develop policies that celebrate diversity, reduce biases, and ensure equitable student opportunities.

Tier 2: Culturally Responsive Targeted Supports

At the targeted level, interventions are tailored for students who require additional support to thrive socially, emotionally, and academically.

- **Small Group Interventions**: Conduct culturally adapted SEL workshops that address specific needs, such as coping strategies or peer relationships.
- **Counseling Sessions**: Provide group counseling services that consider cultural nuances and students' shared experiences.
- **Parental Involvement**: Engage families in the intervention process, leveraging their cultural knowledge to support students' development.

Tier 3: Culturally Responsive Intensive Supports

At the intensive level, interventions focus on individual students with significant challenges, such as those impacted by trauma or systemic inequities.

- **Individualized Plans**: Develop personalized support plans integrating trauma-informed care and culturally relevant therapeutic approaches.
- **Mental Health Services**: Collaborate with culturally competent professionals to provide one-on-one counseling and therapy.
- **Case Management**: Use a team-based approach to coordinate student services involving educators, counselors, and families.

A Holistic Support System

By embedding cultural competence and SEL into each tier of MTSS, schools can create a holistic support system that addresses students' academic and emotional needs in a culturally sensitive manner. This approach ensures that students feel valued, understood, and supported, leading to improved emotional well-being and academic engagement. Key elements of the conceptual framework include:

- **Trauma-Informed Lens**: Recognizing the impact of trauma on learning and integrating practices that promote emotional safety.
- **Cultural Responsiveness**: Ensuring that all interventions are adapted to the cultural contexts of the students being served.
- **Data-Driven Decision-Making**: Using data to identify student needs, monitor progress, and adjust interventions accordingly.
- **Collaboration**: Fostering partnerships among educators, families, and community stakeholders to create a support network.

This conceptual framework demonstrates how cultural competence and SEL can be effectively woven into MTSS to create trauma-informed educational settings. By addressing the unique needs of diverse learners through tiered interventions, schools can promote academic success and emotional well-being, fostering a supportive environment where all students can thrive. This holistic approach mitigates the effects of trauma and celebrates and leverages the rich cultural diversity within the student population.

Research Problem

Despite growing recognition of the importance of **cultural competence** and **social-emotional learning (SEL)** in education, a significant gap exists in their systematic integration within **trauma-informed educational settings**. Current practices often fail to adequately address the unique emotional and academic needs of students from diverse cultural backgrounds, particularly those who have experienced trauma.

Many existing SEL programs are designed with a one-size-fits-all approach, often overlooking students' cultural identities, values, and lived experiences. Similarly, trauma-informed practices frequently lack the cultural sensitivity needed to engage students effectively and foster a sense of belonging. This lack of cultural relevance not only limits the impact of these programs but may also unintentionally reinforce systemic inequities in education. Moreover, while the **multi-tiered system of support (MTSS)** framework provides a structured approach to addressing diverse student needs, it is rarely implemented in ways that fully integrate cultural competence and SEL. The absence of a cohesive framework that combines these elements leaves a critical gap in the ability of schools to create inclusive, supportive, and equitable environments.

As schools become increasingly diverse, educators and policymakers face mounting challenges in meeting the demands of culturally and emotionally responsive teaching. Without targeted interventions that bridge cultural competence and SEL within trauma-informed frameworks, students from marginalized communities risk falling through the cracks, with their emotional well-being and academic success compromised. This research problem underscores the urgent need for a comprehensive framework that embeds cultural competence and SEL into each tier of MTSS. Such a framework would provide educators with practical strategies for addressing the needs of diverse learners, fostering emotional resilience, and promoting academic achievement in trauma-informed settings. Filling this gap is critical for ensuring that all students, regardless of their cultural background or life experiences, have the opportunity to thrive in supportive and inclusive educational environments.

Research Question

How can cultural competence and social-emotional learning (SEL) be effectively integrated into multi-tiered support systems (MTSS) to enhance students' emotional, social, and academic outcomes in trauma-informed educational settings?

Research Objective

The primary objective of this research is to develop a comprehensive framework for integrating cultural competence and social-emotional learning (SEL) into multi-tiered systems of support (MTSS) within trauma-informed educational settings. This framework aims to:

1. **Address Emotional and Academic Needs**: Equip educators with strategies to support students' emotional well-being and academic success of students, particularly those from diverse cultural backgrounds and trauma-affected communities.
2. **Promote Inclusivity and Equity**: Foster inclusive and culturally responsive learning environments that value and respect students' cultural identities.

3. **Provide Practical Tools**: Offer actionable tools and interventions that align with the tiered structure of MTSS, ensuring scalability and adaptability to various educational contexts.
4. **Guide Educators and Policymakers**: Serve as a resource for educators and policymakers to implement culturally competent SEL practices effectively within trauma-informed frameworks.
5. **Encourage Sustainability**: Lay the groundwork for sustainable practices prioritizing diversity, equity, and emotional resilience in education.

By achieving these objectives, the framework seeks to enhance short-term and long-term student outcomes, fostering environments where all learners can thrive.

CULTURAL COMPETENCE IN EDUCATION

Cultural competence in education refers to understanding, appreciating, and effectively interacting with individuals from diverse cultural backgrounds. It involves recognizing the cultural identities, experiences, and values of students and incorporating this awareness into teaching practices, curriculum design, and school policies. Cultural competence is more than just acknowledging diversity; it is about actively embracing and leveraging it to create an equitable and inclusive learning environment that reflects the varied backgrounds of all students (Boutte, Kelly-Jackson, & Johnson, 2017). In the context of trauma-informed care, cultural competence becomes even more critical. Trauma is often shaped by sociocultural factors such as systemic inequities, discrimination, and historical injustices, which disproportionately affect marginalized communities. For students from such backgrounds, schools can be spaces of healing and empowerment or sources of further marginalization. Culturally competent educators ensure that their teaching practices are sensitive to these dynamics, offering support that is both culturally relevant and emotionally safe, thus helping students navigate their trauma.

Cultural competence in education is significant for several reasons. First, when students feel their cultural identities are valued and respected, they are more likely to develop a sense of belonging. This emotional safety is especially important for trauma-affected students, as it can help mitigate the negative effects of their traumatic experiences. In a safe environment, students are empowered to engage with learning and to express themselves without fear of judgment or discrimination. Second, culturally responsive teaching methods that align with students' cultural contexts can increase engagement, motivation, and academic success. When students see their identities reflected in the curriculum, they are more likely to connect to the material and participate actively in their learning. Culturally relevant content can help students see themselves as active agents of knowledge rather than passive recipients of information that may seem disconnected from their realities.

Cultural competence also helps educators recognize and challenge their biases, ensuring equitable disciplinary practices, expectations, and interactions. Educators aware of their biases are less likely to perpetuate systemic inequities in education inadvertently. In a culturally competent environment, students are treated fairly and not subject to unfair disciplinary practices based on cultural misunderstandings or stereotypes. For trauma-affected students, culturally sensitive approaches can facilitate healing by acknowledging and addressing the intersection of cultural identity and trauma. Culturally specific coping mechanisms, storytelling traditions, or community practices can be integrated into the learning environment to support students in processing their experiences. This recognition of cultural differences in coping can be especially powerful for students who come from backgrounds where trauma is an integral part of their community's experience.

Developing cultural competence requires continuous self-reflection, professional development, and openness to learning from students and their communities. Teachers must take the time to understand the unique cultural backgrounds of their students and adapt their instructional approaches to reflect those differences. Schools, too, play a critical role in fostering an institutional culture that prioritizes diversity, equity, and inclusion. A culturally competent school community ensures that every student feels welcomed and valued, regardless of their cultural background (Boutte, Kelly-Jackson, and Johnson 2016). In trauma-informed educational settings, cultural competence is not just an added benefit but a foundational component of the learning environment. By embedding cultural awareness into every aspect of education—from classroom interactions to school policies—educators can create environments where all students, particularly those from marginalized and trauma-affected backgrounds, can thrive both emotionally and academically.

In addition to cultural competence, Social-Emotional Learning (SEL) plays a crucial role in supporting the emotional well-being of students. SEL refers to the process through which individuals develop the skills to understand and manage their emotions, build and maintain positive relationships, demonstrate empathy, set and achieve goals, and make responsible decisions. In educational settings, SEL serves as a cornerstone for fostering emotional well-being and enhancing academic success by equipping students with life skills that extend far beyond the classroom.

SEL is typically organized around five core competencies: self-awareness, self-management, social awareness, relationship skills, and responsible decision-making. Self-awareness involves understanding one's emotions, strengths, and limitations and recognizing how these influence behavior and decisions. Self-management focuses on developing the ability to regulate emotions, cope with stress, and exhibit self-control in challenging situations. Social awareness encourages cultivating empathy and understanding diverse perspectives, particularly in multicultural and inclusive environments. Relationship skills are about building and maintaining healthy, constructive relationships through effective communication, collaboration, and conflict resolution. Finally, responsible decision-making involves making ethical, informed decisions that consider one's well-being and that of others (Borowski, 2019).

Research has consistently demonstrated the transformative impact of SEL on students' emotional and academic outcomes. Students equipped with SEL skills can better manage stress, navigate adversity, and maintain emotional balance, contributing to their overall well-being. SEL has been linked to improved focus, motivation, and problem-solving skills, which often translate into higher academic achievement. Additionally, SEL reduces behavioral issues by teaching students how to express their emotions constructively and interact respectfully with their peers and educators. In trauma-informed educational environments, SEL becomes even more significant. Trauma often disrupts students' ability to regulate emotions, trust others, and engage fully in learning. Schools can help students rebuild their emotional and social capacities by providing SEL tools, creating a foundation for academic and personal growth. SEL offers students the necessary skills to heal from trauma, re-establish trust in others, and navigate life's challenges healthier and more resiliently.

Key aspects of SEL in trauma-informed settings include emphasizing emotional safety and ensuring that students feel secure and supported. This is particularly critical for trauma-affected students who may struggle with vulnerability and fear of judgment. Through relationship-centered approaches, SEL fosters trust between students and educators, helping to break down the barriers that trauma often creates. Additionally, effective SEL programs incorporate cultural competence by recognizing and respecting the diverse cultural contexts of students and their families, which enhances the overall effectiveness of SEL (Osher, Guarino, Jones, & Schanfield, 2024; Smith & Chestnutt, 2020). SEL also encourages students to develop self-efficacy and agency, enabling them to take ownership of their learning and emotional well-being. This sense of control is essential for students who have experienced trauma, as it allows them to regain a sense of power over their lives and decisions. When students feel that they have the tools and support to manage their emotions and relationships, they are more likely to take an active role in their learning and personal development (Peterson 2008).

In trauma-informed educational environments, SEL is not just an isolated intervention but a holistic approach that aligns closely with the goals of trauma-informed education. By addressing the emotional and social dimensions of learning, SEL helps create the conditions necessary for academic success and personal growth. This approach prepares students to navigate the complexities of their lives with confidence and compassion, laying the groundwork for long-term well-being (Al-Hroub & Al-Hroub, 2024; Reed, 2021). As educators and schools increasingly adopt trauma-informed practices, integrating SEL into their frameworks offers a powerful means to support all students, particularly those who have experienced trauma. By prioritizing SEL, schools can create environments that are not only academically enriching but also emotionally sustaining, providing a foundation for students to heal, grow, and succeed in their educational journeys. The combination of cultural competence and SEL offers a comprehensive approach to meeting students' emotional and academic needs, helping them thrive in both the classroom and life.

Integration into Multi-Tiered System of Supports

Multi-Tiered Systems of Support (MTSS) is a comprehensive framework that provides layered, targeted support to students at varying levels of need. The system is designed to address both academic and behavioral challenges by offering a continuum of interventions across three tiers: universal (Tier 1), targeted (Tier 2), and intensive (Tier 3). Integrating cultural competence and social-emotional learning (SEL) into these tiers ensures that students from diverse cultural backgrounds and trauma-affected communities receive holistic support that addresses their emotional, social, and academic needs. Below, we explore how cultural competence and SEL can be woven into each tier of MTSS with practical strategies and examples.

Tier 1: Universal Support

Tier 1 universal support establishes a foundation of inclusivity, cultural competence, and social-emotional learning (SEL) for all students. This tier focuses on prevention and creating a classroom environment that is safe, welcoming, and engaging for every student. By incorporating cultural awareness and SEL into daily practices, educators can create an environment where all students feel valued and equipped to succeed academically and emotionally. One of the primary components of Tier 1 support is the integration of diverse perspectives into the curriculum. This ensures that students are exposed to various voices, histories, and experiences, promoting cultural competence and enhancing their understanding of the world around them. Teachers can include literature, case studies, and materials that reflect various cultures, historical events, and viewpoints. For example, in a social studies lesson, a teacher might present perspectives from indigenous communities, immigrants, and refugees to give students a broader understanding of global and cultural diversity. This approach promotes cultural awareness and allows students to see their own experiences reflected in the classroom, fostering a sense of belonging (Liando & Tatipang, 2021).

In addition to integrating diverse content, it is important to embed social-emotional learning (SEL) into the daily curriculum. SEL focuses on developing essential life skills such as self-awareness, self-management, social awareness, relationship skills, and responsible decision-making. By teaching these competencies early, students gain the tools to navigate social interactions and manage their emotions effectively. A daily "Morning Circle" activity, for instance, can allow students to reflect on their emotions, share their feelings, and discuss ways to resolve conflicts. This practice sets a positive tone for the day, fostering a supportive environment where students feel comfortable expressing themselves and interacting with their peers (Dumbuya, 2023; Lalor, 2023).

Creating a classroom environment that celebrates diversity is another key aspect of Tier 1 support. A classroom should be a place where students feel emotionally safe, respected, and accepted for who they are. Visual displays that reflect the cultural diversity of students, such as posters in multiple languages, help students feel seen and valued. Additionally, using inclusive language during discussions and interactions encourages respect for different cultural norms and values. Teachers can also establish spaces, like a "Cultural Awareness Wall," where students can share stories and artifacts from their own cultural backgrounds. This not only promotes cultural understanding but also reinforces the idea that diversity is something to be celebrated, not just acknowledged.

Incorporating diverse perspectives and SEL practices into daily lessons ensures that all students benefit from a holistic approach to learning. By fostering an environment where students feel both emotionally safe and intellectually engaged, Tier 1 support builds the foundation for students' academic success and well-being. The proactive nature of this support also minimizes the risk of behavioral issues, as students are better equipped to manage their emotions and positively navigate social dynamics. Furthermore, it helps prevent the marginalization of students from diverse backgrounds, ensuring they feel included and represented in their educational experiences.

Finally, Tier 1 support helps educators address the whole child's academic, emotional, and social needs. Teachers can create a classroom environment where all students can thrive by integrating cultural competence and SEL into everyday practices. This universal approach sets the stage for a positive, inclusive learning community where every student's identity and contributions are respected and valued. It also lays the groundwork for more targeted interventions in higher tiers should students need additional support, ensuring that no one is left behind.

Tier 2: Targeted Intervention

Tier 2 interventions are designed to support students who require additional assistance beyond universal strategies, addressing more specific emotional regulation, relationship-building, or cultural understanding needs. While Tier 1 interventions focus on universal approaches that benefit all students, Tier 2 provides more focused, small-group efforts to address particular challenges that some students face. These interventions often involve more personalized strategies and are essential for ensuring that students who may need extra help do not fall through the cracks.

One of the key elements of Tier 2 support is the provision of targeted social-emotional learning (SEL) sessions tailored to the specific needs of students. These sessions are designed to help students cope with particular challenges such as social isolation, anxiety, or difficulty with emotional regulation. A critical aspect of these sessions is ensuring that they are culturally relevant, integrating coping strategies and emotional expression techniques that resonate with students' cultural backgrounds. For example, a small group of students who have experienced trauma might participate in a "Coping Strategies for Stress" session where culturally specific relaxation techniques, like mindfulness practices from students' cultures, are incorporated. This approach makes the interventions more relatable and effective, as it respects the students' unique experiences and cultural identities (Mahfouz et al., 2023; Smith & Chestnutt, 2019).

In addition to providing targeted SEL sessions, it is crucial that the interventions be adapted to meet the cultural needs of the students. This involves recognizing and honoring the cultural values, traditions, and practices of the students receiving support. Tailoring SEL interventions may include adjusting the language used in the sessions, incorporating community-based approaches, and ensuring that the activities align with the cultural norms of the students. For example, in a group of immigrant students, a counselor might incorporate storytelling techniques common in the students' cultures to explore themes of resilience, emotional expression, and coping. Storytelling, as a culturally rich practice, can help students express their emotions in a way that is familiar and comforting, creating a deeper connection with the material and fostering trust between students and educators (Graves Jr. et al., 2017; Heidelburg et al., 2024).

Another effective intervention in Tier 2 is pairing students from diverse backgrounds in structured mentoring relationships. These relationships can foster cross-cultural understanding and provide opportunities for social-emotional growth. Peer mentors can play an essential role in helping mentees navigate social or emotional challenges while also promoting empathy and emotional awareness. These mentoring relationships can help students who may feel isolated or disconnected to develop stronger interpersonal skills, learn new coping strategies, and feel more connected to their school community. For instance, a school could implement a mentoring program where older students from similar cultural backgrounds support younger students in overcoming academic and social challenges. These mentors can share SEL skills, cultural experiences, and guidance, promoting belonging and emotional support (Hairon et al., 2019).

The targeted support in Tier 2 should be carefully crafted to address the emotional and social needs of students and their cultural backgrounds. By tailoring interventions to students' specific needs and cultural contexts, educators can provide meaningful support that resonates with students and helps them develop the skills necessary to manage their emotions, build healthy relationships, and navigate challenges. Moreover, this cultural sensitivity enhances the effectiveness of the interventions, as students are more likely to engage with practices and strategies that reflect their lived experiences.

Ultimately, Tier 2 interventions are a crucial bridge between universal support and more intensive, individualized interventions in Tier 3. By providing focused, culturally relevant support through targeted SEL sessions, mentoring, and culturally adaptive approaches, schools can ensure that students receive the additional assistance they need to thrive emotionally and academically. These interventions address immediate challenges and contribute to building the foundational skills that will help students navigate future challenges with greater resilience and emotional intelligence.

Tier 3: Intensive Support

Tier 3 interventions provide individualized, intensive support for students with significant emotional or academic needs. The support is highly personalized at this level, often requiring one-on-one counseling or therapy. The interventions are carefully crafted to meet the specific needs of each student, particularly those who have experienced trauma or face severe emotional or behavioral challenges. A crucial component of Tier 3 support is the integration of culturally competent practices alongside trauma-informed care. These practices ensure that the interventions not only address the emotional well-being of the students but also respect and incorporate their cultural backgrounds.

One of the primary forms of support in Tier 3 is individualized counseling services that incorporate social-emotional learning (SEL) and cultural competence. Counselors at this level must be trained in trauma-informed care and able to integrate cultural considerations into their therapeutic approaches. This tailored support is crucial for students who may have experienced trauma or have deeply ingrained emotional challenges. For example, a student who struggles with anger management as a result of trauma might receive counseling that focuses on self-regulation strategies. Additionally, the counselor could incorporate culturally relevant techniques, such as community-based healing practices or family involvement, to ensure the intervention resonates with the student's cultural identity and values. This cultural sensitivity fosters a deeper sense of trust and increases the likelihood of positive outcomes for the student (Al-Hroub & Al-Hroub, 2024).

Another valuable approach within Tier 3 is the use of culturally sensitive therapeutic models. These models can include narrative therapy, art therapy, or other culturally specific practices designed to address the emotional needs of trauma-affected students. For instance, art therapy can be particularly effective for students who struggle to express their emotions verbally. A counselor working with a refugee student might use art therapy to help the student express their trauma through painting or drawing. This non-verbal, culturally familiar approach allows students to process difficult emotions in a way that feels both safe and empowering. By tapping into the student's cultural context, these therapies provide a powerful means for healing and emotional expression.

Family and community involvement is another critical aspect of Tier 3 support. Engaging families and community resources ensures that interventions are aligned with students' cultural backgrounds and lived experiences, fostering a stronger sense of support and trust. For example, a counselor working with an African American student who struggles with school engagement might collaborate with the student's family, community leaders, or cultural groups. This collaboration helps tailor the intervention to the student's needs and context, ensuring that the support system around the student is both comprehensive and culturally sensitive. By incorporating community resources, schools can create a more robust support network for the student, enhancing the effectiveness of the intervention (Minch & George, 2007).

Integrating cultural competence and SEL within the Multi-Tiered System of Supports (MTSS) framework is crucial for ensuring that all students, particularly those from diverse cultural backgrounds or who have experienced trauma, receive the necessary emotional and academic support. The multi-tiered approach allows for flexible and scalable interventions, adapting to the unique needs of each student. By embedding cultural awareness into every level of support, schools can create an inclusive and responsive learning environment that fosters academic success and emotional well-being.

Ultimately, the Tier 3 support system in an MTSS framework is designed to provide intensive, personalized interventions that address the most significant needs of students. Students receive the most effective support when these interventions are culturally competent and trauma-informed. Integrating SEL and cultural competence into Tier 3 interventions helps create an environment where all students, especially those with profound challenges, can thrive academically, socially, and emotionally. Schools can help students build resilience and overcome barriers to success through such targeted, culturally responsive interventions, promoting long-term well-being and academic achievement.

RECOMMENDATIONS

Implementing culturally competent Social-Emotional Learning (SEL) practices within a Multi-Tiered Systems of Support (MTSS) framework requires intentional planning, comprehensive professional development, and a sustained commitment from educators, school administrators, and policymakers. By embedding SEL into the MTSS framework, schools can create a robust support system that addresses the academic and emotional needs of all students, particularly those from diverse cultural backgrounds or trauma-affected communities. Below are recommendations and solutions to integrate cultural competence and SEL into trauma-informed educational settings.

One of the first steps in successfully implementing culturally competent SEL is ensuring that teachers and school staff are equipped with the knowledge and skills necessary to incorporate cultural competence and SEL into their everyday practices. Professional development is essential to ensure educators are prepared to meet their students' diverse emotional and academic needs.

Professional development should focus on cultural competence, emphasizing the importance of understanding the unique needs of students from various cultural and socio-economic backgrounds. This training should help teachers recognize the impact of cultural identity on learning, behavior, and emotional well-being. By understanding how cultural factors influence students' emotional expressions and behaviors, educators will be better equipped to foster an inclusive and supportive classroom environment. For example, workshops on culturally responsive pedagogy and anti-bias education can help teachers better understand and respond to cultural differences in the classroom, ensuring that every student feels respected and valued.

In addition to cultural competence, professional development must focus on SEL competencies. Teachers should be trained in fundamental SEL skills, such as emotional regulation, empathy, conflict resolution, and social awareness. These competencies are critical for students' emotional development and for creating a positive classroom environment where students can thrive. SEL workshops for teachers could include role-playing exercises, where educators practice using SEL skills to navigate difficult classroom situations, helping them develop strategies for fostering healthy relationships, managing emotions, and resolving conflicts effectively.

Moreover, training in trauma-informed practices is essential for teachers who work with students who have experienced trauma. Teachers should learn how to identify signs of trauma, create a safe emotional environment, and incorporate trauma-sensitive strategies into their teaching. For example, teachers can be trained to recognize students who may be experiencing trauma and create a classroom atmosphere that promotes safety and trust. This approach ensures that educators can provide the emotional support needed to help students overcome barriers related to past trauma.

Integrating SEL into the curriculum is another key recommendation for fostering a culturally responsive educational environment. The curriculum should be adjusted to reflect the cultural diversity of students and promote SEL competencies across different subjects and grade levels. By embedding SEL in the curriculum, schools can ensure that all students receive consistent messages about emotional growth, empathy, and relationship-building, regardless of the subject being taught.

One effective strategy for integrating SEL into the curriculum is to adopt or develop SEL curricula that reflect students' cultural identities, values, and lived experiences. This ensures that SEL lessons resonate with students and are more likely to be effective in promoting emotional development. For instance, a history curriculum could be designed to incorporate SEL lessons that focus on themes of resilience, community building, and empathy by studying diverse historical figures and events. By highlighting historical examples of resilience and social change, educators can encourage students to develop empathy and reflect on how these themes apply to their lives.

Teachers should also adapt lessons to include perspectives from diverse cultures, ensuring students can see their own experiences reflected in the content. This inclusion promotes cultural pride and emotional engagement, as students are more likely to feel a connection to the material when it speaks to their own cultural experiences. For example, in a literature class, educators can select books written by authors from various cultural backgrounds, allowing students to connect with characters and themes that mirror their own lives. This also encourages students to appreciate different cultural perspectives, fostering greater empathy and understanding.

SEL should not be confined to dedicated SEL programs alone but should be embedded across all academic subjects. For instance, in math and science classes, students can be encouraged to collaborate, manage frustration during challenging tasks, and develop perseverance—key SEL competencies that contribute to their overall emotional and social growth. For example, group projects in science classes can incorporate cooperative learning strategies, promoting teamwork and communication skills—essential components of SEL. By embedding SEL into all aspects of the curriculum, students are given frequent opportunities to develop and practice these vital skills.

School policies are pivotal in creating an environment conducive to integrating culturally competent SEL within the MTSS framework. Policies should be designed to recognize and value cultural diversity while promoting emotional well-being. These policies should ensure that all students, regardless of cultural background, have access to SEL programs and culturally responsive education. One important policy consideration is requiring SEL programs to be reviewed annually for cultural relevance. This ensures that the content of SEL programs remains aligned with the diverse needs of students, particularly in rapidly changing school environments. In addition, diversity training should be a mandatory component of professional development for all school staff, ensuring that educators are consistently exposed to new strategies for promoting cultural competence and inclusivity in the classroom.

Policymakers must also allocate funding to support integrating culturally competent SEL programs. This includes providing resources for professional development, culturally relevant curriculum materials, and support services for students dealing with trauma. For example, schools can receive grants to implement culturally responsive SEL programs or hire experts in cultural competence and SEL to consult with faculty and staff. Schools can ensure that SEL initiatives are adequately supported and sustainable by allocating the necessary resources.

Data collection is another essential component of school policies. Schools should track data on the effectiveness of SEL programs, particularly in promoting emotional and academic success among students from diverse backgrounds. This data will help guide adjustments to the program, ensuring that interventions meet all students' needs. For example, schools could track metrics such as student engagement, behavior referrals, and academic performance in relation to SEL interventions, making adjustments based on outcomes for different cultural groups.

The engagement of families and communities is critical to the success of culturally competent SEL practices. By involving families, schools can ensure that interventions are culturally relevant and aligned with the values and expectations of students' home environments. Family and community engagement strengthens the connection between school and home, promoting a holistic approach to students' emotional and academic well-being.

Schools should create opportunities for families and community members to participate in developing and implementing SEL programs. This could include family workshops on emotional well-being, school events celebrating cultural diversity, or partnerships with local cultural organizations. Schools can also organize community events where students share cultural traditions, stories, and SEL strategies they've learned, fostering a deeper connection between home and school. By involving families in this process, schools can ensure that SEL programs are culturally relevant and supported by the larger community.

Furthermore, communication with families should be culturally sensitive. Schools should offer materials in multiple languages and use culturally appropriate communication channels to ensure all families can access important information about SEL programs. For example, a school newsletter could be translated into several languages, and staff could be trained to use culturally respectful approaches when engaging with parents and caregivers. Culturally sensitive communication helps bridge gaps between home and school, allowing families to support their children's emotional and academic growth more effectively.

Ongoing research and evaluation are necessary to ensure the effectiveness and sustainability of culturally competent SEL practices within the MTSS framework. Research helps schools identify best practices, measure impact, and provide evidence for scaling successful interventions. By continuously assessing the effectiveness of SEL programs, schools can ensure that their strategies meet their students' diverse needs. Schools and districts should engage in action research to assess the impact of culturally responsive SEL interventions on student outcomes, particularly regarding academic achievement and emotional regulation. For example, a school district could implement an action research project to evaluate how culturally responsive SEL interventions affect students' behavior, academic success, and emotional resilience. This data can help schools refine their strategies and implement new practices that better address the needs of diverse student populations.

Collaborations with universities and research organizations can also provide valuable insights into the effectiveness of culturally competent SEL programs. For example, a partnership with a local university could lead to a study on the impact of culturally responsive SEL on improving attendance and academic success among immigrant students. By engaging in research, schools can stay informed about emerging trends and evidence-based practices, ensuring that their SEL programs are continually improving and evolving to meet the needs of all students.

Integrating cultural competence and SEL within an MTSS framework provides a promising approach to supporting the emotional and academic needs of all students, particularly those from diverse backgrounds or trauma-affected communities. By investing in professional development, curriculum adjustments, inclusive policies, and family engagement, schools can create an environment where all students can thrive emotionally and academically. These recommendations offer a clear path forward for educators, administrators, and policymakers committed to fostering inclusive, supportive, and effective learning environments. With sustained effort and collaboration, culturally competent SEL practices can help ensure that every student receives the support they need to succeed.

Future Directions

As the integration of culturally competent Social-Emotional Learning (SEL) within trauma-informed educational settings continues to evolve, future research and practice must address key areas to refine and expand the effectiveness of these practices. The following directions outline critical areas for exploration that will further enhance the implementation of culturally competent SEL within Multi-Tiered Systems of Support (MTSS) in diverse classrooms. While existing studies have examined the immediate effects of

SEL on student well-being and academic performance, there is a need for longitudinal research to assess the long-term impact of culturally competent SEL practices. This type of research will provide valuable insights into the sustained effects of SEL interventions on students' emotional resilience, academic success, and social engagement over time. Longitudinal studies should track the emotional, behavioral, and academic outcomes of students exposed to culturally competent SEL practices throughout their educational journey. This will help identify whether SEL interventions produce lasting positive changes, particularly for students from trauma-affected or marginalized backgrounds.

Example: A study following a cohort of students over five to ten years could examine whether early exposure to culturally responsive SEL improves graduation rates, college readiness, and mental health outcomes.

Research comparing culturally competent SEL practices with traditional SEL methods over a prolonged period could help establish best practices and demonstrate the unique benefits of cultural competence in enhancing SEL outcomes. While cultural competence is widely recognized as a vital component of effective education, there is a lack of standardized, reliable tools for measuring cultural competence within educational settings. Developing such tools is essential for educators and administrators to assess their effectiveness in implementing culturally responsive practices and evaluating student progress. Future research should focus on developing tools for educators and schools to assess their cultural competence. These tools could evaluate educators' awareness of cultural issues, ability to apply culturally responsive teaching strategies, and capacity to create inclusive environments.

Example: A self-assessment tool for teachers could measure their cultural awareness, attitudes toward diversity, and use of culturally relevant teaching practices, helping to identify areas for improvement.

It is equally important to develop mechanisms for gathering feedback from students about their experiences with cultural competence in the classroom. This could include surveys or focus groups to assess students' sense of belonging, emotional safety, and their perception of cultural responsiveness within the school. With the increasing use of technology in education, exploring digital platforms as tools for delivering SEL in diverse classrooms presents an exciting opportunity. Digital platforms can offer personalized, scalable solutions for SEL delivery, especially in classrooms with large students or those with limited access to in-person SEL resources. Research should focus on developing and evaluating digital platforms to deliver culturally competent SEL content. These platforms could provide students with access to SEL lessons, videos, and activities that are culturally relevant and tailored to their individual needs.

Example: A mobile application that offers SEL exercises based on students' cultural backgrounds, with features such as language preferences, cultural stories, and community engagement strategies, could be tested in diverse classrooms.

Virtual Reality (VR) and Augmented Reality (AR) Tools have the potential to create immersive SEL experiences that allow students to navigate social and emotional challenges in a virtual environment. These tools can be customized to reflect diverse cultural perspectives, making SEL more engaging and relevant for students from different backgrounds.

Example: A VR program that simulates real-life situations in culturally diverse settings could help students practice conflict resolution, empathy, and emotional regulation, providing a safe space to develop critical SEL competencies. Incorporating gamified elements into SEL programs can increase student engagement while providing an interactive learning experience. Research into culturally competent SEL games could further enhance student participation and the effectiveness of SEL interventions.

Example: A culturally diverse online game where students navigate emotional scenarios and practice SEL skills in various cultural contexts could be explored to promote emotional intelligence and cultural understanding.

Future research should also explore the potential benefits of collaboration between schools and community organizations, cultural experts, and mental health professionals in implementing culturally competent SEL practices. These partnerships can provide valuable insights into the specific needs of diverse student populations and create more robust support systems. Researchers can explore how schools can partner with local cultural organizations to design and implement SEL programs that reflect the students' communities' values, norms, and traditions.

Example: Community-based SEL workshops could be developed with the input of cultural leaders, mental health professionals, and educators to create tailored interventions that address the unique needs of students from specific cultural backgrounds.

Collaboration with community mental health experts could also help schools address the trauma-informed needs of students while ensuring that SEL practices are culturally sensitive. Mental health professionals can provide support to students who require more intensive interventions, helping to bridge the gap between emotional learning and trauma recovery. Lastly, research should continue to expand the scope of culturally competent SEL by exploring its application across various educational contexts, including early childhood, middle school, high school, and even postsecondary education. Additionally, research should focus on the intersectionality of cultural competence with other identity factors, such as race, ethnicity, socioeconomic status, and ability, to better understand how these dimensions influence SEL outcomes. Expanding research across various age groups and cultural contexts will help uncover the most effective strategies for delivering culturally competent SEL.

Example: Research could compare the effectiveness of SEL practices in elementary schools versus high schools to determine how SEL needs to evolve as students grow and how cultural competence can be integrated across different developmental stages.

Further studies should explore the intersectionality of culture, race, and other identity factors in the context of SEL. Understanding how multiple facets of identity influence students' emotional experiences will allow for more personalized and effective SEL practices. As educational settings become more diverse, culturally competent SEL practices are becoming increasingly essential. By pursuing these future directions—such as longitudinal studies, the development of measurement tools, the use of digital platforms, and community collaborations—research and practice will continue to evolve to better support students from all backgrounds. These innovations hold the potential to create more inclusive, responsive, and effective SEL interventions that promote the emotional and academic success of all students, particularly those from culturally diverse and trauma-affected backgrounds.

Discussion

The integration of cultural competence and Social-Emotional Learning (SEL) within trauma-informed educational settings presents a unique opportunity to enhance the emotional well-being and academic outcomes of students, particularly those from diverse cultural backgrounds and trauma-affected communities. By synthesizing the theoretical and conceptual frameworks discussed throughout this chapter, it becomes evident that these elements, when strategically integrated into Multi-Tiered Systems of Support (MTSS), have the potential to create more inclusive, equitable, and supportive learning environments.

The theoretical foundations of this work, including Vygotsky's Social Development Theory, Bronfenbrenner's Ecological Systems Theory, and Banks' Multicultural Education Theory, provide a robust understanding of how cultural and emotional factors influence learning. These theories emphasize the importance of social interactions, cultural contexts, and environmental factors in shaping students' emotional and academic experiences. By applying these theoretical insights, educators can design and implement SEL interventions that are both emotionally supportive and culturally responsive, thus fostering an environment where students from diverse backgrounds feel seen, valued, and understood.

The conceptual framework, which outlines the integration of cultural competence and SEL within the MTSS model, offers a clear roadmap for educators and policymakers. The multi-tiered approach ensures that SEL is not a one-size-fits-all solution but rather a scaffolded system that provides universal support for all students (Tier 1), targeted interventions for those needing additional assistance (Tier 2), and individualized, intensive support for students with more significant needs (Tier 3). This approach ensures that SEL practices are adaptable and responsive to the varying needs of students, particularly those who have experienced trauma.

Integrating cultural competence into SEL practices is not simply ideal but necessary in today's diverse educational landscape. As highlighted in the background section, the growing recognition of the importance of cultural awareness and emotional intelligence in student success underscores the need for educational practices that reflect the diversity of student populations. Culturally competent SEL practices acknowledge that students' cultural backgrounds shape their emotional responses, learning styles, and social behaviors. These practices help students navigate complex emotional landscapes while fostering a sense of belonging and inclusion.

For educators, this means adopting teaching practices that honor and integrate students' cultural identities into the learning process. Strategies such as culturally relevant SEL curricula, culturally adaptive teaching methods, and diverse teaching materials are essential in ensuring that all students' cultural perspectives are reflected in their educational experiences. By doing so, educators improve students' social-emotional skills and enhance their academic engagement and success. Implementing trauma-informed care within the MTSS framework ensures that students who have experienced trauma receive the emotional and psychological support they need to succeed. Trauma-informed SEL practices are sensitive to the fact that students may carry emotional scars that affect their behavior and learning. By embedding trauma-informed principles into SEL, educators can help students build resilience, regulate emotions, and develop healthier coping mechanisms.

At the policy level, integrating cultural competence and SEL within MTSS necessitates systemic changes to ensure that all students have access to the support they need. Policymakers must prioritize funding for professional development programs that equip educators with the skills to effectively implement culturally competent SEL practices. Such programs should provide teachers with the knowledge and tools to understand the intersectionality of culture, trauma, and emotional learning, ensuring that SEL interventions are inclusive and relevant.

Policies must support the creation of school environments that actively promote diversity, inclusion, and emotional safety. This includes revising school curricula, assessment practices, and disciplinary policies to reflect the needs of diverse student populations. Recognizing cultural competence as a core element of educational practice should be embedded in national and local education policies, ensuring that all students have access to equitable learning opportunities. Incorporating SEL into the broader policy framework also involves integrating it into standards and accountability measures. For example, policies can mandate the inclusion of SEL in the assessment of both student progress and school performance. By making SEL a central educational evaluation component, policymakers can reinforce its importance and ensure that all schools are held accountable for fostering students' emotional and social growth alongside their academic achievements.

While integrating cultural competence and SEL into MTSS holds significant promise, it is not without challenges. One of the main barriers to implementation is the lack of sufficient training and resources for educators to integrate these practices into their classrooms effectively. Many teachers may lack the cultural knowledge or the tools to address the unique needs of students from diverse backgrounds, especially in trauma-affected communities. Additionally, there may be resistance to change from stakeholders who are unfamiliar with the benefits of culturally competent SEL practices or who feel overwhelmed by the complexity of implementing such programs. To overcome these challenges, providing ongoing professional development, support from community organizations, and a collaborative approach to SEL implementation is crucial. Teachers, administrators, counselors, and community leaders must work together to create a shared vision of culturally responsive SEL grounded in the students' needs.

The integration of cultural competence and SEL within trauma-informed educational settings offers a transformative approach to supporting students' emotional well-being and academic success. This chapter provides a roadmap for educators and policymakers to create inclusive and supportive environments by linking theoretical and conceptual frameworks with practical applications. The integration of these practices into MTSS ensures that all students, regardless of their cultural background or experiences with trauma, receive the support they need to thrive emotionally and academically. As research and practice in this area continue to evolve, the potential for creating more equitable and inclusive educational systems remains vast, offering hope for a brighter future for all students.

CONCLUSION

This chapter has explored the intersection of cultural competence and Social-Emotional Learning (SEL) within trauma-informed educational settings, offering a comprehensive framework for integrating these elements into a Multi-Tiered System of Support (MTSS). Through the discussion of key theories, conceptual frameworks, and practical strategies, it is clear that the intentional integration of cultural competence and SEL is essential for fostering emotionally supportive and academically enriching environments, particularly for students from diverse cultural backgrounds and those affected by trauma. Integrating cultural competence into SEL practices ensures that educational settings are responsive to all students' unique needs and backgrounds, honoring their cultural identities and emotional experiences. This, in turn, supports their academic success, emotional well-being, and resilience. By embedding culturally relevant SEL practices within the tiers of MTSS, educators can offer a differentiated approach that provides universal support for all students, targeted interventions for those requiring additional assistance, and individualized care for those with more significant needs.

As discussed, cultural competence and SEL have gained increasing recognition in education, especially in schools that serve diverse student populations. These practices are vital for student success and central to promoting educational equity. Schools prioritizing cultural competence and SEL can help bridge the gap in achievement and emotional well-being, ensuring that all students, regardless of their background or experiences, can thrive. While there are challenges in implementing these practices—such as a lack of resources, insufficient professional development, and resistance to change—the potential benefits of their integration far outweigh these obstacles. With proper support, training, and policy changes, educators and policymakers can create inclusive and trauma-sensitive environments where all students feel supported, valued, and empowered. Integrating cultural competence and SEL into trauma-informed educational settings is a powerful strategy for enhancing student outcomes and promoting equity in education. By embracing these practices, we can create educational systems that address the emotional and academic needs of diverse students and cultivate a more inclusive, compassionate, and resilient future for all learners.

REFERENCES

Al-Hroub, A., & Al-Hroub, R. (2024). Empowering the vulnerable: The impact of SEL on traumatized children's academic and social outcomes in crises. *Current Psychiatry Reports*, *26*(12), 777–781. Advance online publication. DOI: 10.1007/s11920-024-01555-8 PMID: 39523250

Arruzza, E., & Chau, M. (2021). The effectiveness of cultural competence education in enhancing knowledge acquisition, performance, attitudes, and student satisfaction among undergraduate health science students: A scoping review. *Journal of Educational Evaluation for Health Professions*, *18*, 3. DOI: 10.3352/jeehp.2021.18.3 PMID: 33621460

Banks, J. A. (2013). The Construction and Historical Development of Multicultural Education, 1962–2012. *Theory Into Practice, 52*(sup1), 73–82. DOI: 10.1080/00405841.2013.795444

Borowski, T. (2019). *CASEL's Framework for Systemic Social and Emotional Learning. Collaborative for Academic, Social, and Emotional Learning*. CASEL., DOI: 10.4236/ce.2021.121001

Boutte, G., Kelly-Jackson, C., & Johnson, G. L. (2017). Culturally relevant teaching in science classrooms: Addressing academic achievement, cultural competence, and critical consciousness. *Journal of Educational Evaluation for Health Professions*. Advance online publication. DOI: 10.1108/IJGE-01-2016-0001

Dewey, J. (1938). *Experience and Education*. Kappa Delta Pi., DOI: 10.2307/2018929

Dumbuya, E. (2023). Integrating Social and Emotional Learning (SEL) into Curriculum Development: A Pathway to Holistic Education. *SSRN*. DOI: 10.2139/ssrn.5019755

Gay, G. (2018). *Culturally Responsive Teaching: Theory, Research, and Practice* (3rd ed.). Teachers College Press., DOI: 10.1177/0022487108322110

Graves, L., Herndon-Sobalvarro, A., Nichols, K., Aston, C., Ryan, A., Blefari, A., Schutte, K., Schachner, A., Vicoria, L., & Prier, D. (2017). Examining the effectiveness of a culturally adapted social-emotional intervention for African American males in an urban setting. *School Psychology Quarterly*, *32*(1), 62–74. DOI: 10.1037/spq0000145 PMID: 27124505

Hairon, S., Loh, S. H., Lim, S. P., Govindani, S. N., Tan, J. K. T., & Tay, E. C. J. (2019). Structured mentoring: Principles for effective mentoring. *Educational Research for Policy and Practice*, *19*(2), 105–123. DOI: 10.1007/s10671-019-09251-8

Heidelburg, K., Sipior, C., King, J., Cueto Brito, M., & Fredrick, S. (2024). A systematic review of cultural adaptations to social emotional learning interventions for PreK-12th grade Black students. *School Psychology*. Advance online publication. DOI: 10.1037/spq0000676 PMID: 40193512

Hossain, M. N., & Mumu, U. H. (2024). Flood susceptibility modelling of the Teesta River Basin through the AHP-MCDA process using GIS and remote sensing. *Natural Hazards*, *120*(13), 12137–12161. Advance online publication. DOI: 10.1007/s11069-024-06677-z

Jackson, V. H. (2017). The role of cultural Competence in Trauma-Informed Agencies and Services. In *Springer eBooks* (pp. 41–64). DOI: 10.1007/978-3-319-64602-2_4

Katzman, N. F., & Stanton, M. P. (2020). The Integration of Social Emotional Learning and Cultural Education into Online Distance Learning Curricula: Now Imperative during the COVID-19 Pandemic. *Creative Education*, *11*(09), 1561–1571. DOI: 10.4236/ce.2020.119114

Kohli, H. K., Huber, R., & Faul, A. C. (2010). Historical and theoretical development of culturally competent social work practice. *Journal of Teaching in Social Work*, *30*(3), 252–271. DOI: 10.1080/08841233.2010.499091

Lalor, A. D. M. (2023). *For the Greatest Impact on Learning, Embed SEL in the Curriculum*. Edutopia., DOI: 10.3389/feduc.2021.712720

Liando, N. V. F., & Tatipang, D. P. (2021). *Embracing diversity: Culturally responsive curriculum and inclusive pedagogical practices*. Novateur Publication., DOI: 10.3352/np.2021.261

Mahfouz, J., Steed, E. A., & Shapland, D. (2023). Culturally Responsive Social Emotional learning: Perspectives of early childhood teachers. *Early Childhood Education Journal*. Advance online publication. DOI: 10.1007/s10643-023-01599-0

Matalon, M., & Clauss-Ehlers, C. S. (2023c). Creating a multiculturally responsive and Trauma-Informed classroom ecology for diverse learners: Collaboration, classroom community, and identification of systemic barriers. *Adult Literacy Education The International Journal Of Literacy Language And Numeracy*, *5*(1), 55–61. DOI: 10.35847/MMatalon.CClauss-Ehlers.5.1.55

Minch, D., & George, H. P. (2007). *Family and community engagement in tiered systems of support*. Center on PBIS., DOI: 10.1007/s10671-019-09251-8

Osher, D., Guarino, K., Jones, W., & Schanfield, M. (2024). Trauma-Sensitive Schools and Social and Emotional Learning: An Integration. *Edna Bennett Pierce Prevention Research Center*. https://prevention.psu.edu/sel/issue-briefs/trauma-sensitive-schools-and-social-and-emotional-learning-an-integration/

Peterson, T. (2008). Self-efficacy: The foundation of human performance. *Performance Improvement Quarterly*, *21*(2), 7–26. DOI: 10.1002/piq.20008

Ranjbar, N., Erb, M., Mohammad, O., & Moreno, F. A. (2020). Trauma-Informed Care and Cultural Humility in the Mental Health Care of People from Minoritized Communities. *Focus (San Francisco, Calif.)*, *18*(1), 8–15. DOI: 10.1176/appi.focus.20190027 PMID: 32047392

Reed, D., & Sheridan, K. D. (2021). Perceptions of Directly Targeting SEL Learning Skills in Public Education. *Creative Education*, *12*(11), 2765–2779. Advance online publication. DOI: 10.4236/ce.2021.1211204

Smith, A., & Chestnutt, C. (2019). *What's culture got to do with SEL?* Center for Responsive Schools., DOI: 10.1007/s10643-023-01599-0

Smith, A., & Chestnutt, C. (2020). What's Culture Got to Do with SEL? *Center for Responsive Schools*. https://www.crslearn.org/publication/a-sel-for-all/whats-culture-got-to-do-with-sel/

Vygotsky, L. S. (1978). *Mind in Society: Development of Higher Psychological Processes* (Cole, M., Jolm-Steiner, V., Scribner, S., & Souberman, E., Eds.). Harvard University Press., DOI: 10.2307/j.ctvjf9vz4

KEY TERMS AND DEFINITIONS

Cultural Competence: Cultural competence is understanding, communicating, and effectively interacting with people across cultures (citation).

Social-Emotional Learning (SEL): Social-emotional learning is the process through which individuals acquire and effectively apply the knowledge, attitudes, and skills necessary to understand and manage emotions, set and achieve positive goals, feel and show empathy for others, establish and maintain positive relationships, and make responsible decisions.

Trauma-Informed Education: An approach to teaching that acknowledges the presence of trauma in students' lives and incorporates practices that promote healing and learning.

Multi-Tiered Systems of Support (MTSS): A framework that provides different levels of support based on students' needs, integrating academic, behavioral, and social-emotional supports.

Emotional Well-Being: A state in which an individual feel balanced, content, and capable of managing stress.

Inclusive Education: An educational approach that seeks to include all students, regardless of their physical, intellectual, social, emotional, linguistic, or other conditions.

Educational Equity: The principle of fairness in education, ensuring that all students have access to the resources they need to succeed.

Diversity and Inclusion: Practices that recognize and value individual differences and create environments where everyone feels respected and valued.

Chapter 6
Integrating Anti-Racist Education Into Social-Emotional Learning Within a Trauma-Informed MTSS Framework

Andrew Goodman
https://orcid.org/0009-0000-5031-3513
Utah Valley University, USA

ABSTRACT

This chapter explores how anti-racist education can be meaningfully integrated into social-emotional learning (SEL) within a trauma-informed Multi-Tiered System of Support (MTSS). It critiques the Eurocentric foundations of traditional SEL, which often emphasize individualism over community and self-regulation over cultural relevance. By aligning SEL with anti-racist principles, schools can better serve students from historically marginalized communities and foster inclusive, healing-centered environments. Grounded in transformative SEL and critical race theory, this chapter outlines strategies to embed equity across all MTSS tiers, including culturally sustaining practices, educator training, and strong community partnerships. It also addresses the challenges of political resistance and limited resources, offering practical solutions for implementation. The chapter calls on teacher preparation programs to lead this shift by equipping future educators with the tools to disrupt systemic inequities and promote justice-centered SEL.

INTEGRATING ANTI-RACIST EDUCATION INTO SOCIAL-EMOTIONAL LEARNING WITHIN A TRAUMA-INFORMED MTSS FRAMEWORK

The evolving cultural and racial diversity of public school classrooms in the United States presents challenges and opportunities for educators to foster equitable and inclusive learning environments. The National Center for Education Studies (2023) found that 89% of public school elementary teachers identify as female, and in elementary and secondary schools combined, 80% of teachers identify as White while only 46% of students identify as White. With a teaching workforce that remains predominantly White and female, questions about the ability of the current educational system to meet the unique needs of all

DOI: 10.4018/979-8-3693-9020-7.ch006

students equitably arise. Are teachers well-equipped to create and sustain relationships with students, develop their social-emotional well-being, and consistently establish positive classroom management routines in classrooms where so many students have different backgrounds and experiences? Do they have the support they need? Are districts providing the resources for ALL students equitably? Are teachers able to teach marginalized students in a culturally responsive way within the current system? Or do teachers even recognize this to be a problem?

Multiple-Tiered Systems of Support (MTSS) are one way many schools in the United States provide general-tiered support as suggested by the Every Student Succeeds Act of 2015. MTSS is a trauma-informed framework that integrates academic and social-emotional learning through whole-group and targeted interventions as a building-wide approach to improving student achievement and overall well-being. However, are systems like MTSS designed to support a population of diverse students becoming more varied each day? Or, are teachers, likely inadvertently, implementing interventions that fail to reflect diverse students' lived experiences? Without careful attention, gaps like these would surely continue inequities in schools.

Social-emotional learning (SEL) is a foundation for a Tier 1 intervention within the MTSS system. Research shows that consistent and strategic use of SEL significantly enhances students' emotional regulation, improves problem-solving, and helps students learn to build healthy interpersonal relationships (Osher, 2016). Nevertheless, the question remains: How can teachers ensure that SEL interventions are inclusive and responsive to the unique needs of each student, especially those from historically marginalized communities (Chen & Yang, 2022)?

Those who play a pivotal role in advancing equity are the intended audience for this chapter: those who are committed to making schools inclusive and safe for all students. You, readers, have access to challenge system inequities each day. You are the one with the potential to create safe spaces that promote individual well-being for all students - the school psychologists, school social workers, educators, and higher education professionals must be committed to advancing equity. This chapter aims to align SEL and MTSS, advocating for SEL to be a comprehensive approach across all intervention areas. This chapter will delve into the foundational Eurocentric roots of SEL programs, define and critique anti-racist education, and offer strategies for integrating anti-racist approaches into SEL practices. Recognizing that many educators feel unprepared to support diverse student populations (Ukpokodu, 2007), this chapter will address how teachers, schools, and pre-service teacher education programs can strengthen training for anti-racist SEL implementation. The conceptual framework of transformative SEL (Jagers et al., 2019) and seminal writing on critical race theory (Ladson-Billings & Tate, 1995) are the guiding lenses for this chapter. To navigate these questions and support all students equitably, we must explore the foundational theories that guide this work.

CONCEPTUAL FRAMEWORK

This chapter's heart is the conviction that schools must be spaces for healing, inclusion, and equity for all. This chapter is grounded in a synthesis of transformative social-emotional learning (Jagers et al., 2019) that aligns SEL with equity and social justice and critical race theory (Ladson-Billings & Tate, 1995), which explores how racism is embedded within educational systems and practices. Transformative SEL (Jagers et al., 2019) reimagines traditional SEL as more than emotional regulation and interpersonal skills alone. Instead, it explicitly integrates issues of identity, equity, agency, and justice, and it moves

SEL from compliance-based behavior control to a tool for liberation and equity. This approach encourages educators and students to explore how social identity, power, and culture shape emotional experiences and relationships. Rather than teaching students to adapt to systems as they are, transformative SEL asks them to question and reimagine those systems, thereby developing a sense of critical consciousness. It centers real-world issues like racism and inequality as core to emotional growth and school belonging.

When embedded across MTSS tiers, it challenges educators to move from compliance-driven interventions to equity-driven support systems. It also requires that SEL lessons be focused on students' community-connected realities rather than detached from them. Similarly, critical race theory (CRT), introduced to education by scholars like Ladson-Billings and Tate (1995) analyzes how racism is embedded in educational systems and policies. CRT provides more of a structural critique; transformational SEL provides a developmental, relational, and emotional pathway to equity. In tandem, they guide this chapter's call to integrate anti-racist education within SEL practices and use MTSS as a vehicle for meaningful, systemic changes. While these frameworks offer a lens for transformation, they must also be viewed considering the historical development of SEL - particularly the Eurocentric ideologies that have shaped it.

HISTORICAL CONTEXT: THE EUROCENTRIC ROOTS OF SEL PROGRAMS

As established by the Collaborative for Academic, Social, and Emotional Learning (CASEL), the foundational principles of SEL programs emphasize self-awareness, self-management, social awareness, relationship skills, and responsible decision-making (Durlak, 2011). While widely adopted, these competencies reflect Western psychological theories prioritizing individualism, self-regulation, and personal achievement - values not held universally across all cultural contexts (Osher, 2016). These foundations draw heavily from social cognitive theory (Bandura, 1986) and cognitive behavioral theory (Beck, 1976), which stress personal agency and individual behavior change. SEL programs shaped by these theories often encourage practices like goal setting, emotional regulation, and self-efficacy building. While effective in many settings, these strategies may undervalue collective learning processes and relational interdependence that are deeply valued in many non-Western cultural traditions (Chen & Yang, 2022).

Transformative SEL, as previously introduced, addresses these limitations by centering equity, identity, and critical consciousness within emotional learning. A brief overview of this shift provides context for the broader reimagination of SEL frameworks explored in later sections. An expanded historical analysis of anti-racist education also uncovers its roots in movements for educational justice, civil rights, and culturally relevant pedagogy. Pioneers like Gloria Ladson-Billings, Geneva Gay, and James Banks emphasized the critical need for curriculum and instruction to reflect marginalized communities' cultural and historical experiences. These scholars laid the foundation for integrating SEL with justice-oriented education long before SEL became institutionalized by organizations like CASEL. Their work challenged deficit-based narratives and called for schools to become spaces that affirm identity and resist oppression. This legacy informs the need to embed anti-racist education into SEL frameworks today, not as an add-on but as a foundational principle. While the historical critique lays the groundwork, emerging global models and modern political climates add further complexity and urgency to SEL reform.

Global Models and Contemporary Challenges

While CASEL is the most widely recognized framework in the U.S., international SEL initiatives offer culturally adaptive models that may better address diversity and systemic inequities. For example, the Organization for Economic Cooperation and Development (OECD)'s global SEL framework incorporates equity and inclusion as central goals, calling for SEL competencies to reflect cultural and contextual differences (OECD, 2021). Similarly, the United Nations Educational, Scientific, and Cultural Organization (UNESCO)'s Happy Schools framework in the Asia-Pacific region emphasizes emotional well-being, cultural identity, and inclusive pedagogy as critical to learning (UNESCO, 2016). These global frameworks challenge the narrow, individualistic focus of many U.S.-based programs and support the need for anti-racist, community-centered SEL practices that reflect the realities of diverse student populations.

Schools should consider adopting SEL strategies from these international models to strengthen the practical application of the literature. For example, UNESCO's emphasis on well-being as a school-wide goal could translate into integrated SEL-community events that include families and honor cultural celebrations. OECD's call for localized and context-specific SEL can inspire teachers to co-create classroom norms with students and tailor SEL discussions to include local social justice issues. These approaches demonstrate how international insights can be translated into actional practices for equity-driven SEL in diverse classrooms.

Recent trends in U.S. education policy and public sentiment further complicate these efforts. Since 2020, several states have introduced or passed legislation restricting race, equity, and SEL classroom discussions, framing them as politically divisive or ideological (Genao & Mercedes, 2021; Waite, 2021). According to a 2022 RAND Corporation survey, nearly one-quarter of public school teachers reported being directed to limit conversations around race and racism in their classrooms, contributing to widespread uncertainty and fear around implementing anti-racist approaches (Doan et al., 2022). This chilling effect curtails the depth of SEL instruction and discourages schools from embedding culturally relevant practices within MTSS frameworks. Despite this, public support for inclusive and responsive SEL remains strong - especially among parents of color and educators in diverse urban districts - who see SEL as critical to fostering empathy, resilience, and school connectedness (The Education Trust, 2021). These conflicting trends highlight the importance of equipping schools with strategies to implement anti-racist SEL that are contextually responsive and resilient to political pressures.

From Theory to Practice: Localized Implementation of Anti-Racist SEL

For example, Oakland Unified School District in California has implemented district-wide restorative justice circles and culturally responsive SEL through initiatives like African American Female Excellence. These efforts have been linked to stronger improved relationships, greater emotional safety, and stronger engagement among historically underserved student groups (Allbright, n.d.; Kennedy, 2019) Similarly, Chicago Public Schools have adopted an equity-centered SEL approach, aligning emotional learning goals with culturally relevant content and restorative practices. The district's "Equity Framework" guides educators in connecting SEL instruction to students' lived realities and community histories (Forman et al., 2021).

One Chicago Public School principal noted, "We knew that if SEL didn't speak to our students' identities and realities, it wouldn't reach them all. That's why we embedded conversations about race, community struggles, and pride into the curriculum - and we've seen students respond in powerful ways" (Forman et al., 2021, p. 371). Testimonials like this show the potential impact of anti-racist SEL when grounded in lived experience.

It is also critical that anti-racist SEL frameworks be flexible and responsive to regional and local contexts. In politically conservative states where equity language may face scrutiny, educators might adapt the implementation language to focus on belonging, emotional safety, and student engagement - while still centering culturally responsive practices. In contrast, urban districts with histories of racial advocacy may pursue more direct integration of identity-affirming SEL and community engagement.

Conducting local needs assessments and involving students, families, and community members in co-creating SEL content ensures that implementation is inclusive, regionally relevant, and sustainable.

Scaling Anti-Racist SEL Within MTSS

While this framing of Eurocentric ideals is limiting in and of itself, the foundational principle of MTSS is to provide a continuum of supports designed to meet the needs of all students, not just to support the notions of whiteness (Forman, 2021). Therefore, the limitations of Eurocentricity in SEL must be explored alongside a commitment to practical, anti-racist transformation. To achieve meaningful and sustainable change, it is crucial to provide a clear roadmap for scaling anti-racist SEL strategies across all tiers of MTSS. At Tier 1, schools can embed culturally responsive SEL lessons into the core curriculum and integrate school-wide practices like equity-focused community agreements and culturally inclusive celebrations. At Tier 2, targeted support groups can address race-related stress, and restorative practices can serve as culturally relevant alternatives to punitive discipline. Tier 3 interventions should include individualized SEL plans reflecting students' cultural identities and lived experiences while connecting families with culturally competent mental health and mentorship services.

Scaling these practices also requires navigating institutional resistance. Schools can begin by forming equity leadership teams of educators, students, and community members to co-develop and monitor implementation goals. Establishing clear equity policies and offering consistent professional development on anti-racist and trauma-informed pedagogy can build staff capacity and resilience. Data collection that tracks disparities in discipline, engagement, and achievement disaggregated by race can help identify gaps and measure progress. Finally, securing district-level support and allocating funding toward culturally sustaining initiatives are critical to ensure scalability beyond individual classrooms or pilot programs.

Despite promising practices, the persistent influence of Eurocentric frameworks continues to present challenges that must be acknowledged.

LIMITATIONS OF EUROCENTRIC SEL

While traditional SEL programs offer effective tools for fostering emotional and social growth, their Eurocentric underpinnings may limit their effectiveness in multicultural and historically marginalized contexts. These frameworks typically prioritize individual goals and achievement, emotional self-regulation, and self-improvement strategies. However, many non-Western cultures focus on collective well-being, social well-being, and maintaining community interdependence. This cultural disconnect can leave students from collectivist backgrounds disengaged and confused which reduces the impact on SEL programs for those students, where communal priorities often outweigh individual pursuits (Sklad, 2012).

For example, encouraging and rewarding direct verbal communication or public emotional expression may unintentionally marginalize students from cultures where indirect communication or emotional restraint is valued. This cultural bias can lead to misunderstandings and misinterpretations of students' emotional responses, further alienating them from the SEL process. Programs that fail to account for the systemic inequities these students experience may inadvertently downplay the legitimacy of their emotional responses to oppression (Durlak, 2011).

For students of color, whose behaviors may have developed under systemic oppression, trauma, or within specific cultural traditions, expressions of feelings may be misunderstood and characterized as disruptive or problematic within SEL programs and by teachers or school leaders. As such, students may display heightened alertness or resistance to authority as adaptive responses to systemic inequities (Mann & Cheng, 2013). This pathologizing of culturally relevant responses can exacerbate feelings of alienation and disengagement among students of color by sending the message that success is contingent on assimilation to Eurocentric cultural values (Skinner-Dorkenoo, 2021).

In another example, SEL practices that prioritize internal reflection or obedience to authority may manifest through the disproportionate, punitive discipline of Black and Brown students whose cultural norms around expression, identity, and resistance to systemic injustice are more likely to be misinterpreted as defiance or aggression (Nolan, 2021). For this to change, educators need to have a better understanding of culture and anti-racist practices and how to make those understandings change a traditionally oppressive education system.

Understanding the Eurocentric origins and limitations of SEL programs and their impact, especially on students of color, is essential for creating equitable and inclusive programs. While the contributions of traditional SEL cannot be discounted, a critical reexamination of inherent biases is required along with adaptations of SEL principles to reflect the diverse realities of today's students. Only through this reexamination can SEL fulfill its goal of fostering truly inclusive and transformative learning environments (Sklad, 2012). To be fruitful in this work, anti-racist education paired with trauma-informed practices must be included.

Confronting these limitations reaffirms the need to ground SEL in the principles of anti-racist education.

FOUNDATIONS OF ANTI-RACIST EDUCATION IN SEL

Anti-racist education is an intentional proactive approach to dismantling systemic inequities in schools. At its core, anti-racism is guided by three foundational principles: deconstructing systemic inequities, valuing cultural diversity, and fostering critical consciousness among students and educators alike (Lynch, 2017). The goal of anti-racist education is unmasking unequal outcomes for marginalized students by examining and contesting policies, practices, and biases that promote such outcomes to create more equitable learning environments. Often, this work includes analyzing curriculum content, approaches to discipline, and other systemic structures that privilege dominant cultural norms while disadvantaging students of color. Research indicates that educational systems often reflect and reinforce inequities, necessitating a thorough examination of how these structures operate within schools (Karatas & Oral, 2015).

Drawing from the work of educators like Paulo Freire, anti-racist education encourages students and educators to become agents of change by examining and questioning power structures, challenging unjust societal norms, and imagining innovative solutions to injustice. Critical consciousness involves recognizing the interconnectedness of personal experiences and broader social issues, enabling students to engage in meaningful dialogues about race, identity, and equity. This process enables students to understand systemic oppression and become agents of change within their communities. Anti-racist education in SEL is paramount for creating equitable and inclusive learning environments. By consistently deconstructing these inequities as they exist presently and as others arise, teachers and school leaders recognize the unique challenges faced by marginalized students into systems that celebrate all students' cultural identities and lived experiences, ensuring that every student feels seen, heard, and valued.

CHALLENGES AND CRITIQUES OF INTEGRATING ANTI-RACIST EDUCATION INTO SEL

Integrating anti-racist education into SEL frameworks poses distinct challenges to educators, administrators, and policymakers. These challenges often arise from systemic barriers, limited resources, and specific ideological opposition.

As critical race theory highlights, systemic resistance to equity-focused education often stems from a reluctance to confront the embedded nature of racism in institutional structures. Thus, parents, school boards, and community members may misinterpret anti-racist efforts as partisan agendas rather than vital moves toward equity. This resistance can stymie the efforts to implement anti-racist practices in schools, teaching from diluted programs that fail to achieve meaningful change (Forman, 2021). For instance, some stakeholders may argue that discussions around race and equity create discomfort or promote guilt, thus advocating for a more neutral curriculum that avoids these topics altogether (Durlak, 2011). This ideological resistance can significantly hinder the progress of anti-racist initiatives within SEL frameworks, as educators may feel pressured to conform to prevailing attitudes rather than engage in critical discussions about race and equity. School board meetings across the country have seen parents protesting who believe anti-racist education is political indoctrination (Waite, 2021; Genao & Mercedes, 2021). This tension shows how anti-racist education can be misinterpreted and often sparks debates about the purpose and content of school curricula in general. In some cases, resistance may stem from personal or systemic racial biases that go unacknowledged.

Many educators lack access to comprehensive training in equity, cultural competency, and anti-racist teaching practices. Without this foundational knowledge, teachers may struggle to effectively incorporate anti-racist principles into their practice (Day, 2023). Professional development opportunities are often unevenly distributed, leaving underfunded schools and districts with limited access to these resources (Osher, 2016). For educators in under-resourced districts, integrating anti-racist SEL may be further hindered by a lack of access to culturally inclusive material and inconsistent funding for professional development. Studies show that schools serving predominantly marginalized students are least likely to receive targeted SEL support and training (Osher, 2016; Nadeem et al., 2022), perpetuating inequitable implementation. As a result, educators may feel unprepared to navigate discussions on race and equity in their classrooms, leading to a surface-level application of anti-racist principles that fail to connect with students' lived experiences (Taylor, 2017). This gap in training risks reinforcing existing biases, hindering the effectiveness of SEL programs in advancing equity effectively and creating uncertainty about what will be supported versus punished.

Mainstream SEL programs are frequently designed with universal frameworks that do not account for different communities' unique, cultural, historical, and socioeconomic contexts. Educators may find it challenging to adapt these programs to meet the needs of their specific student populations, particularly in communities with complex histories of systemic oppression or significant cultural diversity. For example, a standardized SEL curriculum may not adequately address the challenges faced by students from immigrant backgrounds or those living in poverty, thereby limiting the program's effectiveness in fostering social and emotional growth. This disconnect underscores the necessity for SEL frameworks to be flexible and responsive to the diverse contexts in which they are implemented. Many existing initiatives fail to address systemic inequities, often opting for superficial approaches that lack transformative impact.

Some schools and districts adopt anti-racist language in policies in name only, resulting in performative actions that fall short of driving systemic change. For instance, a curriculum may include a single lesson on diversity or equity without integrating anti-racist principles into the broader SEL framework (Stark, 2021; Forber-Pratt, 2023). This tokenistic approach reduces anti-racism to a checklist item rather than as a core component of educational practice. It can create disconnects between students and educators who are seeking meaningful, authentic engagement with issues of race and equity. Additionally, tokenistic efforts often unintentionally reinforce existing power structures. Many SEL programs rely on standardized, prepackaged curricula marked as 'universally applicable' but fail to meet local needs. These "one-size-fits-all" solutions frequently disregard the unique cultural and historical contexts of the communities they serve. Failure to be critically conscious of students' lived experiences also reinforces inequity. For example, SEL curricula where the voices and perspectives of marginalized communities are not heard risk alienating those students (Chen & Yang, 2022). Integrating anti-racist education into SEL offers substantial promise but also faces considerable obstacles. Opposition from stakeholders, resource constraints, and lack of contextual adaptations can limit its impact. Superficial efforts and generic curricula highlight the urgent need for systemic reforms that integrate anti-racist values into the core principles of SEL frameworks. Achieving true equity requires SEL to directly confront these obstacles and adopt culturally inclusive approaches that honor the diverse experiences of all students. Next, we discuss strategies designed to address these challenges.

A strategic approach is essential for creating meaningful and sustainable change in response to these challenges.

STRATEGIES FOR BUILDING AN INTEGRATED ANTI-RACIST SEL FRAMEWORK

The following strategies are informed by the principles of transformative SEL, which center on collective well-being and critical consciousness, and critical race theory, which calls on educators to disrupt the systemic nature of racism in schooling. Incorporating anti-racist principles into SEL necessitates a deliberate approach, collaborative efforts, and a strong dedication to equity. Rooted in the goals of transformative SEL, this framework seeks to empower students and educators alike by weaving cultural responsiveness, fostering critical reflection, and promoting community engagement into SEL practices.

Below are actionable strategies for developing an integrated, anti-racist SEL framework that prioritizes or centers students' voices and experiences in the design and implementation process.

Centering Student Voice

Centering students' voices means acknowledging and integrating their diverse cultural experiences and perspectives into SEL programs. To achieve this, students must be engaged directly in shaping, designing, and evaluating these programs. Teachers can facilitate meaningful engagement through listening sessions, focus groups, and classroom discussions to better understand students' emotional needs, cultural dynamics, and community values. For example, questions about how emotions are expressed within families or what kinds of support they need to navigate challenges can help SEL practices be more inclusive and culturally relevant (Abrams et al., 2023). Through this participatory approach, students' input is validated, and SEL curricula resonate with their day-to-day lives. Creating a supportive environment that fosters open dialogue about identity, race, and emotions in a supportive way empowers students to express themselves and share their experiences and voices freely without fear of criticism or judgment.

Culturally Sustaining SEL Practices

Culturally sustaining pedagogy goes beyond acknowledging diversity to actively celebrating and weaving it into teaching practices. In doing so, schools can create SEL frameworks that integrate cultural assets into SEL curricula that draw on students' strengths, reflect community values, and foster a strong sense of belonging. Using storytelling traditions from diverse cultures in SEL lessons builds emotional connections and instills cultural pride and cross-cultural understanding. For example, folktales, oral histories, and cultural narratives provide engaging ways to teach emotional intelligence and impart moral lessons that resonate with students (Taylor, 2017). Additionally, restorative justice approaches inspired by Indigenous and community-based traditions can encourage conflict resolution and community healing, reinforcing shared responsibility and interconnectedness principles and the collectivist roots of many marginalized students. To be impactful, SEL programming should align with the values and traditions of the communities it serves. Schools can achieve this by engaging students in community-based initiatives or weaving local cultural events into SEL instruction (Jagers et al., 2019). These types of efforts help students more deeply connect with their environment and promote a sense of belonging, reinforcing the relevance and value of their cultural identities within the educational experience.

Professional Development for Educators

Educators play a pivotal role in the success of SEL programs. Still, many are not adequately trained to understand anti-racist and culturally responsive practices or how to use them within their teaching. Investing in targeted professional development equips educators to do both with confidence and sensitivity. Effective training should delve into implicit bias and explore the historical foundations of systemic racism and its effects on student outcomes. With this deeper understanding, educators can identify and reframe their teaching to promote fairness and inclusivity (Nadeem et al., 2022). Quality professional development must also include practical, ready-to-implement tools and techniques for overcoming bias and creating an inclusive classroom that supports all learners. Professional development should also include self-reflection, encouraging educators to examine their identities, assumptions, and privileges. Tools like journaling, collaborative discussion groups, and workshops on cultural humility can help teachers recognize how their perspectives shape their teaching practices. To sustain these efforts for the long term, schools should offer educators practical resources, such as culturally responsive teaching guides, anti-racist SEL lesson models, and access to mentorship or peer networks. When teachers are equipped with the right resources and support, schools can enhance and strengthen the impact of SEL programs and cultivate a culture of continuous improvement.

Leveraging Community Partnerships

Creating an anti-racist SEL framework requires collaboration with families, cultural organizations, and community leaders to ensure programs are aligned with community needs and strengths. These stakeholders bring essential cultural knowledge and lived experiences that enrich SEL practices. Engaging them in workshops, town halls, or collaborative planning strengthens cultural relevance and broadens support for SEL programs (Bhatti-Sinclair, 2011; Jagers et al., 2019). This collaborative approach fosters shared ownership and investment, enhancing the program's effectiveness. Many marginalized communities often experience generational trauma caused by systemic oppression and historical inequities. Partnering with mental health professionals, cultural organizations, and local advocates enables schools to adopt trauma-informed practices tailored to these realities (Mahoney, 2021). For instance, group therapy sessions and cultural healing practices can equip students with strategies to process and manage their emotional well-being.

Extending SEL beyond classrooms by collaborating with local organizations to establish mentorship programs, extracurricular activities, and service-learning projects. These initiatives build emotional intelligence, strengthen community ties, and help students develop leadership skills in real-world settings (Matias & Mackey, 2015; Allbright, n.d.). By connecting SEL to community resources, schools enhance program relevance and impact. Building an anti-racist SEL framework presents both a challenge and a transformative opportunity. Schools can create SEL programs that drive equity and inclusion by centering student voices, embedding culturally sustaining practices, empowering educators with necessary tools, and leveraging community partnerships. These strategies enable SEL to move beyond traditional approaches, become a powerful tool for systemic change, and empower students to thrive in inclusive, supportive classrooms.

Audit Existing Materials for Bias and Representation

Evaluating SEL content for stereotypes, tokenism, or underrepresentation is vital for creating an inclusive and equitable learning environment. Lessons should intentionally include examples and narratives that authentically reflect the identities and experiences of all students, especially those from historically marginalized communities. For example, replace generic scenarios with culturally specific, real-world scenarios for discussion. Teaching empathy through the lens of pivotal historical or social justice movements, such as the Civil Rights Movement or Black Lives Matter, provides students with relatable, relevant, and impactful content (Mensah, 2019; Schuman & Reynolds, 2023). Diverse literature also serves as a powerful tool; selecting stories that highlight characters from various backgrounds allows educators and students to explore social-emotional competencies while addressing complex social issues like ableism and systemic racism.

Incorporating case studies and cultural narratives further enriches SEL curricula. Exploring topics like immigration on social well-being or examining cultural traditions of emotional expression and conflict resolution deepens students' understandings and connections. Conducting regular audits of SEL materials helps uncover unintentional biases and offers opportunities to incorporate more inclusive practices. Additionally, involving students through collaboration, evaluation, and feedback ensures lessons are relevant to their experiences and resonate with their realities, cultivating a supportive environment where all learners feel seen, valued, and understood.

Center Culturally Responsive Practices

Cultural traditions can be a meaningful foundation for SEL lessons, especially for younger students. Introduce emotional regulation through guided imagery inspired by Indigenous traditions, focusing on breathing patterns linked to natural rhythms or visualizing calming elements like water or wind. Similarly, African diasporic traditions can be explored by using storytelling to process emotions or drumming to relieve stress (Curiel, 2021). Younger students could also participate in a gratitude circle, sharing something they appreciate using prompts tied to their cultural experience.

Integrate SEL competencies within discussions about fairness and equity. Teach self-awareness by helping students identify aspects of their identity, such as their cultural traditions, favorite foods, or family activities, and connect these to their unique strengths. For example, students could create "identity collages" that reflect what makes them special while fostering an appreciation for their classmates' diverse experiences. Build empathy by using books in activities that explore age-appropriate social challenges. For instance, read *Last Stop on Market Street* by Matt de la Peña to explore themes of community and gratitude or *Ada's Violin* by Susan Hood to discuss environmental justice and resourcefulness. After reading, students can reflect on how they might help others in need through group discussions. These activities empower students to see themselves as working together as agents of positive change while enhancing their emotional intelligence and developing critical thinking skills.

Engage Communities in Curriculum Design

Engaging with families, cultural organizations, and students is critical for co-creating SEL content that reflects the community's values and lived experiences. This engagement can take various forms, including organizing community forums or collaborative workshops where families and cultural representatives share their priorities for SEL. For example, educators can invite students to contribute by identifying stories, case studies, or historical events that reflect their realities, making the SEL content more authentic and impactful (Walker, 2022; Kinloch & Dixon, 2017). Community leaders can shape curriculum by sharing their expertise on cultural practices that promote emotional resilience and well-being. Involving local artists, elders, or mental health experts to provide culturally rich activities is an inclusive approach that strengthens cultural responsiveness while fostering a sense of ownership and collaboration among all stakeholders.

By prioritizing input from families and community members, schools build more inclusive environments where students are supported and empowered to thrive. Integrating SEL efforts into the Multi-Tiered System of Support (MTSS), teachers ensure their work toward anti-racist classrooms is embedded within a comprehensive framework that is targeted and culturally relevant. To operationalize these strategies, educators can utilize the following checklists aligned with each tier of MTSS.

MTSS IMPLEMENTATION CHECKLISTS

While anti-racist education is a Tier 1 priority, it must be woven through all levels of the MTSS framework. The MTSS model allows for implementing targeted strategies at various levels to ensure that SEL practices are equitable and culturally responsive. Below are suggestions for including anti-racist and inclusive strategies throughout the MTSS tiers.

Tier 1: Universal Supports

- Equity-Focused Lessons: SEL lessons should center on equity-focused, culturally relevant materials and be aligned with culturally responsive teaching practices. For example, use literature, art, and case studies/scenarios highlighting diverse perspectives. Teachers can also explore how different societies approach conflict resolution. Grounding lessons in global and cultural contexts enhances student engagement and understanding by making the content more relatable and meaningful (Griffin, 2020; Carranza, 2023).
- Inclusive Classroom Norms: Involve students in creating classroom guidelines that integrate respect for diversity and open dialogue within daily routines. Begin the year with a "Community Agreement" activity where students decide on classroom expectations for respectful dialogue and appreciation of different cultural identities as a community of learners. Students, for instance, might agree to listen actively, avoid interrupting, and remain open-minded during discussions with peers or within the larger classroom community.
- Addressing Implicit Bias: Embed implicit bias training directly into SEL lessons. Teachers can introduce the concept through age-appropriate picture books which can then be paired with mindfulness activities, such as "stop and think" exercises, that teach students how to pause before concluding others (Bennouna, 2021). Teachers can also create guided journal activities that prompt students to examine their assumptions about others and reflect on how those assumptions might impact their interactions.

Each of these examples helps lay the foundation for a more inclusive, considerate, and thoughtful classroom environment.

Tier 2: Targeted Interventions

- Small-Group Support: These sessions can be designed in a variety of ways. To develop practice for students' self-advocacy and resilience, group discussions could center on real-world scenarios where students identify and practice advocating for themselves in challenging situations. Students could also study the lives of historical and contemporary figures who have overcome barriers, perhaps finding inspiration from their journeys and achievements.
- Restorative Practices: Restorative practices should serve as an effective alternative to punitive discipline (e.g., taking away privileges, removal from the classroom) through students working together to understand the root causes of conflicts and explore strategies to avoid similar situations moving forward. Within Tier 2 of MTSS, this might look like small groups

sharing personal experiences, brainstorming solutions, or participating in role-playing situations to investigate alternative approaches and outcomes (Forber-Pratt, 2023). Peer mediation programs, where trained student leaders facilitate their peers in resolving conflicts through conversation, show promise. By doing so, relationships are mended through active listening and empathy while contributing to a more supportive and inclusive learning culture.

- Culturally Responsive Collaboration: Collaborating with culturally responsive counselors can provide targeted support for students dealing with identity-based stress or trauma. Through small groups or one-on-one sessions, counselors can design sessions tailored to address the student's specific emotional and cultural needs. For example, a counselor might facilitate discussions on coping strategies for managing microaggressions, helping students build resilience and self-advocacy skills. Collaborative relationships might also extend into creating a mentorship program, where students are paired with someone with similar backgrounds and experiences. Mentors can offer guidance, encouragement, and tools to help students address systemic inequities while strengthening their sense of identity and belonging within the school community.

Tier 3: Intensive Supports

- Individualized Plans: Crafting individualized plans that integrate students' cultural, racial, and historical contexts should provide interventions and accommodations tailored to each student's specific challenges and strengths. Engaging families in the process is one key. Still, holistic support systems may include connecting students with mentors who share the student's cultural background and who can offer and serve as positive role models (Genao & Mercedes, 2021).
- Trauma-Informed Practices: Integrating trauma-informed practices that explicitly recognize and address the emotional and psychological systemic and historical oppression of marginalized students is crucial. Access to mental health professionals who can offer care and strategies appropriate to students' cultural identities and support healing and resilience through culturally relevant support.
- Holistic Support Networks: Establish strong partnerships with community organizations to create comprehensive student needs support systems. This may include offering resources like after-school enrichment programs focused on academic and personal growth, culturally responsive mental health services, and mentorship programs that offer guidance and encouragement. Being a part of supportive and inclusive environments like these (beyond the classroom) promotes overall well-being and success (Kennedy, 2019).

Teacher Self-Reflection Frameworks

Effective anti-racist education begins with educators. Educators engage in critical self-reflection to understand their biases, beliefs, and practices. Structured self-reflection frameworks, journaling prompts, peer discussion groups, and equity audits offer opportunities for introspection and growth (Evans & Knepper, 2020). These activities enable educators to uncover areas for improvement and guide their development as advocates for anti-racist principles and equity. Through this type of self-awareness, educators model the values they aim to teach their students.

To enhance self-reflection within an MTSS framework, educators should embed these practices at every tier:

- Tier 1: Universal Reflection Practices - Incorporate equity audits and classroom observations into the MTSS framework to ensure inclusive SEL practices and challenge implicit biases. These tools provide actionable insight and identify where adjustments are needed to create a more equitable learning environment. When paired with regular journaling prompts for educators to reflect on their interactions with students, teachers can analyze how their approaches support or hinder their work toward anti-racist objectives.
- Tier 2: Targeted Reflection Tools - Educators can participate in small-group or coaching sessions to critically examine how their interventions address marginalized students' cultural and emotional needs. These opportunities for collaboration and critical thinking provide a space to analyze challenges, share insights, and adapt their approaches to develop more inclusive practices (L'Estrange & Howard, 2022)
- Tier 3: Intensive Self-Reflection - As educators provide individualized interventions, we should be reflecting on how personal biases, our own beliefs, and assumptions may shape the interactions and approaches for supporting specific students. Working one-on-one with a coach or supervisor who can provide constructive feedback, or guidance will help educators refine their culturally responsive and trauma-informed approaches. This reflective process promotes individualized supports that are equitable and aligned with students' unique contexts.

To effectively address all these concerns moving forward, teachers' preparation plays a pivotal role in implementing anti-racist SEL practices. Teacher preparation programs provide the foundation for equipping educators with the skills and knowledge to navigate the complexities of anti-SEL practices.

Sustainable change begins not just in practice but in preparation. Teacher training programs are foundational for equipping educators with the knowledge and tools to do this work effectively.

THE ROLE OF TEACHER PREPARATION PROGRAMS

For these reforms to take hold systematically, the next generation of teachers must be prepared with the tools and consciousness to lead this work. Teacher preparation programs are pivotal in providing educators with the skills to implement anti-racist practices effectively. This requires programs to embed anti-racist education and culturally responsive pedagogy as foundational components of all required coursework. Research highlights a gap in teacher training. Candidates lack sufficient training in SEL and its intersection with systemic racism, which limits their ability to address inequities within their classrooms. To address this, future educators must be trained to deeply understand systemic racism, implicit bias, and how culture, identity, and learning intersect (L'Estrange & Howard, 2022).

Equally important is integrating trauma-informed practices within an anti-racist framework. Systemic inequities deeply affect students' emotional and social well-being, affirming spaces that support healing and resilience, particularly for marginalized students. Building critical consciousness among educators - helping them recognize their biases and challenge societal structures that sustain inequities - is essential in enabling them to break down barriers to students' success and creating inclusive, equitable classrooms (Buzard, 2024)

Key Strategies for Teacher Preparation Programs

To prepare educators effectively, teacher preparation programs should implement several key strategies:

1. Courses on Equity and SEL: Teacher preparation curricula must incorporate coursework that examines the intersections of systemic racism, cultural competency, and SEL. These courses should offer actionable strategies for identifying and addressing inequities and fostering an inclusive learning environment. Educators always need to understand the impact of historical and structural disparities that shape the educational system and be equipped with tools to create culturally responsive and equitable teaching strategies.
2. Practical Assignments: Teacher preparation coursework must incorporate assignments that challenge educators to adapt SEL activities to address the unique needs of diverse learners. For example, pre-service teachers could create a lesson plan that draws on students' cultural backgrounds, lived experiences, or community contexts, enabling more authentic engagement. These practical, hands-on tasks help future educators refine their skills and make meaningful connections between themselves and students.
3. Experiential Learning Opportunities: Internships and placements in schools serving culturally and linguistically diverse populations are essential for teacher candidates. These immersive experiences enable future educators to work directly with and connect with diverse communities, gaining a deeper understanding of cultural nuances and practices. To enhance this experiential learning, teacher candidates can collaborate on co-creating inclusive SEL policies that reflect the community values and priorities of the communities they serve.
4. Mentorship and Coaching: Pairing teacher candidates with experienced mentors specializing in anti-racist and trauma-informed SEL practices is essential for their development. Mentors can offer personalized guidance, insights, strategies, best practices, and constructive feedback to help candidates address the challenges and complexities of addressing inequities in education. Reflective supervision should also be embedded in the pre-service teacher experience; incorporating ongoing reflection helps pre-service teachers analyze their experiences, engage in critical self-examination, deepen their self-awareness, and refine their teaching methods in ways that uphold equity-focused and anti-racist goals.

Equipping teachers to implement anti-racist SEL requires a holistic strategy grounded in transformative SEL and CRT, which underscore the need for educators to foster critical consciousness and systemic awareness in both them and their students. Teacher preparation programs must embed anti-racist education, provide experiential learning opportunities, and foster reflective practice so that new teachers are better equipped to create equitable and affirming learning environments supportive of all students. Such an approach is critical for addressing systemic barriers and ensuring that education becomes a tool for social justice.

As teacher preparation programs take on this charge, they anchor the systemic transformation needed to ensure anti-racist SEL becomes the norm, not the exception.

CONCLUSION

Integrating anti-racist education into social-emotional learning within a trauma-informed MTSS framework is not just a moral imperative - it is an urgent educational priority. This chapter has examined the Eurocentric roots of SEL, surfaced systemic barriers, and presented actionable strategies grounded in transformative practice and practitioner wisdom. As schools and districts confront widening inequities and political polarization, anti-racist SEL offers a way forward by fostering identity-affirming, relationship-rich, and justice-centered learning environments.

To realize this vision, educators and leaders must commit to co-creating culturally responsive SEL systems in partnership with students, families, and communities. The work ahead will require courage, creativity, and care. However, by embedding equity into every tier of MTSS and grounding SEL in the lived experiences of all students, schools can shift from transactional compliance to transformational change. In doing so, we prepare not only students - but whole communities - to thrive, heal, and lead in a more just world.

REFERENCES

Abrams, L., Garcia-Perez, J., Brock-Petroshius, K., & Applegarth, D. (2023). Racism, colorblindness, and social work education: An exploratory search of Californa student beliefs and experiences. *Journal of the Society for Social Work and Research, 14*(2), 385–410. DOI: 10.1086/714830

Allbright, T. M., Marsh, J. A., Kennedy, K. E., Hough, H. J., & McKibben, S. (2019, June 11). Social-emotional learning practices: Insights from outlier schools. *Journal of Research in Innovative Teaching and Learning, 12*(1), 35–52. DOI: 10.1108/JRIT-02-2019-0020

Bandura, A. (1986). *Social foundations of thought and action: A social cognitive theory*. Prentice-Hall.

Beck, A. T. (1976). *Cognitive therapy and the emotional disorders*. International Universities Press.

Bennouna, C. B., Brumbaum, H., McLay, M. M., Allaf, C., Wessells, M., & Stark, L. (2021). The role of culturally responsive social and emotional learning in supporting refugee inclusion and belonging: A thematic analysis of service provider perspectives. *PLoS One, 16*(8), e0256743. DOI: 10.1371/journal.pone.0256743 PMID: 34437627

Bhatti-Sinclair, K. A. (2011). *Anti-Racist Practice in Social Work*. Bloomsbury Academic. DOI: 10.1007/978-0-230-34430-3

Buzard, A. (2024). Conceptualizing anti-racist social work pedagogy. *Advances in Social Work, 23*(2), 295–316. DOI: 10.18060/27152

Carranza, P. B. (2023). School-based discrimation and social-emotional learning among Latinx youth: The moderating role of school commitment to diversity equity and inclusion. *Youth & Society, 56*(2), 387–410. DOI: 10.1177/0044118X231170314

Chen, H., & Yang, Y. (2022). The impact of social-emotional learning: A meta-analysis in China. *Frontiers in Psychology, 13*, 13. DOI: 10.3389/fpsyg.2022.1040522 PMID: 36312196

Curiel, L. (2021). Interracial team teaching in social work education. *Advances in Social Work, 21*(2/3), 730–749. DOI: 10.18060/24176

Day, C. P. (2023). Perceptions of social-emotional learning among K-12 teachers in the USA during the Covid-19 pandemic. *School Mental Health, 15*(2), 484–497. DOI: 10.1007/s12310-022-09563-w

Doan, S., Woo, A., Henry, D., & Kaufman, J. H. (2022). *How are teachers talking about race and racism in the classroom?* RAND Corporation., DOI: 10.7249/RRA1108-1

Durlak, J. W., Weissberg, R. P., Dymnicki, A. B., Taylor, R. D., & Schellinger, K. B. (2011). The impact of enhancing students' social and emotional learning: A meta-analysis of school-based univerversal interventions. *Child Development, 82*(1), 405–432. DOI: 10.1111/j.1467-8624.2010.01564.x PMID: 21291449

Evans, M., & Knepper, H. (2020). Building inclusive PA classrooms: The diversity inclusion model. *Teaching Public Administration, 39*(1), 84–106. DOI: 10.1177/0144739420937762

Every, S. S. A. 20 U.S.C. § 6301 (2015). https://www.congress.gov/bill/114th-congress/sentate-bill/1177

Forber-Pratt, A. E., Espelage, D. L., Robinson, L. E., Woolweaver, A. B., Torgal, C., & El Sheikh, A. J. (2023). I'm a security professional, a counselor, a leader, and sometimes a father figure: Transformative social emotional learning through the eyes of school security professionals. *American Journal of Community Psychology, 71*(3-4), 317–331. DOI: 10.1002/ajcp.12640 PMID: 36594880

Forman, S. F., Foster, J. L., & Rigby, J. G. (2021). School leaders' use of social-emotional learning to disrupt whiteness. *Educational Administration Quarterly, 58*(3), 351–385. DOI: 10.1177/0013161X211053609

Genao, S., & Mercedes, Y. (2021). All we need is one mic: A call for anti-racist solidarity to deconstruct anti-black racism in educational leadership. *Journal of School Leadership, 31*(1-2), 127–141. DOI: 10.1177/1052684621993046

Griffin, C. G., Gray, D. L., Hope, E., Metzger, I. W., & Henderson, D. X. (2020). Do coping responses and racial identity promote school adjustment among Black youth? Applying an equit-elaborated social-emotional learning lens. *Urban Education, 57*(2), 198–223. DOI: 10.1177/0042085920933346

Jagers, R. K., Rivas-Drake, D., & Williams, B. (2019). Transformative social and emotional learning (SEL): Toward SEL in service of educational equity and excellence. *Educational Psychologist, 54*(3), 162–184. DOI: 10.1080/00461520.2019.1623032

Karatas, K., & Oral, B. (2015). Teachers' perceptions on culturally responsiveness in education. *Journal of Ethnic and Cultural Studies, 2*(2), 47–57. DOI: 10.29333/ejecs/39

Kennedy, K. (2019). Centering equity and caring leadership for social-emotional learning: Toward a conceptual framework for diverse learners. *Journal of School Leadership, 29*(6), 473–492. DOI: 10.1177/1052684619867469

Kinloch, V., & Dixon, K. (2017). Equity and justice for all. *English Teaching, 16*(3), 331–346. DOI: 10.1108/ETPC-05-2017-0074

L'Estrange, L. &. Howard, J. (August 2022). *Trauma-informed initial teacher education training: A necessary step in a system-wide response to addressing childhood trauma.* ttps://DOI: 10.3389/feduc.2022.929582

Ladson-Billings, G., & Tate, W. F. (1995). Toward a critical race theory of education. *Teachers College Record, 97*(1), 47–68. DOI: 10.1177/016146819509700104

Lynch, I. S., Swartz, S., & Isaacs, D. (2017). Anti-racist moral education: A review of approaches, impact, and theoretical underpinnings from 2000 to 2015. *Journal of Moral Education, 46*(2), 129–144. DOI: 10.1080/03057240.2016.1273825

Mahoney, J. W., Weissberg, R. P., Greenberg, M. T., Dusenbury, L., Jagers, R. J., Niemi, K., Schlinger, M., Schlund, J., Shriver, T. P., VanAusdal, K., & Yoder, N. (2021). Systemic social and emotional learning: Promoting educational success for all preschool to high school students. *The American Psychologist, 76*(7), 1128–1142. DOI: 10.1037/amp0000701 PMID: 33030926

Mann, S., & Cheng, V. (2013). Responding to moral dilemmas: The roles of empathy and collectivist values among the Chinese. *Psychological Reports, 113*(1), 107–117. DOI: 10.2466/17.21.PR0.113x14z6 PMID: 24340805

Matias, C., & Mackey, J. (2015). Breakin' down whiteness in antiracist teaching: Introducing critical whiteness pedagogy. *The Urban Review*, *48*(1), 32–50. DOI: 10.1007/s11256-015-0344-7

Mensah, F. (2019). Finding voice and passion: Critical race theory methodology in science teacher education. *American Educational Research Journal*, *56*(4), 1412–1456. DOI: 10.3102/0002831218818093

Nadeem, E., Shernoff, E., Coccaro, C., & Stoke-Tyler, D. (2022). Supporting teachers during the Covid-19 pandemic: A community-partnered rapid needs assessment. *School Psychology*, *37*(4), 309–318. DOI: 10.1037/spq0000503 PMID: 35482640

National Center for Education Statistics. (2023). *Characteristics of public school teachers.* U.S. Department of Education, Institute of Educatin Sciences. https://nces.ed.gov/prgrams/coe/indicator.clr

Nolan, K. (2021). Urban students' critical race-class narratives: An examination of the relationship between race and class within the context of punitive school disciplineq. *Teachers College Record*, *123*(14), 351–385. DOI: 10.1177/01614681211063965

Organization for Economic Co-operation and Development. (2021). *Beyond acadmic learning: First results from the survey of social and emotional skills.* OECD Publishing. https://doi.org/10.19=787/92a11084-en

Osher, D. K., Kidron, Y., Brackett, M., Dymnicki, A., Jones, S., & Weissberg, R. P. (2016). Advancing the science and practice of social and emotional learning. *Review of Research in Education*, *40*(1), 644–681. DOI: 10.3102/0091732X16673595

Schuman, J., & Reynolds, D. (2023). Attempts at anti-racist teaching by White English teachers of black students. *English Teaching*, *22*(4), 418–432. DOI: 10.1108/ETPC-05-2022-0071

Skinner-Dorkenoo, A. S., Sarmal, A., André, C. J., & Rogbeer, K. G. (2021). How microagressions reinforce and perpetuate systemic racism in the United States. *Perspectives on Psychological Science*, *16*(5), 903–925. DOI: 10.1177/17456916211002543 PMID: 34498526

Sklad, M. D., Diekstra, R., Ritter, M. D., Ben, J., & Gravesteijn, C. (2012). Effectiveness of school-based universal social, emotional, and behavioral programs: Do they enhance students' development in the area of skill, behavior and adjustment? *Psychology in the Schools*, *49*(9), 892–909. DOI: 10.1002/pits.21641

Stark, L. R., Robinson, M. V., Gillespie, A., Aldrich, J., Hassan, W., Wessells, M., Allaf, C., & Bennouna, C. (2021). Supporting mental health and psychosocial wellbeing through social and emotional learning: A participatory study of conflict-affected youth resettled in the U.S. *BMC Public Health*, *21*(1), 21. DOI: 10.1186/s12889-021-11674-z PMID: 34488688

Taylor, R. O., Oberle, E., Durlak, J. A., & Weissberg, R. P. (2017). Promoting positive youth development through school-based social and emotional learning interventions: A meta-analysis of followup effects. *Child Development*, *88*(4), 1156–1171. DOI: 10.1111/cdev.12864 PMID: 28685826

The Education Trust. (2021). *Parents overwhelmingly support social, emotional learning: Findings from a national survey.*https://edtrust.org/resource/parents-overwhelmingly-support social-emotional-learning/

Ukpokodu, O. (2007). Preparing socially conscious teachers: A social justice-oriented teacher education. *Multicultural Education*, *15*(1), 8–15.

United Nationals Education, Scientific and Cultural Organization. (2026). *Happy schools: A framework for learner well-being in the Asia-Pacific*. UNESCO Bangkok. https://unesdoc.unesco.org/ark:/48223/pf0000243980

Waite, S. (2021). Disrupting dysconsciousness: Confronting anti-blackness in educational leadership preparation programs. *Journal of School Leadership, 31*(1-2), 66–84. DOI: 10.1177/1052684621993047

Walker, S. B., Bennett, I., Kettory, P., Pike, C., & Walker, L. (2022). 'deep understading' for anti-racist school transformation: School leaders' professional development inthe context of Black lives matter. *Curriculum Journal, 34*(1), 156–172. DOI: 10.1002/curj.189

ADDITIONAL READING

Anti-Racist Education

DiAngelo, R. (2018). *White fragility: Why it's so hard for White people to talk about racism*. Beacon Press.

Emdin, C. (2016). *For White folks who teach in the hood...and the rest of y'all too: Reality pedagogy and urban education*. Beacon Press.

Hammond, Z. (2015). *Culturally responsive teaching & the brain: Promoting authentic engagement and rigor among culturally and linguistically diverse students*. Corwin.

Kay, M., & Orr, J. (2023). *We're gonna keep on talking: How to lead meaningful race conversations in the elementary classroom*. Stenhouse Publishing. DOI: 10.4324/9781032683058

Sensoy, Ö., & DiAngelo, R. (2017). *Is everyone really equal? An introduction to key concepts in social justice education* (2nd ed.). Teachers College Press.

Tatum, B. D. (2017). *Why are all the Black kids sitting together in the cafeteria?And other conversations about race* (20th anniversary ed.). Basic Books. **Social-Emotional Learning**

Weissberg, R. P., Durlak, J. A., Domitrovich, C. E., & Gullotta, T. P. (Eds.). (2015). *Handbook of social and emotional learning: Research and practice*. The Guilford Press.

Zins, J. E., Weissberg, R. P., Wang, M. C., & Walberg, H. J. (Eds.). (2004). *Building academic success on social and emotional learning: What does the research say?* Teachers College Press.

KEY TERMS AND DEFINITIONS

Anti-Racist Education: A proactive teaching approach that identifies, challenges, and dismantles systemic racism while promoting equity and inclusivity in education.

Critical Consciousness: Analyzing and challenging social inequities and power dynamic structures in society to promote justice and equality.

Culturally Responsive Pedagogy: Teaching practices that incorporate students' cultural backgrounds and lived experiences into classroom teaching to enhance engagement and learning.

Culturally Sustaining Practices: Educational approaches that actively uphold, celebrate, and sustain students' cultural identities to include them in the learning process better.

Equity-Focused SEL: Adaptations of social-emotional learning frameworks tailored to address systemic inequities and cultural diversity.

Eurocentric: A worldview centered on or biased toward Western cultural norms, often disregarding or marginalizing the cultural perspectives of others.

Implicit Bias: Unconscious or subconscious attitudes or stereotypes that influence behavior and decision-making, often resulting in inequitable outcomes.

Multi-Tiered Systems of Support (MTSS): A framework or approach to delivering varying levels of academic, behavioral, and social-emotional support to students based on individual needs.

Social-Emotional Learning (SEL): A framework aimed at fostering and/or enhancing students' emotional awareness, relationship-building, and effective decision-making.

Trauma-Informed Practices: educational strategies that acknowledge the impact of trauma on students and create supportive environments emphasizing emotional safety, healing, and learning.

Chapter 7
Social-Emotional Learning as a Strategy for Addressing Math Anxiety in High School Students

Lori Ilana Barbag
https://orcid.org/0009-0002-6009-0186
National University, USA

ABSTRACT

This chapter examines integrating social-emotional learning (SEL) to mitigate math anxiety among high school students. Drawing on qualitative data, the chapter explores the multifaceted impact of math anxiety, highlighting its cognitive, emotional, and social dimensions. It presents SEL as a transformative approach, emphasizing mindfulness, emotional regulation, and growth mindset development. The chapter highlights the importance of trauma-informed and anti-racist principles, advocating for culturally responsive teaching to address the unique challenges faced by marginalized communities. By situating SEL within a Multi-Tiered System of Supports (MTSS) framework, the chapter outlines practical strategies for educators, including differentiated instruction, restorative practices, and teacher professional development. The findings demonstrate how SEL fosters inclusive classroom environments, enhances student confidence, and improves academic outcomes, offering a comprehensive model to address math anxiety and promote equitable education.

OVERVIEW OF MATH ANXIETY AND ITS IMPACT

Math anxiety is a widespread psychological phenomenon that affects students across all age groups, with high school students facing particularly profound and long-lasting impacts (Khashawneh et al., 2021). Defined by intense feelings of fear, apprehension, and discomfort surrounding mathematical tasks, math anxiety not only undermines academic performance but also creates significant emotional and psychological challenges (Barroso et al., 2021). Research indicates its prevalence, revealing that approximately 40% of high school students report experiencing moderate to severe levels of mathematics anxiety (Luttenberger et al., 2018). These feelings of anxiety often manifest through behavioral avoidance, such as skipping math assignments, procrastinating, or deliberately choosing non-math-related academic and career paths (Cahyawati et al., 2023). Cognitive impairments, such as difficulty concentrating, solving problems under

DOI: 10.4018/979-8-3693-9020-7.ch007

pressure, or recalling previously learned material, frequently accompany these behaviors (Siaw et al., 2021). Emotional distress, characterized by heightened stress, low self-confidence, and even physical symptoms like headaches or nausea, adds another layer of complexity. Together, these symptoms form a destructive feedback loop, where poor performance exacerbates anxiety, which in turn leads to further academic struggles, perpetuating a cycle of fear and failure (Suárez-Pellicioni et al., 2019).

The root causes of math anxiety are multifaceted, involving systemic, social, and individual factors (Caviola et al., 2022). On a systemic level, traditional instructional methods that emphasize rote memorization and repetitive drills over conceptual understanding often foster a fear of failure and hinder deeper learning (Caviola et al., 2022). For example, high-stakes testing environments where students feel pressured to achieve perfection intensify their stress levels, leaving little room for productive mistakes or growth (Cheung et al., 2023). Societal perceptions that portray mathematics as an inherently difficult or exclusive subject, often accompanied by stereotypes about who is "naturally" good at math, reinforce these anxieties (Cosso et al., 2022). Phrases like "I'm just not a math person" or "math is too hard for me" are not only common but also damaging, as they perpetuate a culture of avoidance and resignation (Caviola et al., 2022).

On an individual level, early negative experiences, such as struggling with foundational math skills or encountering overly critical teachers, can leave lasting impressions that shape students' attitudes toward the subject (Luo et al., 2023). Parental influences also play a significant role; parents who express their own math anxieties or inadvertently communicate low expectations can unknowingly pass on these fears to their children (Cosso et al., 2022). Furthermore, marginalized communities, including Black, Indigenous, and people of color (BIPOC), as well as individuals identifying as lesbian, gay, bisexual, transgender, queer or questioning, intersex, and asexual (LGBTQIA+), often face additional stressors stemming from systemic inequities and discrimination (Nenonene et al., 2019). These factors intensify their vulnerability to math anxiety and highlight the intersectionality of this issue. For instance, BIPOC students may face implicit biases in the classroom that affect their access to resources. In contrast, LGBTQIA+ students may encounter exclusionary practices or hostile environments that detract from their focus on academics (Milovanović, 2020).

The consequences of math anxiety extend far beyond academic struggles, impacting students' self-esteem, emotional health, and future aspirations (Soland, 2019). Students with high levels of math anxiety are less likely to participate in advanced math courses or pursue Science, Technology, Engineering, and Mathematics (STEM) related fields, limiting their opportunities in an increasingly technology-driven world (Cribbs et al., 2021). This creates a troubling paradox: while the demand for professionals in STEM fields continues to grow, many students are deterred from pursuing these careers due to their anxiety. For example, studies show that students with math anxiety are significantly underrepresented in fields such as engineering, computer science, and data analytics, perpetuating gender and racial disparities in these areas (Gonzalez-DeHass et al., 2023). The emotional toll of math anxiety also diminishes students' overall well-being, affecting their ability to enjoy learning, form positive relationships, and maintain a healthy sense of self-worth (Khuda & Ikram, 2021). These findings emphasize the need for comprehensive strategies to address math anxiety's complex and interconnected nature (Abín et al., 2020).

One promising approach to mitigating math anxiety is the integration of social-emotional learning (SEL) into math education (Lew & Hwang, 2019). SEL frameworks aim to develop students' self-awareness, emotional regulation, and interpersonal skills, equipping them with the tools to manage anxiety and confidently approach mathematical challenges (CASEL, 2023). Research has shown that SEL strategies, such as fostering a growth mindset, teaching stress-management techniques, and encouraging positive self-talk, can significantly reduce math anxiety while enhancing students' engagement and performance (Ramirez et al., 2018). For example, students taught to reframe mistakes as opportunities for growth rather than failures tend to develop greater resilience and perseverance (Lee & Kwon, 2023). Creating classroom environments where students feel emotionally safe to ask questions and share struggles encourages a positive and supportive learning culture (Karten, 2021). Teachers who employ inclusive practices, such as collaborative problem-solving, peer discussions, and positive reinforcement, contribute to students' sense of belonging and motivation to succeed (Rimm-Kaufman & Sandilos, 2020).

In addition to SEL, trauma-informed practices play a crucial role in addressing the broader emotional and psychological needs of students (Lichtenfeld et al., 2023). Recognizing the impact of adverse childhood experiences and systemic trauma, these practices focus on creating nurturing and responsive educational environments. For instance, teachers trained in trauma-informed methods adapt their strategies to reduce stress and foster resilience, such as offering individualized support, incorporating mindfulness activities, and building strong teacher-student relationships (Humphrey et al., 2020). A teacher might notice a student struggling to stay focused during math class and offer tailored interventions, such as breaking assignments into smaller, more manageable steps (Li et al., 2021). These approaches help alleviate the immediate effects of math anxiety and build students' long-term capacity to cope with challenges in and outside the classroom (Pizzie & Kraemer, 2023).

Moreover, it is important to integrate anti-racist and culturally responsive practices into math education to address the unique challenges faced by marginalized students (Stella, 2022). Educators can create more equitable learning environments by acknowledging and addressing biases in instructional materials, teaching methods, and classroom dynamics. For example, culturally relevant examples and representation in math problems can help students see the relevance of mathematics in their lives and foster a greater sense of inclusion (Teoh et al., 2022). These efforts, combined with SEL, can help dismantle systemic barriers that contribute to math anxiety among underrepresented groups. For instance, a math problem involving budgeting for a community event might resonate more deeply with students than abstract equations, making the subject feel accessible and applicable (Gearty, 2023).

The Multi-Tiered System of Support (MTSS) framework offers a structured and adaptable approach to implement these interventions effectively. MTSS emphasizes providing varying levels of support based on students' individual needs. Universal supports, such as classroom-wide SEL initiatives, aim to benefit all students by promoting emotional resilience and fostering positive peer relationships (Stocker & Gallagher, 2019). Targeted interventions, such as small group activities or peer mentoring, address the specific needs of students showing signs of moderate anxiety. For students requiring intensive support, personalized strategies, including one-on-one counseling, tailored accommodations, or partnerships with school psychologists, are critical for their success (Durlak et al., 2022). This tiered approach ensures that no student is left behind and that resources are allocated effectively to maximize impact.

Professional development for teachers is a cornerstone of these efforts. Educators need training in recognizing the signs of math anxiety, implementing evidence-based SEL and trauma-informed strategies, and fostering inclusive and anti-racist classroom practices (Todd et al., 2022). For example, workshops that teach techniques like differentiated instruction, culturally responsive teaching, and active listening can empower teachers to address the diverse needs of their students better (Boaler, 2015). Additionally, ongoing coaching and peer collaboration among educators can create a culture of continuous improvement, where teachers feel supported in their efforts to create emotionally safe and academically rigorous classrooms (C. Wang et al., 2020). Addressing math anxiety requires a comprehensive, multi-faceted approach that combines SEL, trauma-informed practices, and anti-racist principles within a robust MTSS framework (Y. Wang, 2023). By focusing on these strategies, educators can foster supportive and inclusive learning environments that empower students to overcome their fears, engage deeply with mathematics, and unlock their full potential (Xiao & Sun, 2021). These efforts have the power to transform not only individual student outcomes but also the broader educational landscape, ensuring that math becomes a source of growth, opportunity, and inspiration for future generations (Odak et al., 2023; Özdemir & Babadoğan, 2023). With deliberate action and a commitment to equity, schools can break the cycle of math anxiety and open doors to brighter futures for all learners.

SOCIAL-EMOTIONAL LEARNING AS A KEY INTERVENTION

Social-emotional learning (SEL) has emerged as a transformative approach to addressing math anxiety among high school students (Yuan et al., 2023). Grounded in fostering emotional intelligence, resilience, and interpersonal skills, SEL equips students with the tools to navigate academic challenges and build confidence in their mathematical abilities (CASEL, 2023). While math anxiety has often been regarded as a cognitive problem, SEL reframes it as a multifaceted issue that can be tackled through holistic educational practices (Collie, 2020). Research highlights the critical role of emotional intelligence, self-awareness, and stress management in enabling students to confront and overcome math-related challenges effectively (CASEL, 2023). Teachers incorporating SEL strategies noted that fostering a classroom environment grounded in empathy and mutual respect significantly reduced avoidance behaviors often associated with math anxiety (Luo et al., 2023). Furthermore, integrating SEL competencies like self-regulation and responsible decision-making into instructional practices provided students with cognitive and emotional tools to approach mathematics with confidence and resilience (Barroso et al., 2021). This section explores how teachers leverage SEL strategies to mitigate math anxiety, improve classroom dynamics, and enhance student outcomes, as observed in Lori Barbag's 2024 study.

Managing Math Anxiety

Research indicates that math anxiety stems from a combination of cognitive, emotional, and social factors, including a fear of failure, self-doubt, and negative experiences with mathematics in the past (Klee et al., 2023). Social-emotional learning (SEL) addresses these dimensions by promoting self-awareness, emotional regulation, and relationship-building skills (Keptner et al., 2020). Teachers in Barbag's study reported using SEL techniques to help students identify and manage their emotions during math tasks, enabling them to approach challenges with a calmer and more focused mindset (Caviola et al., 2022; Ramirez et al., 2018). Teachers observed that incorporating SEL strategies like mindfulness and emotional reflection created an environment where students felt safe to acknowledge and work through their anxiety (Caviola et al., 2022). Through positive peer interactions and collaborative learning, SEL helped students build a supportive network, reducing feelings of isolation often associated with math anxiety (Keptner et al., 2020). Participant 5 noted, "When students worked together on problem-solving tasks, their collective confidence grew, and they began to view challenges as opportunities for mutual learning" (Barbag, 2024).

Further examples were found for pre-test preparation strategies, such as deep breathing exercises, visualization techniques, and positive affirmations frequently employed in classrooms (Uhl et al., 2023). These practices reduced test-related stress and instilled a sense of control and readiness in students. Participant 1 in the study shared, "Breathing exercises helped my students enter a test feeling more centered and less overwhelmed by their fears" (Barbag, 2024). Similarly, teachers encouraged students to visualize success, such as imagining themselves solving problems confidently, which helped students counteract their anxiety-driven mental barriers (Uhl et al., 2023). Social-emotional learning also addresses the internalized negative self-talk that often accompanies math anxiety. Teachers taught students to reframe their thoughts from "I'm terrible at math" to "I can improve with practice." (C. Wang et al., 2023). This shift in mindset proved pivotal for many students, as it redirected their focus from fixed limitations to potential growth. Participant 3 described a moment when a student realized their anxiety was rooted in fear rather than actual inability, stating, "Once they learned to calm their emotions, their problem-solving abilities improved dramatically." (Barbag, 2024).

Creating Supportive Classroom Environments

Another critical aspect of social-emotional learning (SEL) is creating supportive and inclusive classroom environments where students feel safe to express their struggles and take academic risks. A key finding from the research emphasized that students with math anxiety often feared judgment and ridicule, which further exacerbated their avoidance behaviors (Yang et al., 2023). Social-emotional learning encourages teachers to foster a culture of empathy, where mistakes are viewed as opportunities for growth rather than failures (Bjälkebring, 2019). This essential element was promoting emotional safety, where students were encouraged to articulate their feelings without adding to their anxiety through emotions of distress, panic, or being mocked (Keptner et al., 2020). In the past, teachers have introduced reflective exercises, such as journaling about their math experiences, to help students process their emotions and identify triggers for anxiety (Bjälkebring, 2019). In Barbag's 2024 study, Participant 2 noted, "By normalizing discussions around struggles and resilience, we've seen students embrace challenges as part of their learning journey" (Barbag, 2024).

The study highlighted specific strategies, including peer collaboration and the "ask 3 before me" rule, which encouraged students to seek help from peers before turning to the teacher. Participant 6 noted, "When students work together, they realize they're not alone in their struggles. This shared experience helps them build confidence and resilience." Peer collaboration also created community and mutual support, helping students form stronger connections (Barbag, 2024). In addition to peer collaboration, teachers utilized structured group activities to ensure balanced participation, enabling all students to contribute and learn from one another (Ramirez et al., 2018). These cooperative learning strategies reduce social barriers and foster a shared sense of accomplishment among students (Yang et al., 2023). Participant 4 observed, "When students collaboratively solve problems, it shifts their focus from individual failure to collective success" (Barbag, 2024).

Individualized accommodations were another important tool. Teachers adapted their instruction to meet the diverse needs of their students by offering quiet testing environments, breaking tasks into smaller, more manageable sections, and providing additional time for assignments. Participant 5 explained, "These small adjustments gave my students the space to focus and succeed without the pressure of keeping up with everyone else." These inclusive practices played a significant role in helping students feel valued and supported (Barbag, 2024). Furthermore, teachers implemented scaffolding techniques, gradually increasing the tasks' complexity. Scaffolding techniques with more complex learning structures help build confidence incrementally, thus minimizing the space for anxiety (Caviola et al., 2022). These differentiated approaches were particularly effective in addressing the unique learning strides of students, enabling them to engage meaningfully with mathematical content (Barroso et al., 2021). Participant 8 shared, "By breaking tasks into achievable steps, students felt a sense of progress that motivated them to persist despite initial difficulties" (Barbag, 2024).

Enhancing Student Outcomes

The impact of social-emotional learning (SEL) on student outcomes extended beyond anxiety reduction, with participants observing notable improvements in engagement, motivation, and academic performance (Ding et al., 2023). Students who engaged in SEL practices were more willing to take risks, ask questions, and persevere through challenges. This behavior shift enhanced their mathematical abilities and fostered a growth mindset (Boaler, 2015). One particularly striking example came from Participant 4, who shared the story of a student who initially avoided math tasks due to fear of failure. After participating in SEL activities, the student began actively engaging in class discussions and volunteering to solve problems on the board (Guo & Liao, 2022). "Seeing this student raise their hand and tackle problems in front of the class was a remarkable transformation," the teacher remarked. This newfound confidence had a ripple effect, inspiring other students to step out of their comfort zones as well (Barbag, 2024). Social-emotional learning also encouraged students to view challenges as learning opportunities (Halme et al., 2022). For example, Participant 2 integrated a "productive failure" exercise into their lessons, where students attempted complex problems without immediate guidance. Although initially met with resistance, the activity helped students develop problem-solving skills and resilience over time (Barbag, 2024). Beyond the classroom, SEL had a lasting impact on students' emotional well-being (Ding et al., 2023). Teachers reported that students who practiced SEL strategies demonstrated improved relationships with peers and a greater ability to manage stress in other areas. These skills translate into higher overall satisfaction with their educational experiences and increased interest in pursuing advanced math courses and Science, Technology, Engineering, and Mathematics (STEM) careers (Cribbs et al., 2021).

Challenges and Recommendations for Implementation

Despite its clear benefits, implementing social-emotional learning (SEL) strategies presents challenges. Teachers in the study consistently highlighted the need for professional development to enhance their ability to integrate SEL effectively into their teaching practices. Participant 7 observed, "While we see the value of SEL, we often lack the training to implement it consistently and effectively." This lack of training, time constraints, and competing curricular demands made it difficult for educators to prioritize SEL in their classrooms (Barbag, 2024). Another challenge noted by teachers was the varying levels of student readiness to engage with SEL activities, which required a tailored approach to ensure inclusivity and effectiveness (Biber, 2020; Burgin et al., 2021). Teachers also reported difficulties balancing mathematics' academic rigor with the time-intensive nature of SEL interventions, often feeling pressured to prioritize content coverage over emotional development (Carisma & Fulgarinas, 2022; Chiu et al., 2020). Participant 2 reflected, "Incorporating SEL often feels like an added task rather than a natural extension of our teaching practice, especially with the constraints of external standardized testing" (Barbag, 2024).

The study recommends incorporating SEL training into teacher professional development programs (Barbag, 2024). Workshops that provide practical tools for integrating SEL into lesson plans, such as facilitating class discussions or designing SEL-infused activities, can empower teachers to make meaningful changes (Dumitrescu, 2023). Participant 8 suggested pairing newer teachers with SEL-trained mentors to provide ongoing support and feedback (Barbag, 2024). Incorporating case studies and real-world scenarios into SEL workshops could provide teachers with relatable and actionable classroom strategies (Ramirez et al., 2018). Furthermore, aligning SEL training with broader school goals, such as improving student engagement or reducing absenteeism, could enhance teacher buy-in and commitment to implementation (Durlak et al., 2022). Participant 6 emphasized, "When we see how SEL connects to measurable outcomes, it's easier to justify integrating it into an already packed curriculum" (Barbag, 2024).

Collaboration among educators is another key factor. By sharing best practices and resources, teachers can learn from one another and create a collective approach to SEL implementation (Kamour & Altakhayneh, 2021; Lau et al., 2022). For example, a school-wide initiative that includes regular SEL-themed assemblies or parent engagement activities could reinforce the importance of emotional well-being at every level of the educational system (McBride, 2019). Collaboration could be further strengthened by creating online platforms where educators share successful SEL practices and challenges, fostering a continuous exchange of ideas (Yang et al., 2023). Establishing interdisciplinary teams that include teachers, counselors, and administrators could also facilitate a more holistic approach to SEL integration (Caviola et al., 2022). Participant 4 noted, "When we work as a team, it becomes easier to see how SEL can fit into the broader framework of student support and achievement" (Barbag, 2024).

Additional recommendations include addressing systemic barriers by advocating for policies that support smaller class sizes, increasing planning time, and enabling access to mental health professionals. These resources would allow teachers to focus more fully on students' needs and ensure that SEL becomes a sustainable part of the educational framework (Durlak et al., 2022). Expanding access to professional development tailored to SEL could also empower teachers with strategies for managing diverse classroom needs effectively (Keptner et al., 2020). Research highlights the importance of providing schools with financial resources to implement systemic changes, such as hiring additional staff to reduce student-to-teacher ratios and creating dedicated time for SEL planning (Obersteiner, 2019; Panayiotou et al., 2019). Participant 3 noted, "With smaller classes and more time to prepare, I can provide the individualized attention my students need to thrive emotionally and academically" (Barbag, 2024; Passolunghi et al., 2020).

Summary

Social-emotional learning (SEL) represents a critical intervention in the battle against math anxiety. By addressing the emotional and social dimensions of learning, SEL empowers students to overcome their fears and engage more fully with mathematical challenges. Barbag's research illustrates that integrating SEL strategies improves academic outcomes and fosters a supportive and inclusive classroom culture (Barbag, 2024). From deep breathing exercises to peer collaboration, SEL equips students with the tools to manage their emotions and develop a positive relationship with mathematics (McLeod & Boyes, 2021). Social-emotional learning also helps students build resilience by teaching them to persist in academic challenges, shifting their mindset from fear of failure to confidence in their ability to improve (Boaler, 2015). Teachers observed that SEL strategies such as reflective journaling allowed students to articulate their anxieties, paving the way for targeted interventions and support (Caviola et al., 2022). Participant

5 shared, "One of my students who struggled with test anxiety began using SEL techniques, and over time, they developed a greater sense of control and self-efficacy in math" (Barbag, 2024).

Moving forward, prioritizing SEL in educational practices will be essential for creating equitable and empowering learning environments for all students (Griggs et al., 2023). Schools must invest in teacher training, foster collaboration, and advocate for systemic changes to ensure the long-term success of SEL initiatives (Hosokawa et al., 2023). By doing so, they can help countless students overcome math anxiety and unlock their full potential in both academics and life (Palestro & Jameson, 2020). Future SEL initiatives should also include family engagement components to extend the benefits of SEL practices beyond the classroom and into students' homes (C. Wang et al., 2023). Research suggests that embedding SEL into school-wide policies, such as incorporating it into mission statements and annual goals, can institutionalize its importance and sustain long-term progress (Durlak et al., 2022). Participant 7 emphasized, "When the entire school community – teachers, administrators, and parents – supports SEL, students feel a consistent message about the value of emotional and academic growth and well-being" (Barbag, 2024).

TRAUMA-INFORMED, ANTI-RACIST SOCIAL-EMOTIONAL LEARNING

Social-emotional learning (SEL) is a powerful tool for fostering students' emotional resilience and academic success (CASEL, 2023). However, to fully address the diverse needs of learners, especially those from marginalized communities, SEL must be implemented through a trauma-informed and anti-racist lens (Keptner et al., 2020). By integrating these frameworks, educators can create safe, equitable, and empowering learning environments that acknowledge and address the systemic barriers many students face (Durlak et al., 2022). Integrating a trauma-informed approach into SEL involved acknowledging the impact of systemic inequities and adverse experiences on students' emotional and cognitive development (Keptner et al., 2020). Teachers who embrace this perspective prioritize creating emotionally safe classrooms that mitigate trauma triggers and promote healing through trust-building and empathy (Caviola et al., 2022). Participant 3 noted, "Recognizing the lived experiences of students from marginalized backgrounds allows us to tailor our SEL strategies to address their unique challenges" (Barbag, 2024). Anti-racist practices further enrich SEL by challenging implicit biases and fostering cultural competency among both educators and students, thereby ensuring that all voices are valued in the learning environment (Durlak et al., 2022; Y. Wang, 2023). Moreover, incorporating culturally responsive teaching within SEL frameworks equips students to navigate and resist systemic barriers while building confidence in their academic potential (Bjälkebring, 2019). This section explores how trauma-informed principles and anti-racist practices enhance the effectiveness of SEL, particularly for students facing systemic inequities and adverse childhood experiences (ACEs) (Caviola et al., 2022).

A Trauma-Informed Approach

Trauma-informed education recognizes that trauma—whether from personal experiences or systemic inequities—profoundly impacts students' cognitive, emotional, and behavioral development (Keptner et al., 2020). Students who have experienced trauma often exhibit heightened anxiety, difficulty concentrating, and challenges in forming positive relationships, which can hinder their academic progress and emotional well-being (Caviola et al., 2022). These issues are particularly pronounced in marginalized students, including Black, Indigenous, and people of color (BIPOC) and lesbian, gay, bisexual, transgender, queer or questioning, intersex, and asexual (LGBTQIA+) youth, who frequently face compounded challenges such as discrimination, poverty, and exclusion from mainstream educational narratives (Perry & Daniels, 2016; SAMHSA, 2023). For instance, a student with food insecurity may struggle to focus on mathematical tasks due to constant worry about basic needs (Caviola et al., 2022). Similarly, an LGBTQIA+ student subjected to bullying might disengage from group activities, fearing judgment or ridicule (Keptner et al., 2020). Trauma-informed SEL addresses these realities by prioritizing safety, trust, and empowerment in the classroom (Caviola et al., 2022).

Teachers in Barbag's study emphasized the importance of creating emotionally secure environments where students feel valued and understood. Participant 3 shared, "When students feel emotionally secure, they're more likely to engage and take risks in their learning" (Barbag, 2024). For example, some educators implemented "calm corners" in their classrooms, where students could self-regulate and practice mindfulness techniques (Sathasivam & Rahim, 2021). These small but impactful changes helped students feel supported and empowered to manage their emotions (Barbag, 2024). Trauma-informed SEL also involves training educators to recognize signs of trauma, such as sudden behavioral shifts or difficulty concentrating (Durlak et al., 2022; Simion, 2023). Teachers in the study reported using daily emotional check-ins to gauge students' well-being. Participant 5 explained, "A simple thumbs-up or thumbs-down during morning meetings helps me identify which students might need extra support that day." This proactive approach ensures that students receive timely interventions tailored to their emotional needs (Barbag, 2024).

Embedding Anti-Racist Practices

Anti-racist education goes beyond acknowledging diversity to actively dismantle systemic biases and promote equity in the classroom (Keptner et al., 2020). In the social-emotional learning (SEL) context, anti-racist practices aim to challenge stereotypes, foster cultural humility, and empower students to celebrate their identities (Mayer et al., 2008). Anti-racist SEL emphasizes the need for educators to critically examine their biases and engage in ongoing professional development to build cultural competence (Keptner et al., 2020). By embedding inclusive narratives and diverse perspectives into curriculum materials, teachers can create a learning environment that validates and uplifts students' lived experiences (CASEL, 2023). Participant 2 shared, "When students see themselves represented in the material, it not only boosts their engagement but also reinforces the message that their identities and histories are valued" (Barbag, 2024).

Culturally responsive SEL strategies were a cornerstone of the practices highlighted in Barbag's study. Participant 6 explained, "I make it a point to include examples and stories that reflect my students' backgrounds. This engages them and affirms their place in the learning environment." For example, math problems were reframed to incorporate culturally relevant contexts, such as budgeting for a community event or analyzing statistical data related to social justice issues (Barbag, 2024). Culturally responsive SEL practices also involve adapting instructional methods to reflect multilingual learners' linguistic and cultural assets, fostering an inclusive atmosphere (Durlak et al., 2022). Participant 8 recalled, "Integrating students' cultural contexts into problem-solving activities has been a game changer in building trust and academic motivation" (Barbag, 2024).

Another critical aspect of anti-racist SEL is addressing the disproportionate impact of punitive disciplinary measures on marginalized students. Research shows that Black and Latinx students are more likely to face suspension or expulsion for behaviors linked to trauma and anxiety, perpetuating cycles of disengagement and academic failure (Skiba et al., 2011). The study's teachers advocated replacing punitive discipline with restorative practices like peer mediation and circle discussions. Participant 4 noted, "Restorative practices allow students to reflect on their actions and repair relationships, rather than feeling punished and alienated" (Barbag, 2024). Restorative practices in SEL reduce disciplinary disparities and cultivate a sense of community and accountability among students (Keptner et al., 2020). These approaches encourage dialogue and mutual understanding, empowering students to resolve conflicts constructively rather than resorting to exclusionary measures (Caviola et al., 2022).

Intersectionality and SEL

An intersectional approach to social-emotional learning (SEL) recognizes that students' identities—such as race, gender, and socioeconomic status—intersect to shape their experiences and challenges (Keptner et al., 2020). For example, a student who identifies as lesbian, gay, bisexual, transgender, queer or questioning, intersex, and asexual (LGBTQIA+) and a person of color may face compounded stressors, including societal discrimination and lack of representation in curriculum materials. An intersectional approach further underscores the importance of creating classroom environments where students' multiple identities are acknowledged and celebrated, reducing feelings of marginalization (CASEL, 2023). Teachers can achieve this by designing activities reflecting diverse cultural and social experiences, helping students see their realities mirrored in the learning process (Durlak et al., 2022). Participant 4 shared, "When students feel represented, their engagement and willingness to participate in discussions significantly improve" (Barbag, 2024).

Teachers in the study emphasized the importance of addressing these complexities through SEL. Participant 8 shared, "Many of my students carry multiple identities, and their experiences shape how they engage with math and learning. SEL helps me connect with them on a deeper level" (Barbag, 2024). For instance, a self-awareness activity might include discussions about how systemic inequities influence students' identities and opportunities, fostering personal reflection and critical thinking (Durlak et al., 2022). By incorporating intersectionality into SEL practices, educators address students' challenges, ensuring that each learner receives equitable support tailored to their unique experiences (Keptner et al., 2020). Teachers reported that introducing case studies featuring diverse figures in mathematics encouraged students to envision broader possibilities for their own futures (Caviola et al., 2022). Participant 6 observed, "Discussing the lives of mathematicians from various backgrounds inspired students to rethink the stereotypes often associated with STEM" (Barbag, 2024). Intersectionality also informs the development of SEL competencies. Social awareness in a trauma-informed, anti-racist framework involves recognizing and challenging societal biases, fostering empathy, and promoting student solidarity (Keptner et al., 2020). Classroom activities like role-playing or storytelling encouraged students to step into others' perspectives, building emotional intelligence and community (Caviola et al., 2022).

Strategies for Implementation

Implementing trauma-informed, anti-racist social-emotional learning (SEL) requires intentionality, collaboration, and systemic support. Key strategies include:

Professional Development. Teachers must have the knowledge and skills to integrate trauma-informed and anti-racist principles into social-emotional learning (SEL) (Keptner et al., 2020). Barbag's research highlighted the need for ongoing training in cultural competency and restorative practices. For example, professional development workshops could include simulations of restorative circles or case studies on implicit bias, providing teachers with actionable tools (Durlak et al., 2022).

Student-Centered Approaches. Co-creating classroom norms with students ensures their voices are heard and respected (CASEL, 2023). Participant 4 described using a class agreement to establish shared expectations, stating, "When students take part in setting the rules, they feel ownership and accountability" (Barbag, 2024). This process often led to unexpected insights, such as students advocating for mental health breaks during long class periods (Caviola et al., 2022).

Restorative Practices. Replacing punitive discipline with restorative approaches fosters accountability and relationship-building (Keptner et al., 2020). Teachers noted that practices such as peer mediation, restorative justice circles, and conflict resolution workshops helped students resolve disputes constructively while developing emotional intelligence (Mayer et al., 2008).

Curriculum Integration. Embedding culturally relevant content into social-emotional learning (SEL) activities ensures that all students see themselves reflected in the material (Caviola et al., 2022). For example, a math teacher might incorporate data analysis related to racial disparities in healthcare outcomes, connecting mathematical concepts to real-world issues that resonate with students.

Parent and Community Engagement. Collaborating with families and community organizations reinforces the principles of trauma-informed, anti-racist social-emotional learning (SEL) beyond the classroom (Durlak et al., 2022). Schools in the study organized parent workshops on SEL strategies, creating a unified support system for students (Barbag, 2024).

Marginalized Groups

The integration of trauma-informed and anti-racist principles in social-emotional learning (SEL) has transformative potential for marginalized students. By addressing the root causes of anxiety, disengagement, and behavioral challenges, this approach creates pathways for both academic and personal growth (CASEL, 2023). Teachers in the study observed significant improvements in students' confidence, participation, and relationships. Participant 2 remarked, "When students feel seen and supported, their whole attitude toward learning changes" (Barbag, 2024). Students who once avoided speaking up in class began taking active roles in group projects, demonstrating newfound self-assurance (Keptner et al., 2020). Trauma-informed SEL provides a critical support system for Adverse Childhood Experiences (ACEs) students. Mindfulness exercises, emotional check-ins, and collaborative activities helped students manage stress and build resilience (Caviola et al., 2022). One educator shared the story of a student who initially struggled with anger outbursts but gradually learned to express their emotions constructively through SEL practices (Durlak et al., 2022). Anti-racist practices ensured that all students had equitable opportunities to thrive regardless of their background. For example, culturally responsive pedagogy enabled students to see the relevance of math in their lives, fostering engagement and pride in their accomplishments (Barbag, 2024).

Summary

Incorporating a trauma-informed, anti-racist lens into social-emotional learning (SEL) is essential for fostering equitable and supportive learning environments. Addressing the unique needs of marginalized students enhances the effectiveness of SEL and contributes to a more just and inclusive educational system (Keptner et al., 2020). Barbag's research emphasizes the importance of these practices in empowering students to overcome barriers and achieve their full potential. As schools embrace these frameworks, they pave the way for a future where every student feels valued, supported, and capable of success (Durlak et al., 2022).

CASE STUDY: TEACHERS' PERCEPTIONS AND PRACTICES

Integrating social-emotional learning (SEL) strategies into high school mathematics classrooms has significantly reduced math anxiety and promoted equitable learning environments (Barbag, 2024; CASEL, 2023). This section uses qualitative data from interviews with high school math teachers to explore practical examples of how SEL strategies have been effectively implemented. These real-world insights highlight how educators address math anxiety, foster equity, and enhance student engagement and performance (Durlak et al., 2022).

Understanding Teachers' Perspectives on Math Anxiety

High school mathematics teachers in the study identified math anxiety as a pervasive challenge that significantly impairs students' academic performance and confidence. Participants consistently observed that students experiencing math anxiety often exhibited emotional, behavioral, and physical symptoms such as avoidance, frustration, and visible distress (Keptner et al., 2020). Participant 2 noted, "Some students will outright refuse to attempt problems because they're convinced they will fail." This highlights the debilitating effects of math anxiety, which often leads to disengagement and reduced academic success (Barbag, 2024).

Teachers emphasized that understanding the root causes of math anxiety was crucial for developing effective interventions. These causes often stemmed from prior experiences, such as struggling with foundational concepts, receiving critical feedback in early grades, or internalizing societal messages that math is inherently difficult (Caviola et al., 2022). Participant 5 shared, "Many students come to us with past experiences of failure in math, and that stays with them. Our job is to rebuild their confidence step by step." Recognizing the emotional baggage students bring to the classroom informed teachers' use of Social-emotional learning strategies to address these challenges (Barbag, 2024).

Implementation of Social-emotional Learning Strategies in Practice

The teachers employed various social-emotional learning (SEL) strategies to support students experiencing math anxiety. These practices centered on building students' self-awareness, self-regulation, and social awareness while fostering a supportive and inclusive classroom environment (CASEL, 2023).

Pre-Test Rituals and Anxiety Reduction Techniques. One of the most common strategies was incorporating pre-test rituals to help students manage their anxiety. Teachers encouraged deep breathing exercises, visualization techniques, and mindfulness before assessments (McLeod & Boyes, 2021). Participant 1 remarked, "I always tell my students to take a moment, breathe, and remind themselves that they've prepared for this. It helps them enter a calmer state of mind" (Barbag, 2024). In addition to mindfulness, teachers employed grounding techniques like writing positive affirmations on index cards or using stress-relief tools such as stress balls (Panayiotou et al., 2019). These rituals reduced immediate anxiety and empowered students to approach challenges with a more positive mindset. Participant 6 observed, "Over time, I've seen students adopt these strategies on their own, even outside of math tests. That's when I know the impact is lasting" (Barbag, 2024).

Relationship-Building and Emotional Safety. Teachers stressed the importance of building strong, trusting relationships with their students. Participant 3 shared, "When students feel that you genuinely care about them, they're more willing to try, even when they're afraid of failing" (Barbag, 2024). To foster emotional safety, teachers engaged in regular one-on-one check-ins with students, allowing them to share their concerns in a nonjudgmental space. These conversations often revealed deeper issues influencing their anxiety, such as fear of disappointing their parents or low self-esteem (Gonzalez-DeHass et al., 2023). Participant 4 noted, "Sometimes, just listening to a student and acknowledging their feelings makes a world of difference" (Barbag, 2024). Creating a culture of trust extended to the entire classroom. Teachers implemented group discussions focused on empathy and support, encouraging students to share their challenges and successes (Li et al., 2021). This sense of community made students feel less isolated in their struggles.

Encouraging a Growth Mindset. Promoting a growth mindset was a cornerstone of the teachers' approaches. By emphasizing effort over immediate correctness, teachers helped students reframe failure as a natural and necessary part of learning (Lichtenfeld et al., 2023). Participant 6 explained, "We celebrate mistakes in my class because they mean you're trying. That shift in perspective makes students less afraid to participate" (Barbag, 2024). Teachers also used concrete examples to illustrate growth. For instance, they highlighted students' progress over time, showing how practice and persistence had improved their skills (Caviola et al., 2022). Visual aids, such as progress charts or portfolios of corrected work, helped students see tangible evidence of their growth, boosting their confidence (Xiao & Sun, 2021).

Addressing Equity Through Social-Emotional Learning

The study's findings also revealed how teachers used social-emotional learning (SEL) to promote equity in the classroom. Recognizing their students' diverse experiences and needs, educators tailored their approaches to ensure that all learners felt supported and included (CASEL, 2023).

Culturally Responsive Practices. Teachers incorporate culturally relevant examples and materials into their lessons to connect with students' experiences. Participant 7 stated, "When students see their own culture or community reflected in the problems we solve, they engage more deeply" (Barbag, 2024). For instance, a teacher designing a lesson on statistics used data from local community issues, such as housing or environmental concerns, to make math feel more meaningful and applicable (Keptner et al., 2020). By celebrating diverse perspectives, teachers fostered a sense of belonging and reduced anxiety linked to feelings of exclusion or alienation (Durlak et al., 2022).

Differentiated Support. Recognizing that students experience math anxiety at different levels, teachers provided differentiated support tailored to individual needs. For example, Participant 4 described offering smaller group sessions for students who needed extra help, while others allowed students to work at their own pace using adaptive learning software (Barbag, 2024). These adaptations extended to assessments as well. Teachers implemented alternative formats, such as oral exams or project-based evaluations, to accommodate different learning styles and reduce test-related stress (Barbag, 2024).

Restorative Approaches to Discipline. Behavioral challenges often arise as manifestations of anxiety, and teachers in the study prioritized restorative practices over punitive measures. Participant 8 shared, "When a student acts out, I try to get to the root of the issue. Often, it's anxiety speaking, not defiance" (Barbag, 2024). Restorative practices included guided reflections, where students could articulate their feelings and work collaboratively with the teacher to develop solutions (Keptner et al., 2020). Circle discussions also allowed students to resolve conflicts and rebuild relationships, fostering a more compassionate and inclusive classroom culture (Durlak et al., 2022).

Outcomes and Reflections

The implementation of social-emotional learning (SEL) strategies led to significant improvements in student outcomes. Teachers observed increased participation, reduced avoidance behaviors, and enhanced academic performance among students who previously struggled with math anxiety (Caviola et al., 2022). Participant 1 shared, "One of my students went from refusing to touch a math problem to volunteering to explain her solutions to the class. That's the power of SEL" (Barbag, 2024). Students also developed greater resilience and a willingness to tackle challenges. Teachers noted that students who initially hesitated to engage in class gradually became more proactive and confident in their abilities (CASEL, 2023). Beyond individual growth, SEL strategies helped cultivate a stronger sense of community within the classroom. Students supported one another, celebrating successes and offering encouragement during setbacks. Participant 5 concluded, "When students know they're supported, they thrive—not just in math, but in everything" (Barbag, 2024).

The case study findings underscore the transformative potential of SEL in addressing math anxiety and promoting equity. Through intentional practices such as pre-test rituals, relationship-building, and culturally responsive teaching, high school math teachers created environments where students could overcome their fears and achieve their full potential (CASEL, 2023). By prioritizing SEL, educators can ensure that all learners have the tools and support they need to succeed. Furthermore, systemic support in the form of professional development and resource allocation will be crucial in sustaining these efforts (Durlak et al., 2022). The collective impact of such practices extends beyond academic achievement, fostering emotional well-being and lifelong confidence in students (Keptner et al., 2020).

Recommendations for Practice

This section provides actionable recommendations for educators and policymakers on integrating social-emotional learning (SEL) into a Multi-Tiered System of Supports (MTSS) framework (Y. Wang, 2023). The emphasis is on prioritizing trauma-informed care and anti-racist principles, highlighting how these approaches can address the multifaceted needs of diverse student populations (Stocker & Gallagher,

2019). Drawing from the findings of Barbag's dissertation, the recommendations aim to equip stakeholders with practical strategies to foster equitable and supportive educational environments (Barbag, 2024).

Develop Comprehensive Professional Development Programs. Educators must receive thorough and ongoing training in social-emotional learning (SEL), trauma-informed care, and anti-racist pedagogy. Professional development should not be limited to one-time workshops. Still, it should include continuous learning opportunities, such as case studies, simulations, and reflective practices, that allow teachers to internalize and apply these principles in their classrooms (Yuan et al., 2023). For example, workshops can guide teachers through real-world scenarios, such as supporting a student with severe math anxiety who avoids participation. Role-playing exercises can help educators practice empathy, active listening, and strategies for de-escalating stress in the moment (Zhou et al., 2020). Additionally, sessions focused on implicit bias can help teachers identify and address unintentional behaviors or language that may alienate marginalized students. Participant 3 in the study highlighted the importance of such training, stating, "Before learning about SEL, I would focus on academics first and emotions second. I realize they're interconnected, and addressing emotions can unlock academic success." By equipping educators with tools to address these interconnections, professional development programs can lay the foundation for more inclusive and supportive classrooms (Barbag, 2024).

Incorporate SEL into the Multi-Tiered System of Supports Framework. Integrating social-emotional learning (SEL) into the Multi-Tiered System of Supports (MTSS) framework ensures that students at all levels of need receive tailored support (Stocker & Gallagher, 2019). At Tier 1, universal SEL strategies should be embedded into daily classroom routines to build foundational skills in self-awareness, self-regulation, and relationship-building (CASEL, 2023). For instance, morning check-ins, class meetings, and mindfulness exercises can help students develop emotional awareness and set a positive tone for learning. Teachers in the study reported using activities like gratitude journals and peer recognition sessions to foster a sense of community and belonging. At Tier 2, small group interventions should target students exhibiting moderate levels of math anxiety. These interventions might include peer support groups where students share strategies and experiences guided by a counselor or teacher (M. Wang et al., 2020). For example, Participant 5 described a "math buddies" program where students worked in pairs to solve problems, building skills and confidence (Barbag, 2024). At Tier 3, students with severe anxiety require intensive, one-on-one support. Trauma-informed approaches, such as individualized counseling and personalized accommodations (e.g., alternative testing environments), are critical at this level (Xiao & Sun, 2021). Teachers in the study noted that involving school psychologists and using SEL-focused apps, like Calm or Headspace, helped students manage extreme anxiety symptoms effectively (Barbag, 2024).

Establish Collaborative School-Wide Practices. A school-wide approach to social-emotional learning (SEL) integration requires collaboration among teachers, administrators, counselors, and families (Durlak et al., 2022). Developing shared goals and consistent practices ensures that all stakeholders contribute to creating a supportive environment. Regular team meetings and professional learning communities (PLCs) are essential for fostering collaboration. For example, teachers might use PLCs to share successful SEL strategies, such as classroom de-escalation techniques or culturally responsive activities. Participant 7 noted, "When we share what works, we're not just helping our students—we're helping each other grow as educators" (Barbag, 2024). Administrators are key in facilitating this collaboration by providing time and resources for these meetings. Schools can also develop shared SEL goals, such as reducing the number of discipline referrals or increasing student self-reports of emotional well-being, to align efforts across all grade levels (Barbag, 2024).

Embed Trauma-Informed Practices into Classroom Management. Trauma-informed practices are essential in addressing the emotional and behavioral challenges that stem from adverse experiences (Keptner et al., 2020). Teachers should create safe, predictable classroom environments by establishing clear routines, demonstrating empathy, and using supportive interventions when addressing disruptions (Halme et al., 2022). For example, rather than using punitive discipline for a student who acts out during a math lesson, teachers can use restorative questioning to uncover the root cause of the behavior. Participant 4 shared, "When I asked a student why he stormed out of class, he told me he felt overwhelmed by a test. That conversation helped me support him better." By responding with understanding rather than punishment, teachers can foster trust and help students feel secure (Barbag, 2024). Predictable routines, such as consistent start-of-class rituals or communicated expectations, also help students with trauma feel more in control of their environment (Halme et al., 2022). Visual schedules and structured transitions are particularly effective for younger students or those with heightened anxiety (Cosso et al., 2022).

Promote Anti-Racist Pedagogy through Social-Emotional Learning. Anti-racist principles should be central to social-emotional learning (SEL) implementation, ensuring all students feel valued and represented in their learning environments (Caviola et al., 2022). Educators must actively address systemic inequities by incorporating culturally responsive teaching materials, facilitating open discussions on race and identity, and challenging stereotypes (Cribbs et al., 2021). For instance, math teachers might integrate lessons that explore historical contributions to mathematics from diverse cultures, such as using algebra problems inspired by the work of Al-Khwarizmi or geometry exercises based on African fractal designs (Caviola et al., 2022). Participant 8 noted, "When students see their culture reflected in the curriculum, they're more engaged and feel like they belong in the classroom" (Barbag, 2024). Additionally, SEL programs should empower students to recognize and resist discrimination. Activities such as role-playing scenarios about standing up to bias or discussing examples of social justice in math contexts (e.g., income inequality data analysis) can foster critical thinking and advocacy skills (Nenonene et al., 2019).

Utilize Data to Drive Decision-Making. Data collection and analysis are vital for assessing the effectiveness of social-emotional learning (SEL) interventions. Schools should use surveys, focus groups, and academic performance metrics to identify trends, monitor progress, and adjust practices accordingly (Gearty, 2023). For example, pre- and post-intervention surveys can measure changes in students' self-reported confidence levels or attitudes toward math (Halme et al., 2022). Participant 2 described using exit tickets to gauge students' emotional states at the end of each lesson, allowing for immediate adjustments to future lessons (Barbag, 2024). Regular data reviews during staff meetings can help identify patterns, such as which interventions are most effective for reducing math anxiety among specific groups of students (Gearty, 2023). This data-driven approach ensures schools remain responsive to students' evolving needs and promote continuous improvement.

Involve Families and Communities. Engaging families and communities in social-emotional learning (SEL) initiatives strengthens student support networks. Schools should provide workshops for parents on SEL strategies, encourage family participation in school events, and collaborate with community organizations to extend resources and support (CASEL, 2023). For example, a school might host a "SEL night" where parents learn mindfulness exercises they can practice at home with their children. Community partnerships, such as bringing in local mental health professionals to lead workshops or creating mentorship programs with local businesses, further extend the impact of SEL beyond the classroom (Durlak et al., 2022). Participant 6 shared, “When parents understand what we’re doing in class and can reinforce those ideas at home, the results are incredible” (Barbag, 2024). This holistic approach ensures that students receive consistent reinforcement of SEL principles both at school and at home.

SUMMARY

Integrating social-emotional learning (SEL) into a Multi-Tiered System of Supports (MTSS) framework, guided by trauma-informed and anti-racist principles, provides a powerful strategy for addressing math anxiety and fostering equitable learning environments (Teoh et al., 2022). By implementing these recommendations, educators and policymakers can create systems that support all students, particularly those from marginalized communities (Griggs et al., 2023). The findings from this study underscore the importance of intentional, inclusive practices in promoting student well-being and academic success. By committing to these approaches, schools can create environments where every student feels valued, supported, and empowered to succeed in mathematics and life (Humphrey et al., 2020).

REFERENCES

Abín, A., Núñez, J. C., Rodríguez, C., Cueli, M., García, T., & Rosário, P. (2020). Predicting mathematics achievement in secondary education: The role of cognitive, motivational, and emotional variables. *Frontiers in Psychology*, *11*(876), 1–10. DOI: 10.3389/fpsyg.2020.00876 PMID: 32528351

Barbag, L. (2024). *Teachers' perceptions of social-emotional learning strategies for high school students experiencing mathematics anxiety* (Publication No. 31558996) [Doctoral dissertation, National University]. ProQuest Dissertations & Theses Global.

Barroso, C., Ganley, C. M., McGraw, A. L., Geer, E. A., Hart, S. A., & Daucourt, M. C. (2021). A meta-analysis of the relation between math anxiety and math achievement. *Psychological Bulletin*, *147*(2), 134–168. DOI: 10.1037/bul0000307 PMID: 33119346

Biber, D. (2020). Social emotional learning for a college classroom. *College Teaching*, *68*(1), 49–52. DOI: 10.1080/87567555.2019.1709408

Bjälkebring, P. (2019). Math anxiety at the University: What forms of teaching and learning statistics in higher education can help students with math anxiety? *Frontiers in Education*, *4*, 1–4. DOI: 10.3389/feduc.2019.00030

Boaler, J. (2015). *Mathematical mindsets*. John Wiley and Sons, Inc.

Burgin, X., Coli, S., & Daniel, M. C. (2021). Exploratory study of Ecuadorian teachers' understanding of social-emotional learning: An examination of primary school teachers. *GIST: Education & Learning Research Journal*, *22*(22), 125–146. DOI: 10.26817/16925777.964

Cahyawati, D., Delima, N., & Gunarto, M. (2023). The impact of undergraduate students' mathematics anxiety and self-concept on their self-regulated learning and academic achievement. *Journal of Elementology*, *9*(1), 183–196. DOI: 10.29408/jel.v9i1.6898

Carisma, M. A. G. Q., & Fulgarinas, J. B. (2022). Community of practice in mathematics for peer tutoring program. *Globus Journal of Progressive Education*, *12*(2), 1–8. 10.DOI: 0.181.24/globus.edu.220222001

CASEL. (2023). https://casel.org/

Caviola, S., Toffalini, E., Giofrè, D., Mercader Ruiz, J., Szűcs, D., & Mammarella, I. C. (2022). Math performance and academic anxiety forms, from sociodemographic to cognitive aspects: A meta-analysis on 906,311 participants. *Educational Psychology Review*, *34*(1), 363–399. DOI: 10.1007/s10648-021-09618-5

Cheung, S. K., Zhang, J., & Wu, C. (2023). Children's performance on untimed and timed algorithmic computation tasks: The roles of executive functioning, maths test anxiety and basic maths fact fluency. *Educational Psychology*, *43*(6), 604–622. DOI: 10.1080/01443410.2023.2225804

Chiu, T. K. F., Jong, M. S., & Mok, I. A. C. (2020). Does learner expertise matter when designing emotional multimedia for learners of primary school mathematics? *Educational Technology Research and Development*, *68*(4), 2305–2320. DOI: 10.1007/s11423-020-09775-4

Collie, R. J. (2020). The development of social and emotional competence at school: An integrated model. *International Journal of Behavioral Development*, *44*(1), 76–87. DOI: 10.1177/0165025419851864

Cosso, J., Ellis, A., O'Rear, C. D., Zippert, E. L., Schmitt, S. A., & Purpura, D. J. (1511). Conceptualizing the factor structure of parents' math anxiety and associations with children's mathematics skills. *Annals of the New York Academy of Sciences*, *1511*(1), 119–132. DOI: 10.1111/nyas.14736 PMID: 35030639

Cosso, J., Ellis, A., O'Rear, C. D., Zippert, E. L., Schmitt, S. A., & Purpura, D. J. (2022).

Cribbs, J., Huang, X., & Piatek, J. K. (2021). Relations of mathematics mindset, mathematics anxiety, mathematics identity, and mathematics self-efficacy to STEM career choice: A structural equation modeling approach. *School Science and Mathematics*, *121*(5), 275–287. DOI: 10.1111/ssm.12470

Ding, Y., Zhang, C., Li, R., Ding, W., Zhu, J., Liu, W., & Chen, N. (2023). The influence of positive co-experience on teacher-student relationship: The mediating role of emotional bonding. *Acta Psychologica Sinica, 55*(5), 726–739. https://doi.org/. 2023.00726DOI: 10.3724/SP.J.1041

Dumitrescu, G. A. (2023). Social emotional learning for students and educators: A framework for pedagogy and classroom management. *Journal of Educational Studies*, *5*(1), 63–99. DOI: 10.55945/jes.v5i1.172

Durlak, J. A., Mahoney, J. L., & Boyle, A. E. (2022). What we know, and what we need to find out about universal, school-based social and emotional learning programs for children and adolescents: A review of meta-analyses and directions for future research. *Psychological Bulletin*, *148*(11-12), 765–782. DOI: 10.1037/bul0000383

Gearty, Z. (2023). *Math anxiety is real; how teachers can help calm the nerves.* Math for All. https://mathforall.edc.org/math-anxiety/#:~:text=Here%20is%20an%20example%20math, experiences%20contribute%20to%20math%20anxiety

Gonzalez-DeHass, A. R., Furner, J. M., Vásquez-Colina, M. D., & Morris, J. D. (2023). Undergraduate students' math anxiety: The role of mindset, achievement goals, and parents. *International Journal of Science and Mathematics Education*, *21*(7), 1–21. DOI: 10.1007/s10763-023-10416-4

Griggs, M. S., Rimm-Kaufman, S. E., Merritt, E. G., & Patton, C. L. (2023). The responsive classroom approach and fifth-grade students' math and science anxiety and self- efficacy. *School Psychology Quarterly*, *28*(4), 360–373. DOI: 10.1037/spq0000026 PMID: 23895315

Guo, S., & Liao, S. (2022). The role of opportunity to learn on student mathematics anxiety, problem-solving performance, and mathematics performance. *Frontiers in Psychology*, *13*, 1–15. DOI: 10.3389/fpsyg.2022.829032 PMID: 35250770

Halme, H., Trezise, K., Hannula-Sormunen, M. M., & McMullen, J. (2022). Characterizing mathematics anxiety and its relation to performance in routine and adaptive tasks. [JNC]. *Journal of Numerical Cognition*, *8*(3), 414–429. DOI: 10.5964/jnc.7675

Hosokawa, R., Matsumoto, Y., Nishida, C., Funato, K., & Mitani, A. (2023). Evaluating the effectiveness of a social and emotional learning program among preschool children in Japan: An experimental cohort study. *Child and Adolescent Psychiatry and Mental Health*, *17*(93), 1–9. DOI: 10.1186/s13034-023-00643-6 PMID: 37537603

Humphrey, N., Lendrum, A., Wigelsworth, M., & Greenberg, M. T. (2020). *Social and emotional learning*. Routledge. DOI: 10.4324/9780429444692

Kamour, M., & Altakhayneh, B. (2021). Impact of a counseling program based on social emotional learning toward reducing math anxiety in middle school students. *International Journal of Curriculum and Instruction, 13*(3), 2026–2038. https://eric.ed.gov/?id= EJ1312987

Karten, T. J. (2021). Inclusion strategies and interventions, *second edition: a user-friendly guide* to instructional strategies that create an inclusive classroom for diverse learners.

Keptner, K. M., Fitzgibbon, C., & O'Sullivan, J. (2020). Effectiveness of anxiety reduction interventions on test anxiety: A comparison of four techniques incorporating sensory modulation. *British Journal of Occupational Therapy*, *84*(5), 289–297. DOI: 10.1177/0308022620935061

Khashawneh, E., Gosling, C., & Williams, B. (2021). What impact does maths anxiety have university students? *BioMedical Central (BMC). BMC Psychology*, *9*(37), 1–9. DOI: 10.1186/s40359-021-00537-2

Khuda, I. E., & Ikram, S. (2021). An investigation into the understanding of anxiety about mathematics learning in the graduating students of karachi. *Pakistan Journal of Society. Education & Language*, *7*(1), 124–135. DOI: 10.54055/pjsel.v7i1.336

Klee, H. L., Miller, A. D., & Buehl, M. M. (2023). Mathematics anxiety, self-concept, and self- efficacy: A multidimensional scaling consideration of measures. *Journal of Experimental Education*, *91*(3), 494–516. DOI: 10.1080/00220973.2021.2024788

Lau, N. T., Hawes, Z., Tremblay, P., & Ansari, D. (2022). Disentangling the individual and contextual effects of math anxiety: A global perspective. *Proceeding of the National Academy of Sciences of the United States of America, 119*(7), 1-11. DOI: 10.1073/pnas.2115855119

Lee, J., & Kwon, K. H. (2023). Promoting sustainable learning in the post-pandemic era: Focused on the role of motivation, growth mindset, self-regulated learning, well-being, and smart device utilization. *Sustainability (Basel), 15*(17), 13247–13268. DOI: 10.3390/su151713247

Lew, K., & Hwang, S. (2019). A study on the correlation between mathematics anxiety and mathematics achievement in high school students. *The Mathematics Educator*, *58*(3), 337–346. DOI: 10.63311/mathedu.2019.58.3.337

Li, Q., Cho, H., Cosso, J., & Maeda, Y. (2021). Relations between students' mathematics anxiety and motivation to learn mathematics: A meta-analysis. *Educational Psychology Review*, *33*(3), 1017–1049. DOI: 10.1007/s10648-020-09589-z

Lichtenfeld, S., Pekrun, R., Marsh, H. W., Nett, U. E., & Reiss, K. (2023). Achievement emotions and elementary school children's academic performance: Longitudinal models of developmental ordering. *Journal of Educational Psychology*, *115*(4), 552–570. DOI: 10.1037/edu0000748

Luo, R., Zhang, A., Wang, Y., Li, H., Xu, Y., Guo, K., & Si, J. (2023). Math attitudes and math anxiety predict students' perception of teacher support in primary school, but not vice versa. *The British Journal of Educational Psychology*, *00*, e12628. DOI: 10.1111/bjep.12628 PMID: 37496095

Luttenberger, S., Wimmer, S., & Paechter, M. (2018). Spotlight on math anxiety. *Psychology Research and Behavior Management*, *11*, 311–322. DOI: 10.2147/PRBM.S141421 PMID: 30123014

Mayer, J. D., Salovey, P., & Caruso, D. R. (2008). Emotional intelligence: New ability or eclectic traits? *The American Psychologist*, *63*(6), 503–517. DOI: 10.1037/0003-066X.63.6.503 PMID: 18793038

McBride, M. R. A. (2019). The character of law: A normative critique of social-emotional learning laws. *Northwestern University Law Review*, *114*(1), 193–239. DOI: 10.2139/ssrn.3357854

McLeod, C., & Boyes, M. (2021). The effectiveness of social-emotional learning strategies and mindful breathing with biofeedback on the reduction of adolescent test anxiety. *Canadian Journal of Education*, *44*(3), 815–847. DOI: 10.53967/cje-rce.v44i3.4869

Milovanović, I. (2020). Math anxiety, math achievement and math motivation in high school students: Gender effects. *Croatian Journal of Education*, *22*(1), 175–206. DOI: 10.15516/cje.v22i1.3372

Nenonene, R. L., Gallagher, C. E., Kelly, M. K., & Collopy, R. M. B. (2019). Challenges and opportunities of infusing social, emotional, and cultural competencies into teacher preparation: One program's story. *Teacher Education Quarterly*, *46*(4), 92–115. DOI: 10.1177/0737532819881846

Obersteiner, A. (2019). Multiple pathways between affect and mathematical competence in young children—Commentary on the studies in the special issue. *Educational Studies in Mathematics*, *100*(3), 317–323. DOI: 10.1007/s10649-018-9853-0

Odak, I., Marušić, I., Bojić, J. M., Puzić, S., Bakić, H., Eliasson, N., Klicpera, B. G., Gøtzsche, K., Kozina, A., Perković, I., Roczen, N., Tomé, G., & Veldin, M. (2023). Teachers' social and emotional competencies: A lever for social and emotional learning in schools. *Sociology & Space / Sociologija i Prostor, 61*(1), 105–122. DOI: 10.5673/sip.61.1.5

Özdemir, E., & Babadoğan, M. C. (2023). Teacher candidates' training needs for social- emotional competencies. (English). *International Journal of Curriculum & Instructional* Studies (IJOCIS). *Uluslararasi Eğitim Programlari & Ögretim Çalışmaları Dergisi*, *13*(1), 95–122. DOI: 10.31704/ijocis.2023.005

Palestro, J. J., & Jameson, M. M. (2020). Math self-efficacy, not emotional self-efficacy, mediates the math anxiety-performance relationship in undergraduate students. *Cognition, Brain, Behavior: An Interdisciplinary Journal*, *24*(4), 379–394. DOI: 10.24193/cbb.2020.24.20

Panayiotou, M., Humphrey, N., & Wigelsworth, M. (2019). An empirical basis for linking social and emotional learning to academic performance. *Contemporary Educational Psychology*, *56*, 193–204. DOI: 10.1016/j.cedpsych.2019.01.009

Passolunghi, M. C., De Vita, C., & Pellizzoni, S. (2020). Math Anxiety and Math Achievement: The Effects of Emotional and Math Strategy Training. *Developmental Science*, *23*(6), e12964. Advance online publication. DOI: 10.1111/desc.12964 PMID: 32159906

Perry, D. L., & Daniels, M. L. (2016). Implementing trauma-informed practices in the school setting: a pilot study. *School Mental Health: A Multidisciplinary Research and Practice Journal, 8*(1), 177–188. DOI: 10.1007/s12310-016-9182-3

Pizzie, R. G., & Kraemer, D. J. M. (2023). Strategies for remediating the impact of math anxiety on high school math performance. *NPJ Science of Learning*, *8*(1), 1–11. DOI: 10.1038/s41539-023-00188-5 PMID: 37779133

Ramirez, G., Hooper, S. Y., Kersting, N. B., Ferguson, R., & Yeager, D. (2018). Teacher math anxiety relates to adolescent students' math achievement. *American Educational Research Association (AERA). AERA Open*, *4*(1), 2332858418756052. Advance online publication. DOI: 10.1177/2332858418756052 PMID: 31069247

Rimm-Kaufman, S., & Sandilos, L. (2020). Improving students' relationships with teachers to provide essential supports for learning. *PsycEXTRA Dataset*. DOI: 10.1037/e501992017-001

SAMHSA. (2023). https://www.samhsa.gov/

Sathasivam, R. V., & Rahim, S. S. (2021). I do better: How social and emotional learning environment enhances assessment for learning strategies in science classrooms. *Journal of International and Comparative Education*, *10*(2), 117–131. DOI: 10.14425/jice.2021.10.2.0913

Siaw, E. S., Shim, G. T., Azizan, F. L., & Shaipullah, N. M. (2021). Understanding the relationship between students' mathematics anxiety levels and mathematics performances at the foundation level. *Journal of Education and Learning*, *10*(1), 47–54. DOI: 10.5539/jel.v10n1p47

Simion, A. (2023). The impact of socio-emotional learning (SEL) on academic evaluation in higher education. *Educatia*, *21*(24), 110–117. DOI: 10.24193/ed21.2023.24.11

Skiba, R. J., Horner, R. H., Chung, C. G., Rausch, M. K., May, S. L., & Tobin, T. (2011). Race is not neutral: A national investigation of African American and Latino disproportionality in school discipline. *School Psychology Review*, *40*(1), 85–107. DOI: 10.1080/02796015.2011.12087730

Soland, J. (2019). Modeling academic achievement and self-efficacy as joint developmental processes: Evidence for education, counseling, and policy. *Journal of Applied Developmental Psychology*, *65*, 101076. Advance online publication. DOI: 10.1016/j.appdev.2019.101076

Stella, M. (2022). Network psychometrics and cognitive network science open new ways for understanding math anxiety as a complex system. *Journal of Complex Networks*, *10*(3), 1–18. DOI: 10.1093/comnet/cnac012

Stocker, S. L., & Gallagher, K. M. (2019). Alleviating anxiety and altering appraisals: Social- emotional learning in the college classroom. *College Teaching*, *67*(1), 23–35. DOI: 10.1080/87567555.2018.1515722

Suárez-Pellicioni, M., Lytle, M., Younger, J. W., & Booth, J. R. (2019). A longitudinal neuroimaging dataset on arithmetic processing in school children. *Scientific Data*, *6*(1), 190040. Advance online publication. DOI: 10.1038/sdata.2019.40 PMID: 30835258

Teoh, S. H., Mohamed, S. R., Mohd, A. H., Rasid, N. S., & Yusof, M. M. (2022). Creating engagement opportunity for math learning. *International Journal of Technology*, *13*(5), 1013. DOI: 10.14716/ijtech.v13i5.5858

Todd, C., Smothers, M., & Colson, T. (2022). Implementing SEL in the classroom: A practitioner perspective. *The Clearing House: A Journal of Educational Strategies, Issues and Ideas*, *95*(1), 18–25. DOI: 10.1080/00098655.2021.2016566

Uhl, J., Eberhardt, S., Schwartz, B., Rafaeli, E., & Lutz, W. (2023). Emotion dynamics of clients with test anxiety before and after an imagery-based treatment. *Journal of Behavior Therapy and Experimental Psychiatry*. Advance online publication. DOI: 10.1016/j.jbtep.2023.101909 PMID: 37714799

Wang, C., Li, X., & Wang, H. J. (2023). The mediating effect of math self-efficacy on the relationship between parenting style and math anxiety. *Frontiers in Psychology*, *14*, 1–10. DOI: 10.3389/fpsyg.2023.1197170 PMID: 37359871

Wang, M., Degol, J. L., Amemiya, J., Parr, A., & Guo, J. (2020). Classroom climate and children's academic and psychological well-being: A systematic review and meta-analysis. *Developmental Review*, *57*, 100912. DOI: 10.1016/j.dr.2020.100912

Wang, Y. (2023). Examining the role of sense of belonging and formative assessment in reducing the negative impact of learning anxiety in mathematics. *European Journal of Psychology of Education: A Journal of Education and Development,* 1–23. DOI: 10.1007/s10212-023-00701-9

Xiao, F., & Sun, L. (2021). Students' motivation and affection profiles and their relation to mathematics achievement, persistence, and behaviors. *Frontiers in Psychology*, *1*(11), 1–15. DOI: 10.3389/fpsyg.2020.533593 PMID: 33519570

Yang, C., Li, J., Zhao, W., Luo, L., & Shanks, D. R. (2023). Do practice tests (quizzes) reduce or provoke test anxiety? A meta-analytic review. *Educational Psychology Review*, *35*(3), 87. Advance online publication. DOI: 10.1007/s10648-023-09801-w

Yuan, Z., Tan, J., & Ye, R. (2023). A cross-national study of mathematics anxiety. *Asia-Pacific Education Researcher (Springer Science & Business Media B.V.), 32*(3), 295–306. DOI: 10.1007/s40299-022-00652-7

Zhou, D., Liu, J., & Liu, J. (2020). The effect of problematic internet use on mathematics

Chapter 8
Heart and Mind — Empathy in Action:
The Power of Social and Emotional Learning

Pamela Gary-Maple
https://orcid.org/0009-0000-8723-6427
National University, USA

ABSTRACT

This chapter, Heart and Mind — Empathy in Action: The Power of Social and Emotional Learning, explores the transformative role of Social and Emotional Learning (SEL) in fostering empathy, resilience, and meaningful human connections. It examines how SEL bridges the gap between cognitive and emotional intelligence, enabling individuals to navigate interpersonal dynamics with greater understanding and compassion. The chapter highlights key components of SEL, including self-awareness, self-regulation, social awareness, relationship skills, and responsible decision-making. Using case studies, educational initiatives, and psychological research, it illustrates how SEL enhances academic performance, mental health, and conflict resolution skills. By integrating heart and mind, SEL empowers individuals to build inclusive communities, address societal challenges, and contribute to a more empathetic and equitable world. The chapter concludes with practical strategies for implementing SEL in schools, emphasizing its potential to inspire meaningful change at both personal and societal levels.

HEART AND MIND — EMPATHY IN ACTION: THE POWER OF SOCIAL AND EMOTIONAL LEARNING

Resolving conflicts constructively and misunderstandings became opportunities for growth rather than barriers to collaboration. Most importantly, this transformation cultivated a sense of belonging—a cornerstone of any thriving community. Empathy in action is the heart of SEL. Recognizing and validating our own and others' emotions unlocks the potential for deeper connections and stronger communities.

DOI: 10.4018/979-8-3693-9020-7.ch008

Adults have just as much to gain from this journey as children do, and when we embrace SEL at all levels, we create a foundation for lasting change.

Reflecting on my journey, I have understood that SEL is not a one-time initiative or a box to check. It is a lifelong process of growth and discovery. By committing to this path, we transform ourselves and pave the way for a more compassionate and inclusive world. And that is a journey worth taking.

The Power of Social-Emotional Learning

Social and Emotional Learning is a process through which children and adults can develop key life skills (Glenn, 2022). SEL has five core competencies:

1. **Self-awareness:** Understanding and recognizing one's emotions, values, and strengths.
2. **Self-management**: Regulating emotions, setting and achieving goals, and staying resilient in facing challenges.
3. **Social awareness:** Empathizing with others, understanding diverse perspectives, and demonstrating compassion.
4. **Relationship skills:** Communication, cooperation, and conflict resolution build healthy relationships.
5. **Responsible decision-making:** Making ethical choices, considering the impact on others, and evaluating consequences.

Self-Awareness

Self-awareness is the ability to reflect on and recognize one's emotions, thoughts, and behaviors (*US* Official *News,* 2021, February 9). It involves understanding how these internal experiences influence actions, relationships, and decisions. Self-awareness also means having an accurate sense of one's strengths, weaknesses, values, and beliefs (NC DOCKS at The University of North Carolina at Greensboro,1987).

The Key Elements (Morie, 2022). It is the first step in emotional regulation and responsible decision-making because it allows individuals to understand their emotional states and how those states can impact others.

1. **Recognizing Emotions:** Being able to identify and name emotions as they arise (e.g., sadness, anger, joy, frustration).
2. **Understanding Triggers:** Knowing what situations, people, or environments provoke specific emotional responses.
3. **Identifying Values and Beliefs:** Understanding what is important to you and how those values influence your actions and decisions.
4. **Recognizing Strengths and Weaknesses:** Being aware of your abilities, talents, and areas for growth.

Why Self-awareness Matters. Self-awareness is the foundation of emotional intelligence (Craig, 2011). When individuals understand their emotions and reasons, they can handle challenging situations and make thoughtful, responsible choices. This skill is essential in school settings, where students constantly face emotional and social challenges. Students with high self-awareness can manage their emotions more effectively, avoid impulsive actions, and form stronger relationships with peers and adults. Furthermore, self-awareness helps individuals understand their values and how these values guide their decisions.

Examples of Self-awareness. When students are clear on their beliefs, they are more likely to make choices that align with their true selves, leading to greater confidence and authenticity (Gali, 2023).

- **Recognizing Emotions in the Moment:**

Scenario: Mia, a 14-year-old student, feels frustrated during a group project because one of her teammates isn't contributing. Mia feels her face becoming hot and her hands clenching. Instead of lashing out at her teammate, Mia pauses and takes a moment to recognize that she's feeling frustrated. She uses this awareness to take a deep breath and express her feelings calmly, explaining how the lack of contribution upsets her.

Explanation: In this example, Mia demonstrates self-awareness by identifying her emotions—frustration—and taking a moment to reflect before reacting. This ability to pause and reflect allows her to respond thoughtfully, which fosters better communication and conflict resolution.

- **Understanding Triggers and Managing Responses:**

Scenario: Devin, a high school student, often feels anxious before exams. He recognizes that his anxiety stems from a fear of failure and the pressure to perform well. By understanding this trigger, Devin develops coping strategies, such as deep breathing exercises, studying in smaller chunks, and talking to his teacher for clarification.

Explanation: Devin's self-awareness helps him identify his anxiety triggers (fear of failure) and enables him to manage his emotions constructively. Rather than becoming overwhelmed by stress, he uses his understanding of his emotions to take proactive steps to manage his anxiety.

- **Recognizing Personal Strengths and Weaknesses:**

Scenario: Nicole, a middle school student, has always been good at art but struggles with math. She acknowledges her artistic talent and admits that math is challenging for her. Instead of avoiding math, Nicole seeks help from a tutor and practices regularly to improve. Meanwhile, she takes pride in her art skills and continues pursuing creative projects outside school.

Explanation: Nicole demonstrates self-awareness by recognizing her strengths (art) and areas for improvement (math). This awareness helps her take a balanced approach to her challenges and fosters a growth mindset where she is willing to try to improve while celebrating her strengths.

- **Understanding Values and Beliefs:**

Scenario: Jaedyn, a 15-year-old, values honesty and integrity above all else. One day, his friend asked him to cover for him by lying about an event that happened. Jaedyn is torn but realizes that lying goes against his core values. He calmly explains to his friend that he cannot lie because it would compromise his integrity.

Explanation: Jaedyn's self-awareness allows him to recognize his core values (honesty and integrity) and make decisions that align with those beliefs. By staying true to his values, Jaedyn shows self-awareness and strengthens his ability to make ethical decisions in the face of peer pressure.

Building Self-awareness. Developing self-awareness is a process that takes time, reflection, and practice. Here are some strategies that can help individuals build greater self-awareness (DeMink-Carthew, 2020):

- **Mindfulness Practices:**

Mindfulness exercises such as meditation, deep breathing, or simply pausing to check in with one's emotions can increase awareness of thoughts and feelings. By being present in the moment, individuals can more easily recognize their emotions and the triggers behind them.

- **Journaling:**

Writing down thoughts, emotions, and experiences can provide valuable insight into one's inner world. Journaling helps individuals process and reflect on their feelings, helping them understand their emotional patterns over time.

- **Seeking Feedback:**

Asking for feedback from trusted friends, family members, or mentors can provide an external perspective on one's strengths and areas for growth. This feedback can help individuals identify blind spots and develop a more accurate self-awareness.

- **Self-reflection:**

Taking time each day to reflect on personal experiences, emotional reactions, and interactions with others can help individuals better understand themselves. Reflection helps identify areas where growth is needed and reinforces personal strengths.

Self-awareness is the cornerstone of social and emotional development. When individuals recognize and understand their emotions, values, and strengths, they are better equipped to navigate challenges, make informed decisions, and build healthy relationships. For students, cultivating self-awareness improves emotional regulation, resilience, and academic success. As part of the broader SEL framework, self-awareness allows students to take control of their emotional well-being and lay the foundation for a fulfilling and balanced life. By actively practicing and nurturing self-awareness, students can unlock their full potential and engage with the world meaningfully and positively (Moran, 2009).

Self-Management

Self-management controls one's emotions, thoughts, and behaviors in different situations. It involves staying calm and focused, especially under pressure, and making decisions that align with one's values and goals. Self-management also includes the capacity to set realistic goals, persistently work towards them, and bounce back from setbacks.

The Key Elements. It is not about suppressing emotions but managing them healthily, positively, and effectively (National Center for Education Evaluation and Regional Assistance (NCEE) (ED/IES), Regional Educational Laboratory Mid-Atlantic (ED), 2021).

1. **Emotional Regulation**: The ability to manage intense emotions such as anger, frustration, or anxiety productively.
2. **Goal Setting and Achievement:** The capacity to set realistic goals and work towards them with perseverance.
3. **Resilience:** The ability to cope with and recover from setbacks, failures, or challenges.
4. **Stress Management:** Techniques to manage stress healthily, such as mindfulness, relaxation exercises, or time management strategies.

Self-management plays a central role in achieving personal and academic success. It allows individuals to stay focused, motivated, and confident, even when facing obstacles.

Why Self-management Matters. Self-management is crucial for emotional well-being, academic success, and personal growth. When individuals can regulate their emotions, they are less likely to act impulsively or get overwhelmed by stress. Emotional regulation helps them make better decisions and maintain positive relationships with others. Setting and achieving goals is also a key aspect of self-management. When individuals break down significant goals into manageable steps and stay motivated, they are more likely to experience a sense of accomplishment and personal satisfaction. Additionally, resilience helps individuals overcome failures and setbacks, allowing them to learn and grow from challenges (Zolkoski, 2021).

Examples of Self-management (Davis, 2024). In a school setting, students who are strong in self-management can better cope with academic pressure, manage relationships with peers and teachers, and remain focused on long-term goals. Outside of school, self-management is essential for personal development and success in many areas of life, including career, health, and relationships.

- **Regulating Emotions During Stressful Situations:**

Scenario: Trinity is preparing for a big presentation in front of her class. As the presentation date draws nearer, she feels increasingly anxious and nervous. Instead of letting her anxiety take over, Trinity practices deep breathing and positive self-talk to calm herself before the presentation. She reminds herself that she has prepared and can do well.

Explanation: In this example, Trinity demonstrates emotional regulation by acknowledging her anxiety and using strategies such as deep breathing and self-talk to manage her emotions. Emotional regulation allows her to stay calm and focused, which ultimately helps her perform well in her presentation.

- **Setting and Achieving Goals:**

Scenario: Devin wants to improve his math grades. He sets a specific goal to raise his grade from a B to an A by the end of the semester. To achieve this, Devin breaks his goal into smaller steps: reviewing class notes every night, seeking extra help from his teacher, and practicing problems independently. Over time, Devin stayed disciplined in following his plan, and by the end of the semester, he successfully earned an A.

Explanation: Devin demonstrates self-management by setting a clear and realistic goal (improving his grade), creating an action plan, and following through with perseverance. His ability to stay focused on his goal despite challenges leads to success.

- **Staying Resilient in the Face of Setbacks:**

Scenario: Nicole is a soccer player who works hard to make the varsity team. After months of training, she finally gets the chance to try out. Unfortunately, Nicole doesn't make the team. Rather than giving up, Nicole takes time to reflect on her performance and identify areas where she can improve. She continued practicing and re-tried out for the team the following year and successfully made the team.

Explanation: Nicole shows resilience by not letting her initial failure define her. She uses the setback as an opportunity for growth, reflects on what she can do better, and continues to work hard towards her goal. Her perseverance and ability to recover from disappointment demonstrate strong self-management.

- **Managing Stress with Time Management:**

Scenario: Jaedyn has a busy week with multiple assignments, a sports practice, and a family event. He feels overwhelmed by the number of tasks he needs to complete. Instead of becoming stressed, Jaedyn creates a schedule that includes time for studying, practicing, and relaxing. By managing his time effectively, Jaedyn can complete his tasks without feeling overwhelmed and still have time for rest and self-care.

Explanation: Jaedyn demonstrates self-management through effective time management. By organizing his schedule and prioritizing tasks, he reduces stress and balances his responsibilities and personal well-being.

- **Coping with Disappointment and Rebounding from Failure:**

Scenario: Aundrea tries out for the lead role in the school play but is not selected. She initially feels disappointed and discouraged, but uses the experience to reflect on what she could do differently next time. She talks to her drama teacher for feedback, practices more, and resolves to try again. By maintaining a positive attitude and learning from the experience, Aundrea becomes more determined to improve.

Explanation: Aundrea demonstrates resilience and emotional regulation by accepting her disappointment and using it as motivation to improve. Her ability to stay positive and continue working towards her goal shows strong self-management.

Building Self-management. Self-management is a skill that develops over time with practice and intention. Here are some strategies that can help individuals build self-management skills (Rothstein, 2023):

- **Develop Emotional Awareness:**

Take time to reflect on emotions and triggers. Practice identifying and naming emotions when they arise. Emotional awareness helps in gaining control over emotional responses.

- **Set SMART Goals:**

Use the SMART goal-setting framework (Specific, Measurable, Achievable, Relevant, Time-bound) to create clear and actionable goals. Break significant goals into smaller steps and celebrate progress along the way.

- **Use Stress Management Techniques:**

Everyone can practice mindfulness, deep breathing, or other relaxation techniques to reduce stress in the classroom. Taking breaks and staying organized can also help manage stress in challenging situations.

- **Cultivate a Growth Mindset:**

Embrace challenges and view setbacks as opportunities to learn and grow. Encourage a mindset that values effort and persistence over perfection.

- **Build Positive Habits:**

Develop routines and habits that support emotional regulation and goal achievement, such as regular physical activity, adequate sleep, and time for relaxation.

Self-management is a critical skill that enables individuals to navigate life's challenges with resilience, focus, and emotional control. Whether regulating emotions during stressful situations, setting and achieving personal goals, or bouncing back from setbacks, self-management empowers individuals to take charge of their feelings and actions. Students and adults can experience tremendous success, improved well-being, and stronger relationships by developing these skills. With the right tools and strategies, self-management becomes a powerful force for positive change, both in and out of the classroom (Taylor, 2024).

Social Awareness

Social awareness is the ability to understand the emotions and viewpoints of others, recognize social and cultural differences, and respond with empathy and compassion. It is an essential skill for fostering healthy relationships, improving communication, and creating inclusive environments. Social awareness involves several key elements:

1. **Empathy:** The ability to understand and share another person's feelings, putting oneself in their shoes.
2. **Perspective-Taking:** The ability to see situations from different viewpoints, especially those different from one's own.
3. **Appreciating Diversity:** Understanding and respecting the differences in people's backgrounds, cultures, and experiences.
4. **Demonstrating Compassion:** Acting with kindness and concern for the well-being of others.

Why Social Awareness Matters. Being socially aware enables individuals to engage with others meaningfully, respecting their emotions, experiences, and backgrounds. It helps create a sense of belonging, reduces conflicts, and promotes cooperation. Social awareness is fundamental for building positive relationships and fostering community. When individuals know others' emotions and perspectives, they are better equipped to communicate effectively and respond in ways that show care and understanding. In school settings, students with strong social awareness can collaborate more effectively, resolve conflicts peacefully, and create a more inclusive and supportive learning environment (Kim, 2011). Additionally, social awareness plays a crucial role in reducing prejudice and discrimination. When individuals can understand and appreciate the differences in others, they are more likely to value diversity and promote inclusivity.

Examples of Social Awareness (Makoelle, 2016). In today's diverse world, social awareness is essential for fostering empathy, tolerance, and mutual respect (Rost, 2021).

- **Empathizing with a Peer's Struggles:**

Scenario: Sonya notices that her friend, Julia, has recently been quiet and withdrawn in class. Instead of ignoring it or assuming Julia is shy, Sonya asks her gently if everything is okay. Julia opens about a difficult situation at home, and Sonya listens attentively, offering support and comfort.

Explanation: Sonya demonstrates social awareness by noticing the changes in her friend's behavior and empathizing with her feelings. She shows compassion and understanding by offering a listening ear, creating a safe space for Julia to express herself.

- **Understanding Diverse Perspectives in a Group Discussion:**

Scenario: Two students have very different opinions on a controversial topic during a class debate. Instead of immediately dismissing the opposing viewpoint, Lucas listens carefully to his classmate's arguments and acknowledges the validity of their perspective. He then respectfully shares his thoughts, fostering a constructive dialogue.

Explanation: Lucas exhibits social awareness by practicing perspective-taking. He understands that people may have different experiences and viewpoints, and he responds with respect and empathy. Social awareness creates an environment where diverse opinions are valued and discussed thoughtfully.

- **Appreciating Cultural Differences in a Multicultural Classroom:**

Scenario: In a classroom with students from various cultural backgrounds, Ms. Lee tries to learn about and celebrate the different traditions, holidays, and customs of her students. She encourages them to share their cultural practices and uses this information to create a more inclusive classroom environment.

Explanation: Ms. Lee demonstrates social awareness by appreciating the diversity in her classroom and promoting an inclusive environment where every student's background is respected. By valuing cultural differences, she helps her students feel seen and admired.

- **Demonstrating Compassion During a Crisis:**

Scenario: After a classmate loses a loved one, Liam notices that many of his peers are unsure how to offer support. He writes a heartfelt note of sympathy, encouraging others to reach out with kind words or gestures. He organizes a group to bring flowers and a card to the grieving student.

Explanation: Liam demonstrates social awareness by recognizing the emotional needs of his classmates and showing compassion through his actions. He encourages others to support their peer, creating a caring and empathetic atmosphere.

- **Responding to Bullying with Empathy:**

Scenario: Mia witnesses a classmate's mistreatment by others for their appearance. Instead of laughing along or ignoring the situation, Mia approaches the student who is being bullied and offers kind words of encouragement. She then reports the bullying to a teacher, advocating for her classmate's well-being.

Explanation: Mia demonstrates social awareness by recognizing the hurt caused by the bullying and empathizing with her classmate's feelings. She helps create a more positive and inclusive environment by acting and showing support.

Building Social Awareness. Social awareness is a skill that develops through practice and intentional reflection. Here are some strategies to build social awareness (Sandilos, 2020):

- **Engage in Active Listening:**

Practice listening attentively to others without interrupting. Focus on understanding their feelings and viewpoints. Ask open-ended questions to encourage deeper conversations and to show genuine interest in their experiences.

- **Practice Perspective-Taking:**

Put yourself in others' shoes and consider how they might feel in different situations. Consider how their background, culture, and personal experiences influence their perspectives. Practice helps increase understanding and empathy.

- **Learn About Different Cultures and Communities:**

Educate yourself about diverse cultures, traditions, and worldviews. Everyone can achieve cultural awareness through books, media, or conversations with people from different backgrounds. Exposure to diverse perspectives helps broaden one's understanding and appreciation of differences.

- **Engage in Acts of Kindness and Compassion:**

Look for opportunities to support others, whether it's offering a helping hand, listening to someone in need, or advocating for those who are marginalized. Small acts of kindness can make a big difference in creating a compassionate community.

- **Reflect on Your Own Biases and Prejudices:**

Take time to reflect on any biases and consider how they might impact your interactions with others. Awareness of your assumptions can help you approach others more openly and clearly.

- **Foster Inclusive Environments:**

Whether in the classroom, workplace, or community, actively work to create spaces where everyone feels included and valued. Encourage diverse perspectives and promote respectful dialogue.

Social awareness is at the heart of creating positive, inclusive, compassionate communities. Individuals can build stronger, more supportive relationships by developing the ability to empathize with others, understand diverse perspectives, and demonstrate compassion. Social awareness helps reduce conflict, fosters cooperation, and promotes mutual respect in schools, workplaces, and communities. As part of the broader Social and Emotional Learning framework, social awareness allows individuals to connect more deeply with others and contribute to a more understanding and empathetic world. By practicing social awareness, we can build a culture of kindness, respect, and inclusion—one interaction at a time (Keedy, 2022).

Relationship Skills

Relationship skills are the abilities that enable individuals to interact positively with others. These skills include effective communication, cooperation, empathy, and conflict resolution. They are vital for creating and maintaining healthy relationships with family, friends, classmates, colleagues, and peers. The key elements of relationship skills are (Mina, 2024):

1. **Effective Communication:** The ability to express thoughts, feelings, and ideas clearly and listen attentively to others.
2. **Cooperation:** The ability to work collaboratively, respect different viewpoints, and find common ground.
3. **Conflict Resolution:** The ability to address disagreements or misunderstandings respectfully and productively.
4. **Empathy and Understanding:** The ability to recognize and respond to the emotions and perspectives of others.
5. **Respect for Boundaries:** The ability to respect personal boundaries and understand the limits and needs of others.

Why Relationship Skills Matter. Developing strong relationship skills is essential for building trust, reducing misunderstandings, and creating positive, supportive environments in both personal and professional settings. Relationship skills are critical for fostering positive social interactions and building meaningful connections. When individuals communicate well, cooperate with others, and handle conflicts respectfully, they create an atmosphere of mutual trust and respect. Relationship skills make collaborating, solving problems, and achieving common goals easier. Strong relationship skills are linked to greater emotional intelligence, allowing individuals to navigate social situations with sensitivity and care. Students with strong relationship skills are likelier to work well in teams, communicate effectively with teachers and peers, and positively handle challenges (Bluth, 2018).

Examples of Relationship Skills. These skills are key to forming lasting relationships, resolving conflicts peacefully, and creating a sense of community in personal and professional settings. Relationship skills also play a crucial role in reducing bullying, promoting inclusivity, and building supportive environments.

- **Effective Communication in a Group Project:**

Scenario: Mia and her classmates are working together on a group project. At the beginning of the project, Mia ensures that everyone has a chance to express their ideas and opinions. She listens attentively to her teammates and encourages open dialogue. When disagreements arise, Mia calmly communicates her thoughts and actively listens to others to find a solution that works for everyone.

Explanation: Mia demonstrates effective communication by fostering an environment where everyone feels heard and respected. Her ability to express herself clearly and listen to others helps the group collaborate effectively and resolve any issues.

- **Cooperating During a Sports Team Practice:**

Scenario: Tyler and his teammates work on a complex play during soccer practice. Tyler notices that one of his teammates is struggling to understand the drill. Instead of getting frustrated, Tyler takes the time to explain the steps so his teammates can understand. He also encourages others to help. As a result, the team can work together and complete the drill.

Explanation: Tyler demonstrates cooperation by supporting his teammate and encouraging a collaborative approach to problem-solving. His willingness to assist others helps the team function smoothly and fosters a sense of teamwork and mutual support.

- **Resolving a Conflict with a Friend:**

Scenario: Sonya and her friend Olivia have been arguing over a misunderstanding. Sonya feels hurt by something Olivia said, but instead of letting the tension grow, she decides to have an open conversation. Sonya expresses her feelings calmly: "I felt hurt when you said that, and I want us to work through it." Olivia listens and apologizes, and the two friends work together to understand each other's perspectives and find a solution.

Explanation: Sonya demonstrates conflict resolution by respectfully approaching the situation and being willing to communicate. She uses "I" statements to express her feelings without blaming Olivia, which helps reduce defensiveness and opens the door for a constructive conversation. Both friends take responsibility for their emotions, and they find a way to repair their relationship.

- **Supporting a Classmate in Need:**

Scenario: Ryan notices that his classmate, Anna, has been feeling down lately. He asks her if she's okay and listens to her concerns. After hearing that Anna is struggling with the workload, Ryan offers to study with her and helps her organize her assignments. Anna feels relieved and grateful for Ryan's support, and the two continue to help each other in the future.

Explanation: Ryan demonstrates empathy and support by recognizing his classmate's struggles and helping. He helps build a stronger relationship based on trust and mutual care by showing kindness and understanding.

- **Navigating Disagreements in a Classroom Discussion:**

Scenario: Two students disagree on an important issue during a class discussion on a controversial topic. Instead of escalating the argument, they calmly explain their viewpoints and ask each other questions to understand their perspectives better. The teacher facilitates the conversation by encouraging respectful listening and helping the students find common ground.

Explanation: In this scenario, the students demonstrate conflict resolution and communication skills by maintaining respect during the disagreement. They listen to each other's points of view, ask clarifying questions, and remain open-minded, allowing for a productive and respectful exchange of ideas.

Building Relationship Skills. Building relationship skills takes time and practice, but it is a process that everyone can develop with intentional effort. Here are some strategies for strengthening relationship skills:

1. Practice Active Listening:

Make an effort to listen attentively to others without interrupting. Focus on understanding their feelings and viewpoints. Respond with empathy by acknowledging their emotions and offering thoughtful feedback.

2. Use "I" Statements:

When discussing sensitive topics or addressing conflicts, use "I" statements to express your feelings and needs without blaming others. For example, "I feel upset when…" instead of "You always…"

3. Be Open to Feedback:

Welcome constructive feedback from others and view it as an opportunity to grow. Accepting input with an open mind shows respect for the opinions and perspectives of others.

4. Build Empathy:

Take the time to consider how others might feel in different situations—imagining yourself in someone else's shoes. Building empathy helps you better understand their emotions and respond with care.

5. Learn Conflict Resolution Techniques:

Develop strategies for resolving conflicts peacefully, such as staying calm, using respectful language, finding common ground, and seeking win-win solutions. Practice compromising and finding mutually beneficial outcomes.

6. Foster Teamwork:

Participate in group activities that require cooperation and collaboration. Whether it's a team project or a sports activity, working with others helps build cooperation and communication skills.

Relationship skills are essential for creating positive, supportive environments where people can connect, collaborate, and resolve conflicts healthily. Effective communication, cooperation, and conflict resolution allow individuals to build and maintain strong relationships, whether at school, work, or in their personal lives. Developing these skills enhances our emotional intelligence and creates a culture of respect, kindness, and understanding (Calderin, 2005). In Social and Emotional Learning, relationship skills enable individuals to connect with others, foster empathy, and build meaningful connections that support personal growth and well-being.

Responsible Decision-Making Skills

Daily decisions can impact ourselves, others, and the world around us. How we make these decisions is deeply influenced by our values, understanding of others, and the ability to consider the consequences of our actions. Responsible decision-making is a cornerstone of Social and Emotional Learning (SEL), allowing individuals to make thoughtful, ethical choices that promote well-being and positive outcomes (Huck, 2023). Responsible decision-making involves making choices that are ethical, respectful, and mindful of their consequences. It means considering how our actions affect ourselves, others, and our environment.

Key Components. This SEL competency requires individuals to reflect on the potential outcomes of their decisions, weigh the pros and cons, and choose the course of action that aligns with their values and promotes the well-being of everyone involved.

1. **Ethical Decision-Making:** The ability to make choices based on ethical principles, such as honesty, fairness, and respect for others.
2. **Evaluating Consequences:** The ability to anticipate and reflect on the short-term and long-term consequences of positive and negative decisions.
3. Considering the Impact on Others: Understanding how one's decisions affect the emotions, well-being, and needs of others.
4. **Choosing the Best Solution:** Weigh different options and select the one that aligns with personal values and benefits all parties involved.
5. **Self-Reflection:** The ability to evaluate past decisions and learn from experiences to improve future choices.

Responsible decision-making is vital for leading a fulfilling and meaningful life. Individuals make thoughtful choices and contribute to a more just, supportive, and harmonious community (Sawchuck, 2021). Making responsible decisions is foundational to personal growth and social harmony. It enables individuals to navigate challenges, solve problems, and build strong relationships based on mutual respect and trust. Responsible decision-making is crucial for success in school, work, and relationships, as it helps individuals avoid harmful consequences and make choices that reflect their values and priorities. In schools, responsible decision-making empowers students to make choices that promote their academic success, personal well-being, and positive relationships with peers and teachers. Responsible decision-making fosters accountability, trust, and cooperation in personal and professional settings.

Examples of Responsible Decision-Making. It helps individuals avoid impulsive decisions that may lead to regret and instead choose paths that reflect their best interests and the needs of others (Price, 2022).

- **Choosing to Speak Up Against Bullying:**

Scenario: During lunch, Emma witnesses a group of students teasing and bullying a classmate. She knows that staying silent would make her complicit, but she is nervous about speaking up. After reflecting on the impact of bullying, Emma decides to approach a teacher and report the incident. She also reaches out to the bullied student to offer support.

Explanation: Emma demonstrates responsible decision-making by considering the ethical choice—standing up for what is right—and evaluating the consequences of her actions. By speaking up, she helps create a safer and more respectful school environment.

- **Deciding to Study Instead of Going to a Party:**

Scenario: Tyler gets invited to a party but has an important test the next day. He wants to go and have fun, but he knows that skipping study time could negatively affect his grades. After weighing the consequences, Tyler decides to stay home and study for the test, understanding that doing well is essential for his long-term academic success.

Explanation: Tyler demonstrates responsible decision-making by evaluating the consequences of his actions. He understands that while attending the party may provide immediate enjoyment, prioritizing his education will lead to better long-term outcomes. This decision reflects his responsibility toward his academic goals.

- **Helping a Friend Who Is Struggling Emotionally:**

Scenario: Mia notices that her friend Nicole has been quiet and withdrawn lately. Instead of ignoring the signs, Mia talks to Nicole and asks if everything is okay. Nicole opens up about feeling overwhelmed with schoolwork and personal issues. Mia listens, offers emotional support, and helps Nicole find resources like tutoring or counseling.

Explanation: Mia demonstrates responsible decision-making by considering the emotional needs of her friend and acting in a way that supports Nicole's well-being. By offering help, Mia reflects on the impact of her actions and chooses to be a compassionate and supportive friend.

- **Making an Honest Choice When Facing Temptation:**

Scenario: Kevin finds a wallet with money and an ID inside on the ground at school. He is tempted to keep the cash but knows it is not the right thing to do. After reflecting on the consequences of his actions, he decides to turn the wallet into the lost and found office, trusting that someone will return it to its rightful owner.

Explanation: Kevin demonstrates ethical decision-making by considering the impact of his actions on the wallet's owner and his integrity. His decision reflects honesty and fairness, reinforcing the value of doing what is right, even when no one is watching.

- **Resolving a Conflict with a Classmate:**

Scenario: Trinity and her classmate David disagree about approaching a group project. Rather than letting the conflict escalate, Trinity takes the time to listen to David's perspective and calmly explains her point of view. They find a compromise that respects both ideas and moves the project forward.

Explanation: Trinity demonstrates responsible decision-making by choosing a peaceful approach to resolving the conflict. She reflects on the impact of the disagreement and seeks a solution that respects both her and David's viewpoints, fostering cooperation and mutual respect.

- **Choosing to Conserve Resources for the Environment:**

Scenario: In class, the teacher presents a project on environmental sustainability. Jaedyn is encouraged to consider the impact of his actions on the environment. He decides to take small steps like reducing waste, recycling, and conserving energy at home, understanding that even small actions can significantly impact the planet.

Explanation: Jaedyn demonstrates responsible decision-making by considering the broader consequences of his actions and choosing to contribute to the environment's well-being. His decisions reflect his commitment to making ethical choices for the greater good.

Building Responsible Decision-Making Skills. Responsible decision-making is a skill that develops over time through practice and reflection. Here are some strategies to strengthen responsible decision-making:

1. **Pause and Reflect:** Before planning, take a moment to pause and consider the possible outcomes. Ask yourself questions like: What are the potential consequences of this decision? How might this choice impact others? Does this decision align with my values?
2. **Weigh the Pros and Cons:** Evaluate each option's potential benefits and risks. Consider how each choice will affect your well-being and the well-being of others. It helps you make an informed and balanced decision.
3. **Consider the Ethical Implications:** Ask yourself if your decision is fair, honest, and respectful. Consider whether your actions align with your core values and principles, such as kindness, fairness, and responsibility.
4. **Seek Advice from Trusted Sources:** When faced with a difficult decision, seek guidance from people you trust, such as family members, friends, or mentors. They can offer valuable perspectives and help you make more informed choices.
5. **Learn from Past Decisions:** Reflect on past decisions, both positive and negative, and consider what you learned from them. This self-reflection helps you make better decisions in the future and avoid repeating mistakes.
6. **Think Long-Term:** Consider the long-term consequences of your decisions, not just the immediate outcomes. Sometimes, making a responsible choice means sacrificing short-term pleasure for long-term benefit.

Responsible decision-making is an essential skill for leading a successful and meaningful life. By making ethical choices, considering the impact on others, and evaluating the consequences of our actions, we contribute to our well-being and that of those around us. In the context of Social and Emotional Learning, responsible decision-making empowers individuals to make thoughtful choices that reflect their values and promote positive outcomes. Whether faced with everyday decisions or more challenging situations, responsible decision-making enables us to navigate life with integrity, empathy, and wisdom.

PROFESSIONAL DEVELOPMENT OPPORTUNITIES FOR EDUCATORS IN SEL

For educators to effectively teach and model SEL, they need access to professional development (PD) opportunities that enhance their understanding and application of SEL principles. These opportunities equip teachers with the tools and strategies to create emotionally intelligent classrooms and support the diverse needs of their students. Below are some of the key professional development avenues available for educators (Baskin, 2022):

1. **Workshops and Seminars**

Many organizations and school districts offer workshops and seminars focusing on SEL. These sessions provide educators with foundational knowledge, practical strategies, and opportunities to practice SEL techniques. Topics often include emotional regulation, building empathy, managing classroom dynamics, and fostering inclusive learning environments.

2. **Online Courses and Certifications**

Numerous online platforms offer SEL-specific courses and certifications, allowing educators to learn independently. Platforms like Coursera, edX, and professional education providers provide comprehensive programs covering SEL frameworks, neuroscience insights, and practical applications. Certification programs, such as those from CASEL (Collaborative for Academic, Social, and Emotional Learning), provide educators with recognized credentials in SEL.

3. **In-School Professional Development Sessions**

Many schools integrate SEL training into their PD schedules. These sessions often focus on applying SEL principles within the school's unique context. Educators collaborate with colleagues to develop consistent strategies for promoting SEL across grade levels and subjects. Having dedicated SEL coaches or trainers can further enhance these sessions.

4. **Conferences and Summits**

Educational conferences and SEL summits bring together experts, researchers, and practitioners to share the latest developments in SEL. Events like the National SEL Conference provide a platform for educators to learn from case studies, participate in hands-on workshops, and network with peers passionate about SEL.

5. **Mentorship and Peer Collaboration**

Informal professional development can be just as impactful. Pairing educators with mentors experienced in SEL or fostering peer collaboration groups allows for the exchange of ideas, challenges, and best practices. Regular team discussions and reflective exercises can deepen understanding and enhance implementation.

6. **Resources from SEL Organizations**

Organizations like CASEL, Second Step, and the Greater Good Science Center provide educators with free and paid resources. These include lesson plans, research articles, webinars, and toolkits to support SEL integration. Leveraging these materials helps educators stay informed about effective practices and emerging trends.

7. **Trauma-Informed Training**

Given the increasing prevalence of trauma among students, many professional development programs incorporate trauma-informed practices into SEL training. These programs help educators recognize and respond to the effects of trauma, creating safer and more supportive learning environments.

8. **Mindfulness and Self-Care Programs**

Educators' ability to teach SEL effectively depends on their emotional well-being. Professional development opportunities focusing on mindfulness, stress management, and self-care provide educators with the tools to manage their emotions and model healthy student behaviors.

Engaging in professional development opportunities enhances educators' SEL expertise and empowers them to create more empathetic and inclusive classrooms (Cavazos, 2024). Educators equipped with SEL knowledge can:

- Better understand and address the emotional needs of their students.
- Foster more substantial relationships with students, colleagues, and parents.
- Implement evidence-based strategies to promote emotional intelligence and resilience.

By investing in their growth, educators set a powerful example for their students and contribute to a school culture prioritizing emotional and social well-being. Professional development in SEL is beneficial and necessary for creating meaningful educational change (Morgan, 2022).

STUDENTS ARE STRUGGLING WITH SEL

Students today face unique challenges that make it difficult for them to engage with SEL fully. The pressures of academic achievement, social dynamics, and digital interactions often overshadow the time and space needed to develop emotional intelligence. Despite integrating SEL into school curricula, many students struggle to apply these skills daily. One significant challenge students face is a lack of emotional awareness. Many young people have difficulty identifying and naming their emotions, let alone understanding how they influence their behavior. Difficulty with emotions can result in impulsive reactions, misunderstandings, and difficulty forming meaningful relationships. The rapid pace of modern life and the distractions of technology often leave little room for introspection, further compounding the issue. Another barrier is the stigma associated with expressing emotions. In many peer groups, showing vulnerability or discussing feelings can be seen as a sign of weakness. This cultural norm discourages students from seeking help or opening up about their struggles, leading to a buildup of unresolved emotions and potential conflicts.

Additionally, students often lack consistent role models for SEL. At the same time, educators and caregivers strive to demonstrate emotional intelligence, but societal pressures undermine efforts, or the absence of SEL in their upbringing. Without clear examples to emulate, students may struggle to translate abstract SEL concepts into real-world applications. The rise of social media and digital communication presents another layer of difficulty. Online interactions can lack the nuance of face-to-face conversations, making it harder for students to practice empathy and interpret emotional cues. Cyberbullying and the pressure to maintain a "perfect" online persona exacerbate feelings of anxiety and inadequacy, further hindering SEL development (Vestal, 2024). Students also face external stressors, such as family dynamics, financial instability, or community violence, which can overshadow their ability to focus on SEL. These challenges often manifest in behaviors mislabeled as defiance or disengagement rather than being recognized as signs of emotional distress.

Addressing Student Struggles with SEL

Schools must take a holistic approach to SEL to support students in overcoming these struggles. First, creating safe and inclusive environments where students feel valued and heard is essential. Encouraging open dialogue about emotions and normalizing vulnerability can help dismantle the stigma around emotional expression. Educators can also incorporate mindfulness practices and reflective exercises into the daily routine, giving students the tools to identify and manage their emotions. Role-playing activities, collaborative projects, and guided discussions allow students to practice empathy and build stronger interpersonal skills. Providing students with relatable role models who demonstrate emotional intelligence is equally important. Whether through mentorship programs, peer-led initiatives, or teacher-led examples, seeing SEL in action helps students understand its value and applicability. Lastly, addressing the external factors that impact students' emotional well-being requires a collaborative effort between schools, families, and communities. Offering resources such as counseling services, after-school programs, and workshops for parents can create a support network that reinforces SEL development at every level.

The Broader Impact

When students overcome their struggles with SEL, the benefits extend beyond the individual. Classrooms become more harmonious, peer relationships improve, and academic performance rises. Moreover, students equipped with emotional intelligence are better prepared to navigate the complexities of adulthood, contributing to healthier and more empathetic communities. Reflecting on these challenges and solutions, it becomes clear that SEL is not just a curriculum, but a vital skill set for life. By addressing students' struggles with empathy and intentionality, we can help them unlock their potential and pave the way for a more compassionate future. To help students build and strengthen their SEL skills, educators can implement various engaging activities tailored to different age groups and learning styles.

Below are some practical activities to support students in developing emotional intelligence, empathy, and interpersonal skills.

1. **Emotion Journaling**

Objective: Develop self-awareness and emotional regulation.

Provide students with journals to record their daily emotions and the situations that triggered them. Please encourage them to describe how they responded and what strategies they used to manage their feelings. Periodically, have students reflect on patterns and discuss positive coping mechanisms in small groups.

2. **Circle Time Discussions**

Objective: Foster open communication and empathy.

Begin or end the day with a circle time where students can share their thoughts and feelings. Use prompts such as "What made you feel happy today?" or "How did you show kindness this week?" Emphasize active listening and respect for others' perspectives.

3. **Role-Playing Scenarios**

Objective: Enhance empathy and problem-solving skills.

Create scenarios based on shared social challenges, such as resolving conflicts or comforting a friend. Have students act out these situations and discuss how different approaches can lead to positive outcomes. Rotate roles to allow students to experience multiple perspectives.

4. **Gratitude Tree**

Objective: Cultivate a positive mindset and social awareness.

Set up a classroom "gratitude tree" where students can write what they are thankful for on paper leaves. Encourage students to add leaves regularly and reflect on the contributions of others. Share the completed tree with the school community as a symbol of positivity.

5. **Mindfulness Exercises**

Objective: Improve focus and stress management.

Guide students through short mindfulness activities like deep breathing, body scans, or visualization exercises. Incorporate mindfulness breaks during transitions to help students refocus. Use apps or videos to introduce new techniques engagingly.

6. **Collaborative Projects**

Objective: Promote teamwork and relationship skills.

Assign group projects that require students to work together toward a common goal. Emphasize the importance of communication, compromise, and celebrating each team member's contributions. Reflect on what went well and how the group could improve its collaboration.

7. **Kindness Challenge**

Objective: Encourage acts of kindness and build a positive classroom culture.

Create a kindness calendar with daily or weekly challenges, such as “compliment a classmate” or “help someone in need.” Celebrate acts of kindness by sharing stories during class or creating a “kindness wall.” Discuss how small gestures can have a significant impact on others.

8. **Emotional Check-Ins**

Objective: Build emotional awareness and self-expression.

Use visual tools like mood meters or emoji charts for students to indicate their feelings. Proactively check in with a student individually to discuss their emotions and provide support when needed. Please encourage students to share strategies that help them manage their feelings.

9. **Community Building Activities**

Objective: Strengthen relationships and inclusivity.

Organize activities such as “Two Truths and a Lie” or “Find someone who...” to help students learn more about each other. Plan classroom traditions or rituals celebrating diversity and building a sense of belonging. Incorporate team-building games that emphasize cooperation and trust.

10. **Digital Citizenship Lessons**

Objective: Teach empathy and respect in online interactions.

Discuss the importance of kindness and respect in digital communication. Role-play scenarios involving cyberbullying or misunderstandings online, and brainstorm positive responses. Create classroom guidelines for responsible technology use.

These activities are most effective when integrated consistently into the school day. SEL is not a one-time lesson but a continuous practice that evolves with students' needs. By providing varied growth opportunities, educators can help students internalize and apply SEL skills in all areas of their lives. Through intentional and engaging activities, educators empower students to navigate their emotions, build meaningful relationships, and contribute to a more empathetic community. The journey of SEL is transformative, fostering growth that extends far beyond the classroom.

Improve SEL for Struggling Students

Educators play a crucial role in shaping students' SEL development. Teachers can help students overcome challenges and build essential emotional and social skills by fostering a supportive and empathetic environment. Below are some strategies educators can use to enhance SEL for struggling students (Romero, 2016). When students feel seen, valued, and understood, they are more likely to engage with

SEL practices. Teachers can establish trust by actively listening, showing genuine interest in students' lives, and creating a safe space for open communication. Simple gestures such as greeting students by name and acknowledging their efforts can make a significant difference in building rapport (Yuan, 2021).

- **Integrate SEL into Everyday Learning**

SEL isn't a standalone lesson or activity but seamlessly woven into daily interactions and academic content. For example, teachers can incorporate group projects that promote collaboration and conflict resolution or use literature and historical events to discuss empathy and perspective-taking. Educators demonstrate its relevance to real-life situations by embedding SEL into various subjects.

- **Model Emotional Intelligence**

Students learn best through observation, and teachers are powerful role models for SEL. By demonstrating self-awareness, empathy, and effective communication, educators can inspire students to emulate these behaviors. Sharing personal stories of overcoming challenges or navigating emotions can make SEL concepts more relatable and accessible.

- **Provide Opportunities for Reflection**

Reflection is a critical component of SEL. Educators can encourage students to pause and think about their emotions, actions, and interactions. Journaling, group discussions, and guided mindfulness exercises effectively foster self-awareness and emotional regulation. These practices help students recognize patterns in their behavior and identify areas for growth.

- **Differentiate SEL Approaches**

Every student has unique needs and learning styles; SEL is no exception. Teachers can adapt their strategies to accommodate diverse learners by offering a variety of activities and supports. For instance, visual learners might benefit from emotion charts, while kinesthetic learners may engage more with role-playing exercises. Providing choices allows students to take ownership of their SEL journey.

- **Create Inclusive and Culturally Responsive Practices**

Cultural background and individual experiences significantly influence how students perceive and engage with SEL. Educators can improve SEL outcomes by acknowledging and valuing students' diverse perspectives. Incorporating culturally relevant materials, celebrating differences, and addressing biases within the classroom create an inclusive environment where all students feel respected and understood.

- **Partner with Families and Communities**

SEL is most effective when reinforced across multiple contexts. Educators can collaborate with families and community organizations to support students' emotional development. Hosting workshops, sharing resources, and maintaining open lines of communication with parents help create a unified approach to SEL. Community programs and mentors can also provide additional support for struggling students.

- **Address Barriers to SEL**

Some students face external challenges, such as trauma, poverty, or unstable home environments, that hinder their ability to engage with SEL. Educators can advocate for resources, such as school counselors or social workers, to address these barriers. Additionally, implementing trauma-informed practices ensures that the classroom remains a safe and supportive space for all learners.

When educators actively support struggling students in their SEL journey, the benefits ripple throughout the school community. Improved emotional intelligence leads to better relationships, reduced behavioral issues, and enhanced academic performance. Moreover, students equipped with SEL skills are more resilient and better prepared to navigate the complexities of life (Victorson, 2021). By embracing these strategies, educators can help their students unlock the full potential of SEL, fostering a more compassionate and connected learning environment. This effort transforms individual lives and lays the groundwork for a more empathetic and inclusive society. Parents are vital to a child's SEL journey, as the home environment significantly influences emotional development (Aziznejad, 2019). Educators can create a more cohesive and supportive network for struggling students by involving parents in SEL initiatives. Here are some strategies to foster this collaboration:

1. **Educate Parents About SEL**

Many parents may be unfamiliar with SEL or its benefits. Hosting informational sessions or workshops can help parents understand the core principles of SEL and how it supports their child's emotional and academic growth. Providing examples of SEL activities and their real-life applications can demystify the process and encourage parental involvement.

2. **Create Open Lines of Communication**

Effective communication is the cornerstone of involving parents in SEL. Regular updates through newsletters, emails, or parent-teacher conferences can keep parents informed about SEL goals, classroom activities, and their child's progress. Encouraging parents to share insights about their child's behavior and emotional needs at home fosters a two-way dialogue that benefits the student.

3. **Offer Practical SEL Strategies for Home**

Providing parents with practical tools and activities to reinforce SEL at home ensures consistency across environments. Simple strategies such as discussing emotions during family meals, practicing mindfulness, or role-playing social scenarios can help parents support their child's emotional growth. Educators can also share resources that align with SEL objectives, such as books, apps, or games.

4. **Involve Parents in School-Based Activities**

Inviting parents to participate in school-based SEL activities strengthens their connection to the program. Events such as family SEL nights, volunteer opportunities in SEL lessons, or collaborative projects between students and parents foster a sense of community and shared responsibility. These experiences also provide parents with firsthand exposure to SEL practices.

5. **Address Parental Concerns and Challenges**

Some parents may hesitate to engage with SEL due to misconceptions, cultural differences, or personal struggles with emotional awareness. Educators can address these concerns by creating a nonjudgmental space for parents to express their views and providing tailored support. Offering workshops on stress management or emotional regulation for parents can also build their confidence in modeling SEL behaviors.

6. **Recognize and Celebrate progress**

Acknowledging parents' efforts and their child's progress reinforces the importance of their involvement. Sharing positive updates, celebrating milestones, or expressing gratitude for parental contributions fosters a sense of partnership. Recognizing even small victories can motivate parents to stay engaged in the SEL journey.

7. **Collaborate with Community Resources**

Schools can partner with community organizations to provide additional support for families. Resources such as counseling services, parenting classes, or SEL-focused community events can help parents navigate challenges and enhance their ability to support their child's emotional development. These partnerships create a more comprehensive support system for struggling students.

When educators and parents work together to support SEL, the impact on students is profound. Consistent reinforcement of SEL skills at home and school creates a stable foundation for emotional growth. Students feel more supported and understood, leading to improved behavior, stronger relationships, and tremendous academic success. Involving parents in SEL is not just about equipping them with tools; it's about building a partnership that prioritizes the child's well-being. By fostering collaboration and empathy, educators and parents can create a unified approach to SEL that empowers students to thrive in and out of the classroom.

Training Parents to Support SEL. Here are some practical professional development activities that can equip parents with the tools they need to support their students' social and emotional growth (PR NEWSWIRE, 2021):

1. SEL 101: Introduction to Social and Emotional Learning

Objective: To introduce parents to the concept of SEL and its importance in their child's development.

Activity: Host a parent workshop that explains the five core competencies of SEL, using videos, real-life examples, and case studies to demonstrate its impact. This session should include interactive discussions where parents can ask questions and share experiences.

Outcome: Parents will gain a foundational understanding of SEL and feel empowered to support their child's emotional and social growth.

2. Empathy at Home: Cultivating Emotional Awareness

Objective: To help parents foster empathy and emotional understanding within the home.

Activity: Create a role-playing exercise where parents practice recognizing and responding to their child's emotions. For example, a parent can simulate a situation where their child is upset, and they must use empathy to guide the conversation.

Outcome: Parents will develop skills to identify emotions in their children, respond empathetically, and model healthy emotional expression.

3. Building Resilience: Self-Management and Goal Setting

Objective: To help parents teach their children how to manage emotions and set realistic goals.

Activity: Lead parents through a session on goal-setting strategies, such as the SMART goals framework (Specific, Measurable, Achievable, Relevant, and Time-bound). Encourage parents to share personal stories of resilience, emphasizing how someone overcame challenges.

Outcome: Parents will feel confident helping their children build resilience and set achievable goals while learning to manage their emotional responses in difficult situations.

4. Active Listening: Strengthening Communication and Relationships

Objective: To help parents improve communication with their children and strengthen relationships.

Activity: Facilitate an interactive listening exercise where parents practice active listening. Listening exercises could involve pairing up and having one person speak about a challenge while the other practices listening without interrupting or offering advice immediately.

Outcome: Parents will understand the importance of active listening in building trust and empathy and will be able to use these skills to strengthen their relationship with their children.

5. Conflict Resolution: Managing Disagreements Effectively

Objective: To teach parents practical strategies for resolving conflicts peacefully and constructively.

Activity: Guide parents through conflict resolution techniques, such as "I" statements (e.g., "I feel frustrated when...") and the importance of compromise. Parents can participate in role-playing activities to practice these techniques.

Outcome: Parents will leave with a toolkit for managing disagreements within the family and their child's social interactions, helping reduce conflict and promote healthier relationships.

6. Creating a SEL-friendly Home Environment

Objective: To help parents create a home environment that supports SEL principles.

Activity: Have parents evaluate their home environment and identify areas where they could incorporate SEL strategies. Discuss ways to model emotional regulation, practice mindfulness, and create a nurturing space for open communication.

Outcome: Parents will gain practical tips for creating a supportive home environment that nurtures their child's social and emotional growth.

7. Check-ins and Follow-up: Ongoing Support and Reflection

Objective: To provide continuous support and opportunities for reflection.

Activity: Organize monthly follow-up meetings or online forums where parents can share their successes, challenges, and insights. Encourage a peer-support network where parents can exchange advice and experiences.

Outcome: Parents will feel supported in their efforts to integrate SEL practices into their family routines, and they will have access to resources for continued learning and growth.

Empathy in action is not just about understanding another's feelings—it's about actively supporting and responding with intention. Social and Emotional Learning provides the foundation for students to thrive emotionally, socially, and academically (Richerme, 2021). When parents have the knowledge and tools to support SEL at home, they can help their children grow into compassionate, resilient, and socially responsible individuals. By working together—school and home—SEL can become a transformative force in shaping a brighter, more emotionally intelligent future for all students. For educators, integrating SEL into the classroom is a powerful way to support students' emotional, social, and academic development. Teachers play a crucial role in creating an environment where SEL can thrive. By modeling SEL skills, providing practice opportunities, and nurturing an emotionally supportive classroom, educators can help students develop the skills they need to succeed in all areas of life. By supporting students in developing these skills, educators prepare them for academic success but also help them build the foundation for a lifetime of positive relationships, responsible decision-making, and personal well-being. As we continue to prioritize SEL, we create communities where empathy is not just a value but a practice that empowers individuals to positively impact the world around them.

Here are a few ways educators can support students with SEL:

- **Model SEL Skills:** Educators should demonstrate self-awareness, self-management, empathy, and responsible decision-making in student interactions. Students learn by example, and when teachers model these skills, they provide real-world examples of navigating their emotions and relationships.
- **Create a Safe and Inclusive Environment:** A classroom where students feel safe, valued, and respected encourages emotional expression and personal growth. Educators can create this environment by promoting inclusivity, encouraging respectful communication, and establishing clear expectations for behavior.
- **Integrate SEL into Daily Practices:** into everyday lessons and activities. Through group work, reflective exercises, or classroom discussions, educators can create moments for students to practice SEL skills. Incorporating SEL into academic subjects helps students apply these skills in various contexts.
- **Encourage Emotional Awareness and Regulation:** Educators can provide students with tools and strategies to understand and regulate their emotions. Mindfulness, breathing exercises, and journaling can help students manage stress, improve focus, and build emotional resilience.
- **Foster Positive Relationships:** Building positive relationships with students is key to supporting their emotional growth. Educators can take time to get to know their students, listen actively, and show empathy for their experiences. When students feel heard and understood, they will likely develop the same skills in their relationships.

- **Collaborate with Families:** The role of families in supporting SEL is essential. Educators can engage parents and caregivers to share strategies for reinforcing SEL at home. Providing resources, hosting workshops, or communicating regularly with families can help ensure that students receive consistent support for their emotional and social development.

REFERENCES

Aziznejad, M., Janmohammadi, S., Farahaninia, M., & Haghani, H. (2019). Self-awareness Skill Training of Mothers as the Head of the Household and the Self-efficacy of Their Sons. *Journal of Client-Centered Nursing Care*, *5*(4), 213–222. DOI: 10.32598/JCCNC.5.4.93.7

Baskin, J. (2022). Understanding the role of educator: Leveraging social-emotional learning in service of equity and inclusion in K-12 public schools [ProQuest Information & Learning]. *Dissertation Abstracts International. B, The Sciences and Engineering*, *83*(11–B), •••.

Bluth, K., Mullarkey, M., & Lathren, C. (2018). Self-Compassion: A Potential Path to Adolescent Resilience and Positive Exploration. *Journal of Child and Family Studies*, *27*(9), 3037–3047. DOI: 10.1007/s10826-018-1125-1 PMID: 34079199

Calderin, R. (2005). *Emotional intelligence in public elementary school principals: Building collegial relations*. ETD Collection for Fordham University.

Cavazos, M. M. (2024). Exploring teacher perceptions and experiences with a social and emotional learning framework in a Title I elementary school: A qualitative study [ProQuest Information & Learning]. *Dissertation Abstracts International. B, The Sciences and Engineering*, *85*(11–B), •••.

Craig, J. B. (2008). *The relationship between the emotional intelligence of the principal and teacher job satisfaction*. Dissertations Available from ProQuest.

Davis, C. (2024). Social–emotional competence: An essential component for building self-help skills in elementary students [ProQuest Information & Learning]. In *Dissertation Abstracts International Section A: Humanities and Social Sciences* (Vol. 85, Issue 12–A). DBT in Schools to Host National Webinar for Educators, School Administrators, and Parents on the Need for Social Emotional Learning (SEL) in a Post-Pandemic World. (2021, May 26). *PR Newswire*.

DeMink-Carthew, J., Netcoh, S., & Farber, K. (2020). Exploring the Potential for Students to Develop Self-Awareness through Personalized Learning. *The Journal of Educational Research*, *113*(3), 165–176. DOI: 10.1080/00220671.2020.1764467

Gali, L. (2023). A Qualitative Study of the Relationship between Self-Compassion, Self-Care, and Self-Efficacy among School Psychologist Leaders. In *ProQuest LLC*. https://doi.org/https://gateway.proquest.com/openurl?url_ver=Z39.88-2004&rft_val_fmt=info:ofi/fmt:kev:mtx:dissertation&res_dat=xri:pqm&rft_dat=xri:pqdiss:30633208

Glenn, D. E.-A. (2022). Social emotional learning: Teachers' perceptions and understandings regarding the five social emotional learning competencies [ProQuest Information & Learning]. *Dissertation Abstracts International. A, The Humanities and Social Sciences*, *83*(10–A), •••.

Huck, C., Jingshun Zhang, Garby, L., & Xiangming Li. (2023). Development of an Instrument to Assess Teacher Perceptions of Social Emotional Learning (SEL) in PK-12 Schools. *New Waves - Educational Research & Development, 26*(1), 24–42.

Kautz, T., Feeney, K., Chiang, H., Lauffer, S., Bartlett, M., & Tilley, C. (2021). Using a Survey of Social and Emotional Learning and School Climate to Inform Decisionmaking. REL 2021-114. In *Regional Educational Laboratory Mid-Atlantic*.

Keedy, A. S. (2022, October 1). WHERE DO WE GO FROM HERE? Tapping the Power of SEL to Navigate New Landscapes: Music educators discuss how Social Emotional Learning has made a difference in their teaching. *Teaching Music*, *30*(2), 28.

Kim, Y.-Y. (2011). *Compassion in Schools: Life Stories of Four Holistic Educators*.

Kristen, P. Morie, Michael J. Crowley, Linda C. Mayes, Marc N. Potenza(2022) The process of emotion identification: Considerations for psychiatric disorders,Journal of Psychiatric Research,Volume 148, Pages 264-274,ISSN 0022-3956, https://doi.org/. jpsychires.2022.01.053.DOI: 10.1016/j

Makoelle, T., & van der Merwe, M. E. (2016). *Inclusive Teaching in South Africa*. African Sun Media., DOI: 10.2307/j.ctv1nzfxs4

Miña, A. A. (2024). The Lived Experiences of Special Education Teachers in Teaching Inclusive Education. *Psychology & Education: A Multidisciplinary Journal, 21*(10), 1072–1090. DOI: 10.5281/zenodo.12731335

Moran, S. (2009). Purpose: Giftedness in intrapersonal intelligence. *High Ability Studies*, *20*(2), 143–159. DOI: 10.1080/13598130903358501

Morgan, L., Close, S., Siller, M., Kushner, E., & Brasher, S. (2022). Teachers' experiences: Social emotional engagement – knowledge and skills. *Educational Research*, *64*(1), 41–59. DOI: 10.1080/00131881.2021.1988865

National Center for Education Evaluation and Regional Assistance (NCEE) (ED/IES), Regional Educational Laboratory Mid-Atlantic (ED), Mathematica.

NC DOCKS at The University of North Carolina at Greensboro, & Phillips, J. B. (1987). Administrative revenge.

Price, K. V. (2022). Public school superintendents' viewpoints on the leadership strategies perceived to guide the culture and climate within a school district [ProQuest Information & Learning]. *Dissertation Abstracts International. A, The Humanities and Social Sciences*, *83*(7–A), •••.

Richerme, L. K. (2021). Every Student Succeeds Act and Social Emotional Learning: Opportunities and considerations for P-12 arts educators. *Arts Education Policy Review*, *122*(3), 151–157. DOI: 10.1080/10632913.2020.1787284

Romero, S. M. (2016). The Awakened Heart of the Mindful Teacher: A Contemplative Exploration. In *ProQuest LLC*. https://doi.org/https://gateway.proquest.com /openurl?url_ver=Z39.88-2004&rft_val_fmt=info:ofi/fmt:kev:mtx:dissertation&res_ dat=xri:pqm&rft_dat=xri:pqdiss:10586430

Rost, L., Eakins, S. A., Gilbert, A., Gallagher, M., Brown, V., Murphy, C. G., Lahayne, S. P., Lewis, S., Bowman, B., Easton, C., & Lopez, M. (2021). What should SEL look like this fall? Educators And Students Weigh In On How To Foster Resilience. *Learning Professional*, *42*(4), 26–29.

Rothstein, S. L. S. (2023). Social-emotional learning and teachers' cultural competency: The relationship between implementation practices and student outcomes [ProQuest Information & Learning]. *Dissertation Abstracts International. A, The Humanities and Social Sciences*, *84*(11–A), •••.

Sandilos, L., Goble, P., & Schwartz, S. (2020). Burnout and Teacher–Child Interactions: The Moderating Influence of SEL Interventions in Head Start Classrooms. *Early Education and Development*, *31*(7), 1169–1185. DOI: 10.1080/10409289.2020.1788331

Sawchuk, S. (2021, October 13). Why High School SEL Programs Feel 'Lame'—And How to Fix Them; Here's how to devise high school SEL opportunities that don't feel preachy and align with adolescents' cognitive and psychological development. *Education Week*, *41*(9), 13.

SEL Lesson - Self Awareness. (2021, February 9). *US Official News*.

Taylor, M. S., & Glavey, E. M. (2024). Harnessing Robotics and Coding to Foster Social- Emotional Learning in Students With Autism. *Journal of Special Education Technology*, *39*(2), 306–313. DOI: 10.1177/01626434231199992

Vestal, B. D. (2024). Cultivating compassion through discussion [ProQuest Information & Learning]. *Dissertation Abstracts International. B, The Sciences and Engineering*, *85*(2–B), •••.

Victorson, M. K., Spears, G., & Foshay, E. (2022). Practical Resources for Dance Educators! Using SEL Strategies in the K–12 Dance Classroom: Practices from Three Chicago Dance Educators. *Dance Education in Practice*, *8*(2), 4–9. DOI: 10.1080/23734833.2022.2059219

Yuan, M., Madrid, S., Khalil, J., Jain, K., Poliakova, P., Keyt, J., & Zhang, H. D. (2021, November 1). Integrating Social Media and SEL for Students: Novel Strategies for Educators and School Staff. *Communique*, *50*(3), 1.

Zolkoski, S. M., Aguilera, S. E., West, E. M., Miller, G. J., Holm, J. M., Sass, S. M., & Stocks, E. L.Staci M. ZolkoskiSamantha Estrada AguileraErin M. WestGary J. MillerJessica M. HolmSarah M. SassEric L. Stocks. (2020). Teacher Perceptions of Skills, Knowledge, and Resources Needed to Promote Social and Emotional Learning in Rural Classrooms. *Rural Educator*, *41*(3), 1–11. DOI: 10.35608/ruraled.v41i3.1098

Section 3
Supporting Diverse and Intersectional Populations Living With Trauma

Chapter 9
A Hidden Oasis of Care:
Trauma-Informed Educational Practices and Teachers of Less Commonly Taught Content Areas (LCTCA)

Maggie Broderick
https://orcid.org/0000-0003-1032-6795
National University, USA

ABSTRACT

Certain special pockets in PK-12 schools are "places of refuge from the hardness of life," as the artist Fernando Botero (Quote.org, n.d.). once described. Trauma-informed educational practices are multifaceted and intersect with issues of culturally responsive teaching (CRT) (Gay, 2018) and diversity, equity, and inclusion. This chapter builds upon previous work by Broderick (2021), which explored the nuanced and unique role of teachers of Less Commonly Taught Content Areas (LCTCA), including the Arts and various other specialized content areas. Teachers of LCTCA may be uniquely positioned to support marginalized students in PK-12 schools, who often face ongoing trauma in and out of school.

A HIDDEN OASIS OF CARE: TRAUMA-INFORMED EDUCATIONAL PRACTICES AND TEACHERS OF LESS COMMONLY TAUGHT CONTENT AREAS (LCTCA)

Art should be an oasis: a place of refuge from the hardness of life. - Fernando Botero

Certain special pockets in PK-12 schools are just such *places of refuge from the hardness of life* that Botero describes above. Botero (quote.org, n.d.) spoke of art and art-making, and these special *places of refuge* can certainly include art-making and art classrooms. However, they go far beyond that single domain and context within our PK-12 schools. Students of all ages and developmental stages often struggle with various social-emotional issues and unrecognized trauma as they go about their day in school (Dietrich Wolf & Scuichetti, 2024). A *place of refuge* within the school may be part of a larger solution for many of today's diverse students.

As the central theme of this book stresses, trauma-informed educational practices are multifaceted and intersect with issues of culturally responsive teaching (CRT) (Gay, 2018), diversity, equity, inclusion, and social justice (Gregory et al., 2016). These values are globally relevant. The United States' politi-

DOI: 10.4018/979-8-3693-9020-7.ch009

cal climate in 2025 necessitates an expansion upon and a refocusing of the ways in which educational systems refer to and implement these inclusive philosophies and practices. One potential avenue has always existed due to the nature of spaces that already exist in many PK-12 schools. This chapter builds upon work exploring the nuanced and unique role of teachers of *Less Commonly Taught Content Areas* (LCTCA) (Broderick, 2021), positing that LCTCA spaces may often serve as *places of refuge* and indeed a potential *hidden oasis of care* for many of today's diverse students.

Researchers and leaders in PK-12 education have established a variety of frameworks to implement multi-tiered systems of support aimed at addressing the needs of all students (Adamson et al., 2019; Novak & Rodriguez, 2023). However, a compelling recognition of the necessity to integrate a trauma-informed approach within these frameworks has emerged in recent years. The impact of the COVID-19 pandemic has underscored this need, as it has affected diverse groups of students in profound and lasting ways. As teachers and support staff wrestle with these challenges, there is an increasing demand for a deeper understanding of the myriad forms of trauma that students may experience. Included are the direct effects of the pandemic—such as loss, isolation, and disruption of learning—and pre-existing traumas that students carry into the classroom. Effectively weaving a trauma-informed perspective into our existing educational frameworks involves training teachers and staff to recognize the signs of trauma, creating safe and supportive environments, and utilizing strategies that promote resilience and healing. By doing so, teachers can ensure that every student feels seen, heard, and supported, setting the stage for academic success and personal growth.

In tandem with school-wide initiatives involving leadership, teachers, and staff, another important facet should be recognized and encouraged. Hidden pockets of nurturing in PK-12 schools often go unseen and are not generally categorized under MTSS or trauma-informed school programs, per se. Some of these hidden pockets are in LCTCA classrooms (Broderick, 2021) and can serve as a *hidden oasis* supporting a trauma-informed approach to PK-12 education. The concept of an oasis speaks to a profound need for rejuvenation, particularly in environments that can feel overwhelming or isolating. Defined as a small fertile area within a vast desert, an oasis acts as a sanctuary, providing essential resources like water and a sense of peace and restoration for weary travelers. In this context, the oasis is more than just a physical space, embodying the idea of a nurturing environment that fosters growth, reflection, and renewal.

Figure 1. Oasis image

Note: Image by Tasfiz Ur Rahman Nabil from Pixabay

For an oasis to thrive, it requires careful maintenance and attention. While nature may initially create these pockets of life, human intervention is crucial to ensure sustainability and vitality. This process mirrors the responsibility of teachers and the wider learning community to cultivate a supportive atmosphere within educational settings. In a PK-12 school, an oasis could manifest as a safe space where students and staff feel valued and understood. It might include designated areas for mindfulness practices, creative expression, or collaborative learning—intentionally designed to promote emotional and mental well-being. By actively tending to these environments, teachers and community members can create a *culture of care* and connection, allowing every individual to feel replenished and empowered. Ultimately, this vision of an oasis within a school underscores the importance of fostering a supportive and inclusive community. Just as travelers seek out an oasis to revitalize their spirits, students, and teachers should have access to nurturing spaces that continuously feed their intellectual and emotional needs, ensuring they can thrive in their educational journey.

BACKGROUND

Broderick (2021) coined the term *Less Commonly Taught Content Areas* (LCTCA) based upon and broadening CARLA's (2020) term of *Less Commonly Taught Languages* (LCTL) and collected anecdotes collected from teachers, allowing for a deep exploration of the challenges and experiences that shape their professional lives. These narratives are drawn from decades of firsthand experiences and keen observations within the classroom, revealing the unique landscape in which LCTCA teachers operate. These teachers often feel like they are a "lone fish" (Broderick, 2021, p. 107), highlighting the isolation that can come with this profession. Teachers often navigate their journeys without colleagues' immediate support or camaraderie, which presents a distinct set of issues and concerns. Each story shares the triumphs that arise despite these struggles, illustrating the resilience and resourcefulness required to thrive in solitude.

Becoming a teacher for the first time is a challenging experience. While teacher preparation programs aim to equip new teachers, the essential skills are often developed through experience and over time. The initial years are particularly significant for establishing a successful teaching career. Statistics highlight a pressing issue: 40-50% of new teachers leave the profession within their first five years, especially in diverse environments like urban or rural schools that cater to at-risk populations (Will, 2018). All new teachers face common hurdles, including classroom management, effective teaching strategies, student engagement, communication with administrators, collaboration with peers, and managing multiple responsibilities. A sense of isolation can make the transition even more difficult for new teachers, particularly those who work in LCTCA (Broderick, 2021). Being one of the few teachers specializing in a particular subject can lead to feeling overwhelmed and unsupported. These teachers face unique challenges navigating an educational landscape dominated by more commonly taught subjects. LCTCA can include the arts, physical education, vocational programs, innovative concepts like STEAM, foreign languages, and other specialized educational areas. In the U.S., subjects typically prioritized include Mathematics, English Language Arts, and Science, leading to a wider perception that other areas, including Physical Education, are less emphasized despite their significance. Teachers in these fields often encounter large class sizes, resource limitations, and pressure from policies that favor core subjects. Thus, their inclusion as LCTCA teachers depends on specific circumstances within their schools. The emphasis on core subjects has intensified since the No Child Left Behind Act of 2001, with legislation like the Every Student Succeeds Act and the Common Core State Standards continuing this trend. Challenges for teachers in LCTCA include budget constraints, program cuts, curriculum narrowing, and a lack of resources. It is crucial for all teachers, especially those early in their careers, to utilize research-based best practices and to receive the necessary support and guidance to evolve from theoretical knowledge to practical application.

The lone fish inspires the idea of an oasis presented in this chapter. Imagine a vast desert where the sun beats down mercilessly, and the horizon shimmers with heat. In this arid expanse, an oasis emerges as a sanctuary, a shimmering pool of life and hope. Just as fish navigate their aquatic world—fluidly darting through currents and seeking the safety of coral—travelers in this parched landscape wander toward the oasis, driven by a primal need for water. Water, a universal need, not only quenches physical thirst but also nourishes the spirit. The oasis represents more than just a source of hydration; it functions as a place of social and emotional replenishment. Here, weary wanderers come together, sharing stories and laughter, their hearts lightened by the companionship found in this respite. The coolness of the water offers them solace, washing away the dust of their journeys and rejuvenating their spirits. Like fish returning to a vibrant reef, the travelers find themselves in a haven where they can restore their strength and renew their bonds. The oasis is a testament to the importance of connection and vitality in our lives, reminding us that just as humans seek sustenance for our bodies, they must nurture their emotions and relationships for true survival. PK-12 schools may often feel like a dessert for some students, especially marginalized groups who may have faced trauma. The next sections will explore systems in PK-12 schools that attempt to address these issues under the umbrella of MTSS, trauma-informed educational practices, culturally responsive teaching, and social-emotional learning (SEL).

Multi-Tiered Systems of Support (MTSS)

Multi-tiered System of Support (MTSS) encompass a comprehensive framework designed to address students' diverse academic and behavioral needs within educational settings. Implementing MTSS integrates academic and behavioral support for all students, recognizing how these aspects are interrelated and work in tandem (Adamson et al., 2019). Novak and Rodriguez (2023) explained how MTSS integration in PK-12 schools helps support today's diverse students in myriad ways. These systems aim to create a widespread and equitable approach that recognizes and values the varied experiences of learners. A crucial element of MTSS is the integration of a trauma-informed lens, which emphasizes the importance of understanding and addressing the effects of trauma on student learning and behavior. This integration is especially relevant to the principles of culturally responsive teaching, as outlined by Gay (2018), and encompasses the broader themes of diversity, equity, inclusion, and social justice in education. Indiana University-Purdue University Indianapolis et al. (2022) stressed the need for *equity-centered MTSS* within PK-12 school systems.

Creating a tiered continuum of behavior support at the classroom level can help enhance schoolwide MTSS. In today's classrooms, diverse PK-12 learners come with a wide range of backgrounds, including varying degrees of trauma. Some may have experienced adverse childhood experiences that affect their emotional well-being, social interactions, and academic performance. Therefore, incorporating MTSS infused with social-emotional learning (SEL) into the curriculum becomes imperative. SEL fosters students' ability to manage emotions and enhances their empathy and interpersonal skills, creating a more supportive learning environment.

A more holistic and responsive approach to education is needed to truly meet these diverse needs. This goal can be achieved by intentionally cultivating strong relationships among students, teachers, and families, which is essential for promoting trust and safety in the academic setting. Community-building initiatives and establishing cultures of care within schools can significantly contribute to this effort. By prioritizing these elements, teachers can create an inclusive atmosphere that recognizes and honors each student's individuality while promoting their overall well-being and academic success.

Implementing MTSS varies significantly across different grade levels, reflecting students' diverse developmental stages and unique needs. In elementary schools, younger children may require more foundational literacy and social-emotional skills support. In contrast, older elementary students may benefit from more targeted interventions that address academic challenges and behavioral issues. Additionally, the nuances in MTSS implementation can be influenced by factors such as the varying levels of instructional experience among teachers, the availability of resources, and the specific issues in different school environments. Majeika et al. (2024) focus on elementary school contexts, highlighting effective strategies for tailoring MTSS to meet students' distinct needs and developmental phases at each grade level. By considering these factors, schools can foster a more supportive and effective educational environment that promotes success for all learners. Recognizing that middle school-aged learners possess differing developmental and social-emotional needs, Hollingsworth (2019) suggested MTSS as a collective work among stakeholders involving all teachers, who may be more siloed at the middle and secondary levels than the elementary level.

Recognizing the intersection and interplay between SEL and MTSS is also crucial (Guest et al., 2024). Similarly, SEL and trauma-informed educational practices naturally go hand-in-hand, involving the quintessentially human elements of compassion and empathy (Lyn & Broderick, 2023). The concept of an *oasis of care* figures naturally, as teachers who embody the human element and empathy may be found in hidden places - particularly the oft-overlooked teachers of LCTCA (Broderick, 2021).

Trauma-Informed Educational Practices

Today's diverse student population is encountering a multitude of challenges, many of which stem from various forms of trauma that can significantly impact their educational experience. These issues can range from individual circumstances, such as abuse or neglect, to broader societal factors like poverty, systemic racism, and community violence. As a result, there is a pressing need for a trauma-informed approach in all aspects of the PK-12 educational system, including frameworks like MTSS.

Marginalized students often experience trauma due to a society that does not always understand and appreciate their differences and diversity. For example, LGBTQIAA+ students may face ongoing bullying and a lack of representation of diverse genders and sexualities in many communities. As Walker-Roberts (2023) stated, a philosophy of inclusion and creating a sense of belonging are key to overcoming these ongoing societal and school patterns. Ethnically and racially diverse students within largely White spaces may similarly face trauma in those communities. Both groups, along with other marginalized groups, additionally face the trauma of historical abuses and neglect toward their communities.

A trauma-informed educational approach recognizes the prevalence of trauma and its effects on learning and behavior. Schools are increasingly understanding that addressing trauma is crucial not only for student well-being but also for fostering a supportive learning environment. This paradigm shift involves training teachers and staff to identify signs of trauma and respond appropriately, ensuring teachers' interactions with students are rooted in empathy, understanding, and support.

Many schools have begun implementing strategies for recognizing and addressing student trauma in recent years. This includes integrating mental health resources, promoting social-emotional learning, and creating safe spaces where students feel secure and valued. Additionally, it is essential to consider the trauma experienced by teachers and staff, as they may also deal with personal and professional challenges that affect their ability to connect with and support students.

Schools can work towards healing students and communities by adopting a comprehensive trauma-informed approach. This commitment transforms educational practices and fosters an environment where all individuals feel empowered, resilient, and ready to engage in their learning journeys. The evolution of educational policies and practices to better recognize and address trauma underscores the importance of creating nurturing, responsive, and inclusive school environments for everyone involved.

The specifics of how teachers of LCTCA (Broderick, 2021) infuse trauma-informed educational practices are becoming increasingly prominent in contemporary literature. This emerging body of work highlights the critical need for integrating trauma-informed practices specifically tailored to teaching LCTCA in its various manifestations. These practices are essential for recognizing the profound impact trauma can have on learning and cognitive processes and the overall educational environment.

Teachers are encouraged to adopt various strategies that address the unique challenges faced by students who have experienced trauma (Norrish & Brunzell, 2023). This practice includes educational leadership creating safe and supportive learning environments that foster resilience and engagement (Dietrich Wolf & Scuichetti, 2024). Teachers can implement interventions that promote healing and enhance learning outcomes by understanding the potential barriers that trauma poses to cognitive development and academic achievement.

The literature underscores the importance of professional development for teachers, equipping them with the necessary knowledge and skills to effectively support all students, particularly those affected by trauma. Recognizing the connection between trauma and learning is crucial, as it empowers teachers to create inclusive spaces that honor their students' diverse experiences and needs. Ultimately, the goal is to harness the potential of LCTCA spaces to transform educational practices, ensuring that all learners can thrive in a nurturing and understanding environment. Jacobson (2021) and Green et al. (2022) highlight how trauma-informed practices augment physical education classrooms and learning experiences. Building trust with students is key (Ellison & Walton-Fisette, 2022) to foster a trauma-informed environment in physical education classrooms.

For many reasons, Broderick (2021) noted that language classrooms are pivotal LCTCA spaces. Teaching and learning a language involve SEL aspects such as relationships and communication. Many language classrooms, especially ESL/ENL classrooms, involve intense and direct work with students who are refugees, immigrants, and other types of language learners who may have faced various traumas. Dunn (2024) examined the human reality of teaching English to marginalized groups who may have faced enduring and ongoing traumas. Giles and Yazan (2020) explained that ESL teachers often feel alone in supporting these marginalized learners, making ESL classrooms a particularly powerful LCTCA space in PK-12 schools.

In visual arts classrooms, students are given a vibrant space to explore their creative expression. The emphasis is on fostering pride in one's work as students experiment with various mediums—painting, sculpture, and digital art. They learn to articulate their thoughts and emotions through their creations, building confidence and a sense of ownership in the artistic process. Collaborative projects also help them to appreciate different perspectives, while reflective critiques promote growth and refinement in their skills.

Music classrooms are unique in fostering students' participation in music-making via ensemble performance. Whether in a choir, band, or orchestra—students develop their musical skills and critical teamwork and communication abilities. The experience of rehearsing and performing together cultivates a deep sense of camaraderie and shared pride in their accomplishments. By exploring various musical styles and instruments, they learn about cultural expression and the power of music to connect with others, enhancing their appreciation for diversity in artistry. Walzer (2021) and Ryals (2022) explained how music classrooms can be ideal places for building community and a sense of belonging, which foster trauma-informed spaces. McEvoy and Salvador (2020) noted that elementary general music teachers have a unique opportunity to infuse culturally responsive and trauma-informed approaches in their schools. These teachers tend to work with students over several years, seeing them throughout the year and throughout their entire time at an elementary school, as do elementary visual art and physical education teachers. The content area of music also brings ample opportunities for self-expression and healing through the power of music, such as Bradley and Hess (2022) discuss in their work regarding "Haunted Melodies" (p. 1). Music classrooms, such as band, orchestra, and choir ensemble spaces, involve unique classroom management and logistical challenges, such as having especially large class sizes for the ensemble rehearsals and needing to foster teamwork among large groups of students who are working on a shared goal. Bauman-Field (2024) posited that music teachers can create a trauma-informed space within this context.

Theater, drama, and creative writing are powerful forms of artistic expression that provide a meaningful outlet for individuals to explore their thoughts, emotions, and experiences. Engaging in these creative practices allows participants to immerse themselves in storytelling, character development, and the nuances of human connection. Within a nurturing community of learners, individuals can share their unique perspectives, fostering an environment of support and collaboration. This community encourages personal growth and celebrates diversity in expression and understanding. Participants can hone their craft through workshops, performances, and writing groups, gain valuable feedback, and build lasting relationships with fellow creatives. Ultimately, theater, drama, and creative writing empower individuals to communicate their truths and connect with others on a deeper level while being part of a caring and inclusive atmosphere. This shared journey of creativity enriches the individual and the community, making it a truly transformative experience. Davis (2020) explained that storytelling aspects, such as those abundant in theater, drama, and creative writing classrooms, provide a powerful human outlet for storytelling.

Trauma-informed educational practices naturally embody the crux of creating a sense of belonging with diversity, equity, inclusion, and social justice in mind. As Williams et al. (2024) expressed, students and teachers can collaborate to enact social change. The type of collaboration nurtured in LCTCA spaces may uniquely suit this purpose for today's diverse students. It can all be wrapped together in teachers' approach, such as within the hidden oasis in certain special pockets, such as the classrooms with teachers of LCTCA.

Culturally Responsive Teaching

Culturally responsive teaching (CRT) (Gay, 2018) naturally intersects with mindfully employed MTSS and trauma-informed educational practices, with diversity, equity, inclusion, and social justice at the intersection. Teachers can work to meet students where they are with empathy and social-emotional understanding. Teachers of LCTCA tend to work with students over longer periods of time and on projects that are especially meaningful to both the students and their teachers. Thus, these teachers may have more of a chance to build relationships and rapport, walk in their students' shoes, so to speak, and recognize our humanness, intersectionality, commonalities, and differences while doing things like creating art and music or working as a team in physical education spaces.

As with trauma-informed approaches for teachers of LCTCA, the research literature is beginning to recognize the role of teachers of LCTCA for CRT. It all goes together to recognize the potential of the hidden oasis living in these special spaces in PK-12 schools. McEvoy and Salvador (2020) noted the intersection between culturally responsive and trauma-informed approaches for elementary music teachers. Salvador and Culp (2022) explained how Universal Design for Learning (UDL) adds an additional layer to this interplay and how music teachers can create powerful community care for their students. In the visual art education arena, Morgan (2018) noted how arts education contributes to students' deeper understanding of citizenship, which naturally aligns with social justice issues. Understanding ourselves and others while embodying our shared humanness, empathy, and interpersonal and intrapersonal facets begets a trauma-informed approach that is culturally responsive and functions as a pillar of effective MTSS. Teachers of LCTCA could foster all of these things while also thinking about social-emotional learning (SEL) in all aspects, as will be further discussed in the next section.

Social-Emotional Learning

Relationships and rapport are central to SEL (Lipscomb et al., 2024). Because many teachers of LCTCA spend longer time with students, such as over the course of years, they may have a greater chance to develop these strong and lasting relationships, leading to trusting and caring rapport that lasts. Students in these special spaces can feel more at ease as they enter these *places of refuge*, as noted at the beginning of this chapter.

Researchers, leaders, and teachers have begun to strongly suggest the meaningful infusion of SEL into MTSS in school systems and classrooms (Guest et al., 2024), which can foster improved mental health for students (Vetter et al., 2024). Teachers' dispositions (Broderick & Lyn, 2022; Clemm von Hohenberg & Broderick, 2020) and ability to form strong relationships and lasting rapport with their students are key and align with the core components of SEL frameworks (CASEL, 2022) and aspects of CRT (Clemm von Hohenberg & Broderick, 2020). Lyn and Broderick (2023) further posited that *radiating compassion* is key when infusing SEL and trauma-informed approaches for students. In LCTCA spaces, teachers can radiate compassion as students work together on longer-term projects, such as music-making, art-making, etc. SEL is indeed powerful within a well-maintained LCTCA oasis. Students may seek out these spaces for comfort during both calm and tumultuous times during their school years. For example, an LGBTQIAA+ student struggling with bullying may find a quiet space with an understanding, empathetic, and compassionate community within the walls of an art classroom. That student may then express themselves via their art-making within that safe and comfortable oasis, resulting in a personal achievement that induces the feelings of pride and self-worth inherent in creation and collaboration. These hidden and oft-overlooked spaces can thus function as fertile areas for social-emotional growth and as a pillar of a well-integrated and mindful MTSS implementation at a school.

A HIDDEN OASIS OF CARE

The discussion of mindful and meaningful MTSS, trauma-informed educational approaches, CRT, and SEL culminates in a culture of care (Lipscomb et al., 2024). Classrooms with teachers of LCTCA at the center can provide an *oasis of care* with a microculture within the larger culture of care in the larger system of the school. LCTCA teachers and classrooms serve as places of learning and sanctuaries, providing a safe haven for diverse student populations. This environment is akin to a hidden oasis where students from various backgrounds—such as LGBTQIAA+, neurodivergent individuals, and racial and ethnic minorities—can find acceptance and belonging. A student who may be facing bullying and marginalization may find a trusting teacher with whom they can develop a lasting and caring relationship within a classroom space where they share like-minded understandings of a content area or experience. A sense of belonging and a *feeling of safety and home* in that space is key.

The concept of a *third space* is foundational here, creating a bridge between home and school where students can express themselves freely and authentically. Within this nurturing environment, connections among students are emphasized, fostering a robust *community of care* that empowers individuals to support one another. As Bergholz and McCarthy (2020) noted, an LCTCA teacher, such as a physical education teacher, can learn to walk in students' shoes and truly become a *student of their own* by adopting a more trauma-informed and culturally responsive approach. A strong commitment to integrating trauma-informed education throughout the curriculum is key, and LCTCA teachers play an integral role in their unique classroom spaces and circumstances. This approach acknowledges some students' challenges and actively works to create additional safe spaces within the school. By prioritizing emotional well-being alongside academic growth, LCTCA cultivates an inclusive atmosphere where every student can thrive.

Creating and Maintaining the Hidden Oasis of Care

Creating and maintaining a *culture of care*, as highlighted by Lipscomb et al. (2024), involves establishing a nurturing environment within the hidden oasis and its surrounding community. This culture emphasizes the importance of respect and support for LCTCA teachers. Recognizing their social and emotional well-being is crucial; when teachers feel valued and cared for, they are better equipped to extend that same level of care to their students.

In this hidden oasis, a holistic approach is essential—implementing strategies that promote mental health, professional development, and peer support among teachers. Programs focusing on mindfulness, stress management, and collaborative teaching practices can create a positive atmosphere. Additionally, creating channels for open communication, where teachers can express their concerns and needs, fosters a sense of belonging and community. School leadership's philosophy toward creating and maintaining that community of care is key.

Prioritizing the well-being of teachers empowers them to nurture their students more effectively and cultivate an environment where every individual feels safe and supported. This reciprocal relationship of care contributes significantly to the overall educational experience, allowing the hidden oasis to thrive as a supportive learning environment for teachers and students. This process inherently involves restorative practices (Lipscomb et al. 2024) and relationships, rapport, teacher dispositions, and teacher self-awareness at the center (Broderick & Lyn, 2022).

Threats to the Hidden Oasis of Care

Various aspects threaten these LCTCA oases of care in PK-12 educational contexts. Most worrisome is that unequal access to LCTCA, particularly arts education (Elpus, 2020), is highly problematic. Affluent suburban schools tend to have more programming in LCTCA, especially in the United States context. In contrast, students of color and/or with lower socioeconomic status tend to have fewer options, hence fewer *oases of care*. Unfortunately, things appear to be moving in the wrong direction, with what Heilig et al. (2010) termed a "devolution of public arts education" (p. 1) potentially inhibiting the role of arts education in aspects such as building a deeper and more meaningful understanding of citizenship (Morgan, 2018).

The realities surrounding logistics and available spaces for LCTCA programs often mirror the broader challenges faced in educational funding and budgeting. Nolte-Yupari (2019) highlighted a pressing issue in visual arts education, pointing out that many art classes frequently lack dedicated physical classrooms. As a result, teachers frequently rely on what has been referred to as "art on a cart"—a logistical workaround that involves transporting supplies and materials from one location to another to facilitate learning. This lack of a stable environment impacts the quality of art education and poses substantial challenges for teachers aiming to provide a cohesive learning experience.

LCTCA areas encompass vital subjects such as music, visual arts, and foreign languages, which often find themselves vulnerable when budgetary constraints arise. These programs are typically the first to be cut or downsized in the face of financial difficulties, reflecting a tendency to prioritize other subjects perceived as more critical to standardized testing and academic performance metrics. This trend is not limited to traditional arts; even LCTCA programs with a STEM focus, such as engineering courses, can be scrutinized during budget evaluations. As districts seek to streamline costs, the valuable contributions made by creative and performing arts fields and interdisciplinary STEM initiatives can be overlooked, undermining the holistic education that fosters innovation and creativity in students.

Overall, the intersection of logistical support, funding, and educational priorities creates significant challenges for the sustainable implementation and growth of LCTCA programs within schools. Addressing these issues requires broader advocacy and a reevaluation of how educational value is perceived in budgeting decisions, ensuring all areas of education receive the support necessary for student success.

Along similar lines, ongoing and sometimes rapid policy changes can impact LCTCA access for students (Beveridge, 2010; Shaw, 2019; Shaw, 2016), Paired with perceptions about LCTCA contexts, such as arts education, as being expendable and not as well understood - perhaps even misunderstood or seen as fluff - abound (Heilig et al., 2010). LCTCA teachers often feel like they are an island (Giles & Yazan, 2020), which can lead to feelings of isolation and a lack of support (Broderick, 2021). The very nature of being more hidden can serve as a double-edged sword, so to speak. While the oasis of care in an LCTCA context benefits from being a safe place for students, it is being more hidden, which makes it potentially seen as more expendable or perhaps simply unnoticed and forgotten.

Emotion(al) labor and burnout are significant issues for teachers working in LCTCA, as highlighted by various studies (Acheson et al., 2016; Ryan et al., 2017). These challenges often manifest in compassion fatigue (Reeves, 2019) and profound teacher burnout, which can severely impact teachers' well-being and effectiveness in the classroom. For instance, Acheson et al. (2016) detail what they call "the burnout spiral" (p. 522) particularly concerning the emotional labor required from rural US foreign language teachers. This concept describes how the continuous demands of emotional engagement with students can lead teachers into a cycle of exhaustion and stress, ultimately affecting their mental health and job performance.

The connection between teacher attrition, stress, and burnout is well-established in the literature, with studies indicating that these factors are intricately linked (Ryan et al., 2017; von Haaren-Mack et al., 2020). In the context of LCTCA, the intensity of the emotional work required to support students can exacerbate feelings of isolation and strain, contributing to a higher likelihood of teachers leaving the profession. Such trends highlight the pressing need for interventions and support systems that address both emotional labor and the risk of burnout, ensuring that teachers remain resilient and effective in their roles.

Renewing, Replenishing, and Re-envisioning the Hidden Oasis

An oasis is a fertile spot in a desert or wasteland where water is found, serving as a crucial refuge for weary travelers. It offers hydration and nourishment in the form of vegetation and sometimes wildlife, creating a thriving environment amidst barren surroundings. The oasis nurtures life and goodness, symbolizing hope and relief for those on a long and arduous journey.

This natural retreat is inherently designed to replenish the weary, providing a space where travelers can physically and mentally rejuvenate. However, the existence of an oasis is delicate; it requires careful maintenance and balance. Various threats loom over this vital resource, including drought, overuse of water, climate change, and environmental degradation. Human activities, such as excessive agricultural practices or urban development, can also jeopardize the fragile ecosystem of the oasis.

To ensure that it remains a sanctuary for future travelers, adopting sustainable practices and conservation efforts is essential. Protecting the oasis involves a collective responsibility to safeguard its water sources, preserve its biodiversity, and maintain the harmony that allows it to flourish in an otherwise inhospitable landscape. Thus, while oases are naturally conducive to replenishing life, they represent a precious balance that must be respected and preserved. Collins (2024) stressed the importance of truly supporting mental health and well-being, especially during the implementation of trauma-informed education and ongoing professional development and growth in trauma-informed practice. The joy of teaching LCTCA is what likely brought teachers to these oases. Hence, as Salvador (2019) noted with powerful examples from the music education arena, joy must be kept and even sometimes reignited. Systems must allow for such joy to flourish if it is to then be there for the students.

Encouraging mindful and ongoing teacher leadership is key. Teacher leaders can share responsibility and augment the voices of teachers of LCTCA in tandem with school and district leadership. The power of teacher leadership is a necessary and oft-missing ingredient (Stein, 2020). It is important to consider how to do this for teachers of LCTCA, specifically by bringing them into the fold and encouraging them, advocating, and so forth.

DIRECTIONS FOR FUTURE RESEARCH, PRACTICE, AND POLICY

Having established the need for more support of teachers of LCTCA and the existence of hidden oases in PK-12 schools, the following sections focus on future directions for research, practice, and policy. Leadership in PK-12 schools can focus on these directions as they consider the role of LCTCA spaces within MTSS, trauma-informed educational environments, and communities of care.

Directions for Future Research

Further research could involve a more specific focus on teachers' experiences participating in LCTCA. Qualitative studies could be implemented to gather in-depth insights into teachers' challenges and successes while engaging in these collaborative activities. This research could include structured interviews, focus group discussions, and observations to capture the nuances of their experiences, motivations, and pedagogical approaches.

Additionally, incorporating a mixed-methods approach that includes both qualitative and quantitative data could provide a more comprehensive understanding of the impact of LCTCA. Statistical analyses could be conducted to measure outcomes such as student engagement, academic performance, and teacher satisfaction before and after the implementation of these collaborative activities. Survey instruments could be developed to collect data from a wider range of participants, allowing for a more expansive view of the role LCTCA plays in educational settings.

Furthermore, exploring the concept of *hidden oases* in LCTCA—those pockets of effective practices and innovation that may not be widely recognized—could reveal valuable insights. This could involve case studies of specific classrooms or schools where LCTCA is thriving, identifying the factors contributing to their success, and documenting the best practices that can be shared with others in the educational community. Overall, this research could significantly enhance our understanding of LCTCA's potential to influence educational experiences for both teachers and students positively.

Directions for Practice and Policy

Practice-based suggestions for school and district leadership and teachers of LCTCA and other content areas are included throughout this chapter. To effectively address the needs of students impacted by trauma, teachers should first focus on understanding trauma-informed practices. This process involves engaging in professional development that emphasizes the principles of trauma-informed care. Teachers can learn to recognize the signs of trauma and understand its profound effects on learning and behavior. Implementing strategies that foster a safe and supportive environment is crucial for students who have experienced trauma.

Fostering a sense of belonging within the classroom is another essential strategy. Teachers should create activities and dynamics that promote inclusion and celebrate diversity. Community-building exercises can facilitate connections among students, allowing them to support one another. Encouraging open communication is vital, as it helps students feel comfortable expressing their thoughts and feelings, thus cultivating a community of trust.

Self-care for teachers is equally important. Promoting self-care practices can help teachers manage the stresses associated with teaching and supporting traumatized students. This may include offering mindfulness sessions, workshops on stress management, or dedicated time for peer support. Integrating SEL strategies into the curriculum is also essential. Teachers should focus on helping students develop emotional intelligence, resilience, and coping skills through engaging and relevant methods. Additionally, teachers should be encouraged to act as advocates for their students' needs. Collaborating with families and community resources, as well as raising awareness among colleagues about the significance of trauma-informed approaches and available resources, is crucial.

For all teachers, training on trauma-informed practices is fundamental. It equips them to understand how trauma affects learning and behavior, enabling them to adapt their teaching strategies accordingly. A school-wide approach to trauma care that promotes understanding among all staff members is vital for creating a supportive environment. Collaboration plays a pivotal role in supporting students with diverse needs. Creating opportunities for interdisciplinary collaboration allows teachers to share strategies and insights. Establishing support networks within the school can facilitate discussions about challenges and successes in implementing trauma-informed approaches, enhancing collective efficacy.

Lastly, advocacy for systemic change is essential. Teachers should be encouraged to advocate for policies and practices at both school and district levels that support trauma-informed education, including access to mental health resources for students. Promoting community engagement to connect with local organizations can further amplify the support available for students experiencing trauma. Schools and districts can create a comprehensive approach by considering the bigger picture, including community, state, and federal factors. This supports students affected by trauma and enhances the overall educational environment for everyone involved.

SUMMARY AND CONCLUSION

In PK-12 schools, specific areas serve as safe havens for students, especially those who are marginalized or struggling. A trauma-informed approach is key, and teachers of LCTCA can serve as a meaningful aspect of a multifaceted approach to trauma-informed educational practices. Students, regardless of age or developmental stage, frequently face various social-emotional challenges and often deal with unseen trauma throughout their school day (Dietrich Wolf & Scuichetti, 2024). A designated safe space within the school can play a crucial role in addressing the needs of today's diverse student population.

The core message of this book emphasizes that trauma-informed educational strategies are complex and interconnected with culturally responsive teaching (CRT) (Gay, 2018), as well as with issues related to diversity, equity, inclusion, and social justice (Gregory et al., 2016). This chapter builds on research examining teachers' essential and distinctive role in Less Commonly Taught Content Areas (LCTCA) (Broderick, 2021), suggesting that LCTCA environments can frequently act as sanctuaries of support and care for many diverse students today.

REFERENCES

Acheson, K., Taylor, J., & Luna, K. (2016). The burnout spiral: The emotion labor of five rural US foreign language teachers. *Modern Language Journal*, *100*(2), 522–537. DOI: 10.1111/modl.12333

Adamson, R. M., McKenna, J. W., & Mitchell, B. (2019). Supporting all students: Creating a tiered continuum of behavior support at the classroom level to enhance schoolwide multi-tiered systems of support. *Preventing School Failure*, *63*(1), 62–67. DOI: 10.1080/1045988X.2018.1501654

Altieri, V., Rooney, M., Guest, J. D., Ross, R. A., Childs, T. M., Ascetta, K. E., Curcio, R., Iachini, A., & Griffiths, L. (2024). Embedding social emotional learning from the bottom up in multi-tiered services and supports frameworks. *Psychology in the Schools*, *61*(7), 2745–2761. DOI: 10.1002/pits.23183

Bauman-Field, B. (2024). Trauma-Informed Classroom Management in Music Education: A Literature Review. Update. *Update - University of South Carolina. Dept. of Music*, *42*(3), 43–51. DOI: 10.1177/87551233231173149

Bergholz, S. L., & McCarthy, J. (2020). Becoming a Student of Your Students: Trauma-Informed, Culturally Relevant Practices for Physical Education Teachers. *Journal of Physical Education, Recreation & Dance*, *92*(1), 8–18. DOI: 10.1080/07303084.2021.1844539

Beveridge, T. (2010). No Child Left Behind and Fine Arts Classes. *Arts Education Policy Review*, *111*(1), 4–7. DOI: 10.1080/10632910903228090

Bradley, D., & Hess, J. (2022). *Trauma and Resilience in Music Education: Haunted Melodies*. Routledge.

Broderick, M. (2021). Navigating the school as a smaller fish: Research-based guidance for teachers of less commonly taught content areas. In Pierce-Friedman, K., & Wellner, L. (Eds.), *Supporting Early Career Teachers with Research-Based Practices*. IGI Global. DOI: 10.4018/978-1-7998-6803-3.ch005

Broderick, M., & Lyn, A. E. (2022). Integrating social emotional learning into the formative development of educator dispositions. In Clemm von Hohenberg, S. (Ed.), *Dispositional Development and Assessment in Teacher Preparation Programs*. IGI Global. DOI: 10.4018/978-1-6684-4089-6.ch004

CARLA. (2020). Less Commonly Taught Languages. https://carla.umn.edu/lctl/

CASEL. (2022). CASEL Framework. https://casel.org/

Clemm von Hohenberg, S., & Broderick, M. (2020). The role of teacher dispositions in a global teaching context. In Ramírez-Verdugo, M. D., & Otcu-Grillman, B. (Eds.), *Interdisciplinary Approaches Toward Enhancing Teacher Education*. IGI Global. DOI: 10.4018/978-1-7998-4697-0.ch012

Collins, A. R. (2024). Supporting teacher mental health during the implementation of trauma-informed education [ProQuest Information & Learning]. *Dissertation Abstracts International. B, The Sciences and Engineering*, *85*(4–B), •••.

Davis, L. (2020). Don't hide the hurt: Using storytelling for trauma-informed teaching. In Ellsworth, A. M. (Ed.), *Cases on emotionally responsive teaching and mentoring* (pp. 13–26). Information Science Reference/IGI Global., DOI: 10.4018/978-1-7998-2971-3.ch002

Dietrich Wolf, L., & Scuichetti, M. B. (2024). Integrating Trauma-Informedness within a Multi-Tiered System of Support: The Critical Role of Administrators. *Journal of Educational Leadership and Policy Studies*, *8*(1).

Dunn, O. (2024). "Who am I to teach you?": Critical reflection in the ESOL classroom. *Language Issues*, *35*(1), 29–38.

Ellison, D. W., & Walton-Fisette, J. (2022). "It's More about Building Trust": Physical Education Teachers' Experiences with Trauma Informed Practices. *European Physical Education Review*, *28*(4), 906–922. DOI: 10.1177/1356336X221096603

Quarmby, T., Sandford, R., & Elpus, K. (2020). Access to arts education in America: The availability of visual art, music, dance, and theater courses in U.S. high schools. *Arts Education Policy Review*, 121.

Gay, G. (2018). *Culturally responsive teaching: Theory, research, and practice* (3rd ed.). Teachers College Press.

Giles, A., & Yazan, B. (2020). "You're Not an Island": A Middle Grades Language Arts Teacher's Changed Perceptions in ESL and Content Teachers' Collaboration. *RMLE Online: Research in Middle Level Education*, *43*(3), 1–15. DOI: 10.1080/19404476.2020.1724045

Green, R., Hooper, O., & Avery, J. (2022). Developing Evidence-Informed Principles for Trauma-Aware Pedagogies in Physical Education. *Physical Education and Sport Pedagogy*, *27*(4), 440–454. DOI: 10.1080/17408989.2021.1891214

Gregory, A., Clawson, K., Davis, A., & Gerewitz, J. (2016). The promise of restorative practices to transform teacher-student relationships and achieve equity in school discipline. *Journal of Educational & Psychological Consultation*, *26*(4), 325–353. DOI: 10.1080/10474412.2014.929950

Heilig, J., Cole, H., & Aguilar, A. (2010). From Dewey to No Child Left Behind: The Evolution and Devolution of Public Arts Education. *Arts Education Policy Review*, *111*(4), 136–145. DOI: 10.1080/10632913.2010.490776

Jacobson, M. R. (2021). An Exploratory Analysis of the Necessity and Utility of Trauma-Informed Practices in Education. *Preventing School Failure*, *65*(2), 124–134. DOI: 10.1080/1045988X.2020.1848776

Lipscomb, S. T., Swander, W., & Mason, E. (2024). Building cultures of care in schools: Centering relationships at the intersection of trauma-informed education and restorative practices. *Contemporary School Psychology*, *28*(4), 653–669. DOI: 10.1007/s40688-023-00481-5

Lyn, A. E., & Broderick, M. (2023). *Radiate Compassion: Educator Dispositions for a Trauma-Sensitive Environment.* Creating Trauma-Sensitive Schools Conference, https://www.attachmenttraumanetwork.org/conference/, February 23, 2023.

Majeika, C. E., Pierce, J., Smith, H., Lembke, E., & Gandhi, A. (2024). Integrated multi-tiered systems of support in elementary schools: Practical applications. Intervention in School and Clinic, 60(1), 53–61. DOI: 10.1177/10534512241254031

McEvoy, C. A., & Salvador, K. (2020). Aligning Culturally Responsive and Trauma-Informed Pedagogies in Elementary General Music. *General Music Today*, *34*(1), 21–28. DOI: 10.1177/1048371320909806

Morgan, I. (2018). Arts Education and Citizenship. *Journal of Distance Education*, *18*(3), 95–102. DOI: 10.1080/15290824.2018.1481964

Nolte-Yupari, S. T. (2019). Facing the Elephant: Let's Talk About Art-on-a-Cart. *Art Education*, *72*(6), 14–19. DOI: 10.1080/00043125.2019.1648142

Norrish, J., & Brunzell, T. (2023). How is Trauma-Informed Education Implemented within Classrooms? A Synthesis of Trauma Informed Education Programs. *The Australian Journal of Teacher Education*, *48*(3), 95–120. DOI: 10.14221/1835-517X.6159

Novak, K., & Rodriguez, K. (2023). In Support of Students: A Leader's Guide to Equitable MTSS. https://doi.org/https://www.wiley.com/enus/In+Support+of+Students%3A+A+Leader%27s+Guide+to+Equitable+MTSS-p-9781119885269

Quote.org. (n.d.). Fernando Botero. https://quote.org/author/fernando-botero-72254

Reeves, A. M. (2019). Compassion Fatigue: Stories/Artworks of an Art Teacher with a Trauma-Informed Pedagogy.

Ryals, L. (2022). A Case Study of One Trauma-Informed Music Education Program. DOI: 10.34944/dspace/7676

Ryan, S. V., Pendergast, L. L., Schwing, S., von der Embse, N. P., Saeki, E., & Segool, N. (2017). Leaving the teaching profession: The role of teacher stress and educational accountability policies on turnover intent. *Teaching and Teacher Education*, *66*, 1–11. DOI: 10.1016/j.tate.2017.03.016

Salvador, K. (2019). Sustaining the Flame: (Re)Igniting Joy in Teaching Music. *Music Educators Journal*, *106*(2), 28–36. DOI: 10.1177/0027432119873701

Sears, C. A. Q. (2016). Professional Notes. *Music Educators Journal*, *102*(3), 18–19. DOI: 10.1177/0027432116630978

Salvador, K., & Culp, M. E. (2022). Intersections in Music Education: Implications of Universal Design for Learning, Culturally Responsive Education, and Trauma-Informed Education for P-12 Praxis. *Music Educators Journal*, *108*(3), 19–29. DOI: 10.1177/00274321221087737

Shaw, R. D. (2016). Music teacher stress in the era of accountability. *Arts Education Policy Review*, *117*(2), 104–116. DOI: 10.1080/10632913.2015.1005325

Shaw, R. D. (2019). Jumping through Hoops: Troubling Music Teacher Dilemmas in the New Era of Accountability. *Music Educators Journal*, *105*(3), 23–29. DOI: 10.1177/0027432118816146

Stein, L. (2020). Teacher Leadership: The Missing Factor in America's Classrooms. *The Clearing House: A Journal of Educational Strategies, Issues and Ideas*, *93*(2), 78–84. DOI: 10.1080/00098655.2020.1716671

Sullivan, A. L., Nguyen, T., & Shaver, E. (2022). Foundations of Equity-Centered MTSS. Equity by Design. Equity Assistance Center Region III, Midwest and Plains Equity Assistance Center.

Vetter, J. B., Fuxman, S., & Dong, Y. E. (2024). A statewide multi-tiered system of support (MTSS) approach to social and emotional learning (SEL) and mental health. *Social and Emotional Learning: Research, Practice, and Policy*, *3*, 100046. Advance online publication. DOI: 10.1016/j.sel.2024.100046 von Haaren-Mack, B., Schaefer, A., Pels, F., & Kleinert, J. (2020). Stress in Physical Education Teachers: A Systematic Review of Sources, Consequences, and Moderators of Stress. *Research Quarterly for Exercise and Sport, 91*(2), 279–297. DOI: 10.1080/02701367.2019.1662878 PMID: 31724912

Walker-Roberts, G. (2023). Creating an Inclusive Learning Environment for LGBTQIAA+ Individuals. *National University Open Educational Resources (OER) Repository*. National University Library. https://repository.nusystem.org/items/69389bca-0457-4d37-9aa5-9a5d6e2c3ba3

Walzer, D. (2021). Fostering Trauma-Informed and Eudaimonic Pedagogy in Music Education. *Frontiers in Education, 6*, 647008. Advance online publication. DOI: 10.3389/feduc.2021.647008

Will, M. (2018, October 23). 5 Things to Know About Today's Teaching Force. https://blogs.edweek.org/edweek/teacherbeat/2018/10/today_teaching_force_richard_ingersoll.html

Williams, H. M. A., Huskic, H., & Noto, C. M. (2024). Disrupting hierarchy in education: Students and teachers collaborating for social change. Teaching for social justice series. https://doi.org/https://www.tcpress.com/disrupting-hierarchy-in-education-9780807769775

DEFINITIONS OF KEY TERMS

Arts Education: Education in content areas such as music, visual arts, drama, and dance.

Compassion Fatigue: The depletion of energy experienced by professionals such as caregivers, healthcare professionals, and teachers due to expending emotion(al) labor and not having their own social-emotional needs replenished.

Content Area: The school subject, such as math or music.

Culturally Responsive Teaching (CRT): Reflective and meaningful teaching practices and philosophies that deeply connect with the lived experiences of diverse learners, taking into account learners' often complex backgrounds and histories (Gay, 2018).

Emotion(al) Labor: Unseen and unnoticed work that a teacher or other member of a helping profession does, especially regarding advocacy within the community and the need to justify their programs.

Less Commonly Taught Content Areas (LCTCA): Content areas taught in US K-12 schools for which there is typically only one to a few teachers in that content area when compared to the more popular content areas that are always taught (i.e. core content areas).

Multi-Tiered Systems of Support (MTSS): A comprehensive framework designed to address students' diverse academic and behavioral needs within educational settings. Implementing MTSS integrates academic and behavioral support for all students, recognizing how these aspects are interrelated and work in tandem (Adamson et al., 2019).

Oasis: A small fertile area within a vast desert that acts as a sanctuary, providing essential resources like water and a sense of peace and restoration for weary travelers.

Social-Emotional Learning (SEL): A framework that fosters students' ability to manage emotions and enhances their empathy and interpersonal skills, creating a more supportive learning environment.

Teacher Burnout: Teachers' feelings of hopelessness and fatigue, due to stress and related issues.

Teacher Isolation: Teachers' feelings of working alone in the professional setting without support and collaboration from administration, colleagues, and community.

Trauma: Lived experiences, including abuse and exposure to danger (such as violence and war), that strongly impact a human's nervous system, personality, and the ways they respond to stimuli throughout life.

Chapter 10
Addressing Commercial Sexual Exploitation of Children:
The Role of Trauma-Informed Practices in Schools

Chisato Hotta
https://orcid.org/0009-0009-4000-0789
National University, USA

ABSTRACT

Commercial sexual exploitation of children encompasses a range of crimes in which a child is sexually abused in exchange for financial gain or other valuables, such as a place to sleep. When a child is commercially sexually exploited, both their mental and physical health is impacted, leading to difficulties in social skills, education, and employment. Unfortunately, exploited children are often viewed negatively, and even when they seek help, their requests may be ignored. Many school officials, including nurses, principals, and teachers, are in a critical position to recognize exploitation and provide support. Trauma-informed practices are strategies designed to address trauma by fostering a safe and supportive environment. Implementing trauma-informed practices in schools is essential to creating safe spaces that provide appropriate support for these children. However, due to a lack of knowledge, there is often a lack of empathy, and trauma-informed practices are not effectively implemented to assist them.

ADDRESSING COMMERCIAL SEXUAL EXPLOITATION OF CHILDREN: THE ROLE OF TRAUMA-INFORMED PRACTICES IN SCHOOLS

The phrase "commercial sexual exploitation of children" (CSEC) often conjures up images of back alley transactions, children chained in basements, and kidnappings on the streets. However, while such scenarios can occur, a study by Kotrla and Wommack (2011) analyzing press releases and online media reports over nine years found that fewer than 10% of cases involved kidnapping. Unfortunately, the lack

DOI: 10.4018/979-8-3693-9020-7.ch010

of knowledge and empathy within various systems, including schools, pushes these children into the shadows, perpetuating the problem of commercial sexual exploitation.

CSEC involves a group of crimes in which a child is sexually abused for financial gain or other benefits, such as a place to sleep (Office of Juvenile Justice and Delinquency Prevention, 2010). When a child is commercially sexually exploited, both their mental and physical health are negatively affected, leading to challenges in social skills, education, and employment. Typically, children are trafficked for an average of 2.2 years, and 68% have only completed elementary or middle school (Counter-Trafficking Data Collaborative, 2018). Research indicates that maladaptive coping skills, aggression, frequent school absences, expulsions, and interactions with peers involved in similar situations are all highly correlated with commercial sexual exploitation and can severely hinder educational progress (Bounds et al., 2015; Deb et al., 2010; Kinnish et al., 2021). Additionally, Bruhns et al. (2018) discovered that adult female survivors of child commercial sexual exploitation often wanted to leave but needed support to meet basic needs, like income, to escape traffickers. They also found that the survivors expressed "access to education or training, which helped some participants identify alternatives and see themselves as capable of something other than sex work" (Bruhns et al., 2018, p. 433). Therefore, struggles with education can manifest both before and after exploitation and can increase the risks of becoming or remaining a commercially sexually exploited child.

In 2016, the International Labor Organization estimated that one million children globally were commercially sexually exploited, including approximately 40,000 in the United States (Rothman et al., 2019). By 2023, out of 22,442 children reported missing from child welfare care, 19% were believed by professionals to be victims of commercial sexual exploitation (National Center for Missing and Exploited Children, 2024). A significant issue is that exploited children continue to be hidden and misunderstood due to a lack of empathy, resulting in increased mental health problems, such as suicidal ideation, and physical health issues, such as unwanted pregnancy (Barnert et al., 2017). Moreover, the life expectancy for these children is only seven years from the point of first exploitation, with homicide and AIDS being the leading causes of death (Walker, 2013). They often endure adverse childhood experiences, including sexual and physical abuse. Unsafe home environments compound their vulnerability, making it difficult for them to resist or escape exploitation (Felitti et al., 1998; McMahon-Howard, 2017). Many children come from backgrounds marked by family disruption, such as divorce, and family dysfunction, such as domestic violence. In 2017 and 2018, the primary risk factors for being sex trafficked included recent immigrant status, substance use, unstable housing, being a runaway or homeless youth, foster care involvement, and mental health concerns (Polaris, n.d.-a, n.d.-b). Additional risks for human trafficking, including the CSEC encompass war, forced migration, poverty, and homelessness (Such et al., 2023). A U.S. study identified racial/ethnic minority status and running away as factors linked to child sex trafficking (Fedina et al., 2019). Factors such as abuse, substance use, poverty, and poor mental health also heighten the risk (Franchino-Olsen, 2021). These vulnerabilities are not confined to children in the United States. Haiti's first nationally representative study on lifetime CSEC revealed that both boys and girls who were victims of child sexual abuse were more likely to experience CSEC, especially those abused at younger ages (Silverman et al., 2021). These risks are interconnected and manifest across individual, family, and societal levels (Such et al., 2023).

Relevant research in the United States is scarce, often leaving schools unaware and unprepared to identify victims of commercial sexual exploitation; many such victims attend school daily, undetected and unsupported (Hannor-Walker et al., 2023). Their behaviors, such as difficulty concentrating, impulse control struggles, and aggression, are frequently misdiagnosed as oppositional defiant disorder or attention-deficit hyperactivity disorder. Yet, these could also be indicators of trauma. This misdiagnosis contributes to the likelihood that children will disengage from school by stopping attendance altogether or attending only sporadically. When they do attend, they often struggle with self-regulation, frustration tolerance, and staying awake in class.

VIEW OF COMMERCIALLY SEXUALLY EXPLOITED CHILDREN

Unfortunately, exploited children are often viewed negatively, and although they may reach out for help, their requests can be ignored. Many police officers and providers mistakenly believe that arresting and detaining children is the best way to help (Musto, 2013). These norms are deeply embedded in multiple systems, including educational systems, which can prevent teachers, school nurses, and other officials from identifying children who are commercially sexually exploited. When identified, these norms also impede their ability to support and assist the traumatized children. For instance, Fraley and Aronowitz (2019) discovered that many children visited school nurses but were perceived as problem students or believed to be engaging in consensual sexual behaviors. The primary theme in their study was "invisibility versus visibility." School nurses often lack awareness of the issue, rendering them unable to recognize or address it (invisibility), whereas exploiters are skilled at identifying and targeting these vulnerable youth (visibility). This invisibility underscores how the risks and signs of youth trafficking are overlooked in schools, with nurses frequently missing these risks and survivors feeling invisible, which leads to a lack of recognition and understanding of their situations.

It has been argued that nurses and school staff should investigate more thoroughly when students frequently report physical issues. For example, when a student visits the school nurse's office with recurring stomach aches, nurses often treat the pain as a menstrual issue without considering other possible causes. A survivor in the study expressed, "I heard what is wrong with you, why are you like this, why are you always complaining about this pain or that pain or that ache... I needed somebody to ask me what happened to you" (Fraley & Aronowitz, 2019, p. 7552). This issue extends beyond school nurses, as many children wished their teachers had inquired as well. However, due to the school staff's lack of knowledge about the appropriate questions to ask, the signs to look for, and the resources available for the youth, many educators do not engage with the students (Deb et al., 2010). Survivors also highlighted clear red flags, such as students possessing hotel keys or pens, which school staff failed to recognize as signs of trafficking (Deb et al., 2010). When school nurses or teachers did notice hotel keys, they often incorrectly assumed the students' families were homeless (Deb et al., 2010).

Furthermore, inadequate monitoring, including exposure through social media, along with a history of abuse and foster care, increases the risk of trafficking (Fraley & Aronowitz, 2019). Traffickers frequently use technology to coordinate with minors before and during trafficking, including scheduling encounters, monitoring activities, and maintaining control (Mitchell & Boyd, 2014). However, school nurses often fail to recognize these factors as potential indicators of trafficking (Fraley & Aronowitz, 2019). Mental health struggles, such as anxiety, and physical signs, such as persistent hunger and excessive sleepiness, are also overlooked as warning signs (Fraley & Aronowitz, 2019). This gap in recognition prevents school officials from identifying risks and symptoms of trafficking, leaving youth more vulnerable.

GENDER THEORY

One way to understand the problem of CSEC is through gender theory, which examines socially constructed perceptions of masculinity, femininity, and queerness (Jule, 2014). Masculinity is highly valued, with males being taught to be strong and in control (Mikkola, 2017). In contrast, femininity is considered secondary to masculinity, encouraging females to be non-sexual and submissive (Mikkola, 2017). A study examining Chinese male student sex workers through 25 online interviews found that the Internet and peer introductions were key entry points into the sex industry (Fang & Tang, 2023). Motivated by both consumption and sexual desire, many participants perceived commercial sex as "transactional hookups" (Fang & Tang, 2023). To manage stigma, they employed strategies such as concealing their work, separating sex from love, and simulating relationships (Fang & Tang, 2023). This study underscores that stigma and CSEC are not limited to the United States. In relation to schools, adolescence is a critical period for gender socialization, with schools and peers playing a significant role in shaping gender norms (Amin et al., 2018; Rosen & Nofziger, 2019). Popularity and social group dynamics further influence this process. Bullying, which varies by gender, also impacts gender socialization—boys are more likely to engage in direct bullying, while girls experience more indirect forms (Rosen & Nofziger, 2019). Deb et al. (2010) found that girls who had been sexually exploited had a high likelihood of exhibiting aggression. One school nurse stated:

Girls are mean very, very mean. There are more girl fights than boy fights . . . over boys . . . my boyfriend . . . your boyfriend, she looked at me the wrong way, or she thinks she can look at me or she called me this name—everything. (Fraley & Aronowitz, 2019, p. 7559)

The aggression exhibited by youth further reinforces the perception that children are the problem rather than victims. This behavior can result in expulsion or suspension, disrupting their education and limiting their academic and personal growth opportunities.

These views also contribute to the normalization and acceptance of pimp culture. Houston-Kolnik et al. (2017) found that many students perceived "being a pimp as glamorous [pimps] make lots of money like he's the man" (p. 1119). Bales and Soodalater (2009) stated, "Pimps have acquired a glitzy, dangerous, 'outlaw' persona" (p. 87). This perception is further reinforced by events such as the "player ball," sometimes backed by mayors, where awards like No. 1 International Pimp of the Year are given. Such events have influenced teenagers to host "pimps and hos" parties, perpetuating the belief that pimps are figures to be admired (Bales & Soodalater, 2009). This perspective influences multiple aspects of the issue, potentially increasing the likelihood that individuals aspire to become pimps or associate with them while also shifting blame onto victims.

Furthermore, societal perceptions of males and masculinity contribute to the continued purchase of children. Bales and Soodalater (2009) noted that there appears to be an implicit societal norm suggesting that men are entitled to purchase sexual services. This notion is reinforced by a statement from Lois Lee, the president of the nonprofit organization Children of the Night: "When the mayor of Syracuse is caught trying to buy sex from a fifteen-year-old girl, or a famous movie star's name appears on the list of a Hollywood brothel, the news is often met with a wink and a nod. It's just guys being guys" (Bales & Soodalater, 2009, p. 86).

HOW COMMERCIAL SEXUAL EXPLOITATION HAPPENS

There are multiple paths for children to get commercially sexually exploited. Hampton and Lieggi (2020) found several themes in the reviewed articles in a literary review. First, most participants shared unsafe environments, such as home and school environments. Many shared a lack of supervision in both settings, such as teachers not being aware of bullying, parents going through domestic violence, and minors being abused without parental knowledge. Unfortunately, this encouraged many of the minors to run away, which was a significant factor that increased the likelihood of being commercially sexually exploited. The second theme was unmet needs like housing, food, and sometimes substances. Several minors also expressed that they had children or siblings they were caring for, which increased the likelihood that they desired stability or some kind of income. Multiple survivors expressed that the traffickers met that unmet need, which made them feel indebted and grateful to their traffickers, resulting in them staying when things became abusive and clinging to the hope that things would become the way they were before. The third theme was a normalization of prostitution and sex work by others around the minors.

UNIQUE POPULATIONS

In a study by Yang et al. (2024) examining sexually diverse and non-sexually diverse girls, meaning those who identify exclusively as heterosexual, in the juvenile justice system, sexually diverse girls faced nearly twice the risk of sexual abuse in non-familial contexts and experienced higher rates of both familial and non-familial abuse. More importantly, sexually diverse girls demonstrated significantly greater involvement in CSEC, with over half of the sample showing CSEC risk. These findings emphasize the need for more comprehensive assessments of sexual victimization and CSEC, as current methods may overlook key vulnerabilities, particularly among sexually diverse youth. Additionally, the study found that sexually diverse girls reported greater trauma exposure and heightened stress responses, which may further contribute to their increased CSEC risk.

Furthermore, Jones et al. (2024) examined youth's understanding of CSE and their willingness to seek help in situations of exploitation. While participants demonstrated some awareness of CSE, many failed to recognize its presence in their own communities. Younger adolescents, gender minorities, and youth in juvenile justice settings exhibited lower levels of knowledge and were less likely to seek help (Jones et al., 2024). Rothman et al. (2024) found that in their study of youth ages 13 to 24 who experienced CSEC before age 18, most had been diagnosed with neurodevelopmental or mood disorders, behavioral issues, or serious mental illness, with 73% having multiple diagnoses. These youths were more likely than the general population to have such conditions.

Lastly, individuals with disabilities, including intellectual disabilities and those who are deaf or hard of hearing, face a higher risk of victimization, including abuse and poverty (Bowman et al., 2024). Factors such as age, gender, communication barriers, and limited resources further increase their vulnerability (Bowman et al., 2024). These studies highlight that marginalized youth face a higher risk of exploitation, emphasizing the need for school staff to receive training on the impact of systemic oppression and to provide culturally sensitive support.

INTERNATIONAL POPULATIONS

Commercial sexual exploitation of children is not a problem that is only in the United States; it is a global problem. Online commercial sexual exploitation of children makes it easier for the problem to be global. Looking at online commercial sexual exploitation by including online child sexual abuse in a questionnaire for child sexual abuse, it was found that including online abuse raised the prevalence from 13.5% to 21.7%, with females at 31.6% and males at 10.8% (Finkelhor et al., 2024). Key factors were non-consensual image sharing and online interactions with older adults, also aiding in identifying survivors with higher distress (Finkelhor et al., 2024). A review by Drejer et al. (2023) found that offenders in the Philippines mainly use outdated platforms like Facebook Live, Skype, and Yahoo Messenger (Napier et al., 2021; Terre des Hommes, 2013). It was also found that many of the research studies, despite rapid tech advancements, show similar results from 2013 and 2021. Live streaming has improved quality, speed, stability, and security, with COVID-19 boosting user adoption. Today, live-streaming services are easy to set up with basic devices, offering free options for smaller broadcasts and privacy features like encryption and private rooms (Drejer et al., 2023). Offenders can also stream videos on cloud platforms like Amazon or Google (Drejer et al., 2023). While these services ban illegal content and set age limits, detecting such content is challenging (Drejer et al., 2023). AI monitoring is underdeveloped, and it's unclear if human checks occur (Drejer et al., 2023). Despite the ease of creating private streams, few systems are detected in the studies that focus on older technologies.

While the Philippines is a major hotspot for LSCSA (Brown, 2016), victims are found worldwide. In Napier et al. (2021), 43 victims were from the Philippines, with others from the UK, China, and Thailand. Australian offenders targeted children in countries like Indonesia, Vietnam, Japan, and Namibia. The Internet Watch Foundation (2018) reported that most victims are white females from wealthy Western backgrounds, highlighting the global nature of victimization.

Looking into Europe, Benavente et al. (2022) highlight that commercial sexual exploitation in Europe affects both sexes and is not solely a gender issue. Interestingly, it is argued that the prevalence is similar for both boys and girls in Europe (Benavente et al., 2022). Like other places, it is driven by power imbalances due to the young age of victims. In most cases, the vulnerability of children and adolescents, linked to their age and unmet needs, is exploited (Finkelhor, 2007). For years, European countries have focused on trafficking minors from developing nations, ignoring the internal sexual exploitation of vulnerable youth (Pereda, 2024). Like the United States and other countries, the legal approach in Europe emphasizes their lack of agency or criminal behavior, overlooking the social inequalities that enable exploitation and ignoring the needs of boys and girls who don't fit victim stereotypes (Pereda, 2024).

In Sub-Saharan Africa, risk factors for CSEC included adverse childhood experiences, victimization, being female (16+), school dropouts, technology use, and alcohol use by children and parents (Amponsah et al., 2024). Protective factors were having more female adolescents in the household, school health screenings, children in school, and strong parental monitoring (Amponsah et al., 2024). This is like many findings in the United States, emphasizing that the problem and protective factors of commercial sexual exploitation of children is truly a global phenomenon.

TYPES OF TRAFFICKERS

Some mass media distract from and normalize the CSEC by portraying pimps as powerful and alluring (Merodio et al., 2020). In the 1970s, American media depicted pimps with flashy cars and designer clothes, creating a misleading image of luxury and influence (Merodio et al., 2020). For example, the song "It's Hard Out Here for a Pimp," from the 2005 film *Hustle & Flow*, won the 2006 Oscar for Best Original Song. Performed by Three 6 Mafia, it glamorizes pimp culture and sexual exploitation. Hip-hop figures such as Bishop Don "Magic" Juan and Snoop Dogg have also publicly celebrated their past involvement in pimping, gaining media attention that reinforces this image (Merodio et al., 2020). Since 1974, the annual Players Ball, led by Bishop Don "Magic" Juan, has further perpetuated this narrative by combining music with the Pimp of the Year award, normalizing and glorifying commercial sexual exploitation and prostitution (Bales & Soodalater, 2009; Merodio et al., 2020). To counter this normalization, it is encouraged to refer to individuals who commercially exploit children as traffickers rather than pimps. There are multiple types of traffickers, including CEO traffickers, familial traffickers, gorilla traffickers, peer traffickers, and Romeo traffickers.

The CEO trafficker lures children into commercial sexual exploitation by posing as a legitimate business owner (Godoy et al., 2016). They cultivate an image of professionalism and wealth, attracting aspiring actresses and entertainers with fraudulent job offers (Godoy et al., 2016). These traffickers may operate an actual business, have connections to legitimate enterprises, or run a deceptive front (Godoy et al., 2016). By leveraging their authority as talent agents, they manipulate victims, often requiring them to complete forms that gather personal information and unknowingly sign agreements facilitating commercial sexual exploitation (Godoy et al., 2016).

The second type of trafficker is the familial trafficker, in which the trafficker is a family member. Mitchell et al. (2010) found that familial trafficking often involves very young victims, with the mother being the trafficker in approximately two-thirds of cases. This pattern contrasts with the more commonly documented profiles of traffickers in the literature (Kotrla, 2010). Raphael et al. (2010) noted that while up to 25% of traffickers are female, only 1% are mothers. The betrayal by a primary caregiver can result in severe trauma, significantly impacting the child's emotional and psychological well-being (Cook et al., 2005). Children subjected to familial trafficking also experience educational disruptions, health risks, early pregnancy, and poor role modeling, all of which negatively affect their development (Rafferty, 2008). Their young age may reduce the likelihood of running away or encountering the juvenile justice system, making them more difficult to identify as trafficking victims. Research indicates that over 60% of child and youth trafficking victims are found in micropolitan or rural areas, where limited awareness, training, and resources further hinder detection (Edwards et al., 2006; Newton et al., 2008; Castañeda, 2000). Sprang and Cole (2018) found that professionals in metropolitan areas were more likely to receive training, understand relevant laws, and recognize trafficking cases. Familial trafficking in isolated, under-resourced areas presents additional challenges for identification and intervention.

The gorilla trafficker exerts control over children through sheer force, using threats, physical violence, and even kidnapping (Kennedy et al., 2007). Unlike other traffickers who may deceive children with false promises, the gorilla trafficker's approach is direct and explicit: the child's role is to work the streets, with severe consequences for non-compliance (Kennedy et al., 2007). Peer traffickers are youths who recruit others into trafficking and may themselves be controlled by another trafficker. In the United States, children are often lured into exploitation by peers who may also be victims (Greenbaum, 2014). Often perceived as popular or mature, these recruiters may offer protection or target vulnerable youth, sometimes in exchange for rewards (Greenbaum, 2014). Some operate independently, enticing others with promises of quick money or inclusion in a network where prostitution is normalized (Greenbaum, 2014). Reed et al. (2019) identified peer influence as a significant factor in commercial sexual exploitation, highlighting two primary influences: peer pressure and role models. Hargreaves-Cormany et al. (2016) found that adolescent female victims were frequently drawn into sex trafficking by peers of similar age whom they perceived as genuine friends. Romeo traffickers use romance to lure the victim into trafficking. According to Polaris (2023), Romeo traffickers use romance targeting individuals that they view as vulnerable. Many times, the trafficker will find and connect with their victims using social media (Polaris, 2023).

TRAUMA-INFORMED PRACTICES

Trauma-informed practices (TIPs) are strategies designed to address trauma by creating a safe and supportive environment. These practices emphasize fostering a secure school culture, nurturing relationships, and enhancing student self-efficacy (National Education Association, 2023). Additionally, a trauma-informed K–12 school system requires all staff to recognize and respond to the effects of trauma on behavior, emotions, and academics. This approach prioritizes avoiding punitive measures, directly addressing trauma, and providing support to help students manage stress, ultimately contributing to a positive school climate (National Child Traumatic Stress Network, n.d.).

Examining the implementation of trauma-informed care in schools, Wassink-de Stigter et al. (2022) found that the primary barriers involved the absence of a facilitator. For example, strong leadership within the school setting facilitated the implementation of trauma-informed care, whereas a lack of leadership acted as a barrier. In exploring key stakeholders and the challenges associated with each, the authors identified mental health professionals and caregivers as crucial contributors. Mental health professionals play a vital role in trauma screening and providing essential support within schools. Their involvement helps establish a trauma-sensitive environment and offers targeted assistance to affected students and staff. However, ensuring student privacy remains a significant challenge in these collaborations.

Additionally, caregivers are key stakeholders in TIPs, and school staff must recognize the diversity of family backgrounds, including biological, foster, and professional caregivers, some of whom may have experienced trauma themselves. Challenges such as stigma, single-parenting, health issues, and substance abuse can hinder caregiver involvement. To be truly trauma-informed, schools must create a safe environment and build trust with caregivers to effectively address trauma, connect them to support services and mitigate the impact of further trauma.

Looking within school settings, staff buy-in is essential for implementing trauma-informed approaches. Key challenges include teachers' lack of trauma awareness, the belief that trauma is solely a home issue, and concerns that TIPs are too lenient. Additionally, general resistance to change can hinder buy-in (Wassink-de Stigter et al., 2022). Pribitkin (2020) further examined these challenges in a study on TIPs within schools in Philadelphia, Nashville, Oakland, San Francisco, and Gladstone, all selected for their recognized TIP programs. The study included interviews with 32 individuals: eight district workers, seven support staff members, six administrators, six teachers, three researchers providing expertise on TIPs, and two trainers. One significant challenge identified was teacher workload. One participant stated, "Our teachers are so highly stressed because of how many trauma-impacted kids are in the classes and how under-resourced and underpaid they are" (Pribitkin, 2020, p. 24). This stress was compounded by the argument that overworked and overwhelmed teachers lack the capacity to implement a new program. Participants also noted that while there is interest in learning about trauma and TIPs, training opportunities remain insufficient (Pribitkin, 2020). Administrators expressed frustration over their inability to offer more professional development training, possibly due to the prioritization of academics over new practices and the lack of recognition that academics and trauma-informed approaches are closely connected (Pribitkin, 2020).

School staff are not the only ones who need to be committed to trauma-informed care; principals must also fully support its implementation. In a survey of 76 principals—57 from traditional schools and 19 from alternative schools—principals were more likely to believe that sex trafficking education should be directed at high school students rather than middle school students, likely due to concerns about age-appropriate content (Rizo et al., 2019). While this concern is understandable, the estimated age of first exploitation is 11–13 years old for males and 12–14 years old for females, highlighting the need to introduce education earlier rather than later (Walker, 2013). Principals also agreed that school staff should be informed about sex trafficking risk factors and trained to address them (Rizo et al., 2019). Similarly, Hornor et al. (2020) examined 286 adolescents referred to a Child Advocacy Center in the Midwest and found that only 33% reported learning about trafficking, including sex trafficking, in their schools.

Overall, principals were uncertain about the likelihood of sex trafficking occurring in their schools. However, principals of alternative schools expressed slightly greater concern about this risk compared to their counterparts in traditional schools (Rizo et al., 2019). This suggests that while principals may acknowledge the importance of understanding of CSEC as a broader societal issue, they may lack the motivation to implement trauma-informed care due to a limited understanding of the likelihood of exploitation occurring within their own schools.

In another study examining high school students' knowledge of sex trafficking and school staff's perspectives on prevention, both groups agreed that schools should provide education on sex trafficking and conduct regular staff training (Kang et al., 2024). Discussions revealed that simply asking students if they have heard of sex trafficking does not accurately capture their understanding. Many students were unclear about the definition of trafficking, particularly in exploitative relationships. School staff also noted the challenges of identifying trafficking cases due to their sensitive nature, emphasizing the need for improved training on recognizing CSEC while balancing sensitivity with trauma-informed practice.

WHAT SCHOOLS CAN DO

A trauma-informed classroom aims to integrate an understanding of how trauma and adverse life experiences affect students into the learning environment (Pickens & Tschopp, 2017). The Substance Abuse and Mental Health Services Administration (2023) outlines four key elements of TIPs. The first is realization, which involves acknowledging that trauma can hinder desired outcomes by affecting mental health and substance use. The second is recognition, which includes identifying trauma-related signs through screenings, employee development, and other strategies. The third is a response, which focuses on creating a safe environment, implementing training, and securing leadership buy-in. The fourth is resistance to re-traumatization, which involves understanding and avoiding actions that may inadvertently reinforce or repeat traumatic experiences for both students and staff. Trauma-informed care ultimately seeks to create a setting that ensures physical and emotional safety, fostering student growth and resilience (Pickens & Tschopp, 2017).

Examining how schools can become more trauma-informed regarding the CSEC involves increasing awareness that CSEC occurs in all communities, recognizing the signs, and understanding its impact on mental and physical health. Hurst (2019) identified a significant lack of awareness within the education system. Key indicators of exploitation include students appearing excessively tired, falling asleep in class, or frequently complaining of physical symptoms such as headaches and stomach aches. Irregular school attendance and possession of expensive items, such as new phones or clothing, may also be warning signs. Regarding mental health, exploited children experience high rates of depressive and anxiety disorders, as well as difficulties with anger, fear, hostility, dissociation, and post-traumatic stress disorder (Los Angeles County Department of Mental Health, n.d.; Office of Juvenile Justice and Delinquency Prevention, 2014). Additionally, they may have suicidal thoughts and exhibit high rates of substance use, either as a coping mechanism or due to traffickers using substances as a means of control (Los Angeles County Department of Mental Health, n.d.).

Recognition requires that schools be educated to increase awareness, understand how to ask students questions and learn how trauma impacts individual students. School staff often lack sufficient knowledge or the necessary procedures and policies to address the issue effectively (Priebe & Suhr, 2005). In research conducted by Hurst (2019), several participants shared that although they did not disclose their experiences to a medical or mental health professional, they confided in a teacher they trusted. Some noted that when a teacher asked once, and they denied the exploitation, there was no follow-up, and they were not asked again. Due to this, it is important for school staff to recognize the signs of commercial sexual exploitation, ask questions from a place of concern rather than judgment, and continue to follow up even if the child initially declines to share. Building connections with students is also essential, as they may not disclose sensitive information if they do not feel comfortable with the adult asking the questions. Some questions that may be helpful to ask students include the following:

- Has someone ever asked you to engage in sexual activity in exchange for something?
- Does someone control you?
- Are your phone, social media, or other communication methods monitored?
- Do you have a boyfriend or girlfriend? Tell me about them. (Listen for factors such as age and controlling behaviors).
- Has anyone ever come to check on your well-being at home?
- When was the last time you ate?
- How often do you eat in a day?

Some questions for staff to ask themselves when assessing risk include the following:

- Do you see any physical bruises or marks on the student's body?
- Does the student exhibit withdrawn behavior, aggression, low self-esteem, or signs of depression or fear?
- Do you see any evidence of self-harm?
- Does the student mention sexual situations that are not typical for their developmental age?

Furthermore, acknowledging the high number of neurodiverse CSEC survivors, implementing TIPs should accommodate sensory, communication, and executive function differences. Using plain language for screening and offering online schooling options may improve accessibility (Rothman et al., 2024). CSEC screening materials incorporating visual aids or social stories could also enhance understanding and support for neurodiverse students (Rothman et al., 2024).

Regarding response, an essential component is ensuring that each student feels understood and heard by creating a safe environment. Kang et al. (2024) found that both students and staff emphasized the need for safe spaces and trust to discuss trafficking. Fear of judgment often prevents youth, particularly those from marginalized backgrounds, from speaking out. Staff require training to respond effectively and sensitively (Kang et al., 2024). In a trauma-informed classroom, educators must explicitly define and model standards for a secure and supportive environment. Establishing guidelines against bullying, promoting respectful communication, and acknowledging positive behaviors are crucial (Pickens & Tschopp, 2017). Managing transitions effectively by providing advance notice and setting clear expectations is also important, as transitions and changes can trigger stress responses in many traumatized children (Pickens & Tschopp, 2017). During behavioral disruptions, educators should maintain a composed approach and focus on actions rather than personal attributes to uphold a respectful and safe classroom climate (Pickens & Tschopp, 2017). For example, instead of becoming frustrated when a student refuses to sit down, a more effective response may be to pull the student aside and ask, "What is stopping you from sitting down?" The answer could reveal underlying issues such as physical pain, anxiety, fear of falling asleep, or other concerns that require support.

The last step is resistance to re-traumatization, which is crucial for ensuring that students who have experienced trauma are not exposed to further harm. This requires schools and staff to take preventive actions to minimize the risk of triggering or exacerbating trauma-related symptoms through their behaviors and procedures (Baker, 2024). Although schools generally aim to support students, especially those affected by trauma, good intentions do not always lead to meaningful outcomes (Presence, 2021). Potentially re-traumatizing responses from schools may include placing students in time-outs, making dismissive or stigmatizing comments such as "You're acting borderline," asserting authority in a way that feels punitive, or labeling students as problems or resistant (Center for Substance Abuse Treatment, 2014). These responses can alienate students and diminish their sense of safety. Another essential aspect of resisting re-traumatization is ensuring that staff have appropriate knowledge of available resources to refer youth to when needed. Hurst (2019) identified a lack of resources provided to youth by teachers and a failure to ask about their safety. A list of accessible resources tailored to students' needs can help address this gap. For example, recognizing that sexually transmitted infections such as chlamydia, gonorrhea, human immunodeficiency virus, and syphilis occur at higher rates among exploited youth, it is important to know which clinics offer private sexually transmitted infections testing and treatment, potentially without requiring parental involvement. This can help reduce students' stigma and shame (Ijadi-Maghsoodi et al., 2016). Additional resources that could be beneficial include the following:

- Mental health resources: individual, group, and family therapy, as well as support groups
- Drop-in services: locations where students can shower, access warm food, and sleep if needed
- Housing resources: temporary housing and youth shelters
- Financial aid resources
- Employment resources
- Tutoring resources

Success Stories and More Recommendations

In a study conducted at a residential facility with 11 current residents, survivors reported numerous negative school experiences, including conflicts with teachers and feelings of failure (Wells et al., 2024). Many faced instability due to frequent school changes, poor attendance, and high failure rates, particularly in middle school (Wells et al., 2024). A significant issue was the discrepancy between their perceived grade level and actual academic records, highlighting a lack of understanding of their academic progress (Wells et al., 2024). Despite these challenges, some students found belonging and motivation through extracurricular activities such as band or track, encouraging them to attend school even when struggling (Wells et al., 2024). The residents emphasized the importance of social connections in education, viewing school as a means of forming friendships (Wells et al., 2024). The residential facility provided educational support through computer-based learning and a full-time certified teacher, and residents acknowledged that they needed more assistance than they had received in previous educational settings. Schools can foster a sense of community and belonging by incorporating interactive learning, ensuring consistent access to special education services, and integrating students' strengths, such as creativity and athletics, into their education to support their growth.

To illustrate TIPs in action, in Canada, the Youth Development Instrument (YDI) research group collaborates with a youth advisory council (YAC) composed of 25 diverse adolescents, including neurodiverse youth, those with mental health challenges, and newcomers to Canada, many of whom joined to create positive change based on their own experiences (Maloney et al., 2024). YDI YAC members, who are compensated, contribute to shaping survey content and mobilizing findings through social media and presentations to students and policymakers (Maloney et al., 2024). In 2023, YDI YAC participated in a retreat focused on social connection and well-being after COVID-19, engaging in activities such as team-building exercises, a cultural walk with a Squamish Nation guide, and a dance party celebrating identity (Maloney et al., 2024). YDI YAC members have presented their findings at conferences and to policymakers, emphasizing equity, youth autonomy, and supportive school environments (Maloney et al., 2024). These insights drive youth-led initiatives, including school clubs to foster belonging (Maloney et al., 2024).

Furthermore, in a study conducted by Aragón et al. (2024), teachers in schools where TIPs were implemented reported strong well-being and low trauma but experienced high burnout. The study found that the most utilized resources included mental health tools, virtual wellness sessions, and social connections, while the most helpful resources were in-person wellness activities, social connections, and training to identify at-risk students.

TIPs can be implemented at any level of education. For example, a Midwestern university offered courses on trauma-informed care, resulting in increased knowledge and skills among participants (Canon et al., 2020). In another study, a survey of 218 primary educators found a connection between trauma knowledge, confidence in using trauma-informed strategies, and building supportive relationships (Bilbrey et al., 2022). While teachers felt confident in offering support, they expressed a need for more training in trauma strategies and increased knowledge of community resources (Bilbrey et al., 2022).

These studies emphasize the importance of training and demonstrate that TIPs can be implemented in various educational settings. They also highlight the significance of social connections for both staff and students, which may help reduce teacher burnout and encourage student engagement. These connections can be fostered through youth-led initiatives like clubs and extracurricular activities like band or track. Additionally, prioritizing mental health care for both students and staff is essential and strongly encouraged.

Bath et al.(2024) found that My Body, My Choice, a sexual health education program for youth with experiences of CSE, was effective for CSE-affected youth, improving knowledge of birth control, attitudes, and confidence in condom use. However, there were no improvements in contraceptive access or guardian communication. This highlights that My Body, My Choice, or similar structured educational programs may be helpful for youth who have been commercially sexually exploited in the past.

Another space that gives hope into change is technology, specifically artificial intelligence, or AI. Singh & Nambiar (2024) highlights AI's potential in combating online child sexual exploitation, with tools like chatbots and machine learning aiding detection. Challenges include privacy, generalization, and personalization (Singh & Nambiar, 2024). Future developments may focus on deep learning and improved predictive analysis, with more research needed on AI's role in prevention.

CONCLUSION

CSEC, in which children are sexually abused in exchange for something valuable, is a crime that occurs in plain sight yet often goes unnoticed. The impact on children is profound, affecting their physical and emotional well-being. Physical consequences include unwanted and multiple pregnancies, sexually transmitted infections, and injuries inflicted by buyers or traffickers, while emotional effects include depression, suicidal ideation, and dissociation (Barnert et al., 2017). These challenges hinder their ability to attend school or focus when they do, often leading to them being mislabeled as problem children.

Many school officials, including nurses, principals, and teachers, are in a crucial position to recognize exploitation and support affected children. However, due to a lack of knowledge, there is often a lack of empathy, and TIPs are not implemented to assist these children. When students struggle, they are not asked the necessary questions; if they are, they are only asked once. Their symptoms may be misattributed to other issues, such as menstrual cramps or oppositional defiant disorder, rather than being recognized as potential indicators of exploitation (Fraley & Aronowitz, 2019; Hannor-Walker et al., 2023).

Tips in schools involve actions and strategies designed to address trauma in children and adults by fostering a safe school environment (National Education Association, 2023). Regarding implementation, barriers often include the absence of a facilitator, such as strong leadership, lack of engagement with stakeholders, and limited caregiver involvement (Wassink-de Stigter et al., 2022). Without these facilitators, traumatized students continue to be retraumatized, increasing their likelihood of returning to their traffickers. Applying the Substance Abuse and Mental Health Services Administration's four elements of TIPs—realization, recognition, response, and resistance to re-traumatization—requires acknowledging that commercial sexual exploitation occurs and understanding its impact, recognizing the warning signs and asking appropriate questions, establishing guidelines to create a safe school environment, and examining school responses that may be retraumatizing, such as time-outs, while developing alternative approaches rooted in curiosity and support. Teachers, particularly in underfunded settings, often take on multiple roles, and the increasing number of traumatized students underscores the need to reassess teacher training on mental health and trauma care (Canon et al., 2020).

REFERENCES

Amin, A., Kågesten, A., Adebayo, E., & Chandra-Mouli, V. (2018). Addressing gender socialization and masculinity norms among adolescent boys: Policy and programmatic implications. *The Journal of Adolescent Health*, *62*(3), S3–S5. DOI: 10.1016/j.jadohealth.2017.06.022 PMID: 29455715

Amponsah, E. B., Abdullah, A., Eltigani, B., & Cluver, L. D. (2024). Risk and protective factors of commercial sexual exploitation of children and adolescents in sub-Saharan Africa: A systematic review. *Trauma, Violence & Abuse*, *25*(4), 3177–3190. DOI: 10.1177/15248380241241021 PMID: 38554071

Aragón, K. M., Mullin, A. C., Felix, E. D., Appel, O., & Sharkey, J. D. (2024). Identifying what educators need to support trauma-informed practices in the schools: A community needs assessment. *School Psychology*, *39*(5), 520–529. DOI: 10.1037/spq0000621 PMID: 38330316

Baker, J. (2024, August 12). Integrating the 4 Rs of trauma-informed care into your practice. *Relias*. https://www.relias.com/blog/4-rs-trauma-informed-care

Bales, K., & Soodalter, R. (2009). *The slave next door: Human trafficking and slavery in America today*. University of California Press. DOI: 10.1525/9780520942998

Barnert, E., Iqbal, Z., Bruce, J., Anoshiravani, A., Kolhatkar, G., & Greenbaum, J. (2017). Commercial sexual exploitation and sex trafficking of children and adolescents: A narrative review. *Academic Pediatrics, 17*(8), 825–829. http://doi.org/. 2017.07.009DOI: 10.1016/j.acap

Bath, E. P., Godoy, S. M., Perris, G. E., Ramos, J., Aralis, H., & Barnert, E. (2024). My body, my choice: An adapted sexual health intervention for youth with histories of commercial sexual exploitation. *Journal of Human Trafficking*, •••, 1–14. DOI: 10.1080/23322705.2024.2332868

Benavente, B., Díaz-Faes, D. A., Ballester, L., & Pereda, N. (2021). Commercial sexual exploitation of children and adolescents in Europe: A systematic review. *Trauma, Violence & Abuse*, *23*(5), 1529–1548. Advance online publication. DOI: 10.1177/1524838021999378 PMID: 33715516

Bounds, D., Julion, W. A., & Delaney, K. R. (2015). Commercial sexual exploitation of children and state child welfare systems. *Policy, Politics & Nursing Practice*, *16*(1–2), 17–26. DOI: 10.1177/1527154415583124 PMID: 25908664

Bowman, E., Kobek, C. M., & Crowe, T. (2024). Deaf populations and human trafficking: Risk and protective factors for consideration. *Journal of Human Trafficking*, *11*(1), 73–89. DOI: 10.1080/23322705.2024.2426936

Brown, R., Napier, S., & Smith, R. (2020). Australians who view: An analysis of financial transactions. *Trends and Issues in Crime and Criminal Justice*, *589*, 1–16.

Bruhns, M. E., del Prado, A., Slezakova, J., Lapinski, A. J., Li, T., & Pizer, B. (2018). Survivors' perspectives on recovery from commercial sexual exploitation beginning in childhood. *The Counseling Psychologist*, *46*(4), 413–455. DOI: 10.1177/0011000018777544

Cannon, L. M., Coolidge, E. M., LeGierse, J., Moskowitz, Y., Buckley, C., Chapin, E., Warren, M., & Kuzma, E. K. (2019). Trauma-informed education: Creating and pilot testing a nursing curriculum on trauma-informed care. *Nurse Education Today*, *85*(85), 104256. DOI: 10.1016/j.nedt.2019.104256 PMID: 31759240

Castañeda, D. (2000). The close relationship context and HIV/AIDS risk reduction among Mexican Americans. *Sex Roles*, *42*(7/8), 551–580. DOI: 10.1023/A:1007095221993

Center for Substance Abuse Treatment. (2014). *Trauma-informed care in behavioral health services.* U.S. Department of Health and Human Services. https://www.ncbi.nlm.nih.gov/books/NBK207201/

Cook, A., Spinazzola, J., Ford, J., Lanktree, C., Blaustein, M., Cloitre, M., & Van der Kolk, B. (2005). Complex Trauma in Children and Adolescents. *Psychiatric Annals*, *35*(5), 390–398. https://psycnet.apa.org/doi/10.3928/00485713-20050501-05. DOI: 10.3928/00485713-20050501-05

Counter-Trafficking Data Collaborative. (2018). Age of victims: Children and adults. *CTDC*. https://www.ctdatacollaborative.org/story/age-victims-children-and-adults

Deb, S., Mukherjee, A., & Mathews, B. (2010). Aggression in sexually abused trafficked girls and efficacy of intervention. *Journal of Interpersonal Violence*, *26*(4), 745–768. DOI: 10.1177/0886260510365875 PMID: 20587459

Des Hommes, T. (2013). *Full screen on view: An exploratory study on the background and psychosocial consequences of webcam child sex tourism in the Philippines*. Terre des Hommes.

Drejer, C., Riegler, M. A., Halvorsen, P., Johnson, M. S., & Baugerud, G. A. (2023). Livestreaming Technology and Online Child Sexual Exploitation and Abuse: A Scoping Review. *Trauma, Violence & Abuse*, *25*(1), 152483802211475. DOI: 10.1177/15248380221147564 PMID: 36727734

Edwards, J. M., Iritani, B. J., & Hallfors, D. D. (2006). Prevalence and correlates of exchanging sex for drugs or money among adolescents in the United States. *Sexually Transmitted Infections*, *82*(5), 354–358. DOI: 10.1136/sti.2006.020693 PMID: 16901917

Fang, Y., & Tang, C. (2023). Transactional desire: Exploring male student sex workers in China. *Journal of Sex Research*, *60*(6), 925–936. DOI: 10.1080/00224499.2023.2181306 PMID: 36826434

Fedina, L., Williamson, C., & Perdue, T. (2019). Risk factors for domestic child sex trafficking in the United States. *Journal of Interpersonal Violence*, *34*(13), 2653–2673. DOI: 10.1177/0886260516662306 PMID: 27470203

Felitti, V. J., Anda, R. F., Nordenberg, D., Williamson, D. F., Spitz, A. M., Edwards, V., & Marks, J. S. (1998). Relationship of childhood abuse and household dysfunction to many of the leading causes of death in adults: The Adverse Childhood Experiences (ACE) Study. *American Journal of Preventive Medicine*, *14*(4), 245–258. DOI: 10.1016/S0749-3797(98)00017-8 PMID: 9635069

Finkelhor, D. (2007). Developmental victimology: The comprehensive study of childhood victimization. In Davis, R. C., Lurigio, A. J., & Herman, S. (Eds.), *Victims of crime* (3rd ed., pp. 9–34). Sage.

Finkelhor, D., Turner, H. A., & Colburn, D. (2024). The prevalence of child sexual abuse with online sexual abuse added. *Child Abuse & Neglect*, *149*, 106634–106634. DOI: 10.1016/j.chiabu.2024.106634 PMID: 38227986

Fraley, H. E., & Aronowitz, T. (2019). Obtaining exposure and depth of field: School nurses "seeing" youth vulnerability to trafficking. *Journal of Interpersonal Violence*, *36*(15–16), 7547–7573. DOI: 10.1177/0886260519836779 PMID: 30879385

Franchino-Olsen, H. (2021). Vulnerabilities relevant for commercial sexual exploitation of children/domestic minor sex trafficking: A systematic review of risk factors. *Trauma, Violence & Abuse*, *22*(1), 99–111. DOI: 10.1177/1524838018821956 PMID: 30712473

Godoy, S., Sadwick, R., & Baca, K. (2016). *Shedding light on sex trafficking*. https://innovation.luskin.ucla.edu/wp-content/uploads/2019/03/Shedding_Light_on_Sex_Trafficking.pdf

Greenbaum, V. J. (2014). Commercial sexual exploitation and sex trafficking of children in the United States. *Current Problems in Pediatric and Adolescent Health Care*, *44*(9), 245–269. DOI: 10.1016/j.cppeds.2014.07.001 PMID: 25131563

Hampton, M. D., & Lieggi, M. (2020). Commercial sexual exploitation of youth in the United States: A qualitative systematic review. *Trauma, Violence & Abuse*, *21*(1), 57–70. DOI: 10.1177/1524838017742168 PMID: 29334030

Hannor-Walker, T. L., Kitchens, S., & Ricks, L. A. (2023). *Commercial sexual exploitation of children in schools: A proposed model for schools*. Georgia Southern Commons. https://digitalcommons.georgiasouthern.edu/nyar_savannah/2023/2023/51/

Hargreaves-Cormany, H. A., Patterson, T. D., & Muirhead, Y. E. (2016). A typology of offenders engaging in the sex trafficking of juveniles (STJ): Implications for risk assessment. *Aggression and Violent Behavior*, *30*, 40–47. DOI: 10.1016/j.avb.2016.06.011

Hornor, G., Sherfield, J., & Tscholl, J. (2020). Teen knowledge of commercial sexual exploitation of children. *Journal of Pediatric Health Care*, *34*(3), 239–245. DOI: 10.1016/j.pedhc.2019.11.006 PMID: 31955901

Houston-Kolnik, J. D., Soibatian, C., & Shattell, M. M. (2017). Advocates' experiences with media and the impact of media on human trafficking advocacy. *Journal of Interpersonal Violence*, *35*(5–6), 1108–1132. DOI: 10.1177/0886260517692337 PMID: 29294657

Hurst, T. E. (2019). Prevention of child sexual exploitation: Insights from adult survivors. *Journal of Interpersonal Violence*, *36*(13–14), NP7350–NP7372. DOI: 10.1177/0886260519825881 PMID: 30688542

Ijadi-Maghsoodi, R., Cook, M., Barnert, E. S., Gaboian, S., & Bath, E. (2016). Understanding and responding to the needs of commercially sexually exploited youth. *Child and Adolescent Psychiatric Clinics of North America*, *25*(1), 107–122. DOI: 10.1016/j.chc.2015.08.007 PMID: 26593123

Internet Watch Foundation. (2018). Trends in online child sexual exploitation: Examining the distribution of captures of live-streamed child sexual abuse. https://www.iwf.org.uk/media/23jj3nc2/distribution-of-captures-of-live-streamed-child-sexual-abuse-final.pdf

Jones, L. M., O'Brien, J. E., Colburn, D., McKinney, K., & Martin, L. (2024). Youth attitudes toward commercial sexual exploitation and help-seeking: An analysis of data collected by the not a number trafficking prevention program. *Research in Human Development*, *21*(2–3), 159–178. DOI: 10.1080/15427609.2024.2412427

Jule, A. (2014). Gender theory. In Michalos, A. C. (Ed.), *Encyclopedia of quality of life and well-being research* (pp. 2464–2466). Springer., DOI: 10.1007/978-94-007-0753-5_1137

Kang, J. S., Dalla, R. L., Nutting, A., & Edwards, K. M. (2024). Sex trafficking perspectives among high school students and school personnel in the Midwest: A focus group study to inform sex trafficking prevention programming. *Research in Human Development*, *21*(2–3), 109–134. DOI: 10.1080/15427609.2024.2410506

Kennedy, M. A., Klein, C., Bristowe, J. T. K., Cooper, B. S., & Yuille, J. C. (2007). Routes of recruitment. *Journal of Aggression, Maltreatment & Trauma*, *15*(2), 1–19. DOI: 10.1300/J146v15n02_01

Kinnish, K., Cohen, J., & Mannarino, A. (2021). *TF-CBT for the commercial sexual exploitation of children (CSEC): An implementation manual.* https://www.tfcbt.org/wp-content/uploads/2021/04/CSEC-Imp-Manual-Final-KK.pdf

Kotrla, K. (2010). Domestic minor sex trafficking in the United States. *Social Work*, *55*(2), 181–187. DOI: 10.1093/sw/55.2.181 PMID: 20408359

Kotrla, K., & Wommack, B. A. (2011). Sex trafficking of minors in the U.S.: Implications for policy, prevention and research. *The Journal of Applied Research on Children*, *2*(1), 5–12. https://files.eric.ed.gov/fulltext/EJ1189039.pdf. DOI: 10.58464/2155-5834.1012

Los Angeles County Department of Mental Health. (n.d.). *Commercial sexual exploitation of children and youth (CSECY).* https://dmh.lacounty.gov/our-services/transition-age-youth/csecy/

Maloney, J. E., Whitehead, J., Long, D., Kaufmann, J., Oberle, E., Schonert-Reichl, K. A., & Samji, H. (2024). Supporting adolescent well-being at school: Integrating transformative social and emotional learning and trauma-informed education. *Social and Emotional Learning: Research, Practice, and Policy*, *4*, 100044. DOI: 10.1016/j.sel.2024.100044

McMahon-Howard, J. (2017). Youth involved in prostitution (YIP): Exploring possible changes in interactions with police and social service agencies and narratives of victimization. *Criminal Justice Review*, *42*(2), 119–145. DOI: 10.1177/0734016817702194

Merodio, G., Duque, E., & Axt Peña, J. C. (2020). They are not Romeo pimps, they are traffickers: Overcoming the socially dominant discourse to prevent the sex trafficking of youth. *Qualitative Inquiry*, *26*(8–9), 1010–1018. DOI: 10.1177/1077800420938881

Mikkola, M. (2017). Feminist perspectives on sex and gender. *Stanford Encyclopedia of Philosophy.* https://plato.stanford.edu/entries/feminism-gender/

Mitchell, K. J., & Boyd, D. (2014, November). Understanding the role of technology in the commercial sexual exploitation of children: The perspective of law enforcement. *Crimes Against Children Research Center.* http://unh.edu/ccrc/pdf/CSEC and technology White Paper_Microsoft.pdf

Mitchell, K. J., Finkelhor, D., & Wolak, J. (2010). Conceptualizing juvenile prostitution as child maltreatment: Findings from the national juvenile prostitution study. *Child Maltreatment*, *15*(1), 18–36. DOI: 10.1177/1077559509349443 PMID: 19926628

Musto, J. (2013). Domestic minor sex trafficking and the detention-to-protection pipeline. *Dialectical Anthropology*, *37*(2), 257–276. DOI: 10.1007/s10624-013-9295-0

Napier, S., Teunissen, C., & Boxall, H. (2021). Live streaming of child sexual abuse: An analysis of offender chat logs (Report no. 639). Australian Institute of Criminology: Trends & issues in crime and criminal justice.

National Center for Missing and Exploited Children. (2024). *Our impact: 2023*. https://www.missingkids.org/ourwork/impact

National Child Traumatic Stress Network. (n.d.). *Trauma-Informed schools for children in K–12: A system framework*. https://www.nctsn.org/sites/default/files/resources/fact-sheet/trauma_informed_schools_for_children_in_k-12_a_systems_framework.pdf

National Education Association. (2023). *Trauma-Informed practices*. https://www.nea.org/professional-excellence/student-engagement/tools-tips/trauma-informed-practices

Newton, P. J., Mulcahy, T. M., & Martin, S. E. (2008). *Finding victims of human trafficking*. University of Chicago. DOI: 10.1037/e540892008-001

Office of Juvenile Justice and Delinquency Prevention. (2010). *Commercial sexual exploitation of children*. https://ojjdp.ojp.gov/programs/commercial-sexual-exploitation-children

Office of Juvenile Justice and Delinquency Prevention. (2014, August). *Commercial sexual exploitation of children and sex trafficking*. https://ojjdp.ojp.gov/sites/g/files/xyckuh176/files/media/document/csecsextrafficking.pdf

Pereda, N. (2024). Invisibilized victims: The sexual exploitation of children and adolescents in the european context / víctimas invisibilizadas: La explotación sexual de niños, niñas y adolescentes en el contexto europeo. Journal for the Study of Education and Development. *Infancia y Aprendizaje*, *47*(2), 243–263. DOI: 10.1177/02103702241253397

Pickens, I. B., & Tschopp, N. (2017). *Trauma-informed classrooms*. National Council of Juvenile and Family Court Judges. https://www.wyschoolpsych.org/wp-content/uploads/NCJFCJ_SJP_Trauma_Informed_Classrooms_Final7213.pdf

Polaris. (2023, March 28). The Tate Brothers and the basics of "Romeo pimping." Polaris. https://polarisproject.org/blog/2023/01/the-tate-brothers-and-the-basics-of-romeo-pimping/

Polaris. (n.d.-a). Growing awareness. Growing impact: 2017 statistics from the National Human Trafficking Hotline and BeFree Textline. https://polarisproject.org/wp-content/uploads/2019/09/2017NHTHStats-1.pdf

Polaris. (n.d.-b). *2018 statistics from the National Human Trafficking Hotline*. https://polarisproject.org/wp-content/uploads/2019/09/Polaris_National_Hotline_2018_Statistics_Fact_Sheet.pdf

Presence. (2021, March 16). Deploying a trauma-informed approach: Use the 4 R's. *Presence*. https://presence.com/insights/deploying-a-trauma-informed-approach-use-the-4-rs/

Pribitkin, T. (2020). *Theory versus practice in educational change: On-the-ground challenges of trauma-informed education practices*. https://knowledge.uchicago.edu/record/2437/files/Pribitkin.pdf

Priebe, A., & Suhr, C. (2005). Hidden in plain view: The commercial sexual exploitation of girls in Atlanta. *Atlanta Women's Agenda, 4*. https://iws.uga.edu/sites/default/files/Child_Prostitution.pdf

Rafferty, Y. (2008). The impact of trafficking on children: Psychological and social policy perspectives. *Child Development Perspectives*, *2*(1), 13–18. DOI: 10.1111/j.1750-8606.2008.00035.x

Raphael, J., Reichert, J. A., & Powers, M. (2010). Pimp control and violence: Domestic sex trafficking of Chicago women and girls. *Women & Criminal Justice*, *20*(1–2), 89–104. DOI: 10.1080/08974451003641065

Reed, S. M., Kennedy, M. A., Decker, M. R., & Cimino, A. N. (2019). Friends, family, and boyfriends: An analysis of relationship pathways into commercial sexual exploitation. *Child Abuse & Neglect*, *90*, 1–12. DOI: 10.1016/j.chiabu.2019.01.016 PMID: 30716650

Rizo, C. F., Klein, L., Chesworth, B. R., Franchino-Olsen, H., Villodas, M. L., Macy, R. J., & Martin, S. L. (2021). Educating students about sex trafficking and responding to students' needs: Principals' perceptions and practices. *Journal of Human Trafficking*, *7*(2), 202–223. DOI: 10.1080/23322705.2019.1698922

Rosen, N. L., & Nofziger, S. (2019). Boys, bullying, and gender roles: How hegemonic masculinity shapes bullying behavior. *Gender Issues*, *36*(3), 295–318. DOI: 10.1007/s12147-018-9226-0

Rothman, E. F., Cusano, J., Wagner, A., Lockwood, S., Cuevas, C. A., & Farrell, A. (2024). Prevalence of neurodevelopmental, mental, and behavioral disorders in a sample of U.S. Commercially sexually exploited youth, and associations with health and health care access. *Journal of Human Trafficking*, *11*(1), 4–19. DOI: 10.1080/23322705.2024.2426943

Rothman, E. F., Farrell, A., Paruk, J., Bright, K., Bair-Merritt, M., & Preis, S. R. (2019). Evaluation of a multi-session group designed to prevent commercial sexual exploitation of minors: The "My Life My Choice" curriculum. *Journal of Interpersonal Violence*, *36*(19–20), 9143–9166. DOI: 10.1177/0886260519865972 PMID: 31354019

Silverman, J. G., Boyce, S. C., Fonseka, R. W., Triplett, D., Chiang, L. F., Caslin, S. S., & Raj, A. (2022). The relationship between commercial sexual exploitation of children (CSEC) and childhood sexual abuse (CSA) among boys and girls in Haiti. *International Journal of Injury Control and Safety Promotion*, *29*(1), 86–92. DOI: 10.1080/17457300.2021.2004430 PMID: 34923923

Sprang, G., & Cole, J. (2018). Familial sex trafficking of minors: Trafficking conditions, clinical presentation, and system involvement. *Journal of Family Violence*, *33*(3), 185–195. DOI: 10.1007/s10896-018-9950-y

Substance Abuse and Mental Health Services Administrative. (2023). *Practical guide for implementing a trauma-informed approach*. https://store.samhsa.gov/sites/default/files/pep23-06-05-005.pdf

Such, E., Gardner, A., Dang, M., Wright, N., Bravo-Balsa, L., Brotherton, V., Browne, H., Esiovwa, N., Jiménez, E., Lucas, B., Wyman, E., & Trodd, Z. (2023). The risks and harms associated with modern slavery during the COVID-19 pandemic in the United Kingdom: A multi-method study. *Journal of Human Trafficking*, •••, 1–21. DOI: 10.1080/23322705.2023.2194760

Walker, K. (2013). *Ending the commercial sexual exploitation of children: A call for multi-system collaboration in California.* California Child Welfare Council. https://youthlaw.org/wp-content/uploads/2015/01/Ending-CSEC-A-Call-for-Multi-System_Collaboration-in-CA.pdf

Wassink-de Stigter, R., Kooijmans, R., Asselman, M. W., Offerman, E. C. P., Nelen, W., & Helmond, P. (2022). Facilitators and barriers in the implementation of trauma-informed approaches in schools: A scoping review. *School Mental Health, 14*(3), 470–484. DOI: 10.1007/s12310-021-09496-w

Wells, S., Goode, G. S., Hogan, K. A., Lavigne, R., Killen, T., & Simmons, M. (2024). "Throw dat hat!": Educational experiences, attainment, and aspirations of adolescent female trafficking survivors in a residential facility. *Social Sciences (Basel, Switzerland), 13*(11), 561–590. DOI: 10.3390/socsci13110561

Yang, R., Beck, A. N., & Lansing, A. E. (2024). Sexual abuse, commercial sexual exploitation, and cumulative adversity among sexually diverse and non-sexually diverse girls in the juvenile justice system. *Journal of Child Sexual Abuse, 33*(6), 765–783. DOI: 10.1080/10538712.2024.2403990 PMID: 39304496

KEY TERMS AND DEFINITIONS

Commercial Sexual Exploitation of Children (CSEC): A group of crimes in which a child is sexually abused for financial gain or other benefits

Gender Theory: Theory which examines socially constructed perceptions of masculinity, femininity, and queerness

Trauma-Informed Practices (TIPs): Strategies designed to address trauma by creating a safe and supportive environment

Youth Advisory Council (YAC): A group of youth who are compensated to contribute to shaping survey content and mobilizing findings through social media and presentations to students and policymakers

APPENDIX

Trauma-Informed Practices CSEC Tool Kit

Realization- Involves acknowledging that trauma can hinder desired outcomes by affecting mental health and substance use

Warning signs to look out for:

- Difficulty concentrating, impulse control struggles, aggression, low frustration tolerance, sleepiness, anger, fear, hostility, dissociation, and post-traumatic stress
- Suicidal thoughts and high rates of substance use
- Possessing hotel keys or pens
- Complaining stomach aches
- Bruises
- Inadequate monitoring, including exposure through social media
- History of abuse
- History or current involvement in foster care
- Younger adolescents
- Gender minorities
- Youth in juvenile justice settings
- Neurodevelopmental or mood disorders, such as autism, ADHD, major depressive disorder
- Behavioral issues
- Serious mental illness
- Individuals with disabilities, including intellectual disabilities
- Deaf or hard of hearing
- Possession of expensive items, such as new phones or clothing

Recognition- Includes identifying trauma-related signs through screenings, employee development, and other strategies

Questions that may be helpful to ask the student:

- Has someone ever asked you to engage in sexual activity in exchange for something?
- Does someone control you?
- Are your phone, social media, or other communication methods monitored?
- Do you have a boyfriend or girlfriend? Tell me about them. (Listen for factors such as age and controlling behaviors).
- Has anyone ever come to check on your well-being at home?
- When was the last time you ate?
- How often do you eat in a day?

Some questions for staff to ask themselves when assessing risk:

- Do you see any physical bruises or marks on the student's body?

- Does the student exhibit withdrawn behavior, aggression, low self-esteem, or signs of depression or fear?
- Do you see any evidence of self-harm?
- Does the student mention sexual situations that are not typical for their developmental age?

Response- Focuses on creating a safe environment, implementing training, and securing leadership buy-in

- Establishing guidelines against bullying
- Promoting respectful communication
- Acknowledge positive behaviors
- Maintain a composed approach and focus on actions during behavioral disruptions
- Managing transitions by providing advance notice and setting clear expectations (Example: "We are going to go to the music room in an hour.)

Resistance to Re-Traumatization- Involves understanding and avoiding actions that may inadvertently reinforce or repeat traumatic experiences for both students and staff

A list of accessible resources tailored to students' needs

- clinics offer private sexually transmitted infections testing and treatment, potentially without requiring parental involvement
- mental health resources: individual, group, and family therapy, support groups
- drop-in services: locations where students can shower, access warm food, and sleep if needed
- housing resources: temporary housing and youth shelters
- financial aid resources
- employment resources
- tutoring resources
- extracurricular activities
- Social connection resources
- youth advisory council (YAC)

A list of accessible resources for teachers

- Mental health resources
- mental health tools
- virtual wellness session
- social connections
- In-person wellness activities
- training to identify at-risk students

Chapter 11
Ensuring Inclusive K-14 Classrooms for LGBTQIAA+ Students When Teachers Implement Equitable Practices by Using the Growth Heartset Theory

Gary Simeon Walker-Roberts
https://orcid.org/0009-0007-6283-6064
National University, USA

ABSTRACT

In this book chapter, the author will discuss what teachers can do to adopt the Growth Heartset Theory so that all LGBTQIAA+ students feel welcome in their classrooms. By applying the Growth Heartset Theory, teachers build an environment conducive to inclusion for LGBTQIAA+ students in K-14 classrooms. By developing empathy, emotion, and inclusive school culture through the lenses of belonging and respect, the Growth Heartset Theory identifies how to support this diverse population in overcoming their specific challenges. By examining these challenges from an interdisciplinary point of view, this chapter calls attention to best practices that assist this student population while validating LGBTQIAA+ identities in educational contexts. It presents practical strategies for teachers and recommendations for curriculum design, classroom management, and teacher training to be consistent with this theory. Implementing these will result in positive educational outcomes.

INTRODUCTION

The ongoing marginalization of students in K-14 classrooms makes it ever more important to develop spaces that embrace equity, respect, and belonging for all, particularly for LGBTQIAA+ students. Still, these students tend to experience unique challenges, such as bullying, discrimination, and a lack

DOI: 10.4018/979-8-3693-9020-7.ch011

of representation in classrooms. This chapter will explore how teachers can adopt an inclusive, social justice-oriented pedagogy for LGBTQIAA+ students, helping them feel seen, supported, and valued, facilitating their academic success and personal well-being.

Teachers have the role of making students feel comfortable so that they can learn what is expected of them. Maslow taught that safety is one of the basic needs that students must fulfill before knowledge transfer begins; without a safe environment, it is almost impossible for students to absorb knowledge (Stocker, 2017). So, this shifts the burden back to teachers, who are the frontline authorities in the classroom, to do everything in their power to make the space a safe and comfortable place for students who identify as LGBTQIAA+.

LGBTQIAA+ students face systemic and social barriers in K-14 public schools. According to the Gay, Lesbian, and Straight Education Network (GLSEN), LGBTQIAA+ students cite staggering statistics; many do not feel safe in school because of their sexual orientation or gender identity. This fear is often reflected in increased absenteeism, lower academic performance, and more significant mental health challenges. This is compounded by peer and teacher discrimination and harassment and the lack of adequate institutional policies that serve to perpetuate the cycle of marginalization.

Before reading the chapter, establishing context is crucial. Basic terms must be defined, and they are critical to the discussion of inclusiveness in K-14 classrooms and the application of the Growth Heartset Theory (see Appendix A). K-14 includes K-12 (high schools) plus two years of post-secondary education (community colleges). The LGBTQIAA+ abbreviation will be shortened to LGBTQ+ for the rest of this chapter.

HISTORICAL CONTEXT FOR MULTI-TIERED SYSTEMS OF SUPPORT

The systemic stigmatization, discrimination, and exclusion of LGBTQ+ people has not always been the case in the history of humans. LGBTQ+ people were once allowed to live in safe and accepting societies worldwide. Unfortunately, safe and accepting societies transitioned to unsafe and unexpecting societies over time. It is important to recognize the generational trauma of people (that still plagues the community today- especially our youth/students) who were once accepted for whom they were to be replaced with a time when they were murdered and imprisoned for living their truth out loud. Here are some historical highlights of acceptance of being marginalized in history:

Indigenous Perspective. Indigenous cultures around the globe have recognized and embraced a diverse spectrum of sexual orientations and gender identities for centuries in ways that are strikingly different from the marginalization of such diversity perpetuated by colonial systems that are heavily Westernized (Bach, 2015; Walker-Roberts, 2024).

Pre-Modern Era. Many ancient societies, including Greece, Rome, and Asia, tolerated other sex partners or non-conforming gender expressions. However, as organized religions such as Christianity and Islam expanded and spread, beliefs shifted, with doctrines defining non-heteronormative behavior as sinful or unnatural. This regulation of morality has provided broader societal foundations for the condemnation of LGBTQ+ identities (Bronski et al., 2023).

The Legal Codification of Colonialism. Similar to the way colonial Western imperial forces imposed legal systems that criminalized same-gender sexualities and non-binary gender expressions on colonized communities, transgender people standing in between colonial powers continue to struggle against these forces of oppression today. Laws like England's Buggery Act of 1533—and the world-spanning enforcement of that law—inscribed homophobia and transphobia into legal codes, many of which persist as law in former colonies today.

Legal Discrimination and Pathologization. The extensive consideration of LGBTQ identities and the existence of same-sex attraction (not as a *sin* but as an authentic human phenomenon) became mainstream in the late 19th century onward, even as both medical and psychological discourses began to pathologize LGBTQ+ identities, framing them as mental illnesses or moral failures. This gave rise to conversion therapy and institutionalization on a large scale. Legal discrimination also ramped up, including laws against same-sex relationships, cross-dressing, and anti-LGBTQ+ public life. Sodomy laws — laws that made homosexual acts illegal — continued to be enforced in the U.S. until nearly the end of the 20th century.

Stigma and Cultural Suppression. LGBTQ+ people faced exclusion from public institutions and ostracism from society during the 20th century. Many lost their jobs, were denied housing, or were abused. The Lavender Scare in the United States in the 1950s resulted in the widespread firing of thousands of federal employees for suspected homosexuality. This moment added deeper levels of marginalization to the community.

Resistance and Advocacy. However, standing up to oppression is nothing new for the LGBTQ+ community, which has continued to resist despite overwhelming oppression and marginalization. The Stonewall Uprising of 1969 was a watershed moment — a catalyst for the modern LGBTQ+ rights movement. Nevertheless, progress has been shadowed by and often entangled with backlash and violence, including anti-LGBTQ+ legislation, stigmatization of the AIDS crisis, and ongoing violence against transgender people (Bronski et al., 2023; Phelps, 2021; Walker-Roberts, 2024).

Contemporary Challenges. While significant gains have been made, including marriage equality in many countries and increased media representation, LGBTQ+ people still face systemic barriers, particularly in areas with strict laws or deep-rooted cultural attitudes. Vulnerabilities such as unequal access to health care, employer discrimination, and high rates of homelessness among LGBTQ+ youth are legacies of a history of marginalization. This history is important if teachers are to understand the structural inequities that are still in place for LGBTQ+ people, particularly in schools. It also underscores the need for implementing equitable and belonging-oriented practices.

CREATING A SENSE OF URGENCY TO BUILD INCLUSIVE CLASSROOMS FOR LGBTQ+ STUDENTS

LGBTQ+ K-14 students are an understudied and widely misunderstood part of K-14 education, but they are also vitally important to our world. The fact that the LGBTQ+ community has faced acts *othering* throughout history that have resulted in mass murder, pathways for unjust bullying, acceptable engaging in unwanted harassment, and lack of social support systems for mental well-being has, needless to say, and rightfully so, should have awakened the 21st-century educational system to acknowledge the trauma that plagues young students today. There is residual trauma that calls for social-emotional learning in classrooms today when teaching LGBTQ+ students in the K-14 educational system. LGBTQ+ students still face a long list of traumatic situations as a direct result of a continuous cycle of being *othered* today (Walker-Roberts, 2024).

1. **Bullying and Harassment:** LGBTQ+ students often experience more bullying and harassment than their heterosexual peers. Research shows they are more vulnerable to both verbal and physical abuse (Bradley et al., 2019; Chan, 2020; Synan, 2023).
2. **Mental Health Risks:** LGBTQ+ youth are at an increased risk for mental health issues like anxiety, depression, and suicidal ideation, often exacerbated by discrimination and lack of support in schools. According to GLSEN (2021), 81.8% of LGBTQ+ students reported they fear being attacked at school by homophobic and transphobic students.
3. **Supportive Environments:** Schools that create inclusive policies and teachers who foster supportive atmospheres—such as Gay-Straight Alliances (GSAs) or LGBTQ+ inclusive visual representation on classroom walls, significantly benefit the well-being and academic success of LGBTQ+ students.
4. **Discrimination Experiences:** Many LGBTQ+ students indicate a history of sexual orientation or gender identity-based discrimination, adversely impacting their academic involvement and achievement.
5. **Acceptance by Family:** Family acceptance is important for the well-being of LGBTQ+ youth. Those who have acceptance from their families tend to fare better from a mental health perspective.
6. **Underperforming Academics:** One approach to increase academic performance is through the benefits of showing up to school or their classroom and feeling safe in an educational environment. Feeling safe and comfortable at school is the right of all students. Students should feel empowered to increase academic performance in this target group. By contrast, people who live through bullying or discrimination often suffer academically (Nduagbo, 2020).
7. **Visibility and Representation:** To have LGBTQ+ individuals incorporated within school curricula and activities can support inclusivity and validation among LGBTQ+ students.
8. **Limited Resource Access:** Some LGBTQ+ students may not have access to resources such as counseling, support groups, and safe spaces, making it difficult to cope with identity-related issues.
9. **Legal Protections:** LGBTQ+ school rights protections vary across states and districts. Some areas have strong anti-discrimination protections, while others may not provide enough legal protections for LGBTQ+ students.
10. **Intersectionality:** Students within the LGBTQ+ community who also identify with other marginalized groups (i.e., students of color and students with disabilities) may face compounded discrimination and challenges, requiring additional considerations in their support.
11. **Building Peer Relationships:** Peer relationships are vital for LGBTQ+ students. Supportive friendships can help buffer against some of the ill effects of bullying and discrimination.
12. **Academic Achievement:** Research demonstrates that LGBTQ+ students in supportive schools with supportive teachers are more likely to attend college and have positive educational outcomes.

Teachers become the front-line support for trauma-informed educational settings from which LGBTQ+ students learn. This chapter will help teachers create support for one of the most underrepresented and most vulnerable minority groups in America. LGBTQ+ students sit at the top layer of the Multi-tiered System framework (MTSS), which is categorized as *the few*. The data on LGBTQ+ student representation in the American education system has been removed from the United States Department of Education at the time of publication (E.D.gov, 2025). However, in the framework of the MTSS, it is safe to claim that LGBTQ+ students are a minority group when compared to non-LGBTQ+ students. Additionally, like any vulnerable minority group, intensified support is needed to create a sense of worth and belonging by focusing on spaces of inclusivity versus exclusion. Time could not be more important than it is right now to support the LGBTQ+ student population.

Teachers must seek training and Professional Development opportunities on LGBTQ+ topics to establish and ensure a more inclusive learning environment. Policies that are inclusive at school and district levels are crucial to preserving LGBTQ+ students' rights and positivity. The suggested intensified support in this chapter points to the unique challenges and needs of LGBTQ+ students in the K-14 educational system and emphasizes the importance of creating supportive and inclusive environments. As seen, once again, the attempt to erase LGBTQ+ topics in literature and visibility in classrooms is in full swing. With the current attacks on LGBTQ+ safety and visibility in academic settings, I recommend that all teachers approach this educational chapter and apply intensified support within the classroom with the Growth Heartset Theory.

GROWTH HEARTSET THEORY

The Growth Heartset Theory is a less familiar relative than the Growth Mindset Theory (Pavlina, 2020; Walker-Roberts, 2024). Growth Heartset Theory offers a different, complementary frame for helping people embrace new ideas, skills, concepts, and beliefs potentially colliding with decades-long personal convictions. While both theories advocate for personal development, the Growth Heartset Theory distinguishes the ability of the individual to foster an empathetic reaction, especially in the role of compassion. The basis of this theory is that individuals must "decide, in their hearts, to desire to learn" about paradigms that are alien to them or else too challenging to comprehend, especially paradigms that "threaten time-honored ideologies" (Walker-Roberts, 2024, p. 247).

In such a context, teachers can adopt the Growth Heartset Theory to nourish inclusivity in themselves and their classrooms, primarily when they advocate for underrepresented groups like our LGBTQ+ students. In short, the Growth Heartset Theory bridges the classical idea of emotional growth with relational growth. It is a construct for designing more inclusive, equitable, and catered environments to foster well-being as individuals and as a collective. The subhead for this chapter is: *Follow your heart, and the mind follows*. Thus, empathy is the emotive key to compassion. Moreover, you see examples of a Growth Heartset in action, understanding the suffering of another human being when they feel unsafe and threatened, even when one do not feel that way. When compassion moves the heart — concern, care, a wish to understand another's point of view — this emotional mix lights the fuse of a Growth Mindset to listen to fresh ideas and respond to them. Before you have a Growth Mindset, you need to have a Growth Heartset.

With the addition of the Growth Heartset Theory to the teacher's toolkit, they will naturally begin to reflect on why they refuse or deny compassion to LGBTQ+ individuals when their existence was almost destroyed at the behest of an entrenched ideology. Practicing self-growth can happen through education, listening to understand, or self-reflection, and world-growing hearts that grow humans emotionally will turn into growing minds (Walker-Roberts, 2024). For classroom environments to be inclusive and affirming for LGBTQ+ students, three components must be approached and prioritized: safety, visibility, and allyship from teachers. This is integral in establishing a climate for all students to flourish academically and socially and feel valued and respected in their educational experience.

THE TEACHER: ALLYSHIP AND SUPPORT FOR LGBTQ+ STUDENTS

Safety is a basic human need available to every student, but for LGBTQ+ students, it is a necessity as they face infamous struggles such as bullying, harassment, and discrimination. Not feeling safe can have a profound impact on students' mental health, self-esteem, and academic performance. *Physical safety* is one of the most important guarantees that should be afforded to LGBTQ+ students. Policies should explicitly articulate unacceptable behavior (such as bullying), and harassment and discrimination against LGBTQ+ students are prohibited. Gender-neutral restrooms and similar facilities contribute to physical safety and should be provided for students. Transgender students have the highest reports of health issues when they retain urine due to fears of using a restroom at school.

Students' *emotional safety* must be protected against verbal attacks, such as the use of homophobic and transphobic slurs (Figures 7 & 8). Teachers need to create an environment of emotional safety among their students so that they can evaluate their identities without fear of being judged, rejected, or hurt. All students deserve to feel like they are seen to create a strong sense of belonging. Visibility is now key to validating and legitimizing LGBTQ+ identities. Students who see themselves represented in curricula, school policies, and the larger school culture feel a sense of belonging instead of isolation. A curriculum with LGBTQ+ representation should be adhered to. If a teacher teaches in a non-LGBTQ+ tolerant school or district, they should find ways to support the student. Later in the chapter, supportive alternatives will be presented.

Teaching students about the history, literature, and contributions of LGBTQ+ people normalizes diverse identities in the classroom and promotes understanding for all students. Suppose this content cannot be taught in the classroom. In that case, teachers can help students find social resources (i.e., Literature, Instagram – where age-appropriate) to help the student feel connected and included. Teachers can role model acceptance and the Growth Heartset Theory through empathy, understanding, and a willingness to learn. Year-round, teachers and school leaders can model visibility by highlighting the contributions and achievements of LGBTQ+ individuals and finding opportunities for students to connect with various role models.

Teachers can use inclusive symbols.

Visual cues of *allyship* — such as pride flags, safe space stickers, and other inclusive symbols and language — indicate to students that their identities matter. Allyship is a strong way to support LGBTQ+ students. As allies, teachers play a key role in making classrooms more inclusive. As allies of LGBTQ+ students, they must remain a steadfast source of education, advocacy, and purposeful action. Teachers should strengthen their knowledge through education. Teachers are life-long learners. With this knowledge, teachers can provide information on LGBTQ+ identity, issues, and experiences. These include understanding terminology, pronouns, and the challenges marginalized groups face. Allies raise their voices to work towards equitable policies and practices (e.g., gender-inclusive dress codes, anti-bullying programs, equitable disciplinary measures). Teachers can actively support inclusion by intervening in acts of discrimination and the use of homophobic and transphobic slurs. They can model inclusive behavior and stand in solidarity with LGBTQ+ students.

When teachers promote *safety, visibility, and allyship* in their classrooms, LGBTQ+ students are more likely to thrive. They also report higher self-esteem, academic engagement, and emotional well-being (Greydanus, 2017). Finally, an inclusive learning environment helps all students by facilitating empathy, diminishing prejudice, and promoting acceptance as a value—a win-win situation for all.

THE CLASSROOM: AN INCLUSIVE AND SAFE SPACE FOR LGBTQ+ STUDENTS AND ALLIES

The teacher set the tone for the classroom environment and the level of support for the students. The classroom is where active learning takes place, and ensuring they are the most inclusive is important for the growth and development of minds. There are several reasons why classrooms should be safe spaces for LGBTQ+ students and their allies. They twist very closely. With physical and emotional safety at the top of mind, a welcoming classroom environment provides a sanctuary for students from bullying, discrimination, and harassment based on their sexual orientation or gender identity. Fostering such emotional safety is vital to their mental health and well-being. When classroom environments are safe, LGBTQ+ students can feel more at home expressing their authentic selves. This sense of authenticity can foster greater self-acceptance and confidence — key personal development factors.

Classrooms must be safe spaces for all students. Safe spaces help to encourage inclusiveness by making sure that all students feel welcome and valid. This setting fosters collaboration and understanding between different communities, adding to the educational experience for all. Students can share their lived experiences comfortably and, through the Growth Heartset Theory, challenge ideology or belief systems bestowed upon them by outside forces: parents, organized religions, and/or peers. Students who experience security and support tend to engage more, participate in class discussions more often, and excel in their academic work. A positive learning environment impacts overall academic success, especially for minority communities in which LGBTQ+ students fall. A safe space empowers allies to confront discrimination or stereotypes they may have learned. Non-LGBTQ+ students can advocate for their LGBTQ+ peers. Allies are vital in creating acceptance and can help disrupt negative attitudes and behaviors.

Safe spaces in the classroom help teachers create a learning environment to discuss identity, diversity, and societal issues. This prompts critical thinking and allows students to gain empathy and develop an understanding of what others have experienced. Safe classrooms can help decrease mental health problems for LGBTQ+ students who experience elevated rates of anxiety, depression, and suicidal thoughts. It is here that a supportive and safe classroom can prevent these by giving them a sense of community and belonging.

Moreover, when they are exposed to this type of learning, it prepares them for life in the outside world. This allows them to thrive and flourish intentionally in a multicultural society. Safe spaces also allow for safe discourse on social justice and equity issues. By learning about these issues, students can work as advocates in the broader culture or support initiatives to change the status quo.

Pride Month: June. LGBTQ+ Pride is a cultural movement and celebration that promotes the belonging, equality, and visibility of LGBTQ+ individuals. It encompasses a range of activities, events, and expressions aimed at raising awareness about the issues faced by LGBTQ+ communities, celebrating their identities, and advocating for their rights.

Pride events often include parades, festivals, and gatherings, typically held in June to commemorate the Stonewall Uprisings of 1969. The Stonewall Uprisings were pivotal in the LGBTQ+ rights movement (Phelps, 2021; Walker-Roberts, 2024). These events provide a platform for LGBTQ+ individuals to express themselves freely, connect with others, and foster a sense of community. Pride also serves as a reminder of the ongoing struggles against discrimination, violence, and inequality faced by LGBTQ+ people worldwide. Students can bring Pride to the classroom in many different ways. Teachers can encourage students to engage in social justice projects, including classroom presentations.

Figure 1. Pride presentations in June

WHICH POSTERS HANG ON THE WALL?

Let us face it. Most likely, the majority of teachers are cisgender and straight. Also, if a teacher is LGBTQ+, they probably do not share all the identities the acronym represents. So teachers can, for example, display posters of important LGBTQ+ people in their classrooms, keeping the focus on representation and visibility in the classroom. There are several important reasons classrooms should have LGBTQ+ posters and materials.

Representation. It is essential to be seen. When students see LGBTQ+ figures represented in their learning environment, it creates a way for them to understand that diverse identities and experiences deserve to be validated and valued. This representation can benefit LGBTQ+ students, creating a sense of belonging.

Inclusivity. LGBTQ+ posters create a sense of inclusion. They indicate that the classroom is a safe environment for all students, regardless of sexual orientation or gender identity. This could help to alleviate feelings of loneliness experienced by LGBTQ+ students.

Education. LGBTQ+ posters can also educate. They can ignite conversations surrounding the history, culture, and contributions of LGBTQ+ individuals, which help to expand students' perspectives and understanding of society.

Reinforcement (Visibility). The exhibition of LGBTQ+ characters can challenge stereotypes and discrimination. It promotes an understanding of and appreciation for diversity and promotes a society with acceptance and respect.

Allies. Students who may not identify as LGBTQ+ but want to support them may recognize the need to speak up when discrimination arises and support their peers.

Mental Health. An affirming environment can benefit LGBTQ+ students' mental health. Having students' identities visually represented, recognized, and respected is a supportive factor in reducing anxiety and depression.

EQUITY AND INCLUSION

Posters supporting LGBTQ+ equality in schools create a more inclusive educational environment for all students. Making a poster of influential LGBTQ+ people can be a great way to celebrate diversity and signal safety to students who are LGBTQ+. Posters can also help create opportunities for discussions and acceptance. Here are some important public figures teachers can find classroom posters on:

Marsha P. Johnson: As a Black trans activist and one of the leaders of the Stonewall uprising, she was the co-founder of the Street Transvestite Action Revolutionaries (STAR).

Harvey Milk: The first openly gay man elected to public office in California, Harvey Milk was a significant advocate for LGBTQ+ rights and is most remembered for his impact on the gay rights movement.

Audre Lorde: This Black, lesbian feminist poet and activist wrote extensively about race, gender, sexuality, and social justice.

Laverne Cox: An actress (most well-known for her role in *Orange Is the New Black*) and transgender rights activist who has fought for visibility and representation of the transgender community in the media.

James Baldwin: A renowned writer and social critic whose works explored the complexities of race, sexuality, and identity.

Kumu Hina Wong-Kalu: A prominent Hawaiian cultural practitioner, educator, and activist for LGBTQ+ rights, especially among Native Hawaiians. Kumu describes herself as *mahu*, a traditional Hawaiian term for embodying or enfolding masculine and feminine qualities. An example of a poster displayed in the classroom to support an affirmation can be seen in Figure 2.

Figure 2. Examples of posters in the classroom

WHAT IS ON THE BOOKSHELF?

Why have LGBTQ+ literature on classroom shelves? The first reason is that the literature will display diversity through representation. For students who identify as part of the LGBTQ+ community, literature reflecting their realities is crucial in fostering a sense of belonging. It allows individuals to see their unique experiences, identities, and challenges mirrored in the narratives they encounter, thus providing both validation and affirmation of their journeys. Secondly, a diverse display of literature will foster authenticity and acceptance. Incorporating LGBTQ+ literature in educational settings empowers all students to understand themselves better and promotes an environment where acceptance is the norm. This exposure broadens their perspectives and nurtures empathy, encouraging acceptance of those who may differ from them, thereby enriching their social consciousness. Thirdly, the books will promote education and awareness of LGBTQ+ subjects. This genre of literature acts as an educational tool, enlightening all readers about the historical context, ongoing struggles, and significant contributions of LGBTQ+ individuals and communities.

By dismantling myths and stereotypes, these narratives pave the way for a more nuanced comprehension of gender and sexuality, fostering a culture of inclusivity within the classroom. Fourthly, purposefully choosing LGBTQ+ books will create inclusive classrooms. Having LGBTQ+ literature readily available in educational environments signals that the space welcomes everyone. It cultivates an atmosphere conducive to open discussions about identity, love, and acceptance, allowing students to engage in meaningful dialogues that enhance their understanding of diverse experiences.

Additionally, LGBTQ+ allies will also have an opportunity to engage through reading. For students who do not identify as LGBTQ+, engaging with LGBTQ+ literature can be a transformative experience. It provides insight into the challenges faced by their peers, empowering them to become allies. This solidarity fosters a collective responsibility to support classmates, promoting a more inclusive and compassionate school community. Lastly, visibility through the literature on the bookshelf can enhance mental health and well-being. Research indicates that literature that resonates with minority experiences positively impacts the mental health of minority students (Drako, 2025). Reading stories reflecting their realities may make them feel more understood and less isolated, contributing significantly to their well-being. Including LGBTQ+ literature in educational curricula is paramount for promoting representation and inclusivity. It educates students while prioritizing all individuals' mental health and well-being, ultimately fostering a more empathetic and informed society.

By embracing these narratives, teachers pave the way for a brighter, more inclusive future for all students. If a teacher teaches at a school that is LGBTQ+ non-tolerant and excludes literature from the curriculum, teachers can house the books in their classroom library. LGBTQ+ literature around the classroom is another way to support inclusion and show an acute awareness of the need for LGBTQ+ equity. Having a diversified bookshelf shows that you care, understand, and are purposeful about contributing to a space where everyone can be represented and visible in the classroom. Including non-gendered words in textbooks, papers, and other learning materials helps ensure that all students can relate and interact with the content (Figure 3).

LITERATURE MATTERS

Literature is the gateway to exploring new knowledge and the opportunity to develop critically as a person. According to research, reading fiction builds empathy and emotional intelligence in students who do so regularly. On the other hand, non-fiction readers tend to gain a more macro-level understanding of issues taking shape in the real world. For this reason, varied exposure is invaluable, as it leads to a well-rounded education; students can connect what they read outside of school with what is being taught inside the classroom (or vice versa), which translates into better grades, success and social acceptance (Drako, 2025). There is a variety of fiction and non-fiction texts that can grace the shelves of the bookcase in the classroom. Here is a list of LGBTQ+ literature that can be appropriate for K-14 era students organized by age group:

Elementary (K-5)

"And Tango Makes Three" by Justin Richardson and Peter Parnell

It is a true story about two male penguins at the Central Park Zoo who build a family when they hatch and raise a chick together. This book is featured on the bookshelf in Figure 3.

"Heather Has Two Mommies" by Lesléa Newman

A story about a little girl named Heather who learns to embrace her two moms and the fact that families come in many different shapes and sizes.

"I Am Jazz" by Jazz Jennings and Jessica Herthel

The story of Jazz, a transgender girl, and her struggles for self-identity are all told through a picture book.

"My Rainbow" by DeShanna Neal and Vanessa Brantley-Newton

A story about a young girl who wants to make a rainbow wig for her transgender daughter, celebrating love and acceptance.

Middle School (6-8)

"George" by Alex Gino

A story about a transgender girl named George who dreams of playing Charlotte in her school's production of "Charlotte's Web."

"The Pants Project" by Cat Clarke

A story about a girl named Liv who feels she is a boy and wishes to wear pants to school for the first time.

"Simon vs. the Homo Sapiens Agenda" by Becky Albertalli

A coming-of-age tale about a gay teenager, Simon, who is blackmailed into coming out and finding love.

"Ash" by Malinda Lo

A queer Cinderella story featuring a strong female protagonist searching for the idea of love and identity. This book is featured on the bookshelf in Figure 3.

High School (9-12)

"Aristotle and Dante Discover the Secrets of the Universe" by Benjamin Alire Sáenz

A coming-of-age story centered on two Mexican-American boys whose friendship transcends typical bounds, covering themes of identity, first love, acceptance, and more.

"They Both Die at the End" by Adam Silvera

A novel about two boys who meet the day they learn they will die and how they spend their last hours together.

"The Hate U Give" by Angie Thomas

Grounding its lens mostly on race and social justice, featuring and exploring themes of identity and activism with LGBTQ+ representation.

"Cemetery Boys" by Aiden Thomas

A paranormal romance about a transgender boy who summons a ghost and grapples with his identity and love.

"Inverse Cowgirl" by Alicia Roth Weigel (Great to follow on Instagram as well)

Weigel depicts her journey as an intersex person through braving the trials of being their true self in a world that demands they be something else. The work explores themes of love and gender identity.

College and Beyond (13-14)

"Fun Home: A Family Tragicomic" by Alison Bechdel

A graphic memoir examining Bechdel's relationship with her father and her coming out as a lesbian.

"The Miseducation of Cameron Post" by Emily M. Danforth

A story about a teenage girl sent to a conversion therapy camp after she is discovered being intimate with another girl.

"Red, White & Royal Blue" by Casey McQuiston

The son of the U.S. president and a British prince fall in love in this romantic comedy with themes of identity and politics.

"Queer, There, and Everywhere: 24 People Who Changed the World" by Sarah Prager

A work of nonfiction showcasing the contributions of LGBTQ+ people throughout history.

"Redefining Realness: My Path to Womanhood, Identity, Love & So Much More" by NY Times best-selling Author Janet Mock.

A nonfiction biography of Janet's coming of age and path to womanhood while startling growing up with her mother on the island of O'ahu, Hawai'i, juxtaposed with her father in Oakland, California. This book is featured on the bookshelf in Figure 3.

This adds to the diversity of experiences and perspectives of the LGBTQ+ community, and these are topics worth studying at every age as part of a broader educational curriculum. According to Drako (2025), "Reading diverse literature also encourages students to explore new concepts and themes, which can enhance their critical thinking and analytical skills" (p. 86). Figure 3 showcases a few LGBTQ+ books that can be placed on the classroom bookshelves.

Figure 3. Examples of bookshelves in the classroom

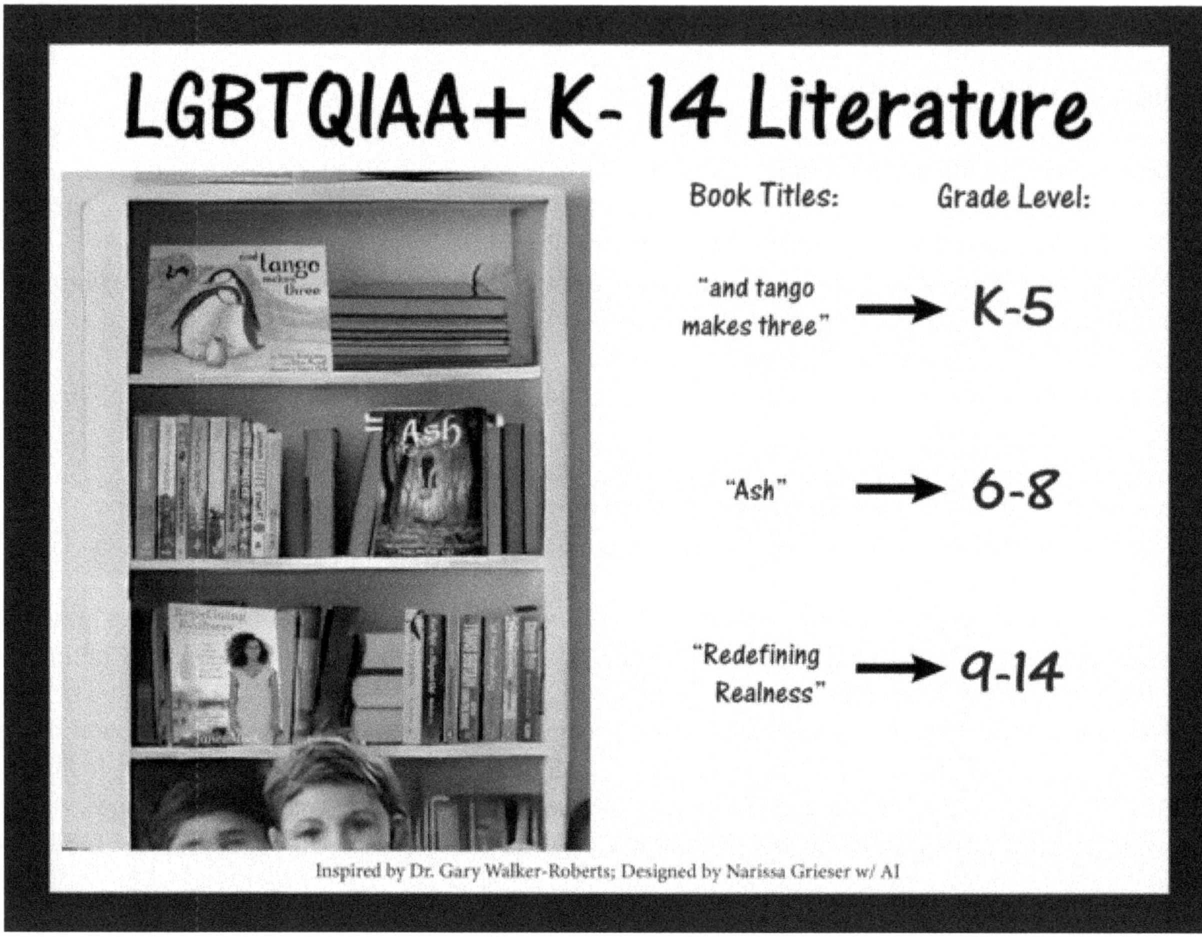

GENDER IDENTITY AND K-14 EDUCATION

Education on loveality/sexuality and gender identity serves as a preventative measure against misinformed perspectives that contribute to social bias, the use of homophobic and transphobic slurs, and microaggressions. Knowing these two independent strands of identity, teachers and students can have an empathetic understanding to guide interactions.

In addition, for people who still have not come out yet (known as *in the closet*), knowledge is a place to explore their potential of being openly LGBTQ+. This exploration may be the first step toward self-acceptance and an asset in overall wellness. Grasping the differences between gender identity and loveality/sexuality improves everyday interactions. Correct language is paramount to avoid miscommunication that ends up causing unwanted pain, fear, or misunderstandings. Using the correct language helps us connect better with one another and ensures everyone feels more included in varied communities.

Clarifying Key Differences

Fundamentally, gender identity is a personal and individual concept determined by how an individual sees themselves internally on the gender spectrum, rather than the traditional methods of gender assignment at birth, which are socially enforced. Now, many are telling stories of feeling wrong in the gender that was assigned to them.

Sexual orientation, on the other hand, refers to the emotional and romantic aspects of the relationships that determine the individuals to whom someone is attracted. This is a realm of feelings and chemistry, not social rules. Crucially, these two strands have no causal relationship; neither subordinates the other. The *Gender Bear* below visually represents how gender identity and loveality/sexuality differ. Remember, gender identity and loveality/sexuality are two different ways individuals identify.

Embracing Diversity

However, there are different ways of expressing identity that go beyond the gender and sexuality binaries our society is used to. Education can be a powerful weapon when it comes to breaking down the fears that often lie at the heart of homophobia and transphobia. Awareness creates more accommodating partners, more loyal friends, and better co-workers.

Developing acceptance and inclusivity starts with knowing the nuances between gender identity and lovealities/sexualities. By pursuing education and respectful communication, teachers can create a society where everyone feels comfortable being themselves.

Gender-Inclusive Language in the Classroom

Using gender-inclusive language encourages an inclusive environment for all students, regardless of gender identity. It recognizes and honors the multiple gender identities that exist beyond the conventional frame of male-female. Students may identify as non-binary, genderqueer, or genderfluid. Using gender-inclusive language affirms their identities and makes them feel recognized and respected in the classroom. Gendered language can perpetuate stereotypes and societal expectations regarding gender roles. Using gender-inclusive language helps challenge these stereotypes and fosters a more equitable approach to gender. Students who feel valued and accepted in the classroom will likely contribute to discussions and share their experiences during lessons. Using gender-inclusive language helps everyone feel included and reinforces everyone's participation in academics. Inclusive language teaches students how to respect other identities and experiences. It pushes them to mind their language and think about how it might impact their peers. This allows room for critical thought and can also help students better comprehend the complexities surrounding gender in society.

Gender Identity Explained: Spectrum of Self

Gender identity: the deeply held sense of being male, female, or something else. This internal sense can differ from that assigned at birth, reflecting the complexity of the human experience. Gender can be male, female, both, or neither, and it is used to describe someone as male, female, both, or neither, and it does not come down to genetics or simply what you are labeled as by society. This innate self-awareness is fundamental to an individual's holistic health and healthy self-image.

The Value of Identity Agency

Another should not minimize the experience of one person. Teachers should also acknowledge the infinite range of gender identities because no single lived experience can account for all human experience. Utilizing the Growth Heartset Theory allows for the emergence of newness and growth as society's language and understanding of gender evolve. Here is a list of gender terminology to help build a foundation for continued education. To add some clarification, there are many other gender identities widely recognized- this list is only a tiny portion of the spectrum:

Agender: Someone who does not identify with any gender or identifies as gender-neutral.
Bigender: Those of two separate genders, either at once or shifting fluidly between the two.
Cisgender: A person whose gender identity corresponds to the binary sex they were assigned at birth (she/her, he/him pronouns).
Genderfluid: A person whose gender identity is not fixed and may change over time.
Intersex: A term for people whose bodies do not fit binary definitions of male or female.
Mahuwahine: A culturally relevant Native Hawaiian term for a person who embodies both male and female spirit.
Non-binary: People who do not fit into the traditional binary of male and female; many non-binary individuals use the pronouns they/them or zi/zem.
Transgender: People whose gender identity does not match the sex assigned to them when they were born.
Two-Spirit: A term used by some Indigenous cultures in North America to describe a diverse range of gender identities that may align more closely with a broader cultural understanding of gender systems.

The labels above are a mere snapshot of the myriad forms of gender. Understanding that every individual's journey is different but valid is essential to what makes us human. This acceptance promotes a community where everyone can be themselves without fear of discrimination. Gender is an ever-evolving spectrum; every experience must be respected.

LOVEALITIES AND SEXUALITIES: A NEW APPROACH

Regarding human relationships, love, and attraction are as varied as people themselves. The idea of *lovealities*, which is a new concept I devised, is a *yin to the yang* of sexualilties. Focusing on romance rather than sexual actions, this tweak of wordplay elevates the importance of an emotional connection rather than focusing on what is happening in the bedroom. Sexual activity that happens in the bedroom is no one else's business other than those involved; however, sharing actions outside of the bedroom when people are in love is welcome in our society all of the time. Point blank, focus on the love between consequential people versus focusing on sexual activities that happen in their private lives, heterosexual, bisexual, and homosexual alike (unless, of course, the situation warrants it- sexual education class, etc.).

The Essence of Love. The love captured in the well-known words of Mitch Albom, *love wins, love always wins*, has always been recited by LGBTQ+ folks, affirming that love conquers all. In this view, it beckons everyone to consider the true nature of love before framing its focus around sexuality (sex acts). Fate, and virtually anything else, pales compared to lovealities — those unique and deeply felt emotions people experience with one another.

What Are Lovealities/Sexualities?

To help navigate the world of love and attraction, the two primary questions one may ask themselves are: Who do I fall in love with?, and *With whom do I want to have sex?* Speaking of lovealities in the K-14 setting is a good way to focus on love versus sexuality. However, it is necessary to engage in conversations about sexuality when the time and situation are appropriate, as mentioned above.

With lovealities, there also is an evolution of sexualities; as societal norms keep shifting, different lovealities and sexualities keep evolving, and they reflect the complexities of our society. What follows is a litany of such lovealities and sexualities that are commonly recognized, perhaps even a launching pad for a deeper understanding.

Heteroloveality (Heterosexual): Interest and emotional attraction toward persons of the opposite gender.
Homoloveality (Homosexual): The attraction and romantic love for members of the same gender.
Biloveality (Bisexual): Romantic love and sexual desire for two or more genders, namely, cisgender men and women.
Panloveality (Pansexual): Romantically love and/or are sexually attracted to people regardless of their sexuality and gender identity.
Aloveality (Asexual): No sexual attraction to others, but still capable of romantic love. Asexual-identifying individuals are born asexual; however, celibacy is a choice not to be sexually or romantically involved with another individual.
Demilovality (Demisexual): Attraction and romantic love that forms exclusively after establishing a deep emotional connection.

However, it should be noted that these lovealities/sexualities are only the tip of the iceberg of the identities people may embody. Everyone's experience is different and worthy of respect. To understand the fullness of the human experience, be cautious, however, as our relationships are an important part of our narratives and deserve extensive respect. By doing this, society continues toward a more inclusive and loving world where love is accepted in all forms.

Gender Bear: A Helpful Visual Tool

One of the best ways to visually explain the differences between Gender Identity and Lovealities/Sexualities is with the help of the *Gender Bear*.

Figure 4. The gender bear (Walker-Roberts, 2023)

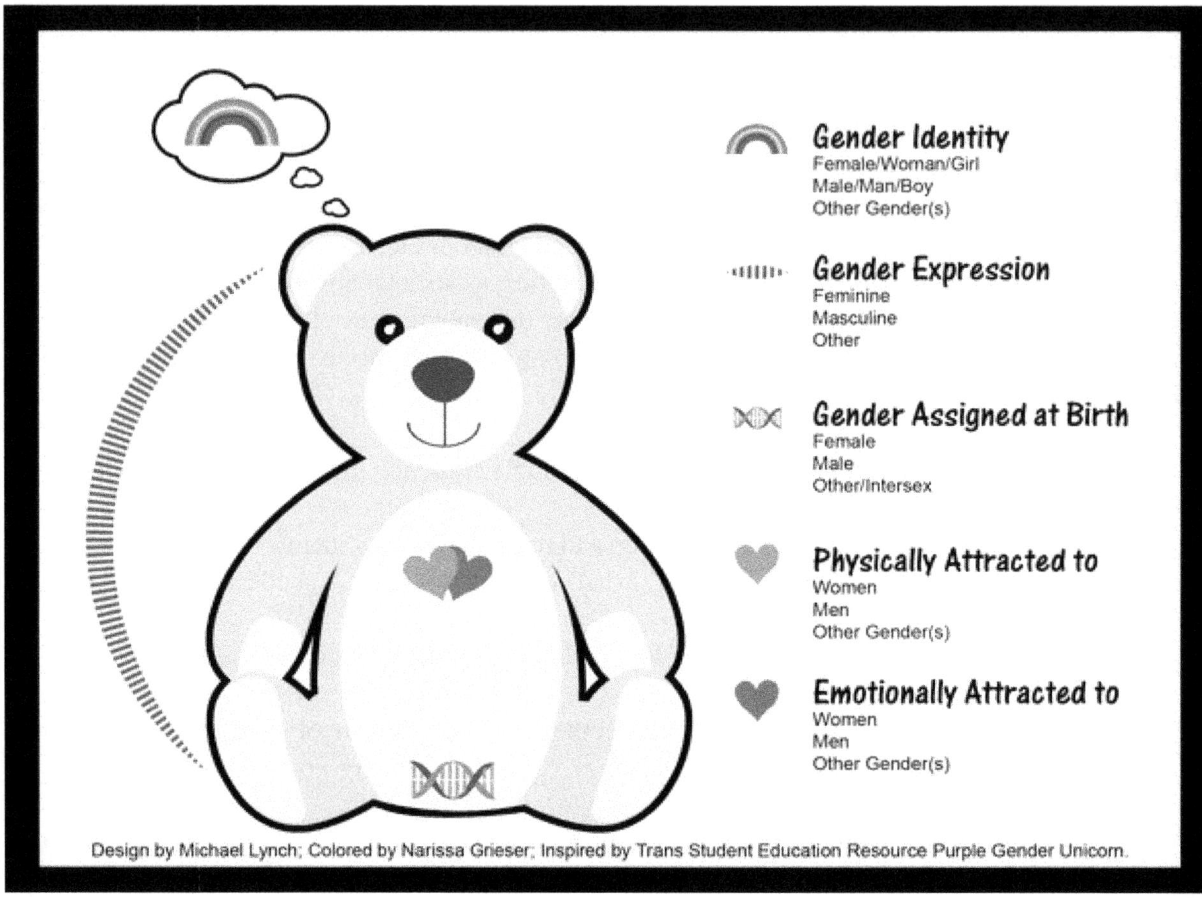

The black-and-white rainbow represents Gender Identity. Gender identity is a complex interplay of individual experience, social factors, and cultural norms. Many researchers and advocates argue that gender is a social construct—which means the roles and expectations society has for a person impact how a person understands their gender and how they express it (Ellemers, 2018; Walker-Roberts, 2024). This consideration reminds us that while biological sex is assigned at birth based on visual characteristics, gender identity is inherently about how someone perceives themselves about masculinity, femininity, and everything in between. *Other Gender (s)* refers to gender non-conforming and gender-neutral identifying individuals outside the binary gender identities.

Gender expression is represented by the individual line arc in the shape of a C to the left of the Gender Bear. Gender expression is how a person's gender identity is seen externally, often through behaviors, clothing, hair, voice, and other forms of presentation. This also encompasses the methods used to express one's gender, which can fall in line with or break from cultural conventions (Ellemers, 2018). Moreover, gender expression can be fluid, evolving to reflect a person's identity and comfort. Importantly, gender expression is not automatically connected with biological sex or gender identity.

The helix DNA between the Gender Bear's legs represents the sex assigned at birth. Sex assigned at birth refers to the gender under which an individual has been classified concerning the physical characteristics observed at birth. Older human research differentiated this typically as either male or female based on external genitalia assigned at birth (Berkowitz et al., 2010). This designation is often recorded on birth certificates and can inform social norms and expectations. It is important to recognize that the sex assigned at birth is not necessarily aligned with someone's gender — a person's internally held sense of their gender.

Whom a person is physically attracted to is represented by the lightest heart on the Gender Bear's chest. Physical attraction is how good one person looks to them in their eyes, primarily based on their appearance. That includes facial features, build, grooming habits, and taste in clothing. This also includes the influence of non-verbal cues, as well as fragrance. Preferences are one of the things that can vary significantly among people and cultures and, of course, are formed by social norms and individual histories. Physical attraction usually causes the initial interest in a romantic or social relationship.

The darkest two hearts on the Gender Bear's chest represent emotional attraction. Emotional attraction is the bond and connection experienced between individuals rooted in shared emotions, experiences, and intimacy. It transcends physical appeal, highlighting the importance of understanding, empathy, and mutual support. This form of attraction typically includes feelings of safety and appreciation within the relationship, nurturing trust, and promoting open communication. Emotional attraction can result in more profound, more significant relationships, motivating individuals to engage more profoundly.

GENDER BINARY LANGUAGE SUBSTITUTIONS: GENDER TRANSFORMATIVE EDUCATION

Gender-inclusive substitution involves replacing a word with a gender-inclusive alternative. This process leads to substituting gendered terms with gender-inclusive terms, making the text more inclusive. The goal is to eliminate making assumptions about a person's gender and loveality/sexuality identity. Using gender-inclusive language can help initiate conversations around gender identity and expression, providing students with a safe and supportive space to explore these aspects of themselves.

When a teacher assumes a student's gender pronoun, they may create an uncomfortable and unsafe environment for the student. A gender-inclusive word or phrase should be used until the individual knows the correct word to use for the individual. In my experience, no student had ever felt uncomfortable or unsafe when I used the gender-inclusive pronouns *they/them.* However, I have created an uncomfortable and/or unsafe environment for a student when I assumed the binary gender pronoun and was incorrect. An additional good rule of thumb is always to use gender-inclusive language when speaking to a crowd of people. It is polite and respectful for a speaker to enact an inclusive environment for everyone in the audience, not just those who identify in the gender binary system (cisgender male and female). Using gender-exclusive language alienates people who identify outside of the gender binary system (gender fluid, genderqueer, gender non-conforming, gender neutral, etc.).

To be clear, substituting gender-inclusive language for gender-binary-specific language does not intend to eliminate the words and phrases stemming from the gender-binary system. Many students, a minority of students, do identify with gender binary language, and when they do, they will be sure to inform you of the correct word to use. A best practice in the classroom is to have students state their correct gender pronouns when they introduce themselves (whether on the first day of class or when entering a situation where new people are involved). An even better practice is for the teacher to lead by example: *Hi, my name is Dr. Walker-Roberts, and my pronouns are they/them.* When introducing yourself to the class, please indicate your correct gender pronoun, as I did.

Additionally, if the teacher were to address the entire classroom with an announcement, they should consciously decide to substitute the binary language for gender-inclusive language. For example, think of a gender-inclusive way to state *boys and girls* with a gender-inclusive phrase when addressing the entire class. If you are having trouble, do not panic; there is an exercise later in the chapter to help everyone with inclusive substitutions. Acknowledging there is a learning curve to changing one's language from binary-specific language to gender-inclusive language. There are some specific ways a teacher can become an expert in using gender-inclusive language in their classroom. Keep two aspects in mind: do not be afraid to be incorrect and be open to correction.

BECOMING A SUPPORTIVE TEACHER USING MULTI-TIERED SYSTEMS OF SUPPORT

Becoming an expert in gender-inclusive language involves a combination of education, patience, self-forgiveness, and more practice. Continue to educate yourself about the importance of gender-inclusive language. Reading this chapter is a significant first step! Additionally, here are actionable steps teachers can take to build up their knowledge in this area:

Learn About Gender Identity. To better understand the spectrum of gender identities, including non-binary, genderqueer, and genderfluid identities. This education will lead teachers to realize why gender-inclusive language is important and necessary for inclusion.

Start Using Gender-Inclusive Pronouns. This begins with using they/them pronouns and practicing using them in sentences. Please do not assume someone's gender based on their name, clothing expression, voice tone, hairstyle, movement mannerisms, etc. Assumptions of someone's gender can hurt people and make the person assuming feel like an idiot when incorrect, so avoid assuming at all costs. Instead, use *they/them* until otherwise informed of the person's correct pronoun. After being informed of a person's correct pronoun, feel free to move forward using the correct pronoun. It is all right to use binary pronouns when the person identifies as them, proving the point that LGBTQ+ people are not trying to eliminate binary pronouns. However, the teachable moment (leaning in with the Growth Heart Theory) is to use the gender-inclusive pronouns they/them when you do not know the correct gender pronoun for the person.

Create or Utilize Inclusive Materials in the Classroom. When you see materials that do not use gender-inclusive language, take a teachable moment (if the text cannot be corrected) and express acknowledgment verbally. Insert gender inclusivity measures where possible. Use materials like the *Gender Bear* and licensed Creative Commons online educational resources (OERs) for teachers and students. For the *Gender Bear*, see Figure 4. Figure 5 illustrates two OERs that are available for teachers and students to access online for free and published by Merlot.

Figure 5. LGBTQ+ OER materials for teachers and students

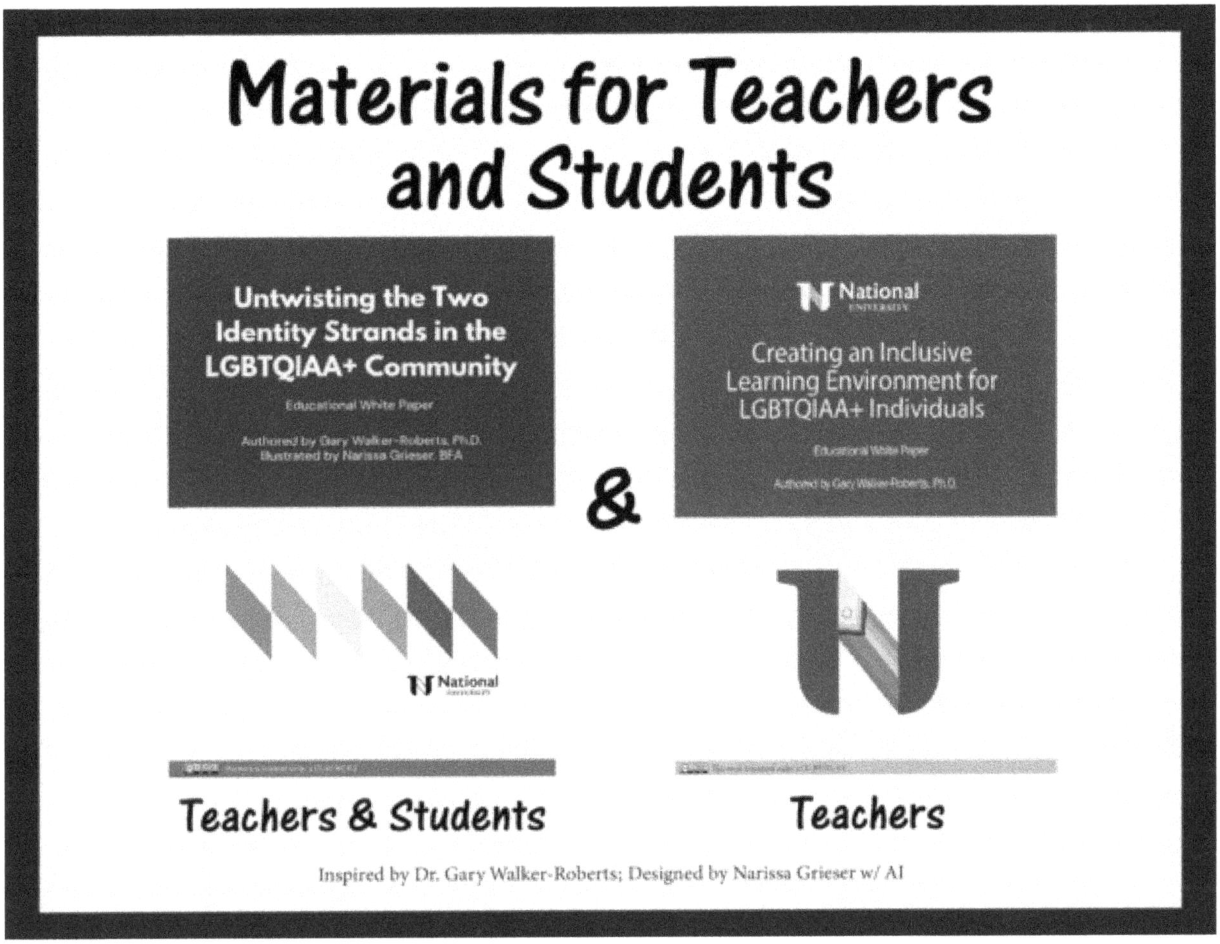

Revise Educational Resources When Possible. Teachers should ensure that the educational resources provided to students use gender-inclusive language. This includes handouts, assignments, presentations, etc (Cempa-Danziger et al., 2022).

Advocate for Gender-Inclusive Policies. In educational institutions, help create and identify policies championing gender-inclusive language in formal communications and documents. This can be in the form of the class roster, in the Learning Management System (LMS), etc.

If Comfortable, Conduct Workshops. Offer workshops or training sessions on the importance of gender-inclusive language and how to implement it effectively in various contexts. Allies are great at leading workshops and trainings to help educate students and teachers.

Model Gender-Inclusive Language. Use gender-inclusive language in both writing and speaking to showcase the effectiveness of this approach (Cempa-Danzinger et al., 2022). Both writing authorities, the Modern Language Association of America (MLA) and the American Psychological Association (APA), stipulate that authors use gender-inclusive language in all papers and publications. Teachers should uphold the gender-inclusive language stipulation of these writing authorities in their and students' work. During the learning process, do not be afraid to be wrong in front of students—students will appreciate the effort and will learn that they, too, can be wrong as long as they make an authentic effort to correct them in the future.

Stay Current and Relevant. Staying current and relevant can be difficult. I have heard many times that the LGBTQ+ acronym is constantly getting long. More and more groups are showing up under the queer umbrella they express. As groups within the community introduce language that describes their group, teachers can enact a growth heartset and a high level of curiosity to learn about the newness. The true essence of education is being introduced to new information. Identity is fluid, and the language used to describe identity is forever changing and growing.

I recommend tempering the emotion of frustration and engaging with the feeling of happiness and wonder when learning new information. When learning new information from a group to which one does not belong, it is important to choose subject matter experts who belong to it. Surround yourself with experts from the group. Social media is a double-edged sword. A person can find negative and positive information about any topic. However, teachers can use the positive side of the sward by following experts on Instagram! Following Instagram influencers (subject matter experts) and people with lived experiences within a group can be very helpful and a great way to learn and stay current on the ever-shifting landscape of the LGBTQ+ community.

It is wise to surround yourself with trustworthy subject matter experts with the information they share. If a teacher teaches at an LGBTQ+ non-tolerant school, they can suggest students follow reputable Instagram subject matter experts to feel less alone and connected to others like them. However, teachers should be aware of the district policies and adhere to Instagram's age rule for users who are 13 years or older (about.instagram.com).

Figure 6 presents a few of many Instagram subject matter experts to follow who can help teachers stay current and relevant in the ever-fast-changing LGBTQ+ community and the inclusive language they use, as well as share with age-appropriate students as an anti-isolation resource.

Figure 6. A few Instagram influencers (SMEs) on social media

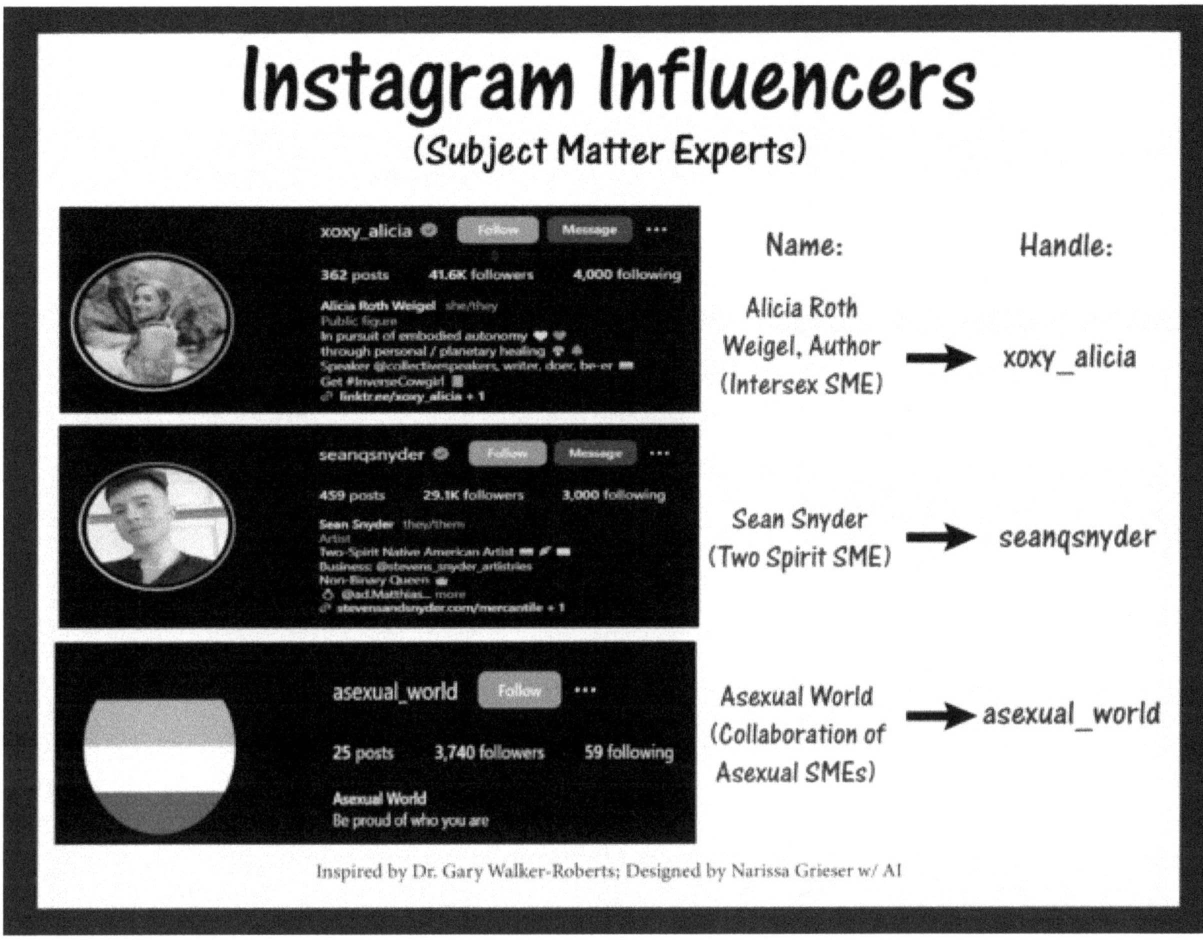

Self-Improvement through Accountability Partners. Regularly evaluate your use of language and identify areas for improvement. Be mindful of how you use language and take responsibility for making changes. Identify an *accountability partner* who will gently hold you accountable when an accidental mistake is made. For example, the accountability partner can gently inform you when they hear you use the word *guys* in verbal communication or see it in your written communication.

ADDRESSING INAPPROPRIATE LANGUAGE AND SLUR INTERVENTION

Speak up if you hear exclusionary language or language you feel is damaging. Intervene when a student uses a homophobic or transphobic slur. Hate crimes typically start with hate speech. Be ready to intervene. Promote respectful conversations about language use. Synan (2023) found that teachers want more professional development (PD) opportunities, stating, "PD is vital to their [teachers] comfort level when it comes to intervening with students who use slurs" (p. 84). The first step in intervening is to acknowledge that homophobic and transphobic slurs used by students are not *typical playground and/*

or classroom taunts; instead, they are the foundation of hate speech, which often leads to hate crimes, suicidal ideation, or suicide. CBS Sacramento reported that a 6th grader, Ronin Shimizu, committed suicide because students taunted him with the homophobic slur *gay* (CBS Sacramento, 2014). Teachers must be familiar with a foundational base of homophobic and transphobic slurs and intervene when they hear students use them. Figure 7 lists a fraction of LGBTQ+ homophobic and transphobic slurs that deem intervention when teachers hear them being used derogatorily at school. Identify the reason and meaning of the slurs in Figure 7. Compare your answers with the answer key in Figure 8.

Figure 7. List of LGBTQ+ slurs

Slurs in Action

Teacher Intervention When Slurs Occur

Slur Words and Phrases	**Reason for Intervention/Meaning**
Faggot/Fag/Faggy	
Tranny/Transgendered	
Dyke	
Hermaphrodite	
Fag Hag	
Homo/No-homo	
Sissy	
Switch Hitter	
Queer	

Inspired by Dr. Gary Walker-Roberts; Designed by Narissa Grieser

Figure 8. List of LGBTQ+ slurs. Answer key. How did you do?

Slurs in Action

Teacher Intervention When Slurs Occur

Slur Words and Phrases	Reason for Intervention/Meaning
Faggot/Fag/Faggy	Degrading, insulting, and hateful to individuals who identify as gay.
Tranny/Transgendered	Degrading, insulting, and hateful to individuals who identify as transgender.
Dyke	Degrading, insulting, and hateful to lesbians.
Hermaphrodite	Degrading, insulting, and hateful to intersex people.
Fag Hag	Degrading, insulting, and hateful to ally women who support LGBTQ+ individuals.
Homo/No-homo	Degrading to the entire community- means the user views LGBTQ+ individuals negatively.
Sissy	Degrading, insulting, and hateful to an effeminate person who does not traffic in masculine toxicity.
Switch Hitter	Degrading, insulting, and hateful to bisexual individuals.
Queer	Term meant to degrade, insult, and be hateful to all individuals identifying as LGBTQ+.

Inspired by Dr. Gary Walker-Roberts; Designed by Narissa Grieser

You can become a leader in gender-inclusive language, thus contributing personally and professionally to more inclusive surroundings and communities. That is why it is vital to recognize the difference between *Gender Identity* and *Lovealities/Sexualities*. A critical aspect of building an inclusive society is understanding the difference between gender and sexual identity. Each element relates to different levels of a person, and differentiation can go a long way in mutual respect and inclusiveness. By separating gender identity from sexual orientation, one begins the process of understanding and validating the lived experiences of individuals.

THE ART OF GENDER-INCLUSIVE LANGUAGE SUBSTITUTION

Practice is so important when learning a new skill. Apply gender-inclusive substitution with language that is used in the classroom. Practice helps take theory and make it a reality. The latest writing guidelines the American Psychological Association set forth emphasize the need for people to utilize gender-nonconforming language in academic writing, promoting inclusivity across diverse audiences. Mastering the art of gender-inclusive substitution—whether through writing or conversation—requires dedication and a willingness to practice. Like learning a new language, a structured scaffolding technique is essential.

Step 1: ***Vocabulary Transformation***. Begin by substituting familiar terms with gender-inclusive alternatives. This exercise allows individuals to acclimate to the new language of inclusivity gradually. As one becomes more comfortable with these substitutions, the language will flow more naturally in written and verbal exchanges.

Step 2: ***Consistent Practice.*** Regularly incorporate these vocabulary adjustments into daily interactions. Just as one would rehearse phrases in a foreign language, consistent use of gender-nonconforming language will solidify understanding and ease of communication.

Step 3: ***Embrace a Growth Heartset***. Recognize that mastery comes with time, and every effort to communicate inclusively is a step toward fostering a more welcoming environment for all. Complete the exercise in Figure 9 by replacing the gender-binary terms and phrases with gender-inclusive terms and phrases. Compare your answers with the answer key in Figure 10.

Figure 9. Art of gender-inclusive substitution exercise

Growth Heartset in Action

Art of Gender Inclusive Substitution

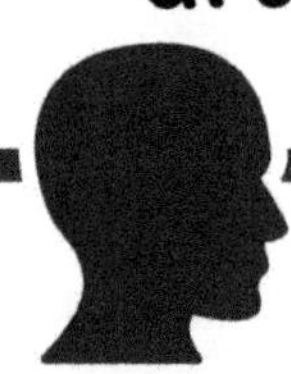

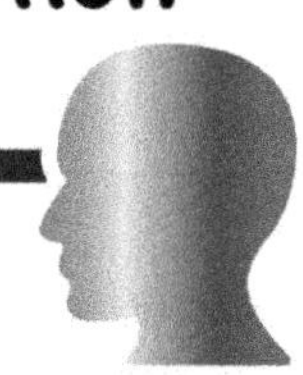

Gender Binary (Fixed Heartset)	Gender Inclusive (Growth Heartset)
Boys and Girls (Classroom)	
Guys/Ladies (addressing a group)	
Words ending in "men" and "women"	
Girlfriend/Boyfriend	
Mom and Dad	
He/Him/His	
She/Her/Hers	
Aunt/Uncle	
Brother/Sister	

Inspired by Dr. Gary Walker-Roberts; Designed by Narissa Grieser

Figure 10. Art of gender-inclusive substitution exercise answer key. How did you do?

Growth Heartset in Action

Art of Gender Inclusive Substitution

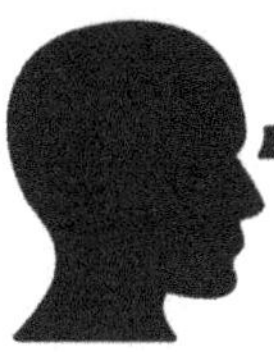

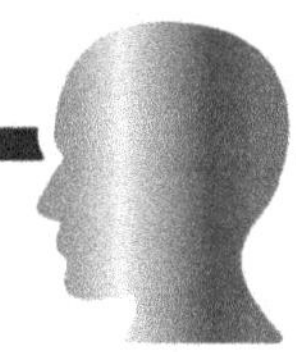

Gender Binary (Fixed Heartset)	Gender Inclusive (Growth Heartset)
Boys and Girls (Classroom)	Students/Crew
Guys/Ladies (addressing a group)	Folks/Y'all/Everyone
Words ending in "men" and "women"	Replace with "Person" at the end
Girlfriend/Boyfriend	Partner
Mom and Dad	Parents/Guardians
He/Him/His	They/Them/Theirs
She/Her/Hers	They/Them/Theirs
Aunt/Uncle	Pibling
Brother/Sister	Sibling

Inspired by Dr. Gary Walker-Roberts; Designed by Narissa Grieser

SAFE SPACE CERTIFIED TEACHER

Begin the journey to becoming a Safe Space certified teacher who helps LGBTQ+ students by learning about LGBTQ+ identities and terminology and understanding the unique challenges faced by LGBTQ+ students. Use training offered by groups like GLSEN or local LGBTQ+ advocacy organizations to gain some helpful knowledge and skills. Teachers earn a certificate and receive a safe space sticker to display on their classroom door (Figure 9).

The certification programs will expand upon the knowledge in this chapter and teach teachers how to create an inclusive classroom by displaying affirming materials (like pride flags, inclusive posters, and safe space stickers) and using gender-inclusive language. Promote and enforce school policies that protect LGBTQ+ students from discrimination, harassment, and bullying, maintaining a safe, supportive environment in the school.

Student Facing Materials. Teachers will be provided with student-facing tools, such as information on LGBTQ+ advocacy groups and relevant reading, to help them gain strength. Finally, it encourages open dialogue by promoting conversations about diversity and helping foster a safe space where students comfortably share their identities. Following these principles is an important way to support LGBTQ+ students and contribute to a more open climate on your campus. After reading this chapter, teachers will have an excellent foundation for earning the certification.

Be sure to display the most current and inclusive Intersex-Inclusive Pride Flag in the classroom (Figure 11). The Intersex-Inclusive Pride Flag is an evolution of the traditional rainbow flag that many identify with the LGBTQ+ community and has represented LGBTQ+ pride since its creation in 1978. The original rainbow flag had six stripes, colored red, orange, yellow, green, blue, and purple, with each color representing different aspects of the LGBTQ+ community and its diversity. The Intersex-Inclusive Pride Flag further expands Daniel Quasar's 2017 Progress Pride Flag to include the intersex community.

Progress Pride Flag. Designer Daniel Quasar created a new version called the Progress Pride Flag. This version of the flag adds a chevron of black and brown rays to symbolize queer people of color and marginalized LGBTQ+ communities. It also includes light blue, pink, and white stripes representing transgender and non-binary people. In 2021, Valentino Vecchietti of Intersex Equality Rights designed the flag that should be used to represent the LGBTQ+ community (Figure 11). The safe space sticker that should be placed on the classroom door to symbolize a safe space should also be the Intersex-Inclusive Pride Flag (Figure 11).

It is increasingly vital to create safe spaces for LGBTQ+ students and allies in the classroom as it helps improve student emotional well-being, academic success, inclusivity, and social justice. It helps not only LGBTQ+ students but the whole school community by promoting understanding, respect, and collaboration. If you unfortunately find yourself at a non-tolerant LGBTQ+ school, replace the Inclusive Flag with any rainbow symbol.

Figure 11. Inclusive flag and safe space sticker

CONCLUSION

The Growth Heartset Theory is a critical methodological approach for teachers looking to develop an environment where LGBTQ+ students matter. Teachers can address this diverse group of individuals' unique needs through a collective focus on empathy, emotional intelligence, and a culture of solidarity and respect. This chapter guides teachers through best practices, strategies for crafting new or updated curricula, classroom management, and teacher training that affirms LGBTQ+ identities. These equitable support systems are to help LGBTQ+ students in classrooms and have transformative potential for changing the face of education worldwide. This chapter serves as a touchstone for teachers committed to fostering inclusivity and improving educational experiences for LGBTQ+ students and as a means of enhancing the larger educational landscape within an increasingly diverse society.

REFERENCES

Bach, J. (2015). Exploring queer pedagogies in the college-level YA literature course. *Discourse (Abingdon), 1071758*. Advance online publication. DOI: 10.1080/01596306.2015

Berkowitz, D., Manohar, N. N., & Tinkler, J. E. (2010). Walk like a man, talk like a woman: Teaching the social construction of gender. *Teaching Sociology*, *38*(2), 132–143. DOI: 10.1177/0092055X10364015

Bronski, M., Heyam, K., & Traub, V. (2023). The LGBTQ+ History Book: Big Ideas Simply Explained. DK.

Cempa-Danziger, D., Kress, T., & Walsh, M. (2022). Integrating gender equity into positive classroom culture. In Alcruz, J., & Blair, M. (Eds.), *Student-centered classrooms : research-driven and inclusive strategies for classroom management* (pp. 135–151). Rowman & Littlefield Publishers.

Darko, G. (2025). Literacy came to a sub-Saharan African village: Ghanaian elementary students' narratives on how access to books influenced their education. ProQuest. Available from Dissertations & Theses @ National University.

Dweck, C. S. (2007). *Mindset: The new psychology of success*. Random House.

Ellemers, N. (2018). Gender stereotypes. *Annual Review of Psychology*, *69*(1), 275–298. DOI: 10.1146/annurev-psych-122216-011719 PMID: 28961059

GLSEN. (2010). The 2009 National School Climate Survey: The Experiences of Lesbian, Gay, Bisexual and Transgender Youth in Our Nation's Schools. https://core.ac.uk/download /71345414.pdf

GLSEN INC. GuideStar Profile. https://www2.guidestar.org/profile/04-3234202

Greydanus, D. (2017). Suicidality and the lesbian, gay, bisexual, and transgender (LGBT) youth: A review. *International Journal of Child Health and Human Development*, *10*(4), 367–376.

Hansford, L., Thomas, F., & Wyatt, K. (2019). The impact of the Work Capability Assessment on mental health: Claimants' lived experiences and GP perspectives in low-income communities. *The Journal of Poverty and Social Justice : Research, Policy, Practice*, *27*(3), 351–368. Advance online publication. DOI: 10.1332/175982719X15637716050550

Lyn, A. E., & Broderick, M. (Eds.). (2023). *Motivation and Momentum in Adult Online Education*. IGI Global., DOI: 10.4018/978-1-6684-7712-0

Nduagbo, K. C. (2020). How gender disparities affect classroom learning. Retrieved from https://www .ascd.org/el/articles/how-gender-disparities-affect-classroom-learning

Open, A. I. (2022). *ChatGPT (Mar 14 version)* [Large language model]. Brainstorm, Ideas, Organizational.

OpenAI. (2023) Justdone. [Large language model]. Image creations.

Pavlina, S. (2020). A growth heartset. https://stevenpavlina.com/blog/2020/a-growth-heatset/

Phelps, C. (2021). The stonewall riots: A document history. *Journal of the History of Sexuality*, *30*(3), 451. https://link.gale.com/apps/doc/A690356795/EAIM?u=pres1571&sid=bookmarkEAIM&xid=3e2f1984

Stocker, R. W. (2017). Chickering's psychosocial theory. University College Advising Manual. (Student Development). Retrieved from http://advisingmanula.uc. iupui.edu/Student DevelopmentTheoris/ChickeringsPsychosocialTheory.aspx

Synan, C. (2023). Intervening when lesbian, gay, bisexual, transgender, and queer/questioning (LGBTQ) slurs happen: a case study of elementary school teachers. ProQuest. Available from Dissertations & Theses @ National University.

Walker-Roberts, G. (2024). Untwisting the two identity strands in the LGBTQIAA+ community. Merlot. https://merlot.org/merlot/viewMaterial.htm?id=773470017

Walker-Roberts, G. S. (2023). Creating an Inclusive and Motivational E-Learning Environment for LGBTQ+ Online Students in Higher Education. In Lyn, A., & Broderick, M. (Eds.), *Motivation and Momentum in Adult Online Education* (pp. 234–249). IGI Global., DOI: 10.4018/978-1-6684-7712-0.ch014

KEY TERMS AND DEFINITIONS

Allyship: The practice of being an ally or socially supporting and advocating for the rights of a marginalized group. This means recognizing the root causes of systemic inequalities, using privilege to uplift the voices of people who have been oppressed, and working to dismantle systems of oppression. This means responding to bias and amplifying the voices of LGBTQ+ students.

LGBTQIAA+: A catch-all abbreviation for Lesbian, Gay, Bisexual, Transgender, Queer/Questioning, Intersex, Asexual, Ally, and persons of any other identity that exists outside the binary, heteronormative, cisgender paradigms (the + at the end of the abbreviation stands for all the other letters in the acronym do not account for). It includes a range of sexual orientations, gender identities, and expressions. The abbreviation is inclusive, adding the A for Allies. For the sake of brevity, the chapter will henceforth refer to LGBTQ+ persons by that abbreviation.

Inclusivity: A practice and philosophy within education that structures environments in which respect, value, and support are extended to anyone, regardless of who they are. Inclusiveness is more than tolerance; it embraces and celebrates differences.

The Theory of Growth Heartset: A theoretical understanding of the influence of empathetic communication, emotional intelligence, and intentionality in creating safe spaces where others can flourish. Building on the Growth Mindset, it highlights emotional growth and relationship-related skills central to connection and belonging.

K-14 Education: The formal continuum of kindergarten through the second year of post-secondary education (i.e., community college, vocational training, etc.). It also broadens the scope of all conversations to include early and the first two years of higher educational experiences.

Microaggressions: These are subtle, usually unintentional remarks or actions that pierce and belittle people. While they may seem insignificant, these interactions together can lead to negative consequences for mental health and well-being. To contextualize this work, this paper is intended to elucidate both approaches of policy discourse surrounding the evolution of inclusive environments in education (Hanford et al., 2019; Walker-Roberts, 2024).

Non-Tolerant LGBTQ+ School: A school environment that is not inclusive of LGBTQ+ individuals is marked by an absence of acceptance and support for students and matters related to LGBTQ+ identities. In this type of atmosphere, students are likely to encounter discrimination, bullying, and harassment due to their sexual orientation or gender identity.

Chapter 12
Beyond the Frontlines:
The Importance of Trauma-Informed Care for Military Children in the K-4 Setting

Nina Sapphira Russell
https://orcid.org/0009-0007-4935-9718
National University, USA

ABSTRACT

The United States operates an all-volunteer military force (AVF), a cornerstone of U.S. defense strategy since its implementation in 1973. Despite its success, challenges such as declining recruitment rates and insufficient support for military families persist. The military lifestyle has its challenges; however, military-connected children face academic, social, and emotional challenges due to frequent PCS moves and parental deployments. A strong support system is necessary for military-connected children. However, research studies on their needs within the K-12 educational system remain scarce. This chapter explores the application of Multi-Tiered Systems of Support (MTSS) and Trauma-Informed Care (TIC) for military-connected children, advocating for targeted interventions that foster resilience, adaptability, and academic success. It examines the intersection of military culture, developmental needs, and the evolving landscape of family support.

INTRODUCTION

The United States operates an all-volunteer military force (AVF), a system officially implemented in 1973 after the Vietnam War (Rostker, 2006; Cunningham, 2023). The AVF is now a cornerstone of U.S. defense strategy. Despite its success, challenges remain, such as declining recruitment rates in recent years (Vergun, 2024), driven by societal trends, eligibility criteria, and insufficient support services for military families. A study conducted by Blue Star Families (2021) reveals that more than one-third of participants do not recommend voluntarily entering military service. One of the primary factors for this reluctance is inadequate support for military spouses and children (IVMF, 2018). According to the 2022 Department of Defense Demographics Report (2022), there are 1.5 million active-duty family members, of whom 49.9% are married and 37% have children. Approximately 40.7% of military children are 11 years old or younger, while 24% are 12-18 (Department of Defense, 2022). While the body of evidence on the mental health and well-being of military families has grown (Gribble et al., 2020), research

DOI: 10.4018/979-8-3693-9020-7.ch012

concerning military-connected children within the K-12 setting is sparse. The chapter aims to explore the Multi-Tiered Systems of Support (MTSS) with Trauma-Informed Care (TIC)for military-connected children in K-12 educational settings. It seeks to address these children's unique challenges, shaped by the demands of an all-volunteer military force (AVF) and the evolving dynamics of military family life. By examining current support systems within the school environment, this chapter aims to highlight the gaps in current research and advocate for targeted interventions to foster adaptability, resilience, and academic success.

OVERVIEW OF MILITARY CHILDREN

When you think of military children, what comes to mind? Perhaps emotional, tear-jerking reunion videos on social media, where a parent surprises their child at school, a sporting event, or homecoming? While these moments are touching, military children are far more than social media fodder. For me, the words adaptability and resilience immediately spring to mind. Military children are shaped by their unique experiences, developing these traits due to frequent relocations across states or countries, starting over at new schools, and making new friends. They also face the challenges of parental deployments and separations. Military-connected children are often proud of their family's service, growing up with a profound understanding of patriotism.

However, life as a military child can feel isolating, particularly without access to a close-knit military community or specialized support systems designed to address their unique needs. Growing up as a "military brat," I vividly recall how transient friendships were, often telling friends, "Don't lose my address" or "Please write!" whenever they moved to a new duty station. Processing difficult moments, such as my father's accident during his deployment in Operation Desert Storm, was another challenge. At the time, I downplayed its impact, only realizing the emotional toll it had taken after his return. With no peers who understood my experiences, I often felt isolated, and structured support systems to help military children navigate these struggles were nonexistent.

The childhood of military-connected children now vastly differs from that of those who grew up in a similar lifestyle. The cultural aspects of the military and the transient lifestyle shape the lived experiences of military families and military-connected children. Understanding the military as a distinct cultural environment with its values, language, and hierarchical structure helps contextualize the challenges faced by the children (Quintana & Cole, 2021). Military children typically experience six to nine moves during their K-12 education (National Military Family Association, 2023), highlighting the need for a strong support system to help them thrive. To illustrate the challenges military children face, let's consider the case of a fictional child, Josie. Due to their parents ' military assignments, Josie has moved five times in the last eight years. Each move has meant starting over in a new school, making new friends, adjusting to different curricula and environments, and adding the layer of the parent deployments looming.

Josie's story exemplifies the main themes:

- Frequent Relocations: The Military lifestyle is transient. Military families may move every 2.5 years (Military Family Advisory Network, 2018) due to a permanent change of station (PCS) - tied to the active-duty service member's assignments (Military Family Advisory Network, 2019). These transitions disrupt their academic, social, and emotional stability as they adapt to new schools, communities, and peer groups.

- Parental Deployments: The absence of a parent during critical periods can lead to feelings of abandonment and increased anxiety.
- Uncertainty and Stress: The unpredictability of military life can cause chronic stress and emotional turmoil.

Proactive communication between parents, schools, and local support organizations, such as those suggested by the National Military Family Association (NMFA), can significantly ease these transitions. Programs specifically designed for military children, like school transition coordinators or peer support groups, foster a sense of belonging and mitigate the difficulties associated with a military lifestyle. While frequent changes can foster adaptability and independence, they can also lead to feelings of isolation or loss. This underscores the importance of trauma-informed care and multi-tiered support systems, crucial for their well-being and development.

As a parent raising military children, I understand firsthand the importance of a robust, multi-tiered support system. Providing the necessary tools and resources to help them navigate the complexities of being a child of an active-duty service member is essential to fostering their emotional and mental health and, ultimately, their success. Children should be viewed individually. A one-size approach to accessing the needs of a military child is not recommended. Today, military children are still viewed as resilient and adaptable, but the narrative has shifted to include more awareness of their challenges. Technology has vastly evolved since I grew up as a military-connected child. Now, military families have greater access to technology, allowing for more consistent connections, social media, and video calls, which helps kids stay in touch with friends and extended family. However, some things remain constant; military children are shaped by their unique experiences, and they develop these traits due to frequent relocations across states or countries, starting over at new schools and making new friends. They also face the challenges of parental deployments and separations. Military children are often proud of their family's service, growing up with a profound understanding of patriotism. The narrative surrounding military children has evolved alongside broader societal conversations about mental health. There is more attention on mental health, particularly around the impact of deployment cycles and the potential for prolonged separations. While resilience and adaptability remain traits of military children, there is increasing recognition of the need to support them as they face diverse challenges, stressors, transitions, and potential traumas. With greater resources available, such as support groups and counselors specialized in military family life, there's an acknowledgment of the unique lifestyle's emotional toll and an effort to help these children process and navigate it in ways that may not have been available in previous decades.

IMPORTANCE OF EARLY EDUCATION IN YOUNG CHILDREN

A key responsibility of early childhood educators is to plan and deliver purposeful, developmentally appropriate learning experiences that support the social, emotional, physical, cognitive, and overall learning development of each child they work with. For this reason, the National Association for the Education of Young Children (NAEYC) created nine principles and guidelines for educators. One of these principles emphasizes the importance of considering individual differences. This principle becomes especially relevant when interacting with and providing services to military-connected children. Development and learning are dynamic processes influenced by the interaction between a child's biological traits and environment, each shaping and impacting future growth patterns. These factors, as well as cultural contexts, experiences, and individual differences, must be considered to shape how children learn and develop. Educators and school administrators must be cognizant of their student population and the unique needs that military-connected children bring to the classroom. Unfamiliarity with the military lifestyle could lead to additional trauma exposures (Rogers, Johnson, Coffey, et al, 2023). Like all cultures, it is shaped by shared beliefs, values, behaviors, norms, symbols, and practices (Heward, Li, Tie, & Waterworth, 2024). For this reason, it is vital for professionals providing services to military members to understand the unique aspects of this culture.

Frequent PCS moves and extended separations from family members are normal parts of military life (Weinstock, 2023). For military-connected children, the cultural characteristics of the military lifestyle often intersect with personal factors such as race, ethnicity, or gender. This intersection can compound military children's challenges in processing and adapting to change, adding complexity to their developmental and emotional needs. The cultural framework offers a roadmap for professionals to take active steps toward becoming more culturally competent (Meyer, Writer & Brim, 2016). Unlike other cultures, military culture is delineated (Meyer et al., 2016) due to specific tenets defined by law. Language plays a significant role in any culture, and the military is no exception. However, military language relies heavily on acronyms, which permeate every aspect of its culture, including military family life. Military families form an essential subculture shaped by the sacrifices they make alongside service members. These shared sacrifices foster a unique set of values and norms specific to military life. Despite the constant flux of deployments and relocations, military communities, like their language, are structured to promote efficiency and adaptability (Meyer et al., 2016).

To civilians unfamiliar with military lifestyles, the extensive use of acronyms can feel like learning a foreign language, often leading to confusion. This linguistic barrier often leads to confusion and misunderstandings, particularly for those who interact with military members and their families in professional or community settings. Detailed descriptions and explanations of commonly used acronyms can help bridge this gap, aiding those unfamiliar with the terminology to understand better and serve military members and their families. Possessing fluency in military culture, stressors, and trauma is critical for educators and administrators working with this population. Military culture encompasses values, norms, and expectations, such as a strong emphasis on discipline, resilience, and service. Understanding these cultural aspects helps educators connect with their students and build trust.

Besides being aware of the potential impacts of deployment-related stressors, the stereotypical military family comprising an active-duty husband and his civilian female spouse is changing due to the military becoming more diverse and shifting societal norms regarding family structures, and an increase in dual-serving couples (Gribble et al, 2020). While most military families are resilient, some families and children experience challenges post-deployment (Gupta, Gerwitz & Gorden, 2023). Awareness of these stressors, including the fear of losing a parent or adjusting to a parent's reintegration post-deployment, allows educators to create tailored interventions to support military-connected students' social and emotional well-being (Paley & Hajal, 2022). By implementing trauma-informed practices, schools can address the needs of military-connected children by prioritizing safety and trust. For instance, educators can integrate social-emotional learning (SEL) curricula that teach coping skills and emotional regulation, benefiting all students while specifically addressing the needs of military-connected children (Chandra et al., 2011). Administrators can also provide professional development opportunities to ensure staff are equipped with the knowledge and tools to support this population.

WHAT IS TRAUMA-INFORMED CARE?

Trauma-informed care (TIC) is a framework used to understand and respond to the effects of trauma on individuals, especially within educational settings. In K-4 settings, TIC is crucial for fostering a supportive environment that nurtures the emotional and psychological development of young children who may have experienced adverse childhood experiences (ACEs). The importance of Trauma-Informed Care in K-4 schools cannot be overstated. Childhood trauma, including physical, emotional, or sexual abuse, neglect, and exposure to domestic violence, can have a profound impact on a child's cognitive, emotional, and social development. Trauma-informed care shifts the focus from "What is wrong with you?" to "What happened to you?". A perspective that encourages empathy and a deeper understanding of a child's behavior (Trauma-Informed Care Implementation Resource Center, 2024). This approach is now embraced by professionals across various fields, including healthcare, education, justice systems, mental health, child welfare, crisis and homeless shelters, and first-response teams like police officers and paramedics (Piotrowski, 2020). ***Originally developed by the Substance Abuse and Mental Services Administration (SAMHSA, 2014), TIC is grounded in six guiding principles.***

1.) Safety
2.) Trustworthiness and Transparency
3.) Peer Support
4.) Collaboration and Mutuality
5.) Empowerment, Voice, and Choice
6.) Historical and Gender Issues

In early childhood education, TIC strategies aim to mitigate the impact of trauma by emphasizing supportive student-teacher relationships, implementing social-emotional learning strategies, and providing targeted interventions when necessary (Baum et al., 2022; Schwartz et al., 2021). A multi-tiered framework comprising universal support for all students, targeted interventions for at-risk groups, and individualized strategies for those with significant needs has proven effective in promoting resilience and academic success, particularly for military-connected students (Gorman et al., 2021).

Trauma Effect on Children

The definition of TIC has evolved; however, it is best described as embracing the approach of what happened to you versus blaming the child. Research has documented the impact of adverse childhood experiences (ACE) on the emotional, mental, physical, social, and behavioral spectrum (Hughes et al, 2017). The American Psychological Association (2024) defines trauma as a psychological response to distressing events, which can result in anxiety, flashbacks, strained relationships, and chronic stress. Constant exposure to trauma in early childhood can interfere with brain development and impair a child's ability to regulate emotions, concentrate, and build positive relationships (NCTSN, 2017). In response to these challenges, trauma-informed educational practices have gained significant attention, aiming to create safe and supportive school environments that recognize and respond to the needs of students who have experienced trauma.

Adverse Childhood Experiences (ACEs) refer to stressful events during childhood that either directly affect the child or disrupt the family environment. These include physical, sexual, or emotional abuse, neglect, and household challenges such as domestic violence, parental imprisonment, substance abuse, mental health issues, or family breakdown (Lester, Lester, Sutcliffe, et al., 2020). Children's responses to trauma differ from adults', and they vary across cultural contexts. During the formative K-4 years, children still develop coping mechanisms and emotional regulation skills, making early interventions crucial for long-term success. Trauma can manifest in various ways in young children, affecting their ability to concentrate, regulate emotions, and form positive relationships. These effects can disrupt a child's sense of safety, making engaging in learning and social activities difficult.

According to the National Institutes of Health (NIH), children and teenagers may exhibit extreme reactions to trauma, and these responses can differ widely. A systematic review and meta-analysis by Hughes et al. (2017) highlighted the detrimental effects of multiple ACEs, such as child abuse, domestic violence, and chronic exposure to trauma and stress. These experiences have been shown to negatively impact health throughout the lifespan (Hughes et al., 2017). Empirical research underscores the importance of early childhood as a critical period for developing social and emotional competencies, which are essential for positive life outcomes. Furthermore, during the formative years, parental environments significantly influence children's long-term development (Cimino & Cerniglia, 2024), and there are links between children's psychopathological, socio-emotional, and behavioral symptoms and traumatic events experienced in utero by their mothers (Colamarino et al., 2024). Without proper support, these children risk falling behind academically and socially, further perpetuating the cycle of trauma (Van der Kolk, 2014).

Relevance of Trauma-Informed Care in K-4 Settings

Research from the past five years demonstrates that the stressors military-connected children face can significantly affect their emotional well-being, mental health, behavior, and academic performance (Esqueda, Astor, & De Pedro, 2012; Lirico, McDonald, McDonald, 2021). A strong MTSS is essential, especially in the critical developmental stage of early education, particularly in the K-4 classroom setting and beyond. Providing military children with the necessary tools and resources to navigate the complexities of their unique circumstances is crucial. Trauma, if unaddressed, can impair a child's ability to focus, regulate emotions, and build relationship skills essential for success in school and beyond (Marans, 2024).

A literature search used peer-reviewed journal articles, emphasizing research published between 2019 and 2024. Search queries included combinations of the terms military children, military families, trauma-informed care, multi-tiered support systems, military-connected students, K-12 setting, and the United States. The results indicate that research related to military children in the K-12 setting is limited and does not address an MTSS for TIC tailored to military-connected children in the K-12 setting. One study discusses the development of the Inventory for School Supports-Youth Report (ISS-YR) to assess school support for military-connected children (Steggerda et al., 2024). However, it does not incorporate an MTSS approach to TIC within the K-12 setting. Additionally, the study has several limitations, as data was collected from a single school district and focused solely on students in grades 3-5 (Steggerda, Cavell, Drew et al., 2024). Similarly, another journal article highlights the need for educational support for military-connected children in Canada (Hill & Cathcart, 2021), and initiatives like the American

Academy of Nursing's "I Serve 2" Call to Action campaign to raise awareness about the unique needs and challenges faced by military connected children past and present (Rossiter et al., 2016). This initiative advocated for foundational support to foster resilience and promote physical, psychological, and behavioral health among these children. While research exists on military-connected children, it often overlooks their experiences in the K-12 educational setting, with much of the focus centered on mental health.

The importance of mental health cannot be understated, as a more holistic approach is necessary. Implementing an MTSS framework for TIC requires collaboration among all healthcare providers, school administrators, school counselors, nurses, and educational staff involved in the lives of military-connected children. A recent study on 9/11 military-connected children highlights the significance of the "I Serve 2" campaign. It reveals that these children are at an increased risk for physical, psychological, and behavioral health issues (Rossiter & Ling, 2022). To address these gaps, it is vital to adopt a holistic approach. To support these efforts, educators are trained to recognize signs of trauma, implement trauma-sensitive teaching strategies, and create classrooms where all children feel safe and supported (Smith & Pollak, 2021). By adopting these practices, schools aim to mitigate the effects of trauma and foster environments that encourage learning and growth for all students.

A critical but often underemphasized factor is military cultural fluency. Professionals working with military-connected children must understand military culture while ensuring that Multi-Tiered Systems of Support (MTSS) are effectively implemented for military families.

Administrators, teachers, and school counselors should cultivate a strong understanding of trauma-informed care (TIC) principles to support the well-being of these children. Collaboration with families is another essential strategy. Engaging military families in the educational process helps create a cohesive support system for children. Educators can foster these connections by maintaining open communication, respecting the unique dynamics of military life, and encouraging parental involvement in school activities whenever possible. Research indicates that when families and schools work together, children are more likely to experience positive academic and social outcomes (Miller, Lines, Sullivan et al., 2013). Schools should consider partnering with community organizations and military support services to enhance resources for military-connected children. Programs such as Military OneSource and the Military Child Education Coalition provide valuable tools and services that can help schools address the unique needs of these students. By leveraging these resources, educators and administrators can ensure that military-connected children receive comprehensive, consistent support, enabling them to academically and personally thrive.

Overview of Multi-Tiered Systems of Support

Unless a parent is an educator, most parents are unfamiliar with what constitutes a Multi-Tiered System of Support (MTSS) within the school system. An MTSS is a comprehensive, evidence-based framework designed to address all students' diverse academic, behavioral, and social-emotional needs within a school setting. The MTSS framework has three tiers: 1.) Universal Support, 2.) Targeted Support, and 3.) Intensive, Individualized Support (Marans, 2024). By integrating data-driven decision-making with a continuum of support, MTSS aims to enhance student outcomes through proactive and preventative measures. Furthermore, MTSS integrates both Response to Intervention (RTI) and Positive Behavioral Interventions and Supports (PBIS), creating a unified approach that simultaneously addresses academic and behavioral challenges, promoting students' holistic development. Additionally, Multi-Tiered Support for Trauma-Informed Care (MTSS-TIC) offers a structured way to provide varying levels of support depending on each child's needs.

Tier 1: Universal Support with Trauma-Informed Care Integration

Tier 1 provides comprehensive, schoolwide programming to meet all students' academic, social, emotional, and behavioral needs. Academically, this includes high-quality instruction using a research-supported curriculum. Social, emotional, and behavioral development is addressed through lessons on schoolwide expectations and the development of essential social-emotional skills (MTSS Center, 2024). When integrated with Trauma-Informed Care (TIC) principles, Tier 1 expands to include Trauma Awareness Training for all staff, enabling them to understand the unique experiences of military children and identify signs of trauma (Trauma Informed Care Resource Center, 2024). Social-emotional learning (SEL) programs are embedded into the daily curriculum to help students build resilience, empathy, and self-regulation skills. Initiatives like buddy systems, peer mentors, and predictable class routines contribute to creating a safe and inclusive environment. Additionally, family engagement efforts ensure regular communication with families about school events and available support services, with sensitivity to challenges like parental deployment or transitions.

Tier 2: Targeted Support

Tier 2 provides targeted interventions designed to support students identified as at-risk in academic, social, emotional, and behavioral areas. Schools use evidence-based programs to implement strategies that align with student needs and are shown to produce positive outcomes. These interventions may include small group sessions, such as counseling or social skills groups, tailored to help students manage social-emotional regulation, which is often challenging for children who have experienced trauma. Peer support groups specifically for military-connected children provide a space to connect, share experiences, and build support networks within the school. Additionally, systems like Check-In/Check-Out pair at-risk students with a designated staff member for regular check-ins, offering consistent positive reinforcement and guidance. Interventions are delivered with appropriate frequency and duration to maximize opportunities for skill practice and constructive feedback (MTSS Center, 2024)

Tier 3: Intensive, Individualized Support

Tier 3 provides highly individualized and intensive interventions for students with significant and persistent academic, social, emotional, or behavioral challenges, including those with disabilities. These supports are tailored to meet the unique needs of each student through a data-driven process emphasizing increased intensity and personalization. Furthermore, since 2011, the National Center on Intensive Intervention (NCII) has supported the implementation of these interventions by equipping educators, university faculty, and other stakeholders with the tools and knowledge needed to address severe learning and behavioral needs (Chandra, 2011). NCII's approach, Data-Based Individualization (DBI), integrates systematic use of assessment data, evidence-based practices, and strategies for intensifying support. (Marans, 2024).

Within the MTSS or special education framework, Tier 3 interventions leverage these principles to ensure effective outcomes. Examples include one-on-one counseling or therapy services provided by school counselors trained in trauma-focused techniques, such as Trauma-Focused Cognitive Behavioral Therapy. Family-based support services also play a critical role, connecting parents with mental health resources like Military Family Life Counselors (MFLCs) available in many military communities. Additionally, individualized trauma-informed learning plans adapt classroom expectations and workloads to the child's unique needs, offering flexibility and reducing stressors.

Trauma-informed care in schools aims to provide a supportive environment that recognizes and responds to the signs of trauma, helping children feel safe and supported (Rogers et al., 2023). Integrating with an MTSS-TIC framework creates a robust support network, enabling military children to thrive academically and emotionally despite the challenges they face. Key to this success is the collaboration between school administrators and military-specific resources, such as local military installations or community organizations that offer additional counseling, financial resources, and academic support. Professional development for staff focused on trauma-informed strategies is also crucial, equipping teachers and counselors with the knowledge to recognize common triggers and responses in military children, ensuring that every child receives the support they need to succeed. Overall, MTSS offers a structured approach to meeting the varied needs of students through integrated academic and behavioral supports. By emphasizing early intervention, data-driven decision-making, and a continuum of support, MTSS aims to enhance educational outcomes and foster a positive school environment. Ongoing research and practice continue to refine its implementation, striving for equitable and effective student support.

Application to Military Children in Early Education

Proactive Measures to Address Potential Trauma. Research has shown that providing integrated and trauma-informed services leads to the development of resilience assets in individuals who have experienced ACEs, and it offsets any negative behaviors or harm (Hughes, Bellis, Hardcastle, Sethi et al, 2018). Military children often face unique stressors due to their active-duty parents. These experiences can lead to emotional distress and potential trauma if not addressed proactively. The MTSS framework offers a structured approach to meet these challenges. At the universal level, school districts with a larger military presence should implement trauma-informed practices that ensure all students, including military children, have access to environments and resources that promote emotional well-being. A good method is to create safe spaces such as “calming corners” in classrooms. This allows children to self-regulate their emotions during distress (Cavanaugh, 2016). It should be noted that different methods exist in implementing support systems. One approach emphasizes identifying at-risk students and directing targeted resources to them (Perry & Daniels, 2016, as cited in Sweetman, 2022). Another strategy is the MTSS approach, where specialist interventions are integrated into mainstream teaching and educators give trauma-awareness training.

This method acknowledges that many students have experienced trauma stemming from both personal and systemic circumstances beyond their control (Koslouski & Chafouleas, 2022).

Children and adolescents spend many hours at school, allowing school administrators and educators to support at-risk students through healthy developmental practices. Unfortunately, many school districts continue to rely on harmful policies, such as suspensions and expulsions, which disrupt students' connection to the learning environment and exacerbate stress for military families (Breedlove et al, 2021). Thus, incorporating curriculum-based social-emotional learning (SEL) programs, such as Second Step or PATHS, teaches coping strategies, emotional regulation, and problem-solving skills, mitigating the impact of trauma (Bethell et al., 2017; Giano et al., 2020).

Additionally, universal screening tools like the Strengths and Difficulties Questionnaire (SDQ) or the Behavioral and Emotional Screening System (BESS) have proven effective in identifying students at risk for mental health and behavioral challenges (Verlenden, Naser, & Brown, 2021). By implementing these measures, educators can identify military children needing support early and provide interventions tailored to their unique circumstances, ensuring they do not fall behind academically or emotionally. At the targeted level, small group interventions can be offered to military children who exhibit signs of moderate distress or struggle with transitions. For instance, peer mentoring programs or group counseling sessions allow students to share their experiences and build resilience in a supportive setting (Smith et al., 2021). Schools can collaborate with military family support organizations, such as Military One-Source or local Family Readiness Groups, to create workshops for children and parents on coping with deployments or relocations.

At the intensive level, schools can provide personalized interventions for military children facing severe trauma, such as those with a parent injured in combat or experiencing parental loss. Individualized counseling sessions with a school psychologist trained in trauma-informed care or referrals to community mental health providers can help address these more complex needs (Williamson et al., 2018; Spencer et al, 2020). Schools can also establish crisis response plans specifically tailored for military-connected students, ensuring they receive immediate and sustained support during challenging times. Humans are inherently social creatures, and relationships play a fundamental role in shaping who we are.

Research consistently highlights the importance of interpersonal connections as a central human necessity (Allen et al., 2021). As a proactive measure, schools may consider creating a "Military Student Ambassador Program" in which incoming students are paired with peers who have navigated similar transitions. This program helps military children acclimate to their new environment and fosters a sense of belonging and community. Additionally, the program can be adapted into a broader school-based mentorship initiative. By matching students with community members based on age, this approach provides practical, non-stigmatizing support for military-connected students facing social and academic challenges (Spencer et al., 2020). Annually celebrating "Military Appreciation Day" also helps to promote a supportive school culture. Furthermore, engaging military families in the school community further enhances inclusivity. In addition to an annual celebration of "Military Appreciation Day, schools can host events such as "Military Family Nights". This allows families to connect with educators, share their experiences, build networks with other military families or families who have successfully transitioned out of the military, and fully understand the stressors of this type of lifestyle. Creating a parent advisory council that includes military families can ensure their voices are represented in school decision-making processes.

Creating Inclusive, Safe, and Flexible Environments. An inclusive, safe, and flexible environment is essential for military children to feel secure and supported within the classroom. MTSS promotes the creation of classrooms that accommodate these needs through a flexible curriculum and school environment that fosters belonging and connection (Williamson et al., 2018; Spencer et al, 2020). Teachers can implement practices allowing military children to express their feelings and experiences in a safe space, ensuring that their emotional needs are addressed while maintaining academic progress. Peer support groups and tailored learning activities that recognize the experiences of military families can further help military children build resilience (Williamson et al., 2018). For example, peer support programs, such as "Student2Student" (S2S), which was developed specifically for military-connected students, offer an excellent opportunity for integrating new students. In this program, current students are trained to welcome and assist military children, helping them build friendships and develop a sense of community within the school (Military Child Education Coalition [MCEC], 2020). P2P and SBM provide military children a platform to share their experiences and validate their emotions in a supportive environment. Studies indicate that peer mentoring is vital in easing anxiety and fostering social connections for new students, especially those navigating frequent transitions. This approach acknowledges that challenges, stress, and adversity are inherent aspects of the human experience (Fullerton et al., 2021).

Creating a welcoming atmosphere starts with nurturing an inclusive school culture and is reinforced by intentional classroom design. Given students' significant time in school, educational institutions must go beyond providing quality education by fostering environments that support students' physical, social, and emotional well-being. Thoughtful seating arrangements, such as desk clusters, beanbag chairs, or standing desks, can encourage collaboration and offer students flexible options to suit their comfort and focus needs. (Kariippanon, 2020). This type of setup is particularly beneficial for military children, who may feel isolated when entering a new school, as it naturally promotes interaction and teamwork. For example, arranging desks in small groups rather than rows facilitates peer-to-peer communication, helping military students form connections more quickly with their classmates. For instance, arranging desks in small groups rather than rows promotes peer-to-peer communication and can help military students establish connections more quickly with their classmates (Williamson et al., 2018). This approach is crucial in reducing isolation often experienced during transitions.

Lastly, teachers can integrate military family experiences into classroom discussions, assignments, and projects to foster a sense of pride and recognition for their contributions. For instance, adopting a deployed soldier or airman as part of a classroom project is an excellent way to show support. In history or social studies classes, teachers can discuss military service and its impact on families, creating opportunities for understanding and connection. By integrating these perspectives into the curriculum, schools validate the unique experiences of military families and promote a culture of inclusivity (Kern et al., 2021).

The Role of Educators and Administrators

Training to Identify and Respond to Signs of Trauma. Educators and administrators play a crucial role in identifying and responding to signs of trauma in military children. Training in trauma-informed practices equips school staff to recognize symptoms of stress, emotional distress, or academic struggles related to trauma (Mellard et al., 2010). In alignment with these efforts, MTSS employs a whole-child approach to education, providing a comprehensive framework that seamlessly integrates academic, behavioral, and social-emotional learning. This cohesive system of support ensures that all aspects of a student's development are addressed in a unified and inclusive manner, fostering both resilience and success (Sailor et al., 2021)

Educators are trained to notice changes in behavior, such as withdrawal, anxiety, or academic decline, and are provided with strategies for addressing these behaviors through targeted interventions. By incorporating trauma-sensitive strategy into their everyday practices, educators can mitigate the impact of trauma on military children's academic and social-emotional development (Bethell et al., 2017). Additionally, training can cover strategies for building trust, using restorative practices to resolve conflicts, and establishing consistent routines that provide stability for students experiencing frequent relocations. Schools using the Multi-Tiered Systems of Support (MTSS) framework can rely on data-driven methods to monitor student progress and provide tiered interventions tailored to their needs.

Cultivating Sensitivity to Military Culture and Experiences. Educators and administrators must also cultivate sensitivity to military culture and the unique experiences of military families. Many educators may not be familiar with military children's challenges, such as dealing with a parent's deployment or adjusting to a new school after a move. Professional development focused on military culture enables educators to understand these stressors better and adopt practices sensitive to military children's needs (Williamson et al., 2018). It can be challenging for educators and administrators in areas without a strong military presence to cultivate military cultural fluency.

However, remote or isolated schools can still access resources and training to build this competency. Organizations like the Military Child Education Coalition (MCEC) offer online training modules, webinars, and toolkits specifically designed to help educators understand the unique dynamics of military life, such as the emotional toll of deployments, frequent relocations, and the reintegration process (MCEC, 2020). By fostering cultural competence, schools are more equipped to provide a supportive environment for military children that acknowledges their unique circumstances and promotes understanding and inclusion within the classroom. Cultural competency training should focus on recognizing and honoring the strengths of military families, such as adaptability, resilience, and a sense of duty, while also addressing the emotional and social challenges these students may face (Williamson et al., 2018).

Administrators can enhance military cultural fluency by establishing partnerships with military-connected organizations, even in remote locations. Virtual collaborations with resources like Military OneSource or School Liaison Officers offer valuable insights, resources, and professional development opportunities. These partnerships also acknowledge that individuals often turn to trusted connections for emotional support when facing adversity. The responsiveness of these support providers to the specific needs of those seeking help significantly impacts outcomes, including the effectiveness of emotional regulation. By fostering these connections, schools can better address military families' unique challenges, creating a more supportive and understanding environment (Gregory, Anderson, Gable, 2020). Additionally, hosting virtual events or guest speaker sessions featuring military family members can help bridge the knowledge gap for educators in isolated communities. Furthermore, the U.S. government established programs such as the Interstate Compact on Educational Opportunity for Military Children, standardizing policies for transferring academic records and adapting to new school requirements. This ensures that military students experience a smoother transition, even in areas with little direct exposure to military culture (Military Interstate Children's Compact Commission [MIC3], 2020).

IMPACT OF TRAUMA-INFORMED CARE

Improved Academic Outcomes

Trauma-informed care plays a crucial role in supporting military children, who often face unique challenges such as frequent relocations, parental deployments, and changes in family structure. Trauma-informed practices help these children feel more secure and engaged in their education by providing a safe, supportive, and understanding environment. This sense of safety allows military children to focus on their studies, leading to improved academic performance. Additionally, trauma-informed approaches prioritize building strong relationships between educators and students, fostering a sense of trust essential for academic success. Research highlights the importance of a secure and nurturing educational setting in fostering academic success. For example, studies have shown that when educators are trained in trauma-informed practices, students experience improved attendance, higher engagement levels, and better academic performance (Overstreet & Chafouleas, 2016). By prioritizing safety and understanding, trauma-informed care helps military children feel more grounded, enabling them to focus on their studies without the burden of unresolved stress. Additionally, trauma-informed approaches emphasize the value of strong relationships between educators and students. These relationships are foundational for building trust, which is often compromised in children who have experienced trauma (Perry & Daniels, 2016). Trust enables students to take academic risks, seek help, and fully engage in learning activities. By addressing both the emotional and cognitive needs of military children, trauma-informed care sets the stage for sustained academic improvement.

Enhanced Emotional Regulation and Resilience

Military children frequently experience high levels of stress and emotional strain due to the unpredictable nature of military life. The constant cycle of transitions, such as moving to new schools and adjusting to different social environments, can exacerbate feelings of anxiety and uncertainty. Trauma-informed care is crucial in supporting these children by teaching them healthy emotional regulation skills and helping them process their feelings constructively. By recognizing the impact of trauma, caregivers and educators can foster resilience, empowering these children to recover from adversity more effectively. As a result, they become better equipped to manage their emotions, cope with stress, and navigate challenges, promoting their overall well-being and long-term success. Educators and caregivers who adopt trauma-informed strategies focus on understanding the underlying causes of behavioral issues rather than merely addressing the symptoms. This shift in perspective allows for interventions that foster resilience—the ability to recover and adapt in the face of adversity (SAMHSA, 2014). Resilient children are better equipped to navigate stressors, build positive relationships, and control their lives. Furthermore, trauma-informed care incorporates practices that encourage mindfulness, self-awareness, and coping strategies. These techniques have been shown to reduce anxiety and improve emotional well-being in children exposed to high levels of stress (Felitti et al., 1998). For military children, developing these skills benefits their immediate well-being and sets a strong foundation for long-term success and adaptability. Research suggests that experiencing stress or adversity early in life can, in certain circumstances, enhance resilience in later years (Crandall et al., 2023).

Broader Implications for Early Education

Creating Inclusive Environments for All Children. Trauma-informed care's principles benefit military children and create a more inclusive and equitable environment for all students. Classrooms that embrace trauma-informed practices equip educators with the tools to recognize and respond to a wide range of student needs, from trauma and mental health challenges to everyday struggles. An understanding and supportive atmosphere ensures that all children can thrive regardless of their background or experiences. Trauma-informed classrooms often incorporate flexible seating, calming areas, and consistent routines, which have been shown to support children with diverse learning needs (Craig, 2016). These strategies ensure that every child, regardless of their background or experiences, feels valued and supported. Moreover, such environments promote a culture of empathy and understanding, reducing stigma and fostering student peer support.

Strengthening Community Ties. Trauma-informed care extends beyond the individual child to impact the larger school community. By promoting empathy, understanding, and collaboration, schools create a network of support that strengthens the bonds between students, teachers, and families. This sense of community helps children feel more connected and less isolated, which is particularly important for military families who may be geographically separated from extended family members. Strong community ties enhance the well-being of military children and contribute to a positive, nurturing school culture that benefits everyone involved. Schools prioritizing trauma-informed care often engage families through workshops, communication strategies, and community-building events. These efforts strengthen the bonds between students, teachers, and families, creating a shared commitment to the well-being of all children. Strong community ties have been linked to increased student engagement, better mental health outcomes, and a more positive school culture overall (Fullerton et al., 2021).

SUMMARY OF KEY POINTS

Challenges Faced by Military Children in K-4. Military children in grades K-4 experience unique challenges that can significantly impact their academic, social, and emotional development. Due to frequent relocations, these children often face schooling disruptions, leading to learning gaps and difficulties adapting to new educational environments (Esqueda et al., 2012). Moreover, the transient nature of military life can result in limited opportunities to form stable peer relationships, exacerbating feelings of isolation and stress (Military One Source, n.d.). Compounding these issues, exposure to parental deployments and the associated uncertainties can lead to increased anxiety and emotional distress, making military children more susceptible to trauma-related symptoms (Chandra et al., 2010). These challenges can hinder their academic and personal success during critical early childhood development stages without adequate support systems. These challenges manifest in several key areas:

Academic Disruptions Frequent relocations—often called Permanent Change of Station (PCS) result in military children attending multiple schools by the time they reach high school (Esqueda et al., 2012). Each transition requires children to adapt to new curricula, standards, and teaching styles, often leading to gaps in learning and inconsistency in academic progress. Furthermore, military children frequently miss critical instructional time during the transition process, compounding the difficulty of keeping up with their peers (Military One Source, n.d.).

Social and Emotional Challenges. Military life can create isolation as children struggle to establish and maintain lasting friendships. This is particularly true for younger children who may lack the emotional maturity to process frequent separations from peers (Military One Source, n.d.). Additionally, parental deployments introduce emotional stress and uncertainty, often leading to anxiety, depression, or behavioral issues (Chandra et al., 2010). Young children may exhibit regressive behaviors, difficulties with attachment, or an inability to concentrate in school.

Lack of Tailored Support. Many schools are not equipped to address the unique needs of military children. Educators may lack awareness of the impact of military life on students, resulting in limited understanding or accommodations. Without tailored support programs, the challenges military children face is further exacerbated, particularly in environments where military families are less prevalent (Crandall et al., 2023; Ross et al., 2021).

Adverse experiences among military children are prevalent, so implementing trauma-informed practices within educational settings is essential. Trauma-informed education focuses on creating a safe, supportive environment that acknowledges and addresses the impact of trauma on learning and behavior (Craig, 2016). Schools must adopt a multi-tiered system of support (MTSS) that integrates academic, behavioral, and social-emotional interventions tailored to the unique needs of military children.

Trauma-informed education recognizes the profound impact of trauma on a child's ability to learn and behave appropriately in school. Schools that embrace this approach focus on creating safe, supportive environments where children feel valued and understood (Craig, 2016). Key components include:

- Establishing trusting relationships between students and educators.
- Providing consistent routines to foster a sense of stability.
- Integrating social-emotional learning (SEL) into the curriculum to help students process and manage emotions effectively (NCTSN, 2017).

MTSS framework provides a structured approach to identify at-risk students early and offer tiered interventions, ranging from universal support for all students to intensive, individualized care (Loftus-Rattan et al., 2023). MTSS offers a framework for addressing the diverse needs of students through a tiered approach:

Tier 1: Universal support for all students, such as SEL programs and positive behavior reinforcement.
Tier 2: Targeted interventions for students exhibiting signs of difficulty, such as small-group counseling sessions.
Tier 3: Intensive, individualized support for students with significant needs, including one-on-one therapy or specialized educational plans (Loftus-Rattan et al., 2023).

For military children, MTSS can be tailored to address specific challenges, such as providing deployment-focused counseling or peer mentoring programs to foster connections and resilience. This might include targeted counseling services, peer support groups, and professional development for educators to recognize and respond effectively to signs of trauma.

Professional Development for Educators. Training educators to recognize and respond to signs of trauma is essential for effective implementation. Professional development programs should include strategies for creating trauma-sensitive classrooms, de-escalation techniques, and building strong teacher-student relationships (Perry & Daniels, 2016).

Call to Action

Advocacy for Policies Prioritizing Trauma-Informed Education. Stakeholders must advocate for policies that prioritize trauma-informed education for military children. This includes allocating resources for mental health services, establishing programs that address the needs of highly mobile student populations, and mandating the integration of trauma-informed approaches in schools located near military installations (National Child Traumatic Stress Network, 2017). Policymakers are crucial in ensuring that military children receive the support they need. Advocacy efforts should focus on:

- Allocating federal and state funding for mental health services in schools near military installations.

- Mandating trauma-informed training for educators in areas with high concentrations of military families.
- Establishing national guidelines for supporting military children in educational settings (Department of Defense Education Activity, 2022c).

Commitment to Professional Development and Systemic Change

Systemic change requires a commitment to ongoing professional development for educators and administrators. Training should encompass strategies for fostering resilience, recognizing trauma indicators, and implementing evidence-based interventions (Perry & Daniels, 2016). Moreover, fostering partnerships between schools, families, and military organizations can enhance the support network available to military children, ensuring they receive comprehensive care across various domains. This includes:

- Partnering with military organizations to provide resources and training.
- Creating peer support programs to connect military children with others who share similar experiences.
- Establishing metrics to evaluate the effectiveness of trauma-informed and MTSS initiatives, ensuring continuous improvement (Fullerton et al., 2021; Sailor et al., 2021)

Community and Family Engagement: Families and communities must be integral to the process. Schools can host workshops to educate parents about trauma-informed practices and resources available to support their children. Additionally, fostering collaboration between schools and military support organizations can enhance the care network available to military children (Chandra et al., 2010).

CONCLUSION

The challenges military children face, particularly in grades K-4, are multifaceted and rooted in the circumstances of military life. These challenges can have long-lasting effects on their academic, social, and emotional well-being. Military families will exist if the U.S. has an all-volunteer force. Thus, the educational system must adapt to meet the needs of this population group. The adverse experiences of military children can contribute to academic struggles, emotional distress, and mental health concerns, all of which can undermine their potential and hinder their ability to succeed in school. Integrating trauma-informed practices and multi-tiered systems of support within schools is essential. Recognizing the needs of military children, educational systems can create environments that promote resilience, foster emotional security, and offer the tailored support necessary for these children to thrive. Trauma-informed education, when implemented with fidelity, not only acknowledges the effects of trauma but also transforms the way schools approach discipline, learning, and support. A multi-tiered support system ensures that all students, particularly those at risk, receive appropriate interventions that address their academic, social, and emotional needs.

There is a need for systemic change. Advocacy is necessary to enact change. Policymakers, educators, administrators, and military leaders must advocate for educational school reform. School systems that prioritize trauma-informed education for military children. Furthermore, school districts must advocate for educators to be trained in trauma-informed care. It is critical to ensure schools can effectively serve military students or any population group that has experienced trauma. Schools near military bases must have the resources and training to provide comprehensive support, including counseling services and peer networks catering to military families. Additionally, educators must be trained to identify signs of trauma and provide the appropriate intervention, possess a professional commitment to understanding the complexities of military life, and trauma can transform schools into safe, supportive spaces where military children can feel secure and valued. The responsibility falls on all stakeholders (i.e., policymakers, educators, military leaders, and families) to collaborate to create an educational landscape supportive of military children. With adequate resources, systemic changes, and a commitment to trauma-informed education, military children will be empowered to overcome their unique obstacles by giving them the tools to grow into resilient, confident, and successful individuals. Making these changes, military children survive and thrive in their educational journeys into their adolescent years and adulthood. Drawing from my childhood as a *military brat*, I am mindful and cognizant of the challenges my children will or could face. I believe acting now can foster a school community that goes above and beyond to support military children and will prevent feelings of isolation and loneliness.

REFERENCES

Allen, K. A., Slatan, C., & Arslan, G. (2021). School belonging among low-income urban youth with disabilities: Testing a theoretical model. *Journal of School Psychology*, *81*, 1–14. DOI: 10.1016/j.jsp.2020.11.001

Bethell, C.D., Davis, M.B., Gombojav, N., Stumbo, S.P., & Powers, K. (2017). A national and across-state profile on Adverse Childhood Experiences among U.S. children and possibilities to heal and thrive.

Breedlove, M., Choi, J., & Zyromski, B. (2021). Mitigating the Effects of Adverse Childhood Experiences: How Restorative Practices in Schools Support Positive Childhood Experiences and Protective Factors. *New Educator*, *17*(3), 223–241. DOI: 10.1080/1547688X.2020.1807078

Cafferky, B. M., Reyes, C. A. D., Beaver, S. L., & Shi, L. (2022). "We'll just draw the curtains!": Military wives' postures toward predeployment emotional preparation. *Family Relations*, *71*(1), 389–407. DOI: 10.1111/fare.12591

Cavanaugh, B. (2016). Trauma-informed classrooms and schools: Perspectives and practices. *Beyond Behavior*, *25*(2), 41–46. DOI: 10.1177/107429561602500206

Center for Health Care Strategies, Inc. (n.d.). What is trauma-informed care? Retrieved from https://www.traumainformedcare.chcs.org/what-is-trauma-informed-care/

Center for Health Care Strategies, Inc. (n.d.). *Childhood trauma*. Retrieved from https://www.traumapolicy.org/topics/childhood-trauma

Chandra, A., Lara-Cinisomo, S., Jaycox, L. H., Tanielian, T., Burns, R. M., Ruder, T., & Han, B. (2010). Children on the homefront: The experience of children from military families. *Pediatrics*, *125*(1), 16–25. DOI: 10.1542/peds.2009-1180 PMID: 19969612

Chandra, A., Lara-Cinisomo, S., Jaycox, L. H., Tanielian, T., Han, B., Burns, R. M., & Ruder, T. (2011). Views from the homefront: The experiences of youth and spouses from military families. *Rand Health Quarterly*, *1*(1). https://www.rand.org/content/dam/rand/pubs/technical_reports/2011/RAND_TR913.pdf PMID: 28083168

Cimino, S., & Cerniglia, L. (2024). The shadow of the past: How paternal traumatic experiences shape early parent-child interactions and offspring's emotional development. *European Journal of Trauma & Dissociation = Revue Européenne du Trauma et de la Dissociation*, *8*(3), 100433. Advance online publication. DOI: 10.1016/j.ejtd.2024.100433

Colamarino, L., Salvagno, C., & Soubelet, A. (2024). The impact on child development of traumatic exposure during pregnancy: A systematic review. *European Journal of Trauma & Dissociation = Revue Européenne du Trauma et de la Dissociation*, *8*(2), 100406. Advance online publication. DOI: 10.1016/j.ejtd.2024.100406

Comptroller of the Department of Defense. (2018). Definitions related to financial management regulations. Retrieved from https://comptroller.defense.gov/Portals/45/documents/fmr/current/09/09_definitions.pdf

Craig, S. E. (2016). *Trauma-Sensitive Schools: Learning Communities Transforming Children's Lives*. Teachers College Press.

Cramm, H., Godfrey, C. M., Murphy, S., McKeown, S., & Dekel, R. (2022). Experiences of children growing up with a parent who has military-related post-traumatic stress disorder: A qualitative systematic review. *JBI Evidence Synthesis*, *20*(7), 1638–1740. DOI: 10.11124/JBIES-20-00229 PMID: 34710888

Crandall, A. A., Magnusson, B. M., Barlow, M. J., Randall, H., Policky, A. L., & Hanson, C. L. (2023). Positive adult experiences as turning points for better adult mental health after childhood adversity. *Frontiers in Public Health*, *11*, 1223953. Advance online publication. DOI: 10.3389/fpubh.2023.1223953 PMID: 37601196

Cunningham, J. (2023). Fifty years strong: The all-volunteer force of the United States. *Army University Press*. https://www.armyupress.army.mil/journals/military-review/online-exclusive/2023-ole/cunningham/

Demographics of the U.S. Military [online]. Retrieved from https://www.cfr.org/backgrounder/demographics-us-military

Department of Defense. (2018). Family readiness group overview. Retrieved from https://media.defense.gov/2018/Sep/10/2001963685/-1/-1/1/FRG_OVERVIEW.PDF

Department of Defense. (2023). Department of Defense instruction 1315.19: *Exceptional family member program (EFMP)*. Retrieved from https://www.esd.whs.mil/Portals/54/Documents/DD/issuances/dodi/131519.pdf

Department of Defense Education Activity. (2022a). *The DoDEA grant program.* https://www.dodea.edu/partnership/grants.cfm

Department of Defense Education Activity. (2022b). The military interstate compact. https://www.dodea.edu/partnership/interstatecompact.cfm

Deployment: An Overview. (2022). https://www.military.com/deployment/deployment-overview.html

DeVoe, E. R., Ross, A. M., Spencer, R., Drew, A., Acker, M., Paris, R., & Jacoby, V. (2020). Coparenting across the deployment cycle: Observations from military families with young children. *Journal of Family Issues*, *41*(9), 1447–1469. DOI: 10.1177/0192513X19894366

Esqueda, M. C., Astor, R. A., & De Pedro, K. M. T. (2012). A call to duty: Educational policy and school reform addressing the needs of children from military families. *Educational Researcher*, *41*(2), 65–70. DOI: 10.3102/0013189X11432139

Felitti, V, Anda, R.F., Nordenberg, D., Williamson, D.R., Spitz, A.M., & Edwards, V.

Giano, Z., Wheeler, D. L., & Hubach, R. D. (2020). The frequencies and disparities of adverse childhood experiences in the U.S. *BMC Public Health*, *20*(1), 1327. DOI: 10.1186/s12889-020-09411-z PMID: 32907569

Gregory, A. J. P., Anderson, J. F., & Gable, S. L. (2020). You don't know how it feels: Accuracy in emotion perception predicts responsiveness of support. *Emotion (Washington, D.C.)*, *20*(3), 343–352. DOI: 10.1037/emo0000608 PMID: 31169372

Gribble, R., Mahar, A. L., Keeling, M., Sullivan, K., McKeowng, S., Burchill, S., Fear, N. T., & Castro, C. A. (2020). Are we family? A scoping review of how military families are defined in mental health and substance use research. *Journal of Military, Veteran and Family Health*, *6*(2), 85–119. DOI: 10.3138/jmvfh-2019-0054

Gupta, A., Gewirtz, A. H., & Borden, L. M. (2023). Post-traumatic stress symptoms and parenting in military families: A systematic integrative review. *Journal of Family Theory & Review*, *15*(4), 822–844. DOI: 10.1111/jftr.12530

Heward, C., Li, W., Tie, Y. C., & Waterworth, P. (2024). A Scoping Review of Military Culture, Military Identity, and Mental Health Outcomes in Military Personnel. *Military Medicine*, *189*(11/12), e2382–e2393. DOI: 10.1093/milmed/usae276 PMID: 38836843

Hill, S., & Cathcart, D. G. (2021). Considerations for supporting Canadian military-connected students in K-12 and higher education. *Journal of Military, Veteran and Family Health*, *7*(3), 114–119. DOI: 10.3138/jmvfh-2020-0070

Hughes, K., Bellis, M. A., Hardcastle, K. A., Sethi, D., Butchart, A., Mikton, C., Jones, L., & Dunne, M. P. (2017). The effect of multiple adverse childhood experiences on health: Asystematic review and meta-analysis. *The Lancet. Public Health*, *2*(8), e356–e366. DOI: 10.1016/S2468-2667(17)30118-4 PMID: 29253477

Jacoby, V. M., Straud, C. L., Tyler, H., Dondanville, K. A., Yarvis, J. S., Mintz, J., Young, M. S., Peterson, A. L., Wachen, J. S., & Resick, P. A. (2024). An evaluation of the associations among posttraumatic stress disorder, depression, and complicated grief in active duty military personnel with traumatic loss. *Journal of Traumatic Stress*, *37*(6), 984–997. DOI: 10.1002/jts.23080 PMID: 39090976

Kariippanon, K. E., Cliff, D. P., Ellis, Y. G., Ucci, M., Okely, A. D., & Parrish, A.-M. (2021). School Flexible Learning Spaces, Student Movement Behavior and Educational Outcomes among Adolescents: A Mixed-Methods Systematic Review. *The Journal of School Health*, *91*(2), 133–145. DOI: 10.1111/josh.12984 PMID: 33368271

Kern, M., Wehmeyer, M., Allen, K., Slaten, C., Arslan, G., Roffey, S., Craig, H., & Vella-Brodrick, D. (2021). School belonging: The importance of student and teacher relationships.

Koslouski, J. B., & Chafouleas, S. M. (2022). Key considerations in delivering trauma-informed professional learning for educators. *Frontiers in Education*, *7*, 853020. DOI: 10.3389/feduc.2022.853020

Lester, S., Khatwa, M., & Sutcliffe, K. (2020). Service needs of young people affected by adverse childhood experiences (ACEs): A systematic review of UK qualitative evidence. *Children & Youth Services Review, 118, N.PAG*. https://doi.org/DOI: 10.1016/j.childyouth.2020.105429

LoBraico, A. L., McDonald, S. E., & McDonald, T. P. (2021). The impact of military-connectedness on academic achievement and behavioral health in children and adolescents: A systematic review. *The Journal of School Health*, *91*(3), 204–213. DOI: 10.1111/josh.12956 PMID: 33438219

Loftus-Rattan, S. M., Wrightington, M., Furey, J., & Case, J. (2023). Multi-Tiered System of Supports: An Ecological Approach to School Psychology Service Delivery. *Teaching of Psychology*, *50*(1), 77–85. DOI: 10.1177/00986283211024262

Maran, S. (2024). Responding to Childhood Trauma: Developing and Learning from Collaborations Beyond the Consulting Room. *Psychoanalytic Inquiry*, *44*(2), 153–165. DOI: 10.1080/07351690.2024.2306099

Marans, S. (2024). Responding to childhood trauma: Developing and learning from collaborations beyond the consulting room. *Psychoanalytic Inquiry*, *44*(2), 153–165. DOI: 10.1080/07351690.2024.2306099

Mellard, D. F., Woods, K. P., & Deshler, D. D. (2010). The role of response to intervention in identifying and addressing reading difficulties. *Learning Disabilities Research & Practice*, *25*(4), 213–223. DOI: 10.1111/j.1540-5826.2010.00310.x

Meyer, E. G., Writer, B. W., & Brim, W. (2016). The Importance of Military Cultural Competence. *Current Psychiatry Reports*, *18*(3), 1–8. DOI: 10.1007/s11920-016-0662-9 PMID: 26830884

Military & Family Life Counseling Program. (2020). The Military and Family Life Counseling (MFLC) Program. Military OneSource._https://www.militaryonesource.mil/confidential-help/non-medical-counseling/military-and-family-life-counseling/the-military-and-family-life-counseling-program/

Military Child Education Coalition. (2022a). MCEC. https://www.militarychild.org/

Military Child Education Coalition. (2022b). Purple star schools. https://www.militarychild.org/purplestarschools

Military Child Education Coalition. (2023). Student2Student. https://www.militarychild.org/programs/student-2-student

Military Child Education Coalition (MCEC). (2020). Online training resources for educators. Retrieved from https://www.militarychild.org

Military Families Learning Network. (2020). Supporting military families: Evidence-informed practices. Retrieved from https://militaryfamilies.psu.edu/wp-content/uploads/2020/01/Supporting-Military-Families_An-Overview-of-Military-Family-Outcomes-and-Evidence-Informed-Practices_29102019.pdf

Military Family Advisory Network. (2018). Moving survey results. Retrieved from https://militaryfamilyadvisorynetwork.org/wp-content/uploads/MFAN-2018-Moving-Survey-1.pdf

Military Family Advisory Network. (2019). Support programming survey results. Retrieved from https://www.mfan.org/research-reports/2019-military-family-support-programming-survey-results/

Military Family Education Coalition. (n.d.). Education revolution: Advocacy booklet. Retrieved from https://militaryfamily.org/wp-content/uploads/Education-Revolution_Advocacy-Booklet.pdf

Military Impacted Schools Association. (n.d.). Military impacted schools association. https://militaryimpactedschoolsassociation.org/

Military Interstate Children's Compact Commission (MIC3). (2020). Interstate compact on educational opportunity for military children. Retrieved from https://www.mic3.net

Military OneSource. (2020). 2020 demographics profile: Active duty families. https://download.militaryonesource.mil/12038/MOS/Infographic/2020- demographics-active-duty-families.pdf

Military OneSource. (2022). View all installations. https://installations.militaryonesource.mil/view-all

Military OneSource. (n.d.). Community capacity building courses. https://www.militaryonesource.mil/training-resources/community-capacity-building/

Military OneSource. (n.d.). Military deployment support. https://www.militaryonesource.mil/military-deployment-support/

Miller, G. E., Lines, C., Sullivan, E., & Hermanutz, K. (2013). Preparing Educators to Partner with Families. *Teaching Education*, *24*(2), 150–163. DOI: 10.1080/10476210.2013.786889

Mulholland, E., Dahlberg, D., & McDowell, L. (2020). A Two-Front War: Exploring Military Families' Battle with Parental Deployment. *Journal of Pediatric Nursing*, *54*, 34–41. DOI: 10.1016/j.pedn.2020.05.019 PMID: 32526614

National Center on Substance Abuse and Child Welfare. (n.d.). Trauma-informed care in substance abuse. Retrieved from https://ncsacw.acf.hhs.gov/userfiles/files/SAMHSA_Trauma.pdf

National Child Traumatic Stress Network (NCTSN). (2017). Trauma-Informed Schools for Children in Military Families.

National Child Traumatic Stress Network (NCTSN). (2018). Creating, supporting, and sustaining trauma-informed schools: A system framework. Retrieved from https://www.nctsn.org

National Council on Family Relations. (2020). Military families executive summary. Retrieved from https://www.ncfr.org/sites/default/files/2020-02/Military-Families-Exec-Sum-Feb-2020.pdf

National Council on Family Relations. (2020). Military families: An overview of military family outcomes and evidence-informed practices. *National Council on Family Relations*. https://www.ncfr.org/sites/default/files/2020-02/Military-Families-Exec-Sum-Feb-2020.pdf

Ormeno, M. D., Roh, Y., Heller, M., Shields, E., Flores-Carrera, A., Greve, M., Hagan, J., Kostrubala, A., & Onasanya, N. (2020). Special Concerns in Military Families. *Current Psychiatry Reports*, *22*(12), 82. Advance online publication. DOI: 10.1007/s11920-020-01207-7 PMID: 33215305

Ortiz, R., Gilgoff, R., & Burke Harris, N. (2022). Adverse Childhood Experiences, Toxic Stress, and Trauma-Informed Neurology. *JAMA Neurology*, *79*(6), 539–540. DOI: 10.1001/jamaneurol.2022.0769 PMID: 35467693

Our Military Kids. (2024). Five-year report. Retrieved from https://www.ourmilitarykids.org/wp-content/uploads/2024/07/5-Year-Report_Final.pdf

Overstreet, S., & Chafouleas, S. M. (2016). Trauma-Informed Schools: Introduction to the Special Issue. *School Mental Health*, *8*(1), 1–6. DOI: 10.1007/s12310-016-9184-1

Paley, B., & Hajal, N. J. (2022). Conceptualizing Emotion Regulation and Coregulation as Family-Level Phenomena. *Clinical Child and Family Psychology Review*, *25*(1), 1. DOI: 10.1007/s10567-022-00378-4 PMID: 35098427

PATHS Program LLC. (n.d.). What is social-emotional learning (SEL)? Retrieved from https://pathsprogram.com/what-is-sel

Perry, B. D., & Daniels, M. L. (2016). *The Boy Who Was Raised as a Dog: And Other Stories from a Child Psychiatrist's Notebook*. Basic Books.

Piotrowski, C., (2020). ACEs and trauma-informed care. Adverse Childhood Experiences, 307-328. *Academic Press: 2020*. .DOI: 10.1016/B978-0-12-816065-7.00015-X

Quintana, T. S., & Cole, R. F. (2021). Forward march: Implementing the ASCA National Model to support military-connected students. *Journal of School Counseling, 19(7)*. http://www.jsc.montana.edu/articles/v19n7.pdf

RAND Corporation. (2018). Key findings on the well-being of military families. Retrieved from https://www.rand.org/pubs/research_reports/RR2304.html

Fullerton, D. J., Zhang, L. M., & Kleitman, S. (2021). An integrative process model of resilience in an academic context: Resilience resources, coping strategies, and positive adaptation. *PLoS One*, *16*(2), 1–22. DOI: 10.1371/journal.pone.0246000

Rogers, M., Johnson, A., Coffey, Y., Fielding, J., Harrington, I., & Bhullar, N. (2023). Parental perceptions of social and emotional well-being of young children from Australian military families. *The Australian Journal of Rural Health*, *31*(6), 1090–1102. Advance online publication. DOI: 10.1111/ajr.13033 PMID: 37622610

Ross, A. M., DeVoe, E. R., Steketee, G., Emmert-Aronson, B. O., Brown, T., & Muroff, J. (2020). Outcomes of a reflective parenting program among military spouses: The moderating role of social support. *Journal of Family Psychology*, *34*(4), 402–413. DOI: 10.1037/fam0000637 PMID: 32027150

Rossiter, A. G., Dumas, M. A., Wilmoth, M. C., & Patrcian, A. P. (2016). "I Serve 2": Meeting the needs of military children in civilian practice. *Nursing Outlook*, *64*(5), 485–490. DOI: 10.1016/j.outlook.2016.05.011 PMID: 27477834

Rossiter, A. G., & Ling, C. G. (2022). Building resilience in US military families: Why it matters. *BMJ Military Health*, *168*(1), 91–94. DOI: 10.1136/bmjmilitary-2020-001735 PMID: 33785586

Rostker, B. D. (2006). The evolution of the all-volunteer force. RAND Corporation. https://www.rand.org/pubs/research_briefs/RB9195.html

Sailor, W., Skrtic, T. M., Cohn, M., & Olmstead, C. (2021). Preparing Teacher Educators for Statewide Scale-Up of Multi-Tiered System of Support (MTSS). *Teacher Education and Special Education*, *44*(1), 24–41. DOI: 10.1177/0888406420938035

Second Step. (n.d.). Our programs: Social-emotional learning. Retrieved from https://www.secondstep.org/our-programs

Smith, K. E., & Pollak, S. D. (2021). Rethinking concepts and categories for understanding the neurodevelopmental effects of childhood adversity. *Perspectives on Psychological Science*, *16*(1), 67–93. DOI: 10.1177/1745691620920725 PMID: 32668190

Spencer, R., Gowdy, G., Herrera, C., Heubach, J., Slep, A. S., & Cavell, T. A. (2020). Web-Based Training for School-Based Mentors of Military-Connected Youth: A Multi-Phase Development Study. *The Journal of Primary Prevention, 41*(6), 567–583. DOI: 10.1007/s10935-020-00616-x PMID: 33146803

Steggerda, J. C., Cavell, T. A., Drew, A. L., Nicholson, J. H., Herrera, C., Gaffney, D., Smith, A. M., & Spencer, R. (2024). Inventory of School Supports--Youth Report (ISS-YR): Development and Validation with Military-Connected Strategy Bridge. (2016). Military and American culture. Retrieved from https://thestrategybridge.org/the-bridge/2016/4/12/military-american-culture

Sweetman, N. (2022). What is a trauma-informed classroom? What are the benefits and challenges involved? *Frontiers in Education, 7*, 450. DOI: 10.3389/feduc.2022.914448

The Education Week. (2023). What is a multi-tiered system of supports (MTSS)? Retrieved from https://www.edweek.org/teaching-learning/mtss-what-is-a-multi-tiered-system-of-supports/2023/10

U.S. Army Morale, Welfare, and Recreation. (n.d.). Exceptional family member program. Retrieved from https://www.armymwr.com/programs-and-services/personal-assistance/exceptional-family-member-program

U.S. Department of Defense. (n.d.). Overview of family readiness programs. Retrieved from https://media.defense.gov/2018/Sep/10/2001963685/-1/-1/1/FRG_OVERVIEW.PDF

U.S. Department of Education. (n.d.). MTSS essential components. Retrieved from https://mtss4success.org/essential-components

USO. (n.d.). A military kid shares his thoughts on family moves. Retrieved From https://www.uso.org/stories/3830-a-military-kid-shares-his-thoughts-on-his-family-s-next-move-and-military-life

Van der Kolk, B. A. (2014). *The body keeps the score: Brain, mind, and body in the healing of trauma*. Penguin Books.

Vergun, D. (2024, January 30). DOD official discusses challenges, solutions to recruiting all-volunteer force. Defense.gov. https://www.defense.gov/News/News- Stories/Article/Article/3660541/dod-official-discusses-challenges-solutions-to-recruiting- all-volunteer-force/

Verlenden, J., Naser, S., & Brown, J. (2021). Steps in the implementation of universal screening for behavioral and emotional risk to support multi-tiered systems of support: Two case studies. *Journal of Applied School Psychology, 37*(1), 69–107. DOI: 10.1080/15377903.2020.1780660

Weinstock, M. (2023, May 4). Staff perspective: Military PCS moves—their impact on military partners. *Center for Deployment Psychology*. https://deploymentpsych.org/blog/staff-perspective-military-pcs-moves-their-impact-military-partners

Williamson, V., Stevelink, S. A. M., Da Silva, E., & Fear, N. T. (2018). A systematic review of wellbeing in children: A comparison of military and civilian families. *Child and Adolescent Psychiatry and Mental Health, 12*(1), 46. DOI: 10.1186/s13034-018-0252-1 PMID: 30443263

KEY TERMS AND DEFINITIONS

Military-Connected Children: (MC): Military-connected children are colloquially known as *military brats*. These military children are also referred to as "military-connected children (MC)" and defined as minors with at least one parent serving in the U.S. Armed Forces as an active-duty member, reservist, or member of the National Guard (DOD, n.d.).

PCS - Permanent Change of Station: A military service member's relocation, including their family, to a new duty station typically lasts between two and four years (Military One Source, 2024).

TDY: -Temporary Duty: Short-term assignments away from the service member's permanent duty station. These are shorter in duration than PCS assignments or deployments. (Military One Source, 2024).

FRG – Family Resource Group: A command-sponsored organization comprising service members, civilian employees, family members, and volunteers within a unit. These groups foster mutual support, aid, and establish a communication network connecting family members, the chain of command, and community resources (DoD, n.d.).

MFLC-Military Family Life Counselors: MFLCs typically work on military installations and are part of the Military and Family Life Counseling Programs, which offer free, confidential, non-medical counseling to service members, their families, and survivors stationed on or near military installations (Military One Source, 2024). MFLCs are specially trained to understand the needs of the military community; These counselors provide essential support through counseling sessions, briefings, and presentations tailored to the unique challenges of military life.

EFMP-Exceptional Family Member Program: EFMP is an executive services directorate created by the Department of Defense (DOD, 2023). Each military branch has its own EFMP. The purpose of this program is to provide support for families with special needs. It is a comprehensive initiative comprising three key components: Family Support, Identification and Enrollment, and Assignment Coordination (Military One Sources, 2024). It helps families by identifying and enrolling members with special medical or educational needs, determining the availability of services at current or future duty stations, and providing information, referrals, and non-clinical case management to facilitate access to necessary resources.

CONUS - Continental United States: Refers to the 48 contiguous states and the District of Columbia

OCONUS - Outside Continental United States: Includes locations such as Alaska, Hawaii, and U.S. territories, including Puerto Rico (Office of the Under Secretary of Defense, 2023).

PTSD – Post-Traumatic Stress Disorder: A mental health condition triggered by experiencing or witnessing traumatic events. In the military context, PTSD can develop from combat, injury, or loss and has far-reaching impacts on family functioning.

Trauma Factors in Military Life: Children in military families face a unique array of stressors. These include: Parental injury or illness (including PTSD), death of a parent, frequent relocations and deployment cycles. This experience can significantly impact a child's mental health, development, and emotional well-being (Mulholland et al., 2020). Family stress is heightened during deployments, with military spouses often assuming the primary responsibility for financial decisions, parenting, and household management (Ormeno et al., 2020). These factors underscore the importance of trauma-informed care approaches when addressing the needs of military families and highlight the necessity of multi-tiered support systems to promote resilience and adaptability (Briggs et al., 2019). A recent systematic review of childhood experiences of living with military-related PTSD parents revealed that family functioning plays a mediating role in child development, with elements such as role fulfillment, emotional expression, and communication shaping processes that sustain healthy family dynamics (Cramm et al., 2022). Further supported by past research, as psychological injuries like PTSD can directly disrupt family functioning, but also do so indirectly through individual, relational, and contextual factors; confounded by PTSD being an invisible injury without outward physical signs, young children may easily internalize its symptoms (Cramm et al., 2022).

Deployment Cycles: Deployment cycles are a hallmark of military life, characterized by repeated separations and reunions. The deployment cycle is divided into three phases: pre-deployment, deployment, and post-deployment/reintegration. Each phase presents unique challenges for military families:

Pre-Deployment Phase: Families experience anticipatory grief, anxiety, and stress. Children may become clingy or show behavioral changes (Cafferky et al., 2020; Mulholland et al., 2020).

Deployment: Families adjust to separation. The parent at home focuses on the children's needs while the deployed parent stays connected despite mission demands (DeVoe et al., 2020).

Post-Deployment/Reintegration: Family reintegration and readjustment periods depend on family dynamics, parental gender roles, and potential injuries. Healthy family functioning supports positive child outcomes, while strained dynamics increase adjustment difficulties (Nicholson et al., 2020; Briggs et al., 2019).

Parental PTSD: Parental PTSD presents distinct challenges for military children, significantly influencing the parent-child relationship. Symptoms such as hypervigilance, emotional numbing, and irritability can impair a parent's ability to provide the emotional availability and responsiveness for a child's emotional security. As a result, children in these environments face an elevated risk of behavioral problems, academic struggles, and emotional dysregulation (Jacoby et al., 2023). Service members, upon reintegration, may struggle due to combat-related losses or injuries, and the unpredictable nature of PTSD symptoms can create a sense of instability, leaving children feeling isolated or confused about their parents' emotional states.

Compounding Effects: Military life encompasses a complex interplay of factors that can compound trauma for military-connected children, including parental PTSD, combat-related injuries, and loss. Navigating a parent's PTSD becomes challenging if their condition impairs the parent's ability to work, causing financial and logistical hardships. Similarly, physical injuries can intensify PTSD symptoms, further destabilizing the family environment. The overlapping and interconnected nature of these stressors highlights the critical need for trauma-informed care and comprehensive support systems designed to address the distinct needs of military children and their families.

Chapter 13
The Evolution of Special Education and the Framework to Support Struggling Students

Crystal Riddick
https://orcid.org/0009-0009-8100-3978
National University, USA

ABSTRACT

This chapter examines the evolution of special education, beginning with Brown v. Board of Education and progressing through contemporary legislation. Through the lens of special education, this chapter will explore a comprehensive approach to learning, identifying fundamental changes, supports, and strategies developed over time to support students effectively. The chapter will focus on equitable practices that foster inclusive and effective educational environments for all learners. The key frameworks and strategies discussed will include the Multi-Tiered System of Supports (MTSS), Positive Behavioral Interventions and Supports (PBIS), Universal Design for Learning (UDL), as well as emerging trends and future directions in special education.

INTRODUCTION

The development of special education has transitioned from an intolerant, exclusive system to an inclusive agency with an equitable lens. Rodrigues-Fee (2023) reported that over time, special education has adopted an inclusive, equitable practice that meets students' needs while providing a free, appropriate education in the student's least restrictive environment. Even though inclusive education practices were only widely adopted in the 1980s, some districts still face significant challenges in implementing this approach. Cornett et al. (2020) deemed that educators have defined inclusion differently. Woodstock &. Hardy's (2020) research concluded that because inclusion is defined so loosely, teachers' pedagogical approach and delivery of inclusive practices vary from school district to school district, creating gaps

DOI: 10.4018/979-8-3693-9020-7.ch013

in education, which could cause the achievement gap that is so frequently associated with students in special education.

The milestones in the history of special education outlined the trajectory of the movement while identifying momentous challenges and highlights that have shaped the field of special education into what we know and use today. It is also important to mention that the changes in legislation have prompted changes in the classroom. It has heightened the awareness of the needs of students as well as the best practices for supporting them. Osborne & Russo's (2020) research concluded that when designing Individualized Education Plans (IEPs) and strength-based IEP goals, they must include an approach that is specific, measurable, achievable, relevant, and time-bound (SMART). By incorporating the philosophy of SMART goals, parents can view the process of the student's goals through the collected and recorded data. Though this chapter's journey about special education can be considered a story, it is much more. It is a testament to how far special education has progressed while implementing strategies that support students in all learning environments through an equitable lens, regardless of their abilities.

HISTORY OF SPECIAL EDUCATION ACROSS THE UNITED STATES

Special education was founded on the philosophy of segregation (Wehmeyer, 2022). According to Smith et al. (2020), this approach was rooted in the medical model of disability, which views disability as a deficit to be remedied through specialized interventions. The special education initiative was created to provide educational opportunities for all students because of the inequities in education while promoting inclusion and diminishing segregation (Wehmeyer, 2022). Special education in the early 20th century was structured differently. Rodrigues-Fee (2023) concluded that students with disabilities received their education in rooms that were in the basement or in the back of the school building, which promoted segregation and created a difference in students and the type of education these students received, if any, structured educational practice at all. Many states refrained from issuing some special education students regular high school diplomas after their academic completion. Kraemer et al. (2022) identified that special education students received a certificate of attendance, which is still valid for some states today. Over time, changes have been made, but Melnick (2024) claimed that the U.S. Supreme Court case of *Brown vs. Board of Education (1954)* was the initial movement that sparked a change in special education. The pivotal movement was enacted to address segregation in public schools as well as highlight the inequities and challenges experienced by students with disabilities. Through this work, *Brown vs Board of Education (1954)* also promoted the right to equal educational opportunities, refuted segregation, and highlighted the importance of education not being based on race or ability. In essence, this act created the framework for access to quality education for all. Nighswander et al. (2024) stated that although *Brown v. Board of Education (1954)* started transforming special education, it was not the last legal case to mandate change. Many other milestones continued to evolve, prompting a change to special education. *Board of Education v. Rowley (1982)* was another infamous court case that has shaped our educational system and contributed to inclusion. The framework for this case outlined inclusive practices for students' success when they received the correct support in a general education classroom.

The Education for All Handicapped Children Act (EAHCA) of 1975 was the following phenomenon that highlighted children with disabilities and their educational needs. This civil rights movement legalized "free appropriate public education" (FAPE) for special education students. Through EAHCA, students received Individualized Education Plans (IEPs), which provided protections and procedural safeguards that prompted schools to include parental involvement when making educational decisions concerning students' education (Wehmeyer, 2022). This widespread movement timestamped what we know today as tailored educational supports or individualized practices to meet the student's needs, which can be attributed to the lack of training for staff and the school's struggles. Francisco et al. (2020) acknowledged that some public educational settings fell short of following through with maintaining compliance or offering a genuinely inclusive environment. It is important to note that the lack of implementation prompted several amendments, which mandated and introduced the Individuals with Disabilities Education Act (IDEA) in 1990. Bleak & Abernathy (2022) examined the expansion of the foundation and scope of EAHCA; IDEA employs a broader perimeter of protection for students with disabilities. Through the Least Restrictive Environment (LRE) approach, students with disabilities have the legal protection to receive their education in an environment with their non-disabled peers while receiving the needed support that will allow them to be successful by refining equity and access.

Although many individuals associate IDEA with students in the school setting, it incorporates mandates to address the needs of students with disabilities before they turn of age to attend school. Osborne & Russo (2020) proclaimed that the Individuals with Disabilities Education Act incorporated early intervention services, offering support to students as early as age three. The core aspect of IDEA is to focus on supporting students early and often. Osborne and Russo (2020) identified another mandate from the IDEA, Child Find, which legally requires all public school districts to locate, identify, and provide evaluations to any child who presents a disability. The importance of the act is to evaluate students early, determine eligibility, and provide the needed support. Even though this philosophical approach was proposed in the updates of IDEA, it is considered one of the most critical mandates in IDEA. In a study on the changes in special education, Sisk (2022) informed readers that the revised process of IDEA also included several other initiatives and mandates to address societal changes to align with equity and students' needs, including the reauthorization that authorized the need for Response to Intervention (RTI). The mandate, later discussed in the chapter, is essential to mention that this approach was the springboard for other strategy-based services, such as PBIS, MTSS, and SEL, which are currently used in public schools today (Yee, 2020).

The reauthorization of IDEA was designed to address new mandates that aligned with current trends associated with students with disabilities; each is the foundation for another societal movement to address equity. For example, Devericks (2024) implies that the Rehabilitation Act of 1973, Section 504, and the Americans with Disabilities Act all advocate for the rights of humans. The core of these movements is equity, inclusion, and the protection of the rights of individuals with disabilities from discrimination, not just in the educational setting but also in all areas of public life. We can contribute these movements to the law in *(I.A. v. Seguin Indep. Sch. Dist.. 881),* which shifted the focus from cognitive impairment to looking at the impact of physical accessibility (Murphy, 2020). Rodrigues-Fee's (2023) research claimed that the profound legislative shifts changed the focus of the core principles from exclusion to education access, equity, and inclusion. Also, through the research conducted by Rodrigus-Fee, it was easy to identify the critical need for systematic support and individualized infrastructures. Still, the important work requires partnerships between all stakeholders to promote thriving environments for every student's success.

In recent years, the philosophy of special education has evolved to emphasize equity over mere inclusion. While inclusion focuses on placing students with disabilities in general education classrooms, equity ensures that these students have access to the resources and support necessary to thrive. Brown et al. (2022) highlight that an equity-driven approach is the best approach to use when addressing systemic barriers, such as funding disparities and implicit biases, that hinder the success of students with disabilities. The shift toward equity has also led to reevaluating assessment and placement practices. Traditional methods of identifying and categorizing disabilities have been criticized for their potential to reinforce stereotypes and perpetuate inequalities. Lopez et al. (2021) argued for adopting culturally responsive assessment tools and practices that reflect students' diverse experiences and backgrounds.

SYSTEMIC BARRIERS

Systemic barriers, such as rigid policies and a lack of accountability, further exacerbate inequities in special education. Policies prioritizing compliance over student outcomes can limit flexibility in addressing individual needs. According to Taylor et al. (2021), schools must shift their focus toward outcome-based accountability systems that prioritize student growth and success. Moreover, the absence of strong advocacy at the policy level contributes to the perpetuation of inequities. Engaging families and communities in advocacy efforts can drive systemic change. Smith et al. (2020) recommend forming coalitions to push for legislative reforms that address funding disparities, implicit biases, and accountability gaps.

Achieving equity in special education is a complex challenge that will require discussions to identify barriers, funding inequities, examine the overrepresentation of minority students, and inadequate support provided to teacher preparation. By prioritizing these issues and implementing targeted solutions, stakeholders can work toward creating a more equitable and inclusive educational system. Continued advocacy and investment in professional development, policy reform, and community engagement are also essential for ensuring all students with disabilities receive the support they need to succeed. However, achieving equity in special education remains challenging despite legal protections and increased awareness.

Resource Disparities: Inequitable funding often leaves schools in low-income areas unable to provide essential services, such as speech therapy or assistive technology (Marsioc, 2021).
Implicit Bias: Educators' unconscious biases can affect referral and placement decisions, leading to overrepresentation of certain groups in special education (Lindsay et al., 2021).
Lack of Training: Many teachers feel unprepared to meet the needs of diverse learners due to limited training in inclusive and culturally responsive practices (Smith et al., 2020).

The Role of Special Education

As students in special education strive to achieve their potential, the services they receive in the educational environment are critical to their accessing the curriculum and achieving their potential. This process must encompass several key aspects to address the needs of very diverse learners. When meeting the specific learning profiles of the students, it is essential to identify how each objective will be provided to support individuals through a tailored educational approach designed for each individual. Rumrill et al. (2020) concluded that the design of this approach is to bridge the gap through an equity lens, as it strives to provide additional pathways for students with disabilities through an educational environment that is not only fair but also inclusive. Rumrill et al. (2020) also identified that not only is the educational environment important, but a cohesive, effective support system that fosters a collaborative partnership among all stakeholders, such as students, parents, and educators, is one of the most critical components when designing special education plans for students. A support system that advocates for the rights of students with disabilities, knowing the safeguards, resources, and opportunities to provide success, is the best support system for all students.

Other key support aspects addressing students' diverse needs include individualized support through tailored educational programs to meet specific learning requirements. Additionally, it ensures equity by bridging gaps in access and outcomes for students with disabilities, thereby promoting a fair and inclusive educational environment (Hott et al., 2021). In addition, Hott et al.'s (2021) research also stated that special education advocates not only for the rights of students with disabilities but also for safeguarding their legal and educational entitlements to ensure they receive Free Appropriate Education (FAPE).

The Rise of Student-Centered Approaches

Another significant philosophical change in special education is the adoption of student-centered approaches. A student-centered philosophy emphasizes the individuality of each student and the importance of tailoring educational experiences to their unique strengths, needs, and interests. Johnson & Rivera (2021) describe this approach as a departure from one-size-fits-all models, advocating for practices such as Universal Design for Learning (UDL) and personalized learning plans. Student-centered philosophies also prioritize the involvement of students in their educational planning. By teaching self-advocacy skills and involving students in developing their Individualized Education Programs (IEPs), educators can empower students to take an active role in their learning. According to Hott et al. (2021), this approach enhances academic outcomes and fosters self-confidence and independence among students with disabilities.

Providing Individualized Support

Developing tailored educational programs to address specific needs provides students access and creates agency. Individualized support addresses students' strengths, weaknesses, and learning styles while incorporating culture. This approach is best used when educators know their students' needs, create personalized learning plans, set realistic and measurable goals, and provide specific interventions such as differentiated instruction and targeted skill-building activities. Teachers and specialists must collaborate to adapt teaching methods, use appropriate technologies, and continuously monitor progress to ensure the strategies meet the evolving needs of the student. Such support enhances academic outcomes and fosters greater independence and confidence in students with disabilities. The concept of individualized support lies at the heart of special education, ensuring that every student has the opportunity to achieve their full potential. Special education classrooms are uniquely positioned to adapt instruction and resources to meet diverse student needs. The strategic strategies and benefits of individualized support in these classrooms emphasize the importance of success using collaborative and evidence-based practices.

Although individualized support can be described differently when examining each student's unique needs, educators can work through a strength-based approach using a growth mindset to develop educational programs. Yell et al.'s (2020) approach to describing individualized planning as a growth mindset confirmed that the program's design must include a personalized plan to set measurable and realistic goals through the identified intervention system and targeted skill activities. Yell et al. (2020) also stated that educators must continuously adapt their education practices and philosophies to ensure progress and meet all students' needs. This approach allows students flexibility through progress monitoring, creating continuous fluidity throughout the learning environment as students make gains and growth. The research on meeting students where they are (Murphy, 2020) stated that a welcoming educational approach provides intensive support that measures outcomes that foster confidence and greater independence in special education students.

Cook et al. (2020) defined individualized instruction as a cornerstone of effective special education. The research highlights that individualized education plans (IEPs) provide a framework for tailoring curriculum to meet the specific needs of students with disabilities. Educators can modify content, pace, and delivery methods by considering students' strengths, weaknesses, and learning goals. For example, visual aids, hands-on activities, and technology can enhance engagement and comprehension for students with varying learning styles. Differentiated instruction further enables teachers to address the diverse academic levels within a single classroom, ensuring equitable access to education (Taylor et al., 2021). Collaboration is vital in implementing individualized support effectively. Teachers, paraprofessionals, therapists, and families must work together to design and deliver comprehensive support plans. Joint planning sessions and regular communication ensure that strategies are consistent across environments. As Hott et al. (2021) highlighted, collaborative teams can identify and address barriers to learning, such as behavioral challenges or sensory sensitivities, through proactive strategies and interventions. Professional development also plays a significant role in enhancing collaboration. Training programs focused on co-teaching models and evidence-based practices equip educators with the skills to provide consistent, high-quality support. According to Brown et al. (2022), schools that invest in collaborative training report improved student outcomes and higher teacher satisfaction.

Implementing evidence-based practices (EBPs) ensures that students' support is practical and scientifically validated. Strategies such as Applied Behavior Analysis (ABA), explicit instruction, and assistive technologies have enhanced learning outcomes for students with disabilities (Smith et al., 2020). For example, ABA techniques can help students develop critical life skills, while assistive technologies, such as speech-to-text software, empower students to overcome communication barriers. Moreover, regular progress monitoring and data collection are essential components of EBPs. By assessing student performance and adjusting interventions accordingly, educators can ensure that individualized support remains dynamic and responsive to changing needs (Johnson & Rivera, 2021). The benefits of individualized support extend beyond academic achievement. Providing tailored instruction fosters a sense of belonging and self-efficacy among students. According to a study by Lopez et al. (2021), students in inclusive classrooms with individualized support demonstrated improved social-emotional skills and greater engagement in learning activities. Additionally, individualized support prepares students for life beyond the classroom by equipping them with the skills to navigate real-world challenges independently. Providing individualized support in special education classrooms is essential for promoting equity and inclusion. By tailoring instruction, fostering collaboration, and utilizing evidence-based practices, educators can address the unique needs of each student effectively. Continued investment in professional development and research will further enhance the ability of special education programs to support diverse learners in achieving their full potential.

Ensuring Equity

Bridging gaps in access and outcomes for students with disabilities. Specific strategies for achieving equity include implementing culturally responsive teaching practices to meet diverse needs and ensuring that all students have access to necessary resources, such as assistive technology and individualized support. Policies such as universal access to inclusive education and targeted funding for underrepresented groups also play a vital role in reducing disparities and promoting fairness within schools. As indicated previously, educators implement strategies to support students as they work to bridge the educational gap. Mensah (2021) stated in his research that the education presented lacks the luster of a personal touch without examining cultural differences. Through culturally responsive teaching, equity is addressed as teaching practices meet students' needs and require equitable resources for all students. Culturally responsive teaching should be approached through the lens of universal design for learning to promote inclusiveness and meet students at their learning levels. Target funding is provided, which helps to reduce disparities and promote fairness for underrepresented groups in the vital role of addressing equity.

Equity in special education is the foundation of an inclusive and fair educational system, ensuring that every student, regardless of ability, has access to resources and opportunities that foster their academic and personal growth. Unlike equality, which focuses on providing the same resources to all students, equity prioritizes tailoring resources and support to meet the unique needs of individual learners. In special education, this principle is critical to bridging achievement gaps and fostering environments where all students can succeed. Equity in special education means that students with disabilities receive the individualized support they need to participate fully in educational settings. It requires addressing systemic barriers that have historically marginalized students with disabilities, including disparities in funding, access to qualified teachers, and availability of assistive technologies. For example, the Individuals with Disabilities Education Act (IDEA) ensures that students with disabilities have access to a free appropriate public education (FAPE) tailored to their needs (Smith et al., 2020). Equity ensures these legal mandates are theoretical and implemented effectively across diverse school contexts.

Challenges to Achieving Equity

Achieving equity in special education remains a significant challenge due to systemic barriers, implicit bias, and resource disparities. This paper examines the key obstacles to equity in special education, focusing on funding inequities, overrepresentation of minority students, and inadequate teacher preparation. By understanding these challenges, stakeholders can develop targeted strategies to address them.

Funding Inequities

One of the primary challenges to achieving equity in special education is the unequal distribution of resources. Schools in low-income areas often lack the funding necessary to provide high-quality special education services. According to Brown et al. (2022), disparities in funding result in larger class sizes, limited access to specialized staff, and outdated instructional materials. These limitations hinder the ability of schools to meet the diverse needs of students with disabilities. Federal and state funding mechanisms often fail to account for the additional costs associated with providing special education services. Taylor et al. (2021) argue that reforming funding models to prioritize equity is essential. For instance, weighted funding formulas that allocate additional resources to schools serving high percentages of students with disabilities can help bridge the resource gap.

Overrepresentation of Minority Students

Another persistent issue in special education is the overrepresentation of minority students in specific disability categories. Implicit biases in referral and evaluation processes often lead to misidentification, resulting in inappropriate placements (Smith et al., 2020). For example, African American and Hispanic students are disproportionately identified with emotional disturbances or intellectual disabilities, which can limit their access to general education classrooms and rigorous academic content. Addressing this challenge requires comprehensive training for educators on culturally responsive practices. Lopez et al. (2021) emphasize the importance of using unbiased assessment tools and involving diverse teams in the evaluation process. Schools must implement ongoing monitoring to ensure that identification practices are equitable and evidence-based. The overrepresentation of minority students in special education is a pervasive issue that highlights systemic inequities within educational systems. This chapter examines the factors contributing to this overrepresentation, the consequences for affected students, and potential solutions to address the disparities. Through a lens of equity, it explores how implicit biases, cultural differences, and inadequate assessment practices contribute to this phenomenon and identifies strategies for fostering more equitable educational environments.

Factors Contributing to Overrepresentation

The overrepresentation of minority students in special education can be traced to a combination of systemic and individual factors. Implicit biases among educators and administrators play a significant role. According to Smith et al. (2020), unconscious stereotypes can influence the referral process, leading to disproportionately high rates of minority students being identified as having disabilities. For instance, African American and Hispanic students are more likely to be labeled with emotional or behavioral disorders, even when their behaviors align with typical developmental norms.

Another contributing factor is the lack of culturally responsive practices in schools. Many assessment tools and educational standards are rooted in dominant cultural norms, which may not accurately reflect the abilities and experiences of students from diverse backgrounds. Lopez et al. (2021) argue that these tools often fail to account for linguistic and cultural differences, resulting in misdiagnoses and inappropriate placements. Socioeconomic disparities further exacerbate this issue. Students from low-income families often attend under-resourced schools with fewer supports, increasing the likelihood of referrals to special education. Taylor et al. (2021) note that these schools may lack access to early intervention programs and other preventative measures that could address learning and behavioral challenges before they necessitate special education services.

Consequences of Overrepresentation

The overrepresentation of minority students in special education has far-reaching consequences for both individuals and communities. Placement in special education programs can stigmatize students, affecting their self-esteem and sense of belonging. According to Johnson & Rivera (2021), students inappropriately placed in restrictive environments may have limited access to general education curricula and fewer opportunities for social interaction with their peers. This overrepresentation also perpetuates cycles of disadvantage. Minority students in special education are less likely to graduate from high school and more likely to experience unemployment or underemployment as adults (Brown et al., 2022).

The systemic nature of these disparities underscores the importance of addressing the root causes of overrepresentation.

Addressing Disparities Through Policy and Practice

Efforts to address the overrepresentation of minority students in special education must focus on systemic change. Implementing culturally responsive teaching practices is a critical step. By integrating students' cultural backgrounds into the curriculum and classroom environment, educators can create more inclusive and equitable learning experiences. Lopez et al. (2021) emphasize the importance of professional development programs that train teachers to recognize and mitigate implicit biases and to use culturally relevant assessment tools. Improving the referral and evaluation processes is also essential. Schools should adopt multidisciplinary team approaches with diverse perspectives when making placement decisions. Hott et al. (2021) recommend using data-driven methods to ensure that referrals are based on objective criteria rather than subjective judgments. Policy reforms are another key component of addressing these disparities. Advocating for equitable funding models that allocate additional resources to under-resourced schools can help reduce the socioeconomic barriers contributing to overrepresentation. Smith et al. (2020) suggest that policies promoting early intervention and preventative services can reduce the need for special education placements by addressing challenges at an earlier stage.

Facilitating Collaboration

Consistent collaboration is essential in education; however, in special education, collaboration promotes student-centered learning as everyone uses a whole-child approach. Ensuring normalcy and consistency leads to a supportive environment that promotes a sense of belonging and contributes to improved educational outcomes for special education students. Promoting partnerships among educators, parents, and service providers. Effective collaboration enhances communication among all stakeholders, ensuring consistency in student support and fostering a shared understanding of the student's needs. This approach leads to developing cohesive strategies and a supportive environment that contributes to improved educational outcomes for students with disabilities.

Policymakers and educators must work together to address these challenges. Legislative efforts, such as increased funding for IDEA and targeted support for underserved communities, are essential. Additionally, schools can adopt equitable practices, such as using multi-tiered support systems (MTSS) to identify and address student needs early and effectively (Sugai et al., 2020). In essence, schools can create environments where all students, including those with disabilities, have the opportunity to thrive. Equity in special education is not just a legal mandate but a moral imperative that reflects the values of fairness and inclusion in society. Disparities in special education access and outcomes persist, disproportionately affecting marginalized communities. Addressing these disparities requires a comprehensive approach that combines equitable policies and inclusive practices. Systemic reforms and evidence-based practices can reduce inequities, emphasizing the importance of equity-focused policies, professional development, and culturally responsive teaching. Equitable policies are critical in addressing disparities in special education. The Individuals with Disabilities Education Act (IDEA) mandates that students with disabilities receive free and appropriate public education (FAPE).

However, implementation often varies based on geographic location, socioeconomic status, and race. According to Taylor et al. (2021), policies that allocate resources equitably and ensure proportional representation of marginalized groups in special education services are essential to closing these gaps. For example, funding models prioritizing underserved communities can improve access to high-quality services and resources. Policy reforms should also address the overrepresentation and underrepresentation of minority students in special education. Smith et al. (2020) highlight that implicit biases in referral and evaluation processes often lead to disproportionate placements. Clear guidelines and training for educators can mitigate these biases, ensuring that all students are accurately identified and supported.

Training

Educator training is pivotal in addressing disparities through practice. Professional development programs focused on cultural competence and inclusive pedagogy equip teachers to meet the diverse needs of their students. Hott et al. (2021) emphasize that ongoing training helps educators recognize and challenge systemic inequities within their classrooms and schools. For instance, Universal Design for Learning (UDL) training enables teachers to create flexible learning environments that accommodate diverse abilities and backgrounds. Collaborative training initiatives involving general and special education teachers can foster inclusive practices. Joint professional development sessions enhance communication and coordination, ensuring consistent and equitable student support. According to Lopez et al. (2021), schools that invest in collaborative training report better student outcomes and greater teacher efficacy. *Culturally responsive teaching (CRT)* is a critical practice in addressing disparities. This approach recognizes and values students' cultural backgrounds, integrating them into the curriculum and classroom environment. Johnson Rivera (2021) argues that CRT fosters a sense of belonging and engagement among marginalized students, reducing achievement gaps. For example, incorporating diverse perspectives and materials into lessons can make learning more relevant and accessible. CRT also involves building strong relationships with students and their families. Engaging families as partners in the educational process ensures that their voices and needs are heard. Taylor et al. (2021) highlight that family engagement is particularly crucial in communities where systemic barriers have historically limited access to education.

Inadequate Teacher Preparation

The lack of adequate preparation for general and special education teachers is another barrier to equity. Many educators feel unprepared to address the diverse needs of students with disabilities, particularly those from culturally and linguistically diverse backgrounds. Hott et al. (2021) highlight that insufficient training in evidence-based practices and inclusive pedagogy contributes to disparities in student outcomes.

Professional development programs can address this issue by equipping teachers with the skills and knowledge needed to create inclusive classrooms. Johnson & Rivera (2021) suggest that training initiatives should focus on Universal Design for Learning (UDL), differentiated instruction, and collaboration between general and special education staff. These approaches promote equitable access to education for all students.

Evidence-Based and Research-Based Best Practices

Evidence-based practices (EBPs) are essential for reducing disparities and improving outcomes in special education. Strategies such as differentiated instruction, assistive technologies, and progress monitoring provide tailored support for diverse learners. Smith et al. (2020) note that EBPs ensure effective and equitable interventions, benefiting students from all backgrounds. Data-driven decision-making allows educators to identify and address disparities in real time. Regular assessment of student progress helps schools adjust interventions and allocate resources where they are most needed.

Brown et al. (2022) highlight that schools using data-driven approaches report significant improvements in equity and inclusion. Addressing disparities in special education requires a multifaceted approach that integrates equitable policies, professional development, culturally responsive teaching, and evidence-based practices. Educators and policymakers can create a more inclusive and equitable educational system by prioritizing these strategies. Continued investment in research and training will be crucial in sustaining progress and ensuring that all students have the opportunity to succeed.

The Role of Family and Community Engagement

Engaging families and communities in the educational process is critical for addressing the overrepresentation of minority students in special education. Building strong partnerships with families ensures that their perspectives and insights are incorporated into decision-making processes. These partnerships should prioritize transparent communication, mutual respect, and shared goals for student success. Taylor et al. (2021) highlight the importance of providing families with resources and training to advocate effectively for their children. Such resources include workshops on navigating special education systems, access to cultural liaisons for non-English-speaking families, and opportunities to participate in school committees or councils that influence policy decisions.

Empowering families in this manner strengthens advocacy and fosters trust and collaboration between schools and the communities they serve. Community organizations can also play a vital role in supporting students and families. Partnerships between schools and community-based organizations can provide additional resources and services, such as tutoring, mentoring, and counseling, to address barriers to academic success (Johnson & River, 2021). The overrepresentation of minority students in special education reflects systemic inequities that require urgent attention. Schools can work toward creating more equitable educational environments by addressing implicit biases, improving assessment practices, and implementing culturally responsive teaching strategies. Engaging families and communities and advocating for policy reforms are essential steps in reducing disparities and ensuring that all students have the opportunity to thrive.

Advocating for and Protecting Rights

Protecting the legal and educational rights of students with disabilities. Key legislation, such as the Individuals with Disabilities Education Act (IDEA) and Section 504 of the Rehabilitation Act, ensures that students with disabilities can access free, appropriate public education (FAPE), accommodations, and procedural safeguards. These laws mandate that schools address the unique needs of students, guaranteeing their right to participate fully in the educational system. Advocating for the rights of students in special education is a critical component of ensuring equitable access to education. Special education services are designed to provide individualized support to students with disabilities, ensuring they can achieve their full potential in academic and social environments. Advocacy is essential in addressing systemic inequities and ensuring compliance with legal mandates such as the Individuals with Disabilities Education Act (IDEA) and Section 504 of the Rehabilitation Act of 1973. This paper explores key aspects of advocating for special education rights, emphasizing collaboration, legislation, and ethical considerations.

Advocating for the rights of students and parents in special education is crucial for ensuring equity and access to quality education. This paper explores key strategies for advocacy, emphasizing the importance of legal protections, collaboration, and empowerment through education. By understanding and leveraging these strategies, stakeholders can work together to create a more inclusive and supportive educational system. The foundation of advocacy in special education lies in understanding the legal protections afforded to students with disabilities.

The Individuals with Disabilities Education Act (IDEA) guarantees the right to a free and appropriate public education (FAPE) for all students with disabilities. According to Taylor et al. (2021), ensuring compliance with IDEA requires vigilance and active participation from parents and educators. For instance, parents have the right to participate in developing their child's Individualized Education Program (IEP), which outlines specific goals, accommodations, and services tailored to their child's needs. Section 504 of the Rehabilitation Act and the Americans with Disabilities Act (ADA) further protect students from discrimination, ensuring equal educational opportunities. Smith et al. (2020) highlight that parents and advocates must be aware of these laws to hold schools accountable and ensure that students receive appropriate accommodations, such as assistive technologies or modified instructional materials.

Effective advocacy depends on strong collaboration between families and educators. Building trusting relationships fosters open communication, ensuring parents' insights about their child's needs are considered in decision-making. Hott et al. (2021) emphasize the importance of involving parents as equal partners in the education process, from initial evaluations to ongoing progress monitoring. Collaborative strategies, such as regular parent-teacher conferences and interdisciplinary meetings, provide a platform for discussing student progress and addressing concerns. Lopez et al. (2021) note that schools implementing collaborative approaches report higher levels of parental satisfaction and improved student outcomes. Additionally, empowering parents with resources and training on special education processes can enhance their ability to advocate effectively.

Educating parents and students about their rights and available resources is critical to advocacy. Workshops, online resources, and support groups can help parents navigate the complexities of special education systems. According to Johnson & Rivera (2021), informed parents are better equipped to identify service gaps and advocate for necessary interventions.

Empowering students to self-advocate is equally important. Teaching students about their rights and involving them in IEP meetings fosters a sense of ownership over their education. Taylor et al. (2021) argue that self-advocacy skills are essential for preparing students with disabilities for post-secondary education and employment. Programs that build confidence, communication skills, and problem-solving abilities can support this goal. Advocacy efforts must also address systemic barriers that hinder equity in special education. Implicit biases, resource disparities, and inadequate educator training can all contribute to inequitable outcomes. Smith et al. (2020) recommend targeted professional development programs to equip teachers with the skills to provide culturally responsive and inclusive instruction. Policy advocacy is another avenue for addressing systemic issues. Engaging with school boards, legislators, and advocacy organizations can drive changes in funding models, staffing ratios, and accountability measures.

Brown et al. (2022) emphasize that collective action at the policy level is essential for creating lasting improvements in special education systems. Advocating for the rights of students and parents in special education is a multifaceted endeavor that requires legal knowledge, collaboration, and systemic change. By fostering strong partnerships, empowering stakeholders through education, and addressing barriers, advocates can ensure that all students with disabilities can access equitable and inclusive educational opportunities. Continued advocacy efforts are essential for upholding the principles of fairness and inclusion in education.

Effective advocacy in special education involves understanding the rights of students and their families and the responsibilities of schools and educators. According to Martin et al. (2021), advocacy encompasses identifying unmet needs, negotiating for services, and monitoring individualized education programs (IEPs) implementation. Parents, educators, and professionals must work collaboratively to address barriers that hinder students' progress. Advocacy ensures that students receive accommodations and modifications tailored to their unique needs, which is particularly critical in inclusive educational settings (Smith et al., 2022).

Parents often serve as the primary advocates for their children, but they may face challenges such as limited knowledge of their rights or the complexity of navigating school systems. To address these barriers, advocacy organizations and professional development programs are essential in empowering families. According to Jones and Taylor (2020), providing parents with training on special education laws and strategies for effective communication can significantly enhance their ability to advocate for their children.

Federal laws like IDEA and Section 504 provide the foundation for advocating for students with disabilities. IDEA mandates that schools provide a Free Appropriate Public Education (FAPE) tailored to students' individual needs through IEPs (U.S. Department of Education, 2021). Additionally, Section 504 ensures that students with disabilities have equal access to educational opportunities and prohibits discrimination in schools receiving federal funding. Advocates must ensure that schools comply with these legal requirements, which include conducting timely evaluations, providing necessary services, and involving families in decision-making processes. For example, a study by Carter et al. (2022) highlights that schools with strong advocacy networks demonstrate higher rates of compliance with IDEA and improved student outcomes. This underscores the importance of advocacy in fostering accountability and supporting the rights of students with disabilities. Advocacy in special education is most effective when it involves collaboration among all stakeholders, including parents, educators, administrators, and specialists. Collaborative advocacy fosters mutual understanding and shared goals, ensuring that the student's best interests remain the central focus. As Nelson and Clark (2023) highlighted, trust and transparent communication are vital in building partnerships that promote positive student outcomes. Ethical considerations are equally important in advocacy efforts. Advocates must respect students' and their families' dignity, autonomy, and cultural backgrounds. Furthermore, they must adhere to ethical guidelines that promote fairness, equity, and confidentiality. For instance, ensuring that advocacy efforts do not prioritize one student's needs at the expense of others' rights is a key ethical principle (Smith et al., 2022). Student rights ensure that they receive a Free Appropriate Public Education (FAPE), and protecting the rights of special education students is a law under the Individuals with Disabilities Act (IDEA). We will explore these laws more deeply later in the text as we dive into mandates, safeguards, and protocols.

BARRIERS SPECIAL EDUCATION STUDENTS FACE IN SCHOOLS

Students with disabilities often encounter barriers that impede their learning and participation, impacting their academic progress and social integration. These barriers can manifest in various forms, including physical, social, cultural, and systematic barriers. Inaccessible school buildings, classrooms, and resources can limit mobility and participation for students with physical disabilities. For instance, schools without ramps, elevators, or adaptive equipment create exclusionary environments that hinder access to learning. Social barriers that students with disabilities may face include stigma, bullying, and a lack of peer understanding, which can lead to feelings of isolation and decreased self-confidence. Such challenges often affect students' emotional well-being and ability to engage in classroom activities. Cultural barriers can be considered as misunderstanding or lack of awareness about disabilities among educators, families, and peers can result in low expectations and improper support. Cultural misconceptions may also prevent students from receiving early interventions or necessary accommodations. Systemic Barriers: Limited funding, inadequate staffing, and insufficient teacher training often impede the implementation of effective special education programs. For example, underfunded schools may lack assistive technologies, specialized staff, or personalized resources to support students with disabilities. Addressing these barriers requires systemic change, including professional development for educators, anti-bullying initiatives, accessible infrastructure, and policies that promote equity and inclusion for all learners.

- Physical Barriers: Inaccessible school facilities and learning environments.
- Social Barriers: Stigmatization, bullying, and social isolation.
- Cultural Barriers: Limited understanding of diverse learning needs among educators and peers.
- Systemic Barriers: Inadequate funding, resources, and training for educators.

Strategies to address these barriers include:

- Implementing Universal Design for Learning (UDL) to create flexible and inclusive learning environments.
- Training educators in culturally relevant teaching to address diverse student needs.
- Promoting anti-bullying programs and fostering an inclusive school culture

INCLUSION THROUGH SCHOOL CULTURE

The philosophical shift to inclusion emerged as the topic of equitable education became the forefront of education. This trending topic conceptualized the idea that students with disabilities must be educated with their nondisabled peers when the proper supports are in place to accommodate the student's needs. Many educational facilities did not accept the idea because of a lack of knowledge, fear, or simply unwillingness to embrace the new educational philosophy. However, new research was being conducted on inclusion and the benefits that all students receive because it enhances the learning experiences of all students. However, the inclusive philosophy continued to be a struggle for some. As educators did not have a concrete understanding of inclusion, some thought they addressed the need by just opening the classroom door and accepting the students into the classroom, which we know today was not inclusion but more acceptance. However, through training and practice, educators began to understand the true foundational philosophy of inclusion, as the definition provided the framework for what inclusion should resemble in the classroom. However, some continued with their old narrative of education, which hindered them from being included, even though it was a federal law.

Providing meaningful inclusion education requires a total school approach and a shift in the mindset of the administration, teachers, parents, and students. Authentic, inclusive practices require a change in the school's culture. This means that every aspect of the school environment is inclusive for all students, not just the physical environment, such as the early efforts of inclusive practices. Inclusion in the classroom has become a cornerstone of modern education. It represents a shift towards equitable learning environments that value diversity and ensure that all students can thrive regardless of their abilities. Embracing inclusion involves integrating students with disabilities into general education settings, fostering a sense of belonging, and tailoring instruction to meet diverse needs. This approach not only benefits students with disabilities but also enriches the educational experiences of all learners by promoting empathy, collaboration, and mutual respect. Inclusion positively impacts both students with disabilities and their peers. Research indicates that inclusive classrooms enhance academic and social outcomes for students with disabilities by providing access to the general curriculum and opportunities for peer interaction (Alquraini & Gut, 2020). For non-disabled peers, inclusion fosters an appreciation for diversity and the development of interpersonal skills. Moreover, inclusive practices prepare all students for participation in a diverse society by challenging stereotypes and encouraging collaborative problem-solving.

Strategies for Implementing Inclusion

To successfully embrace inclusion, schools must adopt strategies that address the diverse needs of students. Key practices include:

1. **Differentiated Instruction**: Teachers can use varied teaching methods to address students' unique learning styles. For instance, visual aids, hands-on activities, and technology-based tools can engage students with different abilities (Tomlinson, 2021).
2. **Universal Design for Learning (UDL)**: UDL provides a framework for creating flexible learning environments accommodating all learners. This involves offering multiple means of engagement, representation, and expression to ensure that students can access and demonstrate knowledge in ways that work best for them (Meyer et al., 2021).
3. **Co-Teaching Models**: Collaboration between general and special education teachers ensures that students with disabilities receive the support they need within the general education classroom. Co-teaching strategies, such as team and station teaching, facilitate individualized instruction without isolating students (Friend et al., 2020).
4. **Positive Behavioral Interventions and Supports (PBIS)**: PBIS helps establish inclusive classroom cultures by promoting positive behavior and preventing disciplinary disparities. This proactive approach encourages consistency in expectations and reduces barriers to participation (Sugai et al., 2020).

While inclusion offers numerous benefits, its implementation can be challenging. Common barriers include limited teacher training, lack of resources, and resistance to change. To address these issues, professional development programs must equip educators with the skills and knowledge necessary for inclusive teaching (Smith et al., 2020). Additionally, schools must allocate resources for assistive technology, classroom aides, and collaborative planning time. Administrative support is crucial in fostering an inclusive culture. School leaders should advocate for policies that prioritize inclusion and encourage community engagement. Parents and caregivers also play a vital role in supporting inclusion by collaborating with educators and advocating for their children's needs (Lindsay et al., 2021). Overcoming challenges requires the commitment of educators, administrators, and the broader school community. As society continues prioritizing diversity and inclusion, the classroom fosters these values and prepares future generations for a collaborative and inclusive world.

ADMINISTRATION SUPPORTING EDUCATORS IN SPECIAL EDUCATION CLASSROOMS

Effective administrative support is critical for empowering educators in special education classrooms. DeMatthews et al. (2021) emphasized that administrators play a key role in creating a supportive environment that fosters professional growth, collaboration, and resource allocation. Providing ongoing professional development is one of the most impactful ways administrators can support special education teachers. Special education often requires educators to adapt to diverse student needs, which demands specialized skills and knowledge. According to Hott et al. (2021), professional development programs focused on evidence-based practices, such as Universal Design for Learning (UDL) and differentiated instruction, equip teachers to create inclusive and effective learning environments. Moreover, administrators should prioritize training that addresses behavioral interventions and assistive technologies. Brown et al. (2022) emphasize that targeted training enhances teacher competence and improves student outcomes. By offering regular workshops, access to online courses, and opportunities for peer collaboration, administrators ensure that educators remain current in their practices.

Resource Allocation

Adequate resource allocation is essential for supporting special education teachers. Schools often face challenges in providing the materials, technology, and personnel necessary to meet the needs of students with disabilities. Taylor et al. (2021) highlight that insufficient resources can lead to teacher burnout and hinder the delivery of quality education. Administrators can address this issue by ensuring special education classrooms have modern assistive technologies, such as speech-to-text software and adaptive learning devices. Hiring paraprofessionals and specialists, such as speech and occupational therapists, also provides teachers with the support needed to address diverse student needs effectively. According to Johnson Rivera (2021), collaborative planning sessions with educators can help administrators identify and prioritize resource gaps.

Building Collaborative Teams

Fostering collaboration among educators, specialists, and families is another critical area where administrators can make a difference. Collaborative teams improve communication, align strategies, and ensure consistency in supporting students with disabilities. Lopez et al. (2021) note that administrators who encourage co-teaching models and interdisciplinary collaboration report higher levels of teacher satisfaction and improved student outcomes. Administrators should also facilitate regular team meetings and provide platforms for sharing best practices. By fostering a culture of collaboration, school leaders can ensure that special education teachers feel supported and valued in their roles.

Advocacy and Policy Support

Advocating for special education teachers at the district and state levels is essential for driving systemic change. Administrators can influence policy decisions regarding funding, staffing ratios, and professional development opportunities. Smith et al. (2020) argue that administrators who actively engage in advocacy create a more equitable and supportive environment for educators and students. For example, advocating for smaller class sizes and increased funding for special education programs directly impacts the workload and effectiveness of teachers. Administrators can also support educators by ensuring compliance with legal requirements, such as those outlined in the Individuals with Disabilities Education Act (IDEA).

Challenges and Future Directions

Despite these philosophical advancements, challenges remain in implementing equitable and student-centered practices. Resource constraints, lack of training for educators, and resistance to change are among the barriers that hinder progress. Smith et al. (2020) emphasize the need for continued advocacy and investment in professional development to address these challenges. Although so much more can be examined regarding the evolution of special education, it is always important to demonstrate flexibility, as educators will need to evaluate their strategies, teaching practices, and student needs through a reflective, equitable lens that allows access and agency for all students. Lastly, some successful tips for achieving success may include the following:

- Promote Inclusion as a Core Value: Foster an environment where all students are respected and valued.
- Engage the Whole School Community: Include teachers, students, parents, and administrators in discussions about inclusion.
- Promote Inclusion as a Core Value: Foster an environment where all students are respected and valued.
- Engage the Whole School Community: Include teachers, students, parents, and administrators in discussions about inclusion.
- Promote Inclusion as a Core Value: Foster an environment where all students are respected and valued.
- Engage the Whole School Community: Include teachers, students, parents, and administrators in discussions about inclusion.
- Promote Inclusion as a Core Value: Foster an environment where all students are respected and valued.
- Engage the Whole School Community: Include teachers, students, parents, and administrators in discussions about inclusion.
- Promote Inclusion as a Core Value: Foster an environment where all students are respected and valued.

- Engage the Whole School Community: Include teachers, students, parents, and administrators in discussions about inclusion.
- Differentiate Instruction: Modify teaching methods and materials to meet diverse learning needs.
- Leverage Technology: Use assistive technology to support learning and accessibility.
- Ensure Physical Accessibility: Make classrooms, hallways, and common areas accessible to all students.
- Accommodate Sensory Needs: Design environments that minimize sensory overload.
- Track Student Progress: Use assessments and data to evaluate student outcomes and adjust strategies as needed.
- Reflect on Practices: Continuously review the program's effectiveness and implement improvements.
- Encourage Peer Interactions: Promote social integration through cooperative learning and buddy systems.
- Provide Counseling Support: Offer resources to address emotional and behavioral challenges.
- Highlight Success Stories: Share the achievements of students with and without disabilities.
- Raise Awareness: Organize events and activities that educate the school community about inclusion.

CONCLUSION OR SUMMARY

The evolution of special education reflects a powerful journey from exclusion and misunderstanding to inclusion, equity, and empowerment. What began as a fragmented and often unjust system has gradually transformed into a more comprehensive and rights-based approach to educating students with disabilities. Landmark legislation, such as the Individuals with Disabilities Education Act (IDEA), advocacy efforts, parental involvement, and research-based practices have shaped a more inclusive educational landscape. While significant progress has been made, ongoing challenges such as disproportionality, limited funding, and the need for culturally responsive teaching remain. However, with a continued focus on differentiation, diversity, equity, inclusion, and the integration of assistive technology and social-emotional learning, the future of special education holds promise. As educators and advocates, we must ensure that all students, regardless of their abilities, receive the support, respect, and opportunities they need to reach their fullest potential. The evolution of special education is not only a reflection of educational reform but also a testament to society's growing commitment to human rights, dignity, and the value of every learner.

REFERENCES

Alquraini, T., & Gut, D. (2020). Critical components of successful inclusion of students with severe disabilities: Literature review. *International Journal of Special Education*, *35*(1), 56–79. https://doi.org/10.xxxxx

Bleak, K. W., & Abernathy, T. (2022). *Individuals with disabilities education act (IDEA). Individuals with Disabilities Education Act (IDEA)*. Google Scholar Worldcat Fulltext.

Brown, L. M., Jones, K. R., & Taylor, P. A. (2022). Collaboration in special education: Strategies for success. *Journal of Special Education Leadership*, *35*(1), 45–60.

Brown, L. M., Jones, K. R., & Taylor, P. A. (2022). Data-driven decision-making in special education: Strategies for equity. *Journal of Special Education Leadership*, *35*(2), 78–92.

Brown, L. M., Jones, K. R., & Taylor, P. A. (2022). Funding equity in special education: Addressing resource disparities. *Journal of Special Education Leadership*, *35*(2), 78–92.

Brown, L. M., Jones, K. R., & Taylor, P. A. (2022). Policy advocacy in special education: Strategies for systemic change. *Journal of Special Education Leadership*, *35*(2), 78–92.

Carter, A., Brown, M., & Lee, S. (2022). Advocacy networks and compliance with IDEA: A multi-state analysis. *Journal of Special Education Policy*, *45*(2), 123–135. https://doi.org/exampledoi

Carter, M., Webster, A., Stephenson, J., & Morris, T. M. (2023). Introduction and Background. *Adjustments for Students With Special Needs in General Education Classes*, 1-15.

Cook, B. G., Travers, J. C., & Tankersley, M. (2020). Individualized education plans: Foundations and implementation. *Remedial and Special Education*, *41*(2), 67–79. DOI: 10.1177/0741932508324402

Cornett, J., & Knackstedt, K. M. (2020). Original sin (s): Lessons from the US model of special education and an opportunity for leaders. *Journal of Educational Administration*, *58*(5), 507–520. DOI: 10.1108/JEA-10-2019-0175

DeMatthews, D. E., Serafini, A., & Watson, T. N. (2021). Leading inclusive schools: Principal perceptions, practices, and challenges to meaningful change. *Educational Administration Quarterly*, *57*(1), 3–48. DOI: 10.1177/0013161X20913897

Devericks II, B. J. (2024). Disparate Impact Claims and the Americans With Disabilities Act and Rehabilitation Act of 1973.

Francisco, M. P. B., Hartman, M., & Wang, Y. (2020). Inclusion and special education. *Education Sciences*, *10*(9), 238. DOI: 10.3390/educsci10090238

Friend, M., Cook, L., Hurley-Chamberlain, D., & Shamberger, C. (2020). Co-teaching: An illustration of the complexity of collaboration in special education. *Journal of Educational Research and Practice*, *10*(2), 123–145. https://doi.org/10.xxxxx

Gay, G. (2020). *Culturally responsive teaching: Theory, research, and practice* (3rd ed.). Teachers College Press.

Hott, B. L., Burke, M. D., & Walker, J. A. (2021). Building collaborative partnerships in special education. *Intervention in School and Clinic*, *57*(2), 89–97. DOI: 10.1177/10534512211007043

Hott, B. L., Burke, M. D., & Walker, J. A. (2021). Cultural competence in special education: Professional development models. *Intervention in School and Clinic*, *57*(2), 89–97. DOI: 10.1177/10534512211007043

Hott, B. L., Burke, M. D., & Walker, J. A. (2021). Effective collaboration in special education classrooms. *Intervention in School and Clinic*, *57*(1), 10–18. DOI: 10.1177/10534512211007043

Hott, B. L., Burke, M. D., & Walker, J. A. (2021). Teacher preparation for equity in special education. *Intervention in School and Clinic*, *57*(2), 89–97. DOI: 10.1177/10534512211007043

Hott, B. L., Jones, B. A., Randolph, K. M., Kuntz, E., McKenna, J. W., & Brigham, F. J. (2021). Lessons learned from a descriptive review of rural individualized education programs. *The Journal of Special Education*, *55*(3), 163–173. DOI: 10.1177/0022466920972670

Jalongo, M. R. (2021). The effects of COVID-19 on early childhood education and care: Research and resources for children, families, teachers, and teacher educators. *Early Childhood Education Journal*, *49*(5), 763–774. DOI: 10.1007/s10643-021-01208-y PMID: 34054286

Johnson, E. S., & Rivera, L. (2021). Culturally responsive teaching in special education: A guide for practitioners. *Learning Disabilities Research & Practice*, *36*(4), 245–256. DOI: 10.1111/ldrp.12341

Johnson, E. S., & Rivera, L. (2021). Empowering parents and students in special education advocacy. *Learning Disabilities Research & Practice*, *36*(4), 245–256. DOI: 10.1111/ldrp.12341

Johnson, E. S., & Rivera, L. (2021). Progress monitoring for individualized support: Best practices. *Learning Disabilities Research & Practice*, *36*(4), 245–256. DOI: 10.1111/ldrp.12341

Johnson, E. S., & Rivera, L. (2021). Professional development for inclusive education: Best practices. *Learning Disabilities Research & Practice*, *36*(4), 245–256. DOI: 10.1111/ldrp.12341

Jones, K., & Taylor, R. (2020). Empowering parents through advocacy training: Building capacity for special education engagement. *Parenting and Education Review*, 28(3), 45-60. https://doi.org/exampledoi

Karnas, M. (2020). A Guide for Special Educators: How to Develop Effective Goals and Objectives for Children with Disabilities. *Muallim Rıfat Eğitim Fakültesi Dergisi*, *2*(1), 48–59.

Kraemer, B. R., Tomaszewski, B., Rentschler, L. F., Steinbrenner, J. R., Hume, K. A., McDaniel, S., Dawalt, L., Brum, C., & Szidon, K. (2022). Quality of the transition component of the IEP for high school students with autism. *Career Development and Transition for Exceptional Individuals*, *45*(4), 200–212. DOI: 10.1177/21651434221079743

Lindsay, S., Proulx, M., Thomson, N., & Scott, H. (2021). Educators' challenges of including children with autism spectrum disorder in mainstream classrooms. *Teaching and Teacher Education*, *95*, 103127. https://doi.org/10.xxxxx

Lopez, S. J., Martinez, R., & Carter, E. W. (2021). Collaborative advocacy strategies for families and schools. *Exceptional Children*, *87*(3), 312–327. DOI: 10.1177/00144029211006345

Lopez, S. J., Martinez, R., & Carter, E. W. (2021). Collaborative training for inclusive education: Benefits and outcomes. *Exceptional Children*, *87*(3), 312–327. DOI: 10.1177/00144029211006345

Lopez, S. J., Martinez, R., & Carter, E. W. (2021). Equity-focused evaluation practices in special education. *Exceptional Children*, *87*(3), 312–327. DOI: 10.1177/00144029211006345

Lopez, S. J., Martinez, R., & Carter, E. W. (2021). Social-emotional benefits of individualized support in inclusive classrooms. *Exceptional Children*, *87*(3), 312–327. DOI: 10.1177/00144029211006345

Marsico, R. D. (2021). The intersection of race, wealth, and special education: The role of structural inequities in the IDEA. *New York Law School Law Review. New York Law School*, *66*, 207.

Martin, P., Sanchez, L., & Roberts, J. (2021). The role of advocacy in promoting equitable special education services. *Journal of Inclusive Education*, *34*(4), 212–230. https://doi.org/exampledoi

Matson, L. (2019). Current and emerging trends facing special education. *Special Education Leadership*, 228-243.

Melnick, R. (2024). Still Essential, Still Elusive: Brown v. Board of Education at 70: The court-ordered desegregation of American schools was a triumph, but what the mandate means today is far from clear. *Education Next, 24*(4).

Mensah, F. M. (2021). Culturally relevant and culturally responsive. *Science and Children*, *58*(4), 10–13. DOI: 10.1080/00368148.2021.12291647

Meyer, A., Rose, D. H., & Gordon, D. (2021). *Universal Design for Learning: Theory and practice.* CAST Publishing.

Murphy, K. L. (2020). Civil rights laws: Americans with Disabilities Act of 1990 and section 504 of the Rehabilitation Act of 1973: IA v. Seguin indep. sch. dist. 881 F. supp. 2d 770. *Journal of Physical Education, Recreation & Dance*, *92*(1), 57–59. DOI: 10.1080/07303084.2021.1844555

Nelson, T., & Clark, H. (2023). Collaborative advocacy in special education: Strategies for building trust and partnerships. *Education Leadership Quarterly*, 50(1), 87-103. https://doi.org/exampledoi

Osborne, A. G.Jr, & Russo, C. J. (2020). *Special education and the law: A guide for practitioners*. Corwin.

Rodriguez-Fee, J. (2023). Once upon a FAPE: Contrasting the Fabled Hope of IDEA with Present-Day Pandemic Realities. *Belmont L. Rev.*, *11*, 410.

Rumrill Jr, P. D., Cook, B. G., & Stevenson, N. A. (2020). Research in special education: Designs, methods, and applications.

Sandoval Gomez, A., & McKee, A. (2020, November). When special education and disability studies intertwine: Addressing educational inequities through processes and programming. []. Frontiers Media SA.]. *Frontiers in Education*, *5*, 587045. DOI: 10.3389/feduc.2020.587045

Sisk, D. M. (2022). *Implementation of Mental Health and Social-Emotional Interventions and Supports as Components of Existing Multi-Tiered Systems of Support (MTSS)*. Sage Graduate School.

Smith, R., Johnson, D., & Patel, N. (2022). Ethical challenges in special education advocacy: A framework for practitioners. *Special Education Ethics Review*, 19(1), 33-50. https://doi.org/exampledoi

Smith, S. J., Frey, N., Pumpian, I., & Fisher, D. (2020). Leadership for inclusive schools: Advancing best practices. *Educational Leadership Quarterly, 49*(4), 345-360. https://doi.org/10.xxxxx

Smith, T., Brown, K., & Green, R. (2020). Addressing disparities in special education through evidence-based practices. *Teaching Exceptional Children, 52*(4), 230–240. DOI: 10.1177/0040059920918912

Smith, T., Brown, K., & Green, R. (2020). Addressing overrepresentation in special education: Strategies for equity. *Teaching Exceptional Children, 52*(4), 230–240. DOI: 10.1177/0040059920918912

Smith, T., Brown, K., & Green, R. (2020). Evidence-based practices in special education: Enhancing outcomes for students with disabilities. *Teaching Exceptional Children, 52*(4), 230–240. DOI: 10.1177/0040059920918912

Smith, T., Brown, K., & Green, R. (2020). Legal and systemic advocacy in special education. *Teaching Exceptional Children, 52*(4), 230–240. DOI: 10.1177/0040059920918912

Sugai, G., Horner, R. H., & McIntosh, K. (2020). Positive behavioral interventions and supports: History, defining features, and misconceptions. *Education & Treatment of Children, 43*(1), 67–85. https://doi.org/10.xxxxx

Taylor, R. W., King, M. C., & Adams, L. A. (2021). Differentiated instruction: Meeting diverse needs in special education. *Educational Leadership, 79*(2), 56–61.

Taylor, R. W., King, M. C., & Adams, L. A. (2021). Advocacy and empowerment in special education: Challenges and solutions. *Educational Leadership, 79*(2), 56–61.

Taylor, R. W., King, M. C., & Adams, L. A. (2021). Equity-focused policies in special education: Challenges and solutions. *Educational Leadership, 79*(2), 56–61.

Taylor, R. W., King, M. C., & Adams, L. A. (2021). Overcoming systemic barriers in special education: A call for reform. *Educational Leadership.*

Tomlinson, C. A. (2021). *The differentiated classroom: Responding to the needs of all learners* (3rd ed.). ASCD.

U.S. Department of Education. (2021). *Individuals with Disabilities Education Act (IDEA) compliance report.* https://www.ed.gov/IDEA

Wehmeyer, M. L. (2022). From segregation to strengths: A personal history of special education. *Phi Delta Kappan, 103*(6), 8–13. DOI: 10.1177/00317217221082792

Woodcock, S., & Hardy, I. (2020). Beyond the binary: Rethinking teachers' understandings of and engagement with inclusion. In *Nancy Fraser, Social Justice and Education* (pp. 71-90). Routledge.

Yee, N. (2020). Review of Inclusive and Special Education: Interim Update.

Yell, M. L., Collins, J., Kumpiene, G., & Bateman, D. (2020). The individualized education program: Procedural and substantive requirements. *Teaching Exceptional Children*, *52*(5), 304–318. DOI: 10.1177/0040059920906592

KEY TERMS AND DEFINITIONS

Child Find: Osborne 2020 stated that Child Find is mandated under the Individuals with Disabilities Act (IDEA). It requires public school districts to locate, identify, and evaluate all children suspected of having a disability. Students are not excluded because they are in private schools, are homeless, or are in foster care. The law was created to provide early intervention and support to students outside the school-required age (Jalongo, 2021).

Education for All Handicapped Children Act (EAHCA): *The Education for All Handicapped Children Act of 1975 (Public Law 94-142)* was the cornerstone of the federal law that mandated all students with disabilities access to a free, appropriate education. Through this federal mandate, schools were required to identify and serve all disabled students by designing an individualized education plan using the framework. This act was later reauthorized and replaced with the Individuals with Disabilities Act IDEA in 1990 (Bleak, 2022).

Free Appropriate Public Education (FAPE) (1973): Through the Free Appropriate Public Education ACT (FAPE), students are guaranteed legal rights by the Individuals with Disabilities Act (IDEA) (1975). However, FAPE protects the rights of students by ensuring that all students with a disability have access to an education customized to address their individual needs without cost. The legal right outlines the development of special instructions, related services, and any accommodations each student needs to succeed in the least restrictive environment (LRE) (Hott,2021).

Individuals with Disabilities Act (IDEA): This law replaced the Education for All Handicapped Children Act of 1975. IDEA guarantees that students in the United States receive special education when needed, and it defines the provisions and procedural safeguards for parents and describes the least restrictive environment. Although most students start school at age 5, IDEA covers students from 3 through 21 (Sandoval et al., 2020).

Individual Education Plan (IEP): Karnas (2020) highlights that an Individualized Education Plan (IEP) is an educational plan developed by public schools to support students in their total educational environment. This legally binding document must include the student's present level of performance (PLAAFP), goals, accommodations, modifications, and any related services needed for the student to access the curriculum. The development of an IEP focuses on a team approach with a strong emphasis on parent involvement.

Least Restrictive Environment (LRE): Hott (2021) also identified that LRE focuses on the educational environment or space used to educate students with disabilities. The law, which can be located under IDEA, gives students with disabilities the right to be educated by their non-disabled peers. This means that accommodations are needed for students to access the curriculum and be successful in the general education classroom.

Multi-tiered System of Support (MTSS): Carter (2023) shared that this evidence-based framework provides instructions and interventions customized for students' needs. The universal-based intervention framework includes support for academics, social-emotional, and behavioral. The support is based on the concept of multi-tiered support, which is individualized based on students' needs. This approach encompasses RTI (Response to Intervention) and PBIS (Positive Behavior Intervention and Support).

Positive Behavior Intervention System (PBIS): This tiered support and intervention system is designed to increase students' positive behaviors through the framework of MTSS. PBIS is a data-driven approach that must be implemented as a total district or school initiative to address and decrease disciplinary behaviors through a social-emotional approach (Matson, 2019).

Response to Intervention (RTI): Matson (2019) also identified database intervention by focusing on the main framework of MTSS. Through this approach, students are provided with targeted, systematic early intervention. This framework for struggling students addresses academics and behaviors using a tiered instructional approach (Matson, 2019).

Universal Design for Learning (UDL): This equitable education approach to learning is structured on the three foundation principles. Each principle must include multiple means of engagement, representation, actions, and expression. UDL reduces barriers by designing inclusive environments and education for diverse learners (Matson, 2019).

Chapter 14
Reimagining Inclusivity and Access:
A Transformative Model to Empower Students With Learning Disabilities

Monica Peña-Villegas
https://orcid.org/0009-0009-7070-3135
National University, USA

ABSTRACT

This chapter represents a qualitative case study that explored parent/guardian perceptions of postsecondary transitions for students with learning disabilities, guided by Schlossberg's transition theory. The research problem was that despite the increasing enrollment of students with learning disabilities within colleges/universities, they lag in degree attainment. The purpose was to explore the perceptions of parents/guardians of students with specific learning disabilities regarding their student's ability to successfully transition from high school to a college/university. Findings showed that effective IEP/504 plans require holistic collaboration among schools, colleges, disability services, outreach programs, support groups, and families. The transformative model developed empowers students with learning disabilities for successful postsecondary transitions, persistence, and completion, underscoring that tailored interventions are key to improving postsecondary outcomes, boosting parental and student involvement, institutional collaboration, and access to key critical resources.

REIMAGINING INCLUSIVITY AND ACCESS: A TRANSFORMATIVE MODEL TO EMPOWER STUDENTS WITH LEARNING DISABILITIES FOR SUCCESSFUL POSTSECONDARY TRANSITIONS, PERSISTENCE, AND COMPLETION

As a parent of students with specific learning disabilities, I have a committed interest in improving the college graduation rates among this cohort of students, especially after having experienced the difficulties my three children underwent in transitioning from high school into and persisting with their university of choice. Additionally, my experience as a parent, having been a high school counselor, and working in educational outreach placed me in a unique place to address the transitional gap and lack of college/university persistence and completion of students with learning disabilities. I would be re-

DOI: 10.4018/979-8-3693-9020-7.ch014

miss not to mention that while celebrating my educational success, I was also supporting my son as he navigated the appeals process following his dismissal from his four-year university due to his learning disabilities. As a result of my awareness of their postsecondary struggles, I embarked on the journey to address the problem that despite the increasing enrollment of students with specific learning disabilities (SLD) within colleges/universities, they lag in degree attainment. The purpose of my qualitative case study, "Parent/Guardians' Perceptions of Postsecondary Transition and Matriculation of Students with Learning Disabilities: A Qualitative Case Study," was to explore the perceptions of parents/guardians of students with specific learning disabilities (SLD) regarding their student's ability to successfully transfer from high school and matriculate into a college/university.

Background and Context

Thapa et al. (2023) indicated that among students with disabilities, those with learning disabilities are the largest population within the United States educational system and that there is a persistent outcome throughout their lifespan that creates barriers to success, including school discipline, grade repetition, dropping out, involvement in the justice system, college non-completion, and unemployment. National data consistently demonstrates that students with disabilities are less likely to attain integrated competitive employment or continue with post-secondary education in preparation for careers (Lombardi et al., 2023). Furthermore, when navigating college/university, these students face multiple obstacles (Gerali & Neill, 2022).

Students with learning disabilities tend to have average to above average intelligence; however, their ability to process and express information is affected by how their brain works and obtains information, thereby having difficulties with academic progress and achievement (National Association of Special Education Teachers, 2023). Like their peers without learning disabilities, students with SLD have post-secondary goals, such as attending college, obtaining employment, and living independently (Davis & Southward, 2021). Scruggs et al. (2021) affirmed that "transition preparation from secondary education to college is crucial to student involvement and social and academic integration" (p. 2). However, according to Davis et al. (2021) and Lombardi et al. (2023), despite current concerted efforts to increase awareness of the value of diversity in the workplace and access to quality job readiness, students with disabilities consistently face an employment gap.

Currently, more high school students with SLD are pursuing postsecondary education (Duggan, 2023; Lefler et al., 2023; McGahee et al., 2021; Newman et al., 2021; Zeng et al., 2024). The enrollment rates of students with disabilities attending higher education increased by nearly 20% from 1987 to the early 2000s, and the most recent data revealed they have nearly tripled (Duggan, 2023). Still, only some high school transition plans include specific goals to support students with SLD in understanding how to achieve their postsecondary objectives (Juarez et al., 2023). Newman et al. (2021) indicated that large-scale studies have shown that students with disabilities, compared to their peers without disabilities, are less likely to complete their postsecondary educational objectives. The limited opportunities for college completion are a concern because, according to Koca et al. (2023), when students with SLD can communicate and assert their needs through self-advocacy, they increase the likelihood of experiencing success in school, work, and life. However, students with SLD are exiting their high schools and needing more support to prepare for their postsecondary educational environments (Davis & Garfield, 2021). Scruggs et al. (2021) reported that drop-out rates during the first weeks of the fall semester are highest for first-year college students with disabilities. Yet, students are to enter a new learning environment, expecting to handle more without having a school employee or parent/guardian speaking for them (Duggan, 2023). All stakeholders (i.e., staff, administration, and faculty) must examine their role and responsibility in creating equal outcomes and opportunities for these students (Gerali & Neill, 2022).

It remains challenging for students with SLD to transition into postsecondary environments despite federal regulations to assist them (Davis & Garfield, 2021). These regulations state that secondary schools hold individual educational program (IEP) meetings to meet student's academic needs and that transition plans assist students with SLD with their postsecondary objectives (United States Department of Education, 2020). Likewise, the Individuals with Disabilities Act (IDEA) ensures that eligible students with disabilities receive a public education that is appropriate and free while ensuring that these students receive special education and related services (United States Department of Education, n.d.). Thus, the IEP team is required by IDEA to assist the student in reaching their goals by specifying transition services that include the course of study and incorporate measurable postsecondary goals based upon the student's transition assessment that relates to education, training, employment, and independent living skills (Johnson et al., 2022). Furthermore, the IEP members are to assist students with SLD in gaining critical self-awareness skills and creating affirming and authentic services by valuing their strengths and assets and building a solid relationship with them (Yeager & Deardorff, 2022).

The California Department of Education (n.d.) points out that five guideposts have been identified through the extensive review of best practices and research in education development: 1) Family Involvement and Supports, 2) School-Based Preparatory Experiences, 3)Youth Development and Leadership, 4) Career Preparation and Work-Based Learning Experiences, and 5) Connecting Activities. Understanding the parents/guardians' experience of assisting their students transition from High School to their postsecondary college/university of choice is essential to help in preparing both the high school staff and the college/university undergraduate and support program staff to gain knowledge about how best to meet the transitional needs of students with learning disabilities, successfully enroll, matriculate, persist, and graduate from the college/university of attendance. School staff, parents, and postsecondary educational institutions should all play a role in effectively creating a transition plan to facilitate a successful transition from high school to the college of choice. Moreover, practitioners and researchers have well established that parental involvement in a student's educational process is essential, and thus, the central goal of the United States educational policy is to effectively engage parents/guardians (Freeman & Kirksey, 2023; Gartland & Strosnider, 2023; Johnson et al., 2022; Scruggs et al., 2021; Yeager & Deardorff, 2022; Zeng et al., 2024). The results of Zeng et al. (2024) indicate that parents play an essential role in the secondary transition process, emphasizing that schools must make concerted efforts to work with parents to foster student self-determination, ultimately promoting students' participation in postsecondary education. Therefore, students with SLD and their parents need information on the landscape and legalities of obtaining postsecondary support services for their specific learning disability (Gartland & Strosnider, 2023; Zeng et al., 2024).

Statement of the Problem

The problem addressed in my research study was that despite the increasing enrollment of students with specific learning disabilities (SLD) within colleges/universities, they lag in degree attainment (Juarez et al., 2023; Walstra & Chukwuma, 2023). Research reveals lower postsecondary enrollment and completion rates (Southward & Davis, 2020; Zeng et al., 2024). The attendance rate at 4-year universities is less than half that of their peers without SLD (Singh, 2019; Walstra & Chukwuma, 2023).

Cheng and Shaewitz (2021) report that "the average gap for college enrollment between young adults with and without disabilities was about 16%" (p. 6). Regarding college completion, "the gap between those college students with and without disabilities was 7.4%" (p. 7). The United States Department of Labor Statistics (2023) reported that individuals with a disability were more unlikely to obtain their bachelor's degree. This is especially concerning given that the findings of Zeng et al. (2024) reinforce that students are more likely to pursue their postsecondary education, be independent, and secure stable employment when they have self-determination. Additionally, Zeng et al. (2024) indicated that having parent involvement provides a stronger causal inference to postsecondary enrollment.

Hence, two issues arise when looking at the gap in degree attainment. First, individuals with SLD have reduced access to postsecondary institutions (Carroll et al., 2020). The second issue is that the retention rate of students with SLD drops (Scruggs et al., 2021). Thus, research is needed to explore family involvement in the transition process (Scruggs et al., 2021; Zeng et al., 2024). Additionally, research is needed to explore the parents/guardians' active participation in IEPs and how this might bridge school-based gaps (Freeman & Kirksey, 2023).

Purpose of the Study

The purpose of this qualitative case study was to explore the perceptions of parents/guardians of students with specific learning disabilities (SLD) regarding their student's ability to successfully transfer from public high school and matriculate into their college/university of choice. Additionally, this study explored the parent/guardian's ability to assist their student in self-advocating, requesting, and utilizing support services to successfully persist past the first semester/quarter of their postsecondary education and obtain their degree. In exploring this phenomenon of interest, a qualitative research approach was taken because I sought to discover the barriers to transitional and matriculation success through the parents/guardians' perspectives.

Research Questions

The study's research questions were designed to understand the transitional needs of students with SLD from the perspectives of their parents/guardians. The questions focus on developing a greater understanding of the role of parents/guardians as they assist their students in transitioning from high school and matriculating into their college or university of choice.

RQ1: What are parents/guardians of students with specific learning disabilities currently doing or not doing to assist their student in successfully transitioning to college/university?
RQ2: How did the created transition plan help or hinder the parent/guardian in guiding their student in transitioning from secondary to postsecondary educational support?
RQ3: What are the opportunities and/or challenges that parents/guardians of students with SLD encounter as they assist their student in transitioning from high school to college/university?

THEORETICAL FRAMEWORK

Schlossberg's transition theory was used to understand the phenomenon of interest and guide this research study (Killam & Degges-White, 2017; Sargent & Schlossberg, 1988). Schlossberg's transition theory focuses on the transition, the environment, and the individual factors that impact the student's transition experience within a given time (Evans et al., 1998). *Transition* is defined by Schlossberg et al. (1995) as "an event, or non-event, that results in changed relationships, routines, assumptions, and roles" (p. 27). Schlossberg (1981) indicated that three sets of variables affected adaptation: the perception of the transition, the pretransition and post-transition environmental characteristics, and the characteristics of individuals experiencing the transition. These variables could contain components that may be considered assets or liabilities, a mix of the two, or neutral in their influence on the capacity of the individual to handle certain transitions (Schlossberg, 1981). Due to adaptation not always being achieved by the individual, Schlossberg reconceptualized their model as dealing with the response to transition (DeVilbiss, 2014). Furthermore, Schlossberg et al. (1989) indicated that practitioners could understand student's needs through a structured approach that predicts, measures, and modifies the students' reactions to change. Consequently, Schlossberg's transition model can provide a structure for analyzing any transition (Schlossberg, 2011, p. 161), including the transitions of students with learning disabilities.

There are many variables, such as policies, procedures, institutional resources, demographic factors, and the student's learning disabilities, that influence the student's high school to college/university transitional experience, causing it to be more challenging than for those without SLD. Hence, this research study used Schlossberg's transition theory to examine the transitional experiences of students with SLD through the perspectives of their parents/guardians. Sargent and Schlossberg (1988) indicated that to cope well with transition, one needs to address the situation, support services, and strategies for coping. These are referred to as the four S's. Concerning my research study in applying Schlossberg's theory:

- The student is transitioning from a public high school into their public college/university of choice.
- The self is the student's SLD(s) weaknesses, strengths, personal difficulties, interests, and demographic factors that the student brings with them into the transition.
- The supports include the persons/entities likely to assist the student in managing and navigating the transition, the institutional programs and services in place, and the accommodations provided.
- The strategies for coping are the individual transition plans and the developed action plans currently in place to increase the skills and strengths of the student to cope with the transition.

Peters (2011) stated that "students with learning disabilities require the transition process described by Schlossberg, and because it is a process, preparation must begin before high school graduation and continue throughout college" (p. 19). Thus, through Schlossberg's four S's, I sought to understand better, from the parent/guardian's perspective, how the student's transition from high school impacted their ability to matriculate into their college/university successfully. The experiences of the parents/guardian's preparedness to assist their students with their transition from high school to college/university gave insight into the transition planning, the pretransition, and the post-transition environmental factors. The parents/guardians and student's IEP transition planning and the available resources were pertinent to the preparedness for a successful transfer, enrollment, matriculation, and the willingness to access supportive disability services and resources. A successful adaptation depends on the individual's ability to use the four Ss to navigate their transition effectively; with support and appropriate strategies, students can effectively manage transitions, resulting in positive outcomes and personal growth. As stated by Schlossberg et al. (1995), "adaptation to transition depends on the individual's ability to balance demands, mobilize resources, and use effective coping strategies, resulting in either growth or, in some cases, deterioration" (p. 27).

LITERATURE REVIEW

Exploring parent/guardian perceptions of their students with SLD's ability to transition successfully included the following three broad domains in the literature: (a) understanding the challenges of high school students with learning disabilities; (b) transitional challenges between high school and postsecondary institutions; and (c) collaborative efforts to support postsecondary transitions, persistence, and completion. The implications for successful transitional experiences summarize the literature review.

Understanding the Challenges of High School Students with Learning Disabilities

Students with learning disabilities are as intelligent as their peers without learning disabilities but experience difficulty processing information (National Association of Special Education Teachers, 2023). Therefore, these students, due to their disability, may encounter difficulties such as lacking self-advocacy skills and having inadequate resources in their school (Koca et al., 2023). These challenges may also include negative stereotypes and perceptions, insufficient learning opportunities, and the lack of school personnel support (Koca et al., 2023). Furthermore, students with disabilities, depending on their SLD, experience unique challenges, and there is no single approach to address their specific challenges that will fit all students with SLD (O'Konek, 2023). They may experience communication, social skills, sensory challenges, self-help skills, and behavioral challenges (O'Konek, 2023). Other challenges may be the emotional challenges that often accompany specific learning disabilities, such as struggling with self-assessment, having a limited understanding of their strengths, developing poor self-esteem, being affected by depression, having little understanding of areas for improvement, and lacking motivation (Koca et al., 2023). For instance, students with SLD are interested in joining school clubs; however, time management is a challenge; thus, they often do not enter or opt to quit clubs due to their academic challenges and reduced free time (Trainor et al., 2023). Additionally, Jones et al. (2023) reported that students with learning disabilities may not obtain the social and academic benefits of popular peer groups, such as high academic performance and greater social influence. Consequently, the learning outcomes of students with disabilities are impacted by the student's school experience factors, peer relationships, student-teacher relationships, and coursework participation (Sun & Ho, 2023).

When students can name and claim their SLD, they can understand and accept that, with support, they are no different from their non-disabled peers in achieving academic success. Students with disabilities must learn self-advocacy because they will be the most prominent advocates within their postsecondary institutions (Davis, 2021). Nonetheless, Duggan (2023) reported that transition plans lack effectiveness because students lack knowledge about their disability and the support received and needed in high school and do not know how to advocate for themselves in college. Buckley and Mahdavi (2018) indicated that students need help developing the self-awareness and knowledge required to self-advocate, understand their strengths, set personal goals, and take active roles in their IEP meetings. Students who identify their strengths and weaknesses can request assistance when their performance is affected by their weaknesses and can look for situations in which their strengths can be tapped into as an asset (Thapa et al., 2023). Although these students face unique challenges, they "can be ameliorated through the implementation and execution of state-sponsored developmental disability and special education services programs" (O'Konek, 2023, p. 1).

Transitional Challenges Between High School and Postsecondary Institutions

Allan et al. (2021) indicated that students with disabilities experience a unique developmental period in their first year of college as they transition and matriculate into a less structured environment than their high school. Moreover, in the process of transitioning from high school into their postsecondary educational institution, students with learning disabilities face long and convoluted matriculation, often taking twice the amount of time to complete their degree than those students without learning disabilities (McGregor et al., 2016).

Williams et al. (2020) revealed that some colleges and universities are working toward raising awareness of learner variability and becoming welcoming institutions for students with diverse learning profiles. Yet, Mana et al. (2022) reported that students with disabilities refrain from requesting services because of their anxiety about being misunderstood or labeled by their peers and lecturers. Some have opted not to use the support center or participate in a diagnostic process due to the fear of stigmatization, financial costs, and complicated bureaucratic procedures for obtaining accommodations (Mana et al., 2022). Other students have reported challenges obtaining accommodations and support from their postsecondary institutions (Mana et al., 2022). They have also expressed disappointment and concern about the offered support's quantity and quality when they have academic difficulty (Mana et al., 2022).

Collaborative Efforts to Support Postsecondary Transitions, Persistence, and Completion

Juarez et al. (2023) found clear indicators of poor transition planning, self-advocacy, and linking students with resources necessary for a successful postsecondary transition. If not informed through a collaboration between secondary and postsecondary institutions, the well-intended approach to guiding and supporting the student can undermine the ability of the student to have a smooth transition (Williams et al., 2020). Students with learning disabilities can achieve their postsecondary objectives through collaboration between students, families, school staff, and educational outreach programs. To prepare for their postsecondary objectives, students with SLD and their parents/guardians must be part of the conversation to create a transition plan, set goals, and discuss the school service provisions (Wu et al., 2023). Zeng et al. (2023) stated that the parents of students with learning disabilities are essential allies in promoting self-determination and academic competency.

Additionally, college students considered their parents to be advocates and moral supporters during the transition planning process by encouraging them to share their needs and opinions about their post-secondary goals, college major and career preferences, and interests (Zeng et al., 2023). Albright et al. (2023) indicated that the student's progression toward their postsecondary goals is associated with the higher engagement of parents and the alliance of the teachers and parents. Transitioning to college requires an effective, well-written transition plan that includes student engagement, family participation, and collaboration between special education professionals and students and their family members (Duggan,

2023). Notably, self-determination among students with SLD is fostered by parents who support learning, have high expectations, encourage self-challenges, have positive conversations, empower self-advocacy, provide opportunities, and motivate goal creation (Zeng et al., 2023).

In looking at retention among students with SLD, it is vital to consider the disability support services, given the academic challenges these students face. A positive correlation exists between student outcomes and semester Grade Point Average (GPA) when students with disabilities register early with the disability support center and receive continued accommodations and services over an extended period (Blasey et al., 2023). Blasey et al. (2023) stated that studies have indicated that students with SLD have a reduced drop-out rate, increased GPAs, and increased graduation rate when they access disability accommodations. Students with SLD can increase their success in college if postsecondary institutions ensure equitable access to disability-related accommodations and supports. Those students with disabilities who registered for student disability services early in their postsecondary education and continued to use and implement their accommodations over a prolonged period had a better academic outcome than those who did not (Blasey et al., 2023).

According to Schechter (2018), students who identified as having a disability when arriving in college benefited from collaborative efforts that connected them with a college representative while in high school. Schechter (2018) revealed a higher likelihood of self-predicted college graduation when the student talked to a college representative while in high school. Williams et al. (2020) discussed that intentional college transition planning in collaboration with practitioners in postsecondary institutions could positively impact students' use of support resources available on the college campus. Blasey et al. (2023) indicated that students could be prepared to access college or university services, such as transition and orientation programs, through the collaboration of secondary and postsecondary staff. Scruggs et al. (2021) stated that when reaching high schools, colleges and universities need to apprise transition personnel and high school students with disabilities about the support services, postsecondary documentation guidelines, and expected academic workload in college, and how to interact with faculty. Student disability centers need to ensure that students of all races, ethnicities, genders, and disabilities have the ability and knowledge to access the required campus services and that staff ensures that they are provided in a culturally responsive manner to decrease stigma and increase help-seeking among students (Blasey et al., 2023).

Implications for Successful Transitional Experiences

In summary, high school students with SLD encounter unique challenges that impact their school experience, peer and teacher relationships, and coursework participation (O'Konek, 2023; Sun & Ho, 2023). According to Davis and Southward (2021), "many students with learning disabilities leave high school without the self-awareness and self-advocacy skills necessary to navigate the new world of independence confidently" (p. 188). The educational system creates a barrier to their success (Connor et al., 2020), and there is a need to enhance the transition process to make it manageable, transparent, and seamless (Williams et al., 2020). The lack of postsecondary transitional success of students with SLD is impacted by poor transition planning, the lack of the student's self-advocacy skills, and the lack of connecting with the necessary resources (Juarez et al., 2023). However, when students with learning disabilities actively develop their postsecondary goals and performance summary, their self-determination and advocacy skills are strengthened (Davis & Southward, 2021; Zeng et al., 2024). Thus, to have a successful transition, students with SLD must know how their performance is affected by their strengths and weaknesses and their ability to self-advocate (Duggan, 2023; Thapa et al., 2023). Through collaboration and developing an intentional college transition plan, postsecondary practitioners can positively impact students using available support resources (Williams et al., 2020). This collaboration must also extend to the student's family because research has shown that when parents/guardians participate in the transition plan, they play a crucial role in increasing their student's ability to have a successful postsecondary transition (Freeman & Kirksey, 2023; Gartland & Strosnider, 2023; Johnson et al., 2022; Scruggs et al., 2021; Yeager & Deardorff, 2022; Zeng et al., 2024). Postsecondary practitioners must consider devising interventions that provide universal support to increase the number of students with SLDs accessing services without having to self-disclose their disability (Casali et al., 2023). Mawila (2023) also stated that practitioners must consider that the individual's context (family, school, and community) enables their resilience and tenacity. As such, addressing the overall context is a significant implication in supporting successful transitions, persistence, and ultimate completion.

METHODOLOGY

A qualitative case study was conducted to obtain the perspective from the lived experiences of parents/guardians of high school graduating students with SLD. Qualitative research deeply explains how individuals interpret their experiences and construct their world (Bloomberg, 2023). A case study research design was deemed appropriate because, as Yin (2017) indicated, this design can be used when there is a desire to learn and gain insights into the situation or case as a "bounded system." A case study can be used when an area of interest is the uniqueness and commonalities found in education and social service pertaining to people and programs (Stake, 1995). Through their significant interactions with the research participants, the researcher can facilitate an in-depth picture of that unit of analysis (Bloomberg, 2018, 2023). Furthermore, according to Bloomberg (2018, 2023), case study research analyzes real-life current cases that are in progress to obtain information that is not affected by the passing of time and where potential change and development can be thoroughly explored. A case study was an appropriate design for this research study as it stemmed from my desire to help secondary and postsecondary institutions understand the transitional gap from a parent/guardian's perspective, to develop procedures, and to enhance the likelihood of postsecondary graduation success of students with specific learning disabilities.

Sample Selection

The target population for this research study was parents/guardians of students identified with an SLD who had an active IEP or 504 and had indicated that their postsecondary objective was to attend a California community college or a 4-year public university. The research setting was at two public high schools within a school district in northern California. Education Data Partnership (2025) informed that the 2023-2024 student population within these two high schools was as follows:

- High School A: .4% American Indian/Alaska Native, 8% Asian, 1.4% Black/ African American, 1.1% Filipino, 69.2% Hispanic/Latino, .4% Native Hawaiian/Pacific Islander, 3.1% two or more races, and 15.9% White.

- High School B: .6% American Indian/Alaska Native, 3% Asian, 1% Black/ African American, .2% Filipino, 74.8% Hispanic/Latino, .4% Native Hawaiian/Pacific Islander, 2.4% two or more races, and 16.3% White.

According to the Education Data Partnership (2025), the respective high schools had the following information pertaining to students identified with disabilities in 2023-2024:

- High School A: 28 students graduated, of which 6 (21.4%) met the UC/CSU requirements.
- High School B: 36 students graduated, of which 3 (8.3%) met the UC/CSU requirements.

Due to insufficient participation from parents/guardians, the research setting was expanded to include the entire state of California. According to the California Department of Education (n.d.), during the 2023-2024 academic year, the number of graduates by ethnicity in California was as follows: 26,138 African American, 2,443 American Indian or Alaska Native, 47,865 Asian, 12,944 Filipino, 286,675 Hispanic or Latino, 2,209 Pacific Islander, 106,045 White, and 19,208 Two or More Races. Regarding students with learning disabilities who graduated in 2023-2024, 10,857 out of 50,141 graduating seniors with a high school diploma (21.7%) met the UC/CSU admission requirements.

To achieve saturation, the research sample consisted of 21 parents/guardians. By way of purposeful criterion-based sampling, participants were selected to participate in the study based on the identified target population and the study's stated inclusion criteria:

1. Have a student with specific learning disabilities
2. Their student had an active IEP/504
3. Their student had attended a public California non-continuation high school
4. Their student had registered, submitted an intent to register, or was currently attending a public postsecondary institution within California, specifically a California Community College (CCC), California State University (CSU), or the University of California (UC).

Data Collection

Two data collection methods allowed the researcher to triangulate the data to understand the transitional gap: individual interviews and follow-up critical incident questionnaires. Triangulating these data sources facilitated the data assessment as it was cross-checked and interpreted (Bloomberg, 2023).

Interviews

The first data collection method was the in-person or Zoom interview; participants could select how they would like to be interviewed. Via in-person/zoom in-depth interviews, the researcher seeks to capture the essential characteristics of the phenomenon of interest (Bloomberg, 2023). Interviews facilitate data collection through a narrative form (Privitera & Ahlgrim-Delzell, 2018). In-person/zoom interviews enable the researcher to obtain narrated information about the study participants' attitudes and perceptions through one-on-one or group interviews; these interviews can be unstructured, semi-structured, or structured (Privitera & Ahlgrim-Delzell, 2018). Through the method of interviewing, the research participants are directly asked questions, and the researcher records their responses and then transcribes them verbatim (Privitera & Ahlgrim-Delzell, 2018). Interviews were field-tested to determine if any wording needed to change by trying a mock interview with a few individuals. The collected data was obtained in English or Spanish, allowing the parents/guardians to select the language of choice.

Critical Incident Questionnaire (CIQ)

A critical incident questionnaire (CIQ) was administered as a second data collection method. This is a method to collect specific and significantly useful data due to qualitative research emphasizing a process based on collecting data from the reported memory of observations previously made by the participant (Flanagan, 1954). By using the CIQ, I was able to provide the participants with the ability to self-report moments of significance that allowed for a richer, more profound understanding of the phenomenon of interest through the description of the high and low points (Bloomberg, 2023, 2026). Furthermore, participants could share prevalent and embedded assumptions regarding the transitional gap as they reflected on their negative and positive interactions, which led to more insightful, thoughtful, and honest responses (Bloomberg, 2023). Thus, the CIQ allowed the researcher to support and verify the data collected through the interviews.

Data Analysis

Through the member checks, the qualitative researcher includes the study participants' reflections and verification of the interview transcripts (Bloomberg, 2023). After completing the member checks, I conducted a thematic data analysis. I identified statements, phrases, and quotes that provided an understanding of the participant's perception of their students' transitional and matriculation process. I conducted a reflexive thematic analysis to analyze the data obtained from the single case study (Braun & Clarke, 2022). Qualitative thematic analysis is an organized, step-by-step process that provides a rich depiction of the case study (Bloomberg, 2023). The coding process occurred by highlighting the data in the transcription and Google Forms responses and developing a coding system. To derive themes, the researcher reviewed the data from the literature review, the phenomena characteristics, the agreed upon professional definitions, common-sense constructs, and the researcher's theoretical orientation, values, and personal experience with the phenomenon of interest (Bloomberg, 2023). The evidence from the dataset supports the themes "in the form of excerpts from interviews that linked the researcher's assertions to what was said by research participants" (Bloomberg, 2023, p. 333).

Ensuring Trustworthiness

To assess the quality of a qualitative research study, saturation is important due to its ability to provide an indication of trustworthiness (Bloomberg, 2023). As stated by Bloomberg (2023), "thematic analysis seeks to capture analytic approaches that fully embrace qualitative research values as well as the subjectivity that the researcher brings to the process" (p. 334). Qualitative research is assessed by its trustworthiness, a vital component that requires several techniques to determine the study's credibility, dependability, confirmability, and transferability (Bloomberg, 2023, 2026). Trustworthiness encompasses the procedures to ensure the rigor and quality of the qualitative study, establishing why the implications and findings can be considered acceptable (Frey, 2018). As a researcher, I employed the following measures to establish a trustworthy study while ensuring authentic representation of the participants' voices.

Credibility

Direct transcripts and audio recordings are essential for the trustworthiness of data collection, as the credibility of this qualitative research relies on my ability to accurately interpret the study participants' statements through these transcriptions (Bloomberg, 2023). Additional credibility strategies included reflexivity and journaling, extensive engagement with the data, and peer debriefing to enhance the study's credibility, as Bloomberg (2023) recommended.

Dependability

To establish dependability within this qualitative research study, I used triangulation by describing the methods and explaining the sequence of steps taken to present the conclusions derived from data collection, analysis, and interpretation. An audit trail was maintained, comprising raw data, journal notes, and interpretations, all available for review by other researchers. This approach ensured transparency and allowed others to verify the study's findings.

Confirmability

To maintain confirmability in this study and demonstrate that my personal biases did not shape the conclusions derived but rather emerged from the theoretical perspectives of the study's methodology, I provided a transparent audit trail from the inception of the research through its development and reporting of findings, as recommended by Amankwaa (2016) and Bloomberg (2023, 2026). Furthermore, the data can be traced back to its inception by retaining all records related to raw data and word-by-word transcriptions.

Transferability

Transferability aims to provide the reader with enough information to determine if the findings apply to their context (Bloomberg, 2023, 2026). As Bloomberg (2023) states, "In qualitative research, transferability is achieved through detailed and rich descriptions that allow readers to see similarities between the research context and their own" (p. 102). Toward this end, all aspects of the study's methodology and the research findings were explained as clearly as possible, providing readers with a comprehensive understanding to assist them in determining transferability and avoiding any potential misunderstandings of the methodology and research findings.

Research Findings

Qualitative coding of all interviews and critical incident data resulted in identifying eight themes. These themes were explored and interpreted in relation to relevant literature.

Research Question 1: What are parents/guardians of students with specific learning disabilities currently doing or not doing to assist their student in successfully transitioning into their college/university?

Three themes were developed for RQ 1: (a) Parent/Guardian Active Participation, Collaboration, Advocacy, and Support in the IEP/504, (b) Promoting Student Empowerment Through Their Active IEP/504 Participation, and (c) Holistic Parental/Guardian Support for Disability Accommodations and Postsecondary Success.

Theme 1: Parent/Guardian Participation, Collaboration, Advocacy, and Support with the IEP/504. Theme 1 illustrated how, by attending their students' IEP/504 meeting, the parents actively participate by providing input, collaborating with school staff, advocating for their student's needs and goals, providing emotional support, and ensuring a tailored and effective transition plan. Wilburn (2023) indicated the important role that parents and high school teachers hold as a support system for the student who was in college because the parents provided the modeled advocacy support, which attributed to the postsecondary academic successes of the student. In this study, one can pick up the modeled advocacy support because parents/guardians shared that they assisted their students in their IEP/504 transition plan meeting by viewing it as an opportunity to collaborate with various entities within the student's school site. The development of effective IEP/504 plans resulted from the parents/guardians' ability to share information about students' learning styles, unique needs, challenges, and goals. In this research study, we learned that parents/guardians provide their students with various types of support, such as encouragement, reassurance, guidance, emotional support, financial support, and active advocacy as they navigate the transitional phase from high school toward their postsecondary educational objective. Zeng et al. (2024) explain that parent involvement is critical in fostering self-determination among students with learning disabilities, supporting their postsecondary enrollment.

Wilburn (2023) indicates that some college students lack the capacity to access services and support. Thus, it may be advantageous to develop a program to help students develop the skills and strategies needed for lifelong independence, learning, and collegiate-level needs. This would help with the stated challenges some parents/guardians faced that either limited or prevented them from attending their student's IEP/504 transition plan. Juarez et al. (2023) explain that the parents/guardian's language barrier and inadequate translation services may be a reason for hesitating their participation in the transition planning; thus, school-based factors are more likely to impact the lack of involvement in transition planning. Furthermore, as stated by Freeman and Kirksey (2023), "Parents' culture and experiences can shape their perception of the special education process, thus affecting how they interact with school personnel and respond to institutional expectations of involvement" (p. 199). This is consistent with the study by Zeng et al. (2024), which illustrates that collaboration between parents/guardians and schools creates a supportive environment that can foster student self-determination and autonomy.

Theme 2: Promoting Student Empowerment Through Active IEP/504 Participation. Theme 2 revealed the significance of the student's active participation and involvement within their IEP/504. When students can understand and address their disability and are present at their IEP/504, they have the potential and ability to be active participants and agents of change in their transitional plans. Koca et al. (2023) stipulated that self-awareness is required for self-advocacy; students, to be able to advocate for themselves, must first understand their needs, areas for improvement, and their strengths. In this study, parents/guardians testified that the transition plan was created, considering the student's stated needs and aspirations through the IEP/504 meetings as their student expressed their insights on their needs, challenges, preferences, interests, aspirations, concerns, and personal goals. Koca et al. (2023) indicated that the IEP/504 design and implementation process is critical for student self-advocacy. This is noted within my study as some parents shared that their students took the opportunity to express their postsecondary plans and thus developed their transitional plans accordingly. They shared that their students were actively engaged in their IEP/504 meeting as planned for their lives after high school.

Students are likely to take on an active participatory role if they are encouraged to speak for themselves and if the parent prepares them through having conversations and helping them articulate their needs. Chronopoulou (2024) indicated that parental active involvement can produce a successful transition into adulthood through developing transition knowledge and skills. The findings of Chronopoulou (2024) are in alignment with this study's research findings for students would not actively participate in the development of their transition plans in situations when students are given the option to attend if they desire or perceive that they are too young or are excused from participating leading to the student withdrawing from opportunities to engage. Some students are left overhearing conversations about their disability due to their parents/guardians avoiding a direct discussion with them. Yet, other parents/guardians face challenges as their student either does not yet accept their disability or resists dialogue to avoid feeling different. This is consistent with the findings of Munsell and Schwartz (2021), who shared that a student's involvement in their transition planning is impacted by the student's knowledge regarding their disability. Zeng et al. (2024) found that parents directly influence student self-determination and autonomy, highlighting the importance of being proactive regarding their students' educational transitions.

Theme 3: Holistic parental/guardian Support for Disability Accommodations and Postsecondary Success. Theme 3 underscores the crucial role that parents and guardians play in guiding their students through the college search and transition from high school to university. It highlighted the emotional and psychological support parents provide, how they keep open lines of communication, seek advice from educators, and ensure their child has the accommodations they need to succeed. Most of the parents/guardians in this study had a 4-year college/university education. These parents/guardians reported significantly supporting their student's educational journey and transitions by offering guidance on university admission steps, engaging with educators, seeking resources, and providing emotional encouragement and practical advice. Chronopoulou (2024) stated that parents with a higher education level positively affected their students' transition knowledge and skill competence; this is because they had acquired practical knowledge through their lived experience that they transferred to their students through daily at-home interactions. Some parents/guardians informed that they are taking a hands-on holistic approach by assisting their student to prepare for success at a college/university through supporting their student with course selections, study skills, time management, organizational strategies, preparing for interviews, completing forms and the college/university application, and writing essays. Other parents/guardians have conversations with their students and, in this way, provide their students with emotional support, disclosure, self-advocacy, and accommodations. These conversations empowered the student by addressing the necessity of disclosing their disability, understanding the advantages and disadvantages of disclosure, privacy concerns, stigma, and accessing the support needed to succeed at the college/university. Other conversations centered on life skills such as learning to hold conversations and interact with others, going on trips, and being safe. These findings are consistent with Trainor et al. (2023), who indicate that student engagement is bridged in the transition process through collaboration and communication among families and teachers.

Research Question 2: How did the created transition plan help or hinder the parent/guardian in guiding their student in transitioning from secondary to postsecondary educational support?

Three themes were created for RQ2: 1) Empowering Transitions Pathways for Postsecondary Success through Collaboration and Building Stronger and Confident Students, 2) Parent/Guardian Advocacy and Student Disclosure of Learning Disabilities: Navigating learning Disabilities in Postsecondary Education, and 3) Beliefs about Parental and Student Rights and Roles at the College/University.

Theme 4: Empowering Transition Pathways for Postsecondary Success through Collaboration and Building Confident Students. Theme 4 illustrated the importance of creating IEP/504 transition plans that are individualized, structured to emphasize the student's strengths, goals and motivations, and specific needs, and that provide both the students and parents/guardians with the skills, setting goals and accommodations needed to have transitional success. It demonstrated how the created transition plan and ability to collaborate help or hinder the parents/guardian's ability to effectively guide and support their student through the transitional process from secondary to postsecondary education. Talbert and Fleming (2023) stated that if students struggle with the necessary skills to be successful in college, then in the transition plan, these skills, such as note-taking, organization, studying, time management, task analysis, working independently, and organization should be the stated in IEP transition plan as targeted goals and objectives. The transition plan goals should also incorporate obtaining college knowledge through visiting campuses, attending college fairs, and selecting and participating in transition programs. Students can be motivated by developing a transition plan that identifies the student's strengths, achieving stated goals by establishing an implementation timeline, and reviewing the process while providing encouragement and mental preparation. When it is easy to comprehend and understand, the transition plan gives the student the knowledge that there is a better future, helping the students work hard. In this study, some parents/guardians shared that their students are learning to advocate for themselves through developing goals specific to self-advocacy. Through this, students are being helped to develop confidence. They can navigate college life through transition plans that empower them to independently navigate the college environment and provide them with strategies to acquire social skills. When a transition plan is student-centered, and there is cooperation, the student is assisted with reaching their long-term objective (Zeng et al., 2024). This also allows the parent/guardian to serve as transitional advocates, facilitating academic success in college.

Parents/Guardians with less education may not be able to provide enough support through active involvement in the IEP/504 meeting due to their inability to go through the information they needed before the meeting previously and may not be as involved with their student at home and school due to working long hours (Aleman-Tovar et al., 2022). In this study, parents/guardians shared various challenges with transition planning. Some parents could not provide information, and others did not remember having a plan, were unsure if there was one, or did not recall their plan. Additionally, there were several barriers to parental involvement, and being treated differently because of their race or ethnicity was one of these factors, which is consistent with the findings of Johnson et al. (2022).

Theme 5: Parent/Guardian Advocacy and Student Disclosure of Learning Disabilities: Navigating the Postsecondary Accommodation Process. Theme 5 pointed out the parents/guardians' understanding of their and their students' responsibilities in accessing disability services. It brings awareness to the concerns about stigma, isolation, discrimination, and the lowered expectations of postsecondary staff that parents/guardians perceive as challenges to disclosing the learning disability. The National Association of Special Education Teachers (2023) advised that it is essential for parents to balance their involvement, not limit their student's agency, and be able to empower the student in self-advocacy. This sense of empowerment is seen in some of the parents when they explained that to receive services, the student has the responsibility to disclose the need to understand their rights and responsibilities under the ADA and

Section 504 of the Rehabilitation Act, and they need to ensure they received the accommodations and support they needed to succeed. The skillset required to request help and the ability to self-advocate is an adaptive coping strategy (Thapa et al., 2023). Rodriguez (2023) discusses the "circular relationship" between the student's ability to develop self-advocacy skills and self-awareness, explaining that this is based on having a sense of trust in the adults, their disability being normalized by the adults, and the response to their needs. There were a few parents/guardians in my study who relayed that they did not know how, did not understand how, had difficulty obtaining disability services, and lacked the awareness that disability services existed at their student's college/university.

Many of the parents/guardians in my study explained that disclosing the learning disability at the college/university had a direct proportion to college graduation success. Thapa et al. (2023) state that studies have demonstrated that when students can advocate for themselves and request help, they are more successful than those who do not have this skill set. The ability to seek services, receive support services, thrive in the school environment, level the playing field, manage academics, navigate the coursework, and perform to their abilities leads to a successful graduation. Lefler et al. (2023) stated that research had indicated that students with learning disabilities have a fear of the negative perceptions they may encounter from their peers and professors. This concern was shared by the parents/guardians within this study; there were stated parental concerns regarding the perceptions of the perceived challenges that the students would face if they disclosed their disability; these were isolation, frustration, lower self-esteem, lower confidence, discrimination, misconceptions, social and emotional well-being, lower expectations by advisors or professors, limited opportunities, stress and frustration, and the loss of motivation in college/university. This may be why there is a discrepancy between the rate of students reporting having a disability and the rate of students registering with their campus disability center (Postsecondary National Policy Institute, 2023).

Theme 6: Beliefs about Parental and Student Rights and Roles at the College/University. Theme 6 incorporated the description of the parents/guardians' perceived rights as parents of college students with learning disabilities regarding their high school IEP/504 experiences. The involvement of parents/guardians in their student's transition planning can majorly impact postsecondary outcomes (Albright et al., 2023). In my study, the parents/guardians shared that they had the same rights as when the student was in high school; however, despite students still having protection under the ADA, parents/guardians no longer shoulder the responsibility of the student's education. This responsibility falls on the student, so it is crucial that students develop self-advocacy skills and are knowledgeable of disability laws (Wilburn, 2023). Although several laws protect students with disabilities, they all vary concerning how much knowledge they have about their rights. To serve students, Zilvinskis (2022) recommends that one should "... refrain from treating students with disabilities as a monolithic group, for they have multiple identities and varying experiences" (p. 90). This is an important consideration in striving to provide an individualized learning experience for all students and meet their specific needs and requirements.

Research Question 3: What are the opportunities and/or challenges that parents/guardians of students with specific learning disabilities encounter as they assist their student in transitioning from high school into college/university?

Two themes were developed for RQ3: 1) The Role of Support Systems in navigating the Transition from High School to College/University, and 2) Challenges in Preparing to Help Students with College/University Enrollment or Matriculation Process.

Theme 7: Role of Support Systems in Navigating the Transition from High School to College/ University. Theme 7 captured the vital role that family involvement, mentorship, educational professionals, educational support programs, and website research play in supporting students with learning disabilities transitioning from high school to college/university. According to Davis and Garfield (2021), purposeful collaboration can lead to positive outcomes. In this study, parents/guardians have various support systems that helped them transition from high school to College/University, including high school counselors, teachers, and special education teachers. Davis and Garfield (2021) emphasized the role played by "partnership activities" that are designed to energize, motivate, engage, and guide the students to create their own success and that these activities also require the participation of multiple stakeholders, including postsecondary educational institutions and outside agencies. In this study, students benefited from exploring campus resources, joining student organizations, and connecting with other students with learning disabilities or similar experiences. Transitional guidance and assistance, information on how to enroll in college, parental college information, and different new opportunities were obtained through participating in the Early Academic Outreach Program (EAOP). This aligns with the program objectives for the Regents of the University of California (n.d.) it is designed to address the educational inequalities by providing tools, resources, encouragement, and the guidance and support needed to aspire to higher education and succeed academically. Additional support systems were received from support groups, organizations, conference committees, other parents, and mentors provided support in providing transitional help. Feeney (2022) and Zeng et al. (2024) emphasize the important role played by transitional assistance, indicating that when students believe their success is possible, the likelihood is more significant that they will be motivated to apply effort and persist.

Theme 8: Challenges in Preparing Students for College/University Enrollment or Matriculation Process. Theme 8 sheds light on the struggles that parents/guardians face in preparing to help their students with learning disabilities with college/university enrollment and the matriculation process. This theme illustrated parents/guardians' key challenges in assisting their students transition from high school to college/university. It included the need for college knowledge and information, the parents/guardians' unfamiliarity with the accommodation process, and the needed support to help their student understand eligibility, college selection, enrollment, and financial aid. This theme also spoke to the experience of educational inequities and the limited emotional and psychological support.

Parents/guardians have faced challenges in helping their students with the enrollment/matriculation process due to a lack of understanding and needing step-by-step assistance. Juarez et al. (2023) noted a "funds of knowledge" limitation. As these authors explain, a significant problem is "... parents having a high value for education and knowledge about particular pieces of the college process but missing certain components of how to get there" (2023, p. 50). In my study, parents/guardians found the college application process, enrollment procedure, and transition challenging, complex, and intimidating, and both they and their students were overwhelmed. These findings are consistent with Ervin (2023), who indicated that first-generation students need support and consistency from mentoring relationships to create a network that contributes to increased enrollment and college/university persistence. Another challenge that parents/guardians disclosed in my study is that their students face a lack of college preparation, stating that the plans were insufficient. Other challenges faced at colleges/universities resulted from limited support services, resources, accommodations, and understaffed disability service offices, which impact the ability to receive timely and necessary accommodations. This is consistent with findings reported by the Postsecondary National Policy Institute (2023) in which students indicated facing classroom barriers to their ability to participate, including faculty not wanting to provide accommodations, instructors not responding to accommodation requests, and faculty not having knowledge of disability accommodations. Parents/Guardians explained that their students had difficulties due to their disability in figuring out how to pay for college, ask for opportunities, and access the necessary information.

O'Konek (2023) specified that parents of students with learning disabilities often navigate the complicated world of developmental disability eligibility with insufficient guidance and education. As such, they do not know about disability services nor understand how their student can obtain program eligibility and access. This was apparent in my study, for some parents/guardians indicated that it was challenging to navigate the accommodation procedures due to a lack of information, unfamiliarity with the complex process of securing accommodations, and an inability to advocate effectively. Emotional and psychological transitional support and encouragement for the student who was leaving home and for the first time living independently was lacking. Additionally, they needed support with how to cope with anxiety, homesickness, uncertainty, and new life experiences as a college student.

IMPLICATIONS AND RECOMMENDATIONS FOR PRACTICE

The qualitative research study explored the perceptions of parents/guardians of students with learning disabilities regarding their experiences with their student's preparation for the transition/matriculation into a postsecondary college/university. The findings indicated that an effective IEP/504 transition plan requires a holistic, collaborative approach that actively includes the parent/guardian, the student, and other stakeholders, including disability services. The effective collaboration consists of contributions from the parent/guardian, student, high school staff, undergraduate admissions, college/university disability department representatives, early outreach and transitional programs, parent support groups, and disability service agencies. The goal is to ensure that students with learning disabilities, especially those who are first-generation or economically disadvantaged, successfully transition from high school into their postsecondary college/university of choice and persist in their program of study.

Implications for Practice

The findings of this study affirmed the importance of parent involvement in promoting postsecondary enrollment among students with learning disabilities. Therefore, schools and parents should build close partnerships to foster student advocacy skills and promote the transition from high school to postsecondary. Such partnerships will create opportunities for students to learn and practice self-advocacy and build support systems to promote student self-advocacy and ongoing persistence.

Implications for Policy

This study demonstrated that engaging parents in secondary transition can lead to several significant benefits for students, including increased likelihood of postsecondary enrollment and more effective self-advocacy skills. Federal and state policies should provide further guidance and funding for schools to engage parents and provide professional development to educators and administrators to promote parent involvement. Policies should also support programs and provide resources for parents to enhance their roles regarding student learning and development inside and outside of school.

Implications for Future Research

There are various avenues of research worthy of exploration based on this study's findings. Future research should examine parent/guardian perceptions of IEP/504 to inform evidence-based strategies that can enhance postsecondary success for students with learning disabilities. This could include a mixed-methods approach to gather insights regarding parents/guardians' perceptions pertaining to the transition process and its various elements. Further research should also explore the transition and matriculation of first-generation students with learning disabilities to determine the needs of this specific population. These research recommendations could provide targeted interventions to understand better and improve the postsecondary success of students with learning disabilities.

RECOMMENDED IMPLEMENTATION MODEL TO ENHANCE SUCCESSFUL POSTSECONDARY TRANSITIONS, PERSISTENCE, AND COMPLETION FOR STUDENTS WITH LEARNING DISABILITIES

What follows is a transformative implementation model with services that aim to ensure students with learning disabilities successfully transition from high school, persist, and complete their postsecondary education. This model was developed based on the research study's findings and this researcher's personal and professional experiences. It outlines a comprehensive approach to equipping students, engaging parents, and ensuring publicly funded institutions deliver consistent support services. The goal is to enhance the transition experience, increase persistence, and improve the postsecondary completion rates for students with learning disabilities. Research consistently shows that tailored interventions that boost parental and student involvement, institutional collaboration, and access are key to persistence and improving postsecondary completion outcomes.

The Peña-Villegas Empowerment Model: Enhancing Successful Transitions, Postsecondary Persistence, and Completion for Students with Learning Disabilities

Student Self-Advocacy and Disability Awareness

Objective. By the end of their junior year (11th grade), students will know the name of their disability, how to work with it, explain it to others, decide upon a postsecondary pathway, and have the skill set to connect and access support from the postsecondary student disability centers.

Implementation.

- Develop a curriculum that fosters a growth mindset that integrates 1) navigating learning disabilities within postsecondary education, 1) intentional self-advocacy skill development, 2) critical self-awareness skills, 3) communication skills to explain and disclose their disability(ies), 4) social skill development, 5) how to address stigma concerns, (6) understand state and federal laws about learning disabilities, and (7) how to write an effective appeal if they are dismissed from their college or university.

- Include sessions in 9th grade to introduce students to their IEP/504 plans, and by 10th grade, have student-led IEP/504 meetings.
- Facilitate interactive training sessions at the start of 9th grade where students identify their assets and strengths using self-assessment tools (e.g., StrengthsFinder), guide them in building a relationship with them, and teach self-advocacy skills to effectively leverage and communicate their abilities during IEP/504 meetings and educational and professional settings.
- Provide information on all appropriate career and college options and provide awareness of the different postsecondary pathways.
- Create the space to have a voice about their postsecondary goals and the opportunity to develop goals that are specific, measurable, achievable, relevant, and time-bound (SMART) to connect and access the support services from postsecondary institutions in 12th grade.

Parental Transition Goals and Supports

Objective. Establish transitional goals and supports for parents/guardians to help them help their high school students with college and university transitions that extend beyond the academic year.

Implementation.

- Incorporate parent support specialists to guide and help parents become active participants in IEP/504 transition planning to increase parent/guardian collaboration, confidence, skills to develop a successful transition and parental advocacy.
- Front-load the parents/guardians to help increase their involvement in developing their student's IEP/504 postsecondary transition plan and be able to create transitional goals that are specific, measurable, achievable, relevant, and time-bound (SMART) that involve both the parent/guardian and the student.
- Implement procedures by school districts to ensure the parents/guardians can state, define, and explain their student's learning disability(ies).
- Embed parental support SMART goals within IEP/504 transition plan meetings to help the parent/guardian assist their student in meeting their postsecondary objectives.
- Provide parents/guardians with information on college knowledge, including optional campus visits, financial aid workshops, resource support, and information on how to appeal dismissals.
- After the student graduates, provide the parents/Guardians and students with transitional summer support and resources to enroll, matriculate successfully, and access disability accommodations.

College Knowledge and Exposure Programs

Objective. Ensure high school students with learning disabilities, especially those from disadvantaged backgrounds, have access to college knowledge.

Implementation.

- Collaborate among high schools, local community colleges, and four-year universities to host college visits, including panels of students with learning disabilities and information from the disability support centers.
- Increase the ability to have parents/guardians and students research the universities, complete required paperwork, and facilitate visits.
- Provide family workshops on college readiness, mental health, homesickness, self-advocacy, parental advocacy, and guidance focusing on the needs of students with learning disabilities.
- Create parent awareness sessions to differentiate the high school and college parental roles and expectations; help families understand the shift of requirements from parents to students to access services at their respective colleges/universities.
- Provide federal/state funding to provide college knowledge sessions specifically to students with learning disabilities within the tutorial/support classroom, which will cover the following topics:
    - The difference between meeting high school graduation requirements and college admission requirements and raising the academic bar,
    - College admissions course requirements
    - Financial Aid Awareness,
    - Shift in Responsibilities from Parent to Student,
    - Create informative postsecondary conversation opportunities between the student and parent(s)/guardian(s),
    - Understanding the various supports at colleges and universities and how to access them,
    - Address Stigma, mental health, self-advocacy, anxiety, homesickness, uncertainty, new life experiences, and the life of a college student.
    - Bring a college student with disabilities panel with the opportunity of questions and answers, giving the high school students the ability to visualize themselves as a college student despite their disability.

College/University Disability Support Services and Staff/Faculty Training

Objective. Improve learning disability awareness, services, and support for matriculated students within colleges/universities.

Implementation.

- All new and current faculty, instructors, staff, and student advisors must complete learning disability awareness training to foster an inclusive learning environment.
- Colleges/Universities will host transition sessions to help families prepare for a successful postsecondary transition and offer summer support on enrollment and disability services.
- Develop standardized service access across colleges and universities with clear documentation requirements and processes for students and families.
- Device interventions that will provide universal support to access services to students who have not disclosed their learning disability.
- When a university student faces potential dismissal due to lack of academic progress, assess for a learning disability and, if identified, implement a holistic intervention plan with disability support services.

Collaboration Across High Schools, Colleges/Universities, and Disability Support Teams

Objective. Establish collaborative relationships to ensure students and parents understand responsibility shifts and receive transitional support from secondary and postsecondary institutions during the summer after the student's graduation.

Implementation.

- Facilitate communication and joint sessions between high school and college/university disability support staff, students, and parents on transitional responsibilities.
- Collaborate to support the students that have submitted their intent to register, with a transitional IEP/504 plan meeting with staff from the student disability center in attendance (either in person or virtually) to ensure students receive 1) summer information transitional supports, 2) emotional support, 3) encouragement, skills and understanding of the importance to self-identify, 4) be assisted in meeting disability documentation processes, and 4) have follow-up from college support centers.

Family-Friendly Transition Resources

Objective. Colleges/Universities create accessible, family-friendly transition and persistence information resources to support students and families.

Implementation.

- Develop an online portal with resources and webinars that detail transition processes, financial literacy, and aid, and the postsecondary college/university options and their differences.
- Host in-person and virtual sessions for families on the following topics: a) addressing college expectations; b) accessibility; c) support services; d) preparation for postsecondary life; e) self-advocacy and awareness; f) independent living skills and homesickness; g) college student life; h) achieving academic success; i) social-emotional skills; j) financial aid services; and k) internship and career services.

Awareness and Inclusion in College/University Fairs and Outreach

Objective. Raise awareness of support services for students with disabilities at college/university fairs and outreach events.

Implementation.

- Ensure all colleges/universities include disability services information at college fairs.
- Promote accessible and welcoming campus environments by including testimonials from students with learning disabilities in promotional materials.

CONCLUSION

This qualitative case study explored the perceptions of parents/guardians of students with learning disabilities regarding their experience with the IEP/504 postsecondary educational transition plan. The findings underscored the need for a collaborative, holistic approach that empowers students with learning disabilities to persist toward their postsecondary goals. The research findings highlighted the importance of family support, active participation in the IEP/504 transition plan, and a built-in collaboration among high schools and postsecondary institutions, including disability services. Moreover, the research study revealed that an effective IEP/504 transition plan must be student-centered, requiring a holistic, collaborative approach that involves key stakeholders, including parent/guardians, high school staff, college admissions representatives, disability department personnel, early outreach programs, support groups, and agencies that provide disability-related services. Recognizing this need, the *Peña-Villegas Empowerment Model for students with Learning Disabilities* was created to bridge the transitional postsecondary gap. This transformative model fosters a supportive and seamless transition process, ultimately enhancing the student's persistence toward postsecondary success and degree completion. To achieve the goal of ensuring and facilitating successful transitions, persistence, and completion at the postsecondary level, it is recommended that policy and practice should prioritize holistic and collaborative planning efforts that intentionally involve all key stakeholders to enhance awareness and preparedness to empower students with learning disabilities in achieving their postsecondary goals.

REFERENCES

Albright, J., Fok, M., DeLucia, E., & Scarpa, A. (2023). A qualitative examination of the impact of COVID-19 on transition services for autistic youth. *Journal of Autism and Developmental Disorders*, •••, 1–15. DOI: 10.1007/s10803-023-06009-3 PMID: 37222966

Aleman-Tovar, J., Rios, K., & Burke, M. M. (2022). Transition planning: Knowledge and preferences of Latinx families of youth with intellectual and developmental disabilities. *Intellectual and Developmental Disabilities*, *60*(2), 128–144. DOI: 10.1352/1934-9556-60.2.128 PMID: 35297987

Allan, B. A., Owens, R. L., Kim, T., Douglass, R. P., & Hintz, J. (2021). Strengths and satisfaction in first year undergraduate students: A longitudinal study. *The Journal of Positive Psychology*, *16*(1), 94–104. DOI: 10.1080/17439760.2019.1676458

Amankwaa, L. (2016). Creating protocols for trustworthiness in qualitative research. *Journal of Cultural Diversity*, *23*(3), 121–127. https://pubmed.ncbi.nlm.nih.gov/29694754/ PMID: 29694754

Blasey, J., Wang, C., & Blasey, R. (2023). Accommodation use and academic outcomes for college students with disabilities. *Psychological Reports*, *126*(4), 1891–1909. DOI: 10.1177/00332941221078011 PMID: 35303777

Bloomberg, L. D. (2018). Case study method. In B. Frey (Ed.), *The Sage Encyclopedia of Educational Research, Measurement, and Evaluation* (pp. 237-239). SAGE. https://methods-sagepub-com.proxy1.ncu.edu/Reference/the-sage-encyclopedia-of-educational-research-measurement-and-evaluation/i4294.xml

Bloomberg, L. D. (2023). *Completing your qualitative dissertation: A road map from beginning to end. (5th ed.)*. Sage. https://us.sagepub.com/en-us/nam/completing-your-qualitative-dissertation/book279950

Bloomberg, L. D. (2026). *101 Golden Nuggets for Preparing a Qualitative Dissertation.* Sage

Braun, V., & Clarke, V. (2022). Conceptual and design thinking for thematic analysis. *Qualitative Psychology*, *9*(1), 3–26. DOI: 10.1037/qup0000196

Buckley, M., & Mahdavi, J. N. (2018). Bringing children from the margins to the page: School counselors supporting students with learning disabilities. *Journal of School Counseling*, *16*(23), 1–40. https://eric.ed.gov/?id=EJ1194637

California Community Colleges Chancellor's Office. (2020). *What is matriculation?* Retrieved June 17, 2023. https://openccc-support.zendesk.com/hc/en-us/articles/15195960217357-What-is-matriculation

California Department of Education. (n.d.). *DataQuest.*, California Department of Education. https://dq.cde.ca.gov/dataquest/

California Department of Education. (n.d.). *Guideposts for success*. Retrieved October 25, 2024, https://www.cde.ca.gov/sp/se/st/guidepostsforsuccess.asp

California Department of Education. (n.d.). *Secondary Transition Planning*. Retrieved February 4, 2025). https://www.cde.ca.gov/sp/se/st/

Carroll, J. M., Pattison, E., Muller, C., & Sutton, A. (2020). Barriers to bachelor's degree completion among college students with a disability. *Sociological Perspectives*, *63*(5), 809–832. DOI: 10.1177/0731121420908896 PMID: 33795909

Casali, N., Meneghetti, C., Tinti, C., Re, A., Sini, B., Passolunghi, M., Valenti, A., Montesano, L., Pellegrino, G., & Carretti, B. (2023). Academic achievement and satisfaction among university students with specific learning disabilities: The roles of soft skills and study-related factors. *Journal of Learning Disabilities*, *222194221150786*. Advance online publication. DOI: 10.1177/00222194221150786 PMID: 36790042

Cheng, L., & Shaewitz, D. (2021). The 2021 youth transition report: Outcomes for youth and young adults with disabilities. Institute for Educational Leadership., https://iel.org/the-2021-youth-transition-report-outcomes-for-youth-and-young-adults-with-disabilities/, Retrieved August 1, 2023, from.

Chronopoulou, E. (2024). Transition skills of youths with disabilities: The impact of individual characteristics, social support and self-esteem. *Journal of Research in Special Educational Needs*, *24*(4), 1060–1072. Advance online publication. DOI: 10.1111/1471-3802.12690

College Futures Foundation. (2015, June). Defining Persistence and Retention https://collegefutures.org/wp-content/uploads/2015/11/defining-foundation-persistence-and-retention.pdf

Connor, D. J., Cavendish, W., Hallaran, A., & Olander, L. (2020). "I'm bright enough to do it, even though sometimes I feel I can't do it": Perspectives of high school students with learning disabilities about existing supports to achieve graduation. *Disability Studies Quarterly*, *40*(2). Advance online publication. DOI: 10.18061/dsq.v40i2.6665

Davis, L. (2021). *Building agency: An assets-based approach to cultivating solidarity with Black students with dis/abilities*https://www.proquest.com/openview/3bd4b68df64dfcd9b3f97b83d87fa6dd/1?pq-origsite=gscholar&cbl=18750&diss=y

Davis, M. T., Cumming, I. K., Park, N. M., & Sheperis, C. J. (2021). Project SEARCH: Analysis of employment outcomes for students with disabilities across two districts. *Journal of Rehabilitation*, *87*(4), 48–57. https://www.researchgate.net/publication/362906313_Davis_M_T_Cumming_I_K_Park_N_M_Sheperis_C_J_2021_Project_SEARCH_Analysis_of_employment_outcomes_for_students_with_disabilities_across_two_school_districts_Journal_of_Rehabilitation_874_48-57

Davis, M. T., & Garfield, T. A. (2021). Transition to adulthood: Preparing students with specific learning disabilities. *Kappa Delta Pi Record*, *57*(2), 64–69. DOI: 10.1080/00228958.2021.1890440

Davis, M. T., & Southward, J. D. (2021). Summary of performance portfolio: Supporting postsecondary transition for students with learning disabilities. *The Clearing House: A Journal of Educational Strategies, Issues and Ideas*, *94*(4), 188–195. DOI: 10.1080/00098655.2021.1891016

DeVilbiss, S. E. (2014). *The transition experience: Understanding the transition from high school to college for conditionally-admitted students using the lens of Schlossberg's transition theory* (Order No. 3618529). Available from ProQuest One Academic. (1530416777). https://www.proquest.com/dissertations-theses/transition-experience-understanding-high-school/docview/1530416777/se-2

Duggan, M. F. (2023). *Struggling to maintain academic success: A phenomenological study of students with disabilities' experiences with limited and/or reduced supports in higher education* (Order No. 30249473). Available from Dissertations & Theses @ Northcentral University; ProQuest One Academic. (2788862270). https://research.ebsco.com/linkprocessor/plink?id=20283c5a-728d-3f83-bbc8-c2f1cfd16240

Education Data Partnership. (2025). *Ed data: Education data partnership.*https://www.ed-data.org/

Ervin, A. (2023, August 12). *How do mentoring relationships affect the college enrollment of first-generation college students?* The chronicle of evidence-based mentoring. Retrieved October 27, 2024, https://www.evidencebasedmentoring.org/how-do-mentoring-relationships-affect-the-college-enrollment-of-first-generation-college-students/

Evans, N. J., Forney, D. S., & Guido-DiBrito, F. (1998). *Student development in college: Theory, research, and practice.* Jossey-Bass. https://eric.ed.gov/?id=ED419456

Feeney, D. M. (2022). Positive self-talk: An emerging learning strategy for students with learning disabilities. *Intervention in School and Clinic, 57*(3), 45–49. DOI: 10.1177/10534512211014881

Flanagan, J. C. (1954). The critical incident technique. *Psychological Bulletin, 51*(4), 327–358. https://www.apa.org/pubs/databases/psycinfo/cit-article.pdf. DOI: 10.1037/h0061470 PMID: 13177800

Freeman, J. A., & Kirksey, J. (2023). Linking IEP status to parental involvement for high school students of first-generation and native-born families. *Exceptional Children, 89*(2), 197–215. DOI: 10.1177/00144029221108402

Frey, B. B. (2018). The SAGE encyclopedia of educational research, measurement, and evaluation. *Sage (Atlanta, Ga.).* Advance online publication. DOI: 10.4135/9781506326139

Gartland, D., & Strosnider, R. (2023). Considerations for transition from high school to postsecondary education. *Learning Disability Quarterly, 46*(3), 230–242. DOI: 10.1177/07319487221111099

Gerali, J., & Neill, L. (2022). *Students With Disabilities Within Academia: Barriers*. Obstacles, Adversity, and Empathy – A Call for Educators to Recognize Their Knowledge and Perception of Disability Identity., DOI: 10.4018/978-1-7998-9746-0.ch011

Hallahan, D. P., Kauffman, J. M., & Pullen, P. C. (2021). *Exceptional learners: An introduction to special education* (14th ed.). Pearson., https://www.pearson.com/en-us/pearsonplus/p/9780136940876

Individuals with Disabilities Education Act, 20 U.S.C. § 1401(3)(A) (2004). https://sites.ed.gov/idea/statute-chapter-33/subchapter-i/1401/3/A

Johnson, D. R., Thurlow, M. L., Wu, Y.-C., Xueqin, Q., Davenport, E., & Matthais, C. (2022). Youth and parent participation in transition planning in the USA: Findings from the national longitudinal transition study 2012 (NLTS 2012). *Journal of International Special Needs Education, 25*(2), 61–73. DOI: 10.9782/JISNE-D-21-00009

Jones, M. H., James, M. T., & Johnson, C. (2023). Social status, popularity goals and students with learning disabilities: An initial investigation. *British Journal of Special Education, 50*(1), 83–103. DOI: 10.1111/1467-8578.12445

Juarez, S. W., Chaparro, G., Rios-Aguilar, C., & Guarneros, N. (2023). Parental expectations of postsecondary outcomes for diverse students with learning disabilities: A funds of knowledge and social capital approach to transition planning. *Journal of Latinos and Education*, *22*(1), 41–56. DOI: 10.1080/15348431.2019.1689136

Judicial Council of California. (2016). *Special education rights for children and families.* Center for Families, Children & the Courts. Retrieved May 21, 2023. https://www.courts.ca.gov/documents/SPED.pdf

Killam, W. K., & Degges-White, S. (2017). *College student development: Applying theory to practice on the diverse campus*. Springer Publishing Company. https://books.google.com/books?hl=en&lr=&id=zpbvDQAAQBAJ&oi=fnd&pg=PP1&ots=QPObFE8Q9B&sig=H6Qrp1Gi1cv-1MDZ15OhlS2ZDZs#v=onepage&q&f=false

Koca, D. B., Sart, Z. H., Sakız, H., & Albayrak-Kaymak, D. (2023). Self-advocacy experiences of students with specific learning disabilities. *Social Psychology of Education*, *26*(3), 709–733. DOI: 10.1007/s11218-023-09771-5

Lefler, E., Alacha, H., Weed, B., Reeble, C., & Garner, A. (2023). Professor and peer perceptions of requests for academic accommodations in college: An examination of ADHD and specific learning disorder. *Psychological Reports, 0*(0), 1–28. 332941231156821. DOI: 10.1177/00332941231156821

Lombardi, A., Rifenbark, G., Rogers, H., Swaminathan, H., Taconet, A., Mazzotti, V., Morningstar, M., Wu, R., & Langdon, S. (2023). Establishing construct validity of a measure of adolescent perceptions of college and career readiness. *Career Development and Transition for Exceptional Individuals*, *46*(1), 4–14. DOI: 10.1177/21651434221081229

Mana, A., Saka, N., Dahan, O., Ben-Simon, A., & Margalit, M. (2022). Implicit theories, social support, and hope as serial mediators for predicting academic self-efficacy among higher education students. *Learning Disability Quarterly*, *45*(2), 85–95. DOI: 10.1177/0731948720918821

Mawila, D. (2023). The mediation role of caregivers and context on individual factors in enabling resilience among learners with specific learning disability. *Interchange: A Quarterly. Interchange*, *54*(1), 81–94. DOI: 10.1007/s10780-022-09484-2

McCabe, G. (2024). *What is GPA? Understanding its calculation, importance and scales.* THE - Times Higher Education. https://www.timeshighereducation.com/student/advice/what-gpa

McGahee, D. W., King-Sears, M. E., & Evmenova, A. S. (2021). High school students with learning disabilities: Requesting accommodations in role-play. *Learning Disabilities Research & Practice*, *36*(2), 82–95. DOI: 10.1111/ldrp.12243

McGregor, K. K., Langenfeld, N., Van Horne, S., Oleson, J., Anson, M., & Jacobson, W. (2016). The university experiences of students with learning disabilities. *Learning Disabilities Research & Practice*, *31*(2), 90–102. DOI: 10.1111/ldrp.12102 PMID: 27667902

Munsell, E. G. S., & Schwartz, A. E. (2021). Youth experiences of the IDEA-mandated transition planning process: A metasynthesis of youth voices. *Review Journal of Autism and Developmental Disorders*, •••, 1–14. DOI: 10.1007/s40489-021-00268-5

National Association of Special Education Teachers. (2023). *Introduction to learning disabilities.* NASET. https://www.naset.org/publications/ld-report/introduction-to-learning-disabilities

Newman, L. A., Madaus, J. W., Lalor, A. R., & Javitz, H. S. (2021). Effect of accessing supports on higher education persistence of students with disabilities. *Journal of Diversity in Higher Education, 14*(3), 353–363. DOI: 10.1037/dhe0000170

O'Konek, J. J. (2023). "I have no voice. May I please borrow yours?" An overture for expanding children's access to intellectual and developmental disability services in the state of North Dakota. *North Dakota Law Review, 98*(1), 1–49. https://law.und.edu/_files/docs/ndlr/pdf/issues/98/1/98ndlr1.pdf

Peña-Villegas, M. (2024). *Parent/Guardians' Perceptions of Postsecondary Transition and Matriculation of Students With Learning Disabilities: A Qualitative Case Study* (Order No. 31769870). Available from Dissertations & Theses @ National University; ProQuest Dissertations & Theses Global. (3174624439). https://go.openathens.net/redirector/nu.edu?url=https://www.proquest.com/dissertations-theses/parent-guardians-perceptions-postsecondary/docview/3174624439/se-2

Peters, J. (2011). *Transition Skills of First-Year College Students with Learning Disabilities* (Order No. 3489342). Available from ProQuest One Academic. (915692476). https://www.proquest.com/docview/915692476

Postsecondary National Policy Institute. (2023, November). *Students with disabilities.* https://pnpi.org/wp-content/uploads/2023/11/StudentswithDisabilities-Nov-2023.pdf

Privitera, G. J., & Ahlgrim-Delzell, L. (2018). *Research methods for education.* Sage. https://collegepublishing.sagepub.com/products/research-methods-for-education-1-245749

Rodriguez, L. R. (2023). Exploring Self-Awareness of Self-Advocacy Skills Among Senior High School Students with Mild to Moderate Learning Disabilities. *Southern New Hampshire University.*https://hdl.handle.net/10474/3729

Sargent, A. G., & Schlossberg, N. K. (1988). Managing adult transitions. *Training and Development Journal, 42*(12), 58. https://eric.ed.gov/?id=EJ381396

Schechter, J. (2018). University students with disabilities: Factors that contribute to their self-predicted likelihood of graduation. *Journal of Postsecondary Education and Disability, 31*(4), 335–349. https://eric.ed.gov/?id=EJ1214186

Schlossberg, N. K. (1981). A model for analyzing human adaptation to transition. *The Counseling Psychologist, 9*(2), 2–18. https://journals.sagepub.com/doi/10.1177/001100008100900202. DOI: 10.1177/001100008100900202

Schlossberg, N. K. (2011). The challenge of change: The transition model and its applications. *Journal of Employment Counseling, 48*(4), 159–162. DOI: 10.1002/j.2161-1920.2011.tb01102.x

Schlossberg, N. K., Lynch, A. Q., & Chickering, A. W. (1989). *Improving higher education environments for adults: Responsive programs and services from entry to departure.* Jossey-Bass. https://eric.ed.gov/?id=ED304057

Schlossberg, N. K., Waters, E. B., & Goodman, J. (1995). *Counseling adults in transition: Linking practice with theory* (2nd ed.). Springer., https://www.abebooks.com/9780826142337/Counseling-Adults-Transition-Linking-Practice-0826142338/plp

Scruggs, S., Dong, S., Ducatt, S., Mitchell, J., & Davis, W. (2021). Impact of high school transition and accommodation experience on student involvement in college. *Journal of Postsecondary Education and Disability*, *34*(2), 179–190. https://files.eric.ed.gov/fulltext/EJ1319194.pdf

Seaman, S. (2024). What Is Our Definition of Post-Secondary Success? *Association of Washington School Principals.* https://awsp.org/connect/blog/blog-detail/awsp-blog/2024/03/14/what-is-our-definition-of-post-secondary-success#:~:text=Post%2Dsecondary%20success%20should%20be,training%2C%20college%2C%20or%20university

Singh, D. K. (2019). Educational rights of college students with disabilities. *College Student Journal*, *53*(2), 243–251. https://eric.ed.gov/?id=EJ1315470

Southward, J. D., & Davis, M. T. (2020). Summary of performance: Bridging the transition from high school to postsecondary education for students with SLD. *Preventing School Failure*, *64*(4), 316–325. DOI: 10.1080/1045988X.2020.1769012

Stake, R. E. (1995). *The art of case study research.* Sage. https://archive.org/details/artofcasestudyre0000stak

Sun, S.-J., & Ho, W.-S. (2023). A follow-up study on the influence of personal, family, and school factors on learning outcomes of students with disabilities in senior high school. *Behavioral Sciences (Basel, Switzerland)*, *13*(7), 554. Advance online publication. DOI: 10.3390/bs13070554 PMID: 37504001

Talbert, L., & Fleming, G. (2023) Transition Planning for College. *Smart Kids with Learning Disabilities.* https://www.smartkidswithld.org/getting-help/know-your-childs-rights/transition-planning-for-college/

Taylor, R. L., Smiley, L. R., & Richards, S. B. (2014). *Exceptional students: Preparing teachers for the 21st Century* (2nd ed.). McGraw Hill Higher Education., https://www.abebooks.com/9780078110504/Exceptional-Students-Preparing-Teachers-21st-0078110505/plp

Thapa, A., Ice, M., Ramdass, J. V., & Cohen, J. (2023). Factors that contribute to post high-school success of young adults with learning disabilities. *Physical Educator*, *13*(1), 26–43. DOI: 10.18666/LDMJ-2022-V27-I2-11473

Trainor, A., Newman, L., & Romano, L. (2023). Contextualizing school engagement during transition for students receiving special education and English learner services. *The Journal of Special Education*, *57*(1), 24–35. DOI: 10.1177/00224669221107089

United States Department of Education. (2020, August). *A transition guide to postsecondary education and employment for students and youth with disabilities.* Office of Special Education and Rehabilitation Services. Retrieved March 18, 2023. https://sites.ed.gov/idea/files/postsecondary-transition-guide-august-2020.pdf

United States Department of Education. (n.d.). *About IDE*A. https://sites.ed.gov/idea/about-idea/

United States Department of Education. (n.d.). *Protecting students with disabilities: Frequently asked questions about Section 504 and the education of children with disabilities*. https://www2.ed.gov

United States Department of Labor Statistics. (2023, February 23). *Persons with a disability: Labor force characteristics – 2022*.https://www.bls.gov/news.release/pdf/disabl.pdf

University of California. (n.d.). *Early Academic Outreach Program (EAOP)*.The Regents of the University of California. https://eaop.universityofcalifornia.edu/

University of California. Berkeley. (n.d.). Undergraduate Education https://guide.berkeley.edu/undergraduate/education/

Walstra, R., & Chukwuma, E. (2023). Inclusion of disability within the spectrum of diversity and the implications for accounting education. *Issues in Accounting Education*, *38*(1), 149–162. DOI: 10.2308/ISSUES-2021-007

Wilburn, M. (2023). *Promoting Retention and Success of Students with Specific Learning Disabilities at the Collegiate Level: A qualitative Case Study on Student Perceptions*. Indiana State University., https://scholars.indianastate.edu/cgi/viewcontent.cgi?article=3040&context=etds

Williams, S. C., Militello, M., & Majewski, D. (2020). Sorting out important elements for successful college transition and completion for students with learning differences. *Preventing School Failure*, *64*(4), 326–338. https://www.tandfonline.com/doi/full/10.1080/1045988X.2020.1776671. DOI: 10.1080/1045988X.2020.1776671

Wu, Y.-C., Thurlow, M., & Johnson, D. (2023). A national view of transition planning participation and post-school goals for English learners with disabilities. *Exceptionality*, *31*(1), 18–35. https://www.tandfonline.com/doi/full/10.1080/09362835.2021.1938060. DOI: 10.1080/09362835.2021.1938060

Yeager, K. H., & Deardorff, M. E. (2022). Strengths-based transition planning: A positive approach for students with learning disabilities. *Intervention in School and Clinic*, *58*(1), 3–8. DOI: 10.1177/10534512211047594

Yin, R. K. (2017). *Case study research and applications: Design and methods*. Sage. https://collegepublishing.sagepub.com/products/case-study-research-and-applications-6-250150

Zeng, W., Ju, S., & Hord, C. (2023). Parental influences on student self-determination: Perspectives of college students with learning disabilities. *Learning Disability Quarterly*, *46*(3), 180–190. DOI: 10.1177/07319487221107890

Zeng, W., Ju, S., & Zhang, D. (2024). The relationships among parent involvement, student self-determination, and postsecondary education enrollment for students with learning disabilities. *Journal of Disability Policy Studies*, *35*(1), 3–13. DOI: 10.1177/10442073221130748

Zilvinskis, J. (2022). The Mediating Effects of Student Services on Engagement among First-Generation and Transfer Students Who Use Disability Services at Community Colleges. *Community College Review*, *50*(1), 71–95. DOI: 10.1177/00915521211047675

ADDITIONAL READING

Cavendish, W., Connor, D. J., Olander, L., & Hallaran, A. (2020). Preparing for their future: Perspectives of high school students with learning disabilities about transition planning. *Exceptionality*, *28*(5), 349–361. DOI: 10.1080/09362835.2019.1625777

Clifton, D. O., Anderson, E. C., & Schreiner, L. A. (2006). *StrengthsQuest: Discover and develop your strengths in academics, career, and beyond* (2nd ed.). Gallup Press.

Daffner, M., DuPaul, G., Anastopoulos, A., & Weyandt, L. (2022). From orientation to graduation: Predictors of academic success for freshmen with ADHD. *Journal of Postsecondary Education and Disability*, *35*(2), 113–130. https://files.eric.ed.gov/fulltext/EJ1364187.pdf

Dangoisse, F., De Clercq, M., Van Meenen, F., Chartier, L., & Nils, F. (2020). When disability becomes ability to navigate the transition to higher education: A comparison of students with and without disabilities. *European Journal of Special Needs Education*, *35*(4), 513–528. DOI: 10.1080/08856257.2019.1708642

Kuriakose, A., & Amaresha, A. C. (2023). Experiences of Students with Learning Disabilities in Higher Education: A Scoping Review. *Indian Journal of Psychological Medicine*, *46*(3), 196–207. DOI: 10.1177/02537176231200912 PMID: 38699764

Landmark, L. J., Roberts, E. L., & Zhang, D. (2013). Educators' Beliefs and Practices About Parent Involvement in Transition Planning. *Career Development and Transition for Exceptional Individuals*, *36*(2), 114–123. DOI: 10.1177/2165143412463047

Mello, M. P., Burke, M. M., Taylor, J. L., Urbano, R., & Hodapp, R. M. (2021). Characteristics of students with disabilities who do and do not receive transition services. *The Journal of Special Education*, *54*(4), 251–259. DOI: 10.1177/0022466920925437

Rossetti, Z., Burke, M. M., Hughes, O., Schraml-Block, K., Rivera, J. I., Rios, K., & Lee, J. D. (2021). Parent perceptions of the advocacy expectation in special education. *Exceptional Children*, *87*(4), 438–457. DOI: 10.1177/0014402921994095

Rowe, D., Mazzotti, V., Fowler, C., Test, D., Mitchell, V., Clark, K. A., & Dean, C. (2021). Updating the secondary transition research base: Evidence-and research-based practices in functional skills. *Career Development and Transition for Exceptional Individuals*, *44*(1), 28–46. DOI: 10.1177/2165143420958674

Tomasello, J., & Brand, B. (2018). *How ESSA and IDEA can support college and career readiness for students with disabilities: Considerations for states.* College and Career Readiness and Success Center. https://eric.ed.gov/?id=ED586419

KEY TERMS AND DEFINITIONS

Section 504 Plan: A 504 plan is tailored for students with learning disabilities, removes barriers to learning, and does not require intensive special education support but provides necessary accommodations (United States Department of Education, n.d.).

Degree Completion: Degree Completion is achieved when students meet the requirements that must be fulfilled: course, unit, grade point, and amount of upper-division work to earn their degree (University of California, Berkeley, n.d.).

Disability: The federal government of the United States under the IDEA defines a disability as: "A child with a disability means a child with intellectual disabilities, hearing impairments (including deafness), speech or language impairments, visual impairments (including blindness), serious emotional disturbance… orthopedic impairments, autism, traumatic brain injury, other health impairments, or specific learning disabilities; and who, by reason thereof, needs special education and related services (Individual with Disabilities Education Act, 2004, § 1401(3)(A)).

Grade Point Average (GPA): An indication of a student's academic achievement at a college or university, calculated as the total number of grade points received over a given period divided by the total number of credits awarded. (McCabe, 2024).

Individual Educational Plan (IEP): If a student is considered eligible for special education services under the Individuals with Disabilities Education Act (IDEA), an Individualized Education Program (IEP) meeting will be held to develop a customized plan. The IEP is the most prominent and significant component of IDEA; it describes the student's educational needs and the services that will be given to meet the student's needs. This plan is created collaboratively by parents, students, and other team members to ensure the student receives appropriate support (Judicial Council of California, 2021).

Individuals With Disabilities Education Act (IDEA): Individuals with Disabilities Act (IDEA) ensures that eligible students with disabilities receive a public education that is appropriate and free while ensuring that these students receive special education and related services (United States Department of Education, n.d.).

Learning Disability (LD): A learning disability is a neurological condition that affects the brain's ability to store, receive, respond, or process information. The disability may impact skills such as listening, speaking, writing, reading, and reasoning (Hallahan et al., 2021). Taylor et al. (2014) further defined a learning disability as difficulty with learning not stemming from environmental disadvantages or sensory deficits. Taylor et al. (2014) additionally state that the Council for Learning Disabilities and the International Reading Association indicated that a learning disability does not stem from other extrinsic causes or incapacities but may coexist.

Matriculation: Matriculation is a process that increases student access to colleges by promoting and sustaining students' efforts to be successful as they pursue their postsecondary educational endeavors (California Community Colleges Chancellor's Office [CCCCO], 2020).

Persistence: Persistence is a student's continuous fall-to-fall enrollment; a student has demonstrated persistence if they successfully matriculated and completed the fall term of the following year (College Futures Foundation, 2015).

Postsecondary Academic Success: Postsecondary success is the achievement of desired outcomes of students following the completion of high school, such as college, university, or vocational training (Seaman, 2024).

Specific Learning Disabilities: Specific learning disability (SLD) is a term used to describe specific learning problems that can cause an individual to have difficulty using certain skills and learning, mainly in the areas of writing, reading, listening, reasoning, speaking, and doing math (National Association of Special Education Teachers, 2023).

Transition: Transition is moving from school to adult life, including training, education, employment, and independent living (California Department of Education, n.d.).

Transition Plan: A transition plan is developed in preparation for the student's adult life by members of the planning team based on the student's needs, abilities, and available services in preparation for the student's "meaningful postsecondary education and/or thriving career" (United States Department of Education, 2020, p. 1). The plan specifies the transition services that includes the course of study and incorporate measurable postsecondary goals based on the student's transition assessment that relates to education, training, employment, and independent living skills (Johnson et al., 2022).

Section 4
Supporting Multilingual Learners, Migrant Students, Newcomer Students, and Refugee Students of Forced Diasporas Living With Trauma

Chapter 15
Frameworks for Multi-Tiered Systems of Support for Trauma-Informed Educational Settings:
Supporting Multilingual Learners

Brandy Shooks
https://orcid.org/0009-0009-5162-1409
Western Michigan University, USA

ABSTRACT

Dr. Brandy Shooks presents a comprehensive exploration of how trauma-informed practices, when integrated with Multi-Tiered Systems of Support (MTSS), can effectively address the unique challenges faced by multilingual learners (MLs). These students often navigate intersecting barriers, including trauma, language acquisition, cultural adjustment, and systemic inequities, making a multifaceted approach essential for fostering resilience and academic success. This chapter delves into the critical need for trauma-informed educational settings that prioritize safety, trust, and collaboration while providing MLs with the tools to thrive academically and emotionally.

1. INTRODUCTION

Trauma-informed educational practices have become essential in addressing the complex challenges faced by multilingual learners (MLs), especially those who have experienced trauma. These students often encounter additional barriers, including language acquisition, cultural adjustment, and the psychological effects of trauma. As educators work to create inclusive and supportive environments, integrating Multi-Tiered Systems of Support (MTSS) with trauma-informed principles is crucial for fostering resilience and academic success among MLs.

This chapter explores a comprehensive approach to supporting MLs through a trauma-informed lens, emphasizing the importance of culturally responsive teaching, structured routines, and emotional regulation strategies. Drawing from insights in *Atomic Habits* by James Clear, *Breath* by James Nestor, *Think Like a Monk* by Jay Shetty and *Atlas of the Heart* by Brene Brown; this work underscores the transformative power of routines, mindfulness, and emotional intelligence in both students and edu-

DOI: 10.4018/979-8-3693-9020-7.ch015

cators. Heather Forbes' *Help for Billy* also provides a framework for addressing behavioral challenges with empathy and understanding. At the same time, the SIOP model offers structured methodologies for supporting language development in trauma-informed settings.

A current study by Dr. Jennifer Foster, Dr. Heidi Cate, and Dr. Brandy Shooks reinforces the centrality of relationships in trauma-informed education. Their study highlights how teacher-student connections and strategies emphasizing safety and resilience can lead to thriving educational communities (Foster et al., under review). Furthermore, trauma-informed practices enhance teacher self-efficacy, empowering educators with tools to navigate challenges, manage classroom dynamics, and foster a holistic sense of well-being for themselves and their students (Shooks, 2020).

Through integrating evidence-based strategies, professional development, and a commitment to empathy, educators can transform classrooms into spaces where multilingual learners overcome barriers and achieve their full potential. This chapter offers a roadmap for creating such environments, blending academic success with emotional and social growth for students and teachers.

2. UNDERSTANDING TRAUMA IN MULTILINGUAL LEARNERS

Trauma refers to the psychological and emotional response to an event or series of deeply distressing or disturbing events. For children and adolescents, trauma can disrupt brain development, impair cognitive functioning, and hinder the ability to form healthy relationships (Van der Kolk, 2014). Multilingual learners may experience various forms of trauma, including but not limited to:

- **Migration and Refugee Experiences:** Exposure to violence, persecution, or natural disasters in their home countries.
- **Family Separation:** Separation from family members during migration or due to deportation.
- **Acculturation Stress:** Challenges adapting to a new cultural environment and balancing cultural identities.
- **Discrimination:** Experiences of racism, xenophobia, or linguistic discrimination in their new communities.

The Impact of Trauma on Language Acquisition and Learning

Trauma can significantly impact language development and academic achievement. Research indicates that trauma affects memory, attention, and executive functioning—all essential components of language learning (Souers & Hall, 2016). Additionally, trauma may lead to behavioral challenges, withdrawal, or heightened anxiety, which can further hinder a student's ability to engage in the classroom.

The Unique Challenges of Trauma for Multilingual Learners

Trauma significantly impacts multilingual learners (MLs) in unique ways, as their experiences often encompass layers of adversity beyond those faced by their monolingual peers. For many MLs, past traumatic experiences are compounded by the challenges of moving to a new country, learning a new language, and navigating an unfamiliar culture. These challenges can create additional struggles that educators must address to support these students effectively.

Past Traumatic Experiences

Many MLs have experienced trauma related to displacement, war, persecution, or natural disasters in their home countries. Such experiences can leave deep psychological scars, including anxiety, hypervigilance, and difficulty trusting others. These preexisting traumas can hinder a student's ability to focus, engage, and form relationships within the classroom.

Challenges of Relocation

The process of moving to a new country itself can be a source of trauma. Students often face separation from loved ones, uncertainty about the future, and the stress of adapting to a new environment. These stressors can manifest as withdrawal, aggression, or disengagement in the classroom. Additionally, the logistical and emotional strain of starting over in a foreign place can exacerbate feelings of isolation and loss.

Learning a New Language and Culture

Acquiring a new language while learning academic content presents a dual challenge for MLs. The pressure to keep up with peers in both language and academics can lead to feelings of inadequacy and frustration. Moreover, cultural differences can create misunderstandings or feelings of alienation. For instance, MLs may struggle to interpret social norms, classroom expectations, or teacher-student dynamics, adding another layer of complexity to their educational experience.

Conscious and Unconscious Bias

Bias, whether explicit or implicit, further compounds the struggles of MLs. Conscious bias may manifest as discrimination or low expectations for MLs' academic and social success. Unconscious bias, though less overt, can influence how teachers and peers perceive and interact with these students. For example, teachers may inadvertently overlook MLs' contributions or assume their language difficulties equate to lower intelligence. Such biases can erode students' confidence and reinforce feelings of exclusion.

3. MULTI-TIERED SYSTEMS OF SUPPORT (MTSS) OVERVIEW

MTSS is a framework designed to provide varying levels of support to students based on their needs. *Tier 1: Universal supports for all students, including high-quality instruction and positive school climate initiatives. Tier 2: Targeted interventions for students who require additional support. Tier 3: Intensive, individualized interventions for students with the most significant needs.* In trauma-informed settings, MTSS integrates principles of safety, trustworthiness, collaboration, empowerment, and cultural responsiveness to address the unique challenges faced by students who have experienced trauma (SAMHSA, 2014).

Tier 1: Universal Supports for Multilingual Learners

Culturally Responsive Teaching

Culturally responsive teaching is foundational to Tier 1 supports. Educators should create inclusive classroom environments that celebrate linguistic and cultural diversity. Strategies include:

- Incorporating Multilingual Materials: Using texts and resources in students' home languages alongside English materials.
- Valuing Students' Backgrounds: Encouraging students to share their cultural traditions and stories.
- Professional Development: Training educators to recognize and address implicit biases and microaggressions.

Social-Emotional Learning (SEL)

Social-emotional learning programs that are trauma-informed and culturally adapted can help MLs build resilience and self-regulation skills. Examples include:

- Mindfulness Practices: Teaching mindfulness to reduce stress and enhance focus.
- Peer Support Systems: Establishing buddy systems that pair MLs with empathetic peers.
- SEL Curriculum Integration: Embedding SEL principles into daily instruction.

Language-Rich Environments

Creating language-rich environments supports both language development and emotional well-being. Teachers can:

- Use visuals, gestures, and bilingual supports to enhance comprehension.
- Foster collaborative learning opportunities where students practice language skills in a supportive context.
- Encourage translanguaging practices, allowing students to use their full linguistic repertoire.

Tier 2: Targeted Interventions for Multilingual Learners

Small Group Interventions

Small group interventions provide MLs with targeted support to address specific academic or emotional challenges. Examples include:

- Language Development Groups: Focused sessions to enhance vocabulary, grammar, and conversational skills.
- Trauma-Informed Counseling Groups: Facilitated by school counselors trained in cultural competency.

Data-Driven Decision Making

Educators should use data to identify MLs who need additional support. Tools include:

- Behavioral Observations: Monitoring changes in behavior that may indicate trauma-related challenges.
- Language Proficiency Assessments: Identifying gaps in language skills that may hinder academic progress.

Collaborative Problem-Solving Teams

Interdisciplinary teams, including teachers, counselors, and language specialists, can collaboratively design interventions tailored to the needs of MLs. Regular meetings and progress monitoring are essential.

Tier 3: Intensive Interventions for Multilingual Learners

Individualized Trauma Support Plans

For MLs with significant trauma-related needs, individualized support plans should integrate academic, social-emotional, and linguistic goals. Key components include:

- Trauma-Informed Therapy: Access to licensed mental health professionals with expertise in trauma and cultural competency.
- One-on-One Tutoring: Intensive academic support tailored to the student's language and learning needs.
- Family Engagement: Collaborating with families to ensure holistic support.

Community Partnerships

Schools can partner with community organizations to provide additional resources, such as:

- Translation and Interpretation Services: Ensuring families can fully participate in their child's education.
- Immigrant and Refugee Support Programs: Legal assistance, housing support, and other essential services.

4. CASE STUDIES

The following case studies are based on fictitious students but provide realistic examples of students' barriers and how educators can support them.

Case Study 1: Supporting a Refugee Student

Amira, a 12-year-old refugee from Syria, arrived at a U.S. middle school with limited English proficiency and a history of trauma stemming from her experiences in a war-torn region. Her school implemented a multi-tiered system of support to address her unique needs.

- Tier 1: Teachers incorporated culturally relevant materials and provided Amira with a peer buddy who spoke Arabic to help her navigate her new environment. Social-emotional learning activities, including mindfulness practices, were integrated into classroom routines to support all students.
- Tier 2: Amira participated in small group interventions focused on language development and trauma-informed counseling sessions facilitated by a bilingual school counselor.
- Tier 3: An individualized trauma support plan was developed, including weekly one-on-one therapy sessions and intensive tutoring to help her catch up academically. The school also engaged Amira's family, providing translation services and connecting them to community resources.

Outcomes: These interventions enabled Amira to make significant progress academically and socially, demonstrating the effectiveness of a trauma-informed MTSS framework.

Case Study 2: Addressing Discrimination in the Classroom

Manuel, a high school student from Guatemala, faced bullying from peers due to his accent and limited English proficiency. This led to a decline in his academic performance and increased social withdrawal.

- Tier 1: The school implemented a cultural competency training program for staff and students to foster an inclusive environment. Classroom activities celebrated linguistic diversity, encouraging students to share their cultural backgrounds.
- Tier 2: Manuel joined a small group focused on building confidence in speaking English. He also participated in peer mentorship programs designed to create supportive relationships.
- Tier 3: A school counselor provided Manuel with trauma-informed counseling to address the emotional impact of bullying. The school worked with his family to ensure ongoing communication and support.

Outcomes: Manuel's sense of belonging improved through these efforts, and his academic performance rebounded. This case underscores the importance of addressing discrimination within a trauma-informed MTSS framework.

Case Study 3: Supporting a Student from a War-torn Country

Khalid, a 15-year-old student from Yemen, arrived at a U.S. high school with limited English proficiency and significant gaps in his education due to the prolonged conflict in his home country. He exhibited signs of trauma, including difficulty concentrating, hypervigilance, and withdrawal from peers.

- *Tier 1: Universal Supports: Teachers implemented culturally responsive teaching practices, incorporating global perspectives and materials that reflected Khalid's cultural background. A peer mentor who spoke Arabic was assigned to help Khalid acclimate to the school environment and build connections with classmates. The school also integrated social-emotional learning (SEL) activities, including stress management techniques, to support Khalid and his peers.*

- *Tier 2: Targeted Interventions: Khalid joined small group language development sessions tailored to multilingual learners. These sessions emphasized conversational English and academic vocabulary, helping Khalid build confidence in both social and classroom interactions. He also participated in group counseling led by a bilingual school counselor, where students shared experiences and developed coping strategies.*
- *Tier 3: Intensive Individualized Support: Recognizing Khalid's specific needs, the school developed an individualized support plan. Khalid received weekly one-on-one therapy sessions with a trauma-informed counselor to address his emotional well-being and develop strategies for managing anxiety and triggers. Additionally, Khalid attended intensive academic tutoring sessions to close gaps in his education, focusing on foundational skills in math and literacy. The school also provided translation services and family outreach, connecting Khalid's parents to community resources for housing, healthcare, and legal assistance.*

Outcomes: With this multi-tiered support system (MTSS), Khalid began to thrive academically and socially. His English proficiency improved significantly, enabling him to participate in class discussions and collaborate with peers actively. Khalid built friendships through extracurricular activities, joining the school's soccer team, where he found a sense of belonging. Over time, Khalid demonstrated increased emotional resilience, better concentration, and a renewed enthusiasm for learning, highlighting the importance of a trauma-informed approach to supporting students from war-torn countries.

Summary

The case studies of Amira, Manuel, and Khalid provide fictional examples that illustrate how trauma-informed and culturally responsive educational strategies can support multilingual learners facing significant challenges. These students, though not based on real individuals, reflect the common experiences of multilingual learners who have been displaced due to war, trauma, or discrimination. Each case study is designed to showcase the practical application of evidence-based frameworks, such as Multi-Tiered Systems of Support (MTSS), social-emotional learning (SEL), and culturally responsive teaching.

Amira's story demonstrates the importance of integrating trauma-informed practices into academic and social settings to support refugee students in overcoming emotional and educational barriers. Manuel's case highlights the role of addressing discrimination through community-building and targeted interventions. Khalid's narrative emphasizes the power of individualized trauma support plans to address the complex needs of students from war-torn regions.

Although these stories are fictional, they are grounded in research and modeled after real-world examples of challenges multilingual learners face. Studies on trauma-informed practices, the effectiveness of MTSS frameworks, and strategies for supporting multilingual learners provided the foundation for these narratives. These case studies serve as valuable tools for educators and policymakers, offering insights into the potential impact of thoughtful, inclusive, and evidence-based educational practices on vulnerable student populations.

5. TRAUMA-INFORMED EDUCATIONAL PRACTICES

The SIOP Method and Multilingual Learners Who Have Experienced Trauma

The Sheltered Instruction Observation Protocol (SIOP) method is a research-based framework designed to support English learners in developing academic language proficiency while accessing grade-level content. Its structured approach provides a supportive environment that can significantly benefit multilingual learners (MLs) who have experienced trauma. The SIOP model has eight interrelated components (Echevarria, Jana, et al., 2017).

1. **Lesson Preparation**: Ensures lessons are carefully designed with clear language and content objectives, incorporating culturally relevant and linguistically appropriate materials for MLs (Echevarria, Jana, et al., 2017).
2. **Building Background**: Connects new learning to students' prior knowledge and experiences, recognizing the diverse backgrounds of MLs and valuing their unique contributions (Echevarria, Jana, et al., 2017).
3. **Comprehensible Input**: Delivers instruction in ways that MLs can understand through visuals, gestures, modeling, and simplified language (Echevarria, Jana, et al., 2017).
4. **Strategies**: Incorporates cognitive and metacognitive strategies to help MLs effectively organize, retain, and apply new information (Echevarria, Jana, et al., 2017).
5. **Interaction**: Promotes meaningful opportunities for students to engage in discussions, collaborative learning, and peer interactions, which can rebuild trust and social skills impacted by trauma (Echevarria, Jana, et al., 2017).
6. **Practice/Application**: Hands-on activities allow MLs to practice language skills in a low-risk, supportive environment (Echevarria, Jana, et al., 2017).
7. **Lesson Delivery**: Ensures instruction is delivered at an appropriate pace, with active engagement and regular checks for understanding (Echevarria, Jana, et al., 2017).
8. **Review/Assessment**: Includes frequent formative assessments to monitor progress and provide feedback, tailoring support to meet individual needs (Echevarria, Jana, et al., 2017).

SIOP is Successful for Multilingual Learners

The SIOP method is particularly effective for multilingual learners because it addresses their unique needs in acquiring language proficiency and academic content knowledge. Its success is attributed to several factors (Echevarria, Jana, et al., 2017):

- **Integration of Language and Content** – By explicitly focusing on both academic content and language development, SIOP ensures that students do not fall behind in either area.
- **Comprehensibility** – Techniques such as scaffolding, visuals, and simplified speech help students access content they might otherwise struggle to understand.
- **Student Engagement** – The emphasis on interaction and active participation encourages students to use and practice language in meaningful contexts, accelerating learning.
- **Cultural Relevance** – The framework encourages teachers to connect instruction to students' backgrounds, making learning more relevant and engaging.

- **Structured Support** – The detailed framework of SIOP helps teachers plan systematic and flexible lessons catering to multilingual learners' varying proficiency levels.

Research has shown that the SIOP model improves academic outcomes for multilingual learners, enhances their language proficiency, and boosts teacher effectiveness. Its structured yet adaptable approach is a powerful tool for supporting multilingual learners in diverse educational settings.

Addressing Trauma Through SIOP

The SIOP method is particularly effective for MLs who have experienced trauma because it integrates principles of clarity, structure, and support, essential for fostering a sense of safety and stability.

- **Creating Predictable Routines**: Trauma can make students feel vulnerable and uncertain. The structured nature of SIOP lessons provides a predictable and consistent framework that helps MLs feel secure.
- **Valuing Cultural Backgrounds**: By building on students' prior knowledge and incorporating culturally relevant materials, SIOP affirms their identities and fosters a sense of belonging.
- **Reducing Cognitive Load**: Trauma often impairs working memory and attention. SIOP's emphasis on clear objectives, comprehensible input, and scaffolded instruction reduces the cognitive demands placed on students.
- **Encouraging Social Interaction**: Trauma can lead to social withdrawal and isolation. SIOP's interactive components promote collaboration and peer support, rebuilding social connections in a safe environment.
- **Fostering Academic Success**: SIOP's dual focus on language development and content mastery enables MLs to achieve academic milestones while gaining the confidence to participate fully in the classroom.

By integrating the SIOP model into a trauma-informed MTSS framework, educators can provide MLs with the structured, supportive, and culturally responsive environment they need to overcome the challenges of trauma and succeed academically.

How Metacognitive Strategies Help Multilingual Learners

Metacognitive strategies, which involve planning, monitoring, and evaluating one's own learning processes, are particularly effective in supporting multilingual learners. These strategies empower students to take an active role in their learning by fostering self-awareness, adaptability, and independent problem-solving. For multilingual learners, metacognition is a powerful tool to navigate the dual challenges of acquiring a new language and mastering academic content.

Benefits of Metacognitive Strategies for Multilingual Learners

1. **Enhancing Language Acquisition**:

Research by Chamot and O'Malley (1994) highlights how metacognitive strategies improve language learning by encouraging students to reflect on their learning processes consciously. For example, a student might aim to focus on understanding new vocabulary in a text, monitor their reading comprehension, and evaluate their success afterward. This reflective approach helps multilingual learners develop better language skills over time.

2. **Improving Academic Achievement**:

Multilingual learners often face challenges in content learning due to language barriers. Metacognitive strategies, such as summarizing information or self-questioning, help students bridge gaps in comprehension. A study by Zhang and Seepho (2013) found that students who used metacognitive strategies performed better academically, as they could plan and adjust their learning to overcome difficulties in both language and content areas.

3. **Fostering Autonomy**:

Metacognition supports the development of learner autonomy, a critical factor for multilingual students who may feel overwhelmed by new academic and linguistic demands. According to Vandergrift and Goh (2012), multilingual learners who employ metacognitive strategies are better equipped to identify their learning strengths and weaknesses, leading to more effective study habits and increased confidence.

4. **Reducing Anxiety and Building Resilience**:

Multilingual learners often experience anxiety when learning a new language. Metacognitive strategies, such as mindfulness of learning progress and reframing challenges as opportunities, can reduce this stress. Flavell (1979) pointed out that metacognition enables learners to understand that learning is a process, which can decrease the pressure to achieve perfection immediately.

Examples of Effective Metacognitive Strategies

- **Planning**: Setting clear goals for a task, such as understanding key ideas in a reading passage.
- **Monitoring**: Asking oneself questions during a task, like "Does this make sense?" or "What can I do to clarify my understanding?"
- **Evaluating**: Reflecting on the effectiveness of strategies used, such as reviewing what worked well or identifying areas for improvement.

Implications for Instruction

Educators can support multilingual learners by explicitly teaching metacognitive strategies. This includes modeling how to plan, monitor, and evaluate learning tasks and integrating tools such as learning journals or graphic organizers to scaffold these skills. By embedding metacognitive strategy instruction into the classroom, teachers can equip multilingual learners with the tools to succeed academically and build lifelong learning skills.

Metacognitive strategies are essential for multilingual learners to navigate the complex language acquisition and academic learning demands. As supported by research, these strategies enhance language proficiency and academic success and empower learners with the confidence and autonomy needed to thrive in diverse educational environments.

6. LEADING VOICES IN TRAUMA-INFORMED EDUCATION: BRACKETT, GREENE, AND FORBES

The growing body of research on trauma-informed strategies in education highlights the critical role of addressing the social, emotional, and psychological needs of students to foster academic success. Trauma, whether stemming from adverse childhood experiences (ACEs), systemic inequities, or external events, profoundly affects a student's ability to learn, engage, and thrive in educational environments. Recognizing this, trauma-informed approaches have become essential for creating supportive, inclusive, and responsive classrooms.

Central to this work are leading experts such as Dr. Marc Brackett, Dr. Ross Greene, and Dr. Heather Forbes, whose research and frameworks have greatly influenced trauma-informed practices. Dr. Marc Brackett, the founder of the Yale Center for Emotional Intelligence, emphasizes the importance of emotional literacy in his RULER framework, which equips educators and students with tools to recognize, understand, label, express, and regulate emotions (Brackett, 2019). His work underscores the value of emotional awareness in creating safe and supportive learning environments that nurture resilience and academic success.

Dr. Ross Greene, renowned for his Collaborative & Proactive Solutions (CPS) model, focuses on addressing the root causes of challenging behavior through collaboration and problem-solving (Greene, 2014). His approach highlights the importance of building strong, empathetic relationships and understanding students' unmet needs rather than resorting to punitive measures (Greene, 2014). This perspective aligns closely with trauma-informed principles, as it centers the student's voice and experience in addressing behavioral challenges.

Dr. Heather Forbes, a leading voice in trauma-informed education, emphasizes the role of connection and empathy in helping students heal from trauma (Forbes, 2012). Through her work, including her books and training programs, Forbes advocates for relationship-based approaches prioritizing emotional safety and understanding (Forbes, 2012). Her emphasis on shifting from reactive to proactive strategies equips educators to create compassionate and effective classrooms (Forbes, 2012).

These experts provide a robust foundation for integrating trauma-informed strategies into education. Their contributions not only enhance students' emotional well-being but also improve academic outcomes by addressing the underlying barriers to learning caused by trauma. This body of research underscores the transformative potential of trauma-informed approaches, ensuring that all students, particularly those impacted by trauma, can succeed academically and emotionally.

7. EMBRACING AND REGULATING EMOTIONS

Based on the work of Dr. Marc Brackett and Dr. Ross Greene, embracing and regulating emotions require critical strategies for addressing emotional and social challenges in the classroom, particularly for students who have experienced trauma. These strategies can be integrated into trauma-informed MTSS frameworks to support MLs effectively.

Emotional Intelligence and Its Role in Education

Emotional intelligence is "the ability to monitor one's own and others' feelings and emotions, to discriminate among them, and to use this information to guide one's thinking and actions" (Salovey & Mayer, 1990). This competency is essential for educators working with MLs who may struggle with emotional regulation due to trauma. Key skills include:

- **Recognizing Emotions**: Identifying and understanding one's own emotions and those of others (Salovey & Mayer, 1990).
- **Labeling Emotions**: Accurately naming emotions to process and address them effectively (Salovey & Mayer, 1990).
- **Regulating Emotions**: Managing emotions to support personal and academic goals (Salovey & Mayer, 1990).

RULER Approach

RULER is an evidence-based framework Dr. Marc Brackett and his team at the Yale Center for Emotional Intelligence developed. The framework is designed to integrate emotional intelligence into schools, helping educators, students, and families develop the skills necessary to recognize, understand, label, express, and regulate emotions effectively. The acronym RULER stands for the five key skills of emotional intelligence (Brackett 2019):

1. **Recognizing emotions** – Identifying emotions in oneself and others, whether through facial expressions, body language, tone of voice, or situational cues (Brackett 2019).
2. **Understanding emotions** – Comprehending the causes and consequences of emotions, including how emotions influence thoughts, behaviors, and decision-making (Brackett 2019).
3. **Labeling emotions** – Accurately identify and name emotions to increase emotional awareness and enhance communication (Brackett 2019).
4. **Expressing emotions** – Appropriately conveying emotions that foster connection and understanding based on context and cultural norms (Brackett 2019).
5. **Regulating emotions** – Effectively managing emotions to promote personal well-being, build healthy relationships, and achieve goals (Brackett 2019).

RULER is implemented through specific tools and practices that integrate emotional intelligence into the fabric of schools:

- **The Charter** – A collaborative document created by students, staff, or families to outline the desired emotional climate of their community and actionable steps to achieve it (Brackett 2019).
- **The Mood Meter** – A visual tool that helps individuals identify and track their emotions based on energy and pleasantness levels (Brackett 2019).
- **The Meta-Moment** – A self-regulation strategy to pause, assess, and respond thoughtfully to emotional situations (Brackett 2019).
- **The Blueprint** – A tool for conflict resolution that fosters empathy and problem-solving.

Research has demonstrated that RULER improves emotional intelligence, enhances academic performance, reduces anxiety, and fosters positive relationships (Brackett 2019). By embedding emotional intelligence into education, RULER supports the creation of safe, inclusive, and engaging learning environments where all students can thrive (Brackett 2019).

Classroom Strategies for Emotional Regulation

Dr. Brackett outlines techniques for helping students to regulate (2019). Here are his actionable strategies for fostering emotional intelligence and regulation among MLs:

1. **Building Relationships**: Positive relationships are foundational for helping students feel safe and valued. This includes staying calm, practicing mindfulness, and affirming students' identities (Brackett 2019).
2. **Creating Predictable Structures**: Routines and clear procedures help reduce anxiety and provide a stable environment for learning (Brackett 2019).
3. **Classroom Environment**: A welcoming environment with flexible seating, calming music, and stress-reducing tools (e.g., fidget toys) can enhance emotional well-being (Brackett 2019).
4. **Avoiding Triggers**: Understanding individual triggers and implementing proactive measures to minimize student stress responses (Brackett 2019).
5. **Emphasizing Positivity**: Praising students often and assigning tasks that build confidence can foster resilience and self-efficacy (Brackett 2019).

Addressing Lagging Skills VS Punishment and Rewards

Dr. Ross Greene's book *Lost in School* presents a transformative approach to understanding and addressing behavioral challenges in students. Greene argues that traditional methods of discipline, such as punishment and rewards, often fail to address the root causes of challenging behaviors. Instead, he emphasizes the importance of understanding the lagging skills and unsolved problems that lead to these behaviors. His Collaborative & Proactive Solutions (CPS) model provides a practical framework for working with students to build the skills they need to succeed while fostering empathy and collaboration (Greene 2014).

Key principles from *Lost in School* include:

1. **Kids Do Well If They Can** – Greene challenges the conventional belief that students misbehave because they lack motivation or choose to act out. Instead, he posits that students want to succeed but may lack the skills—such as emotional regulation, problem-solving, or flexibility—to do so (Greene 2014).
2. **Focus on Lagging Skills and Unsolved Problems** – The CPS approach shifts the focus from diagnosing students or applying punitive measures to identifying specific skills the student needs to develop and the problems that are triggering their behavior (Greene 2014).
3. **Collaborative Problem-Solving** – Greene emphasizes the value of involving students in identifying and addressing their challenges (Greene 2014). This involves three key steps:
    - **Empathy**: Understanding the student's perspective and concerns (Greene 2014).
    - **Define the Problem**: Articulate the adult's concerns about the issue (Greene 2014).
    - **Invitation**: Collaboratively brainstorm solutions that address the student's and the adult's concerns (Greene 2014).
4. **The Role of Relationships** – Greene underscores the importance of strong, trusting relationships between students and adults. These relationships create the foundation for meaningful collaboration and positive change (Greene 2014).

Lost in School is rich with real-world examples and actionable strategies for educators, parents, and school leaders. Greene advocates for a shift in how schools address behavioral challenges, emphasizing a proactive, compassionate, and skill-building approach rather than reactive and punitive measures (Greene 2014). His work highlights the potential for schools to become places of growth and healing, particularly for students who are "lost" in traditional discipline systems (Greene 2014).

By reframing how educators understand and respond to challenging behavior, *Lost in School* provides a roadmap for creating supportive, inclusive learning environments that meet the needs of all students.

By incorporating these insights into trauma-informed MTSS frameworks, educators can better address the complex needs of MLs, creating environments where emotional and academic growth are prioritized.

Insights from Heather Forbes' "Help for Billy"

Heather Forbes' *Help for Billy* offers a compassionate approach to addressing the needs of students affected by trauma, focusing on the importance of relationship-building and understanding behavioral challenges as manifestations of underlying emotional needs. These principles are particularly relevant for multilingual learners (MLs), who may struggle with additional linguistic and cultural barriers (Forbes, 2012).

Key Principles from "Help for Billy"

Forbes emphasizes the need for educators to shift their perspective from punitive discipline to trauma-informed strategies that prioritize connection and understanding. Key strategies include (Forbes 2012):

- **Meeting Students Where They Are**: Recognizing the unique challenges faced by MLs, such as adjusting to a new cultural and linguistic environment and tailoring support to their individual needs (Forbes, 2012).

- **Creating Safe and Predictable Environments**: Establishing routines and clear expectations to reduce anxiety and foster a sense of security (Forbes, 2012).
- **Focusing on Emotional Regulation**: Providing tools and strategies for students to manage their emotions, such as mindfulness practices and calm-down spaces (Forbes, 2012).

Building Relationships

Forbes highlights the critical role of relationships in supporting students who have experienced trauma. For MLs, relationships with educators and peers can help bridge cultural and linguistic gaps, fostering a sense of belonging and safety. Educators can:

- **Develop Trust**: Spend time getting to know students' cultural backgrounds and personal stories.
- **Use Culturally Responsive Practices**: Incorporate students' home languages and cultural references into lessons to validate their identities.
- **Engage Families**: Build partnerships with families to create a holistic support system for MLs.

Addressing Behavioral Challenges

Forbes advocates for understanding behavioral challenges as expressions of unmet needs rather than intentional defiance. For MLs, behavioral issues may stem from frustration, fear, or cultural misunderstandings. Strategies include:

- **Empathy-Driven Discipline**: Address behaviors with curiosity and compassion, seeking to understand the root causes (Forbes, 2012).
- **Collaborative Problem-Solving**: Work with students to identify triggers and develop strategies for challenging situations (Forbes, 2012).
- **Skill-Building**: Teach social-emotional skills explicitly, focusing on communication, self-regulation, and conflict resolution (Forbes, 2012).

Recent Study on Trauma-Informed Training Using Forbes' Work

Heather Forbes' training program, *Beyond Consequences, Logic, and Control*, is based on her work. A school district committed to transforming its approach to student behavior and emotional well-being implemented this training in a year-long program. Forbes' framework emphasizes relationship-based strategies prioritizing connection, understanding, and empathy over traditional punitive measures. This training gave educators the tools to respond to students' underlying emotional needs, fostering a sense of safety and belonging in the classroom (Forbes 2012).

The district-wide adoption of *Beyond Consequences* marked a significant shift in educational practices, creating a foundation for examining its long-term impact on student outcomes, school culture, and teacher efficacy. Building on this foundation, a current study—yet to be published—aims to evaluate the effectiveness of Forbes' trauma-informed strategies in this district (Foster et al., under review). By analyzing qualitative and quantitative data, the study seeks to provide insights into how these practices influence student behavior, emotional regulation, and academic achievement over time (Foster et al., under review).

This recent descriptive case study by Dr. Jennifer Foster, Dr. Heidi Cate, and Dr. Brandy Shooks examined the perspectives of sixteen educators participating in this yearlong trauma-informed training program within a charter school system. Thematic analysis of their experiences revealed five key themes:

1. **The Centrality of Educator-Student Relationships**: Educators identified strong, positive relationships as foundational for creating safe and supportive learning environments (Foster et al., under review). This aligns with Forbes' emphasis on connection and trust as the cornerstone of trauma-informed practices.
2. **Safety**: Both physical and emotional safety were highlighted as critical components of a trauma-informed approach. For MLs, this includes creating linguistically accessible spaces and reducing cultural biases (Foster et al., under review).
3. **Educator Changes**: Participants noted significant shifts in attitudes and practices, including increased empathy and patience when addressing student behaviors (Foster et al., under review).
4. **Resistance**: Some educators resisted implementing trauma-informed practices, underscoring the need for sustained professional development and administrative support (Foster et al., under review).
5. **Thriving**: Many educators reported seeing their students thrive academically and socially because of trauma-informed interventions (Foster et al., under review).

The study underscores the importance of professional development in equipping educators with the tools to support MLs effectively. It also highlights the transformative potential of fostering safe, trusting relationships in trauma-informed educational settings.

By integrating insights from *Help for Billy* and the findings of this study, educators can better understand and address the needs of multilingual learners who have experienced trauma, creating pathways for healing and success.

Expanding the Scope

When working with multilingual students who have experienced trauma, it is crucial to adopt an interdisciplinary approach that extends beyond traditional educational research. While education-focused studies provide valuable insights into pedagogy, language acquisition, and trauma-informed teaching practices, the experiences of these students often intersect with broader aspects of human psychology, resilience, and personal growth. Drawing on the work of thought leaders like Brené Brown, James Nestor, Jay Shetty, and James Clear offers a richer, more holistic perspective.

Brené Brown's exploration of vulnerability, courage, and empathy provides a foundation for understanding the emotional landscapes of students who have endured hardship (Brown, 2021). James Nestor's research into the transformative power of breathing underscores the importance of integrating physical and emotional well-being into teaching practices (Nestor, 2020). Jay Shetty's wisdom on mindfulness and purpose invites educators to create environments that nurture a sense of belonging and healing (Shetty, 2020). Lastly, James Clear's principles of habit formation remind us of the incremental changes that can empower students to build routines fostering both academic and personal growth (Clear, 2018).

By drawing on these diverse perspectives, educators can better support multilingual students who have experienced trauma, addressing not only their academic needs but also their emotional and psychological well-being. This integrative approach creates a more inclusive, compassionate, and effective framework for teaching and learning.

Insights from Brené Brown's "Atlas of the Heart"

Brené Brown's *Atlas of the Heart* offers a profound exploration of emotions and their impact on human connection, resilience, and learning (Brown, 2021). This work is particularly relevant to trauma-informed educational practices, providing tools for understanding and navigating complex emotional landscapes. For multilingual learners (MLs), who may face additional layers of emotional and cultural challenges, the principles in *Atlas of the Heart* can guide educators in creating environments that foster emotional safety and belonging (Brown, 2021).

Naming and Understanding Emotions

Brown emphasizes the importance of accurately naming emotions, enhancing self-awareness and emotional regulation (Brown, 2021). For MLs, this process can be particularly empowering, as they may struggle to express emotions in a new language. Strategies include:

- **Language Development Activities**: Incorporating vocabulary lessons focused on emotions in the students' home languages and English.
- **Visual Aids**: Using emotion charts and multilingual resources to help students identify and articulate their feelings.
- **Modeling Emotional Language**: Educators can model how to express emotions constructively, demonstrating how to navigate emotional experiences effectively.

Fostering Connection

Connection is central to Brown's work, highlighting the role of relationships in healing and learning. For MLs, building connections can mitigate feelings of isolation and displacement. Key approaches include:

- **Culturally Responsive Relationships**: Creating authentic connections by valuing students' cultural and linguistic identities.
- **Peer Collaboration**: Encouraging group work and peer mentorship to build community and shared understanding.
- **Inclusive Storytelling**: Using storytelling to allow MLs to share their experiences and learn from others, fostering empathy and connection.

Embracing Vulnerability and Building Resilience

Brown discusses vulnerability as a pathway to resilience and growth (Brown, 2021). For MLs, creating a safe space to express vulnerability can lead to greater resilience in navigating trauma and academic challenges. Educators can:

- **Normalize Mistakes**: Encourage students to view mistakes as part of learning.
- **Celebrate Small Wins**: Recognize and celebrate incremental progress to build confidence and resilience.

- **Provide Supportive Feedback**: Offer feedback emphasizing growth and effort rather than focusing solely on outcomes.

Creating an Emotionally Safe Classroom

Drawing from Brown's insights, educators can design classrooms that prioritize emotional safety:

- **Set Clear Expectations**: Communicate behavioral and academic expectations while ensuring students feel supported and accepted.
- **Use Restorative Practices**: Address conflicts and challenges through restorative approaches prioritizing understanding and resolution.
- **Encourage Self-Reflection**: Integrate reflective practices like journaling or mood tracking to help students process their emotions.

By integrating the principles from *Atlas of the Heart* into trauma-informed MTSS frameworks, educators can better support the emotional and academic needs of MLs, fostering environments where they can thrive (Brown, 2021).

Insights from "Breath" by James Nestor and "Think Like a Monk" by Jay Shetty

James Nestor's *Breath: The New Science of a Lost Art* and Jay Shetty's *Think Like a Monk* provide transformative insights that can be applied to support multilingual learners (MLs) who have experienced trauma. These works highlight the importance of intentional breathing practices and mindfulness as tools for emotional regulation, resilience, and fostering a sense of well-being in educational settings.

Breathwork for Emotional Regulation

Nestor's research underscores the power of breath to influence physical and emotional health (Nestor, 2020). Trauma often disrupts normal breathing patterns, contributing to heightened anxiety and stress. For MLs, introducing breathwork can provide a simple, accessible strategy for managing these challenges. Key principles include:

- **Slow and Controlled Breathing**: Techniques like diaphragmatic breathing can activate the parasympathetic nervous system, reducing stress and promoting calmness (Nestor, 2020).
- **Nasal Breathing**: Encouraging students to breathe through their noses can improve oxygen efficiency, enhance focus, and stabilize emotions (Nestor, 2020).
- **Box Breathing**: A method of inhaling, holding, exhaling, and holding for equal counts, which can be integrated into classroom routines to help students reset and refocus (Nestor, 2020).

Educators can incorporate these practices through brief breathing exercises during transitions or before challenging tasks, creating a calming environment conducive to learning.

Mindfulness and Purposeful Living

In *Think Like a Monk*, Shetty emphasizes mindfulness, intention, and compassion as tools for personal growth and resilience (Shetty, 2020). These principles can guide educators in fostering supportive environments for MLs:

- **Mindfulness Practices**: Encouraging mindfulness activities, such as guided meditations or gratitude journaling, can help MLs become more present and reduce stress (Shetty, 2020).
- **Purpose-Driven Routines**: Creating routines with a clear purpose, such as starting each day with affirmations or setting intentions, can provide MLs with a sense of stability and direction (Shetty, 2020).
- **Empathy and Connection**: Shetty's emphasis on compassion aligns with trauma-informed practices. Educators can model empathetic communication, validate students' experiences, and build trust (Shetty, 2020).

Practical Applications for Educators

1. **Breathing Breaks**: Integrate short breathing exercises, such as box breathing or alternate nostril breathing, into the school day to help students manage stress and improve focus (Shetty, 2020).
2. **Mindful Transitions**: Use mindfulness activities, such as a moment of silent reflection or a gratitude practice, to ease transitions and create a sense of calm (Shetty, 2020).
3. **Reflective Practices**: Encourage MLs to reflect on their emotions and experiences through journaling or discussions, fostering self-awareness and emotional growth (Shetty, 2020).

By applying *Breath* and *Think Like a Monk principles*, educators can empower multilingual learners to develop tools for resilience and emotional regulation, enhancing their ability to navigate academic and personal challenges.

Insights from "Atomic Habits" by James Clear

James Clear's *Atomic Habits* provides a framework for building effective habits through small, incremental changes (Clear, 2018). This approach can be highly beneficial in supporting multilingual learners (MLs) who have experienced trauma. Clear emphasizes the importance of creating systems for success rather than relying solely on motivation, an approach that aligns with trauma-informed educational practices (Clear, 2018).

Building Positive Habits for MLs

Trauma can disrupt routines and create barriers to consistent learning behaviors. Educators can help MLs establish stability and structure in their daily lives by focusing on habit-building. Key principles include:

- **Start Small**: Introduce manageable changes, such as setting up a daily routine for language practice or mindfulness exercises (Clear, 2018).

- **Make it Obvious**: Use visual cues, such as charts or timers, to remind students of their habits (Clear, 2018).
- **Make it Attractive**: Pair learning activities with positive reinforcement, like celebrating progress or incorporating enjoyable elements into lessons (Clear, 2018).
- **Make it Easy**: Simplify tasks to reduce cognitive load, such as breaking assignments into smaller, achievable steps (Clear, 2018).
- **Make it Satisfy**: Provide immediate feedback and celebrate small victories to encourage consistency (Clear, 2018).

Designing Supportive Routines

Educators can use Clear's habit-building strategies to create routines that enhance learning and emotional regulation for MLs. Examples include:

- **Morning Check-Ins**: Begin the day with a quick activity, such as journaling or a gratitude exercise, to set a positive tone.
- **Structured Study Times**: Establish consistent times for focused learning, supported by visual schedules and clear expectations.
- **Reflection and Goal setting**: Encourage students to reflect on their progress and set achievable goals for the next day or week.

The Role of Environment

Clear emphasizes the impact of the environment on habit formation (Clear, 2018). For MLs, creating a supportive and predictable classroom environment can reinforce positive habits. Strategies include:

- **Decluttering the Learning Space**: Minimize distractions to help students focus on their tasks.
- **Creating Habit-Friendly Zones**: Designate areas for specific activities, such as a quiet reading corner or a collaborative group worktable.
- **Providing Cues and Prompts**: Use visual and auditory cues to guide students through their routines.

Empowering MLs Through Habits

By teaching MLs how to build and maintain positive habits, educators can empower them to take control of their learning and emotional well-being. These habits can help students manage stress, build resilience, and develop a sense of agency in their educational journey.

8. TRAUMA-INFORMED PRACTICES AND TEACHER SELF-EFFICACY

Trauma-informed educational practices do not only benefit students but also significantly impact teachers' sense of self-efficacy. By equipping educators with tools to address the complex needs of students who have experienced trauma, these practices foster a greater sense of confidence, competence, and fulfillment in their roles.

Building Confidence Through Knowledge and Tools

Trauma-informed training provides educators with a deeper understanding of how trauma affects student behavior and learning. This knowledge empowers teachers to:

- **Respond Effectively to Challenging Behaviors**: By understanding the root causes of trauma-related behaviors, educators can implement strategies that de-escalate conflicts and support emotional regulation (Shooks, 2020).
- **Create Structured and Predictable Environments**: Trauma-informed practices emphasize the importance of routines, which not only benefit students but also provide teachers with a framework for consistency in their classrooms (Shooks, 2020).
- **Strengthen Relationships**: Fostering connections with students enhances teachers' ability to build trust and facilitate meaningful learning experiences (Shooks, 2020).

Transformative Impact on Teacher Well-Being

Research, such as the study by Dr. Jennifer Foster, Dr. Heidi Cate, and Dr. Brandy Shooks, highlights trauma-informed practices' profound effect on teachers (Foster et al., under review). Participants in their yearlong training program reported:

- **Increased Empathy and Patience**: Understanding trauma allowed teachers to approach student behaviors with compassion rather than frustration (Foster et al., under review).
- **Improved Job Satisfaction**: Witnessing the positive impact of their interventions reinforced educators' commitment to their profession (Foster et al., under review).
- **Resilience in the Face of Challenges**: Trauma-informed training helped teachers manage stress and navigate resistance within their schools (Foster et al., under review).

Practical Applications for Supporting Educators

Schools can further enhance teacher self-efficacy by:

- **Providing Ongoing Professional Development**: Regular training sessions ensure educators stay informed about best practices.
- **Establishing Collaborative Networks**: Peer support groups and interdisciplinary teams can help teachers share insights and resources.
- **Promoting Self-Care**: Encouraging mindfulness practices, reflection, and work-life balance helps educators maintain their well-being.

By adopting trauma-informed practices, schools create a supportive ecosystem where both students and teachers thrive. Empowered educators are better equipped to meet the needs of multilingual learners, ensuring a holistic approach to trauma-informed education.

9. CONCLUSION

Supporting multilingual learners (MLs) who have experienced trauma requires a multifaceted approach that integrates culturally responsive practices, emotional intelligence, and structured routines. The frameworks and insights explored in this chapter—from Multi-Tiered Systems of Support (MTSS) to trauma-informed strategies—highlight educators' critical role in creating safe and inclusive learning environments. By drawing from James Clear's principles in *Atomic Habits*, educators can help MLs develop routines that foster stability and academic progress. James Nestor's *Breath* provides simple yet powerful breathing techniques that assist students in managing stress and enhancing focus. Jay Shetty's *Think Like a Monk* underscores the importance of mindfulness and purpose, offering educators tools to cultivate calm, resilient classrooms. Heather Forbes' *Help for Billy* emphasizes the necessity of relationship-building and empathy, particularly for students whose behaviors may reflect unmet emotional needs. Brené Brown's *Atlas of the Heart* further enriches this perspective by equipping educators and students with a language for emotions, enabling deeper connections and emotional regulation.

The recent research by Dr. Foster, Dr. Cate, and Dr. Shooks reinforces the centrality of relationships and the transformative impact of trauma-informed training on educators and students alike. It reveals the importance of safety, adaptability, and consistent professional development in overcoming challenges and fostering thriving educational communities.

Ultimately, trauma-informed practices address the immediate needs of MLs and lay the groundwork for long-term academic and emotional success. By combining evidence-based strategies with a commitment to empathy and cultural awareness, educators can empower multilingual learners to navigate their unique challenges and realize their full potential. Furthermore, Trauma-informed practices enhance teacher self-efficacy by equipping educators with the skills, knowledge, and strategies needed to address the multifaceted challenges of supporting multilingual learners who have experienced trauma. These practices enable teachers to foster safe, nurturing environments where students and educators can thrive. By understanding the root causes of trauma-related behaviors and implementing proactive, compassionate interventions, teachers gain confidence to make a meaningful difference in their students' lives. Research has shown that such practices improve student outcomes and contribute to increased job satisfaction and resilience among educators. For instance, professional development opportunities in trauma-informed approaches provide tools for relationship-building, classroom management, and emotional regulation—all critical components of teacher self-efficacy.

In essence, trauma-informed practices create a reciprocal benefit: as educators grow more effective and empowered, their students, particularly multilingual learners navigating the challenges of trauma, are better positioned to succeed academically and socially. This holistic approach underscores the transformative power of empathy, understanding, and structured support in educational settings, fostering a learning environment where students and teachers can achieve growth and resilience together.

REFERENCES

Boomer, L. M., & Hughes, D. A. (2013). *Settling to Learn: Settling Troubled Pupils to Learn: Why Relationships Matter in School*. Worth Publishing.

Brackett, M. (2019). *Permission to Feel*. Celadon Books.

Brown, B. (2021). *Atlas of the Heart: Mapping Meaningful Connection and the Language of Human Experience*. Random House.

Brunzell, T., Stokes, H., & Waters, L. (2015). Trauma-Informed Positive Education: Using Positive Psychology to Strengthen Vulnerable Students. *Contemporary School Psychology*, *20*(1), 63–83. DOI: 10.1007/s40688-015-0070-x

Chamot, A. U., & Michael O'Malley, J. (1994). *The CALLA Handbook: Implementing the Cognitive Academic Language Learning Approach*. Addison-Wesley.

Clear, J. (2018). *Atomic Habits: An Easy & Proven Way to Build Good Habits & Break Bad Ones*. Avery.

Data Resource Center for Child and Adolescent Health. *Child Health Indicators and Subgroups*, 2013. Retrieved from https://www.childhealthdata.org/docs/nsch-docs/sas-codebook_-2011-2012-nsch-v1_05-10-13.pdf

Davidson, J. (2014). Restorative Justice. *Education Digest*, *80*(3), 19–23.

Desilver, D. (2017). "U.S. Students' Academic Achievement Still Lags That of Their Peers in Many Countries." *Pew Research Center*. https://www.pewresearch.org/fact-tank/2017/02/15/u-s-students-internationally-math-science/

Echevarria, J.. (2017). *Making Content Comprehensible for English Learners: The SIOP Model* (4th ed.). Pearson.

Flavell, J. H. (1979). Metacognition and Cognitive Monitoring: A New Area of Cognitive–Developmental Inquiry. *The American Psychologist*, *34*(10), 906–911. DOI: 10.1037/0003-066X.34.10.906

Forbes, H. T. (2012). *Help for Billy: A Beyond Consequences Approach to Helping Challenging Children in the Classroom*. Beyond Consequences Institute.

Greene, R. W. (2014). *Lost at School: Why Our Kids with Behavioral Problems Are Falling Through the Cracks and How We Can Help Them*. Scribner.

Hatch, T. (2001). Incoherence in the system: Three perspectives on the implementation of multiple initiatives in one district. *American Journal of Education*, *109*(4), 407–437.

Ijadi-Maghsoodi, R., Marlotte, L., Garcia, E., Aralis, H., Lester, P., Escudero, P., & Kataoka, S. (2017). Adapting and Implementing a School-Based Resilience-Building Curriculum Among Low-Income Racial and Ethnic Minority Students. *Contemporary School Psychology*, *21*(3), 223–239. DOI: 10.1007/s40688-017-0134-1 PMID: 29686938

Nestor, J. (2020). *Breath: The New Science of a Lost Art*. Riverhead Books.

Plumb, J. L., Bush, K. A., & Kersevich, S. E. (2013). Building Trauma-Informed Schools and Communities. *Children & Schools, 35*(2), 123–126. DOI: 10.1093/cs/cdt007

Protocol, A. T. I. (2014). *Trauma-informed care in behavioral health services.* Substance Abuse and Mental Health Services Administration.

Shetty, J. (2020). *Think Like a Monk: Train Your Mind for Peace and Purpose Every Day*. Scribner.

Shooks, B. (2020). *The Impact of Trauma-Informed Pedagogical Practices on Teacher Self-Efficacy*. Cornerstone University.

Shooks, B. A. *The Impact of Trauma-Informed Pedagogical Practices on Teacher Self-Efficacy*. (Publication No. 28025831) [Doctoral dissertation, Cornerstone University]. ProQuest Dissertations & Theses, 2020.

Souers, K., & Hall, P. (2016). *Fostering Resilient Learners: Strategies for Creating a Trauma-Sensitive Classroom*. ASCD.

Van der Kolk. (2014). *Bessel A. The Body Keeps the Score: Brain, Mind, and Body in the Healing of Trauma*. Viking.

Vandergrift, L., & Goh, C. (2012). *Teaching and Learning Second Language Listening: Metacognition in Action*. Routledge.

Zhang, L., & Seepho, S. (2013). Metacognitive Strategy Use and Academic Reading Achievement: Insights from a Chinese Context. *International Journal of English Linguistics, 3*(5), 15–29. DOI: 10.5539/ijel.v3n5p15

Chapter 16
A Comprehensive Approach Combining the Education System With Family Therapy to Help Immigrant Families With Acculturation: Guide for Educators and Clinicians

Aniek Bradley
https://orcid.org/0009-0007-3101-3727
National University, USA

ABSTRACT

Children of Immigrant parents, regardless of being born in the USA, face additional challenges. Even though young children have a higher level of resilience, some live traumatic events vicariously. Chronic stress of the parents due to language barriers, cultural differences, social influences, and legal status can permeate the children. Clinical interventions with the family can reduce the negative impact of acculturation on the parents and help them understand their children's cultural differences. The challenge is that many of these families are afraid to utilize the available resources, or they are unaware that such resources exist. Promoting such interventions in educational facilities can inform migrant families and help them adjust to a new society.

GUIDE FOR EDUCATORS AND CLINICIANS: A COMPREHENSIVE APPROACH COMBINING THE EDUCATION SYSTEM WITH FAMILY THERAPY TO HELP IMMIGRANT FAMILIES WITH ACCULTURATION

Immigrant families face unique challenges, including social isolation, cultural differences, and language barriers. Children of immigrant parents, regardless of being born in the USA, face additional challenges. Chronic stress of the parents due to language barriers, cultural differences, social influences, and legal status can permeate the children. Even though young children have a higher level of resilience, some

DOI: 10.4018/979-8-3693-9020-7.ch016

live traumatic events vicariously, which can affect their education, development, and future life as adults. Clinical interventions with the family can reduce the negative impact of acculturation on the parents and help them understand their children's cultural differences. The challenge is that many of these families are afraid to utilize the available resources or are unaware that such resources exist. Promoting such interventions in educational facilities can inform immigrant families, help them adjust to a new society, and serve as a preventive measure. Better adjustments mean a better future.

According to the US Census Bureau, the United States had a diversity index of 61.1% in 2020 (Rabe, 2024). Esri Diversity Index reported a national diversity index of 72.5% in 2024, up from 61.0% in 2020, and it is projected to reach 74.0% in 2029 (Esri, 2024). In recent years, children have continued to arrive at different ages or be born into families where the parents are first-time immigrants. School programs should be sensitive to such diversity and an ever-changing multicultural society to have a better educational system and prepare future generations (Karim, 2021). Acculturation-specific interventions for immigrant children and parents can help them, but they can also help society with more prepared and adjusted families. Immigrants go through a process of adaptation involving sociocultural and psychological aspects. Adaptation includes withdrawal, reaction, adjustment, and deculturation. The method depends on how the immigrants acquire elements of the host culture, how much they want to maintain their own, and how they relate to peers of the host culture (Al-Haddad, 2024). Interventions focusing on the Adjustment–Effort–Performance Model, involving positive effort, have shown improved performance. For example, increasing autonomy and variety of tasks and promoting participation, motivation, learning, and efficiency have improved health and well-being (Knight & Parker, 2021).

Children who adjust faster than their parents may feel disengaged and even react negatively to the parents if they try to impose their native culture, values, morals, and principles, more so if they differ from the host culture (Lebrun, 2019). These differences can create problematic communication and affect children's school performance. Providing parents with information and possible programs about the process of acculturation can assist not only in improving the parent-child relationship but also help parents speed up their adjustment and acculturation, reduce their fears, and reduce negative beliefs about the host society's receptivity.

THE ROLE OF CULTURAL VALUES

Cultural values can make a difference in the acculturation process, playing a role in facilitating or hindering immigrants' acculturation experience in the US. Values, principles, and beliefs can influence how individuals balance their native and host cultures (Aldalur et al., 2022). Children from immigrant families may face educational challenges, different expectations, language barriers, and poor parental support, more so if the parents do not speak the host country's language. These can hinder the children's social integration and academic performance. Educational programs, cultural exchange, and mental health can aid the process and improve acculturation.

Key Cultural Values that Impact Acculturation

Acculturation may be impacted by cultural expressions, family structure, religion, values, morals, and communication, among other variables. These are some of the possible cultural differences that can influence the process.

Individualism vs. Collectivism

- Individualism prioritizes self-expression, personal freedom, and independence. Collectivism emphasizes family ties, group goals, and social harmony. These cultural orientations influence people's adaptation to new environments (Triandis, 2001).
- In collectivist societies (e.g., Hispanic, Asian, and African), people may experience more pressure to preserve family ties and community norms when acculturating. On the other hand, individuals from individualistic cultures (e.g., Europe or the US) may feel more inclined to adopt the behaviors and attitudes of the host culture to assert personal autonomy and individual identity (Berry, 2005).

Power Distance

- Power distance refers to acceptable social levels, meaning people with less power expect and accept unequal power distribution. In cultures like many Asian and Hispanic countries with high power distance, there is often a greater emphasis on hierarchy, respect for authority, and the importance of social roles (Hofstede, 2001).
- Individuals from high power-distance cultures acculturated into low power-distance cultures like the US or some European countries may find it challenging to adapt to more egalitarian and informal social structures (Gudykunst & Kim, 2003).

Time Orientation (Monochronic vs. Polychronic)

- Monochronic cultures, like Western societies, emphasize punctuality, scheduling, and completing tasks individually. Polychronic cultures, like Middle Eastern or Latin cultures, are more flexible with time, often prioritizing relationships over strict schedule adherence (Hall, 1983).
- Individuals from monochronic cultures may experience frustration or confusion when acculturating into polychronic cultures, and vice versa. These differing attitudes toward time influence work habits, social interactions, and perceptions of efficiency (P. R., Harris & Moran, 2000).

Language and Communication Style

- Language is a key element of cultural identity and plays a crucial role in the acculturation process. Differences in communication styles (e.g., direct vs. indirect communication) can influence how effectively individuals acculturate (Gudykunst & Ting-Toomey, 1988).
- People may value explicitness and clarity in cultures with direct communication styles, such as Western cultures. In contrast, in cultures with indirect communication, such as Asian cultures, they prioritize preserving harmony and avoiding confrontation. Adapting to a new communication style can be a significant challenge in acculturation (Hofstede, 2001).

Uncertainty Avoidance

- Uncertainty avoidance refers to how individuals in a society feel threatened by ambiguous situations and prefer clear rules and structures (Sparrow, 1996). Some cultures, like Japanese or

Greek, have a high uncertainty avoidance, preferring predictability and avoiding ambiguity. In contrast, low uncertainty avoidance cultures like Sweden or the US are more comfortable with uncertainty and change (Hofstede, 2001).

- Individuals from high uncertainty avoidance cultures may struggle more with the uncertainty of adapting to a new culture, especially if the new culture has different norms or is perceived as more flexible or chaotic (Baker & Carson, 2011).

National Belonging and Ethnic Identity

- Ethnic identity and national belonging strongly influence the acculturation process. Acculturation can be impacted by the conflict of maintaining ethnic identity and adapting to the new culture (Berry, 1997). Some individuals may assimilate entirely into the host culture, abandoning their original cultural practices (assimilation) or refusing to adapt to the new strong identity with their native culture (separation). Others may abandon their cultural values without adopting the values of the new culture (marginalization) or integrate aspects of the new culture and blend them with their own (Berry, 1980).

Religious Beliefs

- Religion can profoundly affect the acculturation process, especially when the host and native cultures have differing religious beliefs or practices. For example, immigrants from Muslim-majority countries may experience challenges in predominantly Christian or secular countries, particularly concerning religious practices such as prayer times, dietary restrictions, or clothing choices.
- Religious values can act as both a source of resistance to acculturation and a way of maintaining a connection to one's cultural heritage, even while adapting to a new society (Moghaddam, 2024).

Cultural Values from Some of the Ethnic Groups in the US

The US is the third-largest and most culturally diverse country in the world, with a population represented by people from every part of the world; it is considered a melting pot where any community can have people from different races, ethnic backgrounds, religions, and cultures. Such diversity needs acceptance and accommodation of other groups. Accepting is understanding that every individual has the right to be; accommodation is understanding those differences through learning. People should be free to have their values and beliefs and not be expected to agree or like different ones, but increasing tolerance and accommodation can improve our society (Verkuyten et al., 2019).

Asian Americans

- Filial Piety: One of the central values in many Asian cultures (e.g., Chinese, Korean, Japanese) is the deep respect for and loyalty to one's family, particularly parents and elders. This value often influences how individuals interact with their family and community and their approach to work, education, and other aspects of life. In the context of acculturation, filial piety may foster strong family ties and social networks, which can support the acculturation process (Lee & Zhou, 2015).

- Collectivism: Many Asian cultures emphasize the importance of the group over the individual. This value can help Asian immigrants adapt by promoting a sense of community and mutual support, making it easier to form tight-knit ethnic communities that provide resources for newcomers (e.g., job opportunities, cultural events, and language support) (Kerr, 2015; Lee & Zhou, 2015).
- Hard Work and Education: Education and diligence are highly valued in many Asian cultures. This cultural emphasis on education and upward mobility often helps Asian immigrants succeed in the US educational system and the workforce (Lee & Zhou, 2015).
- Impact on Acculturation: These values may help Asian immigrants adapt by reinforcing a strong work ethic and a focus on education, which are also valued in American society. Filial piety and collectivism, however, might create tension in more individualistic American environments, especially among younger generations (Lee & Zhou, 2015).

Hispanic/Latino Americans

- Familismo: Familismo is a cultural value that has been found to promote positive attachments, support, loyalty, honor, family relationship quality, obligation to the family, and individual adjustment (Cahill et al., 2021). Familismo, or the importance of family, is a core value in Hispanic/Latino cultures, including the nuclear family and extended family. Familism provides a strong support network for immigrants in the US (Campos et al., 2014).
- Respect: Respect is highly emphasized in Hispanic cultures, especially for authority figures and elders. Showing respect can be seen in interactions with family members and others, aiding with the complex social environments in the US. (Ruiz, 2005).
- Personalismo: This value prioritizes personal relationships and connections. In a US context, personalismo can facilitate acculturation by helping Hispanic/Latino immigrants develop strong social networks and access resources through trust-based relationships (Vargas, 2017).
- Impact on Acculturation: Respect and families can help immigrants find support and navigate the US without losing connection to their cultural roots. However, these values sometimes clash with American individualism, particularly when younger generations adapt or blend with the new culture faster than their parents and seek autonomy. Personalismo can also help Hispanic immigrants navigate social and professional environments in the US, as it emphasizes the importance of relationship-building, which can be vital for success in various domains (Suárez-Orozco & Suárez-Orozco, 2001).

Haitian Americans

- Collectivism and Community Support: Haitians rely on strong community networks, like many other immigrant groups. These networks provide emotional, social, and economic support, which eases the acculturation process by offering a familiar environment and a shared cultural identity (Basch et al., 1994).
- Religion and Spirituality: Haitian culture strongly emphasizes religion, particularly Christianity (Catholicism and Protestantism) and Vodou. This religious orientation can anchor Haitians in the US, providing a sense of belonging and identity in the face of challenges (Basch et al., 1994).
- Resilience and Adaptability: Given the challenges Haitians face, including political instability and economic hardship, a deep sense of resilience is a cultural value, together with highly family-

oriented, hard-working, and friendly attitudes, helps them overcome adversity, increase their adaptation to new environments, and successfully acculturate to the new society (Basch et al., 1994).

- Impact on Acculturation: Support from religious institutions and community networks is critical for Haitian immigrants' acculturation and adjustment to new societies. These social structures offer critical resources like housing, jobs, and emotional support. However, the significant differences between educational systems and language barriers can challenge complete acculturation (Basch et al., 1994).

Middle Eastern Americans (Arab Americans)

- Hospitality and Generosity: Middle Eastern cultures, particularly Arab cultures, emphasize hospitality and generosity. This cultural trait helps foster strong social networks, providing immigrants valuable emotional and financial support (Sobh et al., 2013).
- Family and Honor: Family and maintaining family honor are central to Middle Eastern cultures. Family honor inspires close-knit family relationships and collective decision-making, helping overcome acculturation process challenges (Mechammil & Cruz, 2022).
- Religious Faith (Islam or Christianity): Religion, particularly Islam for many Arab Americans, is an integral part of life and provides a source of identity and community. Religious institutions can provide social networks to help with acculturation (Abi-Hashem, 2007).
- Impact on Acculturation: Strong family networks, religious institutions, and cultural practices can help Middle Eastern immigrants in the US maintain their cultural identity while facing and overcoming acculturation challenges. These factors can also give immigrants the resilience to adapt successfully and deal with discrimination related to religion and ethnicity (Abi-Hashem, 2007).

African Americans (Immigrant Backgrounds)

- Community and Mutual Aid: African immigrants (e.g., from Nigeria and Ethiopia) often bring a strong sense of community, with values emphasizing mutual aid, support, and solidarity. These communal ties help newcomers acculturate by providing a sense of belonging and resources (Agbemenu, 2016).
- Religion and Spirituality: Like other immigrant groups, African immigrants often place a high value on religion (Christianity or Islam), which can offer comfort and a sense of connection in a new country (Agbemenu, 2016).
- Respect for Elders and Family: Respect for elders is a key value in many African cultures, which can help provide a structured and supportive environment for acculturation, especially in familial settings (Agbemenu, 2016).
- Impact on Acculturation: For African immigrants, strong family ties, religious networks, and good community support can improve their adaptation to the US. However, the process can be complex due to discrimination and financial difficulties (Agbemenu, 2016).

Polynesian Americans

- Relationship-oriented: Success depends on good relationships. Prioritizing the community and hospitality builds trust. Cultural traditions are used to develop relationships when people from outside the community are invited as a gesture of trust and good faith (Mayeda et al., 2005).
- Hierarchical Structure: Ranks and seniority are determined, and they have the last word(Mayeda et al., 2005).
- Group-Oriented: They value group assistance, collaboration, and collective effort. They focus on the achievements and dignity of the collective rather than the individual. They aim to achieve group harmony (Mayeda et al., 2005).
- Impact on Acculturation: For Polynesians, strong relationships, respect for hierarchies, good community support, and group value over the individual may conflict with the different approaches in the mainland USA. Studies have shown that forced acculturation into an individualistic and competitive culture severely affects Hawaiian and Samoan families (Mayeda et al., 2005).

Indigenous Peoples of the Americas

- Cooperation: Cooperation has been a key component of survival, but they also respect individual differences and freedom. Therefore, personal advice is avoided because it is implicit that they should know what to do (McCance-Katz, 2018).
- Collectivism: The group is more important than the individual. Self-value is seen as inappropriate. Eye contact may be seen as a challenge; therefore, they avoid it to show respect. They are aware of the importance of words, so their silence may appear as avoidance or poor communication when they are being cautious (McCance-Katz, 2018).
- Harmony: They believe life should be in harmony with nature. Group harmony is also valued and achieved by collective consensus rather than majority rule (McCance-Katz, 2018).
- Respect of the Elders: Their opinions and views are respected and valued, as well as their traditions and spoken words (McCance-Katz, 2018).
- Impact on Acculturation: There are cultural and traditional values that can help adjust to the US individualistic society. Native cultures value generosity and hospitality. Their value is needed over wealth. Therefore, they distribute wealth by giving gifts, which can be helpful when adjusting to a new environment (McCance-Katz, 2018).

HOW FEAR AFFECTS IMMIGRANT FAMILIES IN ACCULTURATION

Fear is a universal emotion shaping human character and temperament. Fear plays an essential role in reactivity or subconscious self-preservation mechanisms and the creation of faulty assumptions or cognitive dissonance, which leads to harmful behaviors. Fear includes feelings of insecurity, vulnerability, and anxiety triggered by past experiences, childhood upbringing, and communication barriers (LeDoux, 2023; Overall et al., 2022; Subba, 2014). Fear can have a profound impact on immigrant families as they navigate the acculturation process. Fear can make a difference in people's perspectives, inner language, emotions, use of stored memory, and behaviors regardless of gender, age, or individuality (Minor & Herzmann, 2019; Otero et al., 2020; Overall et al., 2022). Love and happiness can only exist by letting go of fear (Jampolsky, 2011). Happy people do better in society (Alexander et al., 2021). Happiness makes people more successful and creative, enjoy teamwork, and increases productivity, creating positive feedback loops feeding their happiness (Diener et al., 2020). Fear is involved in the psychological and cultural adjustments immigrants make when integrating into a new society. Fear can arise from discrimination, concerns about their legal status, economic insecurity, and learning new information to adapt to the host culture. Fear can affect their psychological well-being and ability to engage in and benefit from educational and healthcare systems. Fear can develop into trauma and affect the children's biological development. Research shows that children who experience traumatic events during childhood have variations in the amygdala and hippocampus, influencing feelings, thinking, and behaviors detrimental to psychological health (Kılıç et al., 2024).

The amygdala, hippocampus, and prefrontal cortex are involved in memory and releasing stress hormones adrenaline and noradrenaline in the presence of a threat or the thought of a danger (Córdova et al., 2023). Selective attention increases the detection of the threat efficiently and accurately, which is necessary for self-preservation (Wieser & Keil, 2020). People respond to threats in an autonomic response (fear, self-preservation mechanism) or anxiety, assumptions guided by memories (LeDoux, 2023). Memory is activated when presented with stimuli to determine whether the situation is safe (Dozier, 1998). However, a learned fear can be expressed inappropriately in safe situations fueled by assumptions (Sangha et al., 2020). Incorrect judgment of a problem explains why children misunderstand and become upset with their parents or vice versa, creating unnecessary conflicts that later affect how children perform in school and how they acculturate to a new society. Clinicians and educators should be aware of these factors to provide a secure environment for them to thrive and learn. An age-appropriate educational curriculum to promote early knowledge of how fear affects their physical and mental health can help children and their families differentiate not only imminent threats from subjective experiences of fear and anxiety but also help people to differentiate the uniqueness of their fear from those of others (Bradley, 2024, in press). Each person has a "uniquely individual and wholly subjective meaning of the object of such fear, in the context of their unique life history and mode of mentalization" (Etezady, 2013, p.194).

Possible Issues Affecting Acculturation

New immigrants often experience disruption in their sense of belonging, especially in children, since they may not have a sense of belonging to their culture. Cultural practices, religious or spiritual values, and behavior can increase psychological distress as they acculturate to the host culture (Kayama & Yamakawa, 2020). In addition, there are other factors affecting psychological well-being, such as:

Psychological and Emotional Stress: Immigrants with illegal or undocumented status often live with constant anxiety and fear of deportation. Fear can create chronic stress, which has been shown to lead to mental health issues such as post-traumatic stress disorder, depression, and anxiety, and affect overall health. These mental health issues can hinder acculturation by making it harder for families to engage in positive interactions with the new culture (Chavez & Provine, 2009).

Fear of Discrimination and Xenophobia. Fear of discrimination or being mistreated because of race, ethnicity, or immigration status is a common experience for immigrants, particularly in places where anti-immigrant sentiment has risen (Tummala-Narra, 2020). These experiences can slow down, complicate, or stop the acculturation process, as learning the host society's norms, values, and practices becomes harder. Self-discrimination, perspectives of self-value, capacity to adjust to the new culture, and optimistic versus pessimistic views can determine the self-esteem and attitude towards the new society, which can delay the acculturation process. This fear can lead to isolation due to withdrawal from social and community engagement. Isolation can hinder the formation of supportive relationships with native-born citizens (Choy et al., 2021).

Barriers to Educational Engagement. Immigrant families who are fearful of legal repercussions, more so for the undocumented ones, may experience fear of being questioned about revealing their legal status and being reported to the authorities (Gándara & Ee, 2022). Such fear can prevent children from attending schools and parents from accessing resources for their children and engaging with educational institutions (Rodriguez, 2022). This lack of engagement can negatively affect the academic achievement and social adjustment of immigrant children since parents avoid seeking help for their children at school or attending parent-teacher conferences, further hindering their acculturation process (Martin, 2016).

Cultural and Linguistic Barriers. The effects of acculturation on families can be negative or positive due to generational differences, socio-economic status, and degree of acculturation. The acculturation process can significantly change family dynamics, affecting family interactions and children's education. Cultural differences between new cultural values and the native cultural values of the immigrant parents can clash, affecting how they relate and what activities they choose to participate in. These cultural differences can increase avoidance of community or school-related activities, reduce access to beneficial services, and delay their integration and acculturation. Fear of making mistakes in language or cultural practices can also inhibit immigrants from fully participating in their new society. Language barriers are often compounded by fear of being judged or ridiculed for not speaking the dominant language fluently (Gonzalez, 2016).

Impacts on Family Dynamics. Acculturation often changes family dynamics, such as relationships, communication patterns, and roles, particularly between parents and children (Diaz & Bui, 2017). The acculturation process varies in speed and style across family members, increasing generational growth in cultural identification (Birman & Poff, 2011). Children of immigrant parents with limited proficiency in the host language assume the role of family brokers, not just translators; they are mediators or representatives for their parents and sometimes extended family (Araujo, 2008). This shift can alter family dynamics because the children can influence the transmitted information, placing additional responsibilities and some levels of control on children and leading to role reversal, affecting the parent-child relationship hierarchy (Padilla & Perez, 2003).

Generational Differences in Acculturation. Children often acculturate faster than their parents due to their exposure to the host culture through school and peers. These discrepancies can create a generation and acculturation gap between parents and children. Children may adopt the cultural norms and values of the host country, leading to potential conflicts within the family and acculturative stress (Anisman et al., 2024; Qiu, 2025). Parents may struggle and feel pressured to balance their native cultural heritage, values, and practices with the desire to integrate into the host culture and adapt to the new society's expectations (Nesteruk, 2022; Suárez-Orozco & Suárez-Orozco, 2001). Immigrant parents may have higher acculturative stress due to their inability to adapt to the new culture at the same speed as their children, more so when cross-cultural differences contradict their core values and beliefs (Barker & Cornwell, 2019; Renzaho et al., 2017). The struggle often leads to role strain, reduced monitoring, erosion of family hierarchies, and deterioration of family bonds (Marsiglia et al., 2014).

Impacts on Children's Education. The acculturation process plays a role in the effectiveness of children's education. Acculturation can affect children when they struggle to balance their family's cultural expectations and the academic demands of the host society (Vakkai et al., 2020).

Factors to Consider in Children's Education

- Academic Performance: Learning a second language is often challenging and can cause delays in reading, comprehension, and writing skills, affecting overall academic achievement, especially in the early stages of acculturation. Immigrant children often face challenges in language acquisition, more so when they are surrounded by people who do not speak the host culture's language and are forced to use their native language at home. This can negatively affect their academic performance (Portes & Rumbaut, 2001).
- Social Integration and Peer Relationships: Acculturation also impacts children's peer interactions. In some cases, immigrant children may face social isolation or discrimination due to their cultural background, resulting in acculturative stress, which can affect their self-esteem and willingness to engage in school activities (Rudmin, 2009).
- Cultural Differences in Educational Expectations: The educational system and expectations of the native culture can differ significantly from the host culture. Some cultures emphasize learning and memorization, while the US focuses more on critical thinking and active participation. These differences can affect how children perceive and engage with their schooling, adjust to school, and meet teachers' expectations (Suárez-Orozco & Suárez-Orozco, 2001).
- Academic Expectations and Standards: The academic environment should promote every child's unique capacity and skills—children who reach their potential use their unique gifts and capabilities. Maintaining high standards and expectations can help children find their capacity and sense of worth and improve their school performance. Research shows that academic standards and expectations should not be lowered. Educational and parents' educational expectations positively affect children's cognition and reduce depression in both rural and urban environments (M. Liu et al., 2022).
- Parental Involvement: The degree to which parents acculturate can affect their level of involvement in their children's education. More acculturated parents may feel more confident navigating the school system, while less acculturated parents may struggle to engage with teachers and school personnel. Research results show that parental involvement in children's education positively correlates with the parents' level of acculturation; the higher the level of acculturation in parents, the more involved they are in school activities (Valencia, 2002; Youssef, 2023).

Positive Effects of Acculturation

While acculturation can present challenges, there are also positive effects, mainly when the family balances cultural adaptation with preserving heritage. Some positive outcomes are bicultural competence and stronger family resilience. Bicultural competence results from successfully acculturating to a new culture while maintaining the native culture. Bicultural children have several advantages when interacting with their home and host cultures. Research shows that bicultural children have enhanced cognitive flexibility, social adaptability, and higher success in future career opportunities (Berry, 1997). Stronger family resilience assists families navigating acculturation with open communication, mutual support, and shared goals, often experiencing greater cohesion and resilience, facilitating acculturation (Choi & Park, 2012).

Comprehensive approach. Educators and clinicians are crucial in helping children navigate acculturation challenges while maintaining their cultural identity. The process can be a complex and sometimes stressful experience for children, particularly those from immigrant or refugee backgrounds. There are several steps to mitigate the adverse effects of fear on immigrant families and support their acculturation process.

Create a Culturally Responsive Environment. Educators and clinicians should establish an inclusive, safe, and stable environment using regular communication and providing parents and children with sufficient information. Educators should incorporate diverse perspectives into the curriculum to create an inclusive environment. Offer bilingual resources and use culturally relevant teaching methods. Acknowledge and celebrate the cultural backgrounds of all students. Provide parents with enough information so every decision about their child goes through a process where pros and cons are discussed, and their decision-making is not affected by language barriers and misunderstandings (Coleman & Yeh, 2008).

- *Create a Safe and Inclusive Environment:* Educators and clinicians should foster cultural sensitivity by emphasizing safe, inclusive, and accepting environments. Ensuring that immigrant families feel safe and accepted within educational and healthcare settings is crucial. Educators should adapt teaching methods, understand diverse cultural backgrounds, and promote respect for all cultures to improve student engagement and learning. For example, schools and clinics can display materials in multiple languages, employ culturally competent staff, and relocate to areas where immigrant families can feel safe while discussing their concerns without fear of judgment or legal repercussions (Cheetham, 2022).
- *Curriculum and Classroom Practices*: Educators can demonstrate appreciation for diversity by including books, materials, and examples from the children's native cultures in their class. This approach helps children feel valued and understood, which is critical for reducing feelings of alienation (Mittal & Wieling, 2006). Asking for monthly reports written by parents to increase the collaboration between educators and families in their native language, if they do not write in English (translation services should be available for this matter; it does not have to be done at the school level, it could be at a county or city level). Projects and assignments should be focused on strengths and favorite parts of their native culture. Cultural days and celebrations throughout the school year can promote sharing and accepting the positive aspects of their native culture while introducing alternative approaches to the new culture (Gonzalez, 2016).
- *Bilingual Support:* Providing language support, such as ESL (English as a Second Language) programs or bilingual staff, is crucial in helping children understand academic content while learning English (Nieto, 2010)—academic support, guidance in native language through staff, or online services. After-school programs can focus on school work and English language acquisition, which could assist with reducing conflict at home and children taking advantage of the parents' lack of understanding. Resources, activities, and support with a multicultural perspective can encourage children and families to participate and share their backgrounds without fear.

- *Support Language Acquisition:* Helping immigrant families overcome the fear of language barriers is essential for their acculturation. Schools and clinicians can offer language support programs that are culturally sensitive and designed to reduce feelings of shame or embarrassment about not speaking the dominant language. Language classes for adults and children, bilingual counseling, and interpretation services can all be valuable tools for bridging communication gaps and empowering immigrant families (Falicov, 2014).

Social and Emotional Support. Acculturation can cause stress, anxiety, and identity confusion, so clinicians and educators should have sufficient knowledge and skills to provide a social and emotional support-based approach to help children navigate these feelings. Using such an approach can help children increase their coping skills, optimism, positive views, and benefit from adjusting to the new society, increasing the possibility for success (E. Allen, 2021).

- *Provide Psychological Support:* Immigrant families, particularly those dealing with trauma, discrimination, or the fear of deportation, can benefit from mental health support. Educators and clinicians should be able to recognize signs of anxiety, depression, or PTSD and refer families to appropriate mental health services. Trauma-informed care approaches that prioritize safety, trust, and empowerment can help alleviate the psychological stress associated with fear (Subica & Link, 2024).
- *Counseling and Therapy:* Mental health professionals can assist children in managing acculturation stress, identity conflicts, and cultural clashes that may arise in their new environment (Rogers-Sirin et al., 2014). Establishing trust is crucial to encourage openness for effective communication with immigrant children and their families. Clinicians and educators should use active listening, be supportive, demonstrate empathy, and engage in culturally relevant practices.
- *Social Skills Training:* For immigrant children, learning the social norms of the new culture is essential. Clinicians and educators can offer social skills training, role play, and peer mentoring to help students adjust to unfamiliar peer interactions and school settings. Give them specific exercises to increase their coping and resilience. Provide them with information about the value of gratitude. Help children feel proud about their daily activities, progress, and accomplishments, which can promote their self-esteem, capacity for improvement, and a positive view of their future (Silbereisen & Titzmann, 2014).

Promote Peer Support and Integration. Peer relationships can significantly influence a child's sense of belonging and adjustment. Educators and clinicians can encourage cross-cultural interactions, group activities, and inclusive extracurricular programs that facilitate integration. Create clubs where students with a higher level of acculturation provide their insights and what has worked for them to new students.

- *Parent Inclusion*: Including parents in the educational system keeps them informed about their children's progress, can also help them socialize with other parents, and increases their understanding of the differences between the educational system in the US and their native culture. During family nights, immigrant families can be informed about social events, book fairs, workshops, or other activities involving information that can help with acculturation. (Padilla, 2006).
- *Peer Mentorship:* Pairing children with peers with similar backgrounds or who have successfully acculturated can provide emotional and social support. Once immigrant children are

more confident and secure, groups with children from different backgrounds can help them learn about others (Padilla, 2006).

- *Group Activities:* Encouraging participation in sports, arts, or community service activities where children from diverse backgrounds work together helps to promote mutual understanding and acceptance (Padilla, 2006).

Encourage Family Engagement. Family involvement is critical in the acculturation process. Educators and clinicians should work to build strong partnerships with families to provide consistent support across home and school environments (Suárez-Orozco & Suárez-Orozco, 2001).

- *Provide Clear and Accessible Information:* Fear often arises from uncertainty and lack of information, especially about legal status or immigrants' rights. Educators and clinicians should provide clear, accurate, and accessible information about legal rights, available services, and how to navigate institutions (e.g., school systems or healthcare). Information can be shared through multilingual outreach, workshops, or informational pamphlets that address common concerns of immigrant families (Gelatt et al., 2014). Avoid providing parents with their children's negative behaviors; provide solutions and strategies to improve performance to avoid frustration, disappointment, and conflict between parents and children.
- *Parent Education:* Addressing specific needs of the children and parents. Home support in school work and learning is essential. If parents are not well informed or cannot speak or understand school homework, it will affect the child's performance. Provide parents and children with information about resources and programs that help them understand the educational system and cultural expectations. Provide them, when necessary, with detailed information and referrals to professional help, mental health, and family cohesion in their native language. (Suárez-Orozco & Suárez-Orozco, 2001). Distribute brochures with detailed information to help them learn coping strategies to manage acculturation stress.
- *Family Liaison:* Encourage dialogue and multicultural perspectives between the children by encouraging them to do projects with their parents, allowing them to tell their stories and family traditions. This approach can assist children in feeling proud and unique about their background, so acculturation does not involve one's culture and create generational gaps and conflict (H. V. Nguyen et al., 2024). Staff members who act as cultural liaisons or family support specialists can bridge gaps between home and school, facilitating better communication and understanding (O. Harris, 2024). Parents should be invited regularly to meet with teachers to guide them on how they can help their children navigate the school websites so they can stay informed about their child's progress.

Foster Bicultural Competence. Educators and clinicians can help children navigate their home and new cultures by fostering bicultural competence. Counselors and educators should provide appropriate care and support and encourage openness to the new culture, which allows them to balance both identities without feeling pressured to choose one over the other (Berry, 2005).

- *Promote Positive Cultural Identity:* Encourage children to maintain their cultural practices and language while adapting to the new culture. This approach can include allowing students to share their traditions, customs, and language with other children and validating their experiences.
- *Self-Awareness*: Avoid stereotyping and generalizations, even within the same cultural background. Recognize that each child and family has its differences and dynamics. Use a mul-

ticultural lens to incorporate multicultural perspectives by focusing on and using what is beneficial to each culture. Understanding their experiences is critical.

- *Role Models and Mentors:* Offer programs with immigrants who have successfully navigated the acculturation process and are examples of success stories that can provide valuable guidance and support for younger children (Berry, 2005).

Improve the English language acquisition. Educators and clinicians can offer language support, which is critical for immigrant families adjusting to a new culture. Offering translation services, language classes, and bilingual materials helps reduce communication gaps and improve family involvement in the educational process.

- *Language Acquisition*: Introduce the new language through visuals (movies, pictures, games). Avoid highlighting the mispronunciations and repeat the correct way of saying the word—hands-on work and role-play conversational activities between fluent students and immigrant children.
- *Provide Support:* Constantly value the benefits of bilingualism. Foster a sense of belonging with a welcoming attitude to parents and children.
- *Evaluating the efficiency of support strategies*: Tracking academic performance through participation in school activities, family feedback, and self-evaluations. Evaluation of the programs is critical for continuously upgrading them by gathering feedback from immigrant families to assess their needs and adjust programs accordingly for better outcomes.

Provide Trauma-Informed Care. Clinicians, educators, and school personnel should be trained in trauma-informed approaches and the impact of past experiences on acculturation and mental health. The goal is to be able to identify any behavioral or emotional signs of trauma, more so for children who have experienced displacement due to war, violence, or other traumatic events (Burgund Isakov & Markovic, 2024; Van der Kolk, 2014).

- *Create Safe Spaces:* Establish a school environment where children feel physically and emotionally safe. Use trauma-informed practices such as sensitive questioning and empathetic listening. Provide a supportive approach where children can speak about their home environment without pressure, avoid leading questions that make them feel they are betraying their parents, and avoid re-traumatization (Van der Kolk, 2014).
- *Transparent and Open Communication with Parents:* Inform parents about possible physical or emotional signs that are part of mandatory reporting, so that parents know the differences between corporal punishment in their native culture and what is considered problematic in the US. Provide step-by-step information about the protocol for a mandatory report if the children or parents disclose any possible harm. Provide them with referrals to mental health services if necessary.
- *Collaborate with Mental Health Professionals:* Work with clinicians to offer therapy services, particularly for children showing signs of trauma, depression, or anxiety due to their past or acculturation experiences.

Engagement through the community. Educators and clinicians should be cognizant of local organizations, resources, and networks that offer support services so they can forward them to families who need assistance. Using resources and collaboration with established organizations can foster inclusion by providing information about cultural events, community, school activities, legal aid, and counseling (Gelatt et al., 2014).

- *Promote Family and Community Engagement*: Encouraging immigrant families to become involved in community activities can reduce their feelings of isolation and help them form social networks. This approach can also help children develop a stronger sense of belonging, easing their acculturation process. Schools and community organizations should create opportunities for immigrant families to engage in culturally relevant and supportive activities.
- *Resources and Referrals:* Educators and clinicians should have information about available resources to make appropriate referrals depending on the family's needs. Organizations can offer programs and workshops focused on solutions for all possible acculturation challenges.

The Role of Marriage and Family Therapists

Marriage and Family Therapists (MFTs) can offer therapy that focuses on helping immigrant individuals and families facing acculturation challenges navigate these transitions as they adapt to a new culture and society. Below are several ways MFTs can assist immigrant families:

Cultural Adjustment and Acculturation Support

- MFTs can provide significant support for immigrant families, addressing a variety of challenges unique to their experiences, such as cultural adjustment, acculturation stress, language barriers, trauma, and family dynamics (M. Allen et al., 2024; K. T. Nguyen, 2024).
- MFTs can assist immigrant families in understanding the stress of maintaining cultural values while integrating into a new host culture and how this process can affect family, peer, and community relationships (Atkinson & Hackett, 2004).
- MFTs should use culturally competent, responsive treatment strategies that consider cultural differences and respect immigrant families' cultural backgrounds, values, and practices. Culturally responsive therapy focuses on identifying family dynamics within the context of the client's cultural heritage (Hwang & Wood, 2009).
- MFTs must continuously educate themselves about cultural values, beliefs, traditions, morals, and customs that may shape immigrant families' experiences.
- MFTs should use culturally relevant therapeutic techniques and be mindful of cultural norms, such as the role of elders, gender expectations, and the significance of extended family in decision-making processes.
- MFTs can facilitate open dialogues where each family member is encouraged to share their experiences, struggles, and hopes. Encouraging communication styles that reflect the cultural backgrounds of the family members can help bridge generational gaps (Chadwick, 2020; Gursoy et al., 2008).
- MFTs should support families in exploring their cultural identity in a way that allows for integration rather than assimilation. Helping family members find common ground and embrace aspects of both cultures can promote a sense of belonging and self-acceptance (Yampolsky et al., 2013).
- MFTs should build rapport through culturally appropriate greetings, showing empathy, and using culturally familiar metaphors, which can help in making immigrant families feel understood and respected (Souto-Manning, 2007).

- MFTs should provide referrals to culturally competent community organizations, offer group therapy sessions for immigrant families, and encourage participation in community events that help reduce cultural gaps.

Possible Ways MFTs can Mitigate Trauma and Provide Mental Health Support to Help Clients During Acculturation

- MFTs should help clients reframe their experiences and build resilience through strength-based interventions, focusing on their ability to overcome adversity rather than just the deficits and challenges they face, which can lead to more positive outcomes (Hovhannisyan, 2024; Khawaja et al., 2021). This approach acknowledges and builds upon the coping strategies families have developed during their migration journey and highlights their coping strategies, such as community support, religious involvement, and cultural traditions.
- MFTs should emphasize the value of utilizing family dynamics and communication patterns as a source of support to encourage families to work together to overcome adversity (Zigarelli, 2017).
- MFTs can provide trauma-informed therapy to help families cope with the psychological and emotional effects of experienced trauma, whether due to displacement, discrimination, violence, or war, in addition to unique stressors related to cultural adjustment, discrimination, economic hardship, and legal issues. MFTs can use various evidence-based strategies to offer culturally sensitive, trauma-informed care, improving family relationships and mental health outcomes (Atkinson & Hackett, 2004).
- MFTs need to understand the cultural backgrounds of their clients, including traditions, values, and practices, to create a safe, supportive therapeutic environment. Use culturally relevant interventions and consider how trauma may be experienced differently depending on the client's cultural context (Tummala-Narra, 2007).
- MFTs should create a safe space for clients, empowering them to process their trauma at their own pace, avoiding re-traumatization (Medina, 2022), and help clients using culturally strength-based interventions, focusing on their abilities, strong familial bonds, and community support, which can be sources of resilience.
- MFTs should consider immigrant families' struggle with loss, displacement, and cultural dislocation. Narrative therapy can be especially effective in helping these families, allowing them to "rewrite" their stories and helping them create new perspectives for their lives in their new environment (Esquivel et al., 2010).
- MFTs should not work in isolation but rather collaborate with other professionals (e.g., social workers, medical professionals, legal advisors) and community organizations supporting immigrant families. These professionals can offer services that address the social determinants of health, such as housing instability, food insecurity, and legal assistance, facilitating connections between clients and community-based services that provide language classes, legal aid, and support groups for immigrant families.
- MFTs can provide referrals or psychoeducation about the immigration process and guidance on managing new legal and healthcare systems. Help families find coping strategies to manage anxiety, fear, or legal stressors as they process the uncertainty of their immigration status (Garcini et al., 2022).

How MFTs Can Assist with Language and Communication Barriers during Acculturation

- MFTs can help immigrant families navigate language barriers, which are a common issue for immigrant families. The inability to speak a new language can impact family communication, relationship dynamics, and the ability to access education and mental health services (Sue & Sue, 2013).
- MFTs can connect families with interpreters to facilitate better communication with and within the family and even provide references to other needed services.
- MFTs should receive training in addressing differences in communication styles, values around family hierarchy, and gender roles, which are particularly important in immigrant contexts. Understanding the cultural background and practices of the family can increase trust and improve communication (Cole et al., 2016).
- MFTs need to avoid language issues becoming a barrier to effective treatment. Ensure therapy sessions are conducted in the client's preferred language or use an interpreter to bridge communication gaps. Referring clients to bilingual therapists, providing translated materials, and adapting therapeutic methods to be more inclusive can enhance communication and the therapeutic alliance.
- MFTs should be cautious of using family members as interpreters, which can create confidentiality and power dynamics issues (Resera et al., 2015).
- MFTs should address their language barriers and cultural competence. Studies show that immigrants with higher acculturation and language proficiency have a higher use of mental health services (Derr, 2016).
- MFTs should practice active listening. Listening to words and being attuned to emotional cues and non-verbal signals. When language is a barrier, therapists should validate clients' feelings, communicate empathy, and avoid rushing to translate or resolve issues too quickly. Creating a safe environment helps clients feel more comfortable sharing their experiences, even without perfect language fluency (Germer & Neff, 2013).
- MFTs should observe body language, facial expressions, and tone of voice closely. Many immigrant families may struggle with language fluency but may still rely on non-verbal forms of communication to express feelings and thoughts. Additionally, understanding how different cultures use silence, eye contact, and physical proximity can help therapists decode meaning beyond words (Cox et al., 2021).
- MFTs should encourage all family members to participate in therapy and communicate their perspectives, which can be particularly important in immigrant families where communication patterns may be hierarchical or influenced by generational differences. Encouraging younger generations to speak and share their views can help foster more open communication channels, reduce misunderstandings, and enhance resilience against acculturative challenges (Brown & Shay, 2021; Bunn et al., 2022).

MFTs Should Work With Families Focusing on Parent-Child Relationships and Intergenerational Conflict

- MFTs can work with families to improve communication, reduce conflicts, and strengthen parent-child relationships by fostering mutual understanding and respect for cultural values. Immigrant families may be facing intergenerational struggles between parents and children, more so when children are more acculturated to the host country's culture (Choi & Park, 2012).
- MFTs should address acculturation gaps. Immigrant families often experience differing rates of acculturation between parents and children, leading to misunderstandings and conflicts. Therapists can facilitate open dialogues to bridge these gaps, helping family members understand each other's cultural adaptations and perspectives (Renteria, 2017).
- MFTs using Structural Family Therapy (SFT) should be adapted to address the unique dynamics of immigrant families. Guidelines have been developed for therapists working with East Asian American families to modify SFT approaches, considering cultural values and family hierarchies (S. Liu, 2018).
- MFTs can use Contextual Family Therapy, which emphasizes relational ethics and multigenerational processes. This approach offers a framework to address complex dynamics and generational patterns in immigrant families and considers the broader cultural and ethical contexts influencing family relationships (Glebova et al., 2024).
- MFTs are encouraged to develop cultural competence to work with diverse families effectively. Culturally Informed and Flexible Family-Based Treatment for Adolescents (CIFFTA) is one approach that adjusts interventions to the cultural contexts of minority families, increasing engagement and outcome (Santisteban et al., 2012).
- MFTs should differentiate immigrant families from transnational families. Transnational individuals go back and forth between the host nation and their country of origin, maintaining their cultural beliefs and behaviors (Chioneso, 2008). In addition, MFTs should broaden their assumptions about this type of family. Families that have to go back and forth and spend extended periods away from their country, like military families, may show these characteristics (Lucas, 2023; Muruthi et al., 2015).

Addressing Acculturation Stress and Mental Health Disorders

Immigrant families often experience acculturation stress, which can lead to mental health issues such as depression and anxiety. MFTs can assist families by helping them recognize and address the stress's impact, offer coping strategies, and provide a supportive environment to discuss mental health concerns (M. Allen et al., 2024; Nagy et al., 2024).

- MFTs should be flexible and adaptable in their approach to therapy. Understanding that traditional therapeutic models may not always fit the immigrant experience. For example, working with generational differences, different views on mental health, and cultural norms can all shape how therapy should be structured. Culturally relevant interventions can make therapy more accessible and relatable to the family.
- Cognitive Behavioral Therapy (CBT) strategies have been adapted to address acculturative stress among Latin American immigrants and refugees. Therapists emphasize acknowledging accultur-

ative stress, exploring immigration narratives, and employing behavioral activation techniques. These strategies have been effective in treating common mental health conditions such as depression, anxiety, and trauma-related somatization.

- MFTs can employ a systemic framework, allowing them to address the psychological sequelae experienced by immigrants. This approach considers the individual within the broader context of family, community, and societal systems, enabling a comprehensive treatment of acculturative stress. Clinicians can help immigrant clients develop social skills and support networks by using a loss and adaptation framework to address any psychological sequelae experienced during the immigration journey (Beckerman & Corbett, 2008).
- MFTs can help clients navigate the complexities of immigration-related stress, focusing on building resilience through culturally sensitive therapeutic practices. Use tailored approaches for each family to address barriers to mental health services for immigrants, including acculturation stress, fear, and stigma (Jo, 2020; Leong & Lau, 2001).

Ways MFTs Can Help Strengthen Family Bonds and Support Networks

- MFTs can work with immigrant families to strengthen family bonds and enhance their social support systems.
- MFTs can help immigrant families navigate life cycle transitions, manage cultural changes, and promote more muscular family support systems by facilitating discussions about the importance of family cohesion, helping families create support networks, and fostering a sense of community in their new environment (McGoldrick & Hardy, 2008).
- MFTs should use family-based mental health interventions, such as parenting groups, multiple family groups, and home visiting interventions, which have shown potential in improving family functioning and mental health outcomes among refugee families. These interventions often utilize non-specialized or peer providers to deliver culturally sensitive support (Bunn et al., 2022).
- MFTs should enhance family support and cohesion since they protect against acculturation stress. Strengthening family bonds can mitigate the risk of depression and anxiety among first-generation immigrant youth (Bunn et al., 2022; Hertlein, 2023).

Legal and Immigration-Related Stress

The immigration process can be stressful and complex. MFTs can offer emotional support to families dealing with the uncertainty of immigration status, navigating legal processes, and managing the anxiety these issues cause (Garcini et al., 2022). Additionally, they can work with community resources that provide legal assistance (Burnett, 2008).

- MFTs should address legal vulnerabilities and associated trauma to enhance psychological well-being and resilience in these populations (Roberg et al., 2024).
- MFTs should directly address acculturative stress in their clinical practice to improve mental health outcomes for this population. CBT strategies have been found effective in helping immigrant families face and deal with legal issues and acculturative stress (Nagy et al., 2024).

CONCLUSIONS

Navigating acculturation presents both challenges and opportunities for families and children. By fostering trust and strong support systems and promoting cultural integration, professionals can help immigrant families enhance family dynamics, improve educational experiences for future generations, and guide them to thrive and successfully integrate into their new communities. Fear is a significant barrier to the acculturation of immigrant families, impacting their mental health, social integration, educational engagement, and overall ability to navigate the complexities of a new culture (Dail, 1988). By addressing the sources of fear and fostering trust, professionals can help immigrant families by creating supportive environments, offering mental health services, promoting community engagement, providing clear information, and supporting language acquisition, which are strategies. The impact of acculturation on family dynamics and children's education is multifaceted and can lead to challenges and opportunities. While generational differences, cultural conflict, and language barriers can pose obstacles, acculturation can foster resilience, bicultural competence, and greater opportunities for academic and social success.

Understanding these dynamics is crucial for clinicians, educators, policymakers, and community organizations working to support immigrant families and their children through culturally sensitive approaches, emphasizing understanding the unique challenges each child and their family face and fostering healthy environments that promote cultural integration and academic success—building relationships with the family, and encouraging collaboration with the educators. Marriage and family therapists can adopt several strategies to provide comprehensive support to immigrant families dealing with cultural adjustment and acculturation challenges. These strategies foster communication, resilience, and identity integration, leading to healthier family dynamics and better mental health outcomes. Therapists must remain culturally informed and flexible, using diverse approaches tailored to the unique needs of each family they serve.

REFERENCES

Abi-Hashem, N. (2007). Arab Americans: Understanding their challenges, needs, and struggles. In *Ethnocultural perspectives on disaster and trauma: Foundations, issues, and applications* (pp. 115–173). Springer New York.

Agbemenu, K. (2016). Acculturation and health behaviors of African immigrants living in the United States: An integrative review. *The ABNF Journal*, *27*(3), 67–73. https://pubmed.ncbi.nlm.nih.gov/29443470/ PMID: 29443470

Al-Haddad, M. (2024). Facilitating international medical graduates' acculturation: From theory to practice. *Medical Education*, *58*(1), 136–148. DOI: 10.1111/medu.15175 PMID: 37524527

Aldalur, A., Bridgett, T., & Pick, L. H. (2022). Psychological assessment reports for linguistically minoritized clients: Considerations for ethical and professional practice. *Professional Psychology, Research and Practice*, *53*(6), 606–614. DOI: 10.1037/pro0000462 PMID: 37744892

Alexander, R., Aragón, O. R., Bookwala, J., Cherbuin, N., Gatt, J. M., Kahrilas, I. J., Kästner, N., Lawrence, A., Lowe, L., Morrison, R. G., Mueller, S. C., Nusslock, R., Papadelis, C., Polnaszek, K. L., Richter, S. H. L., Silton, R. L., & Styliadis, C. (2021). The neuroscience of positive emotions and affect: Implications for cultivating happiness and wellbeing. *Neuroscience and Biobehavioral Reviews*, *121*, 220–249. DOI: 10.1016/j.neubiorev.2020.12.002 PMID: 33307046

Allen, E. (2021). Promoting the mental health and well-being of first-generation immigrants, asylum seekers and refugee young people in schools: a participatory action research study. University of Salford. ProQuest Dissertations & Theses, 28845227. https://www.proquest.com/openview/9c48e1172ec0f802adf6231855f01114

Allen, M., Armenta, B., Watters, E. R., Aflatooni, L., & Sorenson, L. (2024). Experiences of acculturation stress in first-generation immigrant children: Examining the relationship among acculturation stress, depression, and family dynamics. *Journal of International Migration and Integration*, •••, 1–20. DOI: 10.1007/s12134-024-01210-4

Anisman, H., Doubad, D., Asokumar, A., & Matheson, K. (2024). Psychosocial and neurobiological aspects of the worldwide refugee crisis: From vulnerability to resilience. Neuroscience & Biobehavioral Reviews, 165, 1–33. 105859. https://doi.org/DOI: 10.1016/j.neubiorev.2024.105859

Araujo, L. (2008). A voice: The role of child interpreters in their parents' immigration and settlement experience in Canada. Theses and dissertations. Paper 77. Retrieved from http://digitalcommons.ryerson.ca/dissertations

Atkinson, D. R., & Hackett, G. M. (2004). *Counseling and psychotherapy with culturally diverse clients*. SAGE Publications.

Baker, D. S., & Carson, K. D. (2011). The two faces of uncertainty avoidance: Attachment and adaptation. *Journal of Behavioral and Applied Management*, *12*(2), 128–141. DOI: 10.21818/001c.17633

Barker, G. G., & Cornwell, T. L. (2019). Acculturation, communication, and family relationships: Challenges and opportunities. *Western Journal of Communication, 83*(5), 624–646. DOI: 10.1080/10570314.2019.1620961

Basch, L., Glick Schiller, N., & Szanton Blanc, C. (1994). *Nations unbound: Transnational Projects, postcolonial predicaments, and de-centered Theory*. Routledge.

Beckerman, N. L., & Corbett, L. (2008). Immigration and families: Treating acculturative stress from a systemic framework. *Family Therapy, 35*(2), 63–81. https://psycnet.apa.org/record/2008-16380-001

Berry, J. W. (1980). Acculturation as varieties of adaptation. In Padilla, A. M. (Ed.), *Acculturation: Theory, model, and some new findings* (pp. 9–25). Westview Press.

Berry, J. W. (1997). Immigration, acculturation, and adaptation. *Applied Psychology, 46*(1), 5–34. DOI: 10.1111/j.1464-0597.1997.tb01087.x

Berry, J. W. (2005). Acculturation: Living successfully in two cultures. *International Journal of Intercultural Relations, 29*(6), 697–712. DOI: 10.1016/j.ijintrel.2005.07.013

Birman, D., & Poff, M. (2011). Intergenerational differences in acculturation. Encyclopedia on Early Childhood Development, 11, 1–8. Retrieved from https://www.child-encyclopedia.com/pdf/expert/immigration/according-experts/intergenerational-differences-acculturation

Bradley, A. (2024 in press). *Exploring the relationship between relational fear and romantic relationship quality*.

Brown, C., & Shay, M. (2021). From resilience to wellbeing: Identity-building as an alternative framework for schools' role in promoting children's mental health. *Review of Education, 9*(2), 599–634. DOI: 10.1002/rev3.3264

Bunn, M., Zolman, N., Smith, C. P., Khanna, D., Hanneke, R., Betancourt, T. S., & Weine, S. (2022). Family-based mental health interventions for refugees across the migration continuum: A systematic review. *SSM. Mental Health, 2*, 100153. DOI: 10.1016/j.ssmmh.2022.100153 PMID: 37529116

Burgund Isakov, A., & Markovic, V. (2024). Systematic review of trauma-informed approaches and trauma-informed care for forced migrant families: Concepts and contexts. *Trauma, Violence & Abuse, 25*(5), 3999–4015. DOI: 10.1177/15248380241266161 PMID: 39126194

Burnett, C. (2008). The psychological impact of immigration on the family. *Journal of Family Psychotherapy, 19*(3), 255–270. DOI: 10.1080/08975350802477616

Cahill, K. M., Updegraff, K. A., Causadias, J. M., & Korous, K. M. (2021). Familism values and adjustment among Hispanic/Latino individuals: A systematic review and meta-analysis. *Psychological Bulletin, 147*(9), 947–985. DOI: 10.1037/bul0000336

Campos, B., Ullman, J. B., Aguilera, A., & Dunkel Schetter, C. (2014). Familism and psychological health: The intervening role of closeness and social support. *Cultural Diversity & Ethnic Minority Psychology, 20*(2), 191–201. https://psycnet.apa.org/buy/2014-14452-003. DOI: 10.1037/a0034094 PMID: 24773004

Chadwick, A. (2020). Bridging the generation gap in Higher Education: Intergenerational student challenge and support within families (Doctoral dissertation, University of Central Lancashire). Retrieved from https://clok.uclan.ac.uk/40415/?template=default_internal

Chavez, L. R., & Provine, D. M. (2009). The evolution of immigration enforcement in the United States. *Social Science Quarterly*, *90*(2), 426–445. DOI: 10.1177/0002716208331014 PMID: 24222715

Cheetham, J. (2022). *Social work with immigrants*. Routledge.

Chioneso, N. A. (2008). Expressions of African/Caribbean cultural roots in Canada. *Journal of Black Studies*, *39*(1), 69–84. DOI: 10.1177/0021934706295411

Choi, H. J., & Park, C. H. (2012). Parent-child conflict among immigrant families: A critical review of literature. *Journal of Family Theory & Review*, *4*(3), 211–223. DOI: 10.1111/j.1756-2589.2012.00096.x

Choy, B., Arunachalam, K., Gupta, S., Taylor, M., & Lee, A. (2021). Systematic review: Acculturation strategies and their impact on the mental health of migrant populations. *Public Health in Practice (Oxford, England)*, *2*, 100069. DOI: 10.1016/j.puhip.2020.100069 PMID: 36101596

Cole, M., David, S., & Jiménez, R. (2016). Collaborative translation: Negotiating student investment in culturally responsive p1edagogy. *Language Arts*, *93*(6), 430–443. DOI: 10.58680/la201628636

Coleman, H. L. K., & Yeh, C. (2008). *Handbook of school counseling* (1st ed.). Routledge., DOI: 10.4324/9780203874806

Córdova, A., Caballero-García, A., Drobnic, F., Roche, E., & Noriega, D. C. (2023). Influence of stress and emotions in the learning process: The example of COVID-19 on university students: A narrative review. *Health Care*, *11*(12), 1787. DOI: 10.3390/healthcare11121787 PMID: 37372905

Cox, R. B.Jr, deSouza, D. K., Bao, J., Lin, H., Sahbaz, S., Greder, K. A., Larzelere, R. E., Washburn, I. J., Leon-Cartagena, M., & Arredondo-Lopez, A. (2021). Shared language erosion: Rethinking immigrant family communication and impacts on youth development. *Children (Basel, Switzerland)*, *8*(4), 256. DOI: 10.3390/children8040256 PMID: 33805964

Dail, P. W. (1988). Immigration and migration in America: Social impact and social response. *International Migration (Geneva, Switzerland)*, *26*(4), 441–452. DOI: 10.1111/j.1468-2435.1988.tb00663.x PMID: 12159550

Derr, A. S. (2016). Mental health service use among immigrants in the United States: A systematic review. *Psychiatric Services (Washington, D.C.)*, *67*(3), 265–274. DOI: 10.1176/appi.ps.201500004 PMID: 26695493

Diaz, T., & Bui, N. H. (2017). Subjective well-being in Mexican and Mexican American women: The role of acculturation, ethnic identity, gender roles, and perceived social support. *Journal of Happiness Studies*, *18*(2), 607–624. DOI: 10.1007/s10902-016-9741-1

Diener, E., Thapa, S., & Tay, L. (2020). Positive emotions at work. *Annual Review of Organizational Psychology and Organizational Behavior*, *7*(1), 451–477. DOI: 10.1146/annurev-orgpsych-012119-044908

Dozier, R. W. (1998). *Fear itself: The origin and nature of the powerful emotion that shapes our lives and our world.* St Martin's Press.

ERSI. (2024). Esri Diversity Index data by Region, State, County, and ZIP Code for years 2020, 2024, and 2029. Retrieved from https://storymaps.arcgis.com/stories/171197de105d4e98913d4e551e23407d

Esquivel, G. B., Oades-Sese, G. V., & Jarvis, M. L. (2010). *Culturally sensitive narrative interventions for immigrant children and adolescents.* University Press of America. DOI: 10.5771/9780761850359

Etezady, H. (2013). Fear across the life span. In Akhtar, S. (Ed.), *Fear: A dark shadow across our life span* (pp. 193–219). Taylor & Francis Group.

Falicov, C. J. (2014). *Working with immigrant families: A guide for clinicians.* The Guilford Press.

Gándara, P., & Ee, J. (Eds.). (2022). *Schools under siege: The impact of immigration enforcement on educational equity.* Harvard Education Press.

Garcini, L. M., Rosenfeld, J., Kneese, G., Bondurant, R. G., & Kanzler, K. E. (2022). Dealing with distress from the COVID-19 pandemic: Mental health stressors and coping strategies in vulnerable Latinx communities. *Health & Social Care in the Community, 30*(1), 284–294. DOI: 10.1111/hsc.13402 PMID: 33894080

Gelatt, J., Adams, G., & Huerta, S. (2014). Supporting Immigrant Families' Access to Prekindergarten. Urban Institute. Retrieved from https://eric.ed.gov/?id=ED559309

Germer, C. K., & Neff, K. D. (2013). Self-compassion in clinical practice. *Journal of Clinical Psychology, 69*(8), 856–867. DOI: 10.1002/jclp.22021 PMID: 23775511

Glebova, T., Lal, A., & Gangamma, R. (2024). Relational ethics in immigrant families: The contextual therapy five-dimensional framework. *Family Process, 00*, 1–17. DOI: 10.1111/famp.13071 PMID: 39462970

Gonzalez, M. M. (2016). Preparing teacher candidates for the instruction of English language learners. *Networks (Madison, Wis.), 18*(2), 1–6. DOI: 10.4148/2470-6353.1005

Gudykunst, W. B., & Kim, Y. Y. (2003). *Communicating with strangers: An approach to intercultural communication* (4th ed.). McGraw-Hill.

Gudykunst, W. B., & Ting-Toomey, S. (1988). *Culture and interpersonal communication.* Sage Publications.

Gursoy, D., Maier, T. A., & Chi, C. G. (2008). Generational differences: An examination of work values and generational gaps in the hospitality workforce. *International Journal of Hospitality Management, 27*(3), 448–458. DOI: 10.1016/j.ijhm.2007.11.002

Hall, E. T. (1983). *The dance of life: The other dimension of time.* Anchor Press/Doubleday.

Harris, O. (2024). *Bridging the Gap: Strengthening School-Community Partnerships through Cultural Brokers.* Oscar Harris.

Harris, P. R., & Moran, R. T. (2000). *Managing cultural differences* (5th ed.). Gulf Publishing.

Hertlein, K. M. (2023). *The Routledge international handbook of couple and family therapy* (1st ed.). Routledge., DOI: 10.4324/9781003297871

Hofstede, G. (2001). *Culture's consequences: Comparing values, behaviors, institutions, and organizations across nations*. Sage Publications.

Hovhannisyan, S. (2024). The Acculturation and adaptation of the Armenian Americans: A strength-based approach (Doctoral dissertation, The Chicago School of Professional Psychology).

Hwang, W.-C., & Wood, J. J. (2009). Culturally competent treatment for Asian American families. *Journal of Marital and Family Therapy*, *35*(4), 443–459. DOI: 10.1111/j.1752-0606.2009.00135.x

Jampolsky, G. G. (2011). *Love is letting go of fear*. Random House Digital, Inc.

Jo, Y. (2020). The significance of resilience in mental health promotion of marriage immigrant women: A qualitative study of factors and processes. *BMC Women's Health*, *20*(1), 1–13. DOI: 10.1186/s12905-020-00945-3 PMID: 32345269

Karim, S. (2021). Acculturation in a globalized world: Implications for theory and educational policy and practice. *International Journal of Comparative Education and Development*, *23*(1), 44–58. DOI: 10.1108/IJCED-11-2020-0078

Kayama, M., & Yamakawa, N. (2020). Acculturation and a sense of belonging of children in U.S. Schools and communities: The case of Japanese families. *Children and Youth Services Review*, *119*, 105612. DOI: 10.1016/j.childyouth.2020.105612 PMID: 33082613

Kerr, C. (2015). *Multicultural family art therapy* (1st ed.). Routledge., DOI: 10.4324/9780203366943

Khawaja, N. G., Kamo, R., & Ramirez, E. (2021). Building resilience in transcultural adults: Investigating the effect of a strength-based program. *Australian Psychologist*, *56*(4), 324–334. DOI: 10.1080/00050067.2021.1919489

Kılıç, B. S. S. P., Saltoğlu, S., & Erdoğdu, E. (2024). Effects of early psychological trauma on limbic system structure and function. *Psikiyatride Güncel Yaklasimlar*, *16*(4), 691–706. DOI: 10.18863/pgy.1356857

Knight, C., & Parker, S. K. (2021). How work redesign interventions affect performance: An evidence-based model from a systematic review. *Human Relations*, *74*(1), 69–104. DOI: 10.1177/0018726719865604

Lebrun, C. (2019). Two worlds, one family-acculturation, identity development, and storytelling: Literature review. Expressive Therapies Capstone Theses. 182. Retrieved from https://digitalcommons.lesley.edu/expressive_theses/182

LeDoux, J. E. (2023). The deep history of ourself: How ancient microbes became conscious brains. *Philosophical Psychology*, *36*(4), 704–715. DOI: 10.1080/09515089.2022.2160311

Lee, J., & Zhou, M. (2015). *The asian American achievement paradox*. Russell Sage Foundation.

Leong, F. T. L., & Lau, A. S. (2001). Barriers to providing effective mental health services to Asian Americans. *Mental Health Services Research*, *3*(4), 213–227. DOI: 10.1023/A:1013239606484 PMID: 11859966

Liu, M., Zhang, T., Tang, N., Zhou, F., & Tian, Y. (2022). The effect of educational expectations on children's cognition and depression. *International Journal of Environmental Research and Public Health, 19*(21), 14070. DOI: 10.3390/ijerph192114070 PMID: 36360947

Liu, S. (2018). Guidelines for Adapting Structural Family Therapy Approach for Immigrant Generation East Asian American Families. Graduate School of Professional Psychology: Doctoral Papers and Masters Projects. 309. Retrieved from https://digitalcommons.du.edu/capstone_masters/309

Lucas, K. A. (2023). Transitioning from military to civilian life: An examination of acculturation in veterans previously deployed to warzones. Retrieved from https://core.ac.uk/download/588485656.pdf

Marsiglia, F. F., Nagoshi, J. L., Parsai, M., & Castro, F. G. (2014). The effects of parental acculturation and parenting practices on the substance use of Mexican-heritage adolescents from Southwestern Mexican neighborhoods. *Journal of Ethnicity in Substance Abuse, 13*(3), 288–311. DOI: 10.1080/15332640.2014.905215 PMID: 25176121

Martin, A. (2016). Increasing parental attendance in parent-teacher meetings regarding parents with minority background in schools (Master's thesis). Retrieved from https://vid.brage.unit.no/vid-xmlui/handle/11250/2440140

Mayeda, D. T., Okamoto, S. K., & Mark, G. Y. (2005). Adapting culture in a colonial and capitalized world: Role strain and acculturation in Hawaiian and Samoan families. *Journal of Poverty, 9*(1), 105–120. DOI: 10.1300/J134v09n01_06

McCance-Katz, E. F. (2018). Behavioral health services for American Indians and Alaska Natives. Retrieve from https://www.ncbi.nlm.nih.gov/books/NBK539583/pdf/Bookshelf_NBK539583.pdf

McGoldrick, M., & Hardy, K. V. (2008). *The changing family: Life cycle, gender, and cultural perspectives*. Guilford Press.

Mechammil, M., & Cruz, R. (2022). Greater loss of face and family honor values are associated with greater positive expectancies and substance abuse among Middle Eastern/Northern African US college students. *The American Journal of Drug and Alcohol Abuse, 48*(1), 38–48. DOI: 10.1080/00952990.2021.1954937 PMID: 34582285

Medina, J. M. (2022). Development of a capacity building program to promote trauma-informed services. Walden University. ProQuest Dissertations & Theses, 28967487.

Minor, G., & Herzmann, G. (2019). Effects of negative emotion on neural correlates of item and source memory during encoding and retrieval. *Brain Research, 1718*, 32–45. DOI: 10.1016/j.brainres.2019.05.001 PMID: 31054883

Mittal, M., & Wieling, E. (2006). Training experiences of international doctoral students in marriage and family therapy. *Journal of Marital and Family Therapy, 32*(3), 369–383. DOI: 10.1111/j.1752-0606.2006.tb01613.x PMID: 16933440

Moghaddam, F. M. (2024). *The psychology of multiculturalism, assimilation, and omni-culturalism: Managing diversity in global context*. Springer Nature. DOI: 10.1007/978-3-031-62597-8

Muruthi, B. A., Bermudez, J. M., Chou, J., & Farnham, A. (2015). Neither here nor there: Working with transnational immigrant families in marriage and family therapy. *Family Therapy Magazine, 14*(3), 12–17. Retrieved from https://vtechworks.lib.vt.edu/server/api/core/bitstreams/ef29b8d8-0584-4346-90ff-67ce9d443eaa/content

Nagy, G. A., Zhan, C., Salcedo Rossitch, S., Stafford, A. M., Mendoza, A., Reyes, N. F., & Gonzalez-Guarda, R. (2024). Understanding mental health service needs and treatment characteristics for Latin American immigrants and refugees: A focus on CBT strategies for reducing acculturative stress. *Cognitive Behaviour Therapist, 17*, e12. DOI: 10.1017/S1754470X24000138

Nesteruk, O. (2022). Family dynamics at the intersection of languages, cultures, and aspirations: Reflections of young adults from immigrant families. *Journal of Family Issues, 43*(4), 1015–1038. DOI: 10.1177/0192513X211007527

Nguyen, H. V., Do, Q. A., Schacht, R. L., Yang, J. P., George, W. H., & Pantalone, D. W. (2024). Culture and partner violence: Examining loss of face, acculturation, behavioral intentions, and risk perception among Asian American college women. *Journal of Family Violence, 39*(4), 693–704. DOI: 10.1007/s10896-023-00519-5

Nguyen, K. T. (2024). The experience of ethnic identity and Vietnamese American adolescents' psychological well-being (Doctoral dissertation, The Chicago School of Professional Psychology). ProQuest Dissertations & Theses, 31328550.

Nieto, S. (2010). *The light in their eyes: Creating multicultural learning communities*. Teachers College Press.

Otero, M. C., Wells, J. L., Chen, K.-H., Brown, C. L., Connelly, D. E., Levenson, R. W., & Fredrickson, B. L. (2020). Behavioral indices of positivity resonance associated with long-term marital satisfaction. *Emotion (Washington, D.C.), 20*(7), 1225–1233. DOI: 10.1037/emo0000634 PMID: 31259587

Overall, N. C., Pietromonaco, P. R., & Simpson, J. A. (2022). Buffering and spillover of adult attachment insecurity in couple and family relationships. *Nature Reviews Psychology, 1*(2), 101–111. DOI: 10.1038/s44159-021-00011-1

Padilla, A. M. (2006). Acculturation, social identity, and social cognition: A new perspective. *Hispanic Journal of Behavioral Sciences, 28*(1), 19–23. DOI: 10.1177/0739986303251694

Padilla, A. M., & Perez, W. (2003). Acculturation, social identity, and psychological adjustment. In McGoldrick, R. M., Pearce, J. K., & Giordano, J. (Eds.), *Ethnicity and family therapy* (3rd ed., pp. 156–177). Guilford Press.

Portes, A., & Rumbaut, R. G. (2001). *Legacies: The story of the immigrant second generation*. University of California Press.

Qiu, Y. (2025). Acculturation-related intergenerational conflicts (A-IC) in Chinese immigrant family: A post-intentional phenomenological research Iiquiry (Doctoral dissertation). The George Washington University ProQuest Dissertations & Theses. 31558121.

Rabe, M. (2024). How racially and ethnically diverse is your neighborhood? United States Census Bureau. Retrieved from https://www.census.gov/library/stories/2024/01/racial-ethnic-diversity-neighborhoods.html

Redfield, R., Linton, R., & Herskovits, M. J. (1936). Memorandum on the study of acculturation. *American Anthropologist*, *38*(1), 149–152. https://www.jstor.org/stable/662563. DOI: 10.1525/aa.1936.38.1.02a00330

Renteria, T. (2017). Bridging the Gap Between Non-Spanish Speaking MFTs and Their Spanish Speaking Clients (Doctoral dissertation, California State University, Northridge). Retrieved from https://scholarworks.calstate.edu/downloads/tx31qn10x

Renzaho, A. M., Dhingra, N., & Georgeou, N. (2017). Youth as contested sites of culture: The intergenerational acculturation gap amongst new migrant communities—Parental and young adult perspectives. *PLoS One*, *12*(2), e0170700. DOI: 10.1371/journal.pone.0170700 PMID: 28170406

Resera, E., Tribe, R., & Lane, P. (2015). Interpreting in mental health, roles and dynamics in practice. *International Journal of Culture and Mental Health*, *8*(2), 192–206. DOI: 10.1080/17542863.2014.921207

Roberg, R., Camargo, T., & Marks, A. K. (2024). A mixed-methods exploration of legal vulnerability, trauma, and psychological wellbeing in immigrant caregivers and youth. *Trauma Care*, *4*(1), 60–74. DOI: 10.3390/traumacare4010006

Rodriguez, S. (2022). "Immigration knocks on the door... We are stuck...": A multilevel analysis of undocumented youth's experiences of racism, system Failure, and resistance in policy and school contexts. *Teachers College Record*, *124*(6), 3–37. DOI: 10.1177/01614681221093286

Rogers-Sirin, L., Ryce, P., & Sirin, S. (2014). Acculturation, Acculturative Stress, and Cultural Mismatch and Their Influences on Immigrant Children and Adolescents' Well-Being. In Dimitrova, R., Bender, M., & van de Vijver, F. (Eds.), *Global perspectives on well-being in immigrant families. Advances in immigrant family research* (Vol. 1). Springer., DOI: 10.1007/978-1-4614-9129-3_2

Rudmin, F. (2009). Constructs, measurements and models of acculturation and acculturative stress. *International Journal of Intercultural Relations*, *33*(2), 106–123. DOI: 10.1016/j.ijintrel.2008.12.001

Ruiz, E. (2005). Hispanic culture and relational cultural theory. *Journal of Creativity in Mental Health*, *1*(1), 33–55. DOI: 10.1300/J456v01n01_05

Sangha, S., Diehl, M. M., Bergstrom, H. C., & Drew, M. R. (2020). Know safety, no fear. *Neuroscience and Biobehavioral Reviews*, *108*, 218–230. DOI: 10.1016/j.neubiorev.2019.11.006 PMID: 31738952

Santisteban, D. A., Mena, M. P., & Abalo, C. (2012). Bridging diversity and family systems: Culturally informed and flexible family-based treatment for Hispanic adolescents. *Couple & Family Psychology*, *2*(4), 246–263. DOI: 10.1037/cfp0000013 PMID: 24772378

Sapiro, B., & Ward, A. (2020). Marginalized youth, mental health, and connection with others: A review of the literature. *Child & Adolescent Social Work Journal*, *37*(4), 343–357. DOI: 10.1007/s10560-019-00628-5

Silbereisen, R. K., & Titzmann, P. F. (2014). *The challenges of diaspora migration: Interdisciplinary perspectives on Israel and Germany* (1st ed.). Routledge., DOI: 10.4324/9781315614403

Sobh, R., Belk, R. W., & Wilson, J. A. (2013). Islamic Arab hospitality and multiculturalism. *Marketing Theory*, *13*(4), 443–463. DOI: 10.1177/1470593113499695

Souto-Manning, M. (2007). Immigrant families and children (re) develop identities in a new context. *Early Childhood Education Journal*, *34*(6), 399–405. DOI: 10.1007/s10643-006-0146-3

Sparrow, P. (1996). Careers and the psychological contract: Understanding the European context. *European Journal of Work and Organizational Psychology*, *5*(4), 479–500. Advance online publication. DOI: 10.1080/13594329608414874

Suárez-Orozco, C., & Suárez-Orozco, M. M. (2001). *Children of immigration*. Harvard University Press. DOI: 10.4159/9780674044128

Subba, D. (2014). *Philosophy of Fearism: Life is conducted, directed, and controlled by Fear*. Xlibris Corporation.

Subica, A. M., & Link, B. G. (2024). Mental illness stigma in Black, Latina/o, and Asian Americans. *Journal of Racial and Ethnic Health Disparities*, •••, 1–12. DOI: 10.1007/s40615-024-02259-8 PMID: 39695056

Sue, S., & Sue, D. W. (2013). *Counseling the culturally diverse: Theory and practice*. John Wiley & Sons.

Triandis, H. C. (2001). Individualism-collectivism and personality. *Journal of Personality*, *69*(6), 907–924. DOI: 10.1111/1467-6494.696169 PMID: 11767823

Tummala-Narra, P. (2007). Conceptualizing trauma and resilience across diverse contexts: A multicultural perspective. *Journal of Aggression, Maltreatment & Trauma*, *14*(1-2), 33–53. DOI: 10.1300/J146v14n01_03

Tummala-Narra, P. (2020). The fear of immigrants. *Psychoanalytic Psychology*, *37*(1), 50–61. DOI: 10.1037/pap0000245

Vakkai, R. J. Y., Harris, K., Chaplin, K. S., Crabbe, J. J., & Reynolds, M. (2020). Sociocultural factors that impact the health status, quality of life, and academic achievement of international graduate students: A literature review. *Journal of International Students*, *10*(3), 758–775. . DOI: 10.32674/jis.v10i2.1222

Valencia, R. R. (2002). *Chicano school failure and success: Past, present, and future* (1st ed.). Routledge., DOI: 10.4324/9780203005132

Van der Kolk, B. A. (2014). The body keeps the score: Brain, mind, and body in the healing of trauma. Penguin Books.Ward, C., & Kagitcibasi, C. (2010). Applied acculturation research: Working with, for and beyond communities. *International Journal of Intercultural Relations*, *34*(2), 186–189. DOI: 10.1016/j.ijintrel.2010.02.002

Vargas, K. (2017). The relationship of acculturation, ethnic identity and social support on the psychological well-being of Latino immigrants. University of La Verne. ProQuest Dissertations & Theses, 10160803. Retrieve from https://www.proquest.com/openview/929e9eb0f075d59e2e7a5f485f22eb70

Vera, E. M., Vacek, K., Coyle, L. D., Stinson, J., Mull, M., Doud, K., Buchheit, C., Gorman, C., Hewitt, A., Keene, C., Blackmon, S., & Langrehr, K. J. (2011). An examination of culturally relevant stressors, coping, ethnic identity, and subjective well-being in urban, ethnic minority adolescents. *Professional School Counseling*, *15*(2), 55–66. DOI: 10.1177/2156759X1101500203

Verkuyten, M., Yogeeswaran, K., & Adelman, L. (2019). Intergroup toleration and its implications for culturally diverse societies. *Social Issues and Policy Review*, *13*(1), 5–35. DOI: 10.1111/sipr.12051 PMID: 30930960

Wieser, M. J., & Keil, A. (2020). Attentional threat biases and their role in anxiety: A neurophysiological perspective. *International Journal of Psychophysiology*, *153*, 148–158. DOI: 10.1016/j.ijpsycho.2020.05.004 PMID: 32428525

Yampolsky, M. A., Amiot, C. E., & de la Sablonnière, R. (2013). Multicultural identity integration and well-being: A qualitative exploration of variations in narrative coherence and multicultural identification. *Frontiers in Psychology*, *4*, 126. DOI: 10.3389/fpsyg.2013.00126 PMID: 23504407

Youssef, M. T. (2023). A study of acculturative stress, gender, and age at immigration as predictors of psychological well-being in Middle Eastern youth (Doctoral dissertation). Capella University ProQuest Dissertations & Theses. 30311232

Zigarelli, J. C. (2017). The role of motivation in changing teacher beliefs: an investigation of a strengths-based intervention (Doctoral dissertation, University of Washington Libraries).

KEY TERMS AND DEFINITIONS

Acculturation: Acculturation is learning and adjusting to the views, rules, and ways of life when people come into contact with another culture (Redfield et al., 1936). This process can lead to conflict affecting family interactions, children's development, and education, or adaptation/integration. Changes in a culture can influence changes in a person (Cuellar, 2000). Berry's (1980) acculturation model identifies four methods that explain the different levels of adaptation based on how the individuals follow their native culture, the dominant or host culture, or both. The four methods of acculturation are integration, assimilation, marginalization, and separation (Berry, 1980).

Assimilation: Assimilation happens when minority group members learn and use the values and behaviors of the dominant culture, abandoning their traditional culture (Berry, 1980). Acculturation does not mean losing one's cultural identity to identify with the new host culture. Families should preserve their cultural values and establish a balance with the new ones. Maintaining a strong cultural identity is essential for proper development and emotional well-being (Brown & Shay, 2021).

Integration: Integration is assimilating new information about the host culture through learning about one's own culture. It occurs when immigrants integrate both the new cultural values with their native culture, maintaining their ethnic identity while approving mainstream values as well (Berry, 1980). Integration can reshape family dynamics due to possible role reversals as children are more resilient and have fewer responsibilities and fears; therefore, they adapt quicker than their parents to the new culture. Family dynamics can lead to misunderstandings, affect each family member's role, cause possible conflicts, and cause a disconnect between parents and children, especially if the parents do not speak the new culture's language. Promoting the integration of both cultural values will increase the sense of belonging and maintain a healthy emotional balance between the different systems in which the children interact (Jabbar, 2024).

Separation: Separation occurs when immigrants adhere to their native culture and are reluctant to accept, adapt, change, or even identify with the host culture (Berry, 1980). Separation shows it increases the likelihood of anxiety-related symptoms (Choy et al., 2021). The inability to acculturate can increase social problems such as poverty and unemployment, causing financial difficulties if job search efforts are unsuccessful. Separation can affect education and social functionality due to differences in perceptions between the original and host cultures about the roles and responsibilities among family members and the concepts of fundamental human rights (Dail, 1988).

Marginalization: Marginalization happens when immigrants abandon their cultural values, behaviors, and beliefs but do not adopt the values of the new culture, losing their sense of identity (Berry, 1980). Marginalized families may suffer from social isolation, trauma, poverty, violence, and discrimination, increasing the risk of poor outcomes for the children. Marginalization is associated with the highest depression symptoms (Choy et al., 2021). Children from marginalized families may have lower educational achievement, affecting their future. Poor education is linked to fewer opportunities for full-time employment and higher mental health issues (Sapiro & Ward, 2020). A solid foundation and sense of understanding of ethnic identity can reduce the effects of perceived discrimination and increase life satisfaction (Vera et al., 2011). Integrating the host and native culture is the most adaptive acculturation strategy, whereas separation and marginalization mostly predict adverse outcomes (Diaz & Bui, 2017).

Chapter 17
Whole Human Family Support in K-12 Education:
Exploring the Divide

Samira Galvao
https://orcid.org/0009-0004-8241-094X
National University, USA

ABSTRACT

This chapter delves into several key topics that are essential to understanding and supporting English Language Learners (ELLs) in K-12 education, including the distinctions between adult ELLs and native English speakers, diversity, language diversity, cultural awareness, cultural competence, strengths, challenges, and the complexities of cultural integration. By addressing these areas, the chapter seeks to illuminate the unique needs of ELLs and provide actionable strategies to foster their academic success and overall well-being. This chapter's primary objective is to explore ELLs' critical needs and identify motivational strategies to empower them. These strategies include implementing well-resourced interventions, equipping educators with the necessary tools to support diverse learners, and fostering an inclusive environment where ELLs can thrive. Such efforts are vital for improving attendance, increasing graduation rates, and ensuring that ELLs are prepared for bright, successful futures.

INTRODUCTION

As the number of English Language Learners (ELLs) in the United States in K-12 institutions grows, it becomes increasingly important to address these students and their families' unique needs. ELLs face various challenges, such as language barriers, cultural differences, and adapting to a new educational system. Their families, who may also be adjusting to a new environment, often require additional support to engage effectively in their child's academic journey. Unfortunately, alongside this growth, the number of ELLs who do not graduate from high school is also increasing, largely due to various compounding factors. As Banks (2019) highlights, ELLs represent the fastest-growing demographic in public schools across the United States, yet their success rates lag behind their peers. This gap underscores the urgent need for targeted interventions to support ELLs effectively. However, as Wright (2022) highlights, schools face ongoing challenges in effectively supporting the academic success of ELLs. According to

DOI: 10.4018/979-8-3693-9020-7.ch017

Sheng et al. (2016), school districts that serve large populations of ELLs must implement comprehensive strategies and improved instructional methods to facilitate these students' transition and acquisition of English language skills. Language barriers and cultural adjustment challenges often hinder ELLs' ability to engage fully with academic content. Addressing these barriers requires robust educational support systems and equipping educators with the necessary tools and professional development to effectively meet the diverse needs of their ELL students. Teachers trained in culturally responsive teaching and differentiated instruction can create inclusive classrooms that empower ELLs to achieve their potential.

The scope of this issue is substantial. According to Colorín Colorado (2015), approximately 4.85 million ELLs are enrolled in public schools across the United States, with the majority (62%) of ELL students in grades 6 through 12 being U.S.-born. Despite their domestic roots, these students often face significant obstacles, including limited access to resources and language support programs, making it more difficult for them to succeed academically. For those who struggle to attain English proficiency, the risk of academic disengagement and eventual dropout increases dramatically. The consequences of not addressing these challenges extend beyond the individual students to society. Research by Deussen et al. (2017) indicates that high school dropouts face greater risks of adverse social and economic outcomes, including lower lifetime earnings, reduced access to quality healthcare, and limited opportunities for upward mobility. For ELLs, these risks are exacerbated by the dual challenge of mastering a new language while meeting rigorous academic standards. The long-term implications of these disparities highlight the necessity of implementing systems that support ELLs academically and provide pathways to graduation and future success.

To reverse these trends, a multifaceted approach is essential. This includes increasing investment in ELL-focused programs, such as peer-to-peer mentoring, after-school tutoring, mentorship initiatives, and parental engagement workshops. Schools must also prioritize using evidence-based teaching strategies and provide ongoing professional development for educators. Additionally, fostering a school culture that celebrates linguistic and cultural diversity can assist ELLs feel more valued and supported, reducing their likelihood of disengagement and later dropout García, E. E. (2021). This chapter will explore the unique needs of ELLs in K-12 education and examine motivational strategies designed to empower these students. By implementing strategic, well-resourced interventions and providing educators with the tools to support these learners effectively, we can improve attendance and graduation rates and ensure that ELLs are equipped for brighter futures. Additionally, this chapter will outline a comprehensive plan to support ELL students and their families in K-12 education, helping them achieve academic success while fostering cultural integration and community involvement.

EXPLORING THE DIVIDE: ENGLISH LANGUAGE LEARNERS VS. NATIVE ENGLISH SPEAKERS

English Language Learners (ELLs) represent one of the fastest-growing populations in the United States, especially compared to native English speakers. Despite this increase, these learners face many challenges that set them apart from their native-speaking peers, creating significant barriers to their academic and social success. Many ELLs are immigrants who not only have to master the complexities of a new language but also navigate the difficulties of adjusting to a completely new culture and environment. They often encounter difficulties accessing educational resources and opportunities that would enable them to further their education, whether in K-12 or beyond, which can leave them at a severe disadvantage compared to native-born students (McCracken, 2021). Unlike their native English-speaking counterparts, who have established mechanisms to identify students at risk of academic failure or dropping out, the systems for supporting ELLs are less defined and often overlooked. School districts may not have the infrastructure, resources, or staff trained to adequately meet the unique needs of ELLs, leaving these students without the necessary academic support. This gap in support services can directly impact ELL students' academic progress, often leading to lower test scores, lower high school graduation rates, and limiting future opportunities. The challenges these students face are multifaceted and involve not only language acquisition but also cultural adaptation, social integration, and emotional adjustment to a new educational system.

The legal responsibility to support ELLs is enshrined in the Civil Rights Act of 1964, specifically in Title VI, which prohibits discrimination based on race, color, or national origin in any program or activity receiving federal financial assistance. This law requires that school districts provide equitable services to all students, including ELLs. It ensures that students are not denied access to educational programs or opportunities based on their language or national origin. School districts that fail to offer appropriate educational support to ELLs risk violating their language rights under Title VI, and this noncompliance can lead to severe consequences, including the potential loss of federal funding (Faingold, 2022). Therefore, it is crucial for school districts to ensure that their educational practices and policies are not only inclusive but actively supportive of ELLs. To meet the needs of ELL students, school districts must implement proactive and intentional strategies beyond simply providing basic language instruction. This might include integrating culturally responsive teaching, providing additional academic support in math and science, and ensuring that counselors and language specialists are available to support these students' emotional and social adjustment. Moreover, it is important for schools to offer bilingual staff or language support services to assist in bridging communication gaps between students, families, and educators. Providing an inclusive environment that values diversity, acknowledges cultural differences, and supports language development is key to the success of ELL students.

Furthermore, districts must recognize that the challenges ELLs face are not only about learning English but also about fully integrating into an educational system that may seem unfamiliar and intimidating. Support services should focus on language proficiency and helping these students feel accepted, understood, and confident in their educational journey. As these learners continue to increase, school districts have a moral and legal responsibility to ensure their academic success. As stated by Galvao (2023), by offering tailored programs and adequate resources, districts can better serve their ELL populations and ensure that these students are equipped to succeed both academically and socially in their new environment. Failure to do so deprives these students of their rights and undermines the potential for an inclusive and thriving educational system that benefits all learners.

DIVERSITY

Diversity is crucial to education, especially for English Language Learners (ELLs) navigating a new culture and a second language. For ELLs, the challenges of learning in a new cultural context are compounded by the added complexity of being immersed in a foreign language, which can affect every facet of their educational experience (Galvao, 2020**).** These students come with a wide array of academic and emotional needs. Unfortunately, many school districts struggle to find effective and sustainable solutions to meet those needs Darling-Hammond, L., & Cook-Harvey, C. M. (2018). The lack of comprehensive support structures for ELLs often limits their educational growth and progress, particularly as they transition into different grades. In high schools, ELLs typically benefit from specialized support services designed to assist them in developing their English proficiency, such as English as a Second Language (ESL) programs, language development classrooms, and targeted instructional strategies. Unlike elementary, middle, and high school teachers, who are often trained to understand ELLs' linguistic and cultural needs, they offer tailored support to assist these students in improving their language skills and keeping pace with their peers academically.

Language Diversity

Language plays a central role in diversity, shaping how individuals from different backgrounds interact and understand one another. Dunstan et al. (2018) argue that fostering a shared understanding of language and dialect differences is crucial to promoting inclusivity and social cohesion. The United States, often described as a "melting pot," is home to people from virtually every culture across the globe. More than 20% of residents speak a language other than English at home, reflecting the nation's rich cultural and linguistic diversity. While Spanish is the most common second language spoken by English Language Learners (ELLs) in the U.S., it is not necessarily the dominant foreign language in every state. The linguistic landscape of the U.S. is far more varied, with between 350 and 430 different languages spoken nationwide, making it one of the most linguistically diverse countries in the world (Translators without Borders, 2022). This diversity presents opportunities and challenges regarding communication, cultural integration, and educational success.

For many ELLs, the struggle to communicate in English can create barriers that prevent them and their families from fully participating in various school activities, including extracurricular events. Despite their desire to engage and be part of their school communities, lacking confidence in their English language skills often leaves them feeling isolated or excluded. This linguistic challenge can impede their social integration and lead to frustration. However, strengthening their English proficiency can overcome many of these obstacles. Increased language skills can help ELLs and their families feel more comfortable and capable of engaging in conversations, participating in school events, and building social connections with their peers and their parents (Dorner et al., 2022).

Yet, achieving full proficiency in a second language is a gradual and often lengthy process, especially for the parents. ELLs must be patient with themselves, overcome their frustration, and remain dedicated to their educational goals (Becker & Deris, 2019). According to Cummins (1984), it typically takes five to seven years for an individual to become proficient in a second language. Cummins outlines two distinct levels of language proficiency: Basic Interpersonal Communicative Skills (BICS) and Cognitive Academic Language Proficiency (CALP). BICS refers to the everyday conversational skills that enable a person to interact in common social situations, such as greetings and small talk. In contrast, CALP involves understanding and using language in more complex academic contexts, such as explaining the results of a science experiment or discussing abstract concepts. While BICS may be acquired relatively quickly, CALP takes much longer to develop, requiring a deeper understanding of the language and its academic terminology.

For ELLs, mastering CALP is critical for their academic success. Without a strong grasp of academic language, these students may struggle to keep up with their peers in classroom settings despite their conversational fluency in English. This gap in proficiency can undermine their performance and limit their potential. However, it is important to note that not all ELLs have had the opportunity to become bilingual, and many face challenges that hinder their educational growth. These students may not receive the appropriate support or instructional attention needed to reach their full academic potential (Ortiz & Franquiz, 2019). Too often, linguistic diversity is not viewed as an asset; ELLs may be marginalized or treated as inherently less capable than native English speakers. ELLs deserve the same educational opportunities and support as their native English-speaking peers. It is essential that educators recognize the unique strengths and needs of these students and work to create an inclusive and supportive learning environment that values their linguistic and cultural backgrounds (Claro & Loeb, 2019). By providing ELLs with the proper resources, targeted instruction, and opportunities to develop both BICS and CALP, we can assist them in realizing their full potential and thriving academically, socially, and professionally.

Diversity Within K-12

Darling-Hammond, L., & Cook-Harvey, C. M. (2018) emphasize the continuous growth of English Language Learners (ELLs) in 12 education systems, driven by increasing immigration and the rising number of international students seeking academic opportunities in the United States. This demographic shift brings a wealth of cultural and linguistic diversity to classrooms, allowing educators and students alike to engage in rich, cross-cultural learning experiences. However, this also presents unique challenges, as ELL students come with various educational backgrounds, language proficiencies, and personal experiences. Many ELLs face the dual challenge of acquiring proficiency in their second language (L2) while maintaining and valuing their first language (L1). This balancing act is often misunderstood, leading to misconceptions about their abilities and needs. Fernandez et al. (2017) point out that educators often lack the specialized training required to support these learners effectively, particularly in critical areas such as writing skills, where linguistic and cultural nuances come into play. The need for culturally responsive teaching becomes even more evident when considering the broader issue of personal biases in education. While classrooms are increasingly diverse, overcoming explicit or implicit biases remains a significant hurdle. Though vital, discussions surrounding ethnicity and cultural differences are often approached with hesitation or discomfort, preventing meaningful dialogue. Galvao (2023) highlights the difficulties in addressing cultural diversity concerns and how such conversations frequently miss the opportunity to promote understanding and appreciation of diverse cultural perspectives. Instead, they often expose unexamined biases, creating divisions and inhibiting progress. For instance, cultural differences in communication styles or educational norms are sometimes mistakenly viewed as deficits rather than strengths that enrich the learning environment.

To address these challenges, educators must have the knowledge, skills, and tools to create inclusive and supportive classrooms where ELLs can thrive. This involves providing targeted professional development that focuses on understanding the unique needs of ELLs, fostering cultural competence, and implementing instructional strategies that promote equitable learning opportunities. For example, teacher training programs should include modules on scaffolding writing instruction, integrating students' cultural backgrounds into the curriculum, and recognizing the value of bilingualism as an asset rather than a barrier. Moreover, fostering inclusive environments requires school leaders and policymakers to prioritize initiatives celebrating diversity and encouraging open, respectful discussions about ethnicity and culture. Educators can create spaces where all students feel valued and understood by shifting the focus from disagreement to collaboration. This benefits ELLs and enriches the educational experience for native English speakers, who gain exposure to diverse perspectives and global competencies. Ultimately, the growing presence of ELLs in U.S. classrooms offers an opportunity to redefine and strengthen educational practices. By addressing biases, enhancing teacher training, and embracing the cultural and linguistic diversity that ELLs bring, educators can ensure that all students are empowered to succeed academically, socially, and personally in a multicultural world.

CULTURAL AWARENESS

Jibreel (2015) highlights a critical challenge many English Language Learners (ELLs) face: navigating the complexities of dual cultures. These students often find themselves balancing the customs and traditions of their native culture while simultaneously adapting to a new culture, each with its own unique values, practices, and expectations. This cultural integration process can be enriching and challenging, requiring ELLs to preserve their identity while learning to navigate and succeed in an unfamiliar environment. The American Occupational Therapy Association (2020) defines cultural awareness as recognizing and understanding the differences and similarities between two cultures, particularly when interacting or collaborating with individuals from other cultural backgrounds. It is not merely about observing these differences but developing sensitivity and empathy toward them, fostering meaningful connections that transcend cultural boundaries.

While language is vital for building cultural awareness, fluency alone does not equate to cultural competence. As Presbitero (2020) explains, there are subtle nuances, idiomatic expressions, and contextual meanings within a language that only native speakers fully grasp. These cultural layers cannot be learned solely through textbooks or formal instruction—they are deeply embedded in lived experiences and societal norms. For instance, understanding humor, non-verbal cues, or the cultural significance of certain phrases requires immersion and interaction within the culture. Developing cultural awareness goes beyond linguistic fluency; it necessitates an openness to learning, a willingness to question assumptions, and an ability to see the world through multiple cultural lenses. For ELLs, this process is a critical aspect of their journey, as it enhances their ability to communicate effectively and helps them bridge the gap between their native identity and their evolving identity within a new cultural framework. By fostering cultural awareness, educators and communities can better support ELLs, empowering them to thrive academically and socially in multicultural environments.

Cultural Competence

As defined by López and Davis (2019), *cultural competence* refers to the specific knowledge, understanding, and practices that enable professionals and organizations to navigate cross-cultural situations effectively. It is a framework of reliable behaviors, strategies, and institutional procedures designed to bridge cultural divides, allowing individuals and educational facilities to operate in diverse and multicultural settings. Culture encompasses many factors, including language, beliefs, values, communication styles, and social behaviors, all of which shape individual and group identities. In this context, competence implies acting professionally while respecting and integrating cultural norms and standards.

Guidelines and Values. To achieve meaningful cultural competence, educational institutions must implement clear guidelines, policies, and practices that promote cross-cultural collaboration. This includes fostering an environment of respect, inclusivity, and awareness while ensuring all stakeholders—faculty, staff, and students—are aligned to embrace and support diversity. School districts must cultivate systems that encourage effective cross-cultural interactions and ensure students' unique backgrounds are acknowledged and valued. This commitment directly enhances the quality and impact of services, ultimately improving outcomes for all learners (López & Davis, 2019).

Educational staff must be equipped with key skills to support cultural competence, including respecting diversity, engaging in self-reflection, managing cultural differences effectively, and adapting to the social contexts of their populations. Faculty and staff often find themselves at varying cultural awareness and expertise stages, so district leaders must invest in continuous professional development and cultural sensitivity training. Leaders should integrate cultural competence into all aspects of the institution, from curricula to decision-making processes, ensuring that diverse perspectives are acknowledged and actively incorporated into the educational experience (Peterson, 2022).

Actionable Strategies. Effective cultural competence also requires clear principles and actionable strategies. Bland (2022) outlines several key principles, including respecting the cultural norms of English Language Learners (ELLs), recognizing their language comprehension challenges, fostering collaboration among educators and students, and ensuring inclusive participation in school district events. Additional recommendations include hiring culturally competent staff, offering targeted training programs, and building partnerships with neighboring school districts to share best practices.

However, achieving cultural competence is not without its challenges. Intercultural communication remains a significant barrier, as some educators and staff struggle to collaborate effectively with individuals from diverse backgrounds. This lack of communication can hinder decision-making processes and limit the inclusion of diverse perspectives in curriculum development. Muñiz (2019) highlights the need for district leaders to prioritize culturally responsive pedagogy and ensure faculty members are equipped with the tools and knowledge to engage with diverse learners effectively. To truly embed cultural competence within the school district, leaders must adopt strategies that inspire cultural awareness and celebrate diversity in everyday practices. Pierre et al. (2021) emphasize the importance of culturally relevant coursework, which validates students' cultural identities and enhances their overall academic engagement. Foley (2020) asserts that instructors with the skills, awareness, and willingness to embrace diversity foster a learning environment where all students, regardless of their background, can thrive. The urgency of promoting cultural competence is underscored by shifting demographics in the United States. A recent analysis by Constante et al. (2021) based on U.S. Census Bureau data predicts significant changes in population composition by 2060, including greater racial, ethnic, and cultural diversity. With the increasing diversity of English language learners in K-12 education (Bundick et al., 2021), institutions must position themselves to meet the evolving needs of their students.

According to Gay (2015), cultural diversity is a cornerstone of educational achievement, underscoring its importance for students of all races, ethnicities, cultures, socioeconomic levels, and languages. Embracing diversity in education enriches learning environments and ensures all students feel seen, valued, and empowered to achieve their full potential. However, to fully realize the potential of culturally responsive teaching, it is essential to examine universal ideals and principles and how they can be applied in specific sociocultural, political, economic, geographical, and educational contexts.

Culturally Responsive Teaching. Culturally responsive teaching is not a one-size-fits-all approach. While the overarching goal is to promote equity and inclusivity in education, implementing these principles must align with specific communities' unique needs and challenges. For example, sociocultural contexts demand understanding students' lived experiences, cultural norms, and traditions, which significantly shape their identities and learning styles. Political and economic conditions further influence the resources available to schools, access to quality education, and the priorities that shape curricula and instructional practices. Geographical differences, such as rural versus urban settings, add another layer of complexity, as do variations in educational systems, policies, and historical legacies across regions and countries.

To effectively discuss culturally responsive teaching on an international scale, educators and policy-makers must strike a balance between theory and practice. General ideals, such as fostering respect for diversity, promoting equity, and encouraging the inclusion of multicultural perspectives in curricula, provide a foundation. However, translating these ideals into actionable strategies requires a nuanced understanding of the local context. For instance, culturally responsive teaching might emphasize de-colonizing the curriculum and uplifting indigenous knowledge systems in a region with a history of colonialism. Multilingual societies might prioritize language equity and support students learning a language that is not their native tongue.

Furthermore, implementing culturally responsive teaching requires educators to commit to continuous learning and reflection. Teachers must not only develop cultural competence but also critically evaluate their own biases and assumptions, adapting their teaching methods to meet the diverse needs of their students. This process involves incorporating students' cultural references into all aspects of learning, from instructional materials to classroom interactions, and creating an environment where every student feels respected and empowered to succeed. Cultural competence is no longer optional; it is necessary for educational institutions striving to provide equitable and effective learning experiences. By investing in culturally responsive training, fostering open communication, and embedding cultural awareness into every aspect of the educational process, institutions can create environments where diversity is celebrated and all students are empowered to succeed. Cultural diversity is fundamental to achieving educational equity and excellence, but fostering culturally responsive teaching requires a dual focus on universal principles and localized implementation strategies. By tailoring approaches to diverse educational contexts' unique sociocultural, political, and economic realities, educators can create learning environments that celebrate diversity, promote inclusivity, and empower all students to thrive academically and personally. This comprehensive approach ensures that culturally responsive teaching is not just a theoretical ideal but a transformative practice that drives meaningful change in education systems worldwide.

Cultural Diversity

Cultural diversity is vital in K-12 education, bringing many perspectives, experiences, and ideas that can significantly enhance the academic and social environment. However, if diversity is not actively embraced, celebrated, and managed with sensitivity, it can also become a source of misunderstanding, tension, or even controversy. To truly leverage the potential of cultural diversity, school districts must foster an inclusive and supportive environment where differences are viewed as strengths and opportunities for growth rather than challenges. One of the most transformative aspects of a student in K-12 education journey is the chance to engage with peers and educators from diverse cultural backgrounds—whether from different regions of the country or across the globe. These interactions allow students to broaden their horizons, challenge preconceived notions, and develop a deeper understanding of the world around them. For many students, learning alongside individuals from various cultural, linguistic, and socioeconomic backgrounds fosters empathy, critical thinking, and the ability to work collaboratively in increasingly globalized professional and social settings.

From an educator's perspective, one of the most rewarding experiences is witnessing the dynamic unfolding of cultural diversity within the classroom. When students from different backgrounds come together, they bring unique perspectives, traditions, and approaches to problem-solving. This blending of cultures enriches classroom discussions, encourages innovative thinking, and creates a vibrant learning environment where students learn from the curriculum and each other. Cultural diversity within academic settings also challenges educators to adapt their teaching methods, incorporate culturally relevant materials, and foster an inclusive atmosphere that values all voices (Banks, J., & Banks, C., 2019).

However, the benefits of cultural diversity are not automatic in K-12 education. School districts must intentionally cultivate environments that encourage open dialogue, mutual respect, and a willingness to learn from one another. Without these efforts, the presence of diverse cultural backgrounds can sometimes lead to misunderstandings or even conflict. When cultural differences are ignored or dismissed, it can create feelings of exclusion or marginalization, undermining the potential for collaboration and growth. This is why K-12 institutions must prioritize cultural competence, providing training and resources to help educators and students navigate and embrace diversity effectively. Ultimately, cultural diversity in K-12 institutions is not merely about representation but about creating spaces where differences are celebrated and used as a foundation for academic and social enrichment. By embracing diversity as an asset rather than a challenge, K-12 education institutions can prepare students to thrive in an interconnected world, equipping them with the skills and perspectives needed to contribute meaningfully to a diverse and global society. Through intentional efforts to support and promote inclusivity, scholars and educators can experience the profound benefits of cultural diversity, transforming both the academic experience and the broader educational community.

Strengths. The needs of English Language Learners (ELLs) should be addressed individually, as they vary widely depending on the learner's background, experiences, and educational goals. Developing an effective system to evaluate these diverse needs is crucial in supporting ELLs on their journey to academic success. This approach ensures that each learner's unique strengths and challenges are identified and addressed, enabling them to reach their full potential. Effective evaluation tools and strategies also empower educators to design tailored interventions and instructional approaches, fostering an environment where ELLs can thrive academically and personally (Ee & Gándara, 2020).

English Language Learners bring a wealth of strengths to their educational pursuits. Many possess strong literacy skills in their first language, which serve as a foundation for acquiring proficiency in English. They often have academic knowledge and expertise in specific subject areas developed in their home countries. These strengths provide a valuable starting point for their learning journey, allowing educators to build on their existing knowledge and skills. Moreover, the families of ELLs frequently play an active role in their education, demonstrating a deep commitment to their future. They offer encouragement, instill high levels of personal responsibility, and nurture resilience, resourcefulness, and dedication—essential for academic and lifelong success (Colorado, 2019).

Bilingual English Speakers of Other Languages (ESOL) learners exhibit remarkable cognitive adaptability. They can problem-solve, think critically and creatively, and demonstrate empathy and understanding toward others. These skills enhance their academic performance and position them as valuable contributors to their communities and workplaces. Bilingual ESOL learners often excel in navigating complex social and cultural dynamics, which equips them to endure challenges and succeed in diverse environments. As society becomes increasingly multicultural, these learners have a distinct advantage in adapting to and thriving within culturally diverse settings (Karvonen et al., 2021; Ortiz & Franquiz, 2019).

Several factors positively influence the academic outcomes of bilingual ESOL learners. The time they spend in the K-12 setting, their cultural and social background, and the amount of time they dedicate to adapting to English-speaking environments all play critical roles. Becoming proficient in English is shaped by exposure to and engagement with the language in various academic, social, and professional contexts. Additionally, the support they receive from educators, peers, and their communities further enhances their ability to succeed. Understanding these factors allows educational institutions to design programs and initiatives that better address the needs of ELLs, creating pathways for academic achievement and social integration (Turner, 2020).

To maximize the potential of ELLs, it is essential for educators and 12 institutions to adopt culturally responsive teaching practices. This includes recognizing and valuing learners' diverse linguistic and cultural backgrounds and creating inclusive environments celebrating their unique contributions. Educators can empower ELLs to overcome challenges and achieve academic goals by fostering respect, collaboration, and support. Furthermore, as ELLs succeed in their educational pursuits, they contribute to the broader community, bringing diverse perspectives and skills that enrich society. Investing in the success of ELLs is not only an educational imperative but also a societal one, as it paves the way for a more inclusive and equitable future.

Challenges. Acquiring language skills, especially when learning a foreign language for academic purposes, is a complex and often daunting process for students. English Language Learners (ELLs) face significant challenges as the demands of academic content grow more rigorous, and the language becomes more nuanced and sophisticated (Darling-Hammond, L., & Cook-Harvey, C. M., 2018). As students advance in their studies, they often encounter increased difficulty in mastering academic language, which involves learning new vocabulary and understanding complex syntax and cultural context. This can present an overwhelming barrier to academic success for ELLs, particularly as the language demands become more rigid and formal (Suzuki & DeKeyser, 2017).

According to Fernandez et al. (2017), English language learners face three primary challenges in developing scholarly writing skills: attitudinal, intellectual, and social. These multifaceted challenges require a comprehensive understanding of ELLs' unique obstacles. The attitudinal difficulties often stem from low motivation or a lack of belief in their own abilities. Many ELLs internalize negative perceptions about their writing skills, influenced by their own self-doubt and the critical feedback they receive from others.

Intellectual challenges arise when ELLs struggle to select appropriate topics, engage in scholarly discourse, establish a clear academic voice, and understand the academic register necessary for formal writing. Furthermore, the writing process can be difficult, with many learners finding it hard to structure their thoughts and organize their work in a way that meets academic standards. Socially, ELLs may struggle to communicate effectively with their educators, often feeling disconnected from the academic community due to language barriers and cultural differences. These barriers can hinder their ability to engage with feedback, participate in peer discussions, and connect meaningfully with teachers and classmates (Fernandez et al., 2017).

One of the most significant challenges faced by ELLs, particularly secondary learners, is the stress and anxiety created by immigration issues. Many students live with the constant fear of deportation, which adds an overwhelming layer of emotional distress to their academic lives. This fear can be exacerbated by the trauma of family separations caused by deportation or incarceration, making it even more difficult for ELLs to focus on their studies. For these students, the emotional toll can manifest in various ways, including heightened anxiety, depression, and a sense of hopelessness. Lyn et al. (2023) emphasize that educating the whole student involves integrating social-emotional learning (SEL) with academic instruction. Research on emotional intelligence (EI) highlights that social and emotional competencies are key drivers of personal growth, academic achievement, and professional success.

The constant fear of being separated from their families may lead to a loss of motivation and a decline in academic engagement, as students may struggle to focus on their education when their future in the country is uncertain (Perez & Morrison, 2016). Many educators are unaware of the daily challenges that undocumented students face, which can result in a lack of empathy or support for their unique struggles. This lack of understanding further compounds the difficulties ELLs experience in the classroom (DeLuca-Acconi, Bessaha, Velázquez, & Mendoza, 2022).

The introduction of the Deferred Action for Childhood Arrivals (DACA) program in 2012 provided some relief to undocumented students by offering temporary protections from deportation and work permits. However, the program is only valid for two years and must be renewed, leaving students uncertain about their futures. The limited scope of DACA does not provide long-term security for these students, who may still face the threat of deportation or separation from their families. This uncertainty undermines their stability and makes it even more difficult for them to focus on their education and career goals (United States Citizenship and Immigration Services, 2014). Low socioeconomic status is another pervasive issue for English language learners. Many of these students come from low-income backgrounds, which can severely impact their ability to succeed academically. Financial stress is a significant barrier to learning, as students often struggle to afford necessities such as housing, food, and transportation, let alone textbooks or tuition.

Moreover, the financial instability of their families can increase the pressure on ELLs to contribute to household expenses, further detracting from their focus on their academic responsibilities (Galvao, 2020). The combination of poverty, fear, and social isolation creates a challenging environment for these learners, who must navigate not only the academic demands of their studies but also the emotional and psychological stressors of their circumstances. Discrimination is another persistent challenge faced by ELLs. Many students encounter verbal abuse, bullying, and even hate crimes based on their race, ethnicity, or immigrant status. These forms of discrimination can take a heavy toll on their mental and emotional well-being, leading to feelings of alienation, shame, and fear. Unfortunately, discrimination often extends beyond individual interactions and becomes institutionalized, with ELLs experiencing systemic inequities within educational settings. They may be placed in lower-level courses, overlooked for opportunities, or subject to biased evaluations based on their language proficiency rather than intellectual potential. Additionally, the experience of moving to the United States often exposes ELLs to culture shock. They may have been part of the majority population in their home countries, but upon arriving in the U.S., they are suddenly thrust into the minority role. This shift can be emotionally distressing, as they face new challenges in adapting to a foreign culture while also dealing with the stigma of being labeled as "outsiders." This sense of marginalization can exacerbate feelings of isolation and make it even harder for ELLs to integrate into their academic or social environments (McCracken, 2021).

Despite these numerous obstacles, many ELLs in high school will pursue higher education in the United States because they see it as a crucial step toward assimilating into society and achieving upward mobility. However, this pursuit is fraught with challenges, including prejudice, bigotry, and societal labels. Immigrants often face significant barriers to accessing educational opportunities, and these barriers can limit their ability to succeed academically. These challenges are further compounded by the lack of understanding and support from educational institutions, which may fail to recognize the unique needs and strengths of their immigrant and ELL populations (McCracken, 2021). English language learners face various challenges that extend far beyond language acquisition. They must navigate the complexities of immigration issues, social-emotional stressors, financial hardships, and discrimination, all while striving to succeed in their academic endeavors.

Universal Supports for English Language Learners

It is essential for K-12 institutions and their leaders to recognize and address these challenges, providing the necessary support and resources to help these learners overcome obstacles and achieve their educational and personal goals. By doing so, we can create a more inclusive and equitable educational environment for all students, regardless of their background or circumstances.

Below is a suggested template for a universal Home Language Survey, which can be adapted to suit the needs of any educational facility. This survey serves as a practical and essential tool for creating a welcoming environment and ensuring that ELLs receive the support they need to thrive academically and socially.

Universal Home Language Survey

1. What is your first language or verbal dialect?
   - ____________________________
2. Are you proficient in any other languages?
   - ____________________________
3. What is the primary language used at home?
   - ____________________________
4. What is your level of proficiency in English? (High, Medium, or Low)
   - Read________ Write________ Speak________

Motivation. Motivation is deeply rooted in human behavior and has been a subject of extensive research and analysis. *Motivation* originates from the Latin word *movere*, meaning "to move." It is widely recognized as the driving force behind an individual's actions and perseverance, shaping their path toward future achievements (Galvao, 2020). Motivation is not just a passive state but an active force that directs behavior, choices, and resilience, especially when navigating challenges. According to Shaines (2021), fostering motivation in learners requires a shift from a one-way savior-helper mindset to a two-way mutual learning approach. This shift transforms the learning environment into a collaborative space, allowing English learner scholars to feel empowered to share their struggles and successes openly. This mutual learning mindset enhances motivation by creating a supportive and inclusive atmosphere where learners feel valued and understood.

Motivational theory delves into the *why and how* behind human behavior, offering insights into the processes that activate and sustain actions (Murayama, 2018). It posits that motivation is central to nearly all aspects of life, serving as the foundation for initiating and completing mundane or significant tasks. From simple daily activities like preparing breakfast and exercising to more complex actions like pursuing professional goals or addressing challenges at school, motivation acts as the catalyst that drives individuals forward (Cook et al., 2016). Without motivation, even the most basic tasks can feel insurmountable, emphasizing its critical role in personal and professional success. One of the most influential frameworks in understanding motivation is Maslow's Hierarchy of Needs. First introduced in 1963, Maslow's theory asserts that human motivation is driven by the desire to fulfill a series of hierarchical needs. These needs are organized into seven levels, ranging from the most basic physiological requirements to the more complex pursuit of self-actualization. According to Maslow, individuals must meet their foundational needs before advancing to higher levels of growth and achievement (McLeod,

2018). This progression is essential for understanding why people behave the way they do and what drives their aspirations and actions.

Maslow's Hierarchy of Needs

Physiological Needs. These are the most basic requirements for human survival, including air, water, food, sleep, and reproduction. Individuals cannot function or focus on higher-level needs without these essential elements.

Safety Needs. Once physiological needs are met, safety becomes the priority. This includes physical security, financial stability, health, and well-being. Feeling safe allows individuals to shift their focus toward personal growth and development.

Social Needs. Human beings are inherently social creatures, and the need for love, belonging, and friendship becomes vital. Building meaningful relationships fosters emotional well-being and strengthens motivation.

Esteem Needs. This level encompasses the desire for independence, recognition, and accomplishment. Achieving esteem boosts self-confidence and drives individuals to pursue further challenges.

Cognitive Needs. At this stage, individuals seek intellectual fulfillment and knowledge. Curiosity and the desire to understand the world play a significant role in motivating academic and professional pursuits.

Aesthetic Needs. Beauty, balance, and harmony become important as individuals seek to create or appreciate art, nature, and order.

Self-Actualization. At the pinnacle of the hierarchy, self-actualization represents fulfilling one's potential. Individuals who reach this stage are often characterized by happiness, empathy, and a desire to give back to others.

Maslow's hierarchy demonstrates that most human behavior is influenced by multiple needs operating simultaneously. For example, a person seeking intellectual growth (cognitive needs) may also crave emotional support (social needs) and financial security (safety needs). Understanding this interplay is essential for educators and leaders, as it highlights the importance of addressing the whole individual rather than focusing solely on isolated factors.

In the K-12 settings, motivational theory offers critical insights into how to inspire and sustain learners' engagement. For English Language Learners (ELLs), this means understanding their unique challenges and leveraging motivation to overcome barriers. By addressing both basic needs (such as creating a safe and supportive environment) and higher-order needs (like fostering intellectual curiosity and self-esteem), educators can help ELLs unlock their full potential. Moreover, as Shaines (2021) emphasizes, adopting a mutual learning mindset allows educators to connect with their learners more deeply, building trust and encouraging open dialogue about their experiences.

Motivation is an essential force that drives human behavior and shapes individual and collective outcomes. Whether through motivational theory or Maslow's Hierarchy of Needs, understanding what inspires and sustains action provides valuable tools for personal growth, professional success, and educational advancement. For educators, fostering motivation in learners is not just about imparting knowledge but about creating environments where individuals feel empowered, supported, and inspired to achieve their goals. This holistic approach ensures that motivation remains a driving force in every aspect of life.

Figure 1. Maslow's hierarchy recreated

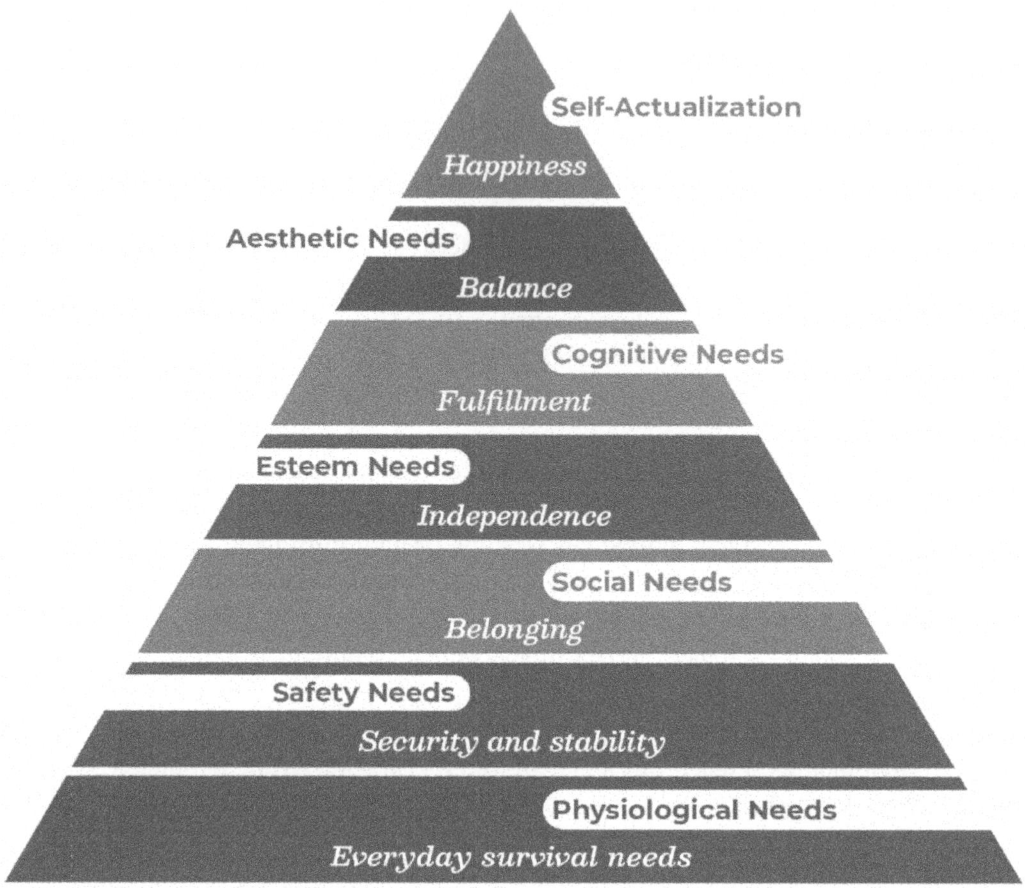

Note: Visual created based on Maslow (1963) Hierarchy of Needs

Here's a more developed and strengthened version of the passage with additional clarity, structure, and supporting ideas:

The Hierarchy of Needs is a foundational motivational theory widely recognized and deeply influential in psychology. This theory, developed by Abraham Maslow, illustrates the progression of human needs and their role in shaping behavior and motivation. According to Cook et. al. (2016), motivational theory emphasizes how individuals perceive their circumstances and manage their thoughts, emotions, and actions. For human beings to avoid negative attitudes or outcomes, their fundamental lower-level needs must be satisfied. As individuals ascend the Hierarchy of Needs, their focus shifts from fulfilling basic survival requirements to achieving self-fulfillment, with each level representing universal human aspirations rooted in societal interactions rather than purely self-centered goals. The hierarchy suggests that human needs are inextricably linked to intrinsic human characteristics, which is critical in motivating behavior. In education, particularly for English for Speakers of Other Languages (ESOL) learners, the hierarchy provides a lens through which educators can understand and support students' unique challenges. ESOL learners must feel a sense of belonging and safety to thrive academically and socially.

This sense of belonging is a motivational driver, encouraging learners to engage in their daily routines and educational endeavors actively.

Below is a detailed exploration of each level in Maslow's hierarchy as it relates to students in K-12:

Physiological Needs

According to Maslow, meeting physiological needs is fundamental to human survival and development (González et al., 2017). These needs include sleep, water, air, food, shelter, clothing, and reproduction—basic requirements that form the foundation of the hierarchy. When these needs are unmet, individuals prioritize them above all else. ELLs' ability to focus on learning diminishes when they lack proper nourishment, rest, or physical security. (González et al., 2017) highlight how students struggling with these unmet needs experience anxiety, which impedes their capacity to engage effectively in school.

Safety Needs

Once physiological needs are satisfied, safety becomes the next priority. Safety encompasses physical security, financial stability, health, and well-being. Maslow observed that safety concerns are often heightened during crises, such as natural disasters or war, but these concerns are equally present for the ELLs navigating new and unfamiliar environments. Many ELLs experience chronic anxiety about financial stability, protection, and the well-being of their families (McLeod, 2018). A lack of safety erodes confidence, making it difficult for learners to trust their surroundings or fully invest in their education. For educators, recognizing and addressing these safety concerns can help alleviate some of the barriers to learning and create an environment where students feel secure and supported.

Social Needs

Social needs represent the desire for love, belonging, and meaningful relationships. Maslow asserts that regardless of one's life stage, the need for connection remains universal. These needs are particularly significant for ELLs as they often face challenges forming social bonds due to language barriers and cultural differences. A sense of isolation can leave students feeling lonely and excluded, hindering their ability to engage and thrive in their communities (Vinney, 2019). Educators are critical in fostering environments where ELLs feel valued, included, and encouraged to form relationships. Encouraging peer collaboration, providing language support, and facilitating cultural exchange activities can help these students overcome social barriers and build a sense of belonging.

Esteem Needs

The need for self-esteem and recognition lies at the heart of Maslow's fourth level. Esteem needs can be divided into two components: self-confidence and the validation of one's achievements by others. Developing self-esteem is crucial for ELLs as it directly impacts their academic performance and personal growth. McLeod (2018) notes that feelings of inferiority can emerge when these needs are unmet, leading to diminished motivation and self-worth. Additionally, independence and language proficiency are vital for ELLs to build self-esteem. Wright (2022) suggests that language acquisition empowers learners and boosts their confidence as they become better equipped to communicate with native speakers.

Krashen's (1984) Monitor Hypothesis within the Second Language Acquisition Theory further supports this idea. It emphasizes that as ELLs develop the ability to self-monitor and correct their language use, their confidence and self-esteem grow, ultimately improving their language proficiency. Educators can support this process by creating a non-judgmental environment that encourages risk-taking and celebrates incremental progress in language learning.

Cognitive Needs

Cognitive needs are centered on intellectual growth, curiosity, and the desire for knowledge and understanding. These needs go beyond formal education, encompassing a broader quest for meaning and coherence in one's experiences (Vinney, 2019). For ELLs, cognitive needs are often intertwined with their efforts to bridge cultural and linguistic gaps. Educators can address these needs by promoting critical thinking, encouraging inquiry, and integrating culturally relevant materials into the curriculum to engage students more deeply.

Aesthetic Needs

Aesthetic needs involve the appreciation of beauty, balance, and harmony. Maslow posited that exposure to art, music, and other forms of creative expression can profoundly impact human well-being (McLeod, 2018). For ELLs, engaging with aesthetic experiences can inspire creativity, foster emotional resilience, and provide a sense of accomplishment. Activities like creating art, writing poetry, or participating in musical performances can be particularly meaningful for learners navigating cultural adjustment challenges (Mastandrea et. al., 2019).

Self-Actualization

At the pinnacle of the hierarchy lies self-actualization, realizing one's fullest potential. For most individuals, self-actualization represents a unique journey through creative pursuits, helping others, or personal achievements. Maslow observed that only a small percentage of individuals reach this stage, but those who do experience profound fulfillment and a sense of purpose (Compton, 2018). For ELLs, self-actualization often involves navigating dual identities—the culture of their home country and the culture of their new environment. This duality can create challenges and offer opportunities for personal growth and self-discovery. Educators can support learners in this journey by celebrating their cultural heritage, encouraging self-expression, and fostering an inclusive environment where their voices are heard and valued.

Intrinsic and Extrinsic Motivation

Motivation can be broadly categorized as intrinsic or extrinsic. Intrinsic motivation arises from internal desires, such as the pursuit of knowledge or personal satisfaction. Activities like reading, exercising, or hobbies often reflect intrinsic motivation (Cherry, 2016). Extrinsic motivation, on the other hand, is driven by external factors, such as financial rewards or social recognition (Locke & Schattke, 2019). Both forms of motivation play essential roles in shaping human behavior, and understanding their interplay can help educators design strategies to inspire and sustain student engagement (Rheinberg, F., & Engeser, S., 2018).

The Role of Educators

Educators have a unique opportunity to support ELLs by addressing their needs across all hierarchy levels. Building connections with students, recognizing their efforts, and providing a safe and inclusive learning environment are critical to fostering motivation and success. As Kakabra (2015) notes, motivation is a key factor influencing the success of ESOL scholars striving to complete advanced degrees. Students who feel supported and empowered will likely overcome challenges and achieve their goals. Maslow's Hierarchy of Needs provides a powerful framework for understanding human motivation and its role in shaping behavior. Meeting these needs is essential for ELLs' academic, social, and personal success. By addressing each level of the hierarchy, educators can create environments where students feel valued, supported, and inspired to reach their full potential (Hopper, E., 2020).

RECOMMENDATIONS

To better support the needs of English Language Learners (ELLs), it is strongly recommended that educational institutions implement mandatory training programs focused on cultural humility for all faculty and staff. With the increasing cultural, racial, ethnic, linguistic, and socioeconomic diversity in today's educational settings, there is a growing need for more comprehensive and effective training models that prepare educators to meet this population's unique challenges (Abdou et al., 2022). By incorporating such training, K-12 institutions can achieve significant potential benefits, including:

1. **Improved Academic Success**: Training on cultural humility can equip faculty and staff with the skills and knowledge necessary to understand and support ELLs' challenges, leading to improved academic outcomes.
2. **Higher Graduation Rates**: Enhanced support systems fostered by trained educators can increase ELLs' persistence, ultimately improving their graduation rates.
3. **Reduced Dropout Rates**: Targeted interventions and culturally responsive practices can assist in reducing the dropout rates for this vulnerable student population by creating a more inclusive and supportive educational environment.

In addition to faculty and staff training, it is also recommended that educational institutions adopt a universal *Home Language Survey (HLS)* as part of their new student registration process. This tool is a simple yet powerful way to identify ELLs and understand their linguistic background upon enrollment. By gathering this information, institutions can develop tailored strategies to meet the unique needs of these students, including language support services, counseling, and academic accommodations. Implementing the HLS as a standard practice can lead to the following benefits:

→ **Early Identification of ELLs**: The HLS allows educational institutions to identify students needing additional language support right from the beginning, enabling a proactive approach to their academic success.

- → **Enhanced Services and Resources**: With clearer insights into the' linguistic and cultural backgrounds of their students, institutions can allocate resources more effectively and design programs that directly address the needs of their ELLs.
- → **Improved Student Engagement**: By recognizing and valuing the linguistic diversity of their student body, institutions foster a sense of belonging and inclusion that encourages active participation and engagement from the ELLs and their parents.
- → **Enhance Language Proficiency**: Provide ELLs with targeted language instruction to improve English proficiency, facilitating access to core academic content and promoting confidence in social settings.
- → **Support Academic Achievement**: Address ELL students' unique learning needs through specialized instructional strategies and individualized support, helping them succeed in meeting academic standards and graduating on time.
- → **Encourage Family Engagement**: Facilitate active family involvement by offering resources, support, and culturally sensitive engagement opportunities, helping families navigate the school system and support their children's learning journey.
- → **Promote Cultural Inclusion**: Create an inclusive school environment where ELL students feel respected, celebrated, and valued for their cultural backgrounds, promoting a sense of belonging within the school community.

Proposed Strategies

1. **Language Development Programs**
    - o **Dedicated ESL Classes**: Offer intensive English as a Second Language (ESL) classes tailored to different proficiency levels, ensuring that each ELL student receives instruction appropriate to their language development needs.
    - o **Bilingual Support Staff**: Employ bilingual educators and paraprofessionals who can assist with instruction and serve as linguistic and cultural bridges for ELL students and their families.
    - o **Language Workshops**: Conduct language workshops for parents, empowering them to improve their English skills, communicate with teachers, and support their children's academic progress.
2. **Academic Support Initiatives**
    - o **Tutoring and Mentorship**: Establish after-school tutoring and mentorship programs where ELL students can receive additional help with coursework, develop study skills, and gain guidance from supportive mentors.
    - o **Culturally Responsive Teaching**: Train educators in culturally responsive teaching techniques, equipping them with strategies to create an inclusive classroom environment that respects diverse backgrounds and adapts learning materials for ELL students.
    - o **Differentiated Instruction**: Incorporate differentiated instruction in mainstream classes to address the varying academic needs of ELL students, ensuring that they can engage with the curriculum effectively alongside their peers.
3. **Family Engagement Programs**
    - o **Family Resource Center**: Establish a resource center where families can access information on school policies, events, and educational resources in multiple languages.

- **Parent Workshops**: Offer workshops on navigating the school system, understanding graduation requirements, and supporting children's academic progress. These sessions can be conducted in families' native languages to facilitate understanding.
- **Regular Communication**: Develop a structured communication plan that provides families with updates, newsletters, and event notifications in accessible formats and languages.

4. **Cultural Inclusion and Awareness Activities**
    - **Cultural Events and Celebrations**: Organize cultural events where ELL students and their families can share and celebrate their heritage, fostering mutual respect and understanding within the school community.
    - **Cultural Competency Training for all Staff**: Conduct training for all school staff on cultural competency, emphasizing strategies for creating an inclusive environment that respects and values the diversity of ELL students and their families.
    - **Student Ambassadors Program**: Develop a program where ELL students serve as ambassadors to educate peers about their cultural backgrounds, creating opportunities for cross-cultural understanding and friendship-building.

Evaluation and Outcomes

This initiative aims to achieve several key outcomes:

- Improved English proficiency and academic performance among ELL students.
- Increased family engagement and satisfaction with the school's support services.
- Enhanced cultural understanding and inclusivity within the school community.
- Higher rates of ELL graduation and successful transition to post-secondary opportunities.

CONCLUSION

English language learners (ELLs) are the fastest-growing population across all 50 states, making it imperative for educational institutions to address their unique needs. Despite their determination and desire to attend higher education to improve their own lives and those of their families, many adult ELLs struggle with a lack of confidence and inadequate institutional support to help them succeed academically. These challenges persist, even as the evidence highlights the significant potential of this group to thrive when provided with the right resources and opportunities. For educational institutions serving many K-12 ELLs, it is necessary and a moral obligation to establish comprehensive systems of support that address their academic, social, and emotional needs. Maslow's Hierarchy of Needs underscores the importance of fulfilling basic human needs before individuals can progress toward higher-level goals. ELLs often find themselves hindered in their ability to meet these foundational needs due to the numerous daily barriers, including linguistic, cultural, financial, and social challenges, among the most significant. Until these basic needs are met, moving toward academic success and self-actualization remains out of reach for many.

Educational administrators, faculty, and policymakers are responsible for collaborating to create and implement strategic, purposeful plans to support and motivate ELLs in K-12. This requires a multifaceted approach that includes:

1. **Providing Targeted Support Services**: Institutions must ensure access to language acquisition programs, academic advising at the secondary level, mental health resources, and culturally responsive counseling to address the unique needs of all ELLs and their families.
2. **Fostering a Welcoming Environment**: Creating a culture of inclusion through faculty training in cultural humility and linguistic diversity can empower ELLs to feel valued and supported.
3. **Breaking Down Barriers**: Policymakers and educators must work to eliminate systemic barriers, such as inflexible academic policies and insufficient financial aid options, that disproportionately affect ELLs.
4. **Promoting Collaborative Efforts**: Administrators and educators should partner with community organizations to create a network of support that extends beyond the classroom and addresses students' broader challenges.

The success of ELLs in the K-12 system depends on a collective commitment to understanding and addressing their needs holistically. By doing so, educational institutions empower ELLs to overcome obstacles, achieve their full potential, and foster a more equitable and inclusive society. Through intentional efforts and strategic planning, the K-12 educational system can serve as a pathway for ELLs to improve their lives and the lives of their families. It is a challenge worth undertaking and a mission that, when fulfilled, benefits not only the individual but the entire community.

REFERENCES

Abdou, A. S., De Pedro, K., De Anda, A., Merced, I., & Mao, K. (2022). Nurturing Cultural Humility and Responsiveness through Restorative Pedagogy in Graduate Education. *International Journal on Teaching and Learning in Higher Education*, *33*(2), 273–284.

Albiladi, W. S. (2019). Teaching English pronunciation revisited: the challenges of teaching EFL in non-English-speaking countries. *European Journal of Foreign Language Teaching*.

American Occupational Therapy Association. (2020). Educator's guide for addressing cultural awareness, humility, and dexterity in occupational therapy curricula. *The American Journal of Occupational Therapy*, 74(Supplement_3), 7413420003p1-7413420003p19.

Artigliere, M. (2019). The Proficiency, Instructional and Affective Domains of Long Term English Language Learners: A Review of the Research. *TESL-EJ*, *23*(1), n1.

Banks, J. A. (2019). An introduction to multicultural education.

Banks, J. A., & Banks, C. A. M. (Eds.). (2019). *Multicultural education: Issues and perspectives*. John Wiley & Sons.

Becker, G. I., & Deris, A. R. (2019). Identification of Hispanic English language learners in special education. *Education Research International*, *2019*, 2019. DOI: 10.1155/2019/2967943

Blakeley, S. (2021). Explore linguistic diversity: What is Linguistic Diversity? https://study.com/learn/lesson/linguistic-diversity.html

Bland, J. (2022). *Compelling Stories for English Language Learners: Creativity, Interculturality and Critical Literacy*. Bloomsbury Publishing. DOI: 10.5040/9781350190016

Bundick, M. J., Remington, K., Morton, E., & Colby, A. (2021). The contours of purpose beyond the self in midlife and later life. *Applied Developmental Science*, *25*(1), 62–82. DOI: 10.1080/10888691.2018.1531718

Cherry, K. (2016). Motivation: Psychological factors that guide behavior. *Pridobljeno*, *15*(12), 2016.

Claro, S., & Loeb, S. (2019). Students with growth mindset learn more in school: Evidence from California's CORE school districts. EdWorkingPaper 19-155 Retrieved Annenberg Inst. Brown Univ. httpwwwedworkingpaperscomai19, 155.

Compton, W. C. (2018). Self-actualization myths: What did Maslow really say? *Journal of Humanistic Psychology*, •••, 0022167818761929.

Constante, K., Cross, F. L., Piceno, V., Medina, M. A., & Rivas-Drake, D. (2021). Latinx adolescents' ethnic-racial discrimination and expected future barriers over time. *Developmental Psychology*, *57*(6), 991–999. DOI: 10.1037/dev0001180 PMID: 34424015

Cook, D. A., & Artino, A. R.Jr. (2016). Motivation to learn: An overview of contemporary theories. *Medical Education*, *50*(10), 997–1014. DOI: 10.1111/medu.13074 PMID: 27628718

Cultural Competence in Education. (2016, September 1). https://study.com/academy/lesson/cultural-competence-in-education.html

Cummins, J. (1984). *Schooling and language minority students: A theoretical framework*. Evaluation, Dissemination and Assessment Center.

Darling-Hammond, L., & Cook-Harvey, C. M. (2018). *Educating the Whole Child: Improving School Climate to Support Student Success*. Learning Policy Institute. DOI: 10.54300/145.655

DeLuca-Acconi, R., Bessaha, M., Velázquez, S. L., & Mendoza, M. R. (2022). How did we get here and where do we go from here? Supporting undocumented students through a pandemic. *School Psychology, 37*(2), 202–211. DOI: 10.1037/spq0000491 PMID: 35225641

Deussen, T., Hanson, H., & Bisht, B. (2017). *Are Two Commonly Used Early Warning Indicators Accurate Predictors of Dropout for English Learner Students? Evidence from Six Districts in Washington State. REL 2017-261*. Regional Educational Laboratory Northwest.

Dictionary, C. (2022). Native English speaker. https://dictionary.cambridge.org/us/dictionary/english/native-speaker?q=native+speakers

Dorner, L. M., Palmer, D., Cervantes-Soon, C. G., Heiman, D., & Crawford, E. R. (Eds.). (2022). *Critical Consciousness in Dual Language Bilingual Education: Case Studies on Policy and Practice*. Taylor & Francis. DOI: 10.4324/9781003240594

Dunstan, S. B., Eads, A., Jaeger, A. J., & Wolfram, W. (2018). The importance of graduate student engagement in a campus language diversity initiative. *Journal of English Linguistics, 46*(3), 215–228. DOI: 10.1177/0075424218783446

Ee, J., & Gándara, P. (2020). The impact of immigration enforcement on the nation's schools. *American Educational Research Journal, 57*(2), 840–871. DOI: 10.3102/0002831219862998

Faingold, E. D. (2022). Language rights in the United States Constitution and the Civil Rights Act of 1964. *Language and Identity, 447*.

Fan, F., & de Jong, E. J. (2019). Exploring professional identities of non-native-English-speaking teachers in the United States: A narrative case study. *TESOL Journal, 10*(4), e495. DOI: 10.1002/tesj.495

Fernandez, R., Peyton, J. K., & Schaetzel, K. (2017). A survey of writing instruction in adult ESL programs: Are teaching practices meeting adult learner needs? *Coabe Journal, 6*(2), 5.

Foley, G. (2020). Introduction: The state of adult education and learning. In Dimensions of adult learning (pp. 3-18). Routledge.

Galvao, S. R. (2020). Addressing the Needs of English Language Learners at the Secondary Level: A Qualitative Single-Case Study (Doctoral dissertation, Northcentral University).

Galvao, S. R. (2023). Addressing the Needs of Adult English Language Learners and Motivational Skills. In *Motivation and Momentum in Adult Online Education* (pp. 266–283). IGI Global. DOI: 10.4018/978-1-6684-7712-0.ch016

García, E. E. (2021). Treating Linguistic and Cultural Diversity as a Resource: The Research Response to the Challenges Inherent in the Improving America's Schools Act and California′ s Proposition 227. In *Language Ideologies* (pp. 90–113). Routledge. DOI: 10.4324/9781315045429-6

Gay, G. The what, why, and how of culturally responsive teaching: international mandates, challenges, and opportunities. Multicultural Education Review, *[s. l.], v. 7, n. 3, p.123-139,2015.*

Glossary, E. S. L. (2022). Glossary of terms relevant to the ESL profession. https://bogglesworldesl .com/glossary/l1.htm

Glossary, E. S. L. (2022). Glossary of terms relevant to the ESL profession. https://bogglesworldesl .com/glossary/l2.htm

González-Cutre, D., Sicilia, Á., Sierra, A. C., Ferriz, R., & Hagger, M. S. (2017). Understanding the need for novelty from the perspective of self-determination theory. *Personality and Individual Differences, 102*, 159–169. DOI: 10.1016/j.paid.2016.06.036

Honigsfeld, A., & Dove, M. G. (2021). *Co-planning: Five essential practices to integrate curriculum and instruction for English learners*. Corwin Press.

Hopper, E. (2020). Maslow's hierarchy of needs explained. ThoughtCo, ThoughtCo, 24.

Jibreel, Z. "Cultural Identity and the Challenges International Students Encounter" (2015). Culminating Projects in English. 23. https://repository.stcloudstate.edu/engl_etds/23

Kakabra, K. K. (2015). English language learning anxiety among foreign language learners in Kurdistan region of Iraq: Soran University as an Example. *International Journal of Education and Research, 3*(1), 485–494.

Karvonen, M., Clark, A. K., Carlson, C., Wells Moreaux, S., & Burnes, J. (2021). Approaches to identification and instruction for students with significant cognitive disabilities who are English learners. *Research and Practice for Persons with Severe Disabilities : the Journal of TASH, 46*(4), 223–239. DOI: 10.1177/15407969211040256

Krashen, S. (1984). *Schooling and language minority students: A theoretical framework*. Evaluation, Dissemination and Assessment Center.

Locke, E. A., & Schattke, K. (2019). Intrinsic and extrinsic motivation: Time for expansion and clarification. *Motivation Science, 5*(4), 277–290. DOI: 10.1037/mot0000116

López, E. J., & Davis, M. T. (2019). A matter of time: English language learners and the RTI process.

Lyn, A. E., Broderick, M., & Spranger, E. (2023). Student well-being and empowerment: SEL in online graduate education. In Rahimi, R., & Liston, D. (Eds.), *Exploring Social Emotional Learning in Diverse Academic Settings*. IGI Global. DOI: 10.4018/978-1-6684-7227-9.ch016

Maine, D. O. E. (n.d.)https://www.maine.gov/doe/learning/multilinguallearner#:~:text=Multilingual %20learners%20are%20students%20with,the%20process%20of%20acquiring%20English. Maine DOE: https://www.maine.gov/doe/learning/multilinguallearner/resources/newcomers SLIFE#:~:text=The%20 Maine%20DOE%20and%20the,skills%20relative%20to%20typical%20peers

Maslow, A. H. (1963). The need to know and the fear of knowing. *The Journal of General Psychology, 68*(1), 111–125. DOI: 10.1080/00221309.1963.9920516 PMID: 13933351

Mastandrea, S., Fagioli, S., & Biasi, V. (2019). Art and psychological well-being: Linking the brain to the aesthetic emotion. *Frontiers in Psychology*, *10*, 739. DOI: 10.3389/fpsyg.2019.00739 PMID: 31019480

McCracken, K. (2021). Barriers, Racism, Discrimination, and Stereotypes Against an Adult Immigrant Pursuing Adult Education: A Case Study.

McLeod, S. A. (2018, May 21). Maslow's hierarchy of needs. Simply Psychology. Retrieved from https://www.simplypsychology.org/maslow.html

Muñiz, J. (2019). *Culturally Responsive Teaching: A 50-State Survey of Teaching Standards*. New America.

Murayama, K., FitzGibbon, L., & Sakaki, M. (2019). Process account of curiosity and interest: A reward-learning perspective. *Educational Psychology Review*, *31*(4), 875–895. DOI: 10.1007/s10648-019-09499-9

Ortiz, A. A., & Fránquiz, M. E. (2019). Co-editors' introduction: Challenges to the success of English learners in the context of language instruction educational programs. *Bilingual Research Journal*, *42*(1), 1–5. DOI: 10.1080/15235882.2019.1598213

Perez, C. P., & Morrison, S. S. (2016). Understanding the challenges of English language learners and increasing college-going culture: Suggestions for school counselors. *Ideas and Research You Can Use: Vistas*, *18*, 1–12.

Peterson, G. (2022). Culturally Responsive Leadership in Bilingual Education: An Exploration of the Practices Implemented by Elementary School Principals in Southern New Mexico (Doctoral dissertation, New Mexico State University).

Pierre, Y., Rathee, N. K., & Rathee, V. S. (2021). Developing cross-cultural competency through multicultural perspective: An exploratory inquiry. *European Scientific Journal*, *17*(27), 324–346. DOI: 10.19044/esj.2021.v17n27p324

Presbitero, A. (2020). Foreign language skill, anxiety, cultural intelligence and individual task performance in global virtual teams: A cognitive perspective. *Journal of International Management*, *26*(2), 100729. DOI: 10.1016/j.intman.2019.100729

Rheinberg, F., & Engeser, S. (2018). Intrinsic motivation and flow. In *Motivation and action* (pp. 579–622). Springer. DOI: 10.1007/978-3-319-65094-4_14

Robinson-Wood, T. (2016). *The convergence of race, ethnicity, and gender: Multiple identities in counseling*. Sage Publications.

Sheng, Z., Sheng, Y., & Anderson, C. J. (2016). Dropping out of school among ELL students: Implications to schools and teacher education. *The Clearing House: A Journal of Educational Strategies, Issues and Ideas*, *84*(3), 98–103. DOI: 10.1080/00098655.2010.538755

Slavin, R. E., Calder, M., & Calderon, M. (2017). *Effective programs for Latino students*. Routledge.

State of South Carolina Department of Education. (2020). South Carolina Adult ESL Handbook. https://ed.sc.gov/instruction/adult-education/english-as-a-second-language/scde-adult-esl-handbook-final/

Suzuki, Y., & DeKeyser, R. (2017). The interface of explicit and implicit knowledge in a second language: Insights from individual differences in cognitive aptitudes. *Language Learning*, *67*(4), 747–790. DOI: 10.1111/lang.12241

Translators without Borders (2022). Language data for the United States of America. https://translatorswithoutborders.org/language-data-for-the-united-states-of-america

Turner, D. L. (2020). Teachers' Perception of Student Engagement when Using Blended Learning: An Exploratory Single-Case Study (Doctoral dissertation, University of Phoenix).

Vinney, C. (2019, November 2). Understanding Maslow's theory of self-actualization. Retrieved from https://www.thoughtco.com/maslow-theory-self-actualization-4169662

Wright, K. (2022). Academic achievement of middle school English language learners based on participation in an English as a second language program (Order No. 28777461). Available from Dissertations & Theses @ Northcentral University. (2624693094). https://go.openathens.net/redirector/ncu.edu?url=https://www.proquest.com/dissertations-theses/academic-achievement-middle-school-english/docview/2624693094/se-2

KEY TERMS AND DEFINITIONS

Cultural Awareness: Recognizing the nuances of your culture and those of others is vital to cultural awareness. It refers to how individuals and organizations interact respectfully, thoughtfully, and effectively with people from diverse ethnicities, languages, cultural groups, and backgrounds. This approach affirms and honors the unique value of individuals, families, and communities, ensuring their dignity is upheld and respected. By embracing cultural differences with sensitivity and understanding, this practice fosters inclusivity, equity, and mutual respect while safeguarding the self-worth and identity of everyone involved (Robinson-Wood, 2016).

Cultural Competence: The ability to engage effectively with individuals from cultures different from one's own relies on a deep understanding and appreciation of cultural differences. This encompasses a combination of behaviors, attitudes, and beliefs that enable professionals to navigate and perform successfully in diverse cross-cultural situations. It reflects a commitment to fostering respectful, inclusive, and productive interactions across cultural boundaries (Cultural Competence in Education, 2016).

Cultural Diversity: Differences in race, culture, ethnicity, socioeconomic status, physical abilities, language, religion, ethics, behavior patterns, and traditions can create significant distinctions among various groups within a larger community, organization, or nation. These distinctions often reflect individuals' diverse backgrounds and experiences, shaping their perspectives, values, and interactions. Such diversity can manifest in numerous ways, from varying social norms and communication styles to different belief systems and customs. Recognizing and understanding these differences is crucial in fostering an environment of inclusivity, respect, and cooperation among individuals and groups from varied backgrounds. (American Occupational Therapy Association, 2020)

:

Diversity: English Language Learners (ELLs) arrive at school with diverse experiences, language abilities, and literacy skills that shape their educational journey. Their academic knowledge and progress are influenced by various factors, including the amount of time they have spent in formal education, the quality and consistency of the instruction they have received, and the stability of their schooling experience. Additional influences such as family circumstances, frequent relocation or transiency, and the emotional impact of prior educational experiences also play a significant role. For some, these experiences may include challenges like interrupted schooling, limited access to resources, or stress from adjusting to a new cultural and linguistic environment. These factors create a complex backdrop that educators must consider to effectively support ELLs in achieving their full academic potential. Recognizing and addressing these influences is essential to creating a learning environment that fosters growth, resilience, and success (Slavin et al., 2017).

Entry Criteria: These criteria function as a structured framework for determining when English Language Learners (ELLs) are prepared to transition out of English as a Second Language (ESL) services. Meeting these benchmarks indicates that learners are ready to integrate fully into mainstream courses and discontinue specialized language support. To be eligible for this transition, students must demonstrate that they have achieved all the language proficiency standards established by the state. This includes mastering reading, writing, listening, and speaking English at levels sufficient to thrive academically in a mainstream educational setting. By ensuring these requirements are met, schools can provide a smoother transition for learners while maintaining the confidence that they can succeed independently in their new learning environments (Colorado, 2017).

English Language Development (ELD): This specific type of instruction was intentionally designed to support English Language Learners (ELLs) in developing their speaking, listening, reading, and writing skills in English. The aim is to provide a comprehensive, immersive learning experience that helps students gain proficiency in all aspects of the language. The instruction includes a variety of strategies and activities tailored to meet the diverse needs of ELLs, ensuring that each student can progress in mastering the language at their own pace. The following components are integral parts of this instructional approach: English as a second language, ESL; English for speakers of other languages, ESOL; English as a new language, ENL; English language learner, ELL; and English learner, EL, Honigsfeld, A., & Dove, M. G. (2021).

English Learners (ELs): Students who are deeply committed to their educational journey, particularly in improving their English language skills, work diligently to achieve academic goals that are on par with those of native English speakers. Their active engagement in the learning process reflects a strong determination to overcome language barriers and excel in reading, writing, speaking, and listening. These learners strive to meet the proficiency standards required in their academic settings and develop the necessary skills to succeed in various disciplines and real-world scenarios. Their dedication helps to ensure that they can compete effectively with their peers, regardless of language differences, and ultimately reach their full potential as students and future contributors to society (Fan & de Jong, 2019).

English Language Learners (ELLs): The term refers to English language instruction designed specifically for students who are non-native speakers of English. The primary goal of an English Language Learner (ELL) program is to equip these individuals with the necessary language skills to communicate effectively in American English. This instruction helps ELLs navigate everyday interactions, engage with local communities, and access various opportunities in mainstream society, including employment, education, and healthcare. By improving their language proficiency, the program enables these learners to better integrate into their new cultural environment, fostering greater independence, social inclusion, and personal empowerment. Ultimately, the ELL program plays a vital role in supporting individuals as they work to overcome language barriers and contribute fully to the communities in which they live (State of South Carolina Department of Education, 2020).

English Language Proficiency (ELP): To achieve proficiency in English, English Language Learners (ELLs) must develop their skills across all four key domains: speaking, listening, reading, and writing. Mastery of these areas is essential for effective communication and academic success. Every state must establish its own English Language Proficiency (ELP) standards to support this development. These standards should clearly define the expectations for what learners can accomplish in each domain at various stages of their language learning journey. Furthermore, these standards must be tailored to reflect the diverse levels of English proficiency among ELLs, ensuring that all learners are provided with appropriate challenges and support based on their individual needs. By establishing these clear, state-specific guidelines, educators can effectively track progress, set achievable goals, and better assist ELLs in advancing toward full language proficiency (Colorado, 2017).

English as a Second Language (ESL): This specialized curriculum was specifically designed for courses focusing on teaching English to English Language Learners (ELLs) with minimal reliance on their native language. These English as a Second Language (ESL) courses aim to immerse students in English, helping them build language proficiency through targeted instruction. Typically, these courses are offered during designated times within the school day. They are often conducted in a pull-out setting, where students are temporarily removed from their mainstream classes to receive focused language support. After completing the ESL sessions, learners are then reintegrated into their regular classroom environments. This model ensures that ELLs receive the intensive language support they need while still participating in their overall academic curriculum, helping them gradually transition into full participation in mainstream classes as they gain proficiency (Galvao, 2020).

English for Speakers of Other Languages (ESOL): The term "English for Speakers of Other Languages" (ESOL) refers to the practice of teaching English to students whose first language is not English. These learners typically reside in an English-speaking country, where English is not the primary language used in daily life, education, and most aspects of their society. ESOL programs are specifically designed to assist these individuals in developing the language skills necessary to communicate effectively in English. ESOL instruction aims to enhance students' ability to navigate academic settings, social interactions, and professional environments by focusing on the four key language domains- speaking, listening, reading, and writing. The goal is to improve linguistic proficiency and ensure that non-native speakers can participate fully and confidently in an English-speaking society. Through tailored teaching methods and support, ESOL programs provide essential tools for learners to thrive in their new environment (Albiladi, 2019).

Entry Criteria: These criteria are crucial in identifying students as English Language Learners (ELLs) and determining their placement in the appropriate educational programs, such as English as a Second Language (ESL) or other support services. The identification process typically begins with a home language survey, which helps to determine if any language other than English is spoken in the student's home environment. This initial step ensures that students requiring language assistance are accurately identified. Following the survey, students are administered an English proficiency test to assess their language skills across key domains such as speaking, listening, reading, and writing. This comprehensive approach ensures that ELLs are placed in the most suitable educational setting, where they can receive the targeted support they need to develop their English language proficiency and succeed academically. By using these criteria, schools can effectively address the diverse needs of English learners and provide them with the appropriate resources for their academic growth (ETS, 2012).

Exit Criteria: These criteria are essential for determining when learners can transition from English as a Second Language (ESL) services and move fully into mainstream academic courses without specialized language support. To qualify for this transition, learners must demonstrate that they have met all the proficiency requirements outlined by the state. This includes showing competence in key language domains, such as speaking, listening, reading, and writing, at a level deemed sufficient for success in general education settings. The criteria ensure that students are linguistically prepared to engage with their peers in regular classrooms and thrive academically in various subject areas. Students can confidently move forward in their educational journey by meeting these standards, fully integrated into the mainstream curriculum and free from additional language assistance. This process helps to guarantee that students have acquired the necessary skills to excel and contribute meaningfully in a diverse, English-speaking educational environment (Colorado, 2017).

Language Diversity: A powerful phrase often used to highlight the wide variety of dialects and the unique ways in which individuals communicate with one another; this expression underscores the linguistic diversity that exists within and across cultures. It serves as a reminder of the intricate differences in speech patterns, vocabulary, pronunciation, and cultural nuances that shape how people express themselves. Beyond just the words spoken, it reflects the deeper cultural, social, and historical contexts that influence communication styles and interpersonal connections. This distinction not only celebrates the diversity of language but also emphasizes the importance of understanding and respecting these differences to foster meaningful interactions and connections across linguistic and cultural boundaries (Blakeley, 2021).

Limited English Proficiency (LEP): This term is commonly utilized by the State Department of Education and school districts to classify students who lack sufficient proficiency in English to participate effectively in English-only instructional settings. These students are identified as requiring additional language support to bridge the gap between their English proficiency and the demands of mainstream academic classes. Typically, these individuals were born outside the United States, and their home language is one other than English, contributing to their need for specialized English language instruction. Using this designation, educational institutions aim to ensure these learners receive the necessary resources, programs, and accommodations to support their linguistic development. This identification process is vital in helping students build the English skills needed to succeed academically while fostering their ability to fully engage in the school community and beyond (Sheng et al., 2016).

Long-Term English Language Learners (LTELLs): These students have been enrolled in English language learning programs for six or more years, yet they continue to demonstrate minimal or no measurable progress in their English language development. Despite the extended support period, their proficiency levels remain comparable to those of learners new to the English language. This ongoing need for services highlights significant challenges in their language acquisition journey, underscoring the importance of addressing potential barriers such as instructional methods, individual learning differences, or external factors impeding their growth. The situation calls for reevaluating strategies and tailored interventions to ensure these learners can achieve meaningful progress and move closer to linguistic and academic success (Artigliere, 2019).

L1: The term refers to an abbreviation for a student's first or native language, acquired naturally in early childhood and used at home or in their community. Recognizing a student's first language is crucial in education, as it helps differentiate it from subsequent languages and supports tailored strategies for second-language learning. This approach respects the student's linguistic and cultural strengths while promoting equitable and inclusive education (ESL Glossary, 2022).

L2: The term refers to a "second language," a language learned in addition to an individual's native one. It helps distinguish between a learner's primary language and the additional language they acquire to adapt to new environments or meet academic or social needs. Recognizing a second language is vital for creating effective educational strategies and addressing challenges like grammar, vocabulary, and cultural nuances. This distinction enables educators to tailor instruction to the learner's needs while valuing their linguistic and cultural strengths, fostering an inclusive environment for multilingual learners to succeed (ESL Glossary, 2022).

Multilingual Learners (MLLs): Multilingual Learners are a term used to describe students acquiring proficiency in multiple languages. These learners are developing fluency in languages beyond their native tongue, with English often being one of those languages. Depending on their language background and educational context, multilingual learners may also be called English Language Learners (ELLs), dual language learners, or long-term English learners. MLLs can have varied linguistic experiences, ranging from those just beginning to learn English to those who have been acquiring English for several years. Their language development may occur through immersion in a bilingual environment or formal language education programs. Understanding the needs of MLLs is critical for educators, as they often face unique challenges in both language acquisition and academic achievement. Therefore, effective instructional strategies are essential to help them develop the skills needed to succeed in all subject areas while becoming proficient in multiple languages (Maine DOE, 2024).

Native English Speakers (NES): A native English speaker is someone born in the United States who learned English as their first language, typically through natural immersion in their home and community. Unlike those who learn English later in life, native speakers acquire the language through everyday interactions from an early age. Native speakers instinctively grasp English grammar, vocabulary, and pronunciation, which enables them to engage easily with cultural and societal norms. Their fluency influences their academic success, literacy development, and integration into various social and professional environments. Recognizing the difference between native English speakers and those learning English as a second language is essential in education, helping to tailor support for English language learners while ensuring native speakers continue to grow in their language development (Cambridge Dictionary, 2022).

Students with Limited or Interrupted Schooling (SLIFE): The term refers to a multilingual learner who meets specific criteria related to their educational and language needs, including their educational background, where they may have experienced no formal schooling (limited or no exposure to structured education), interruptions in schooling (frequent re-enrollments or being at least two years behind their peers), limited schooling outside the U.S. (inconsistent or poor-quality education outside the U. S.), or below-grade-level performance (performing at least two years below peers in literacy or math). This profile highlights the need for specialized support and instructional strategies to help bridge academic and linguistic gaps, empowering the learner to succeed while developing necessary English proficiency. (Maine DOE, 2024).

Chapter 18
Education Without Borders:
Ramping Up Support for Refugee, Migrant, and Immigrant Learners, PK–12

Chigozie Ekpe
https://orcid.org/0009-0001-2036-072X
National University, USA

ABSTRACT

Education is a fundamental right (United Nations, 1948) that should be afforded to all children. To foster academic and personal growth, children must have access to safe, humane, and inclusive learning spaces underpinned by equity and social justice. Approximately 1.6 million children reside in the U.S., with a rising number of minors traveling alone (UNICEF Data Warehouse, 2024). Migrant children in the U.S. experience divergent and unique educational, environmental, health, and socioeconomic barriers and inadequate support which disrupt children's learning and development (Ibrahim et al., 2024). This chapter will clarify the interconnection between different migrant groups. This chapter will adopt a pertinent theoretical lens to explore factors contributing to child migration, the challenges, and different levels of support (or lack thereof) available to these populations. This chapter will culminate in viable suggestions for enhanced support for migrant learners.

INTRODUCTION

Education is a right of every child irrespective of an individual's citizenship, nationality, legal status, or migrant status (Kelcey et al., 2022; United Nations Children's Fund [UNICEF], n.d.). The UN Sustainable Development Goal 4 (SDG4) is committed to "ensure inclusive and equitable quality education and promote lifelong learning opportunities for all" (UN, n.d.a.; n.d.b; United Nations Educational Scientific and Cultural Organization [UNESCO], 2025, para. 3). Against the backdrop of SDG4, all children should have access to quality education despite status or circumstance. The UN's sole education goal is integral to progressive change and education's transformative power to promote a sustainable and equitable environment.

Education is instrumental in ensuring an inclusive culture among learners by upholding ideals of equality, respect, and acceptance (Rentzi, 2024). As a critical humanitarian element, education fosters long-term stability and welfare for refugees (Miri, 2024. The rising number of migrants, refugees, and

DOI: 10.4018/979-8-3693-9020-7.ch018

displaced individuals worldwide, including the 122.6 million reported by the United Nations High Commissioner for Refugees (UNHCR, 2025b), has necessitated intensified studies on refugee education (Miri, 2024; Ungar & Seymour, 2024). Hence, it is imperative to understand the experiences and the academic requirements of migrant, immigrant, and refugee children to ensure both children and youth can continuously flourish in these situations (Mira, 2024). Further, access to standard education empowers immigrants, migrants, and refugees to handle the insecurities of geographical displacement and contribute substantially to their receiving nations' social and economic advancement (Miri, 2024). Of the projected 7.4 million school-aged refugees recorded by the UNHCR, only 61% were enrolled in primary school, compared to a 92% global average enrollment rate.

Children are disturbingly overrepresented among the global refugee headcount (UNICEF, 2024). While children comprise less than a third of the world's population, they account for 40 percent of the worldwide refugee population in 2023 (UNICEF, 2024). In 2020, the international migrant (foreign-born or individuals residing in a nation or setting besides their origin of birth) population comprised nearly 1 to 3 child refugees, while the ratio was less than 1 to 20 for adults (UNICEF, 2024). However, refugees account for a comparatively small fraction of the migrants globally. A more abundant population, albeit generally neglected in publications, is internally displaced persons and the masses who migrate for other motives, including economic stress or climate change. A substantial level of migration activity is mixed, (Kelcey et al., 2022; Mixed Migration Center, 2025) with individuals moving both within and beyond national borderlines for diverse and intersecting reasons such as conflict, poverty, poor leadership, violence, and, progressively, environmental and climate-based stresses (International Organization for Migration ([IOM], 2024; IRC, 2024; Shufutinsky et al., 2022; Ungar & Seymour, 2024; USA for UNHRC, 2025). Granted, in recent times, refugees' education has garnered increased awareness, albeit a dearth of inquiries on how education ties into the other forms and causes of migration (Kelcey et al., 2022).

This chapter provides an overview of the theoretical framework underpinning this review of issues pertinent to migrant and refugee children, the interconnectedness between international immigration, migration, and refugee asylum, and the history of migrants and refugees in the United States. This chapter touches on concepts of diversity, equity, and inclusion related to education and the intersection of social justice and education. Finally, the educational challenges experienced by migrant children and a call to action will be presented in this chapter.

THEORETICAL FRAMEWORK

Researchers adopt multiple theoretical frameworks to foster profound insight into their works or undertakings (Bese & Dali, 2021; Crosby et al., 2006). This chapter is underpinned by the social justice approach posited by Nancy Fraser (2008), David Miller (1999), and John Rawls (1971). The combined lens will clarify the myriad underlying issues surrounding education for migrant, immigrant, and refugee children.

Social Justice Theoretical Framework

Fraser (2008), as paraphrased by Miri (2024), equates justice to "parity of participation" (p.1863) and attributes the emerging viewpoints on justice to globalization. For justice to prevail, social structures must ensure equal participation of all parties in all social interactions (Fraser, 2008; Miri, 2024). Curbing injustice can only be achieved when entrenched deterrents restricting certain individuals or groups from engaging in social activities are eradicated. Fraser (2008) identified three barriers - redistribution, recognition, and representation - which deter people (such as migrants and refugees) from fully engaging in parity of participation (Miri, 2024).

From Fraser's (2008) perspective, according to Miri (2024), redistribution is a facet of economic distribution. If fiscal barriers sabotage the achievement of justice and inclusion, the recourse may require human and material resource reallocation (McIntyre & Neuhaus, 2021), especially regarding education. Miri (2024) verified the significant effect of socioeconomic factors on refugee families' access to educational support. Fraser's (2008) idea of redistribution, according to Mira (2024), echoed Bronfenbrenner's (1997) ecological view of how families' settings and children's learning are affected by changes in societal dispositions and immediate circumstances. Mira (2024) confirmed that refugees' efforts to obtain accommodation and the intricacies of society's dispositions towards them accentuated a dire need for fair allotment of resources and cultural awareness in learning settings. It is imperative to enact guidelines and educational agendas that acknowledge the diverse hardships refugees and their children undergo, ensure they have access to required assistance, and are accorded respect and dignity in the learning settings.

Migrants strive to obtain the necessities of life, compounded by society's disposition towards them, drawing attention to the issue of distributive injustice (Fraser, 2008; Mira, 2024) as Mira (2024) posited, injustice, which typically stems from societal class stratification, results in equality and integration challenges due to limited resources and social status, specifically for refugees - a situation, the author affirms, that can elicit segregation and exclusion. In terms of recognition, people are deterred from interrelating with peers on an equal footing due to the cultural pecking order or chain of command, which exposes them to misrecognition or status inequality, all which stem from the status order (Fraser, 2008). A clear insight into justice can only be attained through the integration of both elements of distribution (class structure) and recognition (status order) (Mira, 2024). Child refugees, despite their academic prowess, can still experience marginalization or misrecognition in school due to entrenched cultural stratification or orders that undermine their cultural heritage. This context depicted the intricate intersection between the elements of recognition (cultural status) and distribution (academic achievement) (Mira, 2024).

The third element of the social justice theory is the political dimension. While power and politics wield an influence over recognition and redistribution, the political angle of the social justice theory is more precise, given it addresses the nation-state jurisdiction's reach and the rulings by which it structures contention (Fraser, 2008). The political element of social justice offers an opening for discourse on issues related to recognition and distribution (Fraser, 2008). The political dimension of justice focuses on representation and is geared towards bureaucratic and belonging issues.

Misrepresentation occurs when political rulings or constraints are unduly enforced or adopted, thereby overlooking the issue of equal opportunity in certain populations' social relations (Fraser, 2008). In addition to enacting policies or rulings, the political element decides how contests are staged and resolved regarding recognition (cultural element) and distribution (economic element). Local education policymakers can sideline a child refugee based on non-citizenship, notwithstanding being a significant entity affected by these rulings, affirming Fraser's stance on misrepresentation within the political element of justice (Mira, 2024). Fraser's social justice theory is an ethical guideline that illuminates how people's opinions impact dominant political narratives (McIntyre, 2021; Mira, 2024). Fraser's theory provides an in-depth insight into refugee children's encounters and hardships faced in educational settings by examining how systemic factors affect how schools and stakeholders address the needs of these young learners.

Other intellectuals opine that social justice is for dismantling all societal structural biases by eroding supremacy and privileges while safeguarding equality for underrepresented individuals (Bese & Dali, 2021). The social justice theory is underpinned by a widespread opinion that social justice efforts must focus on empowering marginalized individuals or populations in educational settings regarding equity, access, and inclusive engagement. Promoting social justice entails examining institutions and their input toward human development, equality, fairness, or whatever society deems ethically acceptable (Campbell, 2021). Social justice translates to a wholesome, equal, and equitable engagement of all individuals in an environment mutually designed to cater to people's needs and safeguard their rights and prospects (Bell, 2013; Bese & Dali, 2021). Hence, social justice must be founded on destabilizing conditions that enable marginalization and exclusive agendas, and critical theorists are crucial to ensuring socially just learning institutions (Bese & Dali, 2021). Ultimately, social justice focuses on reclaiming and promoting the rights of education stakeholders in alignment with access, equity, and inclusive engagement facilitated by all educators' emotional intelligence (EI) dispositions (Bese & Dali, 2021).

INTERNATIONAL IMMIGRATION, MIGRATION, AND REFUGEE ASYLUM

People are constantly on the move, either within or between nations. The underlying circumstances that drive individuals to leave their places of abode for another settlement vary. Children oftentimes neither have control over their movements, and these moves affect their educational attainments and outcomes. The UNHCR (2022) affirms that millions of refugee children and youth remain unsettled for their entire education phase, from pre-elementary to tertiary level. Oftentimes, these children reside in host nations already grappling to provide standard education. To better grasp the education-related issues plaguing foreign-born children in their host or receiving nation, it is critical to differentiate between the various forms or types of movements or pathways.

Refugees are loosely termed as individuals who have been compelled to flee their nations due to violence, war, or persecution (USA for UNHRC, 2025). Refugees, under the UN Convention on the Status of Refugees of 1951, are individuals who, driven by a genuine fear of persecution due to reasons of race, religion, nationality, sexual orientation, gender identity, affiliation with a certain clique, or political view, are outside the nation of their nationality (UNHCR, 1951; 2010; 2025b). Refugees are unable or, owing to such fear, are unwilling to avail themselves of the protection of those countries; or who, not having a nationality and being outside the country of their former habitual residence due to such events, are unable or, owing to such fear, are unwilling to return to it (UNHCR, 1951; 2010; 2025b). Refugees have a well-founded fear of persecution due to factors such as race, religion, nationality, political stance, or social connections (IOM, 2019; USA for UNHRC, 2025a). Usually, refugees are either unable to return home or are terrified of doing so. War and violence due to tribal, religious, and ethnic disputes are the main reasons refugees flee their home nations (USA for UNHCR, 2025a).

While host nations often deem refugees taxing, embracing refugees can be rewarding, particularly if they are well-educated and integrated into their new home (Demir et al., 2024). Refugees outstrip other migrants in labor sectors, tax remittance, and linguistic competence (Demir et al., 2024), and analyses verify the benefits to youth in the receiving nation due to enhanced learning avenues and competition in the employment sector (Tumen, 2021). Unfortunately, most refugees experience bias and exclusion upon arrival in their host nation, including access to education. Migrant is a general term, excluded from international law, which reflects the typical understanding as one who provisionally or permanently leaves one's usual residence, either within a nation or between nation-state borderlines (IOM, 2019). This description took account of specific legal categories of individuals, such as migrant workforces; individuals with legally defined types of movements, such as trafficked migrants; and individuals whose means of movement or status are undefined under international law.

According to the IOM (2024), there are 281 million international migrants (including children) worldwide currently, equating to more than 3.5 percent of the global population. In 2022, IOM (2024) reported 117 million displaced people worldwide, 71.2 million internally displaced individuals, and at least a 30% rise in asylum seekers from 4.1 million in 2020 to 5.4 million in 2022. However, the UNHCR recorded 117.3 million forcibly displaced individuals in 2023 (2024) and 112.6 million in 2024 (2025b).

Most migrants worldwide do not move across international borders; rather, most of these individuals migrate within nations (IOM, 2024). Thus, there are unanticipated worldwide numerical and proportional migrant spikes. While only a minute proportion (3.6%) of the global population is international migrants, there are visible country-level gaps (IOM, 2024). Studies indicated non-uniformity in international migration worldwide spurred by fiscal, demographic, and geographic determinants culminating in distinct migration patterns, among which were migration "corridors" (para.17) accrued over time (IOM, 2024). Migration corridors are an accretion of migratory activities over time, which offer an overview of the evolution of migration patterns into significant foreign-born populations in certain host nations (IOM, 2024).

According to IOM (2024), in 2020, over 40% (115 million) of all international migrants globally were Asian born, about 20% hailing from six Asian nations (Afghanistan, Bangladesh, China, Philippines, as well as India, as the largest nation of origin). Mexico and the Russian Federation are the second and third largest nations of origin, respectively (IOM, 2024). Countries with significant emigrant or migrant populations include Ukraine, the United Kingdom, Romania, Germany, and Poland (IOM, 2024). The United States has remained the primary destination country for international migrants since 1970. Given the nation's history of providing refuge for war and persecution victims, there has been over a fourfold increase (51 million in 2019 from less than 12 million in 1970) in the number of foreign-born individuals residing in the United States (IOM, 2024). The most significant migration corridors are typically from developing nations to larger countries, including the United States, the United Arab Emirates, the Russian Federation, and Saudi Arabia (IOM, 2024).

Immigrants comprise individuals who move into a nation besides their nationality of usual residence so that the nation of destination or receiving nation effectively becomes their new nationality of usual residence (IOM, 2019). Individuals move around globally with diverse intentions. Among the common reasons are ties to their indigenous homes, avenues to apply skills in economic systems when it is unfeasible in their current homes, to evade poverty, to escape conflict and crime, to have the power to be their true selves, and to seek asylum (Hatton, 2020; Shufutinsky et al., 2022). Per migration, the IOM (n.d.) offers a general description, albeit not specified under international law, which borders on the conventional understanding of a person who moves away from his/her place of usual dwelling or abode, be it within a nation or beyond international borderlines, short-term or long-term, and for a host of reasons. This definition embodies certain well-outlined legal groups of individuals, which include migrant workers, smuggled migrants, individuals with legally defined means of movement, as well as individuals whose status or types of movement are not specified under international law, such as international learners.

However, most immigration policies and programs fail to consider the sociocultural workings of immigrant existence beyond the fiscal, hence people are left to contend with bleak and insensitive conditions (Shufutinsky et al., 2022). Many migrants cross international borders to escape insalubrious or menacing conditions or settings, arriving in other countries to seek refuge. Oftentimes termed refugees, these individuals are compelled to flee their home country to avoid conflict, violence, war, or persecution due to factors such as their race, religion, or political affiliation (IOM, 2025; IRC, 2024; Shufutinsky et al., 2022; Ungar & Seymour, 2024; USA for UNHRC, 2025a). For migrants and immigrants, life as they know it is never the same. In a bid to resettle, refugees and their children typically undergo significant anxieties and stress given their uncertain futures and the hardships they endure, ranging from basic survival, getting lost or being captured and detained, or being denied asylum in a receiving nation (Shufutinsky et al., 2022). Challenges prevail even after resettlement, as migrants, immigrants, and refugees face acclimatization issues, which include their host nation's sociocultural and socioeconomic complexities. Inadequate support leaves refugees susceptible to poor outcomes, specifically mental health outcomes, given refugees' cultural and linguistic barriers, traumatic and violent encounters, interrupted learning, and restricted access to resources before migration, among other issues related to their displacement and relocation experiences (Cureton, 2024; Cureton et al., 2024).

Ascertaining refugee status primarily depends on the seeming credibility of individual(s) seeking sanctuary, often leading to drawn-out biased arbitration and even the risk of being detained (Shufutinsky et al., 2022). While legally, detaining an asylum seeker is deemed a type of civil restraint, in many nations, this practice is a criminal confinement, disputably utilized as a deterrence mechanism, potentially culminating in mental health issues such as depression and anxiety (Shufutinsky et al., 2022). Unfortunately, immigrant, migrant, and refugee children are not exempt from these scenarios.

OVERVIEW OF IMMIGRANTS, MIGRANTS, AND REFUGEES IN THE UNITED STATES

To understand the educational issues experienced by immigrants and migrants, such as refugees, it is expedient to provide an overview of the entrance of these diverse populations into the U.S. The highest refugee influx ensued after enacting the 1980 Refugee Act, which occurred that year, with more than 200,000 refugees allowed into the United States (U.S. Immigration and Naturalization Service [INS], 2002). Until 1983, the nation underwent a consistent dip in refugee admission, with the annual entrance rate plateauing between 60,000 and 70,000 individuals (Khuu & Bean, 2022). The U.S. yearly admissions stayed at or a little above 100,000 people between 1989 and 1995, an increase which coincided with the Cold War ceasefire and the dismantling of the Soviet Union (Khuu & Bean, 2022). Between 1980 and 1984, many refugees who attained legal permanent residence status hailed from the Southeast Asian nations of Laos, Cambodia, and Vietnam (Khuu & Bean, 2022). However, over the latter two periods, there was a drop in Southeast Asian arrivals in the U.S., and a converse rise in Cuban and Iranian refugees as well as individuals listed as "other," depicting a growing diversity in refugees' countries of origin (Khuu & Bean, 2022). Further, 1990 to 1995 marked an abrupt refugee spike from nations that had hitherto belonged to the Soviet Union, alluding to the Cold War ceasefire's domino effect.

The U.S. enacted the first refugee bill in 1980- the Refugee Act. This bill focused on two core issues: establishing measures for accepting refugees into the nation and offering standardized federal refugee resettlement aid to foster the entrants' financial autonomy (Khuu & Bean, 2022; U.S. Government Accountability Office [GAO], 2011). The Refugee Act is the nation's sole immigration-centered policy with specifications for immigration integration. Consequently, the United States commenced settlement assistance to this group of migrants, setting the stage for refugees to enjoy more propitious host-community relations than non-refugee migrants (Khuu & Bean, 2022). The Refugee Act set up the Office of Refugee Resettlement (ORR) to oversee cash distribution, health, and complementary income assistance for refugees with disabilities and special needs. The agency also disbursed funding for various support services, among which are English instruction, recruitment services, as well as educating the settlers on the basics of citizenship (Khuu & Bean, 2022). Added to immediate perks and services accessible to new entrant refugees, the U.S. government provided funding for school districts and non-government agencies that served a considerable number or group of refugees (Khuu & Bean, 2022; US ORR 1980). Refugees' citizenship pathway was expedited by way of legal permanent resident status at entry (Martin, 2021; INS, 2002), a development, deemed as an increasingly accepting conduct towards these settlers via enhanced access to vital resources resulted in a setting where refugees and their children could achieve higher levels of integration compared to non-refugee counterparts (Khuu & Bean, 2022).

The Refugee Act was set out as an inclusive, long-term bill. However, the extent of its reach quickly dwindled both in terms of Congress funding for refugee support as well as the eligibility timeline for arrivals to accept monies and healthcare aid (GAO, 2011; Khuu & Bean, 2022). While the U.S. validated these developments to catalyze new settlers to become independent, evidence from research, studies, and government agencies alludes to financial hardships as a deterrent to refugee integration in the nation (U.S. Government Printing Office, 2010). Such alterations indicated that the academic achievement of child refugees would climax for the early 1980s entrants, when refugee aid was at its peak (Khuu & Bean, 2022). Any increments in refugee children's academic achievements, as opposed to their non-refugee peers, were expected to shrink between the late 1980s and the 1990s. Learning gaps between refugee and non-refugee learners would widen due to shifts in the former's education, not changes in non-refugee children's education (Khuu & Bean, 2022). Further, citizenship training and English language education funding were high on the bill's agenda as substantial support accessible to refugees. These tangible supports reflect the receiving nation's commitment to refugees since the act of naturalization and English language competency promote structural access to fiscal prospects and foster social engagement (Khuu & Bean, 2022; Tran & Lara-García, 2020). Advanced English language competency and naturalization are expected to account for a significant part of child refugees' academic edge over their non-refugee peers, who lacked such provisions (Khuu & Bean, 2022).

There are about 1.6 million children aged 18 and below residing in the United States, with a rising number of unaided minors (UNICEF Data Warehouse, 2024). Among the barriers experienced by refugee and migrant children in the United States are protracted nutrition and accommodation insecurity, acute diseases, and lack of access to healthcare (Ibrahim et al., 2024). Not only do these barriers and scant support disrupt children's learning, but they also affect their development. Initial relations between migrants and the receiving nations significantly determine if and to what extent migrants are offered crucial relocation support that may impact children's academic integration (Khuu & Bean, 2022). A positive link exists between a host government's support upon arrival and refugee children's academic output (Khuu & Bean, 2022).

DIVERSITY, EQUITY, AND INCLUSION (DEI) IN EDUCATION

The concept remains ubiquitous in educational and public arenas despite consistent current disputes over definitions and a lack of a distinct accord on the magnitude (and even the proper hierarchy) of diversity, equity, and inclusion (DEI). Diversity refers to physical or sociocultural variations (seeming or real) attributed to individuals and the portrayal of these distinctions in research and institutions (Arsel et al., 2022). Equity is about fair treatment meted out to individuals regarding opportunities and outcomes (Arsel et al., 2022). Inclusion is portrayed as fostering a culture or milieu that promotes belonging and the integration of diverse individuals or populations and is typically operationalized as resistance to marginalization or exclusion. When applied in conjunction, DEI spurs an inclination toward procedural and distributive justice in institutions and organizations (Arsel et al., 2022).

Diversity

Diversity pertains to unique individual disparities or distinctions (Shufutinsky et al., 2022) or groups. Diversity is oftentimes linked to fair and equal treatment in various social cadres (Esty et al., 1995), among which are age, ability, color, culture, diversity of opinion, race, ethnicity, gender, language, nationality, religion, immigrant status, and their interconnection (Arsel et al., 2022; Shufutinsky et al., 2022). Diversity is not always warmly embraced in most settings, especially in the face of entrenched bias, inequity, and inequality (Shufutinsky et al., 2022). Community diversity does not necessarily translate to just and cordial conduct, prospects, or belonging. Additional factors are required to ensure a climate of respect, acceptance, belonging, enhanced output, and strengthened communal relationships.

A vital diversity derivative is multiculturalism which is described as an amalgamation of people of diverse cultural origins or settings, and every cultural attribute that they display, into a group, institution, or societal culture, with a candid sense of safety to engage with peers in any context (Shufutinsky et al., 2022). Multiculturalism juxtaposes assimilation, which assumes individuals should denounce or reject previous cultural attributes or norms to be included in, accepted by, and resemble their host cultures or communities (Shufutinsky et al., 2022). Multiculturalism via inclusion integrates the wealth of diversity among which are various skills, experiences, narratives, intellect, aptitudes, views, creativity, and other abilities, securely to the diverse populations, institutions, or cultures.

Equity

Equity refers to the judicious allotment of needs required to survive and flourish in a community (Eden et al., 2024; Sahlberg & Cobbold, 2021; Shufutinsky et al., 2022) or academic institution. Equity is a critical element of DEI and social justice (to be addressed in a subsequent section) due to the challenges of attaining fair societies and inclusion without it (Shufutinsky et al, 2022; Winters, 2020). Equity ensures fair and equal access to prospects, human development, rights, and all that impacts the adequacy of the determinants of health, power, and resources, devoid of the encumbrances of biased processes, systems, and institutions (Brown, 2019; Shufutinsky et al., 2022). Attaining DEI learning settings does not warrant judging, but institutions and societies must address issues of racism and bias and challenge societal doctrines by donning a social justice lens (Shufutinsky et al., 2022).

Inclusion

Inclusion, which is closely tied to diversity, is exhibited in diverse ways and touches on individuals' access to avenues to engage, contribute, lead, and experience a legitimate sense of belonging, value, and connection to the institution, community, or group (Shufutinsky et al., 2022; UN, n.d.). Migrants, immigrants, and their children comprise diverse populations or multicultural groups. Nation-states and education decision-makers are preoccupied with equity and inclusion in education thanks to various critical emergent global issues, including refugee and migrant crises, demographic shifts, and increasing inequalities (Organization for Economic Cooperation and Development, 2023). Consequently, these issues have led to growing diversity and merit an inquiry into their influence on inclusion and equity in education.

Migrant settlers and refugees are at a disadvantage in host nations compared to their peers who are citizens of these countries. These mobile children, especially refugees who exist at the fringes of society, must be reached to achieve their educational needs. It is imperative to assist numerous children who were not attending school and need to grasp basic socioemotional, literacy, and numerical competence (Pisani & Dowd, 2022). Educational disparities will prevail unless educational systems uphold equity-based policies and practices. Nation-states seek to offer access to quality education but fall short of effectively and comprehensively executing these policies. Though equity-driven policy implementation is feasible, a one-dimensional focus may not be comprehensive enough to raise underprivileged children (Pisani & Dowd, 2022).

Education systems resort to differentiated strategies, considering their learners' diversity while recognizing that certain children undergo unique challenges during their educational journeys. These challenges include separation from family, food insecurity, lack of permanent residence, drop out, or non-enrolment (Pisani & Dowd, 2022). Failure to consider and address the determinants of whether migrant and immigrant children are enrolled, attend, and remain engaged while in school may pave the way to widen the divide between marginalized and advantaged learners. It is critical to note that these issues intersect, and certain dynamics, such as poverty and geographic setting, can exacerbate or hinder the effect of other factors on children's academic output.

Poverty

Poverty is a critical determinant of DEI in education. Poverty and its impact on the learning outcomes of migrant children existing at the fringes of society demand special consideration. Poverty is the primary determinant that spurs academic drawbacks, which can aggravate or ease the connection between other forms of shortcomings and learning outputs (Pisani & Dowd, 2022). Wealth on its own wields a strong influence on school enrollment within and between nations. Low-income nations constantly report higher out-of-school rates than their lower- and upper-middle and high-income counterparts (Pisani & Dowd, 2022).

Within nations, compared to affluent children, indigent children are less likely to be enrolled in school, while poor girls in low-income nations are the least likely across the globe to access education (Pisani & Dowd, 2022). The recent pandemic has intensified these learning barriers as many education systems transitioned to remote instruction. Still, in low- and middle-income settings, only 20% of residences have access to the internet, and about half have access to the media (Carvalho & Hares, 2020; Pisani & Dowd, 2022). Per the related fiscal predicament, it is projected that an additional 90 to 117 million children will exist in poverty, and about 7 to 9.7 million learners will drop out of school (Pisani & Dowd, 2022; Save the Children, 2020).

Poverty also has an irrefutable connection to learning outcomes from a very young age. Multiple analyses identify poverty as a primary contributor to impaired cognitive growth among children ages three to four years living in low- and middle-income nations (Pisani & Dowd, 2022). Relatedly, studies indicate a strong positive link between learning, growth, and family wealth for children aged three to six years, with an effect size of one to three months of development per added family asset (Pisani & Dowd, 2022). The performance of elementary children from different disadvantaged settings also underscores a strong tie between learners' socioeconomic level and their academic output. Thus, poverty fundamentally impacts the equality of learning outcomes for all children or learners. However, there are instances where learners from disadvantaged settings have strong learning outcomes and are closer to performing on par with their privileged co-learners (Pisani & Dowd, 2022). To ensure improved outcomes for migrant, refugee, and immigrant learners amid their disadvantages, it is crucial to grasp how nations and decision-makers prioritize improved learning equity for the children under their charge, and if and how consistent milestones are achieved across the board (Pisani & Dowd, 2022).

Language of Instruction

The education guiding principles in various nations espouse children's right to acquire knowledge in their mother tongue or their home language. However, the reality in classroom settings worldwide is that the language of instruction is typically determined by the agendas of parents, lead instructors, and teachers (Pisani & Dowd, 2022). Indigenous policymakers rule whether their classrooms adopt a foreign language or local dialect(s) for instruction. In many instances, local standpoints and priorities incline towards an international language(s), given their supposed fiscal value and esteem. No matter the language or setting, formal learning occurs in international languages as early as the initial elementary school grades, and in practice typically from the onset, condemning children unable to speak these foreign tongues to the bottom of the ladder.

Typically, the language(s) of instruction learners encounter in the classroom vary from pre-elementary to secondary schooling, such that they receive instruction in multiple languages at various levels and for divergent reasons across their academic paths (Pisani & Dowd, 2022). It is not absolute, even in pre-elementary settings that typically adopt local languages, and these changes in focus and exposure explain the poor overall learning (Pisani & Dowd, 2022). Linguistic barriers were so pervasive that they impacted not only the instructors who acquired an incomplete mastery of the foreign language as they went through the system but also current learners (Pisani & Dowd, 2022). A recent study on seven developing nations revealed that about 10% of fourth graders could read a paragraph in their official (international) language. At the same time, only one in 10 instructors could master their students' language curriculum (Pisani & Dowd, 2022).

SOCIAL JUSTICE AND EDUCATION

Social justice typically alludes to ideal conditions that will accrue beneficially to each community member as having the same fundamental rights, protections, and prospects, upholding a collective cultural identity across the board (Shufutinsky et al., 2022). In a broader sense, social justice can also be construed as an equitable, fair, and benevolent allotment of the profitable fruits of labor that accrue to a community. Thus, the bedrock and groundwork that underpin social justice and set out to make it feasible through dispensation are to guarantee both security and equality for every individual as fundamental and essential liberty, which are political and socioeconomic (Shufutinsky et al., 2022). Shufutinsky et al. (2022) affirmed that social justice is designed to tackle marginalization and exclusion issues and focus on engaging sociopolitical, governmental, corporate, and other systems to foster policies, advocacy, leadership systems, and dreams for an equitable society. Every person and group must be accorded respect and equality for social justice to prevail. People must have equity in access to a fundamental basic level of rights as well as available benefits and resources, enabling full community engagement and the alignment of prospects, benefits, and liabilities, culminating in equitable existence and unbiased societal order.

Education and Power

The issue of power is a critical dimension when tackling social justice in education. Knowledge equates to power, and education is one of the most explored issues in the social justice arena. In most alliances or settings, standard education begets the knowledge oftentimes required to foster, claim, and obtain power (Shufutinsky et al., 2022). From a social justice stance, shared knowledge begets shared power, which aligns with the UN's (1948) declaration of education as a fundamental human right, and even though learning styles and forms vary, they are nevertheless important (Shufutinsky et al., 2022). All children must be afforded opportunities to access, at least, a standard basic education. Education as a social justice concern involves the dimension that embodies humankind. This dimension comprises the education systems and educational inclusivity whereby accessibility is inclusionary and justifiable for all (Shufutinsky et al., 2022; Wong et al., 2020). There is a widespread awareness of the marginalization and exclusion of specific groups or populations in terms of education. Marginalization can come in the form of economic, racial, and other drivers for disparity, affecting not just the provision of education, but the quality of education, educational materials, technologies, facilities, educators, and administrators, among other factors (Shufutinsky et al., 2022).

Education intersects with various social justice issues. Education is a crucial focal point which includes examining academic agendas, among which are access to special needs resources, literacy, institutional health and security, safety from bias, technology, affordability, equitable resource allotment, library availability, school violence and bullying, diversity of subjects, acknowledging ethnic learning styles and knowledge acquisition, as well as parents and caregivers access to teachers and learning requirements (Shufutinsky et al., 2022). Additional salient issues include fair chances at affordable vocational training and higher education, such as universities (including top-ranked institutions), colleges, and trade schools (Shufutinsky et al., 2022). Education can offer immigrant, migrant, and refugee children the necessary knowledge and entryways to a gamut of new journeys and prospects, including gainful employment. For refugee children as well as some disadvantaged migrant and immigrant children, education releases the floodgates of opportunities they all deserve.

CHALLENGES TO IMMIGRANT, MIGRANT, AND REFUGEE CHILDREN'S EDUCATION

Education is the most excellent empowerment tool and is particularly critical for young people, especially refugee youth (USA for UNHCR, 2025a). Education is a shield and symbol of a brighter future for children, especially those affected by disputes and disasters, offers hope, and helps them recuperate, learn, and flourish (IRC, 2024). Besides being a human right, education is vital to ensuring all children reach their full potential (UN Relief and Works Agency for Palestine Refugees in the Near East, n.d.). Armed with education, people have a better chance of a dignified existence. Investing in refugee education accrues colossal and extensive gains. Offering standard education and safe spaces for knowledge acquisition enables refugee children to recover from the impacts of trauma while they prepare for their future. Access to school makes refugee children less susceptible to abusive and perilous child labor and significantly minimizes the risk of premature nuptials for girls (USA for UNHCR, 2023; 2025a; 2025b).

About 50 percent of all refugee children are out of school and are being denied access to learning, jeopardizing the future of an entire generation (USA for UNHCR, 2023; 2025a; 2025b). In 2022, refugee children's primary education average gross enrollment rate at the primary level stood at 68%, which was not significantly different from the year prior (UNHCR, 2022). The pre-primary enrollment rate was 42 percent, while at 37 percent, the rate was low for post-primary level enrollment (UNHCR, 2025b). What is more disconcerting is that refugee girls were even less likely to enroll in school, and even if they do, they only attain a few years of formal learning (UNHCR, 2025b). Access to education is difficult to reclaim once lost (UNHCR, 2022). Reduced or lack of access to education and substandard accessible schools can undercut an individual's prospects (IRC, 2024). In 2020, there were 28 million international child migrants worldwide, equating to 1.4 percent of the global child population (IOM, 2024). About 90% of children worldwide attend primary school, but the numbers are far lower for refugees, a mere 61% (UNHCR, 2024).

As refugee children advance in age, they encounter increasing learning barriers. Only 23% of refugee adolescents receive secondary education, compared to about 85% worldwide (UNHCR, 2024). In low-earning settings, which harbor more than a quarter of the world's refugees, secondary school enrollment is alarming, at barely 10%. With a 36% enrolment rate, UNHCR (2024) affirmed an equally bleak situation for higher education, the learning phase during which future leaders are forged. The increase in enrolment rate for refugees prevails at one percent despite notable increases in total numbers due to investing in scholarships and other initiatives (UNHCR, 2024). Amid the barriers, the pressing question is how to intensify equitable and inclusive education for the target learners.

Amid the burden of academic disadvantages, migrant, immigrant, and refugee children are significantly behind their domestic peers in industrialized host nations such as the United States. Unfortunately, a substantial number of refugee and migrant children are at a disadvantage, having originated from low-income and lower-middle-income nations where they lacked access to adequately trained teachers (Akyeampong, 2022). Consequently, these learners missed the basic learning goals for their level and dropped out of school in the formative years. Beyond their home nations' paucity of teachers, these disadvantaged children were under the tutelage of individuals ill-equipped to address their learning needs. Research revealed these children were not learning despite being in school, depicting them as "silently excluded" (Akyeampong, 2022, p. 78). Further, the schools accessible to the children were blatantly substandard, crushing any hope of education as a means of escape from poverty (Akyeampong, 2022).

CALL TO ACTION: SUPPORT FOR MIGRANT, IMMIGRANT, AND REFUGEE CHILDREN'S LEARNING

Approximately 40 percent of the refugee population comprises children (UNHCR, 2025a), and they are five times more likely to be unenrolled in school (UNICEF, n.d.). Prolonged and frequent intervals in refugee children's learning are worrisome and tend to become permanent, as the turmoil that displaced them shows little or no signs of ebbing shortly (Demir et al., 2024). What is equally disconcerting is the academic interruption within their host nation or community. An example is the resettlement of refugees, immigrants, and migrants from various states in the U.S. to sanctuary states: California, Colorado, Connecticut, Illinois, Massachusetts, New Jersey, New York, Oregon, Rhode Island, Vermont, Wahington, and District of Columbia (Federation for America Immigration Reform, 2025). During this process, these children lose valuable weeks or months of instruction and critical literacy, numerical, and analytical skills. Faced with unemployment, displaced individuals usually spur their children to menial jobs, locking them in a vicious cycle of poverty (Demir et al. 2024). Further, mixed and limited evidence exists on the most effective ways to ensure inclusive educational prospects. How to effectually integrate migrant children into their receiving nations' education systems remains to be addressed. It is imperative to ensure migrant children are provided with the education, emotional support, and training required to thrive and succeed (World Bank Group, 2021). However, Demir et al. (2024) posit that the receiving nation can experience substantial capacity gaps by offering equitable prospects to these vulnerable populations. The authors seek to address these barriers by exploring how receiving nations can foster child refugees' inclusion in their education sector without stretching their capacity.

Student Integration in Education Systems

Integrating migrant children into a host nation's education system is critical lest they miss crucial learning milestones. Host nations must avoid segregating migrant and refugee children and loosen limitations previously created for their domestic peers. Per classroom streamlining, mainstreaming is an inclusive classroom-related integration strategy that entails assigning a few refugee children per classroom and small group instruction (Arar, 2020; Demir et al., 2024). However, these strategies can only succeed in host nations with ample resources and capacity. Host nations must possess adequate educational capacity for new intakes. Further, it is critical to ensure migrant or refugee children sustain attendance after identifying and assigning them to a learning mode. Amplifying learning capacity and continuous access to the education systems is a viable strategy for the seamless integration of migrant children. Analyses unveil refugee children's classroom encounters but fail to offer exhaustive inclusion and applicable capacity expansion guidelines at the national or district level (Demir et al., 2024). Integrating migrant children must not compel them to meet academic bars not created or developed for marginalized or at-risk populations (Demir et al., 2024). Further, a receiving nation's linguistic programs must comprise teachers or instructors adequately trained and certified to educate children in distress. Increased inclusion of migrant children to enhance their sense of belonging in their host community or nation. At the classroom level, teachers and the schools should create activities to help these new entrants integrate into society. Excursions or field trips explicitly designed for migrant and refugee children to visit significant landmarks would help them acclimate themselves to their new environment and host nation. The educators could form community circles and clubs to unite students and share their experiences, cultures, achievements, and challenges. Students can learn from each other, support one another, and prevent feelings of isolation.

At the institutional level, rather than adhering to migrant and refugee children's home indigenous curricula, these children and youth must be immediately enrolled in the receiving nation's schools (Demir et al., 2024). Many teachers, specifically mainstream educators, are not attuned to refugees and migrant children's hardships and consequently fail to support them adequately. Thus, refugee and migrant learners must be assigned to and supported by college-trained and state board licensed special education teachers empowered with relevant pedagogical skills required to work with children in emergency contexts. The teachers must participate in cultural competency training courses and be sensitized to appreciate the learners' diverse language, cultural, and educational backgrounds. Teachers must offer differentiated instruction tailored to meet refugee and immigrant learners' hardships in terms of linguistic impediments, unfamiliar learning styles, and educational systems. Teachers must empathize with the children's traumatic encounters, offer emotional support, and ensure safe learning spaces for them to thrive.

Socioemotional Learning and Emotionally Intelligent Teachers

Teachers are one of the most critical resources and components of a child's education. Access to quality instructors is crucial to attaining SDG4 (Akyeampong, 2022). A learner's knowledge acquisition depends considerably on the person responsible for transferring and imparting knowledge. Migrant children, especially refugees, are vulnerable, new to their host settings, and rely heavily on their teachers to learn. A teacher's approach can elicit support to unleash students' learning capacity and success (Munir et al., 2020). An educator's personality, positionality, ideals, and other qualities influence the teaching approach, instructor-learner ties, and communication mode (Broderick & Lyn, 2022). The teacher's disposition ties into the social justice facet (Saultz et al., 2021) of migrant children's education, particularly since contemporary societies and institutions are typified by diversity. In all this, preparing socially and emotionally intelligent educators who are empathetic toward their learners' plight is imperative.

"A teacher who manages a classroom that includes refugee learners will walk into perhaps the toughest classroom in the world" (USA for UNHCR, 2025b, para.7). This classroom comprises young people from diverse parts of the globe. Some children were forced to behold the destruction or annihilation of their homelands. Among this group of learners are those who experienced the mutilation or demise of their family, friends, and loved ones. These children may be living with disabilities, either from infancy or due to the unrest in their nations of origin (USA for UNHCR, 2025b). Some of the children may have been child soldiers, sexual abuse survivors, or even persons who migrated successfully to safety while their families failed. Indefinite learning interruption compounds the plight of these migrant and refugee children.

It is very likely the classroom will be jam-packed, especially in a public school system, with students from the receiving nation contending for desk space or seating with migrants and refugees. While the seating arrangements make it possible to enroll numerous children in school, the lengthy hours put additional strain on teachers, service providers, and support staff. Further, in certain host nations, migrant and refugee children may have to receive lessons or instruction in a language they are just starting to grasp (USA for UNHCR, 2025b). In all this, one cannot deny the transformative powers of a classroom. In the learning environment, migrant, immigrant, and refugee children can learn to read, write, and do math, the bedrock of lifetime learning. Also, these children can "learn how to learn" (USA for UNHCR, 2025b, para. 10). This foregrounds potential language proficiency as well as development in literature, math, science, history, geography, religious studies, and other subjects as learners progress to post-primary education and further. In addition to academics, migrant and refugee children can be taught fundamental healthcare and sanitation, social responsibility, human rights, and how to seek and access assistance (USA for UNHCR, 2025b). Primary to tertiary education afforded to migrant and refugee children can empower them to be independent, self-reliant, and able to map out their future, in a receiving nation or when they return to their home country. The aforesaid points underscore the vital role and increased need for teachers to provide socioemotional support to migrant, immigrant, and refugee learners. It is necessary for teachers to liaise with counselors or advisors to provide in-transit motivation to these students. Teachers should engage parents, through workshops or surveys, to ascertain what is beneficial to their children and how best to help the learners settle into the community.

Inclusion of Immigrant, Migrant, and Refugee Learners

Decision-makers and education leaders should involve teachers during education scheme planning and must focus on refugee and migrant populations. Educators and agencies at all levels must ensure everyone can learn and attain qualifications from recognized schools, notwithstanding their legal status. Forcibly displaced individuals must be considered during education planning, budgeting, programming, monitoring, and evaluation at the classroom, institution, or government level. Education leaders and instructors should integrate migrant and refugee inclusion into the learning settings and modify curricula to accommodate these populations. All children deserve an education, and no child must be left behind. While migrant and refugee children do not encounter administrative bottlenecks in most receiving nations' education systems, the extent of their inclusion varies significantly. In certain nations, refugees encounter different restrictions while enrolling in schools, and access is limited strictly to questionable institutions. Parallel courses result in examinations or assessments not being recognized by any nation, making subsequent inclusion in national systems at the post-primary and post-secondary levels extremely challenging (USA for UNHCR, 2025b). Migrant and refugee children and youth must be administered certified assessments and gain from authentic, nationally standardized instruction across all learning tiers (USA for UNHCR, 2025b).

However, barring adequate knowledge about the benefits of such inclusion, refugees and migrants may express unease about their children studying a foreign curriculum, especially when it elicits an unsavory possibility of indefinite displacement or appears to sever all connections to their home nations, identities, traditions, and religions (USA for UNHCR, 2025b). It behooves teachers to inform parents of the merits of adapting to their host nation's new learning systems. Teachers should also inform parents that embracing a new learning system or curriculum does not translate to abandoning one's heritage, and refugees and migrants can sustain close ties to their indigenous traditions and vernacular beyond the learning setting.

Schools and educators should create opportunities for the host nation's domestic learners and migrant peers. With the enrollment of migrant and refugee populations come challenges. The learning environment is rife with the complexity of diverse personalities with unique backgrounds and needs, especially refugee children. Hence, the classroom setup is significantly more intricate than what the educators are accustomed to, requiring support to provide fair, safe, and inclusive learning spaces. To better address the migrant and refugee learners' needs, teachers can tap into community resources or public assistance, such as a special supplementary program for women, infants, and children (WIC). Teachers can liaise with their local police department, fire department, faith-based organizations, and medical or healthcare facilities to organize events for these settlers, such as a clothes drive or a food pantry, to provide essentials for them. Also, teachers must contact the school's parent coordinators regularly to discuss migrant and refugee learners' progress. Critical issues to address include the learners' nutrition, medical care access, and housing situations. Teachers and parent coordinators could partner with related agencies to help families secure housing assistance or temporary housing.

In response to the need to expand and fortify the education system to address the global refugee spike, host nations should train and support teachers to provide certified crash education programs specifically for individuals who may have been out of school for extensive periods and find the nation's formal education system challenging (USA for UNHCR, 2025b). Not only will teachers offer new entrants a means to cover the same ground as typical-age students, but they can do so rapidly and more intensively via condensed coursework or syllabi. Institution-based fast-track instruction enables learners to engage in the mainstream setting if they desire (at the appropriate age level), proceed to the next phase (typically secondary), or transition to vocational and technical learning (USA for UNHCR, 2025b).

CONCLUSION

International migration, displacement, and resultant interruptions in education significantly impact learners' social and academic progress. Besides substantial resource allotment and solid coalitions, including migrant, immigrant, and refugee children in education systems warrants human capital, specifically, amply trained and committed teachers. Educators are crucial to new entrants' integration into their host society. The role of socioemotional educators during refugees' and migrants' transition process cannot be overemphasized. Unwavering teacher support, alliances, and investments will empower migrant and refugee learners to thrive in the new system of their host nation, especially with relevant training or coaching in the language of instruction. Not only will these support and investments yield significant returns for immigrants, migrants, and refugees, but also for their receiving nations and beyond. Once again, every child deserves an education; no child must be left behind.

REFERENCES

Akyeampong, K. (2022). Teaching at the bottom of the pyramid: Teacher education in poor and marginalized communities. In Wagner, D. A., Castillo, N. M., & Lewis, S. G. (Eds.), *Learning, marginalization, and improving the quality of education in low-income countries* (pp. 77–111). Open Book Publisher. DOI: 10.11647/OBP.0256.03

Arar, K. (2020). *School leadership for refugees' education: Social justice leadership for immigrant, migrants and refugees*. Routledge. DOI: 10.4324/9780429021770

Arsel, Z., Crockett, D., & Scott, M. L. (2022). Diversity, equity, and inclusion (DEI) in the *Journal of Consumer Research*: A curation and research agenda. *The Journal of Consumer Research, 48*(5), 920–933. DOI: 10.1093/jcr/ucab057

Bell, L. A. (2013). Theoretical foundations. In M. Adams, W.J., Blumenfeld, C., Castaneda, H.W., Hackman, M.L., Peters and Zuniga, *Reading for Diversity and Social Justice*. Routledge, New York, (3) 21- 26.

Bese, S., & Dali, C. (2021). Exploring intrapersonal emotional intelligence consciousness of school leadership in enhancing social justice in schools. *Gender & Behaviour, 19*(2), 18019–18026. https://go.openathens.net/redirector/nu.edu?url=https://www.proquest.com/scholarly-journals/exploring-intrapersonal-emotional-intelligence/docview/2649772534/se-2

Broderick, M., & Lyn, A. E. (2022). Integrating social emotional learning into the formative development of educator dispositions. In *Dispositional Development and Assessment in Teacher Preparation Programs* (pp. 50–75). IGI Global. DOI: 10.4018/978-1-6684-4089-6.ch004

Bronfenbrenner, U. (1977). Toward an experimental ecology of human development. *The American Psychologist, 32*(7), 513–531. DOI: 10.1037/0003-066X.32.7.513

Brown, J. (2019). *How to be an inclusive leader*. Berret-Koehler Publishers.

Campbell, A. C., & Lavallee, C. A. (2020). A community of practice for social justice: Examining the case of an international scholarship alumni association in Ghana. *Journal of Studies in International Education, 24*(4), 409–423. DOI: 10.1177/1028315319842343

Campbell, B. (2021). Social justice and sociological theory. *Society, 58*(5), 355–364. DOI: 10.1007/s12115-021-00625-4 PMID: 34465929

Carvalho, S., & Hares, S. (2020). Six ways COVID-19 will shape the future of education. Center for Global Development. https://www.cgdev.org/blog/six-ways-covid-19-will-shape-future-education

Chaka, C. (2024). Multilingualism, translanguaging, diversity, equity, social justice, and activism: A tenuous nexus and misrepresentations? *International Journal of Language Studies, 18*(1), 7–28. DOI: 10.5281/zenodo.10468173

Crosby, R. A., DiClemente, R. J., & Salazar, L. F. (2006). *Research method in health promotion*. John Willey & Son, Inc.

Cureton, A. (2024). New kids on the block: Refugee students' school-based experiences and engagement in an urban high school. *The Urban Review, 56*(2), 672–697. DOI: 10.1007/s11256-024-00696-7

Cureton, A., Tonui, B. C., Lima Cross, F., & Gonzalez-Benson, O. (2025). 'What's at stake?' An exploration on the merits and drawbacks of the Welcome Corps Program, a private sponsorship of refugees. *International Social Work*, *68*(1), 56–71. DOI: 10.1177/00208728241292051

Demir, S. M., Sahinyazan, F. G., Kara, B. Y., & Buluc, E. (2024). No country for young refugees: Barriers and opportunities for inclusive refugee education practices. *Production and Operations Management*, *0*(0). Advance online publication. DOI: 10.1177/10591478241243382

Federation for America Immigration Reform. (2025). Do you live in one of the 11 sanctuary states or the District of Columbia? https://www.fairus.org/issue/do-you-live-1-11-sanctuary-states

Fraser, N. (2008). *Scales of justice: Reimagining political space in a globalizing world* (Vol. 31). Columbia University Press.

Global Compact, U. N. (n.d.). Diversity, equity, and inclusion. https://unglobalcompact.org/take-action/action/dei

Hatton, T. J. (2020). Asylum migration to the developed world: Persecution, incentives, and policy. *The Journal of Economic Perspectives*, *34*(1), 75–93. DOI: 10.1257/jep.34.1.75

Ibrahim, A., Linton, J. M., & Dawson-Hahn, E. (2024). Providing compassionate, evidence-based care for refugee, immigrant, and migrant children. *Advances in Pediatrics*, *71*(1), 1–16. DOI: 10.1016/j.yapd.2024.01.001 PMID: 38944476

Immigration, U. S. (2002). Statistical yearbook of the immigration and naturalization service, 1999. *Washington, DC: US Government Printing Office.*

International Organization for Migration. (2019). International migration law: Glossary on Migration. https://publications.iom.int/system/files/pdf/iml_34_glossary.pdf

International Organization for Migration. (2024)... *World Migration Report*, *2024*, •••. https://publications.iom.int/books/world-migration-report-2024

International Refugee Committee. (2024). Migrants, asylum seekers, refugees, and immigrants: What is the difference? https://www.rescue.org/article/migrants-asylum-seekers-refugees-and-immigrants-whats-difference

Kelcey, J., Guven, O., & Burde, D. (2022). Education on the move: How migration affects learning outcomes. In Wagner, D. A., Castillo, N. M., & Lewis, S. G. (Eds.), *Learning, Marginalization, and Improving the Quality of Education in Low-income Countries* (pp. 45–76). Open Book Publishers., DOI: 10.11647/OBP.0256.02

Khuu, T. V., & Bean, F. D. (2022). Refugee status, settlement assistance, and the educational integration of migrants' children in the United States. *The International Migration Review*, *56*(3), 780–809. DOI: 10.1177/01979183211057837

Martin, S. F. (2021). *A nation of immigrants*. Cambridge University Press., DOI: 10.1017/9781108900904

McIntyre, J., & Neuhaus, S. (2021). Theorising policy and practice in refugee education: Conceptualising 'safety', 'belonging', 'success' and 'participatory parity' in England and Sweden. *British Educational Research Journal*, *47*(4), 796–816. DOI: 10.1002/berj.3701

Miller, D. (1999). *Principles of Social Justice*. Harvard University Press.

Miri, M. A. (2024). An integrated conceptual model for enhancing refugee education. *British Educational Research Journal*, *50*(4), 1857–1877. DOI: 10.1002/berj.4005

Mixed Migration Center. (2025). What is mixed migration? https://mixedmigration.org/what-is-mixed-migration/

Munir, H., Afzal, A., & Arshad, R. (2020). Influence of teachers' behavior on students' academic achievement at university level. *Journal of Arts & Social Sciences*, *7*(2), 60–69. DOI: 10.46662/jass-vol7-iss2-2020(60-69)

Organization for Economic Co-operation and Development. (2023). *Equity and inclusion in education: Finding strength through diversity*. OECD Publishing., DOI: 10.1787/e9072e21-

Pisani, L., & Dowd, A. J. (2022). Diversity and equity in education: Policy, practice, and options for reaching children at the bottom of the pyramid. In Wagner, D. A., Castillo, N. M., & Lewis, S. G. (Eds.), *Learning, marginalization, and improving the quality of education in low-income countries* (pp. 13–44). Open Book Publisher. DOI: 10.11647/OBP.0256.01

Rawls, J. (1971). *A Theory of Justice*. Harvard University Press. DOI: 10.4159/9780674042605

Rentzi, A. (2024). Social justice in education: Creating an inclusive culture at schools through critical multicultural theory. *European Journal of Education and Pedagogy*, *5*(1), 94–97. DOI: 10.24018/ejedu.2024.5.1.802

Saultz, A., Lyons, A. I., Aronson, B., Sander, S. A., & Malin, J. R. (2021). Understanding preservice teacher dispositions: Implications for social justice and educational policy. *Teacher Education Quarterly*, *48*(1), 7–32. https://www.jstor.org/stable/27094714

Save the Children. (2020). Save our education: Protect every child's right to learn in the COVID-19 response and recovery. Washington, DC: Save the Children International. https://resourcecentre.savethechildren.net/pdf/save_our_education_0.pdf/

Shamieh, J. M., Sawalha, I. H., & Madanat, H. M. (2022). Vulnerability and capacity assessment for refugee education crises. *International Journal of Emerging Markets*, *17*(1), 253–276. DOI: 10.1108/IJOEM-04-2019-0321

Shufutinsky, A., Calvin, J., Shufutinsky, B., Spigel, R., Kravitz, C., Burrel, D. N., Shufutinsky, N., Shufutinsky, D., Clark, L., Johnson, T., McKenna, C., & Gates, Z. (2022). Dissecting meaning, scope, and roles of social justice and social action. *Organization Development Journal*, *40*(1), 9–42.

The UN Refugee Agency. (1951). The refugee convention, 1951. https://www.unhcr.org/media/refugee-convention-1951-travaux-preparatoires-analysed-commentary-dr-paul-weis

The UN Refugee Agency. (2010). Convention and protocol relating to the status of refugees. https://www.unhcr.org/media/convention-and-protocol-relating-status-refugees

The UN Refugee Agency. (2022). UNHCR Education Report 2022 - All inclusive the campaign for refugee education. https://www.unhcr.org/media/unhcr-education-report-2022-all-inclusive-campaign-refugee-education?_gl=1*1wxhalc*_rup_ga*MTg0MTI0Njk2Ni4xNzM2NTM0MTM5*_rup_ga_EVDQTJ4LMY*MTczNjU2MzI4Mi40LjEuMTczNjU2NzYxNC42MC4wLjA

The UN Refugee Agency. (2024). Left behind: Refugee education in crisis. https://www.unhcr.org/leftbehind/#:~:text=As%20refugee%20children%20grow%20up,there%20is%20progress%20to%20report

The UN Refugee Agency. (2025a). Figures at a glance. Figures at a glance | UNHCR

The UN Refugee Agency. (2025b). *Refugee data finder*. Refugee Data Finder - Key Indicators.

Tran, V. C., & Lara-García, F. (2020). A new beginning: Early refugee integration in the United States. *The Russell Sage Foundation Journal of the Social Sciences : RSF*, *6*(3), 117–149. DOI: 10.7758/rsf.2020.6.3.06

Tumen, S. (2021). The effect of refugees on native adolescents' test scores: Quasi-experimental evidence from PISA. *Journal of Development Economics*, *150*, 102633. DOI: 10.1016/j.jdeveco.2021.102633

UN Chief Executive Board. (2023). Annex I: Diversity, equity and inclusion glossary for the United Nations common system. DEI Glossary.pdf

UNESCO. (2022). The right to higher education: A social justice perspective. UNESCO Digital Library. https://unesdoc.unesco.org/ark:/48223/pf0000381750

UNESCO. (2025). Sustainable Development Goal 4 (SDG4). Leading SDG4: Education2030 for Inclusive and Quality Education. https://www.unesco.org/sdg4education2030/en/sdg4#:~:text=SDG4%20is%20a%20commitment%20to,a%20sustainable%20and%20equitable%20world

Ungar, M., & Seymour, A. (2024). Access without borders: A scoping review to identify solutions to creating portable identity, education and health records for refugee children. *Journal of International Migration and Integration*, *25*(4), 1989–2017. DOI: 10.1007/s12134-024-01156-7

UNHCR|USA (2024). Resettlement in the United States. https://www.unhcr.org/us/what-we-do/resettlement-united-states

United Nations. (1948). Universal declaration of human rights. https://documents.un.org/doc/resolution/gen/nr0/043/88/pdf/nr004388.pdf

United Nations. (n.d.a). Identifying social inclusion and exclusion. https://www.un.org/esa/socdev/rwss/2016/chapter1.pdf

United Nations. (n.d.a.). Goal 4: Ensure inclusive and equitable quality education and promote lifelong learning opportunities for all. https://sdgs.un.org/goals/goal4

United Nations. (n.d.b). Sustainable Development Goals. https://www.un.org/sustainabledevelopment/education/

United Nations Children's Fund. (2024). Child displacement. https://data.unicef.org/topic/child-migration-and-displacement/displacement/#data

United Nations Children's Fund. (n.d.). Education solutions for migrant and displaced children and their host communities. https://www.unicef.org/documents/education-solutions-migrant-and-displaced-children-and-their-host-communities

United Nations High Commissioner for Refugees. (2024). Welcome to UNHCR's refugee population statistics database. https://www.unhcr.org/refugee-statistics/

United Nations Office of the High Commissioner for Human Rights. (2025). Convention relating to the status of refugees. https://www.ohchr.org/en/instruments-mechanisms/instruments/convention-relating-status-refugees

United Nations Relief and Works Agency for Palestine Refugees in the Near East. (n.d.). What we do: Education. https://www.unrwa.org/what-we-do/education

U.S. Department of Health and Human Services. (2022). Refugee School Impact Program. https://www.acf.hhs.gov/orr/programs/refugees/school-impact#:~:text=The%20Refugee%20School%20Impact%20(RSI,from%20birth%20to%20age%2018.

U.S. Government Printing Office. (2010). Abandoned upon arrival: Implications for refugees and local communities burdened by a U.S. resettlement system that is not working: A report to the members of the Committee on Foreign Relations, United States Senate, One Hundred Eleventh Congress, second session, July 21, 2010. Washington: U.S. G.P.O. http://purl.access.gpo.gov/GPO/LPS125277

US Governmental Accountability Office. (2011). Refugee assistance: Little is known about the effectiveness of different approaches for improving refugees' employment outcomes. https://www.gao.gov/products/gao-11-369

US Office of Refugee Resettlement. (1980). Annual Report to Congress: Refugee resettlement program. Washington, DC: US Government Printing Office. annual_orr_report_to_congress_1980.pdf

USA for UNHCR. (2025a). Education. https://www.unrefugees.org/what-we-do/education/

USA for UNHCR. (2025b). Starting Out - Why education for refugees matters. https://www.unhcr.org/us/starting-out-why-education-refugees-matters

USA for UNHRC. (2023). What to know about refugee education and why it matters. https://www.unrefugees.org/news/what-to-know-about-refugee-education-and-why-it-matters/

Waghid, Z. (2024). Cultivating critical thinking, social justice awareness and empathy among pre-service teachers through online discussions on global citizenship education. *Journal of Creative Communications*, *19*(1), 74–93. DOI: 10.1177/09732586231194438

Winters, M. (2020). *Inclusive conversations*. Berrett-Koehler Publishers.

Wong, S., Kwok, V., Kwong, T., & Lau, R. (2020). Individuality, accessibility, and inclusivity: Applied education and lifelong learning in revolutionalising education for the 21st century contribution to the futures of education in initiative. UNESCO International Commission of the Futures of education.

World Bank Group. (2021). 10 years on, Turkey continues its support for an ever-growing number of Syrian refugees. https://www.worldbank.org/en/news/feature/2021/06/22/10-years-on-turkey-continues-its-support-for-an-ever-growing-number-of-syrian-refugees

KEY TERMS AND DEFINITIONS

Diversity: Diversity encapsulates the unique differences individuals possess due to determinants such as status, intellectual prowess, academic ability, career and responsibility, age, race, culture, gender, physical size and capacity, sexual orientation, religious denomination, and originalities (UN Global Compact, n.d.).

Equality: Equality denotes a quality or state of being equal. It refers to equivalence in rank, value, ability, degree, quantity, or prospect, such as fostering equality of opportunity in education (UN Chief Executive Board, 2023).

Equity: Equity refers to justice and fairness tenets which ensure all individuals attain their full potential regardless of conditions or milieu (Eden et al., 2024; Sahlberg & Cobbold, 2021; Shufutinsky et al., 2022).

Immigrant: An immigrant is a term for any individual who takes deliberate steps to depart from his or her home country and relocate to a foreign nation with the intent to remain there (International Rescue Committee [IRC], 2024). Immigrants typically undergo prolonged approval processes to move over to a new setting and a significant number of them become legal permanent residents and later citizens (IRC, 2024).

Inclusion: Inclusion refers to the process of addressing the terms of involvement in the community or society for disadvantaged persons due to ethnicity, religious denomination, origin, race, gender affinity, sex, age, disability, fiscal capacity, or other factors, by way of improved prospects, resource availability, and regard for individual rights (United Nations [UN], n.d.a).

Internally Displaced Persons: An internally displaced person is one compelled or mandated to leave or flee one's home or place of customary residence, due to or in a bid to escape the impact of human rights violations, armed conflict, conditions of widespread violence, or natural or man-made disasters, and who have not moved beyond an internationally established borderline (United Nations Children's Fund [UNICEF], 2024).

Migrant: A migrant refers to one who moves from place to place either within one's nation or between international border lines, typically for financial reasons such as seasonal employment (IRC, 2024). Like immigrants, these persons are not compelled to depart from their home nations due to violence or oppression, instead, they are pursuing greener pastures (IRC, 2024).

Mixed Migration: Mixed migration refers to cross-border movements of individuals, including refugees escaping conflict and persecution, trafficking victims, and others seeking improved livelihoods and prospects (Mixed Migration Center, 2025). Mixed migration encompasses the movement of immigrants, migrants, and refugees.

Social Justice: Social justice is a multi-layered construct which touches on various societal concerns which include the community, ableism, gender, fiscal discrimination, misogyny, inequality, racism, race, wealth, property, and racial intolerance (United Nations Education, Science and Cultural Organization [UNESCO], 2022). Social justice addresses the extent or level of justice and equality across diverse social groups (Chaka, 2024), the perpetuation of respect, fairness, and equality (Waghid, 2023), and inclusive community participation, quality service access, and defending human rights (Campbell & Lavallee, 2020).

Refugee: Refugees are individuals compelled to escape their homes due to persecution, conflict, and war, (International Organization for Migration [IOM], 2019; IRC, 2024; United Nations High Commissioner for Refugees [UNHCR], 2024), oftentimes without notice (IRC, 2024). Resettled persons move to other nations willing to admit them and eventually offer permanent stay (UNHCR, 2024). Refugees can only return home when the conditions in their home countries become safe for them (IRC, 2024).

Compilation of References

Abdou, A. S., De Pedro, K., De Anda, A., Merced, I., & Mao, K. (2022). Nurturing Cultural Humility and Responsiveness through Restorative Pedagogy in Graduate Education. *International Journal on Teaching and Learning in Higher Education*, *33*(2), 273–284.

Abi-Hashem, N. (2007). Arab Americans: Understanding their challenges, needs, and struggles. In *Ethnocultural perspectives on disaster and trauma: Foundations, issues, and applications* (pp. 115–173). Springer New York.

Abín, A., Núñez, J. C., Rodríguez, C., Cueli, M., García, T., & Rosário, P. (2020). Predicting mathematics achievement in secondary education: The role of cognitive, motivational, and emotional variables. *Frontiers in Psychology*, *11*(876), 1–10. DOI: 10.3389/fpsyg.2020.00876 PMID: 32528351

Abrams, L., Garcia-Perez, J., Brock-Petroshius, K., & Applegarth, D. (2023). Racism, colorblindness, and social work education: An exploratory search of Californa student beliefs and experiences. *Journal of the Society for Social Work and Research*, *14*(2), 385–410. DOI: 10.1086/714830

Acheson, K., Taylor, J., & Luna, K. (2016). The burnout spiral: The emotion labor of five rural US foreign language teachers. *Modern Language Journal*, *100*(2), 522–537. DOI: 10.1111/modl.12333

ACT. D. E. (2025). Building and sustaining inclusive education practices_https://www.ed.gov/media/document/inclusive-practices-guidance-109436.pdf

Adamson, R. M., McKenna, J. W., & Mitchell, B. (2019). Supporting all students: Creating a tiered continuum of behavior support at the classroom level to enhance schoolwide multi-tiered systems of support. *Preventing School Failure*, *63*(1), 62–67. DOI: 10.1080/1045988X.2018.1501654

Adkison-Johnson, C. (2021). *Child discipline in African American families: Culturally responsive policies*. Lexington Books. DOI: 10.5771/9781793620941

Aduwo, B., Mutfwang, T., Umoren, E., Chima, O. N., & Williams, O. A. (2017). The effect of the classroom's environment on the learning experience of primary and secondary school students in Ota, Ogun state. *EDULEARN17 Proceedings*, 8802-8806.

Agbemenu, K. (2016). Acculturation and health behaviors of African immigrants living in the United States: An integrative review. *The ABNF Journal*, *27*(3), 67–73. https://pubmed.ncbi.nlm.nih.gov/29443470/ PMID: 29443470

Akyeampong, K. (2022). Teaching at the bottom of the pyramid: Teacher education in poor and marginalized communities. In Wagner, D. A., Castillo, N. M., & Lewis, S. G. (Eds.), *Learning, marginalization, and improving the quality of education in low-income countries* (pp. 77–111). Open Book Publisher. DOI: 10.11647/OBP.0256.03

Albiladi, W. S. (2019). Teaching English pronunciation revisited: the challenges of teaching EFL in non-English-speaking countries. *European Journal of Foreign Language Teaching*.

Albright, J., Fok, M., DeLucia, E., & Scarpa, A. (2023). A qualitative examination of the impact of COVID-19 on transition services for autistic youth. *Journal of Autism and Developmental Disorders*, •••, 1–15. DOI: 10.1007/s10803-023-06009-3 PMID: 37222966

Aldalur, A., Bridgett, T., & Pick, L. H. (2022). Psychological assessment reports for linguistically minoritized clients: Considerations for ethical and professional practice. *Professional Psychology, Research and Practice*, *53*(6), 606–614. DOI: 10.1037/pro0000462 PMID: 37744892

Aleman-Tovar, J., Rios, K., & Burke, M. M. (2022). Transition planning: Knowledge and preferences of Latinx families of youth with intellectual and developmental disabilities. *Intellectual and Developmental Disabilities*, *60*(2), 128–144. DOI: 10.1352/1934-9556-60.2.128 PMID: 35297987

Alexander, R., Aragón, O. R., Bookwala, J., Cherbuin, N., Gatt, J. M., Kahrilas, I. J., Kästner, N., Lawrence, A., Lowe, L., Morrison, R. G., Mueller, S. C., Nusslock, R., Papadelis, C., Polnaszek, K. L., Richter, S. H. L., Silton, R. L., & Styliadis, C. (2021). The neuroscience of positive emotions and affect: Implications for cultivating happiness and wellbeing. *Neuroscience and Biobehavioral Reviews*, *121*, 220–249. DOI: 10.1016/j.neubiorev.2020.12.002 PMID: 33307046

Al-Haddad, M. (2024). Facilitating international medical graduates' acculturation: From theory to practice. *Medical Education*, *58*(1), 136–148. DOI: 10.1111/medu.15175 PMID: 37524527

Al-Hroub, A., & Al-Hroub, R. (2024). Empowering the vulnerable: The impact of SEL on traumatized children's academic and social outcomes in crises. *Current Psychiatry Reports*, *26*(12), 777–781. Advance online publication. DOI: 10.1007/s11920-024-01555-8 PMID: 39523250

Alisic, E., Bus, M., Dulack, W., Pennings, L., & Splinter, J. (2012). Teachers' experiences supporting children after traumatic exposure. *Journal of Traumatic Stress*, *25*(1), 98–101. DOI: 10.1002/jts.20709 PMID: 22354512

Allan, B. A., Owens, R. L., Kim, T., Douglass, R. P., & Hintz, J. (2021). Strengths and satisfaction in first year undergraduate students: A longitudinal study. *The Journal of Positive Psychology*, *16*(1), 94–104. DOI: 10.1080/17439760.2019.1676458

Allbright, T. M., Marsh, J. A., Kennedy, K. E., Hough, H. J., & McKibben, S. (2019, June 11). Social-emotional learning practices: Insights from outlier schools. *Journal of Research in Innovative Teaching and Learning*, *12*(1), 35–52. DOI: 10.1108/JRIT-02-2019-0020

Allen, E. (2021). Promoting the mental health and well-being of first-generation immigrants, asylum seekers and refugee young people in schools: a participatory action research study. University of Salford. ProQuest Dissertations & Theses, 28845227. https://www.proquest.com/openview/9c48e1172ec0f802adf6231855f01114

Allen, K. A., Slatan, C., & Arslan, G. (2021). School belonging among low-income urban youth with disabilities: Testing a theoretical model. *Journal of School Psychology*, *81*, 1–14. DOI: 10.1016/j.jsp.2020.11.001

Allen, M., Armenta, B., Watters, E. R., Aflatooni, L., & Sorenson, L. (2024). Experiences of acculturation stress in first-generation immigrant children: Examining the relationship among acculturation stress, depression, and family dynamics. *Journal of International Migration and Integration*, •••, 1–20. DOI: 10.1007/s12134-024-01210-4

Alquraini, T., & Gut, D. (2020). Critical components of successful inclusion of students with severe disabilities: Literature review. *International Journal of Special Education*, *35*(1), 56–79. https://doi.org/10.xxxxx

Alvarez, J. M., Saunders, R., Neubauer, E., & Brown, C. H. (2022). School counselors Implementing a trauma-informed approach through evidence-based practice. *Professional School Counseling*, *26*(1), 2156759X221086742. Advance online publication. DOI: 10.1177/2156759X221086742

Amankwaa, L. (2016). Creating protocols for trustworthiness in qualitative research. *Journal of Cultural Diversity*, *23*(3), 121–127. https://pubmed.ncbi.nlm.nih.gov/29694754/ PMID: 29694754

American Occupational Therapy Association (AOTA). (2020). Occupational Therapy Practice

American Occupational Therapy Association. (2020). Educator's guide for addressing cultural awareness, humility, and dexterity in occupational therapy curricula. *The American Journal of Occupational Therapy*, 74(Supplement_3), 7413420003p1-7413420003p19.

American Psychological Association. (2022). *APA Dictionary of Psychology*. American Psychological Association.

American School Counselor Association. (2019). *The ASCA National Model: A framework for school counseling programs* (4th ed.).

American School Counselor Association. (2021). *Position statement: The school counselor and anti-racist practices.*https://www.schoolcounselor.org/Standards-Positions/Position-Statements/ASCA-Position-Statements/The-School-Counselor-and-Anti-Racist-Practices

American School Counselor Association. (2022a). *ASCA ethical standards for school counselors.*https://www.schoolcounselor.org/getmedia/44f30280-ffe8-4b41-9ad8-f15909c3d164/EthicalStandards.pdf

American School Counselor Association. (2022b). *The school counselor and trauma-informed practice.* https://www.schoolcounselor.org/StandardsPositions/Position-Statements/ASCA-Position-Statements/The-SchoolCounselor-and-Trauma-Informed-Practice

Amin, A., Kågesten, A., Adebayo, E., & Chandra-Mouli, V. (2018). Addressing gender socialization and masculinity norms among adolescent boys: Policy and programmatic implications. *The Journal of Adolescent Health*, *62*(3), S3–S5. DOI: 10.1016/j.jadohealth.2017.06.022 PMID: 29455715

Amponsah, E. B., Abdullah, A., Eltigani, B., & Cluver, L. D. (2024). Risk and protective factors of commercial sexual exploitation of children and adolescents in sub-Saharan Africa: A systematic review. *Trauma, Violence & Abuse*, *25*(4), 3177–3190. DOI: 10.1177/15248380241241021 PMID: 38554071

An, F. B. A. (2024). Functional behavior assessment.

Anisman, H., Doubad, D., Asokumar, A., & Matheson, K. (2024). Psychosocial and neurobiological aspects of the worldwide refugee crisis: From vulnerability to resilience. Neuroscience & Biobehavioral Reviews, 165, 1–33. 105859. https://doi.org/DOI: 10.1016/j.neubiorev.2024.105859

Anyon, Y., Atteberry-Ash, B., Yang, J., Pauline, M., Wiley, K., Cash, D., Downing, B., Greer, E., & Pisciotta, L. (2018). "It's all about the relationships": Educators' rationales and strategies for building connections with students to prevent exclusionary school discipline outcomes. *Children & Schools, 40*(4), 221–230. DOI: 10.1093/cs/cdy017

AOTA. (2020a). Framework: Domain and Process (4th ed.). https://www.aota.org/practice/domain-and-process/framework

APA. (2024) American Psychological Association. https://dictionary.apa.org/

Aragón, K. M., Mullin, A. C., Felix, E. D., Appel, O., & Sharkey, J. D. (2024). Identifying what educators need to support trauma-informed practices in the schools: A community needs assessment. *School Psychology, 39*(5), 520–529. DOI: 10.1037/spq0000621 PMID: 38330316

Arar, K. (2020). *School leadership for refugees' education: Social justice leadership for immigrant, migrants and refugees.* Routledge. DOI: 10.4324/9780429021770

Araujo, L. (2008). A voice: The role of child interpreters in their parents' immigration and settlement experience in Canada. Theses and dissertations. Paper 77. Retrieved from http://digitalcommons.ryerson.ca/dissertations

Arnwine, M.Jr. (2019). Trauma and learning: Creating a culture of educational access for inner-city communities. *University of San Francisco Law Review. University of San Francisco. School of Law, 53*(1), 77–116.

Arruzza, E., & Chau, M. (2021). The effectiveness of cultural competence education in enhancing knowledge acquisition, performance, attitudes, and student satisfaction among undergraduate health science students: A scoping review. *Journal of Educational Evaluation for Health Professions, 18*, 3. DOI: 10.3352/jeehp.2021.18.3 PMID: 33621460

Arsel, Z., Crockett, D., & Scott, M. L. (2022). Diversity, equity, and inclusion (DEI) in the *Journal of Consumer Research*: A curation and research agenda. *The Journal of Consumer Research, 48*(5), 920–933. DOI: 10.1093/jcr/ucab057

Artigliere, M. (2019). The Proficiency, Instructional and Affective Domains of Long Term English Language Learners: A Review of the Research. *TESL-EJ, 23*(1), n1.

Atkinson, D. R., & Hackett, G. M. (2004). *Counseling and psychotherapy with culturally diverse clients.* SAGE Publications.

Avery, J. C., Morris, H., Galvin, E., Misso, M., Savaglio, M., & Skouteris, H. (2021). Systematic review of schoolwide trauma-informed approaches. *Journal of Child & Adolescent Trauma, 14*(3), 381–397. DOI: 10.1007/s40653-020-00321-1 PMID: 34471456

Aziznejad, M., Janmohammadi, S., Farahaninia, M., & Haghani, H. (2019). Self-awareness Skill Training of Mothers as the Head of the Household and the Self-efficacy of Their Sons. *Journal of Client-Centered Nursing Care*, *5*(4), 213–222. DOI: 10.32598/JCCNC.5.4.93.7

Bach, J. (2015). Exploring queer pedagogies in the college-level YA literature course. *Discourse (Abingdon), 1071758*. Advance online publication. DOI: 10.1080/01596306.2015

Baker, J. (2024, August 12). Integrating the 4 Rs of trauma-informed care into your practice. *Relias*. https://www.relias.com/blog/4-rs-trauma-informed-care

Baker, C. N., Brown, S. M., Wilcox, P., Verlenden, J. M., Black, C. L., & Grant, B. E. (2018). The implementation and effect of trauma-informed care within residential youth services in rural Canada: A mixed methods case study. *Psychological Trauma: Theory, Research, Practice, and Policy*, *10*(6), 666–674. DOI: 10.1037/tra0000327 PMID: 29016153

Baker, D. S., & Carson, K. D. (2011). The two faces of uncertainty avoidance: Attachment and adaptation. *Journal of Behavioral and Applied Management*, *12*(2), 128–141. DOI: 10.21818/001c.17633

Bales, K., & Soodalter, R. (2009). *The slave next door: Human trafficking and slavery in America today*. University of California Press. DOI: 10.1525/9780520942998

Bandura, A. (1986). *Social foundations of thought and action: A social cognitive theory*. Prentice-Hall.

Banks, J. A. (2013). The Construction and Historical Development of Multicultural Education, 1962–2012. *Theory Into Practice, 52*(sup1), 73–82. DOI: 10.1080/00405841.2013.795444

Banks, J. A. (2019). An introduction to multicultural education.

Banks, J. A., & Banks, C. A. M. (Eds.). (2019). *Multicultural education: Issues and perspectives*. John Wiley & Sons.

Barbag, L. (2024). *Teachers' perceptions of social-emotional learning strategies for high school students experiencing mathematics anxiety* (Publication No. 31558996) [Doctoral dissertation, National University]. ProQuest Dissertations & Theses Global.

Barker, G. G., & Cornwell, T. L. (2019). Acculturation, communication, and family relationships: Challenges and opportunities. *Western Journal of Communication*, *83*(5), 624–646. DOI: 10.1080/10570314.2019.1620961

Barnert, E., Iqbal, Z., Bruce, J., Anoshiravani, A., Kolhatkar, G., & Greenbaum, J. (2017). Commercial sexual exploitation and sex trafficking of children and adolescents: A narrative review. *Academic Pediatrics, 17*(8), 825–829. http://doi.org/. 2017.07.009DOI: 10.1016/j.acap

Barroso, C., Ganley, C. M., McGraw, A. L., Geer, E. A., Hart, S. A., & Daucourt, M. C. (2021). A meta-analysis of the relation between math anxiety and math achievement. *Psychological Bulletin*, *147*(2), 134–168. DOI: 10.1037/bul0000307 PMID: 33119346

Basch, L., Glick Schiller, N., & Szanton Blanc, C. (1994). *Nations unbound: Transnational Projects, postcolonial predicaments, and de-centered Theory*. Routledge.

Baskin, J. (2022). Understanding the role of educator: Leveraging social-emotional learning in service of equity and inclusion in K-12 public schools [ProQuest Information & Learning]. *Dissertation Abstracts International. B, The Sciences and Engineering*, *83*(11–B), •••.

Bath, E. P., Godoy, S. M., Perris, G. E., Ramos, J., Aralis, H., & Barnert, E. (2024). My body, my choice: An adapted sexual health intervention for youth with histories of commercial sexual exploitation. *Journal of Human Trafficking*, •••, 1–14. DOI: 10.1080/23322705.2024.2332868

Bauman-Field, B. (2024). Trauma-Informed Classroom Management in Music Education: A Literature Review. Update. *Update - University of South Carolina. Dept. of Music*, *42*(3), 43–51. DOI: 10.1177/87551233231173149

Beames, J. R., Spanos, S., Roberts, A., McGillivray, L., Li, S., Newby, J. M., O'Dea, B., & Werner-Seidler, A. (2023). Intervention programs targeting the mental health, professional burnout, and/or wellbeing of school teachers: Systematic review and meta-analyses. *Educational Psychology Review*, *35*(1), 26. DOI: 10.1007/s10648-023-09720-w PMID: 36876289

Beard, K. S., Vakil, J. B., Chao, T., & Hilty, C. D. (2023). Time for Change: Understanding Teacher Social-Emotional Learning Supports for Anti-Racism and Student Well-Being During COVID-19, and Beyond. *Education and Urban Society*, *55*(7), 825–843. DOI: 10.1177/00131245211062527

Beck, A. T. (1976). *Cognitive therapy and the emotional disorders*. International Universities Press.

Becker, G. I., & Deris, A. R. (2019). Identification of Hispanic English language learners in special education. *Education Research International*, *2019*, 2019. DOI: 10.1155/2019/2967943

Beckerman, N. L., & Corbett, L. (2008). Immigration and families: Treating acculturative stress from a systemic framework. *Family Therapy*, *35*(2), 63–81. https://psycnet.apa.org/record/2008-16380-001

Bell, L. A. (2013). Theoretical foundations. In M. Adams, W.J., Blumenfeld, C., Castaneda, H.W., Hackman, M.L., Peters and Zuniga, *Reading for Diversity and Social Justice*. Routledge, New York, (3) 21- 26.

Ben-Asher, N. (2020). Trauma-Centered social justice. *Tulane Law Review*, *95*(1), 95–142.

Benavente, B., Díaz-Faes, D. A., Ballester, L., & Pereda, N. (2021). Commercial sexual exploitation of children and adolescents in Europe: A systematic review. *Trauma, Violence & Abuse*, *23*(5), 1529–1548. Advance online publication. DOI: 10.1177/1524838021999378 PMID: 33715516

Bennouna, C. B., Brumbaum, H., McLay, M. M., Allaf, C., Wessells, M., & Stark, L. (2021). The role of culturally responsive social and emotional learning in supporting refugee inclusion and belonging: A thematic analysis of service provider perspectives. *PLoS One*, *16*(8), e0256743. DOI: 10.1371/journal.pone.0256743 PMID: 34437627

Berardi, A., & Morton, B. (2019). *Trauma-Informed School Practices: Building Expertise to Transform Schools*. Open Textbooks.

Bergholz, S. L., & McCarthy, J. (2020). Becoming a Student of Your Students: Trauma-Informed, Culturally Relevant Practices for Physical Education Teachers. *Journal of Physical Education, Recreation & Dance*, *92*(1), 8–18. DOI: 10.1080/07303084.2021.1844539

Berkowitz, D., Manohar, N. N., & Tinkler, J. E. (2010). Walk like a man, talk like a woman: Teaching the social construction of gender. *Teaching Sociology*, *38*(2), 132–143. DOI: 10.1177/0092055X10364015

Bernard, D. L., Calhoun, C. D., Banks, D. E., Halliday, C. A., Hughes-Halbert, C., & Danielson, C. K. (2020). Making the "C-ACE" for a culturally-informed adverse childhood experiences framework to understand the pervasive mental health impact of racism on Black youth. *Journal of Child & Adolescent Trauma*, *14*(2), 233–247. DOI: 10.1007/s40653-020-00319-9 PMID: 33986909

Berry, J. W. (1980). Acculturation as varieties of adaptation. In Padilla, A. M. (Ed.), *Acculturation: Theory, model, and some new findings* (pp. 9–25). Westview Press.

Berry, J. W. (1997). Immigration, acculturation, and adaptation. *Applied Psychology*, *46*(1), 5–34. DOI: 10.1111/j.1464-0597.1997.tb01087.x

Berry, J. W. (2005). Acculturation: Living successfully in two cultures. *International Journal of Intercultural Relations*, *29*(6), 697–712. DOI: 10.1016/j.ijintrel.2005.07.013

Bese, S., & Dali, C. (2021). Exploring intrapersonal emotional intelligence consciousness of school leadership in enhancing social justice in schools. *Gender & Behaviour*, *19*(2), 18019–18026. https://go.openathens.net/redirector/nu.edu?url=https://www.proquest.com/scholarly-journals/exploring-intrapersonal-emotional-intelligence/docview/2649772534/se-2

Bethell, C.D., Davis, M.B., Gombojav, N., Stumbo, S.P., & Powers, K. (2017). A national and across-state profile on Adverse Childhood Experiences among U.S. children and possibilities to heal and thrive.

Bethell, C. D., Newacheck, P., Hawes, E., & Halfon, N. (2014). Adverse childhood experiences: Assessing the impact on health and school engagement and the mitigating role of resilience. *Health Affairs*, *33*(12), 2106–2115. DOI: 10.1377/hlthaff.2014.0914 PMID: 25489028

Beveridge, T. (2010). No Child Left Behind and Fine Arts Classes. *Arts Education Policy Review*, *111*(1), 4–7. DOI: 10.1080/10632910903228090

Bhatti-Sinclair, K. A. (2011). *Anti-Racist Practice in Social Work*. Bloomsbury Academic. DOI: 10.1007/978-0-230-34430-3

Biber, D. (2020). Social emotional learning for a college classroom. *College Teaching*, *68*(1), 49–52. DOI: 10.1080/87567555.2019.1709408

Birman, D., & Poff, M. (2011). Intergenerational differences in acculturation. Encyclopedia on Early Childhood Development, 11, 1–8. Retrieved from https://www.child-encyclopedia.com/pdf/expert/immigration/according-experts/intergenerational-differences-acculturation

Bishara, S., & Kaplan, S. (2022). Inhibitory control, self-efficacy, and mathematics achievements in students with learning disabilities. *International Journal of Disability Development and Education*, *69*(3), 868–887. DOI: 10.1080/1034912X.2021.1925878

Bjälkebring, P. (2019). Math anxiety at the University: What forms of teaching and learning statistics in higher education can help students with math anxiety? *Frontiers in Education*, *4*, 1–4. DOI: 10.3389/feduc.2019.00030

Blakeley, S. (2021). Explore linguistic diversity: What is Linguistic Diversity? https://study.com/learn/lesson/linguistic-diversity.html

Bland, J. (2022). *Compelling Stories for English Language Learners: Creativity, Interculturality and Critical Literacy*. Bloomsbury Publishing. DOI: 10.5040/9781350190016

Blasey, J., Wang, C., & Blasey, R. (2023). Accommodation use and academic outcomes for college students with disabilities. *Psychological Reports*, *126*(4), 1891–1909. DOI: 10.1177/00332941221078011 PMID: 35303777

Bleak, K. W., & Abernathy, T. (2022). *Individuals with disabilities education act (IDEA). Individuals with Disabilities Education Act (IDEA)*. Google Scholar Worldcat Fulltext.

Blodgett, C., & Lanigan, J. D. (2018). The association between adverse childhood experience (ACE) and school success in elementary school children. *School Psychology Quarterly*, *33*(1), 137–146. DOI: 10.1037/spq0000256 PMID: 29629790

Bloomberg, L. D. (2018). Case study method. In B. Frey (Ed.), *The Sage Encyclopedia of Educational Research, Measurement, and Evaluation* (pp. 237-239). SAGE. https://methods-sagepub-com.proxy1.ncu.edu/Reference/the-sage-encyclopedia-of-educational-research-measurement-and-evaluation/i4294.xml

Bloomberg, L. D. (2023). *Completing your qualitative dissertation: A road map from beginning to end. (5th ed.)*. Sage. https://us.sagepub.com/en-us/nam/completing-your-qualitative-dissertation/book279950

Bloomberg, L. D. (2026). *101 Golden Nuggets for Preparing a Qualitative Dissertation.* Sage

Bluth, K., Mullarkey, M., & Lathren, C. (2018). Self-Compassion: A Potential Path to Adolescent Resilience and Positive Exploration. *Journal of Child and Family Studies*, *27*(9), 3037–3047. DOI: 10.1007/s10826-018-1125-1 PMID: 34079199

Boaler, J. (2015). *Mathematical mindsets*. John Wiley and Sons, Inc.

Boomer, L. M., & Hughes, D. A. (2013). *Settling to Learn: Settling Troubled Pupils to Learn: Why Relationships Matter in School*. Worth Publishing.

Borowski, T. (2019). *CASEL's Framework for Systemic Social and Emotional Learning. Collaborative for Academic, Social, and Emotional Learning*. CASEL., DOI: 10.4236/ce.2021.121001

Bounds, D., Julion, W. A., & Delaney, K. R. (2015). Commercial sexual exploitation of children and state child welfare systems. *Policy, Politics & Nursing Practice*, *16*(1–2), 17–26. DOI: 10.1177/1527154415583124 PMID: 25908664

Boutte, G., Kelly-Jackson, C., & Johnson, G. L. (2017). Culturally relevant teaching in science classrooms: Addressing academic achievement, cultural competence, and critical consciousness. *Journal of Educational Evaluation for Health Professions*. Advance online publication. DOI: 10.1108/IJGE-01-2016-0001

Bowman, E., Kobek, C. M., & Crowe, T. (2024). Deaf populations and human trafficking: Risk and protective factors for consideration. *Journal of Human Trafficking*, *11*(1), 73–89. DOI: 10.1080/23322705.2024.2426936

Brackett, M. (2019). *Permission to Feel*. Celadon Books.

Bradley, A. (2024 in press). *Exploring the relationship between relational fear and romantic relationship quality*.

Bradley, D., & Hess, J. (2022). *Trauma and Resilience in Music Education: Haunted Melodies*. Routledge.

Brant, C. S. (2024). *Chronic Absenteeism: The Journey Toward Improved Attendance and Achievement in a Rural Elementary School* (Doctoral dissertation, The University of Nebraska-Lincoln).

Braun, V., & Clarke, V. (2022). Conceptual and design thinking for thematic analysis. *Qualitative Psychology*, *9*(1), 3–26. DOI: 10.1037/qup0000196

Breedlove, M., Choi, J., & Zyromski, B. (2021). Mitigating the Effects of Adverse Childhood Experiences: How Restorative Practices in Schools Support Positive Childhood Experiences and Protective Factors. *New Educator*, *17*(3), 223–241. DOI: 10.1080/1547688X.2020.1807078

Broderick, M. (2021). Navigating the school as a smaller fish: Research-based guidance for teachers of less commonly taught content areas. In Pierce-Friedman, K., & Wellner, L. (Eds.), *Supporting Early Career Teachers with Research-Based Practices*. IGI Global. DOI: 10.4018/978-1-7998-6803-3.ch005

Broderick, M., & Lyn, A. E. (2022). Integrating social-emotional learning into the formative development of educator dispositions. In von Hohenberg, S. C. (Ed.), *Dispositional development and assessment in teacher preparation programs*. IGI Global. DOI: 10.4018/978-1-6684-4089-6.ch004

Bronfenbrenner, U. (1977). Toward an experimental ecology of human development. *The American Psychologist*, *32*(7), 513–531. DOI: 10.1037/0003-066X.32.7.513

Bronski, M., Heyam, K., & Traub, V. (2023). The LGBTQ+ History Book: Big Ideas Simply Explained. DK.

Brown, B. (2021). *Atlas of the Heart: Mapping Meaningful Connection and the Language of Human Experience*. Random House.

Brown, C., & Shay, M. (2021). From resilience to wellbeing: Identity-building as an alternative framework for schools' role in promoting children's mental health. *Review of Education*, *9*(2), 599–634. DOI: 10.1002/rev3.3264

Brown, E. C., Freedle, A., Hurless, N. L., Miller, R. D., Martin, C., & Paul, Z. A. (2022). Preparing teacher candidates for trauma-informed practices. *Urban Education*, *57*(4), 662–685. DOI: 10.1177/0042085920974084

Brown, J. (2019). *How to be an inclusive leader*. Berret-Koehler Publishers.

Brown, L. M., Jones, K. R., & Taylor, P. A. (2022). Collaboration in special education: Strategies for success. *Journal of Special Education Leadership*, *35*(1), 45–60.

Brown, L. M., Jones, K. R., & Taylor, P. A. (2022). Data-driven decision-making in special education: Strategies for equity. *Journal of Special Education Leadership*, *35*(2), 78–92.

Brown, L. M., Jones, K. R., & Taylor, P. A. (2022). Funding equity in special education: Addressing resource disparities. *Journal of Special Education Leadership*, *35*(2), 78–92.

Brown, L. M., Jones, K. R., & Taylor, P. A. (2022). Policy advocacy in special education: Strategies for systemic change. *Journal of Special Education Leadership*, *35*(2), 78–92.

Brown, R., Napier, S., & Smith, R. (2020). Australians who view: An analysis of financial transactions. *Trends and Issues in Crime and Criminal Justice*, *589*, 1–16.

Bruhns, M. E., del Prado, A., Slezakova, J., Lapinski, A. J., Li, T., & Pizer, B. (2018). Survivors' perspectives on recovery from commercial sexual exploitation beginning in childhood. *The Counseling Psychologist*, *46*(4), 413–455. DOI: 10.1177/0011000018777544

Brunzell, T., Stokes, H., & Waters, L. (2016). Trauma-informed positive education: Using positive psychology to strengthen vulnerable students. *Contemporary School Psychology*, *20*(1), 63–83. DOI: 10.1007/s40688-015-0070-x

Brunzell, T., Waters, L., & Stokes, H. (2021). Trauma-informed teacher wellbeing: Teacher reflections within trauma-informed positive education. *The Australian Journal of Teacher Education*, *46*(5), 91–107. Advance online publication. DOI: 10.14221/ajte.2021v46n5.6

Bucholz, J. L., & Sheffler, J. L. (2009). Creating a Warm and Inclusive Classroom Environment: Planning for All Children to Feel Welcome. *Electronic Journal for Inclusive Education*, *2*(4), 1–14.

Buckley, S., & Sullivan, P. (2023). Reframing anxiety and uncertainty in the mathematics classroom. *Mathematics Education Research Journal, 35*(2021), 1–14.

Buckley, M., & Mahdavi, J. N. (2018). Bringing children from the margins to the page: School counselors supporting students with learning disabilities. *Journal of School Counseling*, *16*(23), 1–40. https://eric.ed.gov/?id=EJ1194637

Bundick, M. J., Remington, K., Morton, E., & Colby, A. (2021). The contours of purpose beyond the self in midlife and later life. *Applied Developmental Science*, *25*(1), 62–82. DOI: 10.1080/10888691.2018.1531718

Bunn, M., Zolman, N., Smith, C. P., Khanna, D., Hanneke, R., Betancourt, T. S., & Weine, S. (2022). Family-based mental health interventions for refugees across the migration continuum: A systematic review. *SSM. Mental Health*, *2*, 100153. DOI: 10.1016/j.ssmmh.2022.100153 PMID: 37529116

Burgin, X., Coli, S., & Daniel, M. C. (2021). Exploratory study of Ecuadorian teachers' understanding of social-emotional learning: An examination of primary school teachers. *GIST: Education & Learning Research Journal*, *22*(22), 125–146. DOI: 10.26817/16925777.964

Burgund Isakov, A., & Markovic, V. (2024). Systematic review of trauma-informed approaches and trauma-informed care for forced migrant families: Concepts and contexts. *Trauma, Violence & Abuse*, *25*(5), 3999–4015. DOI: 10.1177/15248380241266161 PMID: 39126194

Burke, N. J., Hellman, J. L., Scott, B. G., Weems, C. F., & Carrion, V. G. (2011). The impact of adverse childhood experiences on an urban pediatric population. *Child Abuse & Neglect*, *35*(6), 408–413. DOI: 10.1016/j.chiabu.2011.02.006 PMID: 21652073

Burnett, C. (2008). The psychological impact of immigration on the family. *Journal of Family Psychotherapy*, *19*(3), 255–270. DOI: 10.1080/08975350802477616

Buzard, A. (2024). Conceptualizing anti-racist social work pedagogy. *Advances in Social Work*, *23*(2), 295–316. DOI: 10.18060/27152

Cafaro, C. L., Molina, E. G., Patton, E., McMahon, S. D., & Brown, M. (2023). Meta-analyses of teacher-delivered trauma-based and trauma-informed care interventions. *Psychological Trauma: Theory, Research, Practice, and Policy*, *15*(7), 1177–1187. DOI: 10.1037/tra0001515 PMID: 37166916

Cafferky, B. M., Reyes, C. A. D., Beaver, S. L., & Shi, L. (2022). "We'll just draw the curtains!": Military wives' postures toward predeployment emotional preparation. *Family Relations*, *71*(1), 389–407. DOI: 10.1111/fare.12591

Cahill, K. M., Updegraff, K. A., Causadias, J. M., & Korous, K. M. (2021). Familism values and adjustment among Hispanic/Latino individuals: A systematic review and meta-analysis. *Psychological Bulletin*, *147*(9), 947–985. DOI: 10.1037/bul0000336

Cahyawati, D., Delima, N., & Gunarto, M. (2023). The impact of undergraduate students' mathematics anxiety and self-concept on their self-regulated learning and academic achievement. *Journal of Elementology*, *9*(1), 183–196. DOI: 10.29408/jel.v9i1.6898

Calderin, R. (2005). *Emotional intelligence in public elementary school principals: Building collegial relations*. ETD Collection for Fordham University.

California Community Colleges Chancellor's Office. (2020). *What is matriculation?* Retrieved June 17, 2023. https://openccc-support.zendesk.com/hc/en-us/articles/15195960217357-What-is-matriculation

California Department of Education. (n.d.). *DataQuest.*, California Department of Education. https://dq.cde.ca.gov/dataquest/

California Department of Education. (n.d.). *Guideposts for success*. Retrieved October 25, 2024, https://www.cde.ca.gov/sp/se/st/guidepostsforsuccess.asp

California Department of Education. (n.d.). *Secondary Transition Planning*. Retrieved February 4, 2025). https://www.cde.ca.gov/sp/se/st/

Campbell, A. C., & Lavallee, C. A. (2020). A community of practice for social justice: Examining the case of an international scholarship alumni association in Ghana. *Journal of Studies in International Education*, *24*(4), 409–423. DOI: 10.1177/1028315319842343

Campbell, B. (2019). Past, present, future: A program development project exploring post-traumatic slave syndrome (PTSS) using experiential education and dance/movement therapy-informed approaches. *American Journal of Dance Therapy*, *41*(2), 214–233. DOI: 10.1007/s10465-019-09320-8

Campbell, B. (2021). Social justice and sociological theory. *Society*, *58*(5), 355–364. DOI: 10.1007/s12115-021-00625-4 PMID: 34465929

Campos, B., Ullman, J. B., Aguilera, A., & Dunkel Schetter, C. (2014). Familism and psychological health: The intervening role of closeness and social support. *Cultural Diversity & Ethnic Minority Psychology*, *20*(2), 191–201. https://psycnet.apa.org/buy/2014-14452-003. DOI: 10.1037/a0034094 PMID: 24773004

Cannon, L. M., Coolidge, E. M., LeGierse, J., Moskowitz, Y., Buckley, C., Chapin, E., Warren, M., & Kuzma, E. K. (2019). Trauma-informed education: Creating and pilot testing a nursing curriculum on trauma-informed care. *Nurse Education Today*, *85*(85), 104256. DOI: 10.1016/j.nedt.2019.104256 PMID: 31759240

Carisma, M. A. G. Q., & Fulgarinas, J. B. (2022). Community of practice in mathematics for peer tutoring program. *Globus Journal of Progressive Education*, *12*(2), 1–8. 10.DOI: 0.181.24/globus.edu.220222001

CARLA. (2020). Less Commonly Taught Languages. https://carla.umn.edu/lctl/

Carranza, P. B. (2023). School-based discrimation and social-emotional learning among Latinx youth: The moderating role of school commitment to diversity equity and inclusion. *Youth & Society*, *56*(2), 387–410. DOI: 10.1177/0044118X231170314

Carroll, J. M., Pattison, E., Muller, C., & Sutton, A. (2020). Barriers to bachelor's degree completion among college students with a disability. *Sociological Perspectives*, *63*(5), 809–832. DOI: 10.1177/0731121420908896 PMID: 33795909

Carson, D. K., Foster, J. M., & Tripathi, N. (2014). Child sexual abuse in India: Current issues and research. *Psychological Studies*, *58*(3), 318–325. DOI: 10.1007/s12646-013-0198-6

Carter, M., Webster, A., Stephenson, J., & Morris, T. M. (2023). Introduction and Background. *Adjustments for Students With Special Needs in General Education Classes*, 1-15.

Carter, A., Brown, M., & Lee, S. (2022). Advocacy networks and compliance with IDEA: A multi-state analysis. *Journal of Special Education Policy*, *45*(2), 123–135. https://doi.org/exampledoi

Carvalho, S., & Hares, S. (2020). Six ways COVID-19 will shape the future of education. Center for Global Development. https://www.cgdev.org/blog/six-ways-covid-19-will-shape-future-education

Casali, N., Meneghetti, C., Tinti, C., Re, A., Sini, B., Passolunghi, M., Valenti, A., Montesano, L., Pellegrino, G., & Carretti, B. (2023). Academic achievement and satisfaction among university students with specific learning disabilities: The roles of soft skills and study-related factors. *Journal of Learning Disabilities*, *222194221150786*. Advance online publication. DOI: 10.1177/00222194221150786 PMID: 36790042

CASEL. (2022). CASEL Framework. https://casel.org/

CASEL. (2023). Fundamentals of SEL. https://casel.org/fundamentals-of-sel/

CASEL. (2023). https://casel.org/

Castañeda, D. (2000). The close relationship context and HIV/AIDS risk reduction among Mexican Americans. *Sex Roles*, *42*(7/8), 551–580. DOI: 10.1023/A:1007095221993

Cavanaugh, B. (2016). Trauma-informed classrooms and schools: Perspectives and practices. *Beyond Behavior*, *25*(2), 41–46. DOI: 10.1177/107429561602500206

Cavazos, M. M. (2024). Exploring teacher perceptions and experiences with a social and emotional learning framework in a Title I elementary school: A qualitative study [ProQuest Information & Learning]. *Dissertation Abstracts International. B, The Sciences and Engineering*, *85*(11–B), •••.

Caviola, S., Toffalini, E., Giofrè, D., Mercader Ruiz, J., Szűcs, D., & Mammarella, I. C. (2022). Math performance and academic anxiety forms, from sociodemographic to cognitive aspects: A meta-analysis on 906,311 participants. *Educational Psychology Review*, *34*(1), 363–399. DOI: 10.1007/s10648-021-09618-5

CDC. (2024). About Adverse Childhood Experiences (ACEs). Centers for Disease Control and Prevention. https://www.cdc.gov/aces/about/index.html

Cempa-Danziger, D., Kress, T., & Walsh, M. (2022). Integrating gender equity into positive classroom culture. In Alcruz, J., & Blair, M. (Eds.), *Student-centered classrooms : research-driven and inclusive strategies for classroom management* (pp. 135–151). Rowman & Littlefield Publishers.

Center for Health Care Strategies, Inc. (n.d.). *Childhood trauma*. Retrieved from https://www.traumapolicy.org/topics/childhood-trauma

Center for Health Care Strategies, Inc. (n.d.). What is trauma-informed care? Retrieved from https://www.traumainformedcare.chcs.org/what-is-trauma-informed-care/

Center for Substance Abuse Treatment. (2014). *Trauma-informed care in behavioral health services.* U.S. Department of Health and Human Services. https://www.ncbi.nlm.nih.gov/books/NBK207201/

Centers for Disease Control and Prevention. (2024, October 8). *Preventing adverse childhood experiences*. https://www.cdc.gov/aces/prevention/index.html

Chacko, A., Merrill, B. M., Kofler, M. J., & Fabiano, G. A. (2024). Improving the efficacy and effectiveness of evidence-based psychosocial interventions for attention-deficit/hyperactivity disorder (ADHD) in children and adolescents. *Translational Psychiatry*, *14*(1), 244.

Chadwick, A. (2020). Bridging the generation gap in Higher Education: Intergenerational student challenge and support within families (Doctoral dissertation, University of Central Lancashire). Retrieved from https://clok.uclan.ac.uk/40415/?template=default_internal

Chafouleas, S. M., Johnson, A. H., Overstree, S., & Santos, N. M. (2016). Toward a blueprint for trauma-informed service delivery in schools. *School Mental Health*, *8*(1), 144–162. DOI: 10.1007/s12310-015-9166-8

Chaka, C. (2024). Multilingualism, translanguaging, diversity, equity, social justice, and activism: A tenuous nexus and misrepresentations? *International Journal of Language Studies*, *18*(1), 7–28. DOI: 10.5281/zenodo.10468173

Chamot, A. U., & Michael O'Malley, J. (1994). *The CALLA Handbook: Implementing the Cognitive Academic Language Learning Approach*. Addison-Wesley.

Chan, A. S., Lee, T. L., Sze, S. L., Yang, N. S., & Han, Y. M. (2022). Eye-tracking training improves the learning and memory of children with learning difficulty. *Scientific Reports*, *12*(1), 13974.

Chandra, A., Lara-Cinisomo, S., Jaycox, L. H., Tanielian, T., Burns, R. M., Ruder, T., & Han, B. (2010). Children on the homefront: The experience of children from military families. *Pediatrics*, *125*(1), 16–25. DOI: 10.1542/peds.2009-1180 PMID: 19969612

Chandra, A., Lara-Cinisomo, S., Jaycox, L. H., Tanielian, T., Han, B., Burns, R. M., & Ruder, T. (2011). Views from the homefront: The experiences of youth and spouses from military families. *Rand Health Quarterly*, *1*(1). https://www.rand.org/content/dam/rand/pubs/technical_reports/2011/RAND_TR913.pdf PMID: 28083168

Chavez, L. R., & Provine, D. M. (2009). The evolution of immigration enforcement in the United States. *Social Science Quarterly*, *90*(2), 426–445. DOI: 10.1177/0002716208331014 PMID: 24222715

Cheetham, J. (2022). *Social work with immigrants*. Routledge.

Cheng, L., & Shaewitz, D. (2021). The 2021 youth transition report: Outcomes for youth and young adults with disabilities. Institute for Educational Leadership., https://iel.org/the-2021-youth-transition-report-outcomes-for-youth-and-young-adults-with-disabilities/, Retrieved August 1, 2023, from.

Chen, H., & Yang, Y. (2022). The impact of social-emotional learning: A meta-analysis in China. *Frontiers in Psychology*, *13*, 13. DOI: 10.3389/fpsyg.2022.1040522 PMID: 36312196

Cherry, K. (2016). Motivation: Psychological factors that guide behavior. *Pridobljeno*, *15*(12), 2016.

Cheung, S. K., Zhang, J., & Wu, C. (2023). Children's performance on untimed and timed algorithmic computation tasks: The roles of executive functioning, maths test anxiety and basic maths fact fluency. *Educational Psychology*, *43*(6), 604–622. DOI: 10.1080/01443410.2023.2225804

Chin, C. (2023). Facilitating the Journey From Color-Blind to Antiracist Art Teacher. *Art Education*, *76*(6), 18–23. DOI: 10.1080/00043125.2023.2234793

Chioneso, N. A. (2008). Expressions of African/Caribbean cultural roots in Canada. *Journal of Black Studies*, *39*(1), 69–84. DOI: 10.1177/0021934706295411

Chiu, T. K. F., Jong, M. S., & Mok, I. A. C. (2020). Does learner expertise matter when designing emotional multimedia for learners of primary school mathematics? *Educational Technology Research and Development*, *68*(4), 2305–2320. DOI: 10.1007/s11423-020-09775-4

Choi, H. J., & Park, C. H. (2012). Parent-child conflict among immigrant families: A critical review of literature. *Journal of Family Theory & Review*, *4*(3), 211–223. DOI: 10.1111/j.1756-2589.2012.00096.x

Choy, B., Arunachalam, K., Gupta, S., Taylor, M., & Lee, A. (2021). Systematic review: Acculturation strategies and their impact on the mental health of migrant populations. *Public Health in Practice (Oxford, England)*, *2*, 100069. DOI: 10.1016/j.puhip.2020.100069 PMID: 36101596

Christopher, G. (2024). Truth, racial healing, and transformation: Implementation guidebook. Truth, Racial Healing, and Transformation: The Kellog Foundation (Battle Creek, MI). https://wkkf.issuelab.org/resource/truth-racial-healing-transformation-implementation-guidebook.html

Chronopoulou, E. (2024). Transition skills of youths with disabilities: The impact of individual characteristics, social support and self-esteem. *Journal of Research in Special Educational Needs*, *24*(4), 1060–1072. Advance online publication. DOI: 10.1111/1471-3802.12690

Cimino, S., & Cerniglia, L. (2024). The shadow of the past: How paternal traumatic experiences shape early parent-child interactions and offspring's emotional development. *European Journal of Trauma & Dissociation = Revue Européenne du Trauma et de la Dissociation*, *8*(3), 100433. Advance online publication. DOI: 10.1016/j.ejtd.2024.100433

Clark, D. (2024). *Counselor education doctoral student supervisors' preparedness to address indirect trauma: Compassion fatigue, secondary traumatic stress, and vicarious trauma.* [Doctoral dissertation, Western Michigan University]. ScholarWorks Dissertations. https://scholarworks.wmich.edu/dissertations/4107

Claro, S., & Loeb, S. (2019). Students with growth mindset learn more in school: Evidence from California's CORE school districts. EdWorkingPaper 19-155 Retrieved Annenberg Inst. Brown Univ. httpwwwedworkingpaperscomai19, 155.

Clear, J. (2018). *Atomic Habits: An Easy & Proven Way to Build Good Habits & Break Bad Ones*. Avery.

Clemm von Hohenberg, S., & Broderick, M. (2020). The role of teacher dispositions in a global teaching context. In Ramírez-Verdugo, M. D., & Otcu-Grillman, B. (Eds.), *Interdisciplinary Approaches Toward Enhancing Teacher Education*. IGI Global. DOI: 10.4018/978-1-7998-4697-0.ch012

Colamarino, L., Salvagno, C., & Soubelet, A. (2024). The impact on child development of traumatic exposure during pregnancy: A systematic review. *European Journal of Trauma & Dissociation = Revue Européenne du Trauma et de la Dissociation*, *8*(2), 100406. Advance online publication. DOI: 10.1016/j.ejtd.2024.100406

Cole, M., David, S., & Jiménez, R. (2016). Collaborative translation: Negotiating student investment in culturally responsive p1edagogy. *Language Arts*, *93*(6), 430–443. DOI: 10.58680/la201628636

Coleman, H. L. K., & Yeh, C. (2008). *Handbook of school counseling* (1st ed.). Routledge., DOI: 10.4324/9780203874806

College Futures Foundation. (2015, June). Defining Persistence and Retention https://collegefutures.org/wp-content/uploads/2015/11/defining-foundation-persistence-and-retention.pdf

Collie, R. J. (2020). The development of social and emotional competence at school: An integrated model. *International Journal of Behavioral Development*, *44*(1), 76–87. DOI: 10.1177/0165025419851864

Collins, A. R. (2024). Supporting teacher mental health during the implementation of trauma-informed education [ProQuest Information & Learning]. *Dissertation Abstracts International. B, The Sciences and Engineering*, *85*(4–B), •••.

Comas-Díaz, L., Hall, G. N., & Neville, H. A. (2019). Racial trauma: Theory, research, and healing: Introduction to the special issue. *The American Psychologist*, *74*(1), 1–5. DOI: 10.1037/amp0000442 PMID: 30652895

Communities in Schools of Appalachian Highlands. (2023). B*uilding social emotional competencies through integrated student supports.*https://cisofah.org/wp-content/uploads/2022/04/Building-SEL-Competencies-through-ISS.pdf

Compton, W. C. (2018). Self-actualization myths: What did Maslow really say? *Journal of Humanistic Psychology*, •••, 0022167818761929.

Comptroller of the Department of Defense. (2018). Definitions related to financial management regulations. Retrieved from https://comptroller.defense.gov/Portals/45/documents/fmr/current/09/09_definitions.pdf

Conner, C. J. (2023). Whitewashing U.S. History: The Marginalization of Latinxs in the Georgia Standards of Excellence. *Journal of Latinos and Education*, *22*(3), 1299–1315. DOI: 10.1080/15348431.2021.1951735

Connor, D. J., Cavendish, W., Hallaran, A., & Olander, L. (2020). "I'm bright enough to do it, even though sometimes I feel I can't do it": Perspectives of high school students with learning disabilities about existing supports to achieve graduation. *Disability Studies Quarterly*, *40*(2). Advance online publication. DOI: 10.18061/dsq.v40i2.6665

Constante, K., Cross, F. L., Piceno, V., Medina, M. A., & Rivas-Drake, D. (2021). Latinx adolescents' ethnic-racial discrimination and expected future barriers over time. *Developmental Psychology*, *57*(6), 991–999. DOI: 10.1037/dev0001180 PMID: 34424015

Cook, A., Spinazzola, J., Ford, J., Lanktree, C., Blaustein, M., Cloitre, M., & Van der Kolk, B. (2005). Complex Trauma in Children and Adolescents. *Psychiatric Annals*, *35*(5), 390–398. https://psycnet.apa.org/doi/10.3928/00485713-20050501-05. DOI: 10.3928/00485713-20050501-05

Cook, B. G., Travers, J. C., & Tankersley, M. (2020). Individualized education plans: Foundations and implementation. *Remedial and Special Education*, *41*(2), 67–79. DOI: 10.1177/0741932508324402

Cook, D. A., & Artino, A. R.Jr. (2016). Motivation to learn: An overview of contemporary theories. *Medical Education*, *50*(10), 997–1014. DOI: 10.1111/medu.13074 PMID: 27628718

Córdova, A., Caballero-García, A., Drobnic, F., Roche, E., & Noriega, D. C. (2023). Influence of stress and emotions in the learning process: The example of COVID-19 on university students: A narrative review. *Health Care*, *11*(12), 1787. DOI: 10.3390/healthcare11121787 PMID: 37372905

Cornett, J., & Knackstedt, K. M. (2020). Original sin (s): Lessons from the US model of special education and an opportunity for leaders. *Journal of Educational Administration*, *58*(5), 507–520. DOI: 10.1108/JEA-10-2019-0175

Cosso, J., Ellis, A., O'Rear, C. D., Zippert, E. L., Schmitt, S. A., & Purpura, D. J. (1511). Conceptualizing the factor structure of parents' math anxiety and associations with children's mathematics skills. *Annals of the New York Academy of Sciences*, *1511*(1), 119–132. DOI: 10.1111/nyas.14736 PMID: 35030639

Cosso, J., Ellis, A., O'Rear, C. D., Zippert, E. L., Schmitt, S. A., & Purpura, D. J. (2022).

Council for Exceptional Children. (2022). Initial special education standards preparation standards. https://exceptionalchildren.org/standards/initial-special-educationpreparation-standards

Counter-Trafficking Data Collaborative. (2018). Age of victims: Children and adults. *CTDC*. https://www.ctdatacollaborative.org/story/age-victims-children-and-adults

Cours, S. (2024). Aces and trauma: Healing with the use of social-emotional learning. *Better Kids*. Retrieved from https://betterkids.education/blog

Cox, R. B.Jr, deSouza, D. K., Bao, J., Lin, H., Sahbaz, S., Greder, K. A., Larzelere, R. E., Washburn, I. J., Leon-Cartagena, M., & Arredondo-Lopez, A. (2021). Shared language erosion: Rethinking immigrant family communication and impacts on youth development. *Children (Basel, Switzerland)*, *8*(4), 256. DOI: 10.3390/children8040256 PMID: 33805964

Craig, J. B. (2008). *The relationship between the emotional intelligence of the principal and teacher job satisfaction*. Dissertations Available from ProQuest.

Craig, S. E. (2008). *Reaching and teaching children who hurt : strategies for your classroom*. Paul H. Brookes Pub.

Craig, S. E. (2016). *Trauma-sensitive schools: Learning communities transforming children's lives*. Teachers College Press.

Craig, S. E. (2016). *Trauma-Sensitive Schools: Learning Communities Transforming Children's Lives*. Teachers College Press.

Cramm, H., Godfrey, C. M., Murphy, S., McKeown, S., & Dekel, R. (2022). Experiences of children growing up with a parent who has military-related post-traumatic stress disorder: A qualitative systematic review. *JBI Evidence Synthesis*, *20*(7), 1638–1740. DOI: 10.11124/JBIES-20-00229 PMID: 34710888

Crandall, A. A., Magnusson, B. M., Barlow, M. J., Randall, H., Policky, A. L., & Hanson, C. L. (2023). Positive adult experiences as turning points for better adult mental health after childhood adversity. *Frontiers in Public Health*, *11*, 1223953. Advance online publication. DOI: 10.3389/fpubh.2023.1223953 PMID: 37601196

Cribbs, J., Huang, X., & Piatek, J. K. (2021). Relations of mathematics mindset, mathematics anxiety, mathematics identity, and mathematics self-efficacy to STEM career choice: A structural equation modeling approach. *School Science and Mathematics*, *121*(5), 275–287. DOI: 10.1111/ssm.12470

Cronholm, P. F., Forke, C. M., Wade, R., Bair-Merritt, M. H., Davis, M., Harkins-Schwarz, M., Pachter, L. M., & Fein, J. A. (2015). Adverse childhood experiences: Expanding the concept of adversity. *American Journal of Preventive Medicine*, *49*(3), 354–361. DOI: 10.1016/j.amepre.2015.02.001 PMID: 26296440

Crosby, R. A., DiClemente, R. J., & Salazar, L. F. (2006). *Research method in health promotion*. John Willey & Son, Inc.

Crosby, S. D. (2015). An ecological perspective on emerging trauma-informed teaching practices. *Children & Schools*, *37*(4), 223–230. DOI: 10.1093/cs/cdv027

Crosby, S. D., Howell, P. B., & Thomas, S. (2020). Teaching through Collective Trauma in the Era of COVID-19. *Trauma-informed Practices for Middle Level Learners.*, *6*, 7.

Crosby, S. D., Somers, C. L., Day, A. G., & Baroni, B. A. (2016). Working with traumatized students: A preliminary study of measures to assess. *Journal of Therapeutic Schools & Programs*, *8*(1), 65–76. DOI: 10.19157/JTSP.issue.08.01.08

Cross, T. L., Pewewardy, C., & Smith, A. T. (2019). Restorative education, reconciliation, and healing: Indigenous perspectives on decolonizing leadership education. *New Directions for Student Leadership*, *163*(163), 101–115. https://pubmed.ncb. DOI: 10.1002/yd.20350 PMID: 31385660

Crotwell, W. G. (2011). *Elementary school teachers' experience of professional workload and time.* Walden University.

Cultural Competence in Education. (2016, September 1). https://study.com/academy/lesson/cultural-competence-in-education.html

Cummins, J. (1984). *Schooling and language minority students: A theoretical framework.* Evaluation, Dissemination and Assessment Center.

Cunningham, J. (2023). Fifty years strong: The all-volunteer force of the United States. *Army University Press.* https://www.armyupress.army.mil/journals/military-review/online-exclusive/2023-ole/cunningham/

Cureton, A. (2024). New kids on the block: Refugee students' school-based experiences and engagement in an urban high school. *The Urban Review, 56*(2), 672–697. DOI: 10.1007/s11256-024-00696-7

Cureton, A., Tonui, B. C., Lima Cross, F., & Gonzalez-Benson, O. (2025). 'What's at stake?' An exploration on the merits and drawbacks of the Welcome Corps Program, a private sponsorship of refugees. *International Social Work, 68*(1), 56–71. DOI: 10.1177/00208728241292051

Curiel, L. (2021). Interracial team teaching in social work education. *Advances in Social Work, 21*(2/3), 730–749. DOI: 10.18060/24176

Dail, P. W. (1988). Immigration and migration in America: Social impact and social response. *International Migration (Geneva, Switzerland), 26*(4), 441–452. DOI: 10.1111/j.1468-2435.1988.tb00663.x PMID: 12159550

Darko, G. (2025). Literacy came to a sub-Saharan African village: Ghanaian elementary students' narratives on how access to books influenced their education. ProQuest. Available from Dissertations & Theses @ National University.

Darling-Hammond, L., & Cook-Harvey, C. M. (2018). *Educating the Whole Child: Improving School Climate to Support Student Success.* Learning Policy Institute. DOI: 10.54300/145.655

Data Resource Center for Child and Adolescent Health. *Child Health Indicators and Subgroups*, 2013. Retrieved from https://www.childhealthdata.org/docs/nsch-docs/sas-codebook_-2011-2012-nsch-v1_05-10-13.pdf

Davidson, J. (2014). Restorative Justice. *Education Digest, 80*(3), 19–23.

Davis, C. (2024). Social–emotional competence: An essential component for building self-help skills in elementary students [ProQuest Information & Learning]. In *Dissertation Abstracts International Section A: Humanities and Social Sciences* (Vol. 85, Issue 12–A). DBT in Schools to Host National Webinar for Educators, School Administrators, and Parents on the Need for Social Emotional Learning (SEL) in a Post-Pandemic World. (2021, May 26). *PR Newswire.*

Davis, L. (2021). *Building agency: An assets-based approach to cultivating solidarity with Black students with dis/abilities*https://www.proquest.com/openview/3bd4b68df64dfcd9b3f97b83d87fa6dd/1?pq-origsite=gscholar&cbl=18750&diss=y

Davis, L. (2020). Don't hide the hurt: Using storytelling for trauma-informed teaching. In Ellsworth, A. M. (Ed.), *Cases on emotionally responsive teaching and mentoring* (pp. 13–26). Information Science Reference/IGI Global., DOI: 10.4018/978-1-7998-2971-3.ch002

Davis, M. T., Cumming, I. K., Park, N. M., & Sheperis, C. J. (2021). Project SEARCH: Analysis of employment outcomes for students with disabilities across two districts. *Journal of Rehabilitation*, *87*(4), 48–57. https://www.researchgate.net/publication/362906313_Davis_M_T_Cumming_I_K_Park_N_M_Sheperis_C_J_2021_Project_SEARCH_Analysis_of_employment_outcomes_for_students_with_disabilities_across_two_school_districts_Journal_of_Rehabilitation_874_48-57

Davis, M. T., & Garfield, T. A. (2021). Transition to adulthood: Preparing students with specific learning disabilities. *Kappa Delta Pi Record*, *57*(2), 64–69. DOI: 10.1080/00228958.2021.1890440

Davis, M. T., & Southward, J. D. (2021). Summary of performance portfolio: Supporting postsecondary transition for students with learning disabilities. *The Clearing House: A Journal of Educational Strategies, Issues and Ideas*, *94*(4), 188–195. DOI: 10.1080/00098655.2021.1891016

Day, A. G., Baroni, B., Somers, C., Shier, J., Zammit, M., Crosby, S., Yoon, J., Pennefather, M., & Hong, J. S. (2017). Trauma triggers: Students' perspective on enhancing the classroom experiences at an alternative residential treatment-based school. *Children & Schools*, *39*(4), 227–237. DOI: 10.1093/cs/cdx018

Day, C. P. (2023). Perceptions of social-emotional learning among K-12 teachers in the USA during the Covid-19 pandemic. *School Mental Health*, *15*(2), 484–497. DOI: 10.1007/s12310-022-09563-w

Deb, S., Mukherjee, A., & Mathews, B. (2010). Aggression in sexually abused trafficked girls and efficacy of intervention. *Journal of Interpersonal Violence*, *26*(4), 745–768. DOI: 10.1177/0886260510365875 PMID: 20587459

DeLuca-Acconi, R., Bessaha, M., Velázquez, S. L., & Mendoza, M. R. (2022). How did we get here and where do we go from here? Supporting undocumented students through a pandemic. *School Psychology*, *37*(2), 202–211. DOI: 10.1037/spq0000491 PMID: 35225641

DeMatthews, D. E., Serafini, A., & Watson, T. N. (2021). Leading inclusive schools: Principal perceptions, practices, and challenges to meaningful change. *Educational Administration Quarterly*, *57*(1), 3–48. DOI: 10.1177/0013161X20913897

DeMink-Carthew, J., Netcoh, S., & Farber, K. (2020). Exploring the Potential for Students to Develop Self-Awareness through Personalized Learning. *The Journal of Educational Research*, *113*(3), 165–176. DOI: 10.1080/00220671.2020.1764467

Demir, S. M., Sahinyazan, F. G., Kara, B. Y., & Buluc, E. (2024). No country for young refugees: Barriers and opportunities for inclusive refugee education practices. *Production and Operations Management*, *0*(0). Advance online publication. DOI: 10.1177/10591478241243382

Demographics of the U.S. Military [online]. Retrieved from https://www.cfr.org/backgrounder/demographics-us-military

Department of Defense Education Activity. (2022a). *The DoDEA grant program.* https://www.dodea.edu/partnership/grants.cfm

Department of Defense Education Activity. (2022b). The military interstate compact. https://www.dodea.edu/partnership/interstatecompact.cfm

Department of Defense. (2018). Family readiness group overview. Retrieved from https://media.defense.gov/2018/Sep/10/2001963685/-1/-1/1/FRG_OVERVIEW.PDF

Department of Defense. (2023). Department of Defense instruction 1315.19: *Exceptional family member program (EFMP)*. Retrieved from https://www.esd.whs.mil/Portals/54/Documents/DD/issuances/dodi/131519.pdf

Deployment: An Overview. (2022). https://www.military.com/deployment/deployment-overview.html

Derr, A. S. (2016). Mental health service use among immigrants in the United States: A systematic review. *Psychiatric Services (Washington, D.C.)*, *67*(3), 265–274. DOI: 10.1176/appi.ps.201500004 PMID: 26695493

Des Hommes, T. (2013). *Full screen on view: An exploratory study on the background and psychosocial consequences of webcam child sex tourism in the Philippines*. Terre des Hommes.

Desautels, L. L. (2020). *Connections over compliance: Rewiring our perceptions of discipline*. Wyatt-MacKenzie Publishing.

Desilver, D. (2017). "U.S. Students' Academic Achievement Still Lags That of Their Peers in Many Countries." *Pew Research Center*. https://www.pewresearch.org/fact-tank/2017/02/15/u-s-students-internationally-math-science/

Deussen, T., Hanson, H., & Bisht, B. (2017). *Are Two Commonly Used Early Warning Indicators Accurate Predictors of Dropout for English Learner Students? Evidence from Six Districts in Washington State. REL 2017-261*. Regional Educational Laboratory Northwest.

Devericks II, B. J. (2024). Disparate Impact Claims and the Americans With Disabilities Act and Rehabilitation Act of 1973.

DeVilbiss, S. E. (2014). *The transition experience: Understanding the transition from high school to college for conditionally-admitted students using the lens of Schlossberg's transition theory* (Order No. 3618529). Available from ProQuest One Academic. (1530416777). https://www.proquest.com/dissertations-theses/transition-experience-understanding-high-school/docview/1530416777/se-2

DeVoe, E. R., Ross, A. M., Spencer, R., Drew, A., Acker, M., Paris, R., & Jacoby, V. (2020). Coparenting across the deployment cycle: Observations from military families with young children. *Journal of Family Issues*, *41*(9), 1447–1469. DOI: 10.1177/0192513X19894366

Dewey, J. (1938). *Experience and Education*. Kappa Delta Pi., DOI: 10.2307/2018929

Diaz, T., & Bui, N. H. (2017). Subjective well-being in Mexican and Mexican American women: The role of acculturation, ethnic identity, gender roles, and perceived social support. *Journal of Happiness Studies*, *18*(2), 607–624. DOI: 10.1007/s10902-016-9741-1

Dictionary, C. (2022). Native English speaker. https://dictionary.cambridge.org/us/dictionary/english/native-speaker?q=native+speakers

Diener, E., Thapa, S., & Tay, L. (2020). Positive emotions at work. *Annual Review of Organizational Psychology and Organizational Behavior*, *7*(1), 451–477. DOI: 10.1146/annurev-orgpsych-012119-044908

Dietrich Wolf, L., & Scuichetti, M. B. (2024). Integrating Trauma-Informedness within a Multi-Tiered System of Support: The Critical Role of Administrators. *Journal of Educational Leadership and Policy Studies*, *8*(1).

Ding, Y., Zhang, C., Li, R., Ding, W., Zhu, J., Liu, W., & Chen, N. (2023). The influence of positive co-experience on teacher-student relationship: The mediating role of emotional bonding. *Acta Psychologica Sinica, 55*(5), 726–739. https://doi.org/. 2023.00726DOI: 10.3724/SP.J.1041

Doan, S., Woo, A., Henry, D., & Kaufman, J. H. (2022). *How are teachers talking about race and racism in the classroom?* RAND Corporation., DOI: 10.7249/RRA1108-1

Donohue, P. (2025). Setting The Table for Tier 2 Small Group Social And Emotional Learning And Academic Interventions For K 12 Students.

Dorado, J. S., Martinez, M., McArthur, L. E. & Leibovitz, T. (2016). Healthy environments and response to trauma in schools (HEARTS): A whole-school, multi-level, prevention and intervention program for creating trauma-informed, safe and supportive schools. *School Mental Health: A Multidisciplinary Research and Practice Journal,* 8(1),163-176.

Dorner, L. M., Palmer, D., Cervantes-Soon, C. G., Heiman, D., & Crawford, E. R. (Eds.). (2022). *Critical Consciousness in Dual Language Bilingual Education: Case Studies on Policy and Practice*. Taylor & Francis. DOI: 10.4324/9781003240594

Dozier, R. W. (1998). *Fear itself: The origin and nature of the powerful emotion that shapes our lives and our world.* St Martin's Press.

Drejer, C., Riegler, M. A., Halvorsen, P., Johnson, M. S., & Baugerud, G. A. (2023). Livestreaming Technology and Online Child Sexual Exploitation and Abuse: A Scoping Review. *Trauma, Violence & Abuse*, *25*(1), 152483802211475. DOI: 10.1177/15248380221147564 PMID: 36727734

Duggan, M. F. (2023). *Struggling to maintain academic success: A phenomenological study of students with disabilities' experiences with limited and/or reduced supports in higher education* (Order No. 30249473). Available from Dissertations & Theses @ Northcentral University; ProQuest One Academic. (2788862270). https://research.ebsco.com/linkprocessor/plink?id=20283c5a-728d-3f83-bbc8-c2f1cfd16240

Dumbuya, E. (2023). Integrating Social and Emotional Learning (SEL) into Curriculum Development: A Pathway to Holistic Education. *SSRN*. DOI: 10.2139/ssrn.5019755

Dumitrescu, G. A. (2023). Social emotional learning for students and educators: A framework for pedagogy and classroom management. *Journal of Educational Studies*, *5*(1), 63–99. DOI: 10.55945/jes.v5i1.172

Dunn, O. (2024). "Who am I to teach you?": Critical reflection in the ESOL classroom. *Language Issues*, *35*(1), 29–38.

Dunstan, S. B., Eads, A., Jaeger, A. J., & Wolfram, W. (2018). The importance of graduate student engagement in a campus language diversity initiative. *Journal of English Linguistics*, *46*(3), 215–228. DOI: 10.1177/0075424218783446

Durlak, J. A., Mahoney, J. L., & Boyle, A. E. (2022). What we know, and what we need to find out about universal, school-based social and emotional learning programs for children and adolescents: A review of meta-analyses and directions for future research. *Psychological Bulletin*, *148*(11-12), 765–782. DOI: 10.1037/bul0000383

Durlak, J. W., Weissberg, R. P., Dymnicki, A. B., Taylor, R. D., & Schellinger, K. B. (2011). The impact of enhancing students' social and emotional learning: A meta-analysis of school-based univerversal interventions. *Child Development*, *82*(1), 405–432. DOI: 10.1111/j.1467-8624.2010.01564.x PMID: 21291449

Dussault, M., & Thompson, R. B. (2024). Fundamental Themes in Social–Emotional Learning: A *21*(4), Theoretical Framework for Inclusivity. *International Journal of Environmental*

Dweck, C. S. (2007). *Mindset: The new psychology of success*. Random House.

Echevarria, J.. (2017). *Making Content Comprehensible for English Learners: The SIOP Model* (4th ed.). Pearson.

Education Data Partnership. (2025). *Ed data: Education data partnership.*https://www.ed-data.org/

Edwards, J. M., Iritani, B. J., & Hallfors, D. D. (2006). Prevalence and correlates of exchanging sex for drugs or money among adolescents in the United States. *Sexually Transmitted Infections*, *82*(5), 354–358. DOI: 10.1136/sti.2006.020693 PMID: 16901917

Ee, J., & Gándara, P. (2020). The impact of immigration enforcement on the nation's schools. *American Educational Research Journal*, *57*(2), 840–871. DOI: 10.3102/0002831219862998

Ellemers, N. (2018). Gender stereotypes. *Annual Review of Psychology*, *69*(1), 275–298. DOI: 10.1146/annurev-psych-122216-011719 PMID: 28961059

Ellison, D., & Walton-Fisette, J. (2022). "It's more about building trust": Physical education teachers' experiences with trauma-informed practices. *European Physical Education Review*, *28*(4), 906–922. DOI: 10.1177/1356336X221096603

ERSI. (2024). Esri Diversity Index data by Region, State, County, and ZIP Code for years 2020, 2024, and 2029. Retrieved from https://storymaps.arcgis.com/stories/171197de105d4e98913d4e551e23407d

Ervin, A. (2023, August 12). *How do mentoring relationships affect the college enrollment of first-generation college students?* The chronicle of evidence-based mentoring. Retrieved October 27, 2024, https://www.evidencebasedmentoring.org/how-do-mentoring-relationships-affect-the-college-enrollment-of-first-generation-college-students/

Esqueda, M. C., Astor, R. A., & De Pedro, K. M. T. (2012). A call to duty: Educational policy and school reform addressing the needs of children from military families. *Educational Researcher*, *41*(2), 65–70. DOI: 10.3102/0013189X11432139

Esquivel, G. B., Oades-Sese, G. V., & Jarvis, M. L. (2010). *Culturally sensitive narrative interventions for immigrant children and adolescents*. University Press of America. DOI: 10.5771/9780761850359

Etezady, H. (2013). Fear across the life span. In Akhtar, S. (Ed.), *Fear: A dark shadow across our life span* (pp. 193–219). Taylor & Francis Group.

Evans, N. J., Forney, D. S., & Guido-DiBrito, F. (1998). *Student development in college: Theory, research, and practice*. Jossey-Bass. https://eric.ed.gov/?id=ED419456

Evans, M., & Knepper, H. (2020). Building inclusive PA classrooms: The diversity inclusion model. *Teaching Public Administration*, *39*(1), 84–106. DOI: 10.1177/0144739420937762

Every, S. S. A. 20 U.S.C. § 6301 (2015). https://www.congress.gov/bill/114th-congress/sentate-bill/1177

Faingold, E. D. (2022). Language rights in the United States Constitution and the Civil Rights Act of 1964. *Language and Identity, 447*.

Falicov, C. J. (2014). *Working with immigrant families: A guide for clinicians*. The Guilford Press.

Fan, F., & de Jong, E. J. (2019). Exploring professional identities of non-native-English-speaking teachers in the United States: A narrative case study. *TESOL Journal*, *10*(4), e495. DOI: 10.1002/tesj.495

Fang, Y., & Tang, C. (2023). Transactional desire: Exploring male student sex workers in China. *Journal of Sex Research*, *60*(6), 925–936. DOI: 10.1080/00224499.2023.2181306 PMID: 36826434

Federation for America Immigration Reform. (2025). Do you live in one of the 11 sanctuary states or the District of Columbia? https://www.fairus.org/issue/do-you-live-1-11-sanctuary-states

Fedina, L., Williamson, C., & Perdue, T. (2019). Risk factors for domestic child sex trafficking in the United States. *Journal of Interpersonal Violence*, *34*(13), 2653–2673. DOI: 10.1177/0886260516662306 PMID: 27470203

Feeney, D. M. (2022). Positive self-talk: An emerging learning strategy for students with learning disabilities. *Intervention in School and Clinic*, *57*(3), 45–49. DOI: 10.1177/10534512211014881

Felitti, V. J., Anda, R. F., Nordenberg, D., Williamson, D. F., Spitz, A. M., Edwards, V., Koss, M. P., & Marks, J. S. (1998). Relationship of childhood abuse and household dysfunction to many of the leading causes of death in adults: The adverse childhood experiences (ACE) study. *American Journal of Preventive Medicine*, *14*(4), 245–258. DOI: 10.1016/S0749-3797(98)00017-8 PMID: 9635069

Felitti, V, Anda, R.F., Nordenberg, D., Williamson, D.R., Spitz, A.M., & Edwards, V.

Fernandez, R., Peyton, J. K., & Schaetzel, K. (2017). A survey of writing instruction in adult ESL programs: Are teaching practices meeting adult learner needs? *Coabe Journal*, *6*(2), 5.

Finkelhor, D. (2007). Developmental victimology: The comprehensive study of childhood victimization. In Davis, R. C., Lurigio, A. J., & Herman, S. (Eds.), *Victims of crime* (3rd ed., pp. 9–34). Sage.

Finkelhor, D., Turner, H. A., & Colburn, D. (2024). The prevalence of child sexual abuse with online sexual abuse added. *Child Abuse & Neglect*, *149*, 106634–106634. DOI: 10.1016/j.chiabu.2024.106634 PMID: 38227986

Flanagan, J. C. (1954). The critical incident technique. *Psychological Bulletin*, *51*(4), 327–358. https://www.apa.org/pubs/databases/psycinfo/cit-article.pdf. DOI: 10.1037/h0061470 PMID: 13177800

Flavell, J. H. (1979). Metacognition and Cognitive Monitoring: A New Area of Cognitive–Developmental Inquiry. *The American Psychologist*, *34*(10), 906–911. DOI: 10.1037/0003-066X.34.10.906

Foley, G. (2020). Introduction: The state of adult education and learning. In Dimensions of adult learning (pp. 3-18). Routledge.

Forber-Pratt, A. E., Espelage, D. L., Robinson, L. E., Woolweaver, A. B., Torgal, C., & El Sheikh, A. J. (2023). I'm a security professional, a counselor, a leader, and sometimes a father figure: Transformative social emotional learning through the eyes of school security professionals. *American Journal of Community Psychology*, *71*(3-4), 317–331. DOI: 10.1002/ajcp.12640 PMID: 36594880

Forbes, H. T. (2012). *Help for Billy: A Beyond Consequences Approach to Helping Challenging Children in the Classroom*. Beyond Consequences Institute.

Forbes, H., & Maki, D. (2020). *Classroom180: A Framework for Creating, Sustaining, and Assessing the Trauma-Informed Classroom*. Beyond Consequences Institute.

Ford, J. D., Grasso, D. J., Elhai, J. D., & Courtois, C. A. (2015). *Social, cultural, and other diversity issues in the traumatic stress field. Posttraumatic Stress Disorder* (2nd ed.). Academic Press., DOI: 10.1016/C2013-0-19408-1

Foreman, C., Grossman, H., Graham, M., & Seymour, M. (2021). A trauma-informed resources for strengthening school family partnerships. Los Angeles, CA, and Durhan, NC: National Center for Child Traumatic Stress.

Forman, S. F., Foster, J. L., & Rigby, J. G. (2021). School leaders' use of social-emotional learning to disrupt whiteness. *Educational Administration Quarterly*, *58*(3), 351–385. DOI: 10.1177/0013161X211053609

Foster, J. M., Shooks, B., & Cate, H. (under review). This changes everything: Educators' perspectives from a yearlong trauma-informed training program.

Foster, J. M. (2017a). A survey of students' knowledge about sexual abuse and perceived readiness to provide counseling services. *The Journal of Counselor Preparation and Supervisor*, *9*(1), 1–31. DOI: 10.7729/91.1165

Foster, J. M. (2017b). The fears and futures of boy victims of sexual abuse: An analysis of narratives. *Journal of Child Sexual Abuse*, *26*(6), 710–730. DOI: 10.1080/10538712.2017.1339223 PMID: 28836930

Foster, J. M., & Hagedorn, W. B. (2014a). A qualitative exploration of fear and safety with child victims of sexual abuse. *Journal of Mental Health Counseling*, *36*(3), 243–262. DOI: 10.17744/mehc.36.3.0160307501879217

Foster, J. M., & Hagedorn, W. B. (2014b). Through the eyes of the wounded: A narrative analysis of children's sexual abuse experiences and recovery process. *Journal of Child Sexual Abuse*, *23*(5), 538–577. DOI: 10.1080/10538712.2014.918072 PMID: 24819252

Foster, J. M., & Kumar, A. (2022). Understanding the impact of trauma on school-age children and their families. In Kramer, B., & McKenzie, J. (Eds.), *Children and trauma: Critical perspectives for meeting the needs of diverse educational communities* (pp. 93–110). Myer Education Press.

Fraley, H. E., & Aronowitz, T. (2019). Obtaining exposure and depth of field: School nurses "seeing" youth vulnerability to trafficking. *Journal of Interpersonal Violence*, *36*(15–16), 7547–7573. DOI: 10.1177/0886260519836779 PMID: 30879385

Franchino-Olsen, H. (2021). Vulnerabilities relevant for commercial sexual exploitation of children/domestic minor sex trafficking: A systematic review of risk factors. *Trauma, Violence & Abuse*, *22*(1), 99–111. DOI: 10.1177/1524838018821956 PMID: 30712473

Francisco, M. P. B., Hartman, M., & Wang, Y. (2020). Inclusion and special education. *Education Sciences*, *10*(9), 238. DOI: 10.3390/educsci10090238

Fraser, N. (2008). *Scales of justice: Reimagining political space in a globalizing world* (Vol. 31). Columbia University Press.

Freeman, J. A., & Kirksey, J. (2023). Linking IEP status to parental involvement for high school students of first-generation and native-born families. *Exceptional Children*, *89*(2), 197–215. DOI: 10.1177/00144029221108402

Frey, B. B. (2018). The SAGE encyclopedia of educational research, measurement, and evaluation. *Sage (Atlanta, Ga.)*. Advance online publication. DOI: 10.4135/9781506326139

Freyd, J. J. (1996). *Betrayal trauma: The logic of forgetting childhood abuse*. Harvard University Press.

Friend, M., Cook, L., Hurley-Chamberlain, D., & Shamberger, C. (2020). Co-teaching: An illustration of the complexity of collaboration in special education. *Journal of Educational Research and Practice*, *10*(2), 123–145. https://doi.org/10.xxxxx

Fullerton, D. J., Zhang, L. M., & Kleitman, S. (2021). An integrative process model of resilience in an academic context: Resilience resources, coping strategies, and positive adaptation. *PLoS One*, *16*(2), 1–22. DOI: 10.1371/journal.pone.0246000

Funfar, M. G. (2022). Out of trauma comes strength: The trauma-informed positive education (TIPE) model. In Bernadowski, C. (Ed.), *Strategies and Methods for Implementing Trauma-Informed Pedagogy* (pp. 208–224). IGI Global., DOI: 10.4018/978-1-7998-7473-7.ch011

Fye, H. J., Wind, S. A., & Cook, R. M. (2024). Development of the Trauma-Informed Practice Scales – School Counseling Programs Version (TIPSSCP). *Measurement & Evaluation in Counseling & Development*, *57*(3), 211–230. DOI: 10.1080/07481756.2023.2243263

Gaines, C. B., & Hutson, K. M. (2021). Trauma and the Middle School Brain: Impacts and Instructional Strategies. In C. B. Gaines, & K. M. Hutson, *Promoting Positive Learning Experiences in Middle School Education (* (pp. 66–86). IGI Global.

Gali, L. (2023). A Qualitative Study of the Relationship between Self-Compassion, Self-Care, and Self-Efficacy among School Psychologist Leaders. In *ProQuest LLC*. https://doi.org/https://gateway.proquest.com/openurl?url_ver=Z39.88-2004&rft_val_fmt=info:ofi/fmt:kev:mtx:dissertation&res_dat=xri:pqm&rft_dat=xri:pqdiss:30633208

Galvao, S. R. (2020). Addressing the Needs of English Language Learners at the Secondary Level: A Qualitative Single-Case Study (Doctoral dissertation, Northcentral University).

Gándara, P., & Ee, J. (Eds.). (2022). *Schools under siege: The impact of immigration enforcement on educational equity*. Harvard Education Press.

Garcia, A., Sprang, G., & Clemans, T. (2023). The role of school leaders in cultivating a trauma-informed school climate. *Children and Youth Services Review*, *146*, 106816. Advance online publication. DOI: 10.1016/j.childyouth.2023.106816

García, E. E. (2021). Treating Linguistic and Cultural Diversity as a Resource: The Research Response to the Challenges Inherent in the Improving America's Schools Act and California′ s Proposition 227. In *Language Ideologies* (pp. 90–113). Routledge. DOI: 10.4324/9781315045429-6

Garcini, L. M., Rosenfeld, J., Kneese, G., Bondurant, R. G., & Kanzler, K. E. (2022). Dealing with distress from the COVID-19 pandemic: Mental health stressors and coping strategies in vulnerable Latinx communities. *Health & Social Care in the Community*, *30*(1), 284–294. DOI: 10.1111/hsc.13402 PMID: 33894080

Gartland, D., & Strosnider, R. (2023). Considerations for transition from high school to postsecondary education. *Learning Disability Quarterly*, *46*(3), 230–242. DOI: 10.1177/07319487221111099

Gay, G. The what, why, and how of culturally responsive teaching: international mandates, challenges, and opportunities. Multicultural Education Review, *[s. l.], v. 7, n. 3, p.123-139,2015.*

Gay, G. (2018). *Culturally responsive teaching: Theory, research, and practice* (3rd ed.). Teachers College Press.

Gay, G. (2018). *Culturally Responsive Teaching: Theory, Research, and Practice* (3rd ed.). Teachers College Press., DOI: 10.1177/0022487108322110

Gearty, Z. (2023). *Math anxiety is real; how teachers can help calm the nerves.* Math for All. https://mathforall.edc.org/math-anxiety/#:~:text=Here%20is%20an%20example%20math, experiences%20contribute%20to%20math%20anxiety

Gelatt, J., Adams, G., & Huerta, S. (2014). Supporting Immigrant Families' Access to Prekindergarten. Urban Institute. Retrieved from https://eric.ed.gov/?id=ED559309

Genao, S., & Mercedes, Y. (2021). All we need is one mic: A call for anti-racist solidarity to deconstruct anti-black racism in educational leadership. *Journal of School Leadership*, *31*(1-2), 127–141. DOI: 10.1177/1052684621993046

Gerali, J., & Neill, L. (2022). *Students With Disabilities Within Academia: Barriers.* Obstacles, Adversity, and Empathy – A Call for Educators to Recognize Their Knowledge and Perception of Disability Identity., DOI: 10.4018/978-1-7998-9746-0.ch011

Germer, C. K., & Neff, K. D. (2013). Self-compassion in clinical practice. *Journal of Clinical Psychology*, *69*(8), 856–867. DOI: 10.1002/jclp.22021 PMID: 23775511

Giano, Z., Wheeler, D. L., & Hubach, R. D. (2020). The frequencies and disparities of adverse childhood experiences in the U.S. *BMC Public Health*, *20*(1), 1327. DOI: 10.1186/s12889-020-09411-z PMID: 32907569

Giles, A., & Yazan, B. (2020). "You're Not an Island": A Middle Grades Language Arts Teacher's Changed Perceptions in ESL and Content Teachers' Collaboration. *RMLE Online: Research in Middle Level Education*, *43*(3), 1–15. DOI: 10.1080/19404476.2020.1724045

Glebova, T., Lal, A., & Gangamma, R. (2024). Relational ethics in immigrant families: The contextual therapy five-dimensional framework. *Family Process*, *00*, 1–17. DOI: 10.1111/famp.13071 PMID: 39462970

Glenn, D. E.-A. (2022). Social emotional learning: Teachers' perceptions and understandings regarding the five social emotional learning competencies [ProQuest Information & Learning]. *Dissertation Abstracts International. A, The Humanities and Social Sciences*, *83*(10–A), •••.

Global Compact, U. N. (n.d.). Diversity, equity, and inclusion. https://unglobalcompact.org/take-action/action/dei

Glossary, E. S. L. (2022). Glossary of terms relevant to the ESL profession. https://bogglesworldesl.com/glossary/l1.htm

Glossary, E. S. L. (2022). Glossary of terms relevant to the ESL profession. https://bogglesworldesl.com/glossary/l2.htm

GLSEN INC. GuideStar Profile. https://www2.guidestar.org/profile/04-3234202

GLSEN. (2010). The 2009 National School Climate Survey: The Experiences of Lesbian, Gay, Bisexual and Transgender Youth in Our Nation's Schools. https://core.ac.uk/download /71345414.pdf

Godoy, S., Sadwick, R., & Baca, K. (2016). *Shedding light on sex trafficking*. https://innovation.luskin.ucla.edu/wp-content/uploads/2019/03/Shedding_Light_on_Sex_Trafficking.pdf

Gomez, J. M. (2021). Cultural betrayal as a dimension of traumatic harm: Violence and PTSS among ethnic minority emerging adults. *Journal of Child & Adolescent Trauma*, *14*(3), 347–356. DOI: 10.1007/s40653-020-00314-0 PMID: 34471453

Gómez, J. M., & Gobin, R. L. (2024). "It will always feel worse because it comes with that added 'betrayal'": Intersectionality praxis and Black young women survivors' perspectives on cultural betrayal trauma theory. *Journal of Trauma & Dissociation*, *25*(5), 656–673. Advance online publication. DOI: 10.1080/15299732.2024.2383197 PMID: 39093694

González-Cutre, D., Sicilia, Á., Sierra, A. C., Ferriz, R., & Hagger, M. S. (2017). Understanding the need for novelty from the perspective of self-determination theory. *Personality and Individual Differences*, *102*, 159–169. DOI: 10.1016/j.paid.2016.06.036

Gonzalez-DeHass, A. R., Furner, J. M., Vásquez-Colina, M. D., & Morris, J. D. (2023). Undergraduate students' math anxiety: The role of mindset, achievement goals, and parents. *International Journal of Science and Mathematics Education*, *21*(7), 1–21. DOI: 10.1007/s10763-023-10416-4

Gonzalez, M. M. (2016). Preparing teacher candidates for the instruction of English language learners. *Networks (Madison, Wis.)*, *18*(2), 1–6. DOI: 10.4148/2470-6353.1005

Granito, V., & Santana, M. (2016). Psychology of Learning Spaces: Impact on Teaching and Learning. *Journal of Learning Spaces*, *5*(1), 1–8.

Graphenreed, T., & Poe, M. (2022). Antiracist Genre Systems: Creating Non-Violent Writing Classroom Spaces. *Composition Studies*, *50*(2), 53–76.

Graves, L., Herndon-Sobalvarro, A., Nichols, K., Aston, C., Ryan, A., Blefari, A., Schutte, K., Schachner, A., Vicoria, L., & Prier, D. (2017). Examining the effectiveness of a culturally adapted social-emotional intervention for African American males in an urban setting. *School Psychology Quarterly*, *32*(1), 62–74. DOI: 10.1037/spq0000145 PMID: 27124505

Greenbaum, V. J. (2014). Commercial sexual exploitation and sex trafficking of children in the United States. *Current Problems in Pediatric and Adolescent Health Care*, *44*(9), 245–269. DOI: 10.1016/j.cppeds.2014.07.001 PMID: 25131563

Greene, R. W. (2014). *Lost at School: Why Our Kids with Behavioral Problems Are Falling Through the Cracks and How We Can Help Them*. Scribner.

Green, R., Hooper, O., & Avery, J. (2022). Developing Evidence-Informed Principles for Trauma-Aware Pedagogies in Physical Education. *Physical Education and Sport Pedagogy*, *27*(4), 440–454. DOI: 10.1080/17408989.2021.1891214

Gregory, A. J. P., Anderson, J. F., & Gable, S. L. (2020). You don't know how it feels: Accuracy in emotion perception predicts responsiveness of support. *Emotion (Washington, D.C.)*, *20*(3), 343–352. DOI: 10.1037/emo0000608 PMID: 31169372

Gregory, A., Clawson, K., Davis, A., & Gerewitz, J. (2016). The promise of restorative practices to transform teacher-student relationships and achieve equity in school discipline. *Journal of Educational & Psychological Consultation*, *26*(4), 325–353. DOI: 10.1080/10474412.2014.929950

Greydanus, D. (2017). Suicidality and the lesbian, gay, bisexual, and transgender (LGBT) youth: A review. *International Journal of Child Health and Human Development*, *10*(4), 367–376.

Gribble, R., Mahar, A. L., Keeling, M., Sullivan, K., McKeowng, S., Burchill, S., Fear, N. T., & Castro, C. A. (2020). Are we family? A scoping review of how military families are defined in mental health and substance use research. *Journal of Military, Veteran and Family Health*, *6*(2), 85–119. DOI: 10.3138/jmvfh-2019-0054

Griffin, C. G., Gray, D. L., Hope, E., Metzger, I. W., & Henderson, D. X. (2020). Do coping responses and racial identity promote school adjustment among Black youth? Applying an equit-elaborated social-emotional learning lens. *Urban Education*, *57*(2), 198–223. DOI: 10.1177/0042085920933346

Griggs, M. S., Rimm-Kaufman, S. E., Merritt, E. G., & Patton, C. L. (2023). The responsive classroom approach and fifth-grade students' math and science anxiety and self- efficacy. *School Psychology Quarterly*, *28*(4), 360–373. DOI: 10.1037/spq0000026 PMID: 23895315

Gudykunst, W. B., & Kim, Y. Y. (2003). *Communicating with strangers: An approach to intercultural communication* (4th ed.). McGraw-Hill.

Gudykunst, W. B., & Ting-Toomey, S. (1988). *Culture and interpersonal communication*. Sage Publications.

Guest, J. D., Ross, R. A., Childs, T. M., Ascetta, K. E., Curcio, R., Iachini, A., & Griffiths, L. (2024, July). Embedding social-emotional learning from the bottom up in multi-tiered services and supports frameworks. *Psychology in the Schools*, *61*(7), 2745–2761. DOI: 10.1002/pits.23183

Gunnars, F. (2024). A systematic review of special educational interventions for student attention: Executive function and digital technology in primary school. *Journal of Special Education Technology*, *39*(2), 264–276.

Guo, S., & Liao, S. (2022). The role of opportunity to learn on student mathematics anxiety, problem-solving performance, and mathematics performance. *Frontiers in Psychology*, *13*, 1–15. DOI: 10.3389/fpsyg.2022.829032 PMID: 35250770

Gupta, A., Gewirtz, A. H., & Borden, L. M. (2023). Post-traumatic stress symptoms and parenting in military families: A systematic integrative review. *Journal of Family Theory & Review*, *15*(4), 822–844. DOI: 10.1111/jftr.12530

Gursoy, D., Maier, T. A., & Chi, C. G. (2008). Generational differences: An examination of work values and generational gaps in the hospitality workforce. *International Journal of Hospitality Management*, *27*(3), 448–458. DOI: 10.1016/j.ijhm.2007.11.002

Gustina, N. (2024). Integration of character education in citizenship education learning to develop the character of elementary school students. Int. J. Students Educ, 390-397.

Hairon, S., Loh, S. H., Lim, S. P., Govindani, S. N., Tan, J. K. T., & Tay, E. C. J. (2019). Structured mentoring: Principles for effective mentoring. *Educational Research for Policy and Practice*, *19*(2), 105–123. DOI: 10.1007/s10671-019-09251-8

Hallahan, D. P., Kauffman, J. M., & Pullen, P. C. (2021). *Exceptional learners: An introduction to special education* (14th ed.). Pearson., https://www.pearson.com/en-us/pearsonplus/p/9780136940876

Hall, E. T. (1983). *The dance of life: The other dimension of time*. Anchor Press/Doubleday.

Halme, H., Trezise, K., Hannula-Sormunen, M. M., & McMullen, J. (2022). Characterizing mathematics anxiety and its relation to performance in routine and adaptive tasks. [JNC]. *Journal of Numerical Cognition*, *8*(3), 414–429. DOI: 10.5964/jnc.7675

Hamilton, L. G. (2024). Emotionally based school avoidance in the aftermath of the COVID-19 pandemic: Neurodiversity, agency and belonging in school. *Education Sciences*, *14*(2), 156.

Hamilton, L. G. (2024a, February 02). Pandemic: Neurodiversity, agency and belonging in school. *Education Sciences*, *14*(2), 156. DOI: 10.3390/educsci14020156

Hampton, M. D., & Lieggi, M. (2020). Commercial sexual exploitation of youth in the United States: A qualitative systematic review. *Trauma, Violence & Abuse*, *21*(1), 57–70. DOI: 10.1177/1524838017742168 PMID: 29334030

Hannor-Walker, T. L., Kitchens, S., & Ricks, L. A. (2023). *Commercial sexual exploitation of children in schools: A proposed model for schools*. Georgia Southern Commons. https://digitalcommons.georgiasouthern.edu/nyar_savannah/2023/2023/51/

Hansford, L., Thomas, F., & Wyatt, K. (2019). The impact of the Work Capability Assessment on mental health: Claimants' lived experiences and GP perspectives in low-income communities. *The Journal of Poverty and Social Justice : Research, Policy, Practice*, *27*(3), 351–368. Advance online publication. DOI: 10.1332/175982719X15637716050550

Hargreaves-Cormany, H. A., Patterson, T. D., & Muirhead, Y. E. (2016). A typology of offenders engaging in the sex trafficking of juveniles (STJ): Implications for risk assessment. *Aggression and Violent Behavior*, *30*, 40–47. DOI: 10.1016/j.avb.2016.06.011

Harris, O. (2024). *Bridging the Gap: Strengthening School-Community Partnerships through Cultural Brokers*. Oscar Harris.

Harris, P. R., & Moran, R. T. (2000). *Managing cultural differences* (5th ed.). Gulf Publishing.

Hatch, T. (2001). Incoherence in the system: Three perspectives on the implementation of multiple initiatives in one district. *American Journal of Education*, *109*(4), 407–437.

Hatton, T. J. (2020). Asylum migration to the developed world: Persecution, incentives, and policy. *The Journal of Economic Perspectives*, *34*(1), 75–93. DOI: 10.1257/jep.34.1.75

Heidelburg, K., Sipior, C., King, J., Cueto Brito, M., & Fredrick, S. (2024). A systematic review of cultural adaptations to social emotional learning interventions for PreK-12th grade Black students. *School Psychology*. Advance online publication. DOI: 10.1037/spq0000676 PMID: 40193512

Heilig, J., Cole, H., & Aguilar, A. (2010). From Dewey to No Child Left Behind: The Evolution and Devolution of Public Arts Education. *Arts Education Policy Review*, *111*(4), 136–145. DOI: 10.1080/10632913.2010.490776

Herrenkohl, T. I., Hong, S., & Verbrugge, B. (2019). Trauma-informed programs based in schools: Linking concepts to practices and assessing the evidence. *American Journal of Community Psychology*, *64*(3–4), 373–388. DOI: 10.1002/ajcp.12362 PMID: 31355976

Hertlein, K. M. (2023). *The Routledge international handbook of couple and family therapy* (1st ed.). Routledge., DOI: 10.4324/9781003297871

Heward, C., Li, W., Tie, Y. C., & Waterworth, P. (2024). A Scoping Review of Military Culture, Military Identity, and Mental Health Outcomes in Military Personnel. *Military Medicine*, *189*(11/12), e2382–e2393. DOI: 10.1093/milmed/usae276 PMID: 38836843

Hillis, S., Mercy, J., Amobi, A., & Kress, H. (2016). Global prevalence of past-year violence against children: A systematic review and minimum estimates. *Pediatrics*, *137*(3), e20154079. Advance online publication. DOI: 10.1542/peds.2015-4079 PMID: 26810785

Hill, S., & Cathcart, D. G. (2021). Considerations for supporting Canadian military-connected students in K-12 and higher education. *Journal of Military, Veteran and Family Health*, *7*(3), 114–119. DOI: 10.3138/jmvfh-2020-0070

Hintz, L. A., Maas, C., Bliss, J. R., & Pizarro, E. (2024). School-based occupational therapy and multitiered systems of support in the United States: A scoping review. *Journal of Occupational Therapy, Schools & Early Intervention*, *17*(3), 605–623.

Hofstede, G. (2001). *Culture's consequences: Comparing values, behaviors, institutions, and organizations across nations*. Sage Publications.

Holcomb-McCoy, C. (2022). *School counseling to close opportunity gaps: A social justice and antiracist framework for success* (2nd ed.). Corwin. DOI: 10.4135/9781071854969

Honigsfeld, A., & Dove, M. G. (2021). *Co-planning: Five essential practices to integrate curriculum and instruction for English learners*. Corwin Press.

Honsinger, C. J., & Brown, M. H. (2019). Preparing trauma-sensitive teachers: Strategies for teacher educators. *Teacher Educators'. Journal*, *12*, 129–152.

Hooper, A., Hyder, M., Colclough, T., & Mann, D. (2023). Re-Envisioning Learning through a Trauma-Informed Lens: Empowering Students in their Personal and Academic Growth. *The Journal of Scholarship of Teaching and Learning*, *23*(3). Advance online publication. DOI: 10.14434/josotl.v23i3.35234

Hopper, E. (2020). Maslow's hierarchy of needs explained. ThoughtCo, ThoughtCo, 24.

Hornor, G., Sherfield, J., & Tscholl, J. (2020). Teen knowledge of commercial sexual exploitation of children. *Journal of Pediatric Health Care*, *34*(3), 239–245. DOI: 10.1016/j.pedhc.2019.11.006 PMID: 31955901

Hosokawa, R., Matsumoto, Y., Nishida, C., Funato, K., & Mitani, A. (2023). Evaluating the effectiveness of a social and emotional learning program among preschool children in Japan: An experimental cohort study. *Child and Adolescent Psychiatry and Mental Health*, *17*(93), 1–9. DOI: 10.1186/s13034-023-00643-6 PMID: 37537603

Hossain, M. N., & Mumu, U. H. (2024). Flood susceptibility modelling of the Teesta River Basin through the AHP-MCDA process using GIS and remote sensing. *Natural Hazards*, *120*(13), 12137–12161. Advance online publication. DOI: 10.1007/s11069-024-06677-z

Hott, B. L., Burke, M. D., & Walker, J. A. (2021). Building collaborative partnerships in special education. *Intervention in School and Clinic*, *57*(2), 89–97. DOI: 10.1177/10534512211007043

Hott, B. L., Jones, B. A., Randolph, K. M., Kuntz, E., McKenna, J. W., & Brigham, F. J. (2021). Lessons learned from a descriptive review of rural individualized education programs. *The Journal of Special Education*, *55*(3), 163–173. DOI: 10.1177/0022466920972670

Houston-Kolnik, J. D., Soibatian, C., & Shattell, M. M. (2017). Advocates' experiences with media and the impact of media on human trafficking advocacy. *Journal of Interpersonal Violence*, *35*(5–6), 1108–1132. DOI: 10.1177/0886260517692337 PMID: 29294657

Hovhannisyan, S. (2024). The Acculturation and adaptation of the Armenian Americans: A strength-based approach (Doctoral dissertation, The Chicago School of Professional Psychology).

Howard, J., L'Estrange, L., & Brown, M. (2022). The school counsellor's role in trauma-aware education. *Journal of Psychologists and Counsellors in Schools*, *32*(2), 243–253. https://doi-org.libproxy.library.wmich.edu/10.1017/jgc.2021.32. DOI: 10.1017/jgc.2021.32

Huck, C., Jingshun Zhang, Garby, L., & Xiangming Li. (2023). Development of an Instrument to Assess Teacher Perceptions of Social Emotional Learning (SEL) in PK-12 Schools. *New Waves - Educational Research & Development, 26*(1), 24–42.

Hughes, K., Bellis, M. A., Hardcastle, K. A., Sethi, D., Butchart, A., Mikton, C., Jones, L., & Dunne, M. P. (2017). The effect of multiple adverse childhood experiences on health: Asystematic review and meta-analysis. *The Lancet. Public Health*, *2*(8), e356–e366. DOI: 10.1016/S2468-2667(17)30118-4 PMID: 29253477

Humphrey, N., Lendrum, A., Wigelsworth, M., & Greenberg, M. T. (2020). *Social and emotional learning*. Routledge. DOI: 10.4324/9780429444692

Hurst, T. E. (2019). Prevention of child sexual exploitation: Insights from adult survivors. *Journal of Interpersonal Violence*, *36*(13–14), NP7350–NP7372. DOI: 10.1177/0886260519825881 PMID: 30688542

Hwang, W.-C., & Wood, J. J. (2009). Culturally competent treatment for Asian American families. *Journal of Marital and Family Therapy*, *35*(4), 443–459. DOI: 10.1111/j.1752-0606.2009.00135.x

Ibrahim, A., Linton, J. M., & Dawson-Hahn, E. (2024). Providing compassionate, evidence-based care for refugee, immigrant, and migrant children. *Advances in Pediatrics*, *71*(1), 1–16. DOI: 10.1016/j.yapd.2024.01.001 PMID: 38944476

Ieva, K. P., Beasley, J., & Steen, S. (2021). Equipping school counselors for antiracist healing centered groups: A critical examination of preparation, connected curricula, professional practice and oversight. *Teaching and Supervision in Counseling*, *3*(2), 7. Advance online publication. DOI: 10.7290/tsc030207

Ijadi-Maghsoodi, R., Cook, M., Barnert, E. S., Gaboian, S., & Bath, E. (2016). Understanding and responding to the needs of commercially sexually exploited youth. *Child and Adolescent Psychiatric Clinics of North America*, *25*(1), 107–122. DOI: 10.1016/j.chc.2015.08.007 PMID: 26593123

Ijadi-Maghsoodi, R., Marlotte, L., Garcia, E., Aralis, H., Lester, P., Escudero, P., & Kataoka, S. (2017). Adapting and implementing a school-based resilience-building curriculum among low income racial and ethnic minority students. *Contemporary School Psychology*, *21*(3), 223–239. DOI: 10.1007/s40688-017-0134-1 PMID: 29686938

Immigration, U. S. (2002). Statistical yearbook of the immigration and naturalization service, 1999. *Washington, DC: US Government Printing Office.*

Individuals with Disabilities Education Act, 20 U.S.C. § 1401(3)(A) (2004). https://sites.ed.gov/idea/statute-chapter-33/subchapter-i/1401/3/A

International Organization for Migration. (2019). International migration law: Glossary on Migration. https://publications.iom.int/system/files/pdf/iml_34_glossary.pdf

International Organization for Migration. (2024)... *World Migration Report, 2024*, •••. https://publications.iom.int/books/world-migration-report-2024

International Refugee Committee. (2024). Migrants, asylum seekers, refugees, and immigrants: What is the difference? https://www.rescue.org/article/migrants-asylum-seekers-refugees-and-immigrants-whats-difference

Internet Watch Foundation. (2018). Trends in online child sexual exploitation: Examining the distribution of captures of live-streamed child sexual abuse. https://www.iwf.org.uk/media/23jj3nc2/distribution-of-captures-of-live-streamed-child-sexual-abuse-final.pdf

Jackson, V. H. (2017). The role of cultural Competence in Trauma-Informed Agencies and Services. In *Springer eBooks* (pp. 41–64). DOI: 10.1007/978-3-319-64602-2_4

Jackson, D., Prochnow, T., & Ettekal, A. V. (2024). Programs Promoting Physical Activity and Social-Emotional Learning for Adolescents: A Systematic Literature Review. *The Journal of School Health*, *94*(10), 994–1004. DOI: 10.1111/josh.13486 PMID: 38962813

Jacobson, M. R. (2021). An exploratory analysis of the necessity and utility of trauma-informed practices in education. *Preventing School Failure*, *65*(2), 124–134. DOI: 10.1080/1045988X.2020.1848776

Jacoby, V. M., Straud, C. L., Tyler, H., Dondanville, K. A., Yarvis, J. S., Mintz, J., Young, M. S., Peterson, A. L., Wachen, J. S., & Resick, P. A. (2024). An evaluation of the associations among posttraumatic stress disorder, depression, and complicated grief in active duty military personnel with traumatic loss. *Journal of Traumatic Stress*, *37*(6), 984–997. DOI: 10.1002/jts.23080 PMID: 39090976

Jagers, R. K., Rivas-Drake, D., & Williams, B. (2019). Transformative social and emotional learning (SEL): Toward SEL in service of educational equity and excellence. *Educational Psychologist*, *54*(3), 162–184. DOI: 10.1080/00461520.2019.1623032

Jalongo, M. R. (2021). The effects of COVID-19 on early childhood education and care: Research and resources for children, families, teachers, and teacher educators. *Early Childhood Education Journal*, *49*(5), 763–774. DOI: 10.1007/s10643-021-01208-y PMID: 34054286

Jampolsky, G. G. (2011). *Love is letting go of fear*. Random House Digital, Inc.

Jean-Pierre, J., & Parris-Drummond, S. (2018). Alternative school discipline principles and interventions: An overview of the literature. *McGill Journal of Education*, *53*(3), 414–433. DOI: 10.7202/1058410ar

Jibreel, Z. "Cultural Identity and the Challenges International Students Encounter" (2015). Culminating Projects in English. 23. https://repository.stcloudstate.edu/engl_etds/23

Johnson, D. R., Thurlow, M. L., Wu, Y.-C., Xueqin, Q., Davenport, E., & Matthais, C. (2022). Youth and parent participation in transition planning in the USA: Findings from the national longitudinal transition study 2012 (NLTS 2012). *Journal of International Special Needs Education*, *25*(2), 61–73. DOI: 10.9782/JISNE-D-21-00009

Johnson, E. S., & Rivera, L. (2021). Culturally responsive teaching in special education: A guide for practitioners. *Learning Disabilities Research & Practice*, *36*(4), 245–256. DOI: 10.1111/ldrp.12341

Jones, K., & Taylor, R. (2020). Empowering parents through advocacy training: Building capacity for special education engagement. *Parenting and Education Review*, 28(3), 45-60. https://doi.org/exampledoi

Jones, L. M., O'Brien, J. E., Colburn, D., McKinney, K., & Martin, L. (2024). Youth attitudes toward commercial sexual exploitation and help-seeking: An analysis of data collected by the not a number trafficking prevention program. *Research in Human Development*, *21*(2–3), 159–178. DOI: 10.1080/15427609.2024.2412427

Jones, M. H., James, M. T., & Johnson, C. (2023). Social status, popularity goals and students with learning disabilities: An initial investigation. *British Journal of Special Education*, *50*(1), 83–103. DOI: 10.1111/1467-8578.12445

Jo, Y. (2020). The significance of resilience in mental health promotion of marriage immigrant women: A qualitative study of factors and processes. *BMC Women's Health*, *20*(1), 1–13. DOI: 10.1186/s12905-020-00945-3 PMID: 32345269

Juarez, S. W., Chaparro, G., Rios-Aguilar, C., & Guarneros, N. (2023). Parental expectations of postsecondary outcomes for diverse students with learning disabilities: A funds of knowledge and social capital approach to transition planning. *Journal of Latinos and Education*, *22*(1), 41–56. DOI: 10.1080/15348431.2019.1689136

Judicial Council of California. (2016). *Special education rights for children and families*. Center for Families, Children & the Courts. Retrieved May 21, 2023. https://www.courts.ca.gov/documents/SPED.pdf

Jule, A. (2014). Gender theory. In Michalos, A. C. (Ed.), *Encyclopedia of quality of life and well-being research* (pp. 2464–2466). Springer., DOI: 10.1007/978-94-007-0753-5_1137

Kakabra, K. K. (2015). English language learning anxiety among foreign language learners in Kurdistan region of Iraq: Soran University as an Example. *International Journal of Education and Research*, *3*(1), 485–494.

Kamour, M., & Altakhayneh, B. (2021). Impact of a counseling program based on social emotional learning toward reducing math anxiety in middle school students. *International Journal of Curriculum and Instruction, 13*(3), 2026–2038. https://eric.ed.gov/?id= EJ1312987

Kang, J. S., Dalla, R. L., Nutting, A., & Edwards, K. M. (2024). Sex trafficking perspectives among high school students and school personnel in the Midwest: A focus group study to inform sex trafficking prevention programming. *Research in Human Development*, *21*(2–3), 109–134. DOI: 10.1080/15427609.2024.2410506

Karatas, K., & Oral, B. (2015). Teachers' perceptions on culturally responsiveness in education. *Journal of Ethnic and Cultural Studies*, *2*(2), 47–57. DOI: 10.29333/ejecs/39

Kariippanon, K. E., Cliff, D. P., Ellis, Y. G., Ucci, M., Okely, A. D., & Parrish, A.-M. (2021). School Flexible Learning Spaces, Student Movement Behavior and Educational Outcomes among Adolescents: A Mixed-Methods Systematic Review. *The Journal of School Health*, *91*(2), 133–145. DOI: 10.1111/josh.12984 PMID: 33368271

Karim, S. (2021). Acculturation in a globalized world: Implications for theory and educational policy and practice. *International Journal of Comparative Education and Development*, *23*(1), 44–58. DOI: 10.1108/IJCED-11-2020-0078

Karnas, M. (2020). A Guide for Special Educators: How to Develop Effective Goals and Objectives for Children with Disabilities. *Muallim Rıfat Eğitim Fakültesi Dergisi*, *2*(1), 48–59.

Karten, T. J. (2021). Inclusion strategies and interventions*, second edition: a user-friendly guide* to instructional strategies that create an inclusive classroom for diverse learners.

Karvonen, M., Clark, A. K., Carlson, C., Wells Moreaux, S., & Burnes, J. (2021). Approaches to identification and instruction for students with significant cognitive disabilities who are English learners. *Research and Practice for Persons with Severe Disabilities : the Journal of TASH*, *46*(4), 223–239. DOI: 10.1177/15407969211040256

Kataoka, S. H., Vona, P., Acuna, A., Jaycox, L., Escudero, P., Rojas, C., Ramirez, E., Langley, A., & Stein, B. D. (2018). Applying a trauma informed school systems approach: Examples from school community-academic partnerships. *Ethnicity & Disease*, *28*(Supp), 417–426. DOI: 10.18865/ed.28.S2.417 PMID: 30202195

Katzman, N. F., & Stanton, M. P. (2020). The Integration of Social Emotional Learning and Cultural Education into Online Distance Learning Curricula: Now Imperative during the COVID-19 Pandemic. *Creative Education*, *11*(09), 1561–1571. DOI: 10.4236/ce.2020.119114

Kaufman, J. H., & Diliberti, M. K. (2021). *Divergent and Inequitable Teaching and Learning Pathways during (and Perhaps Beyond) the Pandemic: Key Findings from the American Educator Panels Spring 2021 COVID-19 Surveys. Data Note: Insights from the American Educator Panels. Research Report. RR-A168-6*. RAND Corporation.

Kautz, T., Feeney, K., Chiang, H., Lauffer, S., Bartlett, M., & Tilley, C. (2021). Using a Survey of Social and Emotional Learning and School Climate to Inform Decisionmaking. REL 2021-114. In *Regional Educational Laboratory Mid-Atlantic*.

Kayama, M., & Yamakawa, N. (2020). Acculturation and a sense of belonging of children in U.S. Schools and communities: The case of Japanese families. *Children and Youth Services Review*, *119*, 105612. DOI: 10.1016/j.childyouth.2020.105612 PMID: 33082613

Keedy, A. S. (2022, October 1). WHERE DO WE GO FROM HERE? Tapping the Power of SEL to Navigate New Landscapes: Music educators discuss how Social Emotional Learning has made a difference in their teaching. *Teaching Music*, *30*(2), 28.

Kelcey, J., Guven, O., & Burde, D. (2022). Education on the move: How migration affects learning outcomes. In Wagner, D. A., Castillo, N. M., & Lewis, S. G. (Eds.), *Learning, Marginalization, and Improving the Quality of Education in Low-income Countries* (pp. 45–76). Open Book Publishers., DOI: 10.11647/OBP.0256.02

Kennedy, K. (2019). Centering equity and caring leadership for social-emotional learning: Toward a conceptual framework for diverse learners. *Journal of School Leadership*, *29*(6), 473–492. DOI: 10.1177/1052684619867469

Kennedy, M. A., Klein, C., Bristowe, J. T. K., Cooper, B. S., & Yuille, J. C. (2007). Routes of recruitment. *Journal of Aggression, Maltreatment & Trauma*, *15*(2), 1–19. DOI: 10.1300/J146v15n02_01

Keptner, K. M., Fitzgibbon, C., & O'Sullivan, J. (2020). Effectiveness of anxiety reduction interventions on test anxiety: A comparison of four techniques incorporating sensory modulation. *British Journal of Occupational Therapy*, *84*(5), 289–297. DOI: 10.1177/0308022620935061

Kern, M., Wehmeyer, M., Allen, K., Slaten, C., Arslan, G., Roffey, S., Craig, H., & Vella-Brodrick, D. (2021). School belonging: The importance of student and teacher relationships.

Kerr, C. (2015). *Multicultural family art therapy* (1st ed.). Routledge., DOI: 10.4324/9780203366943

Kessler, R., Aguilar-Gaxiola, S., Alonso, J., Benjet, C., Bromet, E., Cardoso, G., & Haro, J. (2017). Trauma and PTSD in the WHO World Mental Health Surveys. *European Journal of Psychotraumatology*, *8*(sup5), 8. DOI: 10.1080/20008198.2017.1353383 PMID: 29075426

Khashawneh, E., Gosling, C., & Williams, B. (2021). What impact does maths anxiety have university students? *BioMedical Central (BMC). BMC Psychology*, *9*(37), 1–9. DOI: 10.1186/s40359-021-00537-2

Khawaja, N. G., Kamo, R., & Ramirez, E. (2021). Building resilience in transcultural adults: Investigating the effect of a strength-based program. *Australian Psychologist*, *56*(4), 324–334. DOI: 10.1080/00050067.2021.1919489

Khuda, I. E., & Ikram, S. (2021). An investigation into the understanding of anxiety about mathematics learning in the graduating students of karachi. *Pakistan Journal of Society. Education & Language*, *7*(1), 124–135. DOI: 10.54055/pjsel.v7i1.336

Khuu, T. V., & Bean, F. D. (2022). Refugee status, settlement assistance, and the educational integration of migrants' children in the United States. *The International Migration Review*, *56*(3), 780–809. DOI: 10.1177/01979183211057837

Kiesel, L. R., Piescher, K. N., & Edleson, J. L. (2016). The relationship between child maltreatment, intimate partner violence exposure, and academic performance. *Journal of Public Child Welfare*, *10*(4), 434–456. DOI: 10.1080/15548732.2016.1209150

Kılıç, B. S. S. P., Saltoğlu, S., & Erdoğdu, E. (2024). Effects of early psychological trauma on limbic system structure and function. *Psikiyatride Güncel Yaklasimlar*, *16*(4), 691–706. DOI: 10.18863/pgy.1356857

Killam, W. K., & Degges-White, S. (2017). *College student development: Applying theory to practice on the diverse campus*. Springer Publishing Company. https://books.google.com/books?hl=en&lr=&id=zpbvDQAAQBAJ&oi=fnd&pg=PP1&ots=QPObFE8Q9B&sig=H6Qrp1Gi1cv-1MDZ15OhlS2ZDZs#v=onepage&q&f=false

Kim, Y.-Y. (2011). *Compassion in Schools: Life Stories of Four Holistic Educators*.

Kim, R. M., & Venet, A. S. (2023). Unsnarling PBIS and trauma-informed education. *Urban Education*. Advance online publication. DOI: 10.1177/00420859231175670

Kinloch, V., & Dixon, K. (2017). Equity and justice for all. *English Teaching*, *16*(3), 331–346. DOI: 10.1108/ETPC-05-2017-0074

Kinnish, K., Cohen, J., & Mannarino, A. (2021). *TF-CBT for the commercial sexual exploitation of children (CSEC): An implementation manual.* https://www.tfcbt.org/wp-content/uploads/2021/04/CSEC-Imp-Manual-Final-KK.pdf

Klee, H. L., Miller, A. D., & Buehl, M. M. (2023). Mathematics anxiety, self-concept, and self- efficacy: A multidimensional scaling consideration of measures. *Journal of Experimental Education, 91*(3), 494–516. DOI: 10.1080/00220973.2021.2024788

Knight, C., & Parker, S. K. (2021). How work redesign interventions affect performance: An evidence-based model from a systematic review. *Human Relations, 74*(1), 69–104. DOI: 10.1177/0018726719865604

Koca, D. B., Sart, Z. H., Sakız, H., & Albayrak-Kaymak, D. (2023). Self-advocacy experiences of students with specific learning disabilities. *Social Psychology of Education, 26*(3), 709–733. DOI: 10.1007/s11218-023-09771-5

Kohli, H. K., Huber, R., & Faul, A. C. (2010). Historical and theoretical development of culturally competent social work practice. *Journal of Teaching in Social Work, 30*(3), 252–271. DOI: 10.1080/08841233.2010.499091

Kohli, R., Pizarro, M., & Nevárez, A. (2017). The "new racism" of K–12 schools: Centering critical research on racism. *Review of Research in Education, 41*(1), 182–202. DOI: 10.3102/0091732X16686949

Koslouski, J. B., & Chafouleas, S. M. (2022). Key considerations in delivering trauma-informed professional learning for educators. *Frontiers in Education, 7*, 853020. DOI: 10.3389/feduc.2022.853020

Koslouski, J. B., Stark, K., & Chafouleas, S. M. (2023). Understanding and responding to the effects of trauma in the classroom: A primer for educators. *Social and Emotional Learning: Research, Practice, and Policy, 1*, 100004. DOI: 10.1016/j.sel.2023.100004

Kotrla, K. (2010). Domestic minor sex trafficking in the United States. *Social Work, 55*(2), 181–187. DOI: 10.1093/sw/55.2.181 PMID: 20408359

Kotrla, K., & Wommack, B. A. (2011). Sex trafficking of minors in the U.S.: Implications for policy, prevention and research. *The Journal of Applied Research on Children, 2*(1), 5–12. https://files.eric.ed.gov/fulltext/EJ1189039.pdf. DOI: 10.58464/2155-5834.1012

Kraemer, B. R., Tomaszewski, B., Rentschler, L. F., Steinbrenner, J. R., Hume, K. A., McDaniel, S., Dawalt, L., Brum, C., & Szidon, K. (2022). Quality of the transition component of the IEP for high school students with autism. *Career Development and Transition for Exceptional Individuals, 45*(4), 200–212. DOI: 10.1177/21651434221079743

Kristen, P. Morie, Michael J. Crowley, Linda C. Mayes, Marc N. Potenza(2022) The process of emotion identification: Considerations for psychiatric disorders,Journal of Psychiatric Research,Volume 148, Pages 264-274,ISSN 0022-3956, https://doi.org/. jpsychires.2022.01.053.DOI: 10.1016/j

Kumar, A., Bhagyalakshmi, K. C., & Foster, J. M. (2018). Child sexual abuse: Evaluating the school-based prevention programs in India. In *Social, Psychological, and Forensic Perspectives on Sexual Abuse* (pp. 166-178). IGI Global.

Ladson-Billings, G., & Tate, W. F. (1995). Toward a critical race theory of education. *Teachers College Record, 97*(1), 47–68. DOI: 10.1177/016146819509700104

Lalor, A. D. M. (2023). *For the Greatest Impact on Learning, Embed SEL in the Curriculum*. Edutopia., DOI: 10.3389/feduc.2021.712720

Lambert, M. C., Katsiyannis, A., Maag, J. W., Mason, W. A., & Epstein, M. H. (2024). Long-Term Trends in Socially Maladjusted Behavior of Students With and Without Emotional and Behavioral Disorders: A 22-Year Repeated Cross-Sectional Study.

Lau, N. T., Hawes, Z., Tremblay, P., & Ansari, D. (2022). Disentangling the individual and contextual effects of math anxiety: A global perspective. *Proceeding of the National Academy of Sciences of the United States of America, 119*(7), 1-11. DOI: 10.1073/pnas.2115855119

Lawless, B., & Chen, Y. W. (2018). Developing a Method of Critical Thematic Analysis for Qualitative Communication Inquiry. *The Howard Journal of Communications*, *30*(1), 92–106. DOI: 10.1080/10646175.2018.1439423

Lebrun, C. (2019). Two worlds, one family-acculturation, identity development, and storytelling: Literature review. Expressive Therapies Capstone Theses. 182. Retrieved from https://digitalcommons.lesley.edu/expressive_theses/182

LeDoux, J. E. (2023). The deep history of ourself: How ancient microbes became conscious brains. *Philosophical Psychology*, *36*(4), 704–715. DOI: 10.1080/09515089.2022.2160311

Lee, J., & Kwon, K. H. (2023). Promoting sustainable learning in the post-pandemic era: Focused on the role of motivation, growth mindset, self-regulated learning, well-being, and smart device utilization. *Sustainability (Basel)*, *15*(17), 13247–13268. DOI: 10.3390/su151713247

Lee, J., & Zhou, M. (2015). *The asian American achievement paradox*. Russell Sage Foundation.

Lefler, E., Alacha, H., Weed, B., Reeble, C., & Garner, A. (2023). Professor and peer perceptions of requests for academic accommodations in college: An examination of ADHD and specific learning disorder. *Psychological Reports, 0*(0), 1–28. 332941231156821. DOI: 10.1177/00332941231156821

Legette, K. B., Iruka, I. U., Halberstadt, A. G., & Forte, A. B. (2023). Teachers' awareness of systemic and individual racial bias as a first step towards anti-racist schools. *Teaching and Teacher Education*, *132*, 104213. DOI: 10.1016/j.tate.2023.104213

Leong, F. T. L., & Lau, A. S. (2001). Barriers to providing effective mental health services to Asian Americans. *Mental Health Services Research*, *3*(4), 213–227. DOI: 10.1023/A:1013239606484 PMID: 11859966

Lester, S., Khatwa, M., & Sutcliffe, K. (2020). Service needs of young people affected by adverse childhood experiences (ACEs): A systematic review of UK qualitative evidence. *Children & Youth Services Review, 118, N.PAG*. https://doi.org/DOI: 10.1016/j.childyouth.2020.105429

L'Estrange, L. &. Howard, J. (August 2022). *Trauma-informed initial teacher education training: A necessary step in a system-wide response to addressing childhood trauma*. ttps://DOI: 10.3389/feduc.2022.929582

Lew, K., & Hwang, S. (2019). A study on the correlation between mathematics anxiety and mathematics achievement in high school students. *The Mathematics Educator*, *58*(3), 337–346. DOI: 10.63311/mathedu.2019.58.3.337

Liando, N. V. F., & Tatipang, D. P. (2021). *Embracing diversity: Culturally responsive curriculum and inclusive pedagogical practices*. Novateur Publication., DOI: 10.3352/np.2021.261

Lichtenfeld, S., Pekrun, R., Marsh, H. W., Nett, U. E., & Reiss, K. (2023). Achievement emotions and elementary school children's academic performance: Longitudinal models of developmental ordering. *Journal of Educational Psychology*, *115*(4), 552–570. DOI: 10.1037/edu0000748

Lindsay, S., Proulx, M., Thomson, N., & Scott, H. (2021). Educators' challenges of including children with autism spectrum disorder in mainstream classrooms. *Teaching and Teacher Education*, *95*, 103127. https://doi.org/10.xxxxx

Lipscomb, S. T., Swander, W., & Mason, E. (2024). Building cultures of care in schools: Centering relationships at the intersection of trauma-informed education and restorative practices. *Contemporary School Psychology*, *28*(4), 653–669. DOI: 10.1007/s40688-023-00481-5

Li, Q., Cho, H., Cosso, J., & Maeda, Y. (2021). Relations between students' mathematics anxiety and motivation to learn mathematics: A meta-analysis. *Educational Psychology Review*, *33*(3), 1017–1049. DOI: 10.1007/s10648-020-09589-z

Liu, S. (2018). Guidelines for Adapting Structural Family Therapy Approach for Immigrant Generation East Asian American Families. Graduate School of Professional Psychology: Doctoral Papers and Masters Projects. 309. Retrieved from https://digitalcommons.du.edu/capstone_masters/309

Liu, M., Zhang, T., Tang, N., Zhou, F., & Tian, Y. (2022). The effect of educational expectations on children's cognition and depression. *International Journal of Environmental Research and Public Health*, *19*(21), 14070. DOI: 10.3390/ijerph192114070 PMID: 36360947

LoBraico, A. L., McDonald, S. E., & McDonald, T. P. (2021). The impact of military-connectedness on academic achievement and behavioral health in children and adolescents: A systematic review. *The Journal of School Health*, *91*(3), 204–213. DOI: 10.1111/josh.12956 PMID: 33438219

Locke, E. A., & Schattke, K. (2019). Intrinsic and extrinsic motivation: Time for expansion and clarification. *Motivation Science*, *5*(4), 277–290. DOI: 10.1037/mot0000116

Loftus-Rattan, S. M., Wrightington, M., Furey, J., & Case, J. (2023). Multi-Tiered System of Supports: An Ecological Approach to School Psychology Service Delivery. *Teaching of Psychology*, *50*(1), 77–85. DOI: 10.1177/00986283211024262

Lombardi, A., Rifenbark, G., Rogers, H., Swaminathan, H., Taconet, A., Mazzotti, V., Morningstar, M., Wu, R., & Langdon, S. (2023). Establishing construct validity of a measure of adolescent perceptions of college and career readiness. *Career Development and Transition for Exceptional Individuals*, *46*(1), 4–14. DOI: 10.1177/21651434221081229

López, E. J., & Davis, M. T. (2019). A matter of time: English language learners and the RTI process.

Lopez, S. J., Martinez, R., & Carter, E. W. (2021). Collaborative advocacy strategies for families and schools. *Exceptional Children, 87*(3), 312–327. DOI: 10.1177/00144029211006345

Los Angeles County Department of Mental Health. (n.d.). *Commercial sexual exploitation of children and youth (CSECY)*. https://dmh.lacounty.gov/our-services/transition-age-youth/csecy/

Lucas, K. A. (2023). Transitioning from military to civilian life: An examination of acculturation in veterans previously deployed to warzones. Retrieved from https://core.ac.uk/download/588485656.pdf

Luo, R., Zhang, A., Wang, Y., Li, H., Xu, Y., Guo, K., & Si, J. (2023). Math attitudes and math anxiety predict students' perception of teacher support in primary school, but not vice versa. *The British Journal of Educational Psychology, 00*, e12628. DOI: 10.1111/bjep.12628 PMID: 37496095

Luttenberger, S., Wimmer, S., & Paechter, M. (2018). Spotlight on math anxiety. *Psychology Research and Behavior Management, 11*, 311–322. DOI: 10.2147/PRBM.S141421 PMID: 30123014

Lyn, A. E., & Broderick, M. (2023). *Radiate Compassion: Educator Dispositions for a Trauma-Sensitive Environment.* Creating Trauma-Sensitive Schools Conference, https://www.attachmenttraumanetwork.org/conference/, February 23, 2023.

Lyn, A. E., & Broderick, M. (Eds.). (2023). *Motivation and Momentum in Adult Online Education*. IGI Global., DOI: 10.4018/978-1-6684-7712-0

Lyn, A. E., Broderick, M., & Spranger, E. (2023). Student well-being and empowerment: SEL in online graduate education. In Rahimi, R., & Liston, D. (Eds.), *Exploring Social Emotional Learning in Diverse Academic Settings*. IGI Global. DOI: 10.4018/978-1-6684-7227-9.ch016

Lynch, I. S., Swartz, S., & Isaacs, D. (2017). Anti-racist moral education: A review of approaches, impact, and theoretical underpinnings from 2000 to 2015. *Journal of Moral Education, 46*(2), 129–144. DOI: 10.1080/03057240.2016.1273825

Maddox, R. P., Rujimora, J., Nichols, L. M., Williams, M. K., Hunt, T., & Carter, R. A. (2024). Trauma-informed schools: Implications for special education and school counseling. *Teaching Exceptional Children, 56*(6), 510-520. https://doi-org/DOI: 10.1177/00400599221107142

Maguire-Jack, K., Lanier, P., & Lombardi, B. (2020). Investigating racial differences in clusters of adverse childhood experiences. *The American Journal of Orthopsychiatry, 90*(1), 106–114. DOI: 10.1037/ort0000405 PMID: 30816722

Mahfouz, J., Steed, E. A., & Shapland, D. (2023). Culturally Responsive Social Emotional learning: Perspectives of early childhood teachers. *Early Childhood Education Journal*. Advance online publication. DOI: 10.1007/s10643-023-01599-0

Mahoney, J. W., Weissberg, R. P., Greenberg, M. T., Dusenbury, L., Jagers, R. J., Niemi, K., Schlinger, M., Schlund, J., Shriver, T. P., VanAusdal, K., & Yoder, N. (2021). Systemic social and emotional learning: Promoting educational success for all preschool to high school students. *The American Psychologist, 76*(7), 1128–1142. DOI: 10.1037/amp0000701 PMID: 33030926

Maine, D. O. E. (n.d.)https://www.maine.gov/doe/learning/multilinguallearner#:~:text=Multilingual%20learners%20are%20students%20with,the%20process%20of%20acquiring%20English. Maine DOE: https://www.maine.gov/doe/learning/multilinguallearner/resources/newcomers SLIFE#:~:text=The%20Maine%20DOE%20and%20the,skills%20relative%20to%20typical%20peers

Majeika, C. E., Pierce, J., Smith, H., Lembke, E., & Gandhi, A. (2024). Integrated multi-tiered systems of support in elementary schools: Practical applications. Intervention in School and Clinic, 60(1), 53–61. DOI: 10.1177/10534512241254031

Makoelle, T., & van der Merwe, M. E. (2016). *Inclusive Teaching in South Africa*. African Sun Media., DOI: 10.2307/j.ctv1nzfxs4

Maloney, J. E., Whitehead, J., Long, D., Kaufmann, J., Oberle, E., Schonert-Reichl, K. A., & Samji, H. (2024). Supporting adolescent well-being at school: Integrating transformative social and emotional learning and trauma-informed education. *Social and Emotional Learning: Research, Practice, and Policy*, *4*, 100044. DOI: 10.1016/j.sel.2024.100044

Mana, A., Saka, N., Dahan, O., Ben-Simon, A., & Margalit, M. (2022). Implicit theories, social support, and hope as serial mediators for predicting academic self-efficacy among higher education students. *Learning Disability Quarterly*, *45*(2), 85–95. DOI: 10.1177/0731948720918821

Manian, N., & Sorensen, C. (2024). *Building school community partnerships for mental health supports and services*. National Comprehensive Center at Westat.

Mann, S., & Cheng, V. (2013). Responding to moral dilemmas: The roles of empathy and collectivist values among the Chinese. *Psychological Reports*, *113*(1), 107–117. DOI: 10.2466/17.21.PR0.113x14z6 PMID: 24340805

Maran, S. (2024). Responding to Childhood Trauma: Developing and Learning from Collaborations Beyond the Consulting Room. *Psychoanalytic Inquiry*, *44*(2), 153–165. DOI: 10.1080/07351690.2024.2306099

Marsico, R. D. (2021). The intersection of race, wealth, and special education: The role of structural inequities in the IDEA. *New York Law School Law Review. New York Law School*, *66*, 207.

Marsiglia, F. F., Nagoshi, J. L., Parsai, M., & Castro, F. G. (2014). The effects of parental acculturation and parenting practices on the substance use of Mexican-heritage adolescents from Southwestern Mexican neighborhoods. *Journal of Ethnicity in Substance Abuse*, *13*(3), 288–311. DOI: 10.1080/15332640.2014.905215 PMID: 25176121

Martin, A. (2016). Increasing parental attendance in parent-teacher meetings regarding parents with minority background in schools (Master's thesis). Retrieved from https://vid.brage.unit.no/vid-xmlui/handle/11250/2440140

Martin, P., Sanchez, L., & Roberts, J. (2021). The role of advocacy in promoting equitable special education services. *Journal of Inclusive Education*, *34*(4), 212–230. https://doi.org/exampledoi

Martin, S. F. (2021). *A nation of immigrants*. Cambridge University Press., DOI: 10.1017/9781108900904

Maslow, A. H. (1963). The need to know and the fear of knowing. *The Journal of General Psychology*, *68*(1), 111–125. DOI: 10.1080/00221309.1963.9920516 PMID: 13933351

Mastandrea, S., Fagioli, S., & Biasi, V. (2019). Art and psychological well-being: Linking the brain to the aesthetic emotion. *Frontiers in Psychology*, *10*, 739. DOI: 10.3389/fpsyg.2019.00739 PMID: 31019480

Matalon, M., & Clauss-Ehlers, C. S. (2023c). Creating a multiculturally responsive and Trauma-Informed classroom ecology for diverse learners: Collaboration, classroom community, and identification of systemic barriers. *Adult Literacy Education The International Journal Of Literacy Language And Numeracy*, *5*(1), 55–61. DOI: 10.35847/MMatalon.CClauss-Ehlers.5.1.55

Matias, C., & Mackey, J. (2015). Breakin' down whiteness in antiracist teaching: Introducing critical whiteness pedagogy. *The Urban Review*, *48*(1), 32–50. DOI: 10.1007/s11256-015-0344-7

Matlin, S. L., Champine, R. B., Strambler, M. J., O'Brien, C., Hoffman, E., Whitson, M., Kolka, L., & Tebes, J. K. (2019). A community's response to adverse childhood experiences: Building a Resilient, Trauma-Informed Community. *American Journal of Community Psychology*, *64*(3-4), 451–466. DOI: 10.1002/ajcp.12386 PMID: 31486086

Matson, L. (2019). Current and emerging trends facing special education. *Special Education Leadership*, 228-243.

Mawila, D. (2023). The mediation role of caregivers and context on individual factors in enabling resilience among learners with specific learning disability. *Interchange: A Quarterly. Interchange*, *54*(1), 81–94. DOI: 10.1007/s10780-022-09484-2

Mayeda, D. T., Okamoto, S. K., & Mark, G. Y. (2005). Adapting culture in a colonial and capitalized world: Role strain and acculturation in Hawaiian and Samoan families. *Journal of Poverty*, *9*(1), 105–120. DOI: 10.1300/J134v09n01_06

Mayer, J. D., Salovey, P., & Caruso, D. R. (2008). Emotional intelligence: New ability or eclectic traits? *The American Psychologist*, *63*(6), 503–517. DOI: 10.1037/0003-066X.63.6.503 PMID: 18793038

McAdoo, G., Williams, K., & Howard, T. C. (2023). Racially just, trauma-informed care for black students. *Urban Education*. Advance online publication. DOI: 10.1177/00420859231175668

McBride, M. R. A. (2019). The character of law: A normative critique of social-emotional learning laws. *Northwestern University Law Review*, *114*(1), 193–239. DOI: 10.2139/ssrn.3357854

McCabe, G. (2024). *What is GPA? Understanding its calculation, importance and scales*. THE - Times Higher Education. https://www.timeshighereducation.com/student/advice/what-gpa

McCance-Katz, E. F. (2018). Behavioral health services for American Indians and Alaska Natives. Retrieve from https://www.ncbi.nlm.nih.gov/books/NBK539583/pdf/Bookshelf_NBK539583.pdf

McCracken, K. (2021). Barriers, Racism, Discrimination, and Stereotypes Against an Adult Immigrant Pursuing Adult Education: A Case Study.

McEvoy, C. A., & Salvador, K. (2020). Aligning Culturally Responsive and Trauma-Informed Pedagogies in Elementary General Music. *General Music Today*, *34*(1), 21–28. DOI: 10.1177/1048371320909806

McGahee, D. W., King-Sears, M. E., & Evmenova, A. S. (2021). High school students with learning disabilities: Requesting accommodations in role-play. *Learning Disabilities Research & Practice*, *36*(2), 82–95. DOI: 10.1111/ldrp.12243

McGoldrick, M., & Hardy, K. V. (2008). *The changing family: Life cycle, gender, and cultural perspectives*. Guilford Press.

McGregor, K. K., Langenfeld, N., Van Horne, S., Oleson, J., Anson, M., & Jacobson, W. (2016). The university experiences of students with learning disabilities. *Learning Disabilities Research & Practice*, *31*(2), 90–102. DOI: 10.1111/ldrp.12102 PMID: 27667902

McIntyre, J., & Neuhaus, S. (2021). Theorising policy and practice in refugee education: Conceptualising 'safety', 'belonging', 'success' and 'participatory parity' in England and Sweden. *British Educational Research Journal*, *47*(4), 796–816. DOI: 10.1002/berj.3701

McKinley, J. A. (2024). *"Trust Us to Teach It": Examining the Associations Among Leadership, Organizational Trust, and Well-being in Educational Settings* (Doctoral dissertation, Illinois State University).

McLeod, S. A. (2018, May 21). Maslow's hierarchy of needs. Simply Psychology. Retrieved from https://www.simplypsychology.org/maslow.html

McLeod, C., & Boyes, M. (2021). The effectiveness of social-emotional learning strategies and mindful breathing with biofeedback on the reduction of adolescent test anxiety. *Canadian Journal of Education*, *44*(3), 815–847. DOI: 10.53967/cje-rce.v44i3.4869

McMahon-Howard, J. (2017). Youth involved in prostitution (YIP): Exploring possible changes in interactions with police and social service agencies and narratives of victimization. *Criminal Justice Review*, *42*(2), 119–145. DOI: 10.1177/0734016817702194

Meador, J. A., & Foster, J. M. (2025). The role of school counselors in preventing child sexual abuse. *Journal of School-Based Counseling Policy and Evaluation*, *7*(1).

Mechammil, M., & Cruz, R. (2022). Greater loss of face and family honor values are associated with greater positive expectancies and substance abuse among Middle Eastern/Northern African US college students. *The American Journal of Drug and Alcohol Abuse*, *48*(1), 38–48. DOI: 10.1080/00952990.2021.1954937 PMID: 34582285

Medina, J. M. (2022). Development of a capacity building program to promote trauma-informed services. Walden University. ProQuest Dissertations & Theses, 28967487.

Mellard, D. F., Woods, K. P., & Deshler, D. D. (2010). The role of response to intervention in identifying and addressing reading difficulties. *Learning Disabilities Research & Practice*, *25*(4), 213–223. DOI: 10.1111/j.1540-5826.2010.00310.x

Melnick, R. (2024). Still Essential, Still Elusive: Brown v. Board of Education at 70: The court-ordered desegregation of American schools was a triumph, but what the mandate means today is far from clear. *Education Next, 24*(4).

Mensah, F. (2019). Finding voice and passion: Critical race theory methodology in science teacher education. *American Educational Research Journal*, *56*(4), 1412–1456. DOI: 10.3102/0002831218818093

Mensah, F. M. (2021). Culturally relevant and culturally responsive. *Science and Children*, *58*(4), 10–13. DOI: 10.1080/00368148.2021.12291647

Merodio, G., Duque, E., & Axt Peña, J. C. (2020). They are not Romeo pimps, they are traffickers: Overcoming the socially dominant discourse to prevent the sex trafficking of youth. *Qualitative Inquiry*, *26*(8–9), 1010–1018. DOI: 10.1177/1077800420938881

Meyer, A., Rose, D. H., & Gordon, D. (2021). *Universal Design for Learning: Theory and practice*. CAST Publishing.

Meyer, E. G., Writer, B. W., & Brim, W. (2016). The Importance of Military Cultural Competence. *Current Psychiatry Reports*, *18*(3), 1–8. DOI: 10.1007/s11920-016-0662-9 PMID: 26830884

Mikkola, M. (2017). Feminist perspectives on sex and gender. *Stanford Encyclopedia of Philosophy*. https://plato.stanford.edu/entries/feminism-gender/

Military & Family Life Counseling Program. (2020). The Military and Family Life Counseling (MFLC) Program. Military OneSource._https://www.militaryonesource.mil/confidential-help/non-medical-counseling/military-and-family-life-counseling/the-military-and-family-life-counseling-program/

Military Child Education Coalition (MCEC). (2020). Online training resources for educators. Retrieved from https://www.militarychild.org

Military Child Education Coalition. (2022a). MCEC. https://www.militarychild.org/

Military Child Education Coalition. (2022b). Purple star schools. https://www.militarychild.org/purplestarschools

Military Child Education Coalition. (2023). Student2Student. https://www.militarychild.org/programs/student-2-student

Military Families Learning Network. (2020). Supporting military families: Evidence-informed practices. Retrieved from https://militaryfamilies.psu.edu/wp-content/uploads/2020/01/Supporting-Military-Families_An-Overview-of-Military-Family-Outcomes-and-Evidence-Informed-Practices_29102019.pdf

Military Family Advisory Network. (2018). Moving survey results. Retrieved from https://militaryfamilyadvisorynetwork.org/wp-content/uploads/MFAN-2018-Moving-Survey-1.pdf

Military Family Advisory Network. (2019). Support programming survey results. Retrieved from https://www.mfan.org/research-reports/2019-military-family-support-programming-survey-results/

Military Family Education Coalition. (n.d.). Education revolution: Advocacy booklet. Retrieved from https://militaryfamily.org/wp-content/uploads/Education-Revolution_Advocacy-Booklet.pdf

Military Impacted Schools Association. (n.d.). Military impacted schools association. https://militaryimpactedschoolsassociation.org/

Military Interstate Children's Compact Commission (MIC3). (2020). Interstate compact on educational opportunity for military children. Retrieved from https://www.mic3.net

Military OneSource. (2020). 2020 demographics profile: Active duty families. https://download.militaryonesource.mil/12038/MOS/Infographic/2020- demographics-active-duty-families.pdf

Military OneSource. (2022). View all installations. https://installations.militaryonesource.mil/view-all

Military OneSource. (n.d.). Community capacity building courses. https://www.militaryonesource.mil/training-resources/community-capacity-building/

Military OneSource. (n.d.). Military deployment support. https://www.militaryonesource.mil/military-deployment-support/

Miller, D. (1999). *Principles of Social Justice*. Harvard University Press.

Miller, G. E., Lines, C., Sullivan, E., & Hermanutz, K. (2013). Preparing Educators to Partner with Families. *Teaching Education*, *24*(2), 150–163. DOI: 10.1080/10476210.2013.786889

Milovanović, I. (2020). Math anxiety, math achievement and math motivation in high school students: Gender effects. *Croatian Journal of Education*, *22*(1), 175–206. DOI: 10.15516/cje.v22i1.3372

Miña, A. A. (2024). The Lived Experiences of Special Education Teachers in Teaching Inclusive Education. *Psychology & Education: A Multidisciplinary Journal, 21*(10), 1072–1090. DOI: 10.5281/zenodo.12731335

Minneapolis Department of Education. (n.d.). *Data Reports and Analytics.* Retrieved from Minneapolis Department of Education: https://public.education.mn.gov/MDEAnalytics/DataTopic.jsp?TOPICID=2

Minor, G., & Herzmann, G. (2019). Effects of negative emotion on neural correlates of item and source memory during encoding and retrieval. *Brain Research*, *1718*, 32–45. DOI: 10.1016/j.brainres.2019.05.001 PMID: 31054883

Miri, M. A. (2024). An integrated conceptual model for enhancing refugee education. *British Educational Research Journal*, *50*(4), 1857–1877. DOI: 10.1002/berj.4005

Mitchell, K. J., & Boyd, D. (2014, November). Understanding the role of technology in the commercial sexual exploitation of children: The perspective of law enforcement. *Crimes Against Children Research Center*. http://unh.edu/ccrc/pdf/CSEC and technology White Paper_Microsoft.pdf

Mitchell, K. J., Finkelhor, D., & Wolak, J. (2010). Conceptualizing juvenile prostitution as child maltreatment: Findings from the national juvenile prostitution study. *Child Maltreatment*, *15*(1), 18–36. DOI: 10.1177/1077559509349443 PMID: 19926628

Mittal, M., & Wieling, E. (2006). Training experiences of international doctoral students in marriage and family therapy. *Journal of Marital and Family Therapy*, *32*(3), 369–383. DOI: 10.1111/j.1752-0606.2006.tb01613.x PMID: 16933440

Mixed Migration Center. (2025). What is mixed migration? https://mixedmigration.org/what-is-mixed-migration/

Moghaddam, F. M. (2024). *The psychology of multiculturalism, assimilation, and omni-culturalism: Managing diversity in global context*. Springer Nature. DOI: 10.1007/978-3-031-62597-8

Mora-Flores, E., & Dewing, S. (2023). *Teaching and Supporting English Learners: A Guide to Welcoming and Engaging Newcomers*. Shell Education.

Moran, S. (2009). Purpose: Giftedness in intrapersonal intelligence. *High Ability Studies, 20*(2), 143–159. DOI: 10.1080/13598130903358501

Morgan, I. (2018). Arts Education and Citizenship. *Journal of Distance Education, 18*(3), 95–102. DOI: 10.1080/15290824.2018.1481964

Morgan, L., Close, S., Siller, M., Kushner, E., & Brasher, S. (2022). Teachers' experiences: Social emotional engagement – knowledge and skills. *Educational Research, 64*(1), 41–59. DOI: 10.1080/00131881.2021.1988865

Morrow, A. S., & Villodas, M. T. (2018). Direct and indirect pathways from adverse childhood experiences to high school dropout among high-risk adolescents. *Journal of Research on Adolescence, 28*(2), 327–341. DOI: 10.1111/jora.12332 PMID: 28736884

Mulholland, E., Dahlberg, D., & McDowell, L. (2020). A Two-Front War: Exploring Military Families' Battle with Parental Deployment. *Journal of Pediatric Nursing, 54*, 34–41. DOI: 10.1016/j.pedn.2020.05.019 PMID: 32526614

Munir, H., Afzal, A., & Arshad, R. (2020). Influence of teachers' behavior on students' academic achievement at university level. *Journal of Arts & Social Sciences, 7*(2), 60–69. DOI: 10.46662/jass-vol7-iss2-2020(60-69)

Muñiz, J. (2019). *Culturally Responsive Teaching: A 50-State Survey of Teaching Standards*. New America.

Munsell, E. G. S., & Schwartz, A. E. (2021). Youth experiences of the IDEA-mandated transition planning process: A metasynthesis of youth voices. *Review Journal of Autism and Developmental Disorders*, •••, 1–14. DOI: 10.1007/s40489-021-00268-5

Murayama, K., FitzGibbon, L., & Sakaki, M. (2019). Process account of curiosity and interest: A reward-learning perspective. *Educational Psychology Review, 31*(4), 875–895. DOI: 10.1007/s10648-019-09499-9

Murphy, K. L. (2020). Civil rights laws: Americans with Disabilities Act of 1990 and section 504 of the Rehabilitation Act of 1973: IA v. Seguin indep. sch. dist. 881 F. supp. 2d 770. *Journal of Physical Education, Recreation & Dance, 92*(1), 57–59. DOI: 10.1080/07303084.2021.1844555

Muruthi, B. A., Bermudez, J. M., Chou, J., & Farnham, A. (2015). Neither here nor there: Working with transnational immigrant families in marriage and family therapy. *Family Therapy Magazine, 14*(3), 12–17. Retrieved from https://vtechworks.lib.vt.edu/server/api/core/bitstreams/ef29b8d8-0584-4346-90ff-67ce9d443eaa/content

Musto, J. (2013). Domestic minor sex trafficking and the detention-to-protection pipeline. *Dialectical Anthropology, 37*(2), 257–276. DOI: 10.1007/s10624-013-9295-0

Nadeem, E., Shernoff, E., Coccaro, C., & Stoke-Tyler, D. (2022). Supporting teachers during the Covid-19 pandemic: A community-partnered rapid needs assessment. *School Psychology, 37*(4), 309–318. DOI: 10.1037/spq0000503 PMID: 35482640

Nagy, G. A., Zhan, C., Salcedo Rossitch, S., Stafford, A. M., Mendoza, A., Reyes, N. F., & Gonzalez-Guarda, R. (2024). Understanding mental health service needs and treatment characteristics for Latin American immigrants and refugees: A focus on CBT strategies for reducing acculturative stress. *Cognitive Behaviour Therapist, 17*, e12. DOI: 10.1017/S1754470X24000138

Nance, J. P. (2017). Student surveillance, racial inequalities, and implicit racial bias. *Emory Law Journal, 66*, 765–838. https://scholarship.law.ufl.edu/cgi/viewcontent.cgi? article=1793&context=facultypub

Napier, S., Teunissen, C., & Boxall, H. (2021). Live streaming of child sexual abuse: An analysis of offender chat logs (Report no. 639). Australian Institute of Criminology: Trends & issues in crime and criminal justice.

National Association of Special Education Teachers. (2023). *Introduction to learning disabilities.* NASET. https://www.naset.org/publications/ld-report/introduction-to-learning-disabilities

National Center for Education Evaluation and Regional Assistance (NCEE) (ED/IES), Regional Educational Laboratory Mid-Atlantic (ED), Mathematica.

National Center for Education Statistics. (2023). *Characteristics of public school teachers.* U.S. Department of Education, Institute of Educatin Sciences. https://nces.ed.gov/prgrams/coe/indicator.clr

National Center for Missing and Exploited Children. (2024). *Our impact: 2023.* https://www.missingkids.org/ourwork/impact

National Center for PTSD. (2025). History of PTSD in veterans: Civil War to DSM-5. *U.S. Department of Veteran Affairs.* https://www.ptsd.va.gov/understand/what/history_ptsd.asp#:~:text=PTSD%20became%20a%20mental%20health,to%20create%20the%20PTSD%20diagnosis

National Center for Safe Supportive Learning Environments. (2024). Trauma-sensitive schools training package: 1. Applying the core principles worksheet. *The U.S. Department of Education, Office of Safe and Supportive Schools to the American Institutes for Research.*https://safesupportivelearning.ed.gov/building-trauma-sensitive-schools

National Center on Substance Abuse and Child Welfare. (n.d.). Trauma-informed care in substance abuse. Retrieved from https://ncsacw.acf.hhs.gov/userfiles/files/SAMHSA_Trauma.pdf

National Child Traumatic Stress Network (NCTSN). (2017). Trauma-Informed Schools for Children in Military Families.

National Child Traumatic Stress Network (NCTSN). (2018). Creating, supporting, and sustaining trauma-informed schools: A system framework. Retrieved from https://www.nctsn.org

National Child Traumatic Stress Network. (2017). *Addressing race and trauma in the classroom: A resource for educators.* National Center for Child Traumatic Stress. Retrieved from: https://www.nctsn.org/sites/default/files/resources//addressing_ race_and_trauma_in_the_classroom_educators.pdf

National Child Traumatic Stress Network. (n.d.). *Essential elements.*https://www.nctsn.org/trauma-informed-care/traumainformed-systems/schools/essentialelements

National Child Traumatic Stress Network. (n.d.). *Trauma-Informed schools for children in K–12: A system framework.* https://www.nctsn.org/sites/default/files/resources/fact-sheet/trauma_informed_schools_for_children_in_k-12_a_systems_framework.pdf

National Child Traumatic Stress Network. Schools Committee. (2017). *Creating, supporting, and sustaining trauma-informed schools: A system framework.* Los Angeles, CA, and Durham, NC: National Center for Child Traumatic Stress. Retrieved from: https://www.nctsn.org/sites/default/files/resources/creating_supporting_sustaining_traum a_informed_schools_a_systems_framework.pdf

National Council on Family Relations. (2020). Military families executive summary. Retrieved from https://www.ncfr.org/sites/default/files/2020-02/Military-Families-Exec-Sum-Feb-2020.pdf

National Council on Family Relations. (2020). Military families: An overview of military family outcomes and evidence-informed practices. *National Council on Family Relations.* https://www.ncfr.org/sites/default/files/2020-02/Military-Families-Exec-Sum-Feb-2020.pdf

National Education Association. (2023). *Trauma-Informed practices.* https://www.nea.org/professional-excellence/student-engagement/tools-tips/trauma-informed-practices

National Policy Board for Educational Administration. (2018). *National Educational Leadership Preparation (NELP) program recognition standards building level.* https:// www.npbea.org/wp-content/uploads/2018/11/NELP-Building-Standards.pdf

NC DOCKS at The University of North Carolina at Greensboro, & Phillips, J. B. (1987). Administrative revenge.

Nduagbo, K. C. (2020). How gender disparities affect classroom learning. Retrieved from https://www.ascd.org/el/articles/how-gender-disparities-affect-classroom-learning

Nelson Christensen, A. C. (2025). Rethinking trauma-sensitive schools from an anti-racist lens. International Journal of School &amp. *Educational Psychology, 13*(2), 156–169. DOI: 10.1080/21683603.2025.2483931

Nelson, T., & Clark, H. (2023). Collaborative advocacy in special education: Strategies for building trust and partnerships. *Education Leadership Quarterly*, 50(1), 87-103. https://doi.org/exampledoi

Nenonene, R. L., Gallagher, C. E., Kelly, M. K., & Collopy, R. M. B. (2019). Challenges and opportunities of infusing social, emotional, and cultural competencies into teacher preparation: One program's story. *Teacher Education Quarterly, 46*(4), 92–115. DOI: 10.1177/0737532819881846

Nesteruk, O. (2022). Family dynamics at the intersection of languages, cultures, and aspirations: Reflections of young adults from immigrant families. *Journal of Family Issues, 43*(4), 1015–1038. DOI: 10.1177/0192513X211007527

Nestor, J. (2020). *Breath: The New Science of a Lost Art.* Riverhead Books.

Neves, I. C., Amorim, F. F., & Ribeiro Salomon, A. L. (2020). Burnout syndrome on teachers and its relation to nutrition: An integrative review. *Current Psychiatry Research and Reviews, 16*(1), 31–41. DOI: 10.2174/1573400515666191202113523

Newman, L. A., Madaus, J. W., Lalor, A. R., & Javitz, H. S. (2021). Effect of accessing supports on higher education persistence of students with disabilities. *Journal of Diversity in Higher Education, 14*(3), 353–363. DOI: 10.1037/dhe0000170

Newton, P. J., Mulcahy, T. M., & Martin, S. E. (2008). *Finding victims of human trafficking*. University of Chicago. DOI: 10.1037/e540892008-001

Nguyen, K. T. (2024). The experience of ethnic identity and Vietnamese American adolescents' psychological well-being (Doctoral dissertation, The Chicago School of Professional Psychology). ProQuest Dissertations & Theses, 31328550.

Nguyen, H. V., Do, Q. A., Schacht, R. L., Yang, J. P., George, W. H., & Pantalone, D. W. (2024). Culture and partner violence: Examining loss of face, acculturation, behavioral intentions, and risk perception among Asian American college women. *Journal of Family Violence, 39*(4), 693–704. DOI: 10.1007/s10896-023-00519-5

Nickerson, A., & Jimerson, S. R. (2015). *Supporting students experiencing childhood trauma: Tips for parents and educators.* National Association of School Psychologists. https://www.nasponline.org/resources-and-publications/resources-and-podcasts/school-climate-safety-and-crisis/mental-health-resources/trauma/supporting-students-experiencing-childhood-trauma-tips-for-parents-and-educators

Nieto, S. (2010). *The light in their eyes: Creating multicultural learning communities*. Teachers College Press.

Nikolašević, Ž., Krstić, T., Rajšli, A., & Bugarski Ignjatović, V. (2024, June). The Relationship Between Behavior Aspects of Executive Functions and Personality Traits in Healthy Young Adults. *Psychological Reports, 127*(3), 1317–1335. DOI: 10.1177/00332941221132996

Nolan, K. (2021). Urban students' critical race-class narratives: An examination of the relationship between race and class within the context of punitive school disciplineq. *Teachers College Record, 123*(14), 351–385. DOI: 10.1177/01614681211063965

Nolte-Yupari, S. T. (2019). Facing the Elephant: Let's Talk About Art-on-a-Cart. *Art Education, 72*(6), 14–19. DOI: 10.1080/00043125.2019.1648142

Norrish, J., & Brunzell, T. (2023). How is Trauma-Informed Education Implemented within Classrooms? A Synthesis of Trauma Informed Education Programs. *The Australian Journal of Teacher Education, 48*(3), 95–120. DOI: 10.14221/1835-517X.6159

Novak, K., & Rodriguez, K. (2023). In Support of Students: A Leader's Guide to Equitable MTSS. https://doi.org/https://www.wiley.com/enus/In+Support+of+Students%3A+A+Leader%27s+Guide+to+Equitable+MTSS-p-9781119885269

O'Donnell, K. E., Shen, L., Stratford, D. C., Candelaria, P. Y., & Clemens, N. H. (2024). Integrating a Self-Regulation Intervention Within a Tier-2 Academic Intervention. *Intervention in School and Clinic, 60*(1), 17–27.

O'Konek, J. J. (2023). "I have no voice. May I please borrow yours?" An overture for expanding children's access to intellectual and developmental disability services in the state of North Dakota. *North Dakota Law Review*, *98*(1), 1–49. https://law.und.edu/_files/docs/ndlr/pdf/issues/98/1/98ndlr1.pdf

Obersteiner, A. (2019). Multiple pathways between affect and mathematical competence in young children—Commentary on the studies in the special issue. *Educational Studies in Mathematics*, *100*(3), 317–323. DOI: 10.1007/s10649-018-9853-0

Odak, I., Marušić, I., Bojić, J. M., Puzić, S., Bakić, H., Eliasson, N., Klicpera, B. G., Gøtzsche, K., Kozina, A., Perković, I., Roczen, N., Tomé, G., & Veldin, M. (2023). Teachers' social and emotional competencies: A lever for social and emotional learning in schools. *Sociology & Space / Sociologija i Prostor, 61*(1), 105–122. DOI: 10.5673/sip.61.1.5

Office of Juvenile Justice and Delinquency Prevention. (2010). *Commercial sexual exploitation of children.* https://ojjdp.ojp.gov/programs/commercial-sexual-exploitation-children

Office of Juvenile Justice and Delinquency Prevention. (2014, August). *Commercial sexual exploitation of children and sex trafficking.* https://ojjdp.ojp.gov/sites/g/files/xyckuh176/files/media/document/csecsextrafficking.pdf

Open, A. I. (2022). *ChatGPT (Mar 14 version)* [Large language model]. Brainstorm, Ideas, Organizational.

OpenAI. (2023) Justdone. [Large language model]. Image creations.

Organization for Economic Co-operation and Development. (2021). *Beyond acadmic learning: First results from the survey of social and emotional skills.* OECD Publishing. https://doi.org/10.19=787/92a11084-en

Organization for Economic Co-operation and Development. (2023). *Equity and inclusion in education: Finding strength through diversity.* OECD Publishing., DOI: 10.1787/e9072e21-

Ormeno, M. D., Roh, Y., Heller, M., Shields, E., Flores-Carrera, A., Greve, M., Hagan, J., Kostrubala, A., & Onasanya, N. (2020). Special Concerns in Military Families. *Current Psychiatry Reports*, *22*(12), 82. Advance online publication. DOI: 10.1007/s11920-020-01207-7 PMID: 33215305

Ortiz, A. A., & Fránquiz, M. E. (2019). Co-editors' introduction: Challenges to the success of English learners in the context of language instruction educational programs. *Bilingual Research Journal*, *42*(1), 1–5. DOI: 10.1080/15235882.2019.1598213

Ortiz, R., Gilgoff, R., & Burke Harris, N. (2022). Adverse Childhood Experiences, Toxic Stress, and Trauma-Informed Neurology. *JAMA Neurology*, *79*(6), 539–540. DOI: 10.1001/jamaneurol.2022.0769 PMID: 35467693

Osborne, A. G.Jr, & Russo, C. J. (2020). *Special education and the law: A guide for practitioners.* Corwin.

Osher, D., Guarino, K., Jones, W., & Schanfield, M. (2024). Trauma-Sensitive Schools and Social and Emotional Learning: An Integration. *Edna Bennett Pierce Prevention Research Center*. https://prevention.psu.edu/sel/issue-briefs/trauma-sensitive-schools-and-social-and-emotional-learning-an-integration/

Osher, D. K., Kidron, Y., Brackett, M., Dymnicki, A., Jones, S., & Weissberg, R. P. (2016). Advancing the science and practice of social and emotional learning. *Review of Research in Education, 40*(1), 644–681. DOI: 10.3102/0091732X16673595

Osta, K., & Vasquez, H. (2024). Implicit bias and structural racialization. National Equity Project. https://www.nationalequityproject.org/frameworks/implicit-bias-structural-racialization

Osuch, E., & Engel, J. (2004). Research on the treatment of trauma spectrum responses: the role of the optimal healing environment and neurobiology. *Journal of Alternative and Complementary Medicine*, S-211 - S-221.

Otero, M. C., Wells, J. L., Chen, K.-H., Brown, C. L., Connelly, D. E., Levenson, R. W., & Fredrickson, B. L. (2020). Behavioral indices of positivity resonance associated with long-term marital satisfaction. *Emotion (Washington, D.C.), 20*(7), 1225–1233. DOI: 10.1037/emo0000634 PMID: 31259587

Our Military Kids. (2024). Five-year report. Retrieved from https://www.ourmilitarykids.org/wp-content/uploads/2024/07/5-Year-Report_Final.pdf

Overall, N. C., Pietromonaco, P. R., & Simpson, J. A. (2022). Buffering and spillover of adult attachment insecurity in couple and family relationships. *Nature Reviews Psychology, 1*(2), 101–111. DOI: 10.1038/s44159-021-00011-1

Overstreet, S., & Chafouleas, S. M. (2016). Trauma-Informed Schools: Introduction to the Special Issue. *School Mental Health, 8*(1), 1–6. DOI: 10.1007/s12310-016-9184-1

Özdemir, E., & Babadoğan, M. C. (2023). Teacher candidates' training needs for social- emotional competencies. (English). *International Journal of Curriculum & Instructional* Studies (IJOCIS). *Uluslararasi Eğitim Programlari & Ögretim Çalışmaları Dergisi, 13*(1), 95–122. DOI: 10.31704/ijocis.2023.005

Padilla, A. M. (2006). Acculturation, social identity, and social cognition: A new perspective. *Hispanic Journal of Behavioral Sciences, 28*(1), 19–23. DOI: 10.1177/0739986303251694

Padilla, A. M., & Perez, W. (2003). Acculturation, social identity, and psychological adjustment. In McGoldrick, R. M., Pearce, J. K., & Giordano, J. (Eds.), *Ethnicity and family therapy* (3rd ed., pp. 156–177). Guilford Press.

Palestro, J. J., & Jameson, M. M. (2020). Math self-efficacy, not emotional self-efficacy, mediates the math anxiety-performance relationship in undergraduate students. *Cognition, Brain, Behavior: An Interdisciplinary Journal, 24*(4), 379–394. DOI: 10.24193/cbb.2020.24.20

Paley, B., & Hajal, N. J. (2022). Conceptualizing Emotion Regulation and Coregulation as Family-Level Phenomena. *Clinical Child and Family Psychology Review, 25*(1), 1. DOI: 10.1007/s10567-022-00378-4 PMID: 35098427

Panayiotou, M., Humphrey, N., & Wigelsworth, M. (2019). An empirical basis for linking social and emotional learning to academic performance. *Contemporary Educational Psychology, 56*, 193–204. DOI: 10.1016/j.cedpsych.2019.01.009

Parameswaran, U. D., Molloy, J., & Kuttner, P. (2024). Healing Schools: A Framework for Joining Trauma-Informed Care, Restorative Justice, and Multicultural Education for Whole School Reform. *The Urban Review*, *56*(1), 186–209. DOI: 10.1007/s11256-023-00666-5

Passolunghi, M. C., De Vita, C., & Pellizzoni, S. (2020). Math Anxiety and Math Achievement: The Effects of Emotional and Math Strategy Training. *Developmental Science*, *23*(6), e12964. Advance online publication. DOI: 10.1111/desc.12964 PMID: 32159906

PATHS Program LLC. (n.d.). What is social-emotional learning (SEL)? Retrieved from https://pathsprogram.com/what-is-sel

Pavlina, S. (2020). A growth heartset. https://stevenpavlina.com/blog/2020/a-growth-heatset/

Peña-Villegas, M. (2024). *Parent/Guardians' Perceptions of Postsecondary Transition and Matriculation of Students With Learning Disabilities: A Qualitative Case Study* (Order No. 31769870). Available from Dissertations & Theses @ National University; ProQuest Dissertations & Theses Global. (3174624439). https://go.openathens.net/redirector/nu.edu?url=https://www.proquest.com/dissertations-theses/parent-guardians-perceptions-postsecondary/docview/3174624439/se-2

Pereda, N. (2024). Invisibilized victims: The sexual exploitation of children and adolescents in the european context / víctimas invisibilizadas: La explotación sexual de niños, niñas y adolescentes en el contexto europeo. Journal for the Study of Education and Development. *Infancia y Aprendizaje*, *47*(2), 243–263. DOI: 10.1177/02103702241253397

Perez, C. P., & Morrison, S. S. (2016). Understanding the challenges of English language learners and increasing college-going culture: Suggestions for school counselors. *Ideas and Research You Can Use: Vistas*, *18*, 1–12.

Perry, B. D. (2009). *Born for love: Why empathy is essential—and endangered*. HarperCollins.

Perry, B. D., & Daniels, M. L. (2016). *The Boy Who Was Raised as a Dog: And Other Stories from a Child Psychiatrist's Notebook*. Basic Books.

Perry, D., & Daniels, M. (2016). Implementing trauma-informed practices in the school setting: A pilot study. *School Mental Health*, *8*(1), 177–188. DOI: 10.1007/s12310-016-9182-3

Peters, J. (2011). *Transition Skills of First-Year College Students with Learning Disabilities* (Order No. 3489342). Available from ProQuest One Academic. (915692476). https://www.proquest.com/docview/915692476

Peterson, G. (2022). Culturally Responsive Leadership in Bilingual Education: An Exploration of the Practices Implemented by Elementary School Principals in Southern New Mexico (Doctoral dissertation, New Mexico State University).

Peterson, T. (2008). Self-efficacy: The foundation of human performance. *Performance Improvement Quarterly*, *21*(2), 7–26. DOI: 10.1002/piq.20008

Phelps, C. (2021). The stonewall riots: A document history. *Journal of the History of Sexuality*, *30*(3), 451. https://link.gale.com/apps/doc/A690356795/EAIM?u=pres1571&sid=bookmarkEAIM&xid=3e2f1984

Pickens, I. B., & Tschopp, N. (2017). *Trauma-informed classrooms.* National Council of Juvenile and Family Court Judges. https://www.wyschoolpsych.org/wp-content/uploads/NCJFCJ_SJP_Trauma_Informed_Classrooms_Final7213.pdf

Pierre, Y., Rathee, N. K., & Rathee, V. S. (2021). Developing cross-cultural competency through multicultural perspective: An exploratory inquiry. *European Scientific Journal, 17*(27), 324–346. DOI: 10.19044/esj.2021.v17n27p324

Piotrowski, C., (2020). ACEs and trauma-informed care. Adverse Childhood Experiences, 307-328. *Academic Press: 2020*. .DOI: 10.1016/B978-0-12-816065-7.00015-X

Pizzie, R. G., & Kraemer, D. J. M. (2023). Strategies for remediating the impact of math anxiety on high school math performance. *NPJ Science of Learning*, *8*(1), 1–11. DOI: 10.1038/s41539-023-00188-5 PMID: 37779133

Plumb, J. L., Bush, K. A., & Kersevich, S. E. (2013). Building Trauma-Informed Schools and Communities. *Children & Schools*, *35*(2), 123–126. DOI: 10.1093/cs/cdt007

Plumb, J., Kersevich, S. E., & Bush, K. A. (2016). Trauma-sensitive schools: An evidence-based approach. *School Social Work Journal*, *40*(2), 37–60.

Polaris. (2023, March 28). The Tate Brothers and the basics of "Romeo pimping." Polaris. https://polarisproject.org/blog/2023/01/the-tate-brothers-and-the-basics-of-romeo-pimping/

Polaris. (n.d.-a). Growing awareness. Growing impact: 2017 statistics from the National Human Trafficking Hotline and BeFree Textline. https://polarisproject.org/wp-content/uploads/2019/09/2017NHTHStats-1.pdf

Polaris. (n.d.-b). *2018 statistics from the National Human Trafficking Hotline*. https://polarisproject.org/wp-content/uploads/2019/09/Polaris_National_Hotline_2018_Statistics_Fact_Sheet.pdf

Portes, A., & Rumbaut, R. G. (2001). *Legacies: The story of the immigrant second generation*. University of California Press.

Postsecondary National Policy Institute. (2023, November). *Students with disabilities*. https://pnpi.org/wp-content/uploads/2023/11/StudentswithDisabilities-Nov-2023.pdf

Presbitero, A. (2020). Foreign language skill, anxiety, cultural intelligence and individual task performance in global virtual teams: A cognitive perspective. *Journal of International Management*, *26*(2), 100729. DOI: 10.1016/j.intman.2019.100729

Presence. (2021, March 16). Deploying a trauma-informed approach: Use the 4 R's. *Presence*. https://presence.com/insights/deploying-a-trauma-informed-approach-use-the-4-rs/

Pribitkin, T. (2020). *Theory versus practice in educational change: On-the-ground challenges of trauma-informed education practices*. https://knowledge.uchicago.edu/record/2437/files/Pribitkin.pdf

Price, K. V. (2022). Public school superintendents' viewpoints on the leadership strategies perceived to guide the culture and climate within a school district [ProQuest Information & Learning]. *Dissertation Abstracts International. A, The Humanities and Social Sciences*, *83*(7–A), •••.

Priebe, A., & Suhr, C. (2005). Hidden in plain view: The commercial sexual exploitation of girls in Atlanta. *Atlanta Women's Agenda, 4.* https://iws.uga.edu/sites/default/files/Child_Prostitution.pdf

Privitera, G. J., & Ahlgrim-Delzell, L. (2018). *Research methods for education.* Sage. https://collegepublishing.sagepub.com/products/research-methods-for-education-1-245749

Protocol, A. T. I. (2014). *Trauma-informed care in behavioral health services.* Substance Abuse and Mental Health Services Administration.

Qiu, Y. (2025). Acculturation-related intergenerational conflicts (A-IC) in Chinese immigrant family: A post-intentional phenomenological research Iiquiry (Doctoral dissertation). The George Washington University ProQuest Dissertations & Theses. 31558121.

Quarmby, T., Sandford, R., & Elpus, K. (2020). Access to arts education in America: The availability of visual art, music, dance, and theater courses in U.S. high schools. *Arts Education Policy Review*, 121.

Quintana, T. S., & Cole, R. F. (2021). Forward march: Implementing the ASCA National Model to support military-connected students. *Journal of School Counseling, 19(7)*. http://www.jsc.montana.edu/articles/v19n7.pdf

Quote.org. (n.d.). Fernando Botero. https://quote.org/author/fernando-botero-72254

Rabe, M. (2024). How racially and ethnically diverse is your neighborhood? United States Census Bureau. Retrieved from https://www.census.gov/library/stories/2024/01/racial-ethnic-diversity-neighborhoods.html

Rafferty, Y. (2008). The impact of trafficking on children: Psychological and social policy perspectives. *Child Development Perspectives*, *2*(1), 13–18. DOI: 10.1111/j.1750-8606.2008.00035.x

Ramirez, G., Hooper, S. Y., Kersting, N. B., Ferguson, R., & Yeager, D. (2018). Teacher math anxiety relates to adolescent students' math achievement. *American Educational Research Association (AERA). AERA Open*, *4*(1), 2332858418756052. Advance online publication. DOI: 10.1177/2332858418756052 PMID: 31069247

RAND Corporation. (2018). Key findings on the well-being of military families. Retrieved from https://www.rand.org/pubs/research_reports/RR2304.html

Ranjbar, N., Erb, M., Mohammad, O., & Moreno, F. A. (2020). Trauma-Informed Care and Cultural Humility in the Mental Health Care of People from Minoritized Communities. *Focus (San Francisco, Calif.)*, *18*(1), 8–15. DOI: 10.1176/appi.focus.20190027 PMID: 32047392

Raphael, J., Reichert, J. A., & Powers, M. (2010). Pimp control and violence: Domestic sex trafficking of Chicago women and girls. *Women & Criminal Justice*, *20*(1–2), 89–104. DOI: 10.1080/08974451003641065

Rawls, J. (1971). *A Theory of Justice*. Harvard University Press. DOI: 10.4159/9780674042605

Ray, S. A., Hollenbeck, J. K., Ankomahjr, P., Giacopelli, T., Link, G., Ruckdaschel, T., & Runge, J. (2024). Effects of Occupational Therapy Professional Development Training on School-Based Practice. *Journal of Occupational Therapy, Schools & Early Intervention*, *17*(4), 979–993. DOI: 10.1080/19411243.2024.2326212

Redfield, R., Linton, R., & Herskovits, M. J. (1936). Memorandum on the study of acculturation. *American Anthropologist, 38*(1), 149–152. https://www.jstor.org/stable/662563. DOI: 10.1525/aa.1936.38.1.02a00330

Reed, D., & Sheridan, K. D. (2021). Perceptions of Directly Targeting SEL Learning Skills in Public Education. *Creative Education, 12*(11), 2765–2779. Advance online publication. DOI: 10.4236/ce.2021.1211204

Reed, S. M., Kennedy, M. A., Decker, M. R., & Cimino, A. N. (2019). Friends, family, and boyfriends: An analysis of relationship pathways into commercial sexual exploitation. *Child Abuse & Neglect, 90*, 1–12. DOI: 10.1016/j.chiabu.2019.01.016 PMID: 30716650

Reeves, A. M. (2019). Compassion Fatigue: Stories/Artworks of an Art Teacher with a Trauma-Informed Pedagogy.

Renteria, T. (2017). Bridging the Gap Between Non-Spanish Speaking MFTs and Their Spanish Speaking Clients (Doctoral dissertation, California State University, Northridge). Retrieved from https://scholarworks.calstate.edu/downloads/tx31qn10x

Rentzi, A. (2024). Social justice in education: Creating an inclusive culture at schools through critical multicultural theory. *European Journal of Education and Pedagogy, 5*(1), 94–97. DOI: 10.24018/ejedu.2024.5.1.802

Renzaho, A. M., Dhingra, N., & Georgeou, N. (2017). Youth as contested sites of culture: The intergenerational acculturation gap amongst new migrant communities—Parental and young adult perspectives. *PLoS One, 12*(2), e0170700. DOI: 10.1371/journal.pone.0170700 PMID: 28170406

Resera, E., Tribe, R., & Lane, P. (2015). Interpreting in mental health, roles and dynamics in practice. *International Journal of Culture and Mental Health, 8*(2), 192–206. DOI: 10.1080/17542863.2014.921207

Rheinberg, F., & Engeser, S. (2018). Intrinsic motivation and flow. In *Motivation and action* (pp. 579–622). Springer. DOI: 10.1007/978-3-319-65094-4_14

Richerme, L. K. (2021). Every Student Succeeds Act and Social Emotional Learning: Opportunities and considerations for P-12 arts educators. *Arts Education Policy Review, 122*(3), 151–157. DOI: 10.1080/10632913.2020.1787284

Rimm-Kaufman, S., & Sandilos, L. (2020). Improving students' relationships with teachers to provide essential supports for learning. *PsycEXTRA Dataset.* DOI: 10.1037/e501992017-001

Rizo, C. F., Klein, L., Chesworth, B. R., Franchino-Olsen, H., Villodas, M. L., Macy, R. J., & Martin, S. L. (2021). Educating students about sex trafficking and responding to students' needs: Principals' perceptions and practices. *Journal of Human Trafficking, 7*(2), 202–223. DOI: 10.1080/23322705.2019.1698922

Roberg, R., Camargo, T., & Marks, A. K. (2024). A mixed-methods exploration of legal vulnerability, trauma, and psychological wellbeing in immigrant caregivers and youth. *Trauma Care, 4*(1), 60–74. DOI: 10.3390/traumacare4010006

Robinson-Wood, T. (2016). *The convergence of race, ethnicity, and gender: Multiple identities in counseling*. Sage Publications.

Rodriguez, L. R. (2023). Exploring Self-Awareness of Self-Advocacy Skills Among Senior High School Students with Mild to Moderate Learning Disabilities. *Southern New Hampshire University.*https://hdl.handle.net/10474/3729

Rodriguez-Fee, J. (2023). Once upon a FAPE: Contrasting the Fabled Hope of IDEA with Present-Day Pandemic Realities. *Belmont L. Rev.*, *11*, 410.

Rodriguez, S. (2022). “Immigration knocks on the door... We are stuck...”: A multilevel analysis of undocumented youth’s experiences of racism, system Failure, and resistance in policy and school contexts. *Teachers College Record*, *124*(6), 3–37. DOI: 10.1177/01614681221093286

Rogers, M., Johnson, A., Coffey, Y., Fielding, J., Harrington, I., & Bhullar, N. (2023). Parental perceptions of social and emotional well-being of young children from Australian military families. *The Australian Journal of Rural Health*, *31*(6), 1090–1102. Advance online publication. DOI: 10.1111/ajr.13033 PMID: 37622610

Rogers-Sirin, L., Ryce, P., & Sirin, S. (2014). Acculturation, Acculturative Stress, and Cultural Mismatch and Their Influences on Immigrant Children and Adolescents’ Well-Being. In Dimitrova, R., Bender, M., & van de Vijver, F. (Eds.), *Global perspectives on well-being in immigrant families. Advances in immigrant family research* (Vol. 1). Springer., DOI: 10.1007/978-1-4614-9129-3_2

Romero, S. M. (2016). The Awakened Heart of the Mindful Teacher: A Contemplative Exploration. In *ProQuest LLC*. https://doi.org/https://gateway.proquest.com /openurl?url_ver=Z39.88-2004&rft_val_fmt=info:ofi/fmt:kev:mtx:dissertation&res_ dat=xri:pqm&rft_dat=xri:pqdiss:10586430

Roseby, S., & Gascoigne, M. (2021). A systematic review on the impact of trauma-informed education programs on academic and academic-related functioning for students who have experienced childhood adversity. *Traumatology*, *27*(2), 149–167. DOI: 10.1037/trm0000276

Rosen, N. L., & Nofziger, S. (2019). Boys, bullying, and gender roles: How hegemonic masculinity shapes bullying behavior. *Gender Issues*, *36*(3), 295–318. DOI: 10.1007/s12147-018-9226-0

Ross, A. M., DeVoe, E. R., Steketee, G., Emmert-Aronson, B. O., Brown, T., & Muroff, J. (2020). Outcomes of a reflective parenting program among military spouses: The moderating role of social support. *Journal of Family Psychology*, *34*(4), 402–413. DOI: 10.1037/fam0000637 PMID: 32027150

Rossiter, A. G., Dumas, M. A., Wilmoth, M. C., & Patrcian, A. P. (2016). “I Serve 2”: Meeting the needs of military children in civilian practice. *Nursing Outlook*, *64*(5), 485–490. DOI: 10.1016/j.outlook.2016.05.011 PMID: 27477834

Rossiter, A. G., & Ling, C. G. (2022). Building resilience in US military families: Why it matters. *BMJ Military Health*, *168*(1), 91–94. DOI: 10.1136/bmjmilitary-2020-001735 PMID: 33785586

Rostker, B. D. (2006). The evolution of the all-volunteer force. RAND Corporation. https://www.rand.org/pubs/research_briefs/RB9195.html

Rost, L., Eakins, S. A., Gilbert, A., Gallagher, M., Brown, V., Murphy, C. G., Lahayne, S. P., Lewis, S., Bowman, B., Easton, C., & Lopez, M. (2021). What should SEL look like this fall? Educators And Students Weigh In On How To Foster Resilience. *Learning Professional*, *42*(4), 26–29.

Rothman, E. F., Cusano, J., Wagner, A., Lockwood, S., Cuevas, C. A., & Farrell, A. (2024). Prevalence of neurodevelopmental, mental, and behavioral disorders in a sample of U.S. Commercially sexually exploited youth, and associations with health and health care access. *Journal of Human Trafficking*, *11*(1), 4–19. DOI: 10.1080/23322705.2024.2426943

Rothman, E. F., Farrell, A., Paruk, J., Bright, K., Bair-Merritt, M., & Preis, S. R. (2019). Evaluation of a multi-session group designed to prevent commercial sexual exploitation of minors: The "My Life My Choice" curriculum. *Journal of Interpersonal Violence*, *36*(19–20), 9143–9166. DOI: 10.1177/0886260519865972 PMID: 31354019

Rothstein, S. L. S. (2023). Social-emotional learning and teachers' cultural competency: The relationship between implementation practices and student outcomes [ProQuest Information & Learning]. *Dissertation Abstracts International. A, The Humanities and Social Sciences*, *84*(11–A), ●●●.

Rudmin, F. (2009). Constructs, measurements and models of acculturation and acculturative stress. *International Journal of Intercultural Relations*, *33*(2), 106–123. DOI: 10.1016/j.ijintrel.2008.12.001

Ruiz, E. (2005). Hispanic culture and relational cultural theory. *Journal of Creativity in Mental Health*, *1*(1), 33–55. DOI: 10.1300/J456v01n01_05

Rumrill Jr, P. D., Cook, B. G., & Stevenson, N. A. (2020). Research in special education: Designs, methods, and applications.

Ryals, L. (2022). A Case Study of One Trauma-Informed Music Education Program. DOI: 10.34944/dspace/7676

Ryan, S. V., Pendergast, L. L., Schwing, S., von der Embse, N. P., Saeki, E., & Segool, N. (2017). Leaving the teaching profession: The role of teacher stress and educational accountability policies on turnover intent. *Teaching and Teacher Education*, *66*, 1–11. DOI: 10.1016/j.tate.2017.03.016

Sailor, W., Skrtic, T. M., Cohn, M., & Olmstead, C. (2021). Preparing Teacher Educators for Statewide Scale-Up of Multi-Tiered System of Support (MTSS). *Teacher Education and Special Education*, *44*(1), 24–41. DOI: 10.1177/0888406420938035

Salvador, K. (2019). Sustaining the Flame: (Re)Igniting Joy in Teaching Music. *Music Educators Journal*, *106*(2), 28–36. DOI: 10.1177/0027432119873701

Salvador, K., & Culp, M. E. (2022). Intersections in Music Education: Implications of Universal Design for Learning, Culturally Responsive Education, and Trauma-Informed Education for P-12 Praxis. *Music Educators Journal*, *108*(3), 19–29. DOI: 10.1177/00274321221087737

SAMHSA. (2023). https://www.samhsa.gov/

Sandilos, L., Goble, P., & Schwartz, S. (2020). Burnout and Teacher–Child Interactions: The Moderating Influence of SEL Interventions in Head Start Classrooms. *Early Education and Development*, *31*(7), 1169–1185. DOI: 10.1080/10409289.2020.1788331

Sandoval Gomez, A., & McKee, A. (2020, November). When special education and disability studies intertwine: Addressing educational inequities through processes and programming. [). Frontiers Media SA.]. *Frontiers in Education*, *5*, 587045. DOI: 10.3389/feduc.2020.587045

Sangha, S., Diehl, M. M., Bergstrom, H. C., & Drew, M. R. (2020). Know safety, no fear. *Neuroscience and Biobehavioral Reviews*, *108*, 218–230. DOI: 10.1016/j.neubiorev.2019.11.006 PMID: 31738952

Santisteban, D. A., Mena, M. P., & Abalo, C. (2012). Bridging diversity and family systems: Culturally informed and flexible family-based treatment for Hispanic adolescents. *Couple & Family Psychology*, *2*(4), 246–263. DOI: 10.1037/cfp0000013 PMID: 24772378

Sapiro, B., & Ward, A. (2020). Marginalized youth, mental health, and connection with others: A review of the literature. *Child & Adolescent Social Work Journal*, *37*(4), 343–357. DOI: 10.1007/s10560-019-00628-5

Sargent, A. G., & Schlossberg, N. K. (1988). Managing adult transitions. *Training and Development Journal*, *42*(12), 58. https://eric.ed.gov/?id=EJ381396

Sathasivam, R. V., & Rahim, S. S. (2021). I do better: How social and emotional learning environment enhances assessment for learning strategies in science classrooms. *Journal of International and Comparative Education*, *10*(2), 117–131. DOI: 10.14425/jice.2021.10.2.0913

Saultz, A., Lyons, A. I., Aronson, B., Sander, S. A., & Malin, J. R. (2021). Understanding preservice teacher dispositions: Implications for social justice and educational policy. *Teacher Education Quarterly*, *48*(1), 7–32. https://www.jstor.org/stable/27094714

Save the Children. (2020). Save our education: Protect every child's right to learn in the COVID-19 response and recovery. Washington, DC: Save the Children International. https://resourcecentre.savethechildren.net/pdf/save_our_education_0.pdf/

Sawchuk, S. (2021, October 13). Why High School SEL Programs Feel 'Lame'—And How to Fix Them; Here's how to devise high school SEL opportunities that don't feel preachy and align with adolescents' cognitive and psychological development. *Education Week*, *41*(9), 13.

Schechter, J. (2018). University students with disabilities: Factors that contribute to their self-predicted likelihood of graduation. *Journal of Postsecondary Education and Disability*, *31*(4), 335–349. https://eric.ed.gov/?id=EJ1214186

Schlossberg, N. K., Lynch, A. Q., & Chickering, A. W. (1989). *Improving higher education environments for adults: Responsive programs and services from entry to departure*. Jossey-Bass. https://eric.ed.gov/?id=ED304057

Schlossberg, N. K. (1981). A model for analyzing human adaptation to transition. *The Counseling Psychologist*, *9*(2), 2–18. https://journals.sagepub.com/doi/10.1177/001100008100900202. DOI: 10.1177/001100008100900202

Schlossberg, N. K. (2011). The challenge of change: The transition model and its applications. *Journal of Employment Counseling*, *48*(4), 159–162. DOI: 10.1002/j.2161-1920.2011.tb01102.x

Schlossberg, N. K., Waters, E. B., & Goodman, J. (1995). *Counseling adults in transition: Linking practice with theory* (2nd ed.). Springer., https://www.abebooks.com/9780826142337/Counseling-Adults-Transition-Linking-Practice-0826142338/plp

School Health Assessment and Performance Evaluation System. (2023). *Trauma responsive schools: What is the TSR-IA*.https://theshapesystem.com/trauma/

Schuman, J., & Reynolds, D. (2023). Attempts at anti-racist teaching by White English teachers of black students. *English Teaching*, *22*(4), 418–432. DOI: 10.1108/ETPC-05-2022-0071

Schwind, D. B., & Handley-More, D. (2024). Utilizing MTSS for the occupation of feeding: A case study. *Journal of Occupational Therapy, Schools & Early Intervention*, *17*(2), 193–200.

Scruggs, S., Dong, S., Ducatt, S., Mitchell, J., & Davis, W. (2021). Impact of high school transition and accommodation experience on student involvement in college. *Journal of Postsecondary Education and Disability*, *34*(2), 179–190. https://files.eric.ed.gov/fulltext/EJ1319194.pdf

Seaman, S. (2024). What Is Our Definition of Post-Secondary Success? *Association of Washington School Principals*.https://awsp.org/connect/blog/blog-detail/awsp-blog/2024/03/14/what-is-our-definition-of-post-secondary-success#:~:text=Post%2Dsecondary%20success%20should%20be,training%2C%20college%2C%20or%20university

Sears, C. A. Q. (2016). Professional Notes. *Music Educators Journal*, *102*(3), 18–19. DOI: 10.1177/0027432116630978

Second Step. (n.d.). Our programs: Social-emotional learning. Retrieved from https://www.secondstep.org/our-programs

SEL Lesson - Self Awareness. (2021, February 9). *US Official News*.

Shamieh, J. M., Sawalha, I. H., & Madanat, H. M. (2022). Vulnerability and capacity assessment for refugee education crises. *International Journal of Emerging Markets*, *17*(1), 253–276. DOI: 10.1108/IJOEM-04-2019-0321

Shaw, R. D. (2016). Music teacher stress in the era of accountability. *Arts Education Policy Review*, *117*(2), 104–116. DOI: 10.1080/10632913.2015.1005325

Shaw, R. D. (2019). Jumping through Hoops: Troubling Music Teacher Dilemmas in the New Era of Accountability. *Music Educators Journal*, *105*(3), 23–29. DOI: 10.1177/0027432118816146

Sheng, Z., Sheng, Y., & Anderson, C. J. (2016). Dropping out of school among ELL students: Implications to schools and teacher education. *The Clearing House: A Journal of Educational Strategies, Issues and Ideas*, *84*(3), 98–103. DOI: 10.1080/00098655.2010.538755

Shetty, J. (2020). *Think Like a Monk: Train Your Mind for Peace and Purpose Every Day*. Scribner.

Shooks, B. A. (2020). *The impact of trauma-informed pedagogical practices on teacher self efficacy.* (Publication No. 28025831) [Doctoral dissertation, Cornerstone University]. ProQuest Dissertations & Theses.

Shooks, B. A. *The Impact of Trauma-Informed Pedagogical Practices on Teacher Self-Efficacy*. (Publication No. 28025831) [Doctoral dissertation, Cornerstone University]. ProQuest Dissertations & Theses, 2020.

Shooks, B. (2020). *The Impact of Trauma-Informed Pedagogical Practices on Teacher Self-Efficacy.* Cornerstone University.

Shufutinsky, A., Calvin, J., Shufutinsky, B., Spigel, R., Kravitz, C., Burrel, D. N., Shufutinsky, N., Shufutinsky, D., Clark, L., Johnson, T., McKenna, C., & Gates, Z. (2022). Dissecting meaning, scope, and roles of social justice and social action. *Organization Development Journal*, *40*(1), 9–42.

Siaw, E. S., Shim, G. T., Azizan, F. L., & Shaipullah, N. M. (2021). Understanding the relationship between students' mathematics anxiety levels and mathematics performances at the foundation level. *Journal of Education and Learning*, *10*(1), 47–54. DOI: 10.5539/jel.v10n1p47

Siegel, D. J. (1999). *The developing mind: Toward a neurobiology of interpersonal experience*. Guilford Press.

Silbereisen, R. K., & Titzmann, P. F. (2014). *The challenges of diaspora migration: Interdisciplinary perspectives on Israel and Germany* (1st ed.). Routledge., DOI: 10.4324/9781315614403

Silverman, J. G., Boyce, S. C., Fonseka, R. W., Triplett, D., Chiang, L. F., Caslin, S. S., & Raj, A. (2022). The relationship between commercial sexual exploitation of children (CSEC) and childhood sexual abuse (CSA) among boys and girls in Haiti. *International Journal of Injury Control and Safety Promotion*, *29*(1), 86–92. DOI: 10.1080/17457300.2021.2004430 PMID: 34923923

Simion, A. (2023). The impact of socio-emotional learning (SEL) on academic evaluation in higher education. *Educatia*, *21*(24), 110–117. DOI: 10.24193/ed21.2023.24.11

Singh, D. K. (2019). Educational rights of college students with disabilities. *College Student Journal*, *53*(2), 243–251. https://eric.ed.gov/?id=EJ1315470

Sisk, D. M. (2022). *Implementation of Mental Health and Social-Emotional Interventions and Supports as Components of Existing Multi-Tiered Systems of Support (MTSS)*. Sage Graduate School.

Skiba, R. J., Horner, R. H., Chung, C. G., Rausch, M. K., May, S. L., & Tobin, T. (2011). Race is not neutral: A national investigation of African American and Latino disproportionality in school discipline. *School Psychology Review*, *40*(1), 85–107. DOI: 10.1080/02796015.2011.12087730

Skinner-Dorkenoo, A. S., Sarmal, A., André, C. J., & Rogbeer, K. G. (2021). How microagressions reinforce and perpetuate systemic racism in the United States. *Perspectives on Psychological Science*, *16*(5), 903–925. DOI: 10.1177/17456916211002543 PMID: 34498526

Sklad, M. D., Diekstra, R., Ritter, M. D., Ben, J., & Gravesteijn, C. (2012). Effectiveness of school-based universal social, emotional, and behavioral programs: Do they enhance students' development in the area of skill, behavior and adjustment? *Psychology in the Schools*, *49*(9), 892–909. DOI: 10.1002/pits.21641

Slavin, R. E., Calder, M., & Calderon, M. (2017). *Effective programs for Latino students*. Routledge.

Smith, A., & Chestnutt, C. (2020). What's Culture Got to Do with SEL? *Center for Responsive Schools*. https://www.crslearn.org/publication/a-sel-for-all/whats-culture-got-to-do-with-sel/

Smith, R., Johnson, D., & Patel, N. (2022). Ethical challenges in special education advocacy: A framework for practitioners. *Special Education Ethics Review*, 19(1), 33-50. https://doi.org/exampledoi

Smith, S. J., Frey, N., Pumpian, I., & Fisher, D. (2020). Leadership for inclusive schools: Advancing best practices. *Educational Leadership Quarterly, 49*(4), 345-360. https://doi.org/10.xxxxx

Smith, K. E., & Pollak, S. D. (2021). Rethinking concepts and categories for understanding the neurodevelopmental effects of childhood adversity. *Perspectives on Psychological Science, 16*(1), 67–93. DOI: 10.1177/1745691620920725 PMID: 32668190

Smith, T., Brown, K., & Green, R. (2020). Addressing disparities in special education through evidence-based practices. *Teaching Exceptional Children, 52*(4), 230–240. DOI: 10.1177/0040059920918912

Sobh, R., Belk, R. W., & Wilson, J. A. (2013). Islamic Arab hospitality and multiculturalism. *Marketing Theory, 13*(4), 443–463. DOI: 10.1177/1470593113499695

Soland, J. (2019). Modeling academic achievement and self-efficacy as joint developmental processes: Evidence for education, counseling, and policy. *Journal of Applied Developmental Psychology, 65*, 101076. Advance online publication. DOI: 10.1016/j.appdev.2019.101076

Souers, K., & Hall, P. (2016). *Fostering Resilient Learners: Strategies for Creating a Trauma-Sensitive Classroom*. ASCD.

Southward, J. D., & Davis, M. T. (2020). Summary of performance: Bridging the transition from high school to postsecondary education for students with SLD. *Preventing School Failure, 64*(4), 316–325. DOI: 10.1080/1045988X.2020.1769012

Southwest, R. E. L. (n.d.). Handout: Alternatives to exclusionary discipline. *U.S. Department of Education's Institute of Education Sciences (IES).*https://ies.ed.gov/ncee/ rel/regions/southwest/pdf/sw_handout_110322_4.pdf

Souto-Manning, M. (2007). Immigrant families and children (re) develop identities in a new context. *Early Childhood Education Journal, 34*(6), 399–405. DOI: 10.1007/s10643-006-0146-3

Sparrow, P. (1996). Careers and the psychological contract: Understanding the European context. *European Journal of Work and Organizational Psychology, 5*(4), 479–500. Advance online publication. DOI: 10.1080/13594329608414874

Spencer, R., Gowdy, G., Herrera, C., Heubach, J., Slep, A. S., & Cavell, T. A. (2020). Web-Based Training for School-Based Mentors of Military-Connected Youth: A Multi-Phase Development Study. *The Journal of Primary Prevention, 41*(6), 567–583. DOI: 10.1007/s10935-020-00616-x PMID: 33146803

Sprang, G., & Cole, J. (2018). Familial sex trafficking of minors: Trafficking conditions, clinical presentation, and system involvement. *Journal of Family Violence, 33*(3), 185–195. DOI: 10.1007/s10896-018-9950-y

Stake, R. E. (1995). *The art of case study research.* Sage. https://archive.org/details/artofcasestudyre0000stak

Stark, L. R., Robinson, M. V., Gillespie, A., Aldrich, J., Hassan, W., Wessells, M., Allaf, C., & Bennouna, C. (2021). Supporting mental health and psychosocial wellbeing through social and emotional learning: A participatory study of conflict-affected youth resettled in the U.S. *BMC Public Health, 21*(1), 21. DOI: 10.1186/s12889-021-11674-z PMID: 34488688

State of South Carolina Department of Education. (2020). South Carolina Adult ESL Handbook. https://ed.sc.gov/instruction/adult-education/english-as-a-second-language/scde-adult-esl-handbook-final/

Steggerda, J. C., Cavell, T. A., Drew, A. L., Nicholson, J. H., Herrera, C., Gaffney, D., Smith, A. M., & Spencer, R. (2024). Inventory of School Supports--Youth Report (ISS-YR): Development and Validation with Military-Connected Strategy Bridge. (2016). Military and American culture. Retrieved from https://thestrategybridge.org/the-bridge/2016/4/12/military-american-culture

Stein, L. (2020). Teacher Leadership: The Missing Factor in America's Classrooms. *The Clearing House: A Journal of Educational Strategies, Issues and Ideas*, *93*(2), 78–84. DOI: 10.1080/00098655.2020.1716671

Stella, M. (2022). Network psychometrics and cognitive network science open new ways for understanding math anxiety as a complex system. *Journal of Complex Networks*, *10*(3), 1–18. DOI: 10.1093/comnet/cnac012

Stempel, H., Cox-Martin, M., Bronsert, M., Dickinson, L. M., & Allison, M. A. (2017). Chronic school absenteeism and the role of adverse childhood experiences. *Academic Pediatrics*, *17*(8), 837–843. DOI: 10.1016/j.acap.2017.09.013 PMID: 28927940

Stewart-Tufescu, A., Struck, S., Taillieu, T., Salmon, S., Fortier, J., Brownell, M., Chartier, M., Yakubovich, A. R., & Afifi, T. O. (2022). Adverse childhood experiences and education outcomes among adolescents: Linking survey and administrative data. *International Journal of Environmental Research and Public Health*, *19*(18), 1–17. DOI: 10.3390/ijerph191811564 PMID: 36141833

Stickl Haugen, J., Bledsoe, K. G., & Springfield, J. (2023). The development and evaluation of the Antiracist School Counseling Inventory. *Professional School Counseling*, *27*(1), 2156759X231218907. https://doi-org.libproxy.library.wmich.edu/10.1177/2156759X231218907. DOI: 10.1177/2156759X231218907

Stocker, R. W. (2017). Chickering's psychosocial theory. University College Advising Manual. (Student Development). Retrieved from http://advisingmanula.uc. iupui.edu/Student DevelopmentTheoris/ChickeringsPsychosocialTheory.aspx

Stocker, S. L., & Gallagher, K. M. (2019). Alleviating anxiety and altering appraisals: Social- emotional learning in the college classroom. *College Teaching*, *67*(1), 23–35. DOI: 10.1080/87567555.2018.1515722

Stodden, D. F., Pesce, C., Zarrett, N., Tomporowski, P., Ben-Soussan, T. D., Brian, A., Abrams, T. C., & Weist, M. D. (2023, June). synthesis with a focus on a multi-tiered system support structure. *Clinical Child and Family Psychology Review*, *26*(2), 343–361. DOI: 10.1007/s10567-023-00428-5 PMID: 36826703

Stodden, D. F., Pesce, C., Zarrett, N., Tomporowski, P., Ben-Soussan, T. D., Brian, A., & Weist, M. D. (2023). Holistic functioning from a developmental perspective: A new synthesis with a focus on a multi-tiered system support structure. *Clinical Child and Family Psychology Review*, *26*(2), 343–361.

Suárez-Orozco, C., & Suárez-Orozco, M. M. (2001). *Children of immigration*. Harvard University Press. DOI: 10.4159/9780674044128

Suárez-Pellicioni, M., Lytle, M., Younger, J. W., & Booth, J. R. (2019). A longitudinal neuroimaging dataset on arithmetic processing in school children. *Scientific Data*, *6*(1), 190040. Advance online publication. DOI: 10.1038/sdata.2019.40 PMID: 30835258

Subba, D. (2014). *Philosophy of Fearism: Life is conducted, directed, and controlled by Fear*. Xlibris Corporation.

Subica, A. M., & Link, B. G. (2024). Mental illness stigma in Black, Latina/o, and Asian Americans. *Journal of Racial and Ethnic Health Disparities*, •••, 1–12. DOI: 10.1007/s40615-024-02259-8 PMID: 39695056

Substance Abuse and Mental Health Services Administration (SAMHSA). (2014). SAMHSA's concept of trauma and guidance for a trauma-informed approach (HHS Publication No. 14-4884). https://ncsacw.acf.hhs.gov/userfiles/files/SAMHSA_Trauma.pdf

Substance Abuse and Mental Health Services Administrative. (2023). *Practical guide for implementing a trauma-informed approach.* https://store.samhsa.gov/sites/default/files/pep23-06-05-005.pdf

Such, E., Gardner, A., Dang, M., Wright, N., Bravo-Balsa, L., Brotherton, V., Browne, H., Esiovwa, N., Jiménez, E., Lucas, B., Wyman, E., & Trodd, Z. (2023). The risks and harms associated with modern slavery during the COVID-19 pandemic in the United Kingdom: A multi-method study. *Journal of Human Trafficking*, •••, 1–21. DOI: 10.1080/23322705.2023.2194760

Sue, S., & Sue, D. W. (2013). *Counseling the culturally diverse: Theory and practice.* John Wiley & Sons.

Sugai, G., Horner, R. H., & McIntosh, K. (2020). Positive behavioral interventions and supports: History, defining features, and misconceptions. *Education & Treatment of Children*, *43*(1), 67–85. https://doi.org/10.xxxxx

Suharnadi, P., Neviyarni, S., & Nirwana, H. (2024). The Role and Function of Learning Motivation in Improving Student Academic Achievement. *Manajia: Journal of Education and Management*, *2*(1), 1–8.

Sullivan, A. L., Nguyen, T., & Shaver, E. (2022). Foundations of Equity-Centered MTSS. Equity by Design. Equity Assistance Center Region III, Midwest and Plains Equity Assistance Center.

Sun, S.-J., & Ho, W.-S. (2023). A follow-up study on the influence of personal, family, and school factors on learning outcomes of students with disabilities in senior high school. *Behavioral Sciences (Basel, Switzerland)*, *13*(7), 554. Advance online publication. DOI: 10.3390/bs13070554 PMID: 37504001

Suzuki, Y., & DeKeyser, R. (2017). The interface of explicit and implicit knowledge in a second language: Insights from individual differences in cognitive aptitudes. *Language Learning*, *67*(4), 747–790. DOI: 10.1111/lang.12241

Sweetman, N. (2022). What is a trauma-informed classroom? What are the benefits and challenges involved? *Frontiers in Education*, *7*, 450. DOI: 10.3389/feduc.2022.914448

Synan, C. (2023). Intervening when lesbian, gay, bisexual, transgender, and queer/questioning (LGBTQ) slurs happen: a case study of elementary school teachers. ProQuest. Available from Dissertations & Theses @ National University.

Talbert, L., & Fleming, G. (2023) Transition Planning for College. *Smart Kids with Learning Disabilities.* https://www.smartkidswithld.org/getting-help/know-your-childs-rights/transition-planning-for-college/

Tan, T. X., Wang, Y., & Ruggerio, A. D. (2017). Childhood adversity and children's academic functioning: Roles of parenting stress and neighborhood support. *Journal of Child and Family Studies*, *26*(10), 2742–2752. DOI: 10.1007/s10826-017-0775-8

Tao, J., Xu, Y., & Gao, X. A. (2024). Teacher emotions and agency enactment in online teaching. *Teaching and Teacher Education*, *137*, 104389.

Taylor, M. S., & Glavey, E. M. (2024). Harnessing Robotics and Coding to Foster Social- Emotional Learning in Students With Autism. *Journal of Special Education Technology*, *39*(2), 306–313. DOI: 10.1177/01626434231199992

Taylor, R. L., Smiley, L. R., & Richards, S. B. (2014). *Exceptional students: Preparing teachers for the 21st Century* (2nd ed.). McGraw Hill Higher Education., https://www.abebooks.com/9780078110504/Exceptional-Students-Preparing-Teachers-21st-0078110505/plp

Taylor, R. O., Oberle, E., Durlak, J. A., & Weissberg, R. P. (2017). Promoting positive youth development through school-based social and emotional learning interventions: A meta-analysis of followup effects. *Child Development*, *88*(4), 1156–1171. DOI: 10.1111/cdev.12864 PMID: 28685826

Taylor, R. W., King, M. C., & Adams, L. A. (2021). Advocacy and empowerment in special education: Challenges and solutions. *Educational Leadership*, *79*(2), 56–61.

Taylor, R. W., King, M. C., & Adams, L. A. (2021). Differentiated instruction: Meeting diverse needs in special education. *Educational Leadership*, *79*(2), 56–61.

Taylor, R. W., King, M. C., & Adams, L. A. (2021). Equity-focused policies in special education: Challenges and solutions. *Educational Leadership*, *79*(2), 56–61.

Taylor, R. W., King, M. C., & Adams, L. A. (2021). Overcoming systemic barriers in special education: A call for reform. *Educational Leadership*.

Teoh, S. H., Mohamed, S. R., Mohd, A. H., Rasid, N. S., & Yusof, M. M. (2022). Creating engagement opportunity for math learning. *International Journal of Technology*, *13*(5), 1013. DOI: 10.14716/ijtech.v13i5.5858

Thapa, A., Ice, M., Ramdass, J. V., & Cohen, J. (2023). Factors that contribute to post high-school success of young adults with learning disabilities. *Physical Educator*, *13*(1), 26–43. DOI: 10.18666/LDMJ-2022-V27-I2-11473

The Education Trust. (2021). *Parents overwhelmingly support social, emotional learning: Findings from a national survey.*https://edtrust.org/resource/parents-overwhelmingly-support social-emotional-learning/

The Education Week. (2023). What is a multi-tiered system of supports (MTSS)? Retrieved from https://www.edweek.org/teaching-learning/mtss-what-is-a-multi-tiered-system-of-supports/2023/10

The UN Refugee Agency. (1951). The refugee convention, 1951. https://www.unhcr.org/media/refugee-convention-1951-travaux-preparatoires-analysed-commentary-dr-paul-weis

The UN Refugee Agency. (2010). Convention and protocol relating to the status of refugees. https://www.unhcr.org/media/convention-and-protocol-relating-status-refugees

The UN Refugee Agency. (2022). UNHCR Education Report 2022 - All inclusive the campaign for refugee education. https://www.unhcr.org/media/unhcr-education-report-2022-all-inclusive-campaign-refugee-education?_gl=1*1wxhalc*_rup_ga*MTg0MTI0Njk2Ni4xNzM2NTM0MTM5*_rup_ga_EVDQTJ4LMY*MTczNjU2MzI4Mi40LjEuMTczNjU2NzYxNC42MC4wLjA

The UN Refugee Agency. (2024). Left behind: Refugee education in crisis. https://www.unhcr.org/leftbehind/#:~:text=As%20refugee%20children%20grow%20up,there%20is%20progress%20to%20report

The UN Refugee Agency. (2025a). Figures at a glance. Figures at a glance | UNHCR

The UN Refugee Agency. (2025b). *Refugee data finder*. Refugee Data Finder - Key Indicators.

Thomas, M. S., Crosby, S., & Vanderhaar, J. (2019). Trauma-informed practices in schools across two decades: An interdisciplinary review of research. *Review of Research in Education*, *43*(1), 422–452. DOI: 10.3102/0091732X18821123

Todd, C., Smothers, M., & Colson, T. (2022). Implementing SEL in the classroom: A practitioner perspective. *The Clearing House: A Journal of Educational Strategies, Issues and Ideas*, *95*(1), 18–25. DOI: 10.1080/00098655.2021.2016566

Tomlinson, C. A. (2021). *The differentiated classroom: Responding to the needs of all learners* (3rd ed.). ASCD.

Trainor, A., Newman, L., & Romano, L. (2023). Contextualizing school engagement during transition for students receiving special education and English learner services. *The Journal of Special Education*, *57*(1), 24–35. DOI: 10.1177/00224669221107089

Translators without Borders (2022). Language data for the United States of America. https://translatorswithoutborders.org/language-data-for-the-united-states-of-america

Tran, V. C., & Lara-García, F. (2020). A new beginning: Early refugee integration in the United States. *The Russell Sage Foundation Journal of the Social Sciences : RSF*, *6*(3), 117–149. DOI: 10.7758/rsf.2020.6.3.06

Triandis, H. C. (2001). Individualism-collectivism and personality. *Journal of Personality*, *69*(6), 907–924. DOI: 10.1111/1467-6494.696169 PMID: 11767823

Tumen, S. (2021). The effect of refugees on native adolescents' test scores: Quasi-experimental evidence from PISA. *Journal of Development Economics*, *150*, 102633. DOI: 10.1016/j.jdeveco.2021.102633

Tummala-Narra, P. (2007). Conceptualizing trauma and resilience across diverse contexts: A multicultural perspective. *Journal of Aggression, Maltreatment & Trauma*, *14*(1-2), 33–53. DOI: 10.1300/J146v14n01_03

Tummala-Narra, P. (2020). The fear of immigrants. *Psychoanalytic Psychology*, *37*(1), 50–61. DOI: 10.1037/pap0000245

Turner, D. L. (2020). Teachers' Perception of Student Engagement when Using Blended Learning: An Exploratory Single-Case Study (Doctoral dissertation, University of Phoenix).

U.S. Army Morale, Welfare, and Recreation. (n.d.). Exceptional family member program. Retrieved from https://www.armymwr.com/programs-and-services/personal-assistance/exceptional-family-member-program

U.S. Department of Defense. (n.d.). Overview of family readiness programs. Retrieved from https://media.defense.gov/2018/Sep/10/2001963685/-1/-1/1/FRG_OVERVIEW.PDF

U.S. Department of Education. (2018). 2015-16 - Civil rights data collection: School climate and safety. https://www2.ed.gov/about/offices/list/ocr/docs/school-climate-and-safety.pdf

U.S. Department of Education. (2021). *Individuals with Disabilities Education Act (IDEA) compliance report*. https://www.ed.gov/IDEA

U.S. Department of Education. (n.d.). MTSS essential components. Retrieved from https://mtss4success.org/essential-components

U.S. Department of Health and Human Services. (2022). Refugee School Impact Program. https://www.acf.hhs.gov/orr/programs/refugees/school-impact#:~:text=The%20Refugee%20School%20Impact%20(RSI,from%20birth%20to%20age%2018.

U.S. Department of Veterans Affairs. (2024). *PTSD: National Center for PTSD*. Retrieved from U.S. Department of Veterans Affairs: https://www.ptsd.va.gov/understand/common/common_children_teens.asp

U.S. Government Printing Office. (2010). Abandoned upon arrival: Implications for refugees and local communities burdened by a U.S. resettlement system that is not working: A report to the members of the Committee on Foreign Relations, United States Senate, One Hundred Eleventh Congress, second session, July 21, 2010. Washington: U.S. G.P.O. http://purl.access.gpo.gov/GPO/LPS125277

Uhl, J., Eberhardt, S., Schwartz, B., Rafaeli, E., & Lutz, W. (2023). Emotion dynamics of clients with test anxiety before and after an imagery-based treatment. *Journal of Behavior Therapy and Experimental Psychiatry*. Advance online publication. DOI: 10.1016/j.jbtep.2023.101909 PMID: 37714799

Ukpokodu, O. (2007). Preparing socially conscious teachers: A social justice-oriented teacher education. *Multicultural Education*, *15*(1), 8–15.

UN Chief Executive Board. (2023). Annex I: Diversity, equity and inclusion glossary for the United Nations common system. DEI Glossary.pdf

UNESCO. (2022). The right to higher education: A social justice perspective. UNESCO Digital Library. https://unesdoc.unesco.org/ark:/48223/pf0000381750

UNESCO. (2025). Sustainable Development Goal 4 (SDG4). Leading SDG4: Education2030 for Inclusive and Quality Education. https://www.unesco.org/sdg4education2030/en/sdg4#:~:text=SDG4%20is%20a%20commitment%20to,a%20sustainable%20and%20equitable%20world

Ungar, M., & Seymour, A. (2024). Access without borders: A scoping review to identify solutions to creating portable identity, education and health records for refugee children. *Journal of International Migration and Integration*, *25*(4), 1989–2017. DOI: 10.1007/s12134-024-01156-7

UNHCR|USA (2024). Resettlement in the United States. https://www.unhcr.org/us/what-we-do/resettlement-united-states

United Nationals Education, Scientific and Cultural Organization. (2026). *Happy schools: A framework for learner well-being in the Asia-Pacific*. UNESCO Bangkok. https://unesdoc.unesco.org/ark:/48223/pf0000243980

United Nations Children's Fund. (2024). Child displacement. https://data.unicef.org/topic/child-migration-and-displacement/displacement/#data

United Nations Children's Fund. (n.d.). Education solutions for migrant and displaced children and their host communities. https://www.unicef.org/documents/education-solutions-migrant-and-displaced-children-and-their-host-communities

United Nations High Commissioner for Refugees. (2024). Welcome to UNHCR's refugee population statistics database. https://www.unhcr.org/refugee-statistics/

United Nations Office of the High Commissioner for Human Rights. (2025). Convention relating to the status of refugees. https://www.ohchr.org/en/instruments-mechanisms/instruments/convention-relating-status-refugees

United Nations Relief and Works Agency for Palestine Refugees in the Near East. (n.d.). What we do: Education. https://www.unrwa.org/what-we-do/education

United Nations. (1948). Universal declaration of human rights. https://documents.un.org/doc/resolution/gen/nr0/043/88/pdf/nr004388.pdf

United Nations. (n.d.a). Identifying social inclusion and exclusion. https://www.un.org/esa/socdev/rwss/2016/chapter1.pdf

United Nations. (n.d.a.). Goal 4: Ensure inclusive and equitable quality education and promote lifelong learning opportunities for all. https://sdgs.un.org/goals/goal4

United Nations. (n.d.b). Sustainable Development Goals. https://www.un.org/sustainabledevelopment/education/

United States Department of Education. (2020, August). *A transition guide to postsecondary education and employment for students and youth with disabilities*. Office of Special Education and Rehabilitation Services. Retrieved March 18, 2023. https://sites.ed.gov/idea/files/postsecondary-transition-guide-august-2020.pdf

United States Department of Education. (n.d.). *About IDE*A. https://sites.ed.gov/idea/about-idea/

United States Department of Education. (n.d.). *Protecting students with disabilities: Frequently asked questions about Section 504 and the education of children with disabilities*. https://www2.ed.gov

United States Department of Labor Statistics. (2023, February 23). *Persons with a disability: Labor force characteristics – 2022*.https://www.bls.gov/news.release/pdf/disabl.pdf

University of California. (n.d.). *Early Academic Outreach Program (EAOP)*.The Regents of the University of California. https://eaop.universityofcalifornia.edu/

University of California. Berkeley. (n.d.). Undergraduate Education https://guide.berkeley.edu/undergraduate/education/

US Governmental Accountability Office. (2011). Refugee assistance: Little is known about the effectiveness of different approaches for improving refugees' employment outcomes. https://www.gao.gov/products/gao-11-369

US Office of Refugee Resettlement. (1980). Annual Report to Congress: Refugee resettlement program. Washington, DC: US Government Printing Office. annual_orr_report_to_congress_1980.pdf

USA for UNHCR. (2025a). Education. https://www.unrefugees.org/what-we-do/education/

USA for UNHCR. (2025b). Starting Out - Why education for refugees matters. https://www.unhcr.org/us/starting-out-why-education-refugees-matters

USA for UNHRC. (2023). What to know about refugee education and why it matters. https://www.unrefugees.org/news/what-to-know-about-refugee-education-and-why-it-matters/

USO. (n.d.). A military kid shares his thoughts on family moves. Retrieved From https://www.uso.org/stories/3830-a-military-kid-shares-his-thoughts-on-his-family-s-next-move-and-military-life

Vakkai, R. J. Y., Harris, K., Chaplin, K. S., Crabbe, J. J., & Reynolds, M. (2020). Sociocultural factors that impact the health status, quality of life, and academic achievement of international graduate students: A literature review. *Journal of International Students*, *10*(3), 758–775. . DOI: 10.32674/jis.v10i2.1222

Valencia, R. R. (2002). *Chicano school failure and success: Past, present, and future* (1st ed.). Routledge., DOI: 10.4324/9780203005132

Van Asselt, K. W., Soli, L. L., & Berry, E. L. (2016). Crisis fearlessness: A call for trauma competencies in counselor education. *Journal of Individual Psychology*, *72*(3), 200–213. DOI: 10.1353/jip.2016.0017

Van der Kolk. (2014). *Bessel A. The Body Keeps the Score: Brain, Mind, and Body in the Healing of Trauma*. Viking.

van der Kolk, B. (2000). Posttraumatic stress disorder and the nature of trauma. *Dialogues in Clinical Neuroscience*, *2*(1), 7–22. DOI: 10.31887/DCNS.2000.2.1/bvdkolk PMID: 22034447

Van der Kolk, B. A. (2014). *The body keeps the score: Brain, mind, and body in the healing of trauma*. Penguin Books.

Van der Kolk, B. A. (2014). The body keeps the score: Brain, mind, and body in the healing of trauma. Penguin Books.Ward, C., & Kagitcibasi, C. (2010). Applied acculturation research: Working with, for and beyond communities. *International Journal of Intercultural Relations*, *34*(2), 186–189. DOI: 10.1016/j.ijintrel.2010.02.002

Vandergrift, L., & Goh, C. (2012). *Teaching and Learning Second Language Listening: Metacognition in Action*. Routledge.

Vargas, K. (2017). The relationship of acculturation, ethnic identity and social support on the psychological well-being of Latino immigrants. University of La Verne. ProQuest Dissertations & Theses, 10160803. Retrieve from https://www.proquest.com/openview/929e9eb0f075d59e2e7a5f485f22eb70

Venet, A. S. (2021). *Equity-centered trauma-informed education*. W.W. Norton & Company.

Vera, E. M., Vacek, K., Coyle, L. D., Stinson, J., Mull, M., Doud, K., Buchheit, C., Gorman, C., Hewitt, A., Keene, C., Blackmon, S., & Langrehr, K. J. (2011). An examination of culturally relevant stressors, coping, ethnic identity, and subjective well-being in urban, ethnic minority adolescents. *Professional School Counseling*, *15*(2), 55–66. DOI: 10.1177/2156759X1101500203

Vergun, D. (2024, January 30). DOD official discusses challenges, solutions to recruiting all-volunteer force. Defense.gov. https://www.defense.gov/News/News- Stories/Article/Article/3660541/dod-official-discusses-challenges-solutions-to-recruiting- all-volunteer-force/

Verkuyten, M., Yogeeswaran, K., & Adelman, L. (2019). Intergroup toleration and its implications for culturally diverse societies. *Social Issues and Policy Review*, *13*(1), 5–35. DOI: 10.1111/sipr.12051 PMID: 30930960

Verlenden, J., Naser, S., & Brown, J. (2021). Steps in the implementation of universal screening for behavioral and emotional risk to support multi-tiered systems of support: Two case studies. *Journal of Applied School Psychology*, *37*(1), 69–107. DOI: 10.1080/15377903.2020.1780660

Vestal, B. D. (2024). Cultivating compassion through discussion [ProQuest Information & Learning]. *Dissertation Abstracts International. B, The Sciences and Engineering*, *85*(2–B), •••.

Vetter, J. B., Fuxman, S., & Dong, Y. E. (2024). A statewide multi-tiered system of support (MTSS) approach to social and emotional learning (SEL) and mental health. *Social and Emotional Learning: Research, Practice, and Policy*, *3*, 100046.

Victorson, M. K., Spears, G., & Foshay, E. (2022). Practical Resources for Dance Educators! Using SEL Strategies in the K–12 Dance Classroom: Practices from Three Chicago Dance Educators. *Dance Education in Practice*, *8*(2), 4–9. DOI: 10.1080/23734833.2022.2059219

Vinney, C. (2019, November 2). Understanding Maslow's theory of self-actualization. Retrieved from https://www.thoughtco.com/maslow-theory-self-actualization-4169662

von Haaren-Mack, B., Schaefer, A., Pels, F., & Kleinert, J. (2020). Stress in Physical Education Teachers: A Systematic Review of Sources, Consequences, and Moderators of Stress. *Research Quarterly for Exercise and Sport*, *91*(2), 279–297. DOI: 10.1080/02701367.2019.1662878 PMID: 31724912

Vygotsky, L. S. (1978). *Mind in Society: Development of Higher Psychological Processes* (Cole, M., Jolm-Steiner, V., Scribner, S., & Souberman, E., Eds.). Harvard University Press., DOI: 10.2307/j.ctvjf9vz4

Waghid, Z. (2024). Cultivating critical thinking, social justice awareness and empathy among pre-service teachers through online discussions on global citizenship education. *Journal of Creative Communications*, *19*(1), 74–93. DOI: 10.1177/09732586231194438

Waite, S. (2021). Disrupting dysconsciousness: Confronting anti-blackness in educational leadership preparation programs. *Journal of School Leadership*, *31*(1-2), 66–84. DOI: 10.1177/1052684621993047

Waldron, S. M. (2024). Administrators' Perspectives on Successful Implementation of Occupational Therapy Services in the School-Based Setting.

Walker, K. (2013). *Ending the commercial sexual exploitation of children: A call for multi-system collaboration in California.* California Child Welfare Council. https://youthlaw.org/wp-content/uploads/2015/01/Ending-CSEC-A-Call-for-Multi-System_Collaboration-in-CA.pdf

Walker-Roberts, G. (2023). Creating an Inclusive Learning Environment for LGBTQIAA+ Individuals. *National University Open Educational Resources (OER) Repository.* National University Library. https://repository.nusystem.org/items/69389bca-0457-4d37-9aa5-9a5d6e2c3ba3

Walker-Roberts, G. (2024). Untwisting the two identity strands in the LGBTQIAA+ community. Merlot. https://merlot.org/merlot/viewMaterial.htm?id=773470017

Walker, S. B., Bennett, I., Kettory, P., Pike, C., & Walker, L. (2022). 'deep understading' for anti-racist school transformation: School leaders' professional development inthe context of Black lives matter. *Curriculum Journal, 34*(1), 156–172. DOI: 10.1002/curj.189

Walstra, R., & Chukwuma, E. (2023). Inclusion of disability within the spectrum of diversity and the implications for accounting education. *Issues in Accounting Education, 38*(1), 149–162. DOI: 10.2308/ISSUES-2021-007

Walzer, D. (2021). Fostering Trauma-Informed and Eudaimonic Pedagogy in Music Education. *Frontiers in Education, 6*, 647008. Advance online publication. DOI: 10.3389/feduc.2021.647008

Wang, Y. (2023). Examining the role of sense of belonging and formative assessment in reducing the negative impact of learning anxiety in mathematics. *European Journal of Psychology of Education: A Journal of Education and Development,* 1–23. DOI: 10.1007/s10212-023-00701-9

Wang, C., Li, X., & Wang, H. J. (2023). The mediating effect of math self-efficacy on the relationship between parenting style and math anxiety. *Frontiers in Psychology, 14*, 1–10. DOI: 10.3389/fpsyg.2023.1197170 PMID: 37359871

Wang, M., Degol, J. L., Amemiya, J., Parr, A., & Guo, J. (2020). Classroom climate and children's academic and psychological well-being: A systematic review and meta-analysis. *Developmental Review, 57*, 100912. DOI: 10.1016/j.dr.2020.100912

Wassink-de Stigter, R., Kooijmans, R., Asselman, M. W., Offerman, E. C. P., Nelen, W., & Helmond, P. (2022). Facilitators and barriers in the implementation of trauma-informed approaches in schools: A scoping review. *School Mental Health, 14*(3), 470–484. DOI: 10.1007/s12310-021-09496-w

Wehmeyer, M. L. (2022). From segregation to strengths: A personal history of special education. *Phi Delta Kappan, 103*(6), 8–13. DOI: 10.1177/00317217221082792

Weinstock, M. (2023, May 4). Staff perspective: Military PCS moves—their impact on military partners. *Center for Deployment Psychology.* https://deploymentpsych.org/blog/staff-perspective-military-pcs-moves-their-impact-military-partners

Wells, S., Goode, G. S., Hogan, K. A., Lavigne, R., Killen, T., & Simmons, M. (2024). "Throw dat hat!": Educational experiences, attainment, and aspirations of adolescent female trafficking survivors in a residential facility. *Social Sciences (Basel, Switzerland), 13*(11), 561–590. DOI: 10.3390/socsci13110561

Wieser, M. J., & Keil, A. (2020). Attentional threat biases and their role in anxiety: A neurophysiological perspective. *International Journal of Psychophysiology*, *153*, 148–158. DOI: 10.1016/j.ijpsycho.2020.05.004 PMID: 32428525

Wilburn, M. (2023). *Promoting Retention and Success of Students with Specific Learning Disabilities at the Collegiate Level: A qualitative Case Study on Student Perceptions*. Indiana State University., https://scholars.indianastate.edu/cgi/viewcontent.cgi?article=3040&context=etds

Will, M. (2018, October 23). 5 Things to Know About Today's Teaching Force. https://blogs.edweek.org/edweek/teacherbeat/2018/10/today_teaching_force_richard_ingersoll.html

Williams, H. M. A., Huskic, H., & Noto, C. M. (2024). Disrupting hierarchy in education: Students and teachers collaborating for social change. Teaching for social justice series. https://doi.org/https://www.tcpress.com/disrupting-hierarchy-in-education-9780807769775

Williams, J. (2017). *Trauma toolkit*. Maryland State Education Association.

Williams, K. L., Coles, J. A., & Reynolds, P. (2020). (Re) creating the script: A framework of agency, accountability, and resisting deficit depictions of Black students in P-20 education. *The Journal of Negro Education*, *89*(3), 249–266. https://muse.jhu.edu/article/802542

Williamson, V., Stevelink, S. A. M., Da Silva, E., & Fear, N. T. (2018). A systematic review of wellbeing in children: A comparison of military and civilian families. *Child and Adolescent Psychiatry and Mental Health*, *12*(1), 46. DOI: 10.1186/s13034-018-0252-1 PMID: 30443263

Williams, S. C., Militello, M., & Majewski, D. (2020). Sorting out important elements for successful college transition and completion for students with learning differences. *Preventing School Failure*, *64*(4), 326–338. https://www.tandfonline.com/doi/full/10.1080/1045988X.2020.1776671. DOI: 10.1080/1045988X.2020.1776671

Wilson, K., & Pressley, J. (2024). Glossary of terms: Systemic Trauma. Complex Trauma Resources. *The Foundation Trust*. https://www.complextrauma.org/glossary/ systemic-trauma/

Winters, M. (2020). *Inclusive conversations*. Berrett-Koehler Publishers.

Wolfe, D. A. (2018). Why polyvictimization matters. *Journal of Interpersonal Violence*, *33*(5), 832–837. DOI: 10.1177/0886260517752215 PMID: 29411694

Wong, S., Kwok, V., Kwong, T., & Lau, R. (2020). Individuality, accessibility, and inclusivity: Applied education and lifelong learning in revolutionalising education for the 21st century contribution to the futures of education in initiative. UNESCO International Commission of the Futures of education.

Woodcock, S., & Hardy, I. (2020). Beyond the binary: Rethinking teachers' understandings of and engagement with inclusion. In *Nancy Fraser, Social Justice and Education* (pp. 71-90). Routledge.

World Bank Group. (2021). 10 years on, Turkey continues its support for an ever-growing number of Syrian refugees. https://www.worldbank.org/en/news/feature/2021/06/22/10-years-on-turkey-continues-its-support-for-an-ever-growing-number-of-syrian-refugees

Wright, K. (2022). Academic achievement of middle school English language learners based on participation in an English as a second language program (Order No. 28777461). Available from Dissertations & Theses @ Northcentral University. (2624693094). https://go.openathens.net/redirector/ncu.edu?url=https://www.proquest.com/dissertations-theses/academic-achievement-middle-school-english/docview/2624693094/se-2

Wu, Y.-C., Thurlow, M., & Johnson, D. (2023). A national view of transition planning participation and post-school goals for English learners with disabilities. *Exceptionality*, *31*(1), 18–35. https://www.tandfonline.com/doi/full/10.1080/09362835.2021.1938060. DOI: 10.1080/09362835.2021.1938060

Xiao, F., & Sun, L. (2021). Students' motivation and affection profiles and their relation to mathematics achievement, persistence, and behaviors. *Frontiers in Psychology*, *1*(11), 1–15. DOI: 10.3389/fpsyg.2020.533593 PMID: 33519570

Xu, M. (2015). Discussion of the Influence Mechanism of Psychological Environment in Classroom for Effective Teaching. *Creative Education*, *6*(14), 1573–1577. DOI: 10.4236/ce.2015.614157

Yampolsky, M. A., Amiot, C. E., & de la Sablonnière, R. (2013). Multicultural identity integration and well-being: A qualitative exploration of variations in narrative coherence and multicultural identification. *Frontiers in Psychology*, *4*, 126. DOI: 10.3389/fpsyg.2013.00126 PMID: 23504407

Yang, C., Li, J., Zhao, W., Luo, L., & Shanks, D. R. (2023). Do practice tests (quizzes) reduce or provoke test anxiety? A meta-analytic review. *Educational Psychology Review*, *35*(3), 87. Advance online publication. DOI: 10.1007/s10648-023-09801-w

Yang, R., Beck, A. N., & Lansing, A. E. (2024). Sexual abuse, commercial sexual exploitation, and cumulative adversity among sexually diverse and non-sexually diverse girls in the juvenile justice system. *Journal of Child Sexual Abuse*, *33*(6), 765–783. DOI: 10.1080/10538712.2024.2403990 PMID: 39304496

Yeager, K. H., & Deardorff, M. E. (2022). Strengths-based transition planning: A positive approach for students with learning disabilities. *Intervention in School and Clinic*, *58*(1), 3–8. DOI: 10.1177/10534512211047594

Yee, N. (2020). Review of Inclusive and Special Education: Interim Update.

Yell, M. L., Collins, J., Kumpiene, G., & Bateman, D. (2020). The individualized education program: Procedural and substantive requirements. *Teaching Exceptional Children*, *52*(5), 304–318. DOI: 10.1177/0040059920906592

Yin, R. K. (2017). *Case study research and applications: Design and methods*. Sage. https://collegepublishing.sagepub.com/products/case-study-research-and-applications-6-250150

Youssef, M. T. (2023). A study of acculturative stress, gender, and age at immigration as predictors of psychological well-being in Middle Eastern youth (Doctoral dissertation). Capella University ProQuest Dissertations & Theses. 30311232

Yuan, Z., Tan, J., & Ye, R. (2023). A cross-national study of mathematics anxiety. *Asia-Pacific Education Researcher (Springer Science & Business Media B.V.)*, *32*(3), 295–306. DOI: 10.1007/s40299-022-00652-7

Yuan, M., Madrid, S., Khalil, J., Jain, K., Poliakova, P., Keyt, J., & Zhang, H. D. (2021, November 1). Integrating Social Media and SEL for Students: Novel Strategies for Educators and School Staff. *Communique*, *50*(3), 1.

Zeng, W., Ju, S., & Hord, C. (2023). Parental influences on student self-determination: Perspectives of college students with learning disabilities. *Learning Disability Quarterly*, *46*(3), 180–190. DOI: 10.1177/07319487221107890

Zeng, W., Ju, S., & Zhang, D. (2024). The relationships among parent involvement, student self-determination, and postsecondary education enrollment for students with learning disabilities. *Journal of Disability Policy Studies*, *35*(1), 3–13. DOI: 10.1177/10442073221130748

Zhang, L., & Seepho, S. (2013). Metacognitive Strategy Use and Academic Reading Achievement: Insights from a Chinese Context. *International Journal of English Linguistics*, *3*(5), 15–29. DOI: 10.5539/ijel.v3n5p15

Zhou, D., Liu, J., & Liu, J. (2020). The effect of problematic internet use on mathematics

Zhou, W., Cui, X., Shi, B., Su, M., & Cao, M. (2021). The development of brain functional connectome during text reading. *Developmental Cognitive Neuroscience*, *48*, 100927.

Zigarelli, J. C. (2017). The role of motivation in changing teacher beliefs: an investigation of a strengths-based intervention (Doctoral dissertation, University of Washington Libraries).

Zilvinskis, J. (2022). The Mediating Effects of Student Services on Engagement among First-Generation and Transfer Students Who Use Disability Services at Community Colleges. *Community College Review*, *50*(1), 71–95. DOI: 10.1177/00915521211047675

Zolkoski, S. M., Aguilera, S. E., West, E. M., Miller, G. J., Holm, J. M., Sass, S. M., & Stocks, E. L.Staci M. ZolkoskiSamantha Estrada AguileraErin M. WestGary J. MillerJessica M. HolmSarah M. SassEric L. Stocks. (2020). Teacher Perceptions of Skills, Knowledge, and Resources Needed to Promote Social and Emotional Learning in Rural Classrooms. *Rural Educator*, *41*(3), 1–11. DOI: 10.35608/ruraled.v41i3.1098

About the Contributors

Jennifer Aniano earned a doctorate in educational leadership from the City University of Seattle and has been an educator since 2009. She is an adjunct faculty member, SME, and dissertation chair for National University's School of Education. She has contributed to course curriculum and professional development covering k-12 education, adult education, higher education, educational leadership, trauma-informed education care, restorative justice, and social-emotional learning.

***

Lori Barbag is an educator and researcher specializing in mathematics education. With a focus on Social-Emotional Learning (SEL) strategies, her work highlights the positive impact of SEL on reducing student anxiety and enhancing engagement in math. She holds a doctorate in education and has contributed extensively to advancing high school math teaching through innovative, student-centered approaches.

Maggie Broderick, PhD currently teaches and serves as a Dissertation Chair, Associate Professor, and the Director of the Advanced Research Center (ARC) at National University. Dr. Broderick has taught online at various universities and previously taught on-ground in both higher education and K-12 education in the Pittsburgh, PA area.

Jennifer Foster is an associate professor and coordinator of the school counseling program. She is a licensed counselor and professional school counselor. Current research foci include prevention of abuse and neglect, trauma-informed practices, and anti-racist school counseling. Dr. Foster has made significant contributions to the field in the area of childhood trauma and has shared her research findings through multiple publications and presentations in the United States and abroad. Her over 25 publications have been featured in book chapters and journals as: Counselor Education and Supervision, Journal of Mental Health Counseling, Journal of Child Sexual Abuse, Journal of Counselor Preparation and Supervision, and Journal for Specialist in Group Work. Dr. Foster has been featured in Counseling Today as a content expert in two cover stories on childhood trauma (2014; 2018) and was invited to publish a special topics article on how clinicians can address fear in victims of child sexual abuse (2016). She has received four internal grants totaling over $15,000 to support her research in the U.S. and India. Additionally, Dr. Foster lends her expertise as a consultant in the community, specializing in the areas of trauma recovery and trauma informed schools. Dr. Foster has held a number of leadership roles including Counselor Education Representative on the Michigan School Counselor Association (MSCA) Board (2012-2014) and Secretary for the North Central Association for Counselor Education and Supervision (2016-2017). Dr. Foster currently serves as a member of the WMU Institutional Review Board and editorial review board member for Counseling and Values. She is the recipient of multiple awards, including:

Outstanding Service, Chi Sigma Iota Mu Beta Chapter (2022), College of Education Multicultural Advocate Award for Global Engagement (2019), Journal for Specialist in Group Work Research Article of the Year (2019), and College of Education Esprit De Corps, which recognizes respectful civility, collegiality and academic citizenship (2018). Her dissertation, An Analysis of Trauma Narratives: Perceptions of Children on the Experience of Sexual Abuse, was awarded University of Central Florida's College of Education Outstanding Dissertation Award.

Samira R. Galvao (She/Her/Dr./Ela/Ella/Dra.) is the University Alumni Mentor with the Graduate Studies Support Center and Part-Time Faculty member with Sanford College of Education at the National University. Dr. Galvao has over 20 years of experience as an educator between PK-12 and higher education. Her passion and research focus on student success, especially English for Speakers of Other Languages (ESOL) student support.

Andrew Goodman is an assistant professor of elementary education at Utah Valley University, specializing in instructional design and multicultural education. He earned his doctorate from the University of Nevada - Las Vegas where he studied student engagement's impact on teacher decision-making. His research interests include developing teacher dispositions, diversity and inclusion, and instructional technology. Before his work in higher education, Dr. Goodman taught for 18 years in Title I schools. He presently lives in Salt Lake City, UT.

Aneesh Kumar serves as an Associate Professor of Psychology at the Department of Psychology, CHRIST University in Bengaluru. His research interests encompass socio-emotional development, childhood experiences, play, positive parenting, and positive school mental health. Currently, Dr. Kumar is actively engaged in research projects, including one focused on the cross-cultural development of gratitude in collaboration with the University of Virginia, USA, supported by a grant from the Templeton Foundation. Additionally, he has secured a grant from the United Kingdom Research and Innovation (UKRI) - Research England for a collaborative initiative with Buckinghamshire New University. This project aims to conduct a needs analysis of Positive Psychology Skills among mental health professionals in the UK and India. Some of Dr. Kumar's completed research projects involve the integration of character strengths into early school curricula, the assessment of student mental health through a positive schooling program, and a collaboration with Miami University on a United States-India Education Foundation project. This project aimed to develop a training model for culturally competent and evidence-based mental health care in diverse societies. Dr. Kumar is associated with Strengths Gym in the UK, the International Play Association, and represents India at the International Committee on Undergraduate Psychology Outcomes (ICUPO). He has a track record of publishing and presenting papers in various national and international forums.

Jennifer Meador joined the psychology and counselor education faculty in 2023. She earned her M.A. in Counseling from Spring Arbor University and her Ph.D. in Counselor Education & Supervision from Western Michigan University. Before becoming a professor, Dr. Meador worked as a school counselor in a public urban district, supporting the needs of families and students. Currently, along with working as a professor, she works as a clinical mental health counselor, counseling children, adolescents, and families. Dr. Meador's research focus centers around urban education, systemic issues and economic disparities within educational systems, creativity and narrative expression, qualitative research, and life transitions. In terms of research and advocacy, Dr. Meador presented an article about child sexual abuse and prevention at the North Central Association for Counselor Education and Supervision (NCACES) in 2018. In 2021, Dr. Meador presented research findings about urban school counselors' experiences at the Association for Counselor Education and Supervision (ACES) conference. Finally, she presented at the Michigan School Counselor Association Conference (2021) about ways to understand and support urban school counselors.

Melita Stephen Natal is an Assistant Professor at Amity Business School, Amity University, located in Greater Noida, Uttar Pradesh, India. With a keen interest in research and teaching, she contributes to the academic development of students in business studies. Through her work, she actively engages in advancing knowledge and fostering a collaborative learning environment.

Monica Peña-Villegas received her EdD with a specialization in Special Education from National University in December 2024. Her doctoral research study, "Parent/Guardians' Perceptions of Postsecondary Transition and Matriculation of Students with Learning Disabilities: A Qualitative Case Study," was nominated for the Dissertation of the Year Award. She received her MSW from California State University, Sacramento, and her BS from the University of California, Davis. She is currently employed by the UC Davis Early Academic Outreach Program and is currently the Associate Director. She is a Council for Exceptional Children member and participates in the Yolo County Special Education Local Plan Area Community Advisory Committee. One of her life goals is to make visible and attainable the doors that are open to underrepresented students so that they, too, can achieve their postsecondary goals by providing middle and high school students and their parents/guardians the knowledge and skills they need to persist beyond a high school education and to achieve success at the postsecondary level.

Mibi Riba earned her undergraduate degree from JNC Pasighat in Arunachal Pradesh's East Siang District and completed her higher education at Rajiv Gandhi University, Itanagar. As a dedicated Social Anthropologist, she completed her M.Phil in 2006. Following this, she served as a government school teacher from 2006 to 2015. During her PhD studies from 2015 to 2020, Dr Riba also contributed to the Institute of Distance Education at RGU as a counsellor, guiding numerous distance learners for four years. Since October 2021, she has been an Assistant Professor (Guest) at Dera Natung Government College. She actively supervises students' fieldwork research in villages, assisting them with their dissertations, a key requirement in their final Anthropology semester.

Ranjit Singha is a Doctorate Research Fellow at Christ (Deemed to be University) and holds a prestigious membership in the American Psychological Association (APA). With a strong background in Research and Development, he has significantly contributed to various fields such as Mindfulness, Addiction Psychology, Women Empowerment, UN Sustainable Development Goals, and Data Science. With over 15 years of experience in Administration, Teaching, and Research, both in Industry and Higher Education Institutions (HEI), Mr Ranjit has established himself as a seasoned professional. Mr Ranjit is dedicated to research and teaching endeavours, primarily focusing on mindfulness and compassion-based interventions. His work in these areas aims to promote well-being and foster positive change in individuals and communities.

Surjit Singha is an academician with a broad spectrum of interests, including UN Sustainable Development Goals, Organizational Climate, Workforce Diversity, Organizational Culture, HRM, Marketing, Finance, IB, Global Business, Business, AI, K12 & Higher Education, Gender and Cultural Studies. Currently a faculty member at Kristu Jayanti College, Dr. Surjit also serves as an Editor, reviewer, and author for prominent global publications and journals, including being on the Editorial review board of Information Resources Management Journal and contributor to various publications. With over 15 years of experience in Administration, Teaching, and Research, Dr. Surjit is dedicated to imparting knowledge and guiding students in their research pursuits. As a research mentor, Dr. Surjit has nurtured young minds and fostered academic growth. Dr. Surjit has an impressive track record of over 150+ publications (SCOPUS Indexed 79+), including articles, book chapters, and textbooks, holds two US Copyrights, and has successfully completed and published two fully funded minor research projects from Kristu Jayanti College.

Jishamol Thomas is a PhD Research Scholar at the Department of Social Work, Christ University, Bengaluru, and an Assistant Professor at the Department of Social Work, Christ College of Science and Management.

Gary Simeon Walker-Roberts, Ph.D. (they/them/theirs), is a proud LGTBQIAA+ scholar who began their educational journey at the local community college in California. After earning an Associates of Arts in Arts and Humanities at Los Medanos College, Dr. Gary earned a Bachelor of Arts in Ethnic Studies, Gender and Sexualities at California State University, East Bay (CSUEB). Thereafter, they earned a Master of Arts in English at Arizona State University and obtained a Doctor of Philosophy in Education with a specialization in E-Learning at legacy Northcentral University, now known as National University (NU). Dr. Gary is a Professor in the Advanced Graduate Studies Department of the Sanford College of Education at NU. Dr. Gary enjoys their role as Professor, Dissertation Committee Chair, and Subject Matter Expert where they successfully facilitate doctoral candidates to reach their terminal degrees. Lastly, Dr. Gary is a proud inaugural member of National University System's Social Justice, Equity, Diversity, and Inclusion (S-JEDI) Office where they champion the Inclusive Excellence Framework with a focus on LGTBQIAA+ inclusion and equity at NU.

Index

A

C

D

E

F

G

I

S

T

V

www.ingramcontent.com/pod-product-compliance
Ingram Content Group UK Ltd.
Pitfield, Milton Keynes, MK11 3LW, UK
UKHW050952290926
15470UKWH00005B/1786

9 798369 390207